Guided by Spirits

Connecting with Your Spirit Allies

Alex McCann Johnson

GUIDED BY SPIRIT
PUBLISHING

Guided by Spirits
Connecting with Your Spirit Allies

Alex McCann Johnson

Published by Guided by Spirit Publishing

Guided by Spirit Publishing
203 Main St.
Williston, ND, 58801, USA
www.guidedbyspiritpublishing.com
info@guidedbyspiritpublishing.com

Guided by Spirit Publishing
203 Main St.
Williston, ND, 58801, USA

The information in this book is provided for informational purposes only. The author and publisher make no representations as to the accuracy or completeness of any information in this book and are not liable for any errors or omissions or for the results obtained from the use of such information.

ISBN: 979-8-9913133-1-5

Printed in the United States of America

Cover Design by Eugine Johnson

Contents

Ascended Masters   705

Galactic Guides

Acknowledgments

This book would not have been possible without the guidance, support, and love of many incredible beings, both seen and unseen. First and foremost, I want to express my deepest gratitude to the spirit guides who have walked with me throughout my journey. Your wisdom and presence have been the foundation of this work, and I am eternally grateful for your unwavering support.

To my beloved partner, Eugine, thank you for your endless encouragement, love, and understanding. Your belief in me and in this work has been a constant source of strength. Together, we have created a life of exploration and connection, and for that, I am deeply thankful.

I also want to thank my friends, family, and colleagues who have supported me along the way. Your encouragement, feedback, and shared experiences have enriched this book and made it what it is today.

A special thank you to the many clients and students I have had the privilege of working with over the years. Your openness, trust, and commitment to your own spiritual journeys have inspired me and reaffirmed the importance of this work.

Finally, to every reader who picks up this book, thank you for allowing me to be a part of your spiritual journey. I hope that Guided By Spirits serves as a source of inspiration and guidance as you connect with the spiritual realms and uncover the wisdom that is always available to you.

With deepest gratitude,
Alex McCann Johnson

Alex McCann Johnson

Chapter 1
Guided by the Unseen

My journey with spirit guides began long before I had any understanding of what they were or the roles they played in our lives. One of my earliest memories of this mysterious connection was when I was about five or six years old. Our neighbor, a woman who was so friendly and caring, had recently been diagnosed with cancer. At that tender age, I didn't understand what cancer was or grasp the seriousness of her situation. One day, feeling an inexplicable urge, I walked over to her house and knocked on her door. When she answered, I looked up at her with the conviction only a child could have and said, "The angels will take care of you." It was only later that I learned she had received the devastating news of her illness that very day.

This seemingly small encounter was a significant moment, though I didn't realize it then. It wasn't until my twenties that I began piecing together my life's puzzle, seeing the intricate threads of connection to the spirit world that had always been there. Through years of reflection, study, and experience, I understood that I had been communicating with spirit guides all along. These unseen companions, who had watched over me, guided me, and sometimes nudged me in directions I hadn't planned, were essential in navigating my life's journey. Looking back, I am filled with gratitude for their constant presence and guidance. Their influence has been profound, and I am continually awed by how they have shaped my path.

Understanding what spirit guides are is essential to appreciating their impact. Spirit guides are non-physical entities existing in the spiritual realm whose purpose is to assist us in our earthly journey. They can be ancestral spirits, animal spirits, angelic beings, or even ascended masters. Though many have at least one main guide, we are believed to have several. These guides may remain with us throughout our lives or come and go as our needs and the lessons we are meant to learn evolve.

The essence of spirit guides is their respect for our free will. They do not impose their will upon us or dictate our actions. Instead, they offer subtle nudges, intuitive insights, and synchronicities to help us make informed decisions. Their guidance is always loving, supportive, and non-judgmental. They are like gentle teachers who provide us with the tools and encouragement to navigate our path while leaving the ultimate choices up to us.

Spirit guides play a multifaceted role in our lives. They provide guidance and insight, particularly in times of need. Whether facing a difficult decision, grappling with a personal issue, or seeking a deeper understanding of our purpose, our guides offer clarity and direction. They communicate through various means—dreams, meditation, signs, and the everyday miracles of synchronicity.

Protection is another significant aspect of their role. While they focus on guidance, spirit guides also help shield us from negative energies and influences, ensuring we stay aligned with a path of light and love. This protective role is subtle but powerful, often operating in the background of our lives.

In moments of emotional turmoil or when we feel overwhelmed, spirit guides offer emotional and spiritual support. They remind us that we are never truly alone, comforting us in our darkest times and encouraging us to keep moving forward. Their presence is a beacon of hope, reassuring us of the unending support from the spiritual realm.

One of the most important roles of spirit guides is facilitating our personal and spiritual growth. They help us recognize and overcome our fears, limitations, and negative patterns. By gently pushing us beyond our comfort zones, they enable us to evolve and reach our highest potential. They are teachers who share wisdom, helping us understand complex spiritual concepts and navigate life's lessons. Often, their teachings encourage us to expand our awareness and consciousness, bringing knowledge that transcends our immediate understanding.

Connecting with spirit guides can also deepen our connection to the Divine. Acting as intermediaries, they help us strengthen our bonds with higher realms and understand our place in the universe. Through their guidance, we can enrich our spiritual practice and experience a profound sense of oneness with all that is.

A pivotal moment in my understanding of spirit guides came in my late teens. Desperate for answers about my future, particularly in love, I visited a psychic. At that time, I was secretly grappling with my identity and the longing for a love I had yet to experience. The psychic told me that I would find love in the early fall when the leaves were falling, and the wind picked up. I clung to this prophecy, expecting it to come true that year. Yet, as the seasons passed without any sign of romance, my hope began to fade. This pattern repeated year after year, leading me to doubt the validity of the message and falling into despair.

Then, just as I had given up hope, something remarkable happened. In a moment of synchronicity, I met my future husband, who happened to be my neighbor. One day, as he walked toward me, the wind picked up, and a flurry of leaves swirled around us. It was as if the spirit was reminding me not to lose faith, that they had been working behind the scenes all along, waiting for the perfect moment. This experience reinforced my belief in the guidance of spirit and taught me an invaluable lesson about patience and trust.

My journey with spirit guides has been transformative. In my twenties, my exploration of spirituality deepened. I immersed myself in books, workshops, and meditation practices. Gradually, I began to recognize the signs and messages from my guides. They would appear in dreams, leave feathers as signs, and orchestrate synchronicities too in-my-face to ignore.

One of the most significant lessons my guides have taught me is the importance of trust. Trusting their guidance, even when challenging my logic or comfort zone, has led me to incredible opportunities and insights. They have shown me that I can navigate life's challenges with grace and confidence by trusting in the unseen.

This lesson was particularly evident when I decided to run for city commissioner in my hometown. Early in my campaign, I received the message that I would not win but that the experience would teach me invaluable lessons. Initially, this was confusing—why pursue something destined to fail? However, the journey taught me the importance of resilience and public humility. Despite the close race and eventual loss, I was surrounded by support and learned crucial lessons about perseverance and grace. My guides had prepared me for this outcome, emphasizing the growth and learning rather than the result itself.

As you begin your journey to connect with your spirit guides, remember that it is a personal and unique experience. There is no right or wrong way to establish this connection. What matters most is your openness, willingness, and trust in the process. Your guides are always with you, ready to assist and support you on your path. By building a relationship with them, you can unlock a wealth of wisdom, love, and guidance that will enrich your life in ways you never imagined.

In the following chapters, we will explore the various types of spirit guides, their roles, and how to connect with them. From angelic guides to animal spirits, from ancestral guides to ascended masters, we will delve into the rich tapestry of spiritual assistance available to us. By understanding the different aspects of spirit guides and their purpose, you will be better equipped to recognize their presence in your life and embrace their profound support.

Chapter 2

Preparing for Connection

Embarking on the journey to connect with your spirit guides is akin to setting off on an epic adventure. Like any significant journey, it requires thoughtful preparation. This process is not just about the act of connection but about creating an environment—both physical and mental—that fosters deep and meaningful interactions with your guides. For me, this journey began with a commitment to clear my energy and elevate my vibration, recognizing that my openness and clarity would be crucial in establishing a true connection.

The first and most vital step in preparing for this spiritual adventure is setting a clear intention. Intention acts as the cornerstone of your practice, guiding your energy and focus toward the desired outcome. When I set my intentions, I often feel like I'm casting a line into the vast universe, signaling to my guides that I am ready and open to receive their wisdom and guidance. Even if you are not a fisherman, this is your opportunity to reel in the big one. This clarity not only aligns my energy with my goals but also signals to my spirit guides that I am committed and serious about our connection.

Setting intentions starts with a deep reflection on my desires and goals. I ask myself why I want to connect with my spirit guides and what I hope to gain from this relationship. Do I seek guidance for a specific issue, or am I looking to deepen my spiritual practice overall? Being clear about my motivations helps me to formulate a focused and powerful intention. For instance, when dealing with uncertainty in my career, I intended to receive clarity and direction from my guides about the best path forward.

Visualization is another powerful tool I used to strengthen my intention. Each day, I take a few moments to visualize my desired outcome. I see myself in a calm, sacred space, feeling the presence of my guides around me. I imagine the clarity and comfort their guidance brings, and I allow myself to experience these feelings fully. This practice not only reinforces my intention but also creates a positive and welcoming energy that draws my guides closer.

Affirmations also play a crucial role in embedding my intentions into my daily life. By repeating my intentions—either silently or aloud—I reaffirm my commitment to this journey and align my subconscious mind with my conscious goals. I often start my day with affirmations like, "I am open and receptive to the guidance of my spirit guides," or "My spirit guides are always with me, providing wisdom and support." These affirmations help to keep my intentions front and center, guiding my thoughts and actions throughout the day.

While setting clear intentions is essential, releasing any attachment to how or when these intentions will manifest is equally important. Trusting in the timing and methods of the spirit guides allows for a more profound and relaxed connection. I remind myself to stay open and flexible, trusting that my guides will respond in the best way possible, even if it's not in the manner I initially envisioned.

Creating a sacred space is the next step in this preparation process. This space serves as a sanctuary where I can retreat, meditate, and connect with my spirit guides without the distractions of daily life. It is a place imbued with energy that supports my spiritual practice, enhancing my ability to receive and interpret the guidance of my guides.

Choosing a location for my sacred space is a deeply personal decision. I look for a place in my home where I feel most comfortable and at peace—a quiet corner or even a spot outdoors. Once chosen, I cleanse this space to remove any negative or stagnant energy. I use methods to purify the area by cleansing with sage or palo santo, using sound vibrations from a singing bowl, or simply visualizing white light filling the space. As an energy healer, I often employ Reiki to clear and infuse the space with positive energy.

Setting up an altar is another way to personalize and energize my sacred space. My altar is a small table adorned with items that hold spiritual significance to me. Crystals, candles, incense, and images of deities or spiritual beings are all elements that I include. Each object on my altar has a purpose and meaning, contributing to the overall energy of the space. For instance, I might place a rose quartz crystal to attract love and compassion or light a white candle to symbolize purity and clarity.

Comfort is key to creating a space that I look forward to spending time in. I add cushions, blankets, or a comfortable chair to make the space inviting. Personal touches, such as meaningful artwork, photographs, or spiritual books, further enhance my connection to this sacred space. The more the space reflects my personality and spiritual journey, the more powerful it becomes as a tool for connecting with my guides.

Establishing a routine for using my sacred space is crucial for building a consistent and potent connection with my spirit guides. Whether it's a daily meditation session, a weekly ritual, or simply a few moments of quiet reflection each day, consistency strengthens the energy of the space and deepens my connection with my guides. Over time, the repeated use of this sacred space amplifies its energy, making it a potent focal point for my spiritual practice.

Maintaining my sacred space is an ongoing process. I keep it clean and tidy, regularly refreshing the energy by cleansing it of any negativity. I also periodically rearrange or add new items to keep the space vibrant and alive. This upkeep ensures that my sacred space remains a powerful and supportive environment for my spiritual work.

I lay a solid foundation for connecting with my spirit guides by setting clear intentions and creating a sacred space. These preparations signal my commitment to this spiritual journey and demonstrate my readiness to receive the wisdom and support my guides offer.

As you prepare to embark on your own journey to connect with your spirit guides, remember that this process is deeply personal and unique. There is no right or wrong way to prepare; what matters most is creating an environment that feels sacred and supportive to you. By cultivating a space that resonates with your energy and setting intentions that align with your goals, you invite your spirit guides into your life in a profound and meaningful way. This journey, filled with discovery, growth, and guidance, will undoubtedly enrich your life in ways you never imagined.

Chapter 3
Methods of Communication

Connecting with spirit guides is a very personal journey, and the ways they communicate with us can vary widely. Often, we may feel tempted to compare our experiences to others or expect our guides to communicate in specific ways we've read about or heard from others. However, each of us is unique, and so too are our connections with the spirit world. In this chapter, I'll explore several methods of communication—including meditation, dreams, signs, and synchronicities—that have proven effective for myself and others. By understanding and practicing these methods, you can open yourself to the profound guidance and wisdom your spirit guides offer.

One of the most significant lessons I've learned over years of teaching and mentoring is that everyone's experience with spirit communication is different. As you begin this journey, it's essential to remain open-minded and willing to experiment with various methods. Even if a particular approach, like dreamwork, doesn't initially resonate with you, give it a chance. When the mind is at rest, the quiet hours of the night often provide a fertile ground for deep and meaningful connections with spirit.

Meditation

Meditation is perhaps one of the most powerful and direct methods for connecting with your spirit guides. It allows you to quiet the mind, open your heart, and create a receptive state for communication. People often find meditation intimidating, fearing that they can't quiet their minds. But meditation doesn't require a perfectly still mind; it simply requires presence and intention. Here's how you can start:

- **Find a Quiet Space:** Choose a place where you can sit or lie down comfortably without interruptions. Ideally, use your sacred space, as discussed in the previous chapter. This could be a corner of your room, a spot in nature, or any place where you feel at peace.

- **Set Your Intention:** Before beginning, clearly state your intention to connect with your spirit guides. You might say, "I invite my spirit guides to communicate with me and provide their guidance and wisdom." This intention acts as a beacon, signaling to your guides that you are open and ready to receive their messages.

- **Focus on Your Breath:** Close your eyes and take several deep, calming breaths. Pay attention to the sensation of the air entering and leaving your body. This focus helps to calm your mind and anchors you in the present moment, making it easier to connect with your guides.

- **Enter a Meditative State:** As you continue to breathe deeply, allow your body to relax completely. Imagine releasing all tension and stress, feeling a wave of relaxation wash over you. Envision yourself surrounded by a warm, loving light, which acts as a protective barrier and a channel for communication.

- **Open to Communication:** In this relaxed state, remain open and receptive. You might visualize meeting your spirit guides in a serene, beautiful place or simply sitting in stillness, waiting for any impressions, thoughts, or feelings to arise. Trust whatever comes to you, even if it doesn't make immediate sense.

- **Record Your Experience:** After your meditation, take a few moments to write down any messages, images, or sensations you received. Over time, you might notice patterns or recurring themes in these communications, providing deeper insights into your guides' messages.

Meditation requires patience and practice. As you continue this practice, you will likely find that your ability to connect with your spirit guides deepens and becomes more natural. I remember when I first started meditating, my mind was full of chatter. But with persistence, I learned to find the stillness where my guides' voices could be heard.

Dreams

Dreams are another common medium through which spirit guides communicate with us. Our subconscious mind is more open to spiritual messages when we are in the dream state. Utilizing dreams as a method of communication can be both enlightening and comforting. Here's how to use dreams to connect with your guides:

- **Set an Intention Before Sleep:** Each night, before you go to bed, set a clear intention to receive guidance from your spirit guides in your dreams. You might say, "I invite my spirit guides to communicate with me in my dreams and provide their guidance." This prepares your subconscious mind to be alert to the messages during sleep.

- **Keep a Dream Journal:** Place a notebook and pen by your bed to record your dreams as soon as you wake up. Dreams can fade quickly upon waking, so it's essential to jot down any memories immediately, no matter how fragmented they may seem.

- **Look for Symbols and Patterns:** Pay attention to any symbols, characters, or recurring themes in your dreams. Spirit guides often use symbols to convey their messages. Reflect on what these symbols might mean to you personally. Over time, you may start recognizing familiar symbols that your guides used to communicate specific messages.

- **Reflection Your Dreams:** Take time each day to reflect on your dreams and any messages you might have received. Consider how these messages relate to your current life situation. Spirit guides often use dreams to provide insights or guidance that we might not be open to during waking hours.

- **Ask for Clarity:** If a dream message is unclear, don't hesitate to ask your spirit guides for clarification. You can do this through meditation or by setting another intention before sleep, asking for more detailed or understandable guidance.

Dreams can serve as a profound source of guidance and insight. By paying close attention to your dreams and actively seeking communication through them, you can uncover valuable messages from your spirit guides that might otherwise remain hidden.

Signs

Spirit guides often communicate through signs, which can be subtle or overt but are always meaningful. Recognizing and interpreting these signs can deepen your connection with your guides. Here's how to become attuned to these spiritual messages:

- **Stay Present and Aware:** Being mindful and present in your daily life is crucial for noticing signs from your spirit guides. These signs can take many forms—a feather on your path, a particular animal appearing frequently, or a recurring number sequence.

- **Trust Your Intuition:** When you encounter something unusual or out of the ordinary, trust your intuition. If a specific sign captures your attention and evokes a strong feeling, it is likely a message from your spirit guides.

- **Ask for Specific Signs:** If you need confirmation or guidance on a particular issue, ask your spirit guides for a specific sign. For example, you might ask to see a butterfly to signify you are on the right path. Be clear in your request and open to how the sign might appear.

- **Be Open to Interpretation:** Signs often require personal interpretation. Consider what the sign means to you and how it relates to your current life circumstances. What thoughts or feelings arise when you see the sign? How does it connect to your questions or concerns?

- **Express Gratitude:** When you receive a sign, acknowledge it and express your gratitude to your spirit guides. This helps to strengthen your connection and shows your appreciation for their guidance.

Recognizing and interpreting signs is a powerful way to receive guidance from your spirit guides. By staying open and aware, you can develop a clearer understanding of the messages they are sending you.

Synchronicities

Synchronicities are meaningful coincidences that often provide guidance and validation from our spirit guides. These events are orchestrated in ways that transcend ordinary causality and offer significant insights. Here's how to recognize and work with synchronicities:

- **Notice the Patterns:** Pay attention to patterns and coincidences in your life. These might include meeting the right person at the perfect time, repeatedly hearing the same phrase, or experiencing a series of related events. These patterns are often the subtle work of your spirit guides.

- **Reflect on the Meaning:** Take time to consider what the synchronicity might mean for you. How does it relate to your current situation or question? What message might your spirit guides be conveying through this sequence of events?

- **Trust the Timing:** Synchronicities often occur at pivotal moments in our lives. Trust that the timing is perfect and that your spirit guides are providing guidance exactly when you need it. These moments are often orchestrated to guide you toward or away from certain paths.

- **Take Action:** If a synchronicity provides a clear message or direction, take action on it. Responding to these signs demonstrates to your spirit guides that you are listening and willing to follow their guidance. This can lead to more frequent and clear communications.

Synchronicities reveal the interconnectedness of our lives and the spiritual realm. By paying attention to these meaningful coincidences, you can receive profound insights and guidance from your spirit guides.

Personal Experience and Advice

In my own journey, I've found that spirit guides communicate in a variety of ways, each tailored to the individual's needs and circumstances. Many times, people are surprised by how spirit manifests for them once they open up to the possibility. They often start noticing signs and messages they had previously overlooked or dismissed.

One particularly experience stands out from my time in Hawaii. It was the day I was leaving, and as I drove towards the airport, I felt a deep need for reassurance that I was on the right path. I asked the universe for a sign. On the way, I felt an irresistible urge to stop at a cliffside scenic spot for one last look at the ocean. As my friend and I stood there, gazing over the vast expanse of water, something incredible happened. Out of the blue, a pod of orcas appeared, gliding gracefully through the waves. Orcas are a rare sight off the coast, and seeing them felt like a magical moment.

This sighting was meaningful because I had previously asked for whales as a sign of reassurance from my guides. A year before, while working at a bar, I had requested whales as my sign. Not long after, the ESPN channel inexplicably showed a program featuring whales on the TV above the bar. It was an odd but powerful sign. Standing on that cliff seeing those orcas, I felt reassurance. It was as if the universe was speaking directly to me, confirming that I was exactly where I needed to be.

This experience is just one example of the many ways our spirit guides can communicate with us. As you begin your journey to connect with your spirit guides, give yourself grace and be patient. Embrace this opportunity to learn more about yourself and your spiritual connections. Remember, there is no single "correct" way to communicate with spirit. What matters most is your openness, willingness, and trust in the process. With time and practice, your connection with your spirit guides will deepen, enriching your life in ways you never imagined.

Alex McCann Johnson

Chapter 4
Developing Intuition

Developing intuition and enhancing psychic abilities is a journey filled with excitement and challenge. These abilities are not reserved for a select few; they are within everyone's reach, given the right practice and awareness. The key to unlocking these gifts lies in understanding how you naturally sense and interact with the world around you. By honing your awareness of your senses and paying attention to subtle shifts, you can become more attuned to the messages and guidance from your spirit guides.

In my mentorship program, one of the foundational lessons I teach is to engage with the world through all your senses fully. This immersive experience is crucial for developing your intuition. It's important to recognize that you may receive messages through senses you might not typically rely on during readings or spiritual sessions. For example, you might suddenly pick up on smells even if you usually don't have strong clairgustance (clear tasting). Conversely, you might not receive messages through your dominant senses in every session. This variability is a natural part of the process and reflects how the spirit communicates in diverse ways depending on the context.

Understanding Your Senses

The journey to developing your intuition begins with a deep understanding of how you sense the world. This might seem straightforward, but it forms the essential foundation for more advanced psychic development. Each of us experiences the world through our senses—sight, sound, touch, taste, and smell. By becoming more attuned to these senses, you can start to recognize when a message or subtle shift is occurring.

Spend a week immersing yourself in sensory awareness. Pay close attention to how you experience the world around you. For instance, when you look at a tree, do you first notice its vibrant colors and intricate shapes, or do you feel its energy and presence more than its visual details? When listening to music, are you more drawn to the melody or the emotions it stirs within you? Understanding your primary ways of perceiving helps you identify which senses are most dominant and how they might be utilized to receive messages from your spirit guides.

The Clair Senses

The psychic senses, often referred to as the "Clair" senses, extend beyond our physical senses. These include clairvoyance (clear seeing), clairaudience (clear hearing), clairsentience (clear feeling), claircognizance (clear knowing), clairgustance (clear tasting), and clairsalience (clear smelling). Everyone has a unique combination of these abilities, with some being more prominent than others. For me, claircognizance is the strongest, manifesting as sudden insights or knowledge. Here's a deeper look at each of the clair senses:

- **Clairvoyance (Clear Seeing):** This ability involves seeing images, symbols, or visions that are not physically present. These can appear in your mind's eye or through physical sight. Those with strong clairvoyance might see colors, lights, or even spirit beings during meditation or intuitive sessions.

- **Clairaudience (Clear Hearing):** This ability allows you to hear messages from the spirit world, which can manifest as a voice in your mind or external sounds. Clairaudient individuals might hear words, music, or other sounds that convey specific messages from guides or spirits.

- **Clairsentience (Clear Feeling):** This sense involves feeling emotions or physical sensations from the spirit realm. It often includes sensing others' emotions or feeling the presence of spirit through physical sensations like chills or pressure. It's a deeply empathetic connection that can provide rich, emotional insights.

- **Claircognizance (Clear Knowing):** This ability is characterized by knowing something without any physical evidence. It's an intuitive understanding that often arrives suddenly and with a strong sense of certainty. People with claircognizance frequently receive insights or answers spontaneously, as if the knowledge just appears in their minds.

- **Clairgustance (Clear Tasting):** This less common ability involves tasting something that isn't physically present. It can be significant when it happens, providing symbolic messages or connections to specific memories or experiences.

- **Clairsalience (Clear Smelling):** Also less common, this ability involves smelling scents that are not physically present. It can be a powerful sense, with those experiencing clairsalience often smelling flowers, smoke, or other scents associated with spirits or loved ones who have passed.

Enhancing Your Psychic Abilities

Enhancing your psychic abilities requires consistent practice, patience, and a willingness to explore your senses. Here are several steps to help you develop your intuition:

- **Meditation:** Regular meditation is fundamental for quieting the mind and opening your awareness to subtle energies. During meditation, focus on each of your senses and notice any shifts or messages. This practice helps to strengthen your connection to your inner guidance and your spirit guides. Try different meditation techniques to find what resonates best with you, whether it's guided meditation, mindfulness, or silent meditation.

- **Mindfulness:** Being fully present and engaging with your senses in everyday life enhances your intuitive abilities. Practice mindfulness by paying attention to your surroundings, thoughts, and emotions without judgment. This heightened awareness allows you to catch subtle messages from the spirit that you might otherwise miss.

- **Journaling:** Keeping a journal of your experiences and any messages you receive helps reinforce your connection to your psychic abilities. Write down your thoughts, dreams, and intuitive insights regularly. Over time, reviewing your journal can reveal patterns and progress in your intuitive development.

- **Exercises for Each Clair Sense:** Specific exercises can help strengthen each of your clair senses. For clairvoyance, practice visualizing different images or colors in your mind's eye. For clairaudience, focus on the sounds around you and notice any subtle nuances. For clairsentience, pay attention to your physical sensations and emotions in various environments. For claircognizance, trust, and to act on your gut feelings and insights without overanalyzing. For clairgustance and clairsalience, try to recall or imagine distinct tastes and smells and see how they evoke memories or emotions.

- **Working with Tools:** Tools like tarot cards, oracle cards, or pendulums can enhance your intuitive abilities. These tools provide a tangible way to receive and interpret messages from your spirit guides. They can serve as a focal point for your intuition, helping to clarify and strengthen the guidance you receive.

- **Trusting Your Intuition:** Developing psychic abilities hinges significantly on learning to trust your intuition. When you receive a message or have an intuitive hit, trust it without second-guessing. The more you trust and act on your intuition, the stronger and more reliable it will become. Building this trust takes time and practice, but it's essential for deepening your intuitive skills.

Guided by Spirits

I've discovered that my strongest ability is claircognizance. I often receive sudden insights or knowledge that seem to come out of nowhere, providing me with guidance and understanding. Clairsentience follows closely, allowing me to feel emotions or physical sensations that give additional information. Although clairvoyance is less frequent for me, it still plays a significant role in my spiritual connections.

I've also had moments when clairgustance and clairsalience have provided unexpected but meaningful insights. For example, during a meditation session, I once smelled the distinct scent of roses, which I later discovered was associated with a specific spirit guide. These experiences taught me the importance of remaining open to all sensory inputs, as spirit communication can manifest through any of the clair senses.

We begin to learn more about the universe and how it communicates when we start to understand how we perceive it. Everyone's journey is unique, and it's vital to remember that you won't perceive things the same way as others do. I used to believe that I needed to receive messages just like famous mediums or psychics, but I realized that trying to emulate their methods only distracted me from discovering my unique approach. While exploring various techniques is beneficial, you should ultimately follow what resonates most with you.

Developing your intuition and enhancing your psychic abilities is a journey that requires patience, practice, and an open mind. Enjoy the process and allow yourself to explore without pressure or rigid expectations. You might notice everything feels different—colors seem more vibrant, the texture of everyday objects becomes more significant, and even simple touches convey a deeper meaning.

Give yourself grace and patience as you learn. Embrace the opportunity to discover more about yourself and your unique abilities. Remember, everyone has the potential to develop their intuition and connect with spirit. The key is to stay open, practice regularly, and trust in your own inner guidance.

Alex McCann Johnson

Chapter 5
Overcoming Doubts and Fears

Trusting the guidance from your spirit guides can be one of the most challenging aspects of developing your intuitive abilities. It's easy to get caught up in your own thoughts, doubting the messages you receive and questioning your own capabilities. So, cultivating a positive mindset is crucial. Without it, you may spiral into self-doubt and fear, which can block the flow of communication with your guides.

When I am relaxed and free from concern about others' opinions, the guidance I receive flows naturally. However, if I'm tense or worried about how others will perceive me, connecting with my guides becomes significantly more difficult. This is a common experience, particularly for those new to working with spirit guides. The key to overcoming this is to set aside your ego and trust in the process—though this is often easier said than done.

One of the most valuable lessons I learned early in my journey was to trust the messages I received, even when they were difficult to share. I recall an experience at an expo where I was offering readings. I kept receiving the word "divorce" for a particular individual. As a novice in a public setting, this was a heavy message to deliver. I hesitated, fearing the impact of sharing such news. I was in my head, worried about causing distress.

Yet the message persisted, growing louder and more insistent. Finally, I mustered the courage to tell the woman that I was hearing "divorce." To my surprise, she broke down in tears, not out of sorrow but relief.

She thanked me because no one else had been willing to address the issue directly. She was in the midst of seeking a divorce lawyer due to an abusive relationship, and my message gave her the validation she needed.

This experience emphasized the importance of trusting the guidance that comes through, no matter how daunting it may be. It also emphasized the need to deliver such messages with sensitivity and responsibility. While it's crucial to trust and share the insights you receive, it's equally important to consider how to convey them effectively and compassionately.

Building Trust in the Guidance

Overcoming doubts and fears is a gradual journey that requires practice and patience. Here are some strategies to help build trust in the guidance you receive from your spirit guides:

Acknowledge Your Fears: Recognize that it is normal to have doubts and fears, especially when stepping into new or unfamiliar territory. These feelings are a natural part of the growth process. Acknowledging them without judgment is the first step toward overcoming them.

Practice Self-Compassion: Treat yourself with kindness as you navigate this journey. Self-compassion helps to quiet the inner critic that often fuels doubt and fear. Remind yourself that making mistakes is part of learning, and each experience offers a valuable lesson.

Reflect on Past Experiences: Look back on times when you trusted your intuition or guidance from your spirit guides and found it to be accurate. Reflecting on these moments can reinforce your confidence and trust in your abilities.

Stay Grounded: Regular grounding practices can help calm your mind and reduce anxiety. Techniques such as deep breathing, spending time in nature, and mindfulness exercises can help you stay centered and connected to your inner wisdom.

Ask for Clarity: If you receive a confusing or overwhelming message, don't hesitate to ask your spirit guides for more clarity. They can provide additional insights or help you understand the message more fully. You can also ask for signs or confirmations to validate the guidance you're receiving.

Build a Support System: Surround yourself with supportive and like-minded individuals who understand and respect your journey. Having a community or a mentor can provide encouragement and perspective and help you navigate doubts and fears.

Trust the Process: Trust that your spirit guides have your best interests at heart. They are here to support and guide you, even when the messages are challenging. Trusting the process means letting go of the need for control and allowing the guidance to unfold naturally.

Set Boundaries: It's important to establish boundaries with yourself and with spirit. If you feel overwhelmed, communicate your need for space or a break. Your spirit guides will respect and understand your boundaries, ensuring that the communication remains healthy and manageable.

I've learned to trust the messages that come through, even when they push me outside my comfort zone. Spirit guides provide guidance that is ultimately for the highest good, even if it isn't immediately clear or easy to accept. By setting aside my ego and embracing the process, I've been able to deliver messages that bring clarity, relief, and healing to others.

Trusting in the guidance from your spirit guides is a journey of faith. It involves letting go of the need to control or fully understand every aspect of the communication. It means being open to the unknown and embracing the mystery of the spiritual realm. By doing so, you can deepen your connection with your spirit guides.

Navigating Challenges

As you move forward, it's crucial to give yourself grace. Celebrate your progress, however small, and learn from each experience. Trust that you are exactly where you need to be on your journey and that your spirit guides are always there to support you. With time and practice, overcoming doubts and fears will become more manageable, and the guidance you receive will flow more freely and clearly.

Overcoming doubts and fears is an essential part of developing your intuitive abilities. Each step you take in facing these challenges strengthens your connection and deepens your trust in the guidance you receive.

Embrace Progress Over Perfection: The path to overcoming doubts and fears isn't about achieving perfection but about celebrating progress and learning. Each moment of doubt is an opportunity to strengthen your faith and deepen your connection with your spirit guides. Your intuitive abilities will flourish with patience and perseverance, and your spiritual practice will become a source of guidance and inspiration.

Practice Self-Awareness: Regularly check in with yourself to assess how you feel about the guidance you are receiving and your comfort level in sharing it. Self-awareness can help you address any emerging doubts or fears before they become significant obstacles.

Learn from Each Experience: Every experience, whether it feels successful or challenging, is a learning opportunity. Reflect on what worked, what didn't, and how you can apply these insights to future interactions with your guides.

You can navigate this journey with greater ease and confidence by practicing self-compassion, staying grounded, and building a supportive network. Trust that your spirit guides are always with you, offering the guidance you need. Embrace the journey, and allow yourself to grow and evolve with each experience.

Remember, the journey of overcoming doubts and fears is continuous and dynamic. Each step forward, no matter how small, is a victory in deepening your trust and connection with your spirit guides. Through dedication and openness, your intuitive abilities will thrive, and your relationship with your guides will become a source of empowerment

Guided by Spirits
and enlightenment.

Alex McCann Johnson

Chapter 6

When Ego Steps In

Embarking on a journey of deep spiritual connection and service requires confronting and understanding a crucial aspect of our being: the ego. The ego, often seen as a hindrance to spiritual growth, is fundamentally a tool for survival. It shapes our identity, helps us navigate the complexities of the world, and protects us. However, to connect effectively with spirit and live a life dedicated to service, we must learn to understand and manage the ego, knowing when to set it aside.

The ego, at its core, is our sense of self. It defines our individuality, preferences, and boundaries. This self-awareness is vital for survival; it helps us recognize danger, pursue our goals, and assert our needs. Yet, the ego can become a barrier when it dominates our thoughts and actions. It can foster separation, competition, and fear—attitudes that are counterproductive to spiritual growth and the ethos of service.

Understanding the role of the ego is the first step in learning to manage it. The ego is not inherently negative; it is simply a part of our human experience. It becomes problematic when it controls us and dictates our actions based on fear, pride, or a craving for recognition. Such ego-driven motives can lead us astray from our true purpose and obstruct our connection with spirit.

One of the most important lessons on the spiritual path is learning to recognize when the ego is influencing our thoughts and actions. This awareness allows us to pause and evaluate whether we are acting from a

29

place of love and service or from self-interest and fear. Developing this self-awareness allows us to choose our responses consciously and align our actions with our higher purpose.

To set the ego aside, particularly when working with spirit, we must cultivate humility. Humility is not about devaluing ourselves; it's about understanding that we are part of something much larger. It involves acknowledging our limitations and being open to guidance from higher sources. When we approach our spiritual practice with humility, we create a space for spirit to work through us without the interference of our ego.

Another crucial aspect of managing the ego is practicing detachment. Detachment does not imply a lack of concern; rather, it means releasing our need to control outcomes and being open to whatever unfolds. When we detach from the need for recognition, success, or approval, we free ourselves from the ego's grip and allow our true selves to emerge. This detachment fosters a deeper connection with spirit and enables us to act with genuine compassion and a spirit of service.

Service, by its very nature, transcends the ego. When we serve others, we move beyond our self-centered concerns and focus on the needs of those around us. This shift in focus helps to quiet the ego and aligns us with the flow of universal love. Acts of service, no matter how small, are powerful tools for keeping the ego in check and reinforcing our connection to the spirit.

Mindfulness is another valuable practice for managing the ego. By staying present in the moment, we can observe our thoughts and feelings without becoming entangled in them. This practice helps us recognize when the ego is asserting itself and gently redirect our focus back to our higher intentions. Mindfulness cultivates a state of inner peace and clarity, making it easier to connect with the spirit and act from a place of love and service.

It's also essential to develop a sense of inner security and self-worth that is not reliant on external validation. When we depend on external achievements or approval for our sense of worth, we give the ego control over our happiness. Cultivating a strong sense of self-worth from within makes us less susceptible to the ego's demands and more aligned with our true purpose.

Incorporating practices such as meditation, journaling, and reflective contemplation can help us understand and manage the ego. These practices provide a space for introspection and self-exploration, allowing us to uncover the deeper motivations behind our actions and realign ourselves with our spiritual goals.

Ultimately, learning to manage the ego is an ongoing process. It requires patience, self-compassion, and a commitment to growth. As we develop this skill, we become more adept at setting the ego aside and allowing our true selves to shine through. This alignment with our higher selves fosters a deeper connection with spirit and enhances our ability to live a life of service.

The ego is an integral part of our human experience, but it must be understood and managed to facilitate our spiritual growth and service to others. By cultivating humility, practicing detachment, staying mindful, and developing inner security, we can learn to control the ego and set it aside when working with the spirit. This process allows us to live more authentically, connect more deeply with the universe, and make a meaningful impact on the world around us. Embracing this journey of managing the ego is crucial for anyone committed to living a life of spiritual depth and dedicated service.

Alex McCann Johnson

Chapter 7

Discerning Your Way Through It

As you deepen your connection with your spirit guides and begin to receive their messages more frequently, developing the ability to discern these messages becomes crucial. Discernment is the process of distinguishing between true spiritual guidance and other thoughts, feelings, or influences that might cloud your perception. It involves cultivating a keen sense of awareness and judgment to ensure that the guidance you follow is accurate, benevolent, and aligned with your highest good.

In the realm of spiritual communication, not all messages are created equal. Just as in everyday life, where we must evaluate the reliability of the information we receive, spiritual discernment is essential for navigating the guidance provided by your spirit guides. Discernment helps you to identify true guidance, ensuring that the messages you receive are from your authentic spirit guides and not influenced by your own subconscious fears, desires, or external energies. It also helps maintain spiritual integrity by adhering to guidance that promotes growth, healing, and positivity while preventing misunderstandings or misapplications that could lead to confusion or harm.

Developing discernment is an ongoing process that requires practice and self-awareness. Regular grounding and centering practices are foundational in this process. These practices help to clear your mind and connect you to the present moment. When you are grounded, you are less likely to be swayed by extraneous thoughts and more capable of receiving clear, authentic guidance. Grounding can be achieved through simple techniques like deep breathing, visualization, or spending time in nature. Centering yourself in the present moment also creates a stable platform from which you can evaluate the messages you receive.

Another key aspect of discernment is setting a clear intention before seeking guidance. This intention acts as a filter, aligning your energy with the type of guidance you seek and helping to attract messages that resonate with your true purpose. For example, you might set an intention to receive guidance on a particular area of your life or to connect with a specific type of spirit guide. Setting this intention helps to focus your energy and open you to the appropriate communication channels.

Understanding the role of the ego is crucial in the discernment process. The ego can sometimes interfere with spiritual communication by projecting fears, doubts, or desires onto the messages you receive. It's important to recognize when your ego is at play and to set it aside to allow for clearer, more authentic guidance. This doesn't mean suppressing the ego but rather acknowledging its presence and choosing to listen to the deeper, more intuitive aspects of your being. The ego often speaks with a voice of urgency or anxiety, while true spiritual guidance typically brings a sense of peace and clarity.

Paying attention to your emotional responses to messages is also important. True guidance from your spirit guides usually brings a sense of calm, clarity, and upliftment, even if the message itself is challenging. If a message evokes fear, confusion, or negativity, it may be influenced by other sources and require further evaluation. Reflect on how the guidance makes you feel at a deeper level. Genuine messages often resonate with a sense of inner truth and alignment, even if they challenge you to step out of your comfort zone.

Cross-referencing the guidance you receive with other known truths or experiences can be helpful when in doubt. Spirit guides often provide consistent messages that align with your overall spiritual path. If a new message contradicts previous guidance or established truths, it warrants closer scrutiny. Look for patterns and themes in the guidance you receive over time. True spiritual guidance tends to be coherent and aligned with the overarching principles of your life and growth.

Seeking confirmation is another effective practice. If you are uncertain about a message, ask your spirit guides for additional signs or messages to validate their guidance. Spirit guides understand the importance of clarity and are usually willing to provide further confirmation. This might come through repeated signs, synchronicities, or other forms of affirmation in your daily life. Pay attention to how these confirmations manifest and whether they reinforce the initial guidance.

Consulting trusted sources, such as a spiritual mentor or community, can provide valuable insights and help you discern the authenticity of a message. Be selective about who you consult, ensuring they have a strong track record of integrity and spiritual wisdom. Engaging with a supportive spiritual community can also offer different perspectives and deepen your understanding of the messages you receive.

In my own journey, discernment has been a vital skill I've had to develop through experience. There have been times when I received messages that felt conflicting or unclear. For example, I once received guidance that seemed to encourage a significant life change, but it brought a sense of unease. By taking time to ground myself, reflect on the message, and seek additional confirmation, I realized that the guidance was influenced by my own fears rather than my spirit guides. This process taught me to trust my intuition and take the necessary steps to ensure the clarity and authenticity of the guidance I follow.

Discernment is not a onetime skill to be mastered but a lifelong practice to be cultivated. As you continue to grow and evolve on your spiritual path, your ability to discern will deepen, enhancing your connection with your spirit guides and enriching your spiritual journey. Embrace discernment with an open heart and mind, and allow it to guide you towards greater clarity, wisdom, and alignment with your highest good. Remember, the journey of connecting with spirit guides is deeply personal and unique to each individual. Trust in your own abilities, be patient with yourself, and continue to seek the highest truth in all the guidance you receive. Your spirit guides are here to support you every step of the way, helping you navigate your path with confidence and clarity.

Discerning your way through the guidance from your spirit guides is a crucial part of your spiritual journey. It involves grounding yourself, setting clear intentions, understanding the ego's influence, and seeking confirmation and support when needed. By developing and practicing discernment, you ensure that the guidance you follow is truly aligned with your highest good and the path you are meant to walk. This ongoing practice not only strengthens your connection with your spirit guides but also enriches your life with wisdom, clarity, and a deeper understanding of your spiritual purpose.

Chapter 8
Spirit Guide Mediumship

I'm going to throw this out there: if you're reading this, chances are you're interested in learning more about connecting with your spiritual guides. Let me encourage you to take a deep dive into what I call spirit guide mediumship. You won't regret it. For a long time, I was focused on connecting with those who had passed, often overlooking the powerful presence of guides who are always here to help. Once I began to focus on spirit guide mediumship, it became clear that these beings are invaluable allies on our journey.

What Is Spirit Guide Mediumship?

Spirit guide mediumship involves connecting with spiritual guides who offer guidance, protection, and wisdom. Unlike traditional mediumship, which often focuses on communicating with departed loved ones, spirit guide mediumship centers on building relationships with higher beings dedicated to assisting us in our spiritual evolution. These guides can be from various realms, including angels, ascended masters, ancestors, and even galactic entities.

This practice is not about escaping the human experience but enriching it. Spirit guides are always ready to help us navigate life's challenges, provide insights into our purpose, and support our growth. By engaging in spirit guide mediumship, we open ourselves to a broader spectrum of spiritual assistance and deepen our understanding of our place in the universe.

Embracing the Journey of Spirit Guide Mediumship

Spirit guide mediumship is a transformative journey of building a connection with your spiritual allies. These guides are ever-present, ready to assist and support you in ways that are often beyond your immediate awareness. As you embark on this journey, you will discover that each guide brings a unique perspective and set of skills tailored to help you on your path.

For me, this journey has been about recognizing and honoring the diverse forms of guidance available to us. I've encountered spirit guides in many forms—some as ancestors who provide a sense of continuity and support, others as angelic beings offering protection and healing. Each guide has contributed to my growth in distinct ways, helping me to navigate different phases of my life.

Transformative Power of Spirit Guide Mediumship

Engaging with spirit guides through mediumship can transform your life. Here's how:

- Connection and Belonging: One of the most immediate benefits of spirit guide mediumship is the deep sense of connection it fosters. Knowing that you have a team of spiritual allies constantly supporting you can bring immense comfort and reassurance. This awareness is particularly comforting during challenging times, providing a sense of belonging and security.

- Enhanced Intuition and Awareness: Regularly connecting with your guides sharpens your intuition and heightens your spiritual awareness. You become more attuned to subtle energies and synchronicities, allowing you to navigate life with greater clarity. This enhanced awareness helps you make decisions that align with your highest good, leading to a more harmonious and fulfilling life.

- Healing and Wholeness: Spirit guides can facilitate healing. They offer perspectives that help you address and release emotional, mental, and spiritual blockages. This healing process can lead to greater self-acceptance and inner peace, allowing you to move forward with a sense of wholeness and freedom.

- Personal Growth and Self-Discovery: Spirit guides provide invaluable wisdom that aids in understanding your purpose, strengths, and potential. Their guidance helps you gain a clearer sense of direction and motivation to pursue your goals and dreams. Connecting with your guides can inspire you to explore new spiritual practices, expand your consciousness, and deepen your understanding of the universe.

- Enhanced Relationships: As you cultivate qualities like compassion, empathy, and understanding through your connection with spirit guides, these qualities naturally extend into your relationships with others. This leads to more meaningful, authentic, and harmonious interactions. Your guides can also provide insights on navigating interpersonal challenges, helping you communicate more effectively and resolve conflicts with greater ease.

Finding Your Primary Guides

Exploring Different Types of Guides

The journey to identifying your primary guides involves exploring the various types of guides and understanding which ones resonate most with you. Here's a brief overview of the different types of spirit guides you might encounter:

- **Spirit Guides:** Personal guides who offer tailored guidance and support throughout your spiritual journey. They often appear in forms that are significant or familiar to you, like that imaginary friend when you were younger that was your main spirit guide or child guide.

- **Angelic Guides**: Divine beings who provide unconditional love, protection, and healing. Angels are often associated with specific qualities, such as strength, wisdom, or compassion.

- **Animal Guides:** Working alongside the animal kingdom, these guides embody the characteristics and wisdom of different animals. They offer insights into your instincts, strengths, and challenges.

- **Nature and Elemental Guides:** Spirits connected to the natural world and the elements (earth, water, fire, air, and ether). They promote balance and grounding by helping you align with the rhythms of nature.

- **Ancestor Guides:** Spirits of those who have come before you, offering wisdom, protection, and a connection to your heritage. They help you understand and heal family patterns.

- **Deities:** Gods and goddesses from various pantheons provide powerful archetypal energy and guidance related to their domains, such as love, wisdom, or transformation.

- **Ascended Masters:** Enlightened beings who offer wisdom and teachings that transcend individual cultures and religions. They guide you towards higher states of consciousness and spiritual mastery.

- **Galactic Guides:** Extraterrestrial beings from various star systems and dimensions. They offer advanced knowledge, healing, and insights into the interconnectedness of the universe.

Trusting Your Resonance

As you explore different types of guides, pay attention to which ones you feel most drawn to. This resonance is a key indicator of your primary guides. Trust your intuition and the subtle nudges from your spirit. Your guides often communicate through feelings, thoughts, or signs that align with your deepest desires and aspirations.

For me, the journey of spirit guide mediumship has been about recognizing which guides resonate most with my soul's purpose.

Guided by Spirits

Whether it's the nurturing presence of an angelic guide, the grounded wisdom of an ancestor, or the advanced knowledge of a galactic being, each guide's energy offers something unique to my spiritual growth.

Spirit guide mediumship is an ongoing adventure filled with discovery, growth, and transformation. Embrace the journey with an open heart and mind. Be willing to explore and connect with the diverse array of guides available to you. Remember, each guide you encounter is a powerful ally ready to support you on your path.

As you continue to deepen your connection with your guides, you will find that their wisdom and guidance enrich your spiritual practice and help you navigate the complexities of your journey with greater clarity and grace. Trust in the process and allow your guides to lead you toward a more connected, purposeful, and enlightened existence.

Chapter 9

Back Yourself Up to the Basics

Spirit guide mediumship is an ancient practice that involves communicating with non-physical entities known as spirit guides. These guides are considered benevolent beings who offer wisdom, guidance, and support to individuals throughout their lives. The concept of spirit guides transcends cultures and religions, with each tradition having its own understanding and interpretation of these spiritual helpers. Going back to the basics of spirit guide mediumship involves understanding who these guides are, their roles, and the transformative impact they can have on our lives.

Spirit guides are often described as souls who have evolved beyond the need for physical incarnation. They exist in higher planes of consciousness, where they have access to universal knowledge. These guides come in various forms and may include ancestors, angels, ascended masters, nature spirits, and even animal spirits. Each type of guide brings its own unique energy and perspective, offering different kinds of support and guidance depending on the individual's needs and spiritual path.

The primary role of spirit guides is to assist us in our spiritual journey. They provide guidance on our life purpose, help us navigate challenges, and support our personal and spiritual growth. Spirit guides communicate through various means, including intuition, dreams, synchronicities, and inner knowing. While they may not always provide direct answers, their influence can help us gain clarity and make decisions that align with our highest good.

One of the most fundamental aspects of spirit guide mediumship is the recognition that we are never alone. From birth to death and even beyond, our spirit guides are with us, offering their support and love. This constant companionship can be a source of immense comfort, particularly during times of uncertainty and difficulty. Knowing that we have spiritual allies who are dedicated to our well-being can foster a sense of security and inner peace.

Spirit guides also play a crucial role in helping us develop our intuition and spiritual awareness. By tuning into their guidance, we can enhance our ability to perceive and interpret subtle energies and messages. This heightened sensitivity can lead to greater self-awareness and a deeper connection with the divine. Over time, we may find that our intuition becomes a reliable source of guidance in our daily lives, helping us to navigate our path with confidence and clarity.

Another essential function of spirit guides is to facilitate healing. They can assist us in addressing and releasing emotional, mental, and spiritual blockages that hinder our growth. Through their support, we can gain a deeper understanding of our wounds and traumas, allowing us to heal and move forward. This healing process often involves confronting and integrating aspects of ourselves that we may have suppressed or ignored. By doing so, we can achieve a greater sense of wholeness and inner harmony.

Spirit guides also help us understand and embrace our life purpose. They provide guidance on our unique gifts and talents, encouraging us to pursue paths that align with our soul's mission. This sense of purpose can be incredibly empowering, giving us the motivation and direction needed to achieve our goals. As we align with our true calling, we may find that our lives become more fulfilling and meaningful.

Furthermore, spirit guides can offer valuable insights into our relationships. They help us navigate the complexities of human connections, offering guidance on how to communicate effectively, resolve conflicts, and build harmonious relationships. By fostering compassion and empathy, our guides can enhance our interactions with others, leading to more authentic and supportive connections.

Guided by Spirits

In addition to their guidance and support, spirit guides can also inspire us to explore new spiritual practices and expand our consciousness. Their influence can lead us to discover different modalities of healing, meditation, and self-discovery, enriching our spiritual journey. This exploration can open us up to new perspectives and experiences, deepening our understanding of ourselves and the universe.

The transformative impact of spirit-guide mediumship cannot be overstated. By developing a relationship with our spirit guides, we can experience personal and spiritual growth. Their wisdom can help us navigate the challenges of life with greater ease and grace, fostering a sense of purpose and inner peace. Through their guidance, we can achieve healing, clarity, and a deeper connection with the divine.

In my personal understanding, spirit guide mediumship is a deeply empowering practice that offers invaluable guidance throughout our lives. By understanding who these guides are and the roles they play, we can begin to appreciate the impact they have on our spiritual journey. Whether through providing guidance, facilitating healing, or inspiring personal growth, spirit guides are ever-present allies dedicated to helping us realize our highest potential. Embracing their presence and wisdom can lead to a more connected, purposeful, and enlightened existence.

Alex McCann Johnson

Chapter 10

Religion vs. Spirituality

Religion and spirituality are two distinct yet interwoven paths that people often explore in their quest to understand the divine and connect with a higher power. Each path offers unique approaches, practices, and experiences that cater to different aspects of the human need for meaning, purpose, and connection. As you embark on your spiritual journey, understanding the differences and similarities between religion and spirituality can help you navigate these paths and find what resonates most deeply with your soul.

Religion: Structure and Community

Religion is typically defined by its structured framework, which includes organized institutions, established doctrines, and communal practices. It provides a systematic way of worship, moral guidance, and a sense of belonging to a larger community. Many people find comfort in the rituals, teachings, and traditions that religions offer, as they provide stability and a connection to a long-standing heritage.

For example, attending regular services, participating in sacraments, or following a liturgical calendar are all aspects of religious practice that help individuals feel part of something larger than themselves. These communal experiences reinforce shared beliefs and values, creating a sense of unity and continuity among followers. Religion also often offers clear guidelines on how to live a righteous life, addressing moral and ethical questions with prescribed teachings and rules.

However, the structured nature of religion can sometimes feel restrictive to those who seek a more personal or fluid approach to the divine. The doctrines and dogmas may not always align with individual experiences or evolving personal beliefs. Yet, for many, the community, shared rituals, and the sense of connection to something greater than oneself provide profound meaning and fulfillment.

Spirituality: Personal and Transformative

In contrast, spirituality is more individualized and less confined by structures. It emphasizes a personal connection with the divine, seeking direct experiences and inner transformation. Spirituality is often seen as a journey of self-discovery and enlightenment, where individuals explore their inner world, seek higher consciousness, and cultivate a personal relationship with spirit guides, the universe, or a higher power.

Spirituality encourages flexibility and personal freedom, allowing individuals to tailor their practices to their unique experiences and inner callings. This might involve meditation, yoga, mindfulness, or any number of personal rituals that foster a deep sense of connection and inner peace. Spiritual seekers often pursue their path through introspection, seeking direct encounters with the divine rather than adhering to established doctrines.

The appeal of spirituality lies in its adaptability and personal relevance. It allows for a dynamic and evolving relationship with the divine that can change as one's understanding and experiences grow. However, this freedom can also pose challenges, such as the absence of communal support or clear guidelines that are typically found in religious frameworks.

The Intersection of Religion and Spirituality

Despite their differences, religion and spirituality often intersect and complement each other. Many people find themselves drawn to elements of both, creating a hybrid approach that incorporates structured practices with personal, transformative experiences. This blend allows individuals to enjoy the stability and community offered by religion while embracing the personal growth and direct connection provided by spirituality.

For instance, one might regularly attend church services for communal worship while also practicing meditation or mindfulness to cultivate a personal relationship with the divine. This integration can lead to a richer and more fulfilling spiritual life, balancing the external practices of religion with the internal journey of spirituality.

Embracing Your Unique Path

As you explore your spiritual path, it's essential to recognize that both religion and spirituality have their unique strengths. Religion can offer a strong community, shared beliefs, and a collective experience of the divine. It provides established practices that can help guide your spiritual development and offer a sense of belonging. On the other hand, spirituality offers flexibility, personal freedom, and the opportunity to tailor your practices to your unique experiences and inner calling.

Reflect on your background and experiences, including any religious upbringing you may have had. This conditioning shapes how you perceive and engage with the divine. Embracing your history, whether it includes religious practices or not, can provide a foundation for your spiritual growth.

One of the most beautiful aspects of exploring spirituality is the realization that it's okay to create a belief system that resonates with you. Whether you attend church every Sunday, practice meditation daily, or blend various practices from different traditions, your spiritual path is uniquely yours. What matters most is your intention and the authenticity of your connection with the divine.

The Role of Faith and Intention

Faith is a powerful element that both religion and spirituality share. It's the trust and belief in something greater than yourself. This faith can be a guiding force, providing strength, comfort, and direction in your life. Whether your faith is rooted in religious teachings or personal spiritual experiences, it can be a source of inspiration and growth.

Connecting with spirit guides and loving beings transcends religious boundaries. These connections are about opening your heart and mind to the higher frequencies of love, wisdom, and guidance that the universe offers. Spirit encourages us to connect deeply and recognize the divine presence in all aspects of life, whether through religious practices, spiritual exploration, or both.

Intention plays a crucial role in your spiritual journey. Your intention shapes your experiences and interactions with the divine. When you intend to connect deeply, seek truth, and grow spiritually, you align yourself with higher energies supporting your journey. Whether your practices are religious or spiritual, what matters is the sincerity and purity of your intention.

Respecting Diverse Paths

In my experience, I have encountered individuals from various belief systems, each finding power and meaning in their faith. Some find solace and guidance within the structure of religion, while others thrive in the freedom of spirituality. Both paths can lead to profound experiences of the divine and deep inner transformation.

It's also important to respect and honor the paths of others. Everyone's journey is unique; what resonates deeply with one person might not be for another. By embracing a mindset of openness and respect, we can learn from each other and expand our understanding of the divine.

Navigating the interplay between religion and spirituality is a personal journey. There is no right or wrong path, only what feels true and resonant for you. Whether you find your connection to the divine through religious practices, personal spiritual exploration, or a blend of both, what matters most is your intention, authenticity, and the love and wisdom you cultivate along the way.

Embrace your journey with an open heart, trust in your inner guidance, and allow yourself the freedom to explore and grow. Your connection with the divine is uniquely yours, and as you deepen this connection, you contribute to the collective awakening and the greater good of all beings. Each step you take, whether through the structured rituals of religion or the expansive journey of spirituality, brings you closer to the divine essence within and around you.

Alex McCann Johnson

Chapter 11
Major Religions Today

The world is a mosaic of diverse religious beliefs, each offering a unique lens through which to understand spirituality, morality, and the purpose of life. Major religions significantly influence their followers' cultural and spiritual lives, offering guidelines for daily living and ways to connect with the divine. This chapter examines the core beliefs and practices of eight influential religions in contemporary society.

Christianity

Christianity, the world's largest religion, with over two billion adherents, is centered on the life and teachings of Jesus Christ. Christians believe Jesus is the Son of God and the Savior of humanity, whose life and resurrection offer salvation to all who believe. The core tenets of Christianity include the belief in the Trinity—God as Father, Son, and Holy Spirit—and the importance of the Bible, consisting of the Old and New Testaments, as sacred scripture.

Christian practices vary widely but commonly include worship services, prayer, sacraments such as baptism and communion, and the observance of significant religious holidays like Christmas and Easter. Christian communities emphasize living according to the teachings of Jesus, which stress love, compassion, forgiveness, and service to others.

Islam

Islam, the second-largest religion with over 1.8 billion followers, is based on the belief in one God, Allah, and the teachings of the Prophet Muhammad, who is regarded as the last prophet in a line that includes figures like Abraham, Moses, and Jesus. The Quran, Islam's holy book, and the Hadith, collections of Muhammad's sayings and actions, form the basis of Islamic teachings and law.

Muslims follow the Five Pillars of Islam, which guide their faith and practices: Shahada (declaration of faith), Salah (prayer five times a day), Zakat (almsgiving), Sawm (fasting during Ramadan), and Hajj (pilgrimage to Mecca). These pillars are fundamental to Muslim life, emphasizing the importance of devotion, charity, and self-discipline.

Hinduism

Hinduism, with over a billion adherents, is one of the oldest religions and is characterized by a rich tapestry of beliefs and practices. It has no single founder and encompasses a wide variety of traditions and philosophies. Key texts include the Vedas and Upanishads, which provide spiritual insights and guidance.

Central to Hindu belief are the concepts of Dharma (duty/ethics), Karma (the law of cause and effect), Samsara (the cycle of rebirth), and Moksha (liberation from the cycle of rebirth). Hindus worship multiple deities, each representing different aspects of the divine, with prominent gods including Brahma, Vishnu, and Shiva. Practices often include rituals, meditation, yoga, and pilgrimages to sacred sites.

Buddhism

Founded by Siddhartha Gautama, known as the Buddha, in the 5th century BCE, Buddhism has over 500 million followers. It teaches the Four Noble Truths: the reality of suffering (Dukkha), the cause of suffering (Tanha or craving), the cessation of suffering (Nirvana), and the path leading to the end of suffering (the Eightfold Path).

The Eightfold Path encompasses the right understanding, intention, speech, action, livelihood, effort, mindfulness, and concentration. Buddhists practice meditation and mindfulness to cultivate wisdom and compassion and aim to achieve enlightenment by overcoming desire and ignorance. Buddhism also emphasizes ethical living and the development of moral virtues.

Judaism

Judaism, with about 14 million adherents, is one of the oldest monotheistic religions. It is based on the belief in one God and the teachings of the Torah, the first five books of the Hebrew Bible. Jews view their relationship with God as a covenant, emphasizing justice, morality, and ethical behavior.

Key practices include observing the Sabbath, following dietary laws (Kashrut), prayer, and participating in rituals associated with life events and Jewish festivals. The Talmud, a comprehensive compilation of rabbinic teachings and interpretations, provides further guidance on Jewish law and tradition. Jewish life is deeply rooted in community and the observance of commandments that foster a righteous and ethical way of living.

Sikhism

Sikhism, founded by Guru Nanak in the 15th century in Punjab, India, has around 25 million followers. Sikhs believe in one God and follow the teachings of the ten Sikh Gurus, compiled in the Guru Granth Sahib, their central religious scripture. The core principles of Sikhism include the equality of all people, selfless service (Seva), and devotion to God through prayer and honest living.

Sikhs practice daily prayers, meditate on God's name (Naam Japna), and engage in community service. They also adhere to the Five Ks—Kesh (uncut hair), Kara (steel bracelet), Kanga (wooden comb), Kachera (cotton undergarment), and Kirpan (ceremonial sword)—which are physical symbols of their faith and commitment.

Bahá'í Faith

The Bahá'í Faith, established in the 19th century by Bahá'u'lláh, has over seven million adherents. Bahá'ís believe in the unity of all religions and the oneness of humanity, viewing Bahá'u'lláh as the latest in a line of divine messengers that includes Abraham, Moses, Buddha, Jesus, and Muhammad.

The Bahá'í Faith emphasizes principles such as the elimination of prejudice, the equality of men and women, universal education, and the harmony of science and religion. Bahá'ís practice daily prayer and meditation and actively participate in community-building activities that promote social justice and unity.

Taoism

Taoism, originating in China, is both a religious and philosophical tradition with millions of followers. It is based on the teachings of Laozi, as encapsulated in the Tao Te Ching, and emphasizes living in harmony with the Tao (the Way), which represents the fundamental essence and natural order of the universe.

Key Taoist concepts include Wu Wei (effortless action), simplicity, and alignment with nature. Taoist practices often involve meditation, Tai Chi, and rituals that promote spiritual and physical well-being, aiming to cultivate balance and harmony within oneself and with the world.

Diversity of Beliefs

The diversity of religious beliefs and practices across the globe highlights the myriad ways in which humans seek to understand and connect with the divine. Each of these major religions provides a unique path to spiritual fulfillment and offers insights into the nature of existence and our place within the universe. Whether through the structured rituals of organized religion or the personal exploration of spirituality, the quest for meaning, purpose, and connection to a higher power is a universal aspect of the human experience. By learning about and respecting different religious traditions, we can foster greater understanding, tolerance, and unity in our global community, enriching our own spiritual journeys in the process.

Chapter 12
Spirit Guides in Major Religions

Spirit guides are mystical beings that provide wisdom, support, and guidance to individuals on their spiritual paths. While not all religions explicitly mention the term "spirit guides," many faiths acknowledge the presence of spiritual beings who assist and guide humanity. These guides come in various forms—angels, deities, enlightened beings, or revered ancestors—and their roles vary across different religious traditions. Understanding how spirit guides function within various religions can offer deeper insights into the universal nature of spiritual support and guidance.

Christianity

In Christianity, the concept of spirit guides is closely linked to angels and saints. Angels are seen as messengers and servants of God who provide protection, guidance, and comfort to believers. The Bible recounts numerous instances where angels intervened in human affairs, such as the angel Gabriel announcing the birth of Jesus to Mary. Many Christians believe in guardian angels, who are assigned to protect and guide individuals throughout their lives.

Saints, who are venerated for their holy lives and miracles, also act as intercessors and guides. Christians often pray to saints for their intercession and guidance, believing that these holy figures can help them align their lives with God's will. For example, Saint Anthony is called upon to help find lost items, and Saint Jude is invoked in desperate situations. Through prayer and devotion, Christians seek to connect with these spiritual beings to receive their guidance and support.

Islam

In Islam, spirit guides are associated with angels (Mala'ika) and the prophets. Angels in Islam are created by Allah to perform various tasks, such as delivering messages, protecting individuals, and recording human deeds. Each person is believed to have two guardian angels who record their good and bad actions. The Quran and Hadith frequently mention angels, such as the archangel Gabriel (Jibril), who is known for delivering revelations to the Prophet Muhammad.

The prophets, especially Muhammad, are also seen as guides who provide a model for righteous living. Muslims seek guidance through prayer (Salah), supplication (Dua), and reading the Quran, often asking for the intercession of these holy figures to help them stay on the path of righteousness and faith.

Hinduism

Hinduism, with its rich pantheon of deities, offers a multitude of spiritual guides. Deities such as Vishnu, Shiva, and Lakshmi are invoked for their wisdom, protection, and guidance. Each deity represents different aspects of the divine and offers unique support depending on the worshiper's needs. For example, Ganesha is called upon to remove obstacles, while Saraswati is invoked for wisdom and learning.

In addition to deities, Hinduism also honors gurus (spiritual teachers) and ancestral spirits as guides. Gurus play a crucial role in imparting spiritual wisdom and guiding disciples on their paths. Ancestors, revered through rituals and ceremonies, are believed to continue offering support and blessings. Hindus seek the guidance of these spiritual beings through devotion (Bhakti), meditation, and various rituals that connect them to the divine.

Buddhism

In Buddhism, spirit guides are often viewed as enlightened beings, such as Buddhas and Bodhisattvas, who assist others on the path to enlightenment. Bodhisattvas, like Avalokiteshvara (the Bodhisattva of Compassion), are beings who have attained enlightenment but choose to remain in the cycle of rebirth to help all sentient beings achieve liberation.

The teachings of the historical Buddha, Siddhartha Gautama, serve as a foundational guide for Buddhists. His insights into the nature of suffering and the path to enlightenment provide a roadmap for spiritual practice. Buddhists connect with these enlightened beings through meditation, chanting, and studying sacred texts, seeking their wisdom to cultivate compassion, mindfulness, and insight.

Judaism

In Judaism, spirit guides are often associated with angels (Mal'akhim) and revered ancestors. Angels in Jewish tradition are seen as messengers of God who deliver divine messages and provide protection. The Hebrew Bible describes many angelic encounters, such as Jacob wrestling with an angel and the angel Gabriel's messages to Daniel.

Revered ancestors, such as the patriarchs Abraham, Isaac, and Jacob, are considered spiritual guides whose stories and teachings offer wisdom and moral direction. Jewish tradition emphasizes learning from the examples set by these figures and seeking guidance through prayer, the study of the Torah, and observance of mitzvot (commandments).

Sikhism

In Sikhism, the primary spiritual guides are the ten Sikh Gurus and the Guru Granth Sahib, the central religious scripture. The Gurus, especially Guru Nanak, the founder of Sikhism, provide spiritual teachings that guide Sikhs in living a life of righteousness, equality, and devotion.

The Guru Granth Sahib is considered the eternal living Guru, offering guidance through its hymns and teachings. Sikhs engage with this sacred text by reading, singing, and reflecting on its verses. Practices such as attending Gurdwara services, performing Seva (selfless service), and meditating on God's name (Naam Japna) are ways Sikhs connect with their spiritual guides.

Bahá'í Faith

In the Bahá'í Faith, the Manifestations of God, including Bahá'u'lláh, the Báb, and other recognized prophets, serve as the primary spiritual guides. These Manifestations are believed to reveal divine teachings suited to the needs of humanity at different times and places, guiding spiritual and moral development.

Bahá'ís seek guidance from the writings of Bahá'u'lláh and other central figures, engaging in prayer, meditation, and community-building activities to align their lives with the principles of unity, justice, and service to humanity.

Taoism

Taoism recognizes various spiritual guides, including immortals (Xian) and deities who embody the principles of the Tao (the Way). Laozi, the author of the Tao Te Ching, is revered as a spiritual guide whose teachings promote harmony with the natural order of the universe.

Taoists also honor deities like the Jade Emperor and the Eight Immortals, who offer protection and wisdom. Practices such as meditation, Tai Chi, and rituals that align with the Tao help Taoists connect with these guides and cultivate balance and spiritual health.

The Common Thread

Spirit guides are a common thread across many of the world's major religions, providing a source of wisdom, protection, and support. Whether they are seen as angels, deities, enlightened beings, or revered ancestors, these guides play a vital role in helping individuals navigate their spiritual journeys. Understanding the role of spirit guides in different religious traditions can deepen our appreciation for the diverse ways people connect with the divine. By honoring these guides and seeking their wisdom, we can enrich our own spiritual practices and foster a greater sense of connection with the universal forces that transcend cultural and religious boundaries.

Alex McCann Johnson

Chapter 13

Guides of All Types: Exploring the Rich Diversity of Spirit Guides

When I first embarked on my journey into the world of mediumship, my initial focus was on connecting people with their departed loved ones. Like many, I was drawn to the idea of bridging the gap between this world and the next, helping someone connect with a beloved relative like "Betty's aunt." However, as I delved deeper, I discovered a vast, under-explored realm within mediumship—spirit guide mediumship. It was here that I found my true calling. When I began receiving messages from guides, my entire perspective shifted. I realized these guides could offer insights and support, not just for the individuals I was reading for, but for my own spiritual growth as well. This discovery marked the beginning of an epic journey into the diverse world of spirit guides.

This book is designed to be your gateway into this expansive domain. As you read through the following chapters, you will encounter a wide variety of guides, each with unique characteristics, roles, and ways of assisting us on our spiritual paths. The main categories we will explore include Spirit Guides, Angelic Guides, Animal Guides, Nature and Elemental Guides, Ancestor Guides, Ascended Masters, Deities, and Galactic Guides. Each of these categories contains numerous subcategories, and it's important to remember that there are likely many more types of guides beyond what we can cover here.

Spirit Guides

Spirit Guides are perhaps the most familiar type of guide. These non-physical entities assist us throughout our earthly journey, offering guidance, support, and wisdom tailored to our specific needs. They come in many forms, each serving a unique purpose in our lives.

- Life Guides are with us from birth until death, providing consistent support and direction. They help us navigate the complexities of life and grow from our experiences.

- Gatekeepers protect us from negative energies and manage our interactions with the spiritual realm, ensuring our spiritual experiences are safe and positive.

- Akashic Guides assist us in accessing the Akashic Records, a vast compendium of all universal events and experiences. They help us understand our soul's journey and the lessons we are here to learn.

- Child Guides bring a playful, innocent energy into our lives, helping us reconnect with our inner child and find joy in the everyday.

- Learning Guides are focused on our personal growth, aiding us in acquiring new knowledge and skills throughout our lives.

These guides can appear at different times depending on what we need, and their guidance can profoundly impact our personal and spiritual development.

Angelic Guides

Angelic Guides are divine beings from the spiritual realm who offer protection, comfort, and guidance. They encompass various types of angels, each with specific roles and attributes.

- Archangels, such as Michael, Raphael, and Gabriel, are known for their immense power and authority. They oversee large groups of angels and provide significant assistance in times of need.

- Guardian Angels are assigned to individuals, offering personal protection and guidance throughout their lives.

- Cherubim is associated with wisdom and divine knowledge, often assisting us in understanding deeper spiritual truths.

- Seraphim are beings of purity, believed to be closest to the divine source, radiating love and light.

Angelic Guides are often called upon in moments of crisis or when we seek divine intervention. Their presence can be incredibly comforting and reassuring.

Animal Guides

Animal Guides, also known as spirit animals, power animals, or totem animals, connect us to the natural world and bring the wisdom of the animal kingdom into our spiritual journeys. Each animal guide embodies specific attributes and lessons that can teach us about ourselves and help us harness particular strengths.

- A wolf might symbolize strength, loyalty, and intuition.

- An eagle could represent vision, freedom, and a higher perspective.

- A bear might bring lessons of strength and introspection.

- A deer could teach gentleness and intuition.

Animal guides often appear in our lives when their particular qualities are needed. By observing and learning from these animals, we can gain valuable insights and grow in our personal and spiritual lives.

Nature and Elemental Guides

Nature and Elemental Guides are spirits connected to the natural world and the elements of earth, air, fire, and water. These include beings like faeries, mermaids, nymphs, trolls, gnomes, sylphs, salamanders, sprites, and dryads. They offer insight into the natural rhythms and energies that influence our lives.

- Faeries are known for their playful, sometimes mischievous nature, helping us see the magic in everyday life.

- Mermaids connect us with the emotional depths of the water element, offering guidance on emotional healing and intuition.

- Nymphs and dryads are associated with trees and forests, providing wisdom about growth, stability, and connection to nature.

- Sylphs are air spirits that bring clarity, communication, and inspiration.

- Salamanders are fire spirits linked to transformation, passion, and creativity.

These guides can help us attune to the natural world and understand the elemental forces that shape our existence.

Ancestor Guides

Ancestor Guides are the spirits of those who have come before us, both within our direct lineage and from the broader human collective. They offer the wisdom and experiences of the past, helping us understand our roots and guiding us through familial and cultural challenges.

- Direct ancestors are family members from our lineage, providing support based on shared heritage and experiences.

- Indirect ancestors may not be related by blood but are connected through cultural or spiritual lineage, offering guidance rooted in shared traditions.

- Spiritual ancestors are those who have contributed to our spiritual path, often revered teachers or figures who have influenced our beliefs.

- Past life ancestors are those with whom we have shared previous lifetimes, bringing lessons and wisdom from those experiences.

Connecting with ancestor guides can provide insights into our personal and collective histories, helping us navigate our present challenges with the wisdom of the past.

Ascended Masters

Ascended Masters are enlightened beings who have transcended the physical plane and now offer their wisdom and guidance to humanity. They include well-known figures such as Jesus, Buddha, Saint Germain, and Kuan Yin. Each brings unique teachings and qualities that can aid in our spiritual growth and healing.

- Jesus teaches lessons in unconditional love, forgiveness, and compassion.

- Buddha guides us on the path to enlightenment, detachment, and inner peace.

- Saint Germain is associated with transformation, alchemy, and the Violet Flame of spiritual purification.

- Kuan Yin embodies compassion, mercy, and the power of nurturing and healing.

Ascended Masters often appear when we are ready to take significant steps in our spiritual evolution, offering insights and support.

Deities

Deities are divine entities from various cultural and religious pantheons around the world. They include gods and goddesses from traditions such as Hindu, Greek, Roman, Norse, Celtic, Egyptian, Native American, African Yoruba, Japanese Shinto, Chinese, Australian Aboriginal, Peruvian, and Philippine.

- Hindu deities like Shiva and Lakshmi offer teachings on destruction and renewal, as well as abundance and prosperity.

- Greek gods such as Zeus and Athena provide insights into leadership and wisdom.

- Norse deities like Odin and Freya guide us in matters of war, love, and spiritual insight.

Each pantheon offers a rich tapestry of divine energies to explore, with each deity bringing specific attributes and lessons that can help us connect with the divine in its many forms.

Galactic Guides

Galactic Guides are beings from other realms and dimensions, often associated with extraterrestrial intelligence. They include entities such as Arcturians, Pleiadians, Sirians, Andromedans, Orions, Lyrans, Vegans, Zetas, Blue Avians, Reptilians, and Cosmic Masters. These guides help us understand our connection to the broader universe and offer insights into the cosmic aspects of our existence.

- Arcturians are known for their advanced technology and deep spiritual wisdom.

- Pleiadians teach about love, healing, and the harmonious mind and spirit integration.

- Sirians bring ancient knowledge and star wisdom, often associated with deep cosmic mysteries.

These guides expand our understanding of the universe and our place within it, offering unique perspectives that can greatly enhance our spiritual journey.

Exploring and Connecting with Guides

As you journey through this book, you will delve into each of these categories in detail. Each chapter is crafted to help you understand and connect with different types of guides. I encourage you to try engaging with each type as you explore the chapters. Each guide offers unique insights and assistance, enriching your spiritual path in distinct ways.

Embrace their connections and allow them to support your spiritual growth. If you find it challenging to connect with a particular type of guide or if understanding them feels difficult, that's perfectly okay. Each person's spiritual journey is unique, and it's natural to resonate more with certain guides than others. Feel free to revisit chapters later or skip sections that don't resonate with you at the moment.

This book is your introduction to the many types of guides available to you. It provides a foundation upon which you can build your practice and deepen your connection with the spiritual realm. Remember, the relationship with your guides is personal and ever-evolving. As you grow, so too will your connections with them. Stay open, curious, and patient, and you will uncover the profound support and wisdom these guides offer.

May your journey with your guides be filled with light, love, and endless discovery.

Alex McCann Johnson

Spirit Guides

Alex McCann Johnson

Chapter 14

Spirit Guides: A Journery of Connection and Discovery

Welcome to a journey that has profoundly changed my life and has the potential to transform yours as well. The world of spirit guides is rich with wisdom, support, and unseen connections that can enhance our everyday experiences and spiritual growth. My path to discovering and connecting with spirit guides began with curiosity and a desire for deeper understanding. Over time, I've come to realize that these guides are always with us, ready to assist, guide, and protect. At first, I might have mistaken them for the spirits of departed loved ones, but I soon learned that spirit guides and deceased relatives serve different roles in our lives.

Spirit guides are not a new concept. Various cultures and traditions throughout history have recognized and revered these benevolent beings. They are often seen as messengers, protectors, and teachers who offer guidance from the spiritual realm. Their roles can vary widely, and they may present themselves in different forms, but their ultimate purpose is to support our journey through life.

Connecting with spirit guides can be a personal and rewarding experience. It's a relationship that requires openness, trust, and a willingness to explore the unknown. In my experience, spirit guides communicate in subtle ways—through signs, symbols, dreams, and intuitive feelings. Recognizing and interpreting these messages has been a key part of my spiritual practice.

The journey to understanding and connecting with spirit guides involves patience and practice. It's about tuning into your intuition, being mindful of the signs around you, and maintaining an open heart and mind. Each guide has a unique way of communicating and a specific role to play in our lives. Some may help with daily challenges, while others offer spiritual insights or protection.

Types of Spirit Guides

Throughout this journey, I have encountered various types of spirit guides, each with distinct characteristics and purposes.

Life Guides: Life guides assist with our life's journey, offering wisdom and direction. They provide insight into our life path and help us make decisions that align with our highest good.

Gatekeepers: Gatekeepers protect our spiritual gateway, ensuring that only positive influences enter our energy field. They serve as a shield against negative energies and unwanted spiritual interference.

Akashic Guides: Akashic guides help us access the Akashic Records, a repository of all knowledge and experiences. These guides assist us in understanding our soul's journey and the lessons we are meant to learn in this lifetime.

Child Guides: Child guides bring joy and innocence, reminding us of the importance of play and creativity. They encourage us to embrace our inner child and find delight in the simple pleasures of life.

Learning Guides: Learning guides support our growth and the acquisition of new skills and knowledge. They help us navigate our educational pursuits and encourage continuous learning and development.

Shadow Guides: Shadow guides help us confront and integrate our shadow aspects, those parts of ourselves that we might reject or hide. They assist us in understanding and healing deep-seated fears, traumas, and negative patterns.

Building a Relationship with Spirit Guides

Building a relationship with your spirit guides is an ongoing process. It requires dedication, respect, and gratitude. Regular meditation, setting clear intentions, and creating a sacred space can significantly enhance this connection. Over time, this relationship can bring about changes, offering clarity, support, and a deeper sense of purpose.

Meditation: Regular meditation helps to quiet the mind and open your awareness to the presence of your guides. It creates a space for communication and allows you to receive messages more clearly.

Setting Intentions: Setting clear intentions signals to your guides that you are open to their guidance. Whether you seek advice on a specific issue or general support, clearly stating your intention can facilitate a stronger connection.

Creating a Sacred Space: A sacred space is a designated area where you can focus on your spiritual practice. It can be a corner of a room, an altar, or any space where you feel comfortable and at peace. This space helps to create a conducive environment for connecting with your guides.

When I first started this work, my focus was on mediumship, primarily connecting people with their departed loved ones. However, I soon discovered a whole underutilized field—spirit guide mediumship. When I began receiving messages from guides, everything changed for me. I found my niche.

I remember the initial stages of my journey when the idea of spirit guides was both exciting and intimidating. The first time I consciously connected with a guide was through a meditative practice. I set a clear intention, asking for guidance on a personal matter. During the meditation, I felt a gentle presence and received a vivid image of an older man with kind eyes. He conveyed a sense of peace and offered simple but needed advice. This experience was a turning point, affirming that I was not alone and that these guides were ready to assist me.

Over the years, I have developed a deeper relationship with my spirit guides. I have learned to trust their guidance, even when it challenges my understanding or comfort zone. There have been times when the messages were subtle and required me to pay close attention to my surroundings and inner feelings. Other times, the guidance was clear and direct, providing immediate clarity and support.

One particularly memorable experience involved a life guide who appeared during a difficult period. I was struggling with a major life decision and felt overwhelmed by the choices before me. Through meditation, I connected with this guide, who presented a vision of a path lined with bright lights. The message was to follow the lighted path, symbolizing the direction that aligned with my highest good. This guidance gave me the confidence to make a decision that ultimately led to significant positive changes in my life, the very life of becoming a guiding light you see now.

As you embark on your own journey to connect with spirit guides, remember that it's a unique experience. There is no right or wrong way to do it; you can only do what feels right for you. Embrace the process with an open heart and a curious mind, and be prepared to be amazed by the wisdom and guidance that these spiritual beings can offer.

Welcome to the world of spirit guides. May your journey be filled with wonder, discovery, and profound connection. Stay open, curious, and patient, and you will discover the profound support and wisdom that these guides offer.

Chapter 15

Overview of Spirit Guides

Spirit guides are ethereal beings existing in the spiritual realm, dedicated to assisting us on our earthly journey. These guides are not limited by physical form and can manifest in various ways, often appearing as human figures, animals, or even pure energy. Their primary purpose is to support our spiritual growth, provide guidance, and offer protection throughout our lives. We often have multiple spirit guides at any given time, forming a kind of a spiritual entourage that we might not even be aware of. If you have the gift of clairvoyance, you might see them accompanying you, silently guiding and protecting.

Some spirit guides are with us for specific moments or periods in our lives. They may appear during challenging times or significant transitions and leave once their guidance is no longer needed. For example, a guide might come to support you during a hospital stay or a traumatic event and depart once you have recovered. Similarly, some guides are linked to particular relationships or jobs, and they move on when those phases end. You might have a heartbreak guide who appears during a difficult breakup, helping you heal, and then leaves once you have mended.

Most of us have at least one guide who remains with us throughout our entire lives. These lifelong guides provide ongoing support, helping to highlight our talents, guide us toward our purpose, and offer light during our darkest moments. Occasionally, as we grow and evolve, we may outgrow our original guide and welcome a new one, much like transitioning from one mentor to another as our needs and circumstances change.

While spirit guides can offer insights and guidance, the ultimate choice to follow their advice rests with us. They respect our free will and understand that we must make our own decisions. This dynamic underscores the importance of setting intentions and boundaries in our relationship with our guides. If you feel the need for a new guide or wish to release one, you have the power to call in or let go of these spiritual allies.

What Are Spirit Guides?

Spirit guides are likewise friends with a deep understanding of our souls and life paths. They can see beyond the physical realm, offering insights that help us navigate life's challenges and celebrate our victories. Their guidance is often subtle, delivered through signs, symbols, dreams, and intuitive feelings. Recognizing and interpreting these messages is a vital part of building a relationship with them.

Spirit guides are not confined to anyone's form and can appear in ways that resonate most deeply with us. They might manifest as a person, an animal, or simply a presence or energy that we feel. Regardless of their form, their ultimate goal is to help us align with our higher purpose and navigate our lives with greater clarity and wisdom.

Historical and Cultural Perspectives

The concept of spirit guides is universal, with roots in various cultures and traditions throughout history. Indigenous cultures frequently honor animal guides or totems, believing that these spirits embody the wisdom and strength of the animal kingdom. In ancient Greece, the idea of a 'daemon' closely resembles personal guardian spirits that provide inspiration and protection. Christianity introduces the concept of guardian angels, divine beings assigned to protect and guide individuals throughout their lives.

Despite the different names and attributes, the core belief remains consistent across cultures: spirit guides are here to help us. They serve as intermediaries between the physical and spiritual worlds, ensuring we receive the guidance and support needed to fulfill our life's purpose.

The Multifaceted Role of Spirit Guides

Spirit guides play diverse roles in our lives, acting as mentors, protectors, and healers. Their guidance can manifest in various ways, from intuitive nudges and vivid dreams to seemingly coincidental events that provide clarity and direction.

Guidance: One of the primary roles of spirit guides is to offer guidance. This can come in the form of subtle suggestions, intuitive feelings, or through more direct messages during meditation or dreams. They might also communicate through synchronicities—those moments of perfect timing that feel too significant to be mere coincidence.

Protection: Spirit guides also serve as protectors, guarding us against negative energies and influences. This protective aspect can be especially comforting in challenging situations or environments. Calling on your guides for protection can provide a sense of peace and security, knowing that you are supported by these benevolent beings.

Healing: Another crucial role of spirit guides is to assist in healing. They can help us work through emotional, mental, and even physical pain, guiding us toward balance and well-being. By inviting their healing energy, we can address past traumas, overcome fears, and experience personal transformations.

How to Connect with Your Spirit Guides

Connecting with spirit guides is a deeply personal and enriching experience. It starts with an open heart and a willingness to explore the spiritual realm. Here are some initial steps and common practices to help establish and deepen your connection with your guides:

Set Clear Intentions: Begin your journey by setting a clear intention to connect with your spirit guides. This can be expressed through a simple prayer or affirmation, clearly stating your desire to build a relationship with them.

Create a Sacred Space: Dedicate a specific area in your home for spiritual practices. This could be a small altar adorned with meaningful objects such as crystals, candles, or images that resonate with you. Creating a sacred space signals your commitment to this spiritual journey and provides a conducive environment for connecting with your guides.

Meditation and Mindfulness: Regular meditation is one of the most effective ways to connect with spirit guides. It helps quiet the mind and opens your awareness to the subtle energies and messages from your guides. Begin with short meditation sessions and gradually extend them as you become more comfortable and attuned to their presence.

Pay Attention to Signs and Synchronicities: Spirit guides often communicate through signs and synchronicities. Be mindful of repeating numbers, finding feathers or coins, or encountering other symbols that seem significant. These are often messages from your guides, providing guidance and reassurance.

Journal Your Experiences: Keep a journal to document your experiences and any messages you receive. Writing down your thoughts and feelings can help you recognize patterns and gain deeper insights into the offered guidance.

Ask for Guidance: Don't hesitate to ask your guides for help. Whether you need assistance with a specific issue or general support, vocalize your request and remain open to the responses. Trust that they are always ready to assist you.

Trust Your Intuition: Trust is crucial in building a relationship with your spirit guides. Believe in the messages and feelings you receive, even if they don't immediately make sense. Doubt can hinder the connection, so have faith in your intuition and guidance from your guides.

Building a Relationship with Spirit Guides

Building a relationship with your spirit guides is an ongoing journey that requires patience, trust, and a genuine desire to connect. Incorporating these practices into your daily life can strengthen your bond with your guides and allow you to benefit from their wisdom and support.

As you continue on this path, remember that each experience with your spirit guides is unique and personal. There is no right or wrong way to connect; what matters most is your openness and willingness to engage with them. Stay curious, be patient, and you will find that your spirit guides are always there, ready to guide you towards a deeper understanding of yourself and your life's purpose.

Alex McCann Johnson

Chapter 16
Life Guides

Imagine standing on the stage of life, surrounded by a team of invisible supporters who are always there to guide, protect, and inspire you. These are your life guides, spiritual beings assigned to you before birth, carefully selected to accompany you through every experience, challenge, and triumph. Life guides are some of the most intimate and dedicated spirit guides we can encounter. They are with us from the moment we take our first breath, overseeing our life's journey and ensuring we stay aligned with our highest purpose.

I felt an immense sense of companionship and reassurance from the moment I became aware of my life guides. They are always present, ready to offer wisdom and insight, no matter how big or small the issue at hand. Their purpose is to help us make decisions that align with our true selves and to encourage us to pursue our dreams and aspirations. Whether it's a gentle nudge toward a new opportunity or a comforting presence during a difficult time, life guides are deeply invested in our growth and well-being.

Life guides are ethereal beings assigned to us to provide continuous support and guidance throughout our lives. Unlike other types of spirit guides who may come and go, life guides remain with us for the long haul, often accompanying us from birth to death. They are chosen based on their unique abilities and experiences, which align with the lessons we are meant to learn and the goals we are meant to achieve in this lifetime.

These guides act as mentors, offering wisdom that goes beyond our physical experience. They see our life's path with the clarity we often lack, guiding us toward opportunities and experiences that promote our growth and happiness. Life guides are intimately aware of our soul's purpose and work tirelessly to keep us on track, even when we feel lost or uncertain.

Roles and Responsibilities: How Life Guides Assist in Your Life's Journey

Life guides play a complex role in our lives, encompassing various aspects of support and guidance. One of their primary responsibilities is to help us recognize and fulfill our life's purpose. They gently steer us towards paths that resonate with our true selves, whether that's nudging us toward a new career, helping us heal from past traumas, or encouraging us to take a leap of faith.

In my journey, I've noticed that life guides often communicate through intuitive feelings and gut instincts. When faced with a difficult decision, those subtle nudges—like a feeling of unease or a sudden burst of clarity—are often the whispers of our life guides, guiding us toward choices that serve our highest good.

Life guides also help us navigate challenges and obstacles. When life throws unexpected hurdles our way, our guides provide the strength and resilience needed to overcome them. They remind us of our inner power and encourage us to keep moving forward, even when the path seems uncertain. During times of grief, loss, or confusion, they offer emotional and spiritual support, helping us see the bigger picture and understand that every experience, whether positive or negative, contributes to our soul's growth.

Another crucial role of life guides is to provide ongoing encouragement and motivation. They are our cheerleaders, celebrating our victories and gently pushing us to continue striving for our goals. They help us cultivate self-belief and remind us of our innate capabilities, fostering a sense of confidence and purpose.

Historical Significance

The concept of life guides has been acknowledged and revered across various cultures and traditions throughout history. In ancient Greece, for instance, the idea of a personal 'daemon' was widely accepted. These daemons were seen as benevolent spirits or guiding forces that provided wisdom, inspiration, and protection throughout a person's life. The philosopher Socrates famously spoke of his 'daimonion,' an inner voice that guided his actions and decisions.

In many indigenous cultures, life guides are often perceived as ancestral spirits who continue to watch over their descendants. These ancestral guides are believed to provide wisdom and protection, ensuring that their knowledge and experiences are passed down through generations. They serve as a bridge between the past and the present, helping individuals navigate their lives with the guidance of those who came before them.

Eastern traditions such as Hinduism and Buddhism also recognize the role of spiritual guides. In Hinduism, deities like Ganesha, known as the remover of obstacles, often serve as guides who help devotees overcome challenges and achieve their goals. In Buddhism, bodhisattvas like Avalokiteshvara (Kuan Yin) are revered as compassionate guides who assist in the spiritual journey toward enlightenment. While these figures are often classified as deities or ascended beings, their role closely aligns with that of life guides, offering continuous support and guidance.

Understanding the historical significance of life guides can deepen our appreciation for their role in our lives. These guides have been acknowledged and honored for centuries, providing a timeless source of wisdom and support. By connecting with our life guides, we tap into a rich tradition of spiritual guidance that transcends cultural and temporal boundaries.

How to Connect with Life Guides: Practical Steps and Tips

Connecting with life guides is a deeply personal experience, but some practical steps and tips can help foster this connection:

Set Clear Intentions: Begin by setting a clear intention to connect with your life guides. This can be through a simple prayer or affirmation. Here's a specific prayer you can use:

"Dear Life Guide, I invite your presence into my life. Please help me to see and understand your guidance. Assist me in making choices that align with my highest good and true purpose. Thank you for your constant support and wisdom. I am open to receiving your messages and guidance with love and gratitude."

Meditate Regularly: Meditation is a powerful tool for connecting with life guides. Find a quiet space where you won't be disturbed and focus on calming your mind. As you enter a meditative state, invite your life guides to join you. Pay attention to any sensations, thoughts, or images that arise. The more often you connect with your life guide through meditation, the more you will notice their influence in your daily life.

Create a Sacred Space: Dedicate a space in your home for spiritual practice. This can be a small altar with items that hold personal significance, such as crystals, candles, or photos. Creating a sacred space helps you focus and enhances your connection with your guides. To connect specifically with life guides, you might include symbols of longevity, such as evergreen branches or stones, representing their enduring presence in your life.

Pay Attention to Intuition: Life guides often communicate through intuitive feelings and gut instincts. Pay attention to those subtle nudges and trust your inner voice. Over time, you'll learn to distinguish the guidance of your life guides from other thoughts and feelings. You might also develop a specific "calling card"—a unique sensation or feeling in your body that signals their presence.

Ask for Signs: Don't hesitate to ask your life guides for signs. Whether you need confirmation about a decision or reassurance during a challenging time, ask your guides to send you a clear sign. Be specific in your request and open to receiving their messages in unexpected ways. Signs might come through repeating numbers, meaningful songs, or other synchronistic events.

Practice Gratitude: Show appreciation for the guidance and support your life guides provide. Regularly expressing gratitude can strengthen your bond and enhance your connection. Thank your guides for their presence and the wisdom they offer, acknowledging the profound role they play in your life.

Embracing the Role of Life Guides

Building a relationship with your life guides is an ongoing journey that requires patience, trust, and a genuine desire to connect. By taking these practical steps and understanding their historical significance, you can deepen your relationship with these benevolent beings and enhance your spiritual growth.

Remember, connecting with your life guides is a unique and personal journey. It requires an open heart and a willingness to explore the spiritual realm. Embrace the process, remain open to their guidance, and allow yourself to be amazed by the wisdom and support they offer.

Alex McCann Johnson

Chapter 17

Gatekeepers

In the realm of spiritual exploration and mediumship, gatekeepers play a crucial and often understated role. These protective spirit guides act as vigilant bouncers of the spiritual world, ensuring that our energy fields remain secure and that we are shielded from negative influences. Their primary responsibility is to guard our spiritual gateways, maintaining the integrity of our energetic boundaries. Through my journey with mediumship, I've come to rely heavily on my gatekeeper, whether it's during meditation or when connecting with other spirits. They not only manage the flow of spirits and energies around us but also create a safe space for us to delve deeper into our spiritual practices.

Gatekeepers are unique among spirit guides due to their specific focus on protection. Their main job is to guard our spiritual gateways—the entry points to our spiritual and energetic selves. By doing so, they ensure that only beneficial energies and influences can access our personal space. This is especially crucial during spiritual practices such as meditation, prayer, or mediumship, where we might be more vulnerable to external influences.

When I first became aware of my gatekeeper, I was immediately struck by the sense of security she brought into my life. Knowing that these protective beings were always watching over me allowed me to explore my spiritual path with confidence and peace of mind. Whether acting as a stern gatekeeper or a gentle guide, they ensure that our spiritual experiences are safe and positive.

Roles and Responsibilities: Guarding Your Spiritual Gateway

The primary responsibility of gatekeepers is to protect our spiritual gateways. These gateways can be thought of as the doors through which spiritual energies and influences enter and exit our lives. Gatekeepers stand guard at these entrances, making sure that only those energies that align with our highest good are allowed through.

Filtering Energies: Gatekeepers are adept at discerning between positive and negative influences. When new guides or energies approach us, gatekeepers act as the first line of defense, filtering out anything that might be harmful or distracting. This filtering process is vital, especially for those of us who are sensitive to energy or frequently engage in spiritual practices.

Providing Safe Space: During times of heightened spiritual activity, such as deep meditation or ritual, gatekeepers strengthen their protective presence. They create a safe and sacred space, allowing us to focus entirely on our practice without the concern of unwanted intrusions.

Managing Spirit Traffic: For those involved in mediumship, gatekeepers play an essential role in managing the flow of spirits. They act much like bouncers, ensuring that only appropriate and welcome spirits are allowed to communicate with us. This helps prevent overwhelming or negative experiences and maintains the orderliness of our spiritual interactions.

In my spiritual journey, I've found that gatekeepers are especially active during times of significant spiritual growth or challenge. They provide the necessary protection to allow us to explore our spiritual boundaries safely and to receive the guidance and support we need without interference from negative energies.

How to Identify Gatekeepers: Signs and Symbols They Might Use

Identifying gatekeepers can be a unique experience for each individual. They often communicate through specific signs and symbols that convey their protective nature. Here are some common ways you might recognize their presence:

Symbols of Protection: Gatekeepers frequently use universal symbols associated with protection. These can include images like shields, gates, locks, or even specific animals known for their guarding instincts, such as lions, wolves, or owls.

Intuitive Feelings of Safety: A heightened sense of safety and security is a clear indicator of your gatekeeper's presence. If you suddenly feel a sense of peace and protection, especially during or after invoking their presence, it's likely your gatekeeper is near.

Dreams and Visions: Gatekeepers may appear in your dreams or meditative visions as guardians standing at a threshold or doorway. This visual representation underscores their role in guarding your spiritual entry points.

Repetitive Signs: Pay attention to recurring symbols or imagery in your daily life. If you frequently encounter protective symbols, such as a shield or a gate, it might be your gatekeeper trying to communicate.

Physical Sensations: Many people report feeling specific physical sensations, such as a warm or tingling feeling, when their gatekeepers are present. These sensations can serve as a confirmation of their protective presence.

Connecting with Gatekeepers: Techniques and Practices

Establishing a strong connection with your gatekeepers is crucial for maintaining a protected and balanced spiritual life. Here are some techniques and practices that can help you connect with your gatekeepers:

Meditation: Regular meditation is one of the most effective ways to connect with your gatekeepers. During meditation, invite your gatekeepers to join you. Visualize them standing guard at your spiritual gateway, offering their protection and ensuring that your space remains secure.

Set Intentions: Before engaging in any spiritual activity, set a clear intention to invite your gatekeepers to provide protection. This can be done through a simple prayer or affirmation. Here's a specific prayer you can use:

"Dear Gatekeeper, I invite you to stand guard at my spiritual gateway. Please protect me from any negative energies and ensure that only love and light enter my space. I trust in your guidance and thank you for your unwavering protection."

Create a Sacred Space: Dedicate a part of your home to spiritual practice. This space can include protective symbols, crystals, or other objects that resonate with the energy of your gatekeepers. For instance, placing black tourmaline in your sacred space can help enhance your connection with your gatekeeper by absorbing negative energies.

Ask for Signs: Don't hesitate to ask your gatekeepers for signs of their presence. Be specific in your requests and remain open to the ways they might communicate with you. Whether through symbols, physical sensations, or intuitive feelings, trust that they will provide the confirmation you seek.

Express Gratitude: Regularly expressing gratitude to your gatekeepers can strengthen your bond. Thank them for their protection and guidance, and acknowledge their role in maintaining your spiritual gateway's security. This practice not only reinforces their presence but also deepens your connection.

Historical Significance

The concept of spiritual guardians or gatekeepers is embedded in various cultural and religious traditions throughout history. These protective entities have been revered as essential figures responsible for guarding sacred spaces and ensuring the safety of individuals from malevolent forces.

In ancient Greek mythology, the role of gatekeepers was often attributed to gods and goddesses who guarded the entrances to sacred temples and the underworld. For example, Hades, the god of the underworld, was often depicted with Cerberus, a three-headed dog guarding the gates to prevent the dead from escaping and the living from entering without permission.

Similarly, in ancient Egypt, certain deities were believed to protect the gates to the afterlife. Anubis, the god of mummification and the afterlife was often depicted as a guardian of the gates, ensuring that only those deemed worthy could pass through to the realm of the dead.

In indigenous cultures, many tribes believed in protective spirits or ancestors who guarded their communities and sacred spaces. These spirits were called upon to maintain harmony and balance within the tribe, safeguarding against spiritual threats and ensuring the well-being of the community.

Eastern traditions, such as Hinduism and Buddhism, often depict fierce deities who protect temple entrances and sacred sites. These guardians ensure that only those with pure intentions can enter and receive the blessings within.

Today, the concept of gatekeepers continues to hold significant importance in spiritual practices. Many people recognize the need for spiritual protection and call upon their gatekeepers to provide it. Understanding the historical significance of gatekeepers can deepen our appreciation for their role and reinforce the importance of maintaining a strong connection with these protective guides.

Embracing the Role of Gatekeepers

Gatekeepers are essential allies in our spiritual journey. Their vigilant protection of our spiritual gateways ensures we remain safe and secure from negative influences. By recognizing and connecting with our gatekeepers, we can enhance our spiritual practices and navigate our paths with greater confidence and security.

Embracing their presence and understanding their historical significance allows us to appreciate the invaluable support they provide fully. Remember, connecting with your gatekeepers is a personal and ongoing journey. It requires an open heart, trust, and a genuine desire to build a relationship with them. As you continue to explore this connection, you will find that your gatekeepers offer a sense of safety and guidance, empowering you to pursue your spiritual path with greater peace and assurance.

Chapter 18
Akashic Guides

Among the various types of spirit guides, Akashic guides hold a unique and profound role. They are the keepers and guardians of the Akashic Records—a vast, ethereal repository of all knowledge, experiences, and potential futures. These guides assist us in accessing the records, offering invaluable insights into our past, present, and future. My journey with Akashic guides began with a sense of awe and curiosity. The notion that a spiritual library exists holding the wisdom of the universe, was both fascinating and inspiring. With the guidance of my Akashic guide, Angela, I have been able to delve into this cosmic library, uncovering layers of my soul's history and potential.

Understanding the Akashic Records

The Akashic Records are often described as a cosmic or spiritual library containing the energetic imprint of every thought, action, emotion, and experience that has ever occurred or will ever occur. These records transcend time and space and are believed to exist in a higher dimension. They are not physical in nature but can be accessed through spiritual practices, often with the help of Akashic guides.

The significance of the Akashic Records lies in their ability to provide deep insights into our lives. Accessing these records can help us understand our soul's purpose, uncover karmic patterns, and gain clarity on life lessons. The records can reveal past life experiences that influence our current circumstances, shed light on relationships, and offer guidance for future decisions. In my personal journey, exploring the Akashic Records has been akin to reading a book where each chapter reveals a different aspect of my soul's journey, filled with lessons and insights.

Roles and Responsibilities: How Akashic Guides Assist with Accessing the Records

Akashic guides are essential facilitators in our exploration of the Akashic Records. Their responsibilities are multifaceted and aligned with our spiritual growth and understanding.

Gatekeeping: Akashic guides act as gatekeepers to the Akashic Records. They ensure we approach the records with respect and the right intentions. They guard the records, allowing access only to the information we are ready to receive and understand, thus preventing us from becoming overwhelmed or confused by the vast knowledge within.

Interpretation: Once we access the records, Akashic guides assist in interpreting the complex and multi-layered information we receive. The records often contain symbolic and abstract data that can be difficult to comprehend. Our guides help us make sense of these insights and apply them to our lives meaningfully.

Healing and Integration: Akashic guides support our healing by helping us understand and integrate the lessons from the records. They provide comfort and guidance as we process past traumas and karmic patterns. Their presence is particularly vital during emotional or spiritual healing processes, offering insights that lead to huge transformations.

Spiritual Growth: These guides contribute significantly to our spiritual growth and development by facilitating access to the Akashic Records. They encourage us to learn from our past, live fully in the present, and align with our highest potential for the future. Their guidance helps us navigate our soul's journey with greater clarity and purpose.

In my experience, Akashic guides provide a sense of security and clarity when navigating the records. Their presence ensures that the insights I receive are not only meaningful but also manageable, allowing me to integrate the knowledge into my daily life effectively.

Methods to Connect with Akashic Guides: Meditation and Visualization Practices

Connecting with Akashic guides and accessing the Akashic Records requires practice and patience. Here are some methods that have helped me establish a strong connection with these guides:

Meditation: Meditation is a powerful tool for connecting with Akashic guides and accessing the records. Start by finding a quiet and comfortable space where you won't be disturbed. Focus on your breath to calm your mind. Once centered, set the intention to connect with your Akashic guides and access the records. Visualize a door or portal opening to the Akashic library and invite your guides to join you. Be open to any images, thoughts, or sensations that arise during this process.

Visualization: Visualization exercises can be very effective in connecting with Akashic guides. Imagine yourself walking through a serene landscape until you reach a grand library. Visualize entering this library, where your Akashic guides are waiting to assist you. Trust in the images and messages that come through, and don't hesitate to ask your guides for clarity and guidance as you explore the records.

Prayer and Intention Setting: Begin your practice with a prayer or affirmation, expressing your desire to connect with your Akashic guides. Clearly state your intention to access the records for insight, healing, and growth. This sets a clear and respectful tone for your session. Here's a specific prayer you can use:

"Dear Akashic Guide, I invite you to join me and help me access the Akashic Records. Please provide me with clarity, insight, and understanding of my soul's journey. Guide me in interpreting the information and integrating the lessons I learn into my life. Thank you for your wisdom and support."

Journaling: After your meditation or visualization session, take time to journal about your experience. Write down any messages, insights, or images that you received. Journaling helps you process and integrate the information and provides a valuable record to refer back to in the future.

Regular Practice: Consistency is key when connecting with Akashic guides. Regular practice strengthens your connection and makes it easier to access the records over time. Dedicate a specific time each week for this practice and be patient with the process.

Historical Significance

The concept of the Akashic Records has deep roots in various spiritual traditions and philosophies. The term "Akasha" is derived from a Sanskrit word meaning "ether" or "sky," referring to the fifth element in Eastern cosmology, believed to be the substance that holds all universal knowledge.

In Hindu philosophy, the Akashic Records are thought to be a universal storehouse of knowledge, accessible to those with heightened spiritual awareness. This concept also parallels the idea of a cosmic memory found in ancient Egyptian and Greek traditions, where sacred archives held the wisdom of the gods and the universe.

The modern understanding of the Akashic Records has been significantly influenced by Theosophy, a spiritual and religious movement founded in the late 19th century by Helena Petrovna Blavatsky. Theosophists believe in the interconnectedness of all souls and the ability to access divine truth through personal enlightenment. Blavatsky introduced Western audiences to the idea of the Akashic Records, describing them as a cosmic memory that can be tapped into for spiritual insight.

In the early 20th century, the American clairvoyant Edgar Cayce, often referred to as the "Sleeping Prophet," brought further attention to the Akashic Records. Cayce claimed to access the records during trance-like states, using this source for his numerous psychic readings. His work played a crucial role in popularizing the concept of the Akashic Records within the Western spiritual community.

Guided by Spirits

Many indigenous cultures also hold beliefs similar to the concept of the Akashic Records. Native American traditions, for example, often speak of a "Great Spirit" that contains the wisdom of all time and can be accessed through vision quests and other spiritual practices.

Understanding the historical significance of the Akashic Records enriches our practice by connecting us to a long lineage of spiritual seekers who have explored this profound source of wisdom. By accessing the records with the help of our Akashic guides, we continue this ancient tradition of seeking knowledge and understanding beyond the physical realm.

Embracing the Journey with Akashic Guides

Akashic guides are invaluable allies on our spiritual journey. They help us access the Akashic Records, providing insights that can transform our understanding of ourselves and our lives. By connecting with these guides through meditation, visualization, and other practices, we open ourselves to a wealth of wisdom and guidance. Embracing the historical significance of the Akashic Records further enriches our experience, allowing us to tap into a timeless source of universal knowledge.

As you embark on your journey with Akashic guides, remember that patience, openness, and regular practice are key. Each session with your guides is an opportunity to delve deeper into your soul's journey and uncover the rich tapestry of your existence. Trust in the process, and allow your Akashic guides to illuminate the path to greater understanding and spiritual growth.

Alex McCann Johnson

Chapter 19

Child Guides

In the world of spirit guides, child guides hold a special place with their unique blend of innocence, joy, and boundless creativity. They often appear as children, embodying the qualities that remind us to reconnect with our inner child. For me, having a child guide has been a joyous experience that brought lightness and happiness into my life. Even amidst the depths of inner child work, which involves healing old wounds and nurturing unexpressed needs, my child guide has been a constant source of joy and comfort. These guides help us embrace the simplicity of life and find the joy and wonder that often gets lost in adulthood.

Child guides are spirit guides that appear as children. They bring with them an energy that is light, playful, and filled with wonder. Their presence encourages us to engage with life in a more carefree and joyful manner. When I first met my child guide, I was immediately struck by the sheer happiness that filled the surrounding space. It was as if all the worries and burdens of adulthood had momentarily vanished, replaced by the pure joy of being alive. I needed this before what I was about to delve into.

Child guides are particularly important for those of us who carry inner child wounds. These wounds can manifest from various childhood experiences and often continue to influence our relationships and behavior into adulthood. Whether we experience abandonment, guilt, neglect, or trust issues, our child guides can help us address and heal these deep-seated wounds. They remind us of the importance of nurturing our inner child and embracing the parts of ourselves that long for love, joy, and acceptance.

Roles and Responsibilities: How Child Guides Help Us

Child guides play several essential roles in our lives, each centered around bringing innocence and joy. Here's how they contribute to our well-being and spiritual growth:

Encouraging Playfulness: One of the primary roles of child guides is to encourage us to embrace playfulness. They remind us that life doesn't always have to be serious and that engaging in playful activities can rejuvenate our spirit. Whether it's dancing, drawing, or simply playing games, child guides urge us to find joy in the simple things.

Promoting Creativity: Child guides are closely associated with creativity. They inspire us to explore our creative passions without fear of judgment or failure. When I feel stuck or uninspired, connecting with my child guide often brings a burst of creative energy and fresh ideas. They help us to tap into the boundless imagination that we often lose touch with as we grow older.

Healing the Inner Child: Many of us carry wounds from our childhood that can affect our adult lives. Child guides help us heal these wounds by reconnecting us with our inner child. Through their guidance, we can address past traumas, embrace our authentic selves, and find healing. They provide the love and support that our younger selves need but may not have received.

Instilling a Sense of Wonder: Child guides help us see the world with fresh eyes. They remind us of the wonder and awe that we experienced as children, encouraging us to find beauty and magic in everyday moments. This sense of wonder can enrich our lives and deepen our spiritual practice, making each day an adventure filled with possibilities.

Offering Emotional Support: During challenging times, child guides provide emotional support and comfort. Their pure, loving energy can help soothe our worries and bring a sense of peace. In my darkest moments, my child guide's presence has often been a source of comfort and reassurance, reminding me that joy and innocence are always within reach.

Connecting with Child Guides: Practical Steps and Visualization

Building a connection with child guides can be a joyful and rewarding experience. Here are some practical steps and visualization techniques that have helped me connect with my child guide:

Set the Intention: Begin by setting a clear intention to connect with your child guide. You can do this through a simple prayer or affirmation. Express your desire to invite their joyful and playful energy into your life. Here's a specific prayer you can use:

"Dear Child Guide, I invite you to join me and fill my life with your light, joy, and innocence. Help me reconnect with my inner child and embrace the wonder and creativity that you bring. Thank you for your loving presence and guidance. I welcome you with open arms and an open heart."

Create a Playful Environment: Surround yourself with objects and activities that evoke a sense of playfulness. This could include toys, art supplies, music, or anything that brings you joy. Creating a playful environment can help you tune into the energy of your child guide and make the connection feel more natural.

Visualization: One effective way to connect with your child guide is through visualization. Find a quiet and comfortable space where you won't be disturbed. Close your eyes and take a few deep breaths to center yourself. Imagine a beautiful, vibrant playground filled with laughter and joy. Visualize yourself entering this playground and inviting your child guide to join you. Be open to any images, sensations, or messages that come through during this time.

Engage in Playful Activities: Engage in activities that you enjoyed as a child. This could be anything from drawing and coloring to playing games or spending time in nature. Allow yourself to fully immerse in the activity and be open to the presence and guidance of your child guide. These activities can help you reconnect with the playful and creative aspects of yourself.

Pay Attention to Signs: Child guides often communicate through playful and whimsical signs. Pay attention to moments of synchronicity, such as finding a feather, hearing a song from your childhood, or encountering animals and objects that remind you of your inner child. These signs can be a confirmation of your child guide's presence and their encouragement for you to embrace joy and play.

Express Gratitude: Regularly express gratitude to your child guide for their presence and guidance. Thank them for bringing joy, creativity, and healing into your life. Showing appreciation can strengthen your connection and invite more of their positive energy into your daily experiences.

Historical Significance

The concept of child-like spirits and guides is prevalent in various cultures and spiritual traditions throughout history. In many indigenous cultures, child spirits are seen as messengers of joy and play, often associated with fertility and the renewal of life. These cultures recognize the importance of maintaining a child-like perspective and the healing power of play and innocence.

In ancient mythology, child deities often represented new beginnings, purity, and the potential for growth. For instance, in Greek mythology, Eros, the god of love, is depicted as a playful child, symbolizing the innocence and joy of love and connection. Similarly, in Hindu mythology, Krishna is often portrayed as a mischievous and playful child, bringing joy and divine love to those around him.

In more recent spiritual practices, the concept of the "inner child" has gained significant prominence. This idea emphasizes the importance of reconnecting with the child-like aspects of ourselves to heal emotional wounds and rediscover joy. Many therapeutic practices encourage individuals to engage with their inner child as a means of healing and personal growth. Understanding the historical significance of child guides helps us appreciate their role in connecting us to a timeless tradition of valuing innocence, play, and the healing power of joy.

Embracing the Journey with Child Guides

Child guides are invaluable allies on our spiritual journey. They bring innocence, joy, and creativity into our lives, helping us heal and reconnect with our inner child. By taking practical steps to connect with them and understanding their historical significance, we can deepen our relationship with these playful and loving guides. Embracing their presence allows us to approach life with a sense of wonder, playfulness, and profound joy.

As you embark on your journey with child guides, remember to nurture the playful and creative aspects of yourself. Allow your child guide to lead you into moments of joy and wonder, and trust in their ability to bring healing and light into your life. Through their guidance, you can rediscover the simple pleasures and boundless possibilities that come from viewing the world through the eyes of a child.

Alex McCann Johnson

Chapter 20

Shadow Guides

In the realm of spirit guides, there is a particular type that often evokes curiosity and sometimes fear—the Shadow Guide. Unlike other spirit guides that embody light, joy, or protection, Shadow Guides delve into the darker aspects of our psyche. They guide us through our fears, traumas, and the hidden parts of ourselves that we may not wish to confront. Working with a Shadow Guide is not about inviting negativity but rather about embracing the full spectrum of our human experience and fostering deep, transformative healing.

Shadow Guides are spirit guides that help us navigate the darker, often hidden parts of our consciousness. These guides are not inherently dark or negative; instead, they specialize in bringing our attention to the aspects of ourselves that need healing, understanding, and integration. They help us confront our fears, traumas, and the unresolved emotions that we have pushed into the shadows of our minds.

When I first encountered my Shadow Guide, I was initially apprehensive. The idea of confronting my deepest fears and darkest emotions was daunting. However, as I allowed myself to engage with my Shadow Guide, I realized that their presence was not one of judgment or malice but of profound compassion and wisdom. They guided me gently through my inner turmoil, helping me to understand and integrate the parts of myself I had long ignored or denied.

Shadow Guides teach us that true healing and self-discovery require us to face all aspects of our being, including those we find uncomfortable or painful. By working with these guides, we can achieve a deeper level of self-awareness and transformation.

Roles and Responsibilities: How Shadow Guides Assist in Personal Growth

Shadow Guides play a crucial role in our personal and spiritual development. They help us explore and understand the darker aspects of our psyche, leading to healing and growth. Here's how they contribute to our well-being:

Confronting Fears: One of the primary roles of Shadow Guides is to help us confront our fears. They bring to light the things we have avoided or repressed, allowing us to face and understand them. This process can be challenging, but it is essential for overcoming our fears and moving forward in our lives.

Healing Past Traumas: Shadow Guides assist in healing past traumas by bringing them into our awareness. They guide us through the process of revisiting painful memories and emotions, providing the support needed to heal and integrate these experiences. Their presence helps us to see our traumas not as burdens but as opportunities for growth and understanding.

Integrating the Shadow Self: The concept of the "shadow self" refers to the parts of our personality that we reject or deny. Shadow Guides help us acknowledge and integrate these aspects, fostering a sense of wholeness and self-acceptance. By embracing our shadow self, we can understand our true nature more fully and live more authentically.

Transforming Negative Patterns: Shadow Guides bring our attention to negative patterns and behaviors that may be holding us back. They help us understand the root causes of these patterns and guide us in transforming them into positive actions and beliefs. This transformation leads to greater personal freedom and empowerment.

Fostering Deep Self-Awareness: By working with Shadow Guides, we develop a deeper understanding of ourselves. They help us explore the complexities of our psyche, revealing insights that lead to profound self-awareness and growth. This self-awareness is the foundation for lasting personal transformation.

In my journey, my Shadow Guide has been an invaluable ally in navigating the darker aspects of my life. Their guidance has led to significant healing and a deeper understanding of myself. Through their support, I have learned to embrace all parts of my being and to view my challenges as opportunities for growth. This is some deep work and it is not easy at all.

Connecting with Shadow Guides: Techniques and Practices

Connecting with Shadow Guides requires courage and a willingness to explore the darker aspects of your psyche. Here are some techniques and practices that have helped me build a strong connection with my Shadow Guide:

Set the Intention: Begin by setting a clear intention to connect with your Shadow Guide. You can do this through a simple prayer or affirmation. Express your willingness to explore and heal the darker aspects of yourself. Here's a specific prayer you can use:

"Dear Shadow Guide, I invite you to join me on this journey of self-discovery and healing. Help me confront my fears, heal my past traumas, and embrace the shadow aspects of myself. Guide me with compassion and wisdom as I navigate the depths of my inner darkness. Thank you for your presence and support."

Meditation: Meditation is a powerful tool for connecting with your Shadow Guide. Find a quiet and comfortable space where you won't be disturbed. Close your eyes and focus on your breath to calm your mind. As you enter a meditative state, invite your Shadow Guide to join you. Visualize them appearing before you and ask them to show you the aspects of your shadow self that you need to explore. Be open to any images, thoughts, or feelings that arise during this process.

Shadow Work Journaling: Journaling is an effective way to explore the themes and insights that arise from working with your Shadow Guide. After your meditation or visualization session, write down any messages, emotions, or memories that surfaced. Reflect on these entries and consider how they relate to your current experiences and challenges. Journaling can help you process and integrate the insights you receive from your Shadow Guide.

Visualization Exercises: Visualization can be a powerful method for connecting with your Shadow Guide. Imagine yourself walking through a dark yet inviting forest. As you journey deeper, you come across a clearing where your Shadow Guide awaits. Visualize engaging with them, asking questions, and seeking their guidance on the aspects of your life that need healing and understanding. Trust in the images and feelings that come to you during this exercise.

Emotional Release Practices: Engaging in practices that facilitate emotional release can help you connect with your Shadow Guide. This can include activities like breathwork, dancing, or even crying. Allow yourself to experience and express your emotions fully. Your Shadow Guide can provide support and guidance as you release the pent-up emotions and energies that you have been carrying.

Pay Attention to Nightmares and Negative Emotions: Shadow Guides often communicate through our dreams and emotions, particularly through nightmares or intense feelings. Pay attention to recurring themes or symbols in your dreams, as these can provide clues about the aspects of your shadow self that need attention. Similarly, notice any strong emotional reactions you have during the day, as these can be indications of unresolved issues that your Shadow Guide wants you to explore.

Historical Significance

The concept of confronting one's shadow self and integrating the darker aspects of our being is deeply rooted in various psychological and spiritual traditions. Carl Jung, a renowned Swiss psychiatrist, introduced the concept of the "shadow" as part of his work on the human psyche. Jung believed that the shadow represents the unconscious parts of ourselves that we reject or deny. He argued that personal growth and self-awareness require confronting and integrating our shadows.

In many indigenous cultures, the idea of facing one's shadow is a critical aspect of spiritual and emotional healing. Shamans often guide individuals through rituals and journeys to confront their fears, traumas, and darker aspects of themselves. These practices are seen as essential for achieving balance and harmony within oneself.

Similarly, in various mythological and religious traditions, the journey into darkness or the underworld is a common motif. For example, in Greek mythology, the hero's journey often involves descending into the underworld to confront and overcome challenges. This descent symbolizes facing and integrating the darker aspects of oneself.

The concept of the shadow is also present in alchemical traditions, where the process of transforming base materials into gold is a metaphor for personal and spiritual transformation. This transformation involves confronting and purifying the darker aspects of one's being to achieve enlightenment and self-realization.

Understanding the historical and cultural significance of shadow work enriches our appreciation for the role of Shadow Guides in our lives. These guides help us engage in a timeless process of self-discovery and healing, leading to profound personal transformation.

Embracing the Journey with Shadow Guides

In conclusion, Shadow Guides are powerful allies in our journey of self-discovery and healing. They help us navigate the darker aspects of our psyche, providing insights and support as we confront our fears, traumas, and unresolved emotions. By connecting with these guides through meditation, visualization, and other practices, we can achieve a deeper level of self-awareness and transformation.

Embracing the presence of Shadow Guides allows us to integrate all aspects of our being, leading to greater wholeness and personal freedom. As you embark on your journey with Shadow Guides, remember to approach this process with courage, compassion, and an open heart. Trust in their guidance, and allow them to illuminate the path to greater understanding and healing.

Chapter 21

Learning Guides

As someone who is always in a course or learning something new, I find myself frequently accompanied by learning guides. These spirit guides are dedicated to aiding us in acquiring knowledge, developing skills, and fostering personal growth. Learning guides are like wise teachers, mentors, and coaches who assist us in our educational and professional endeavors. When I first connected with my learning guide, I felt an immense sense of encouragement and clarity, especially when tackling challenging subjects or skills. Learning guides are invaluable allies in our quest for understanding and mastery.

In my experience, learning guides have a unique ability to illuminate complex topics, making them easier to grasp. They inspire us to be curious, diligent, and open-minded, transforming the learning process into an exciting and fulfilling journey. Whether we are pursuing formal education, learning a new hobby, or seeking spiritual knowledge, our learning guides are always ready to support and guide us.

Learning guides are spirit guides dedicated to helping us gain knowledge and skills. They embody the qualities of wisdom, patience, and encouragement. When I first encountered my learning guide, I felt an overwhelming sense of support, particularly when dealing with difficult or complex subjects. These guides are like personal mentors, always ready to assist us in our educational pursuits and personal development.

Learning guides are not just limited to academic endeavors. They also help us develop practical skills, artistic talents, and spiritual knowledge.

Their presence can transform the learning process from a daunting task into an enriching experience filled with growth and discovery. They inspire us to remain curious, to ask questions, and to explore new areas of interest without fear of failure.

Roles and Responsibilities: How They Assist in Learning and Growth

The primary role of learning guides is to facilitate our learning and growth. Here are some of the key responsibilities they undertake:

Providing Insight and Clarity: Learning guides help us gain deeper insights into the subjects we are studying. They can clarify complex concepts, making them easier to understand. Whenever I struggle with a topic, I often ask my learning guide for help, and soon enough, I find myself having a moment of clarity.

Encouraging Curiosity: These guides inspire a sense of curiosity and a love for learning. They encourage us to ask questions, explore new areas of interest, and seek out knowledge. Their presence can ignite a passion for lifelong learning.

Supporting Skill Development: Whether it's learning a new language, mastering an instrument, or honing a craft, learning guides assist in the development of practical skills. They provide guidance and support, helping us stay motivated and focused.

Offering Encouragement: Learning can be challenging, and there are times when we may feel discouraged. Learning guides offer emotional support and encouragement, reminding us of our capabilities and potential. Their reassuring presence helps us persevere through difficult times.

Facilitating Personal and Spiritual Growth: Learning guides also help us grow personally and spiritually beyond academic and practical knowledge. They offer wisdom and insights that foster self-awareness, emotional intelligence, and spiritual enlightenment.

Guided by Spirits

In my journey, my learning guide has been a constant source of inspiration and support. They have helped me navigate academic challenges, encouraged me to pursue new interests, and provided invaluable insights that have contributed to my personal and spiritual growth.

How to Recognize Learning Guides: Identifying Their Presence

Recognizing the presence of learning guides can be a unique and personal experience. Here are some ways to identify when your learning guide is present:

Sudden Clarity or Insight: If you experience sudden moments of clarity or understanding, especially when grappling with a difficult topic, it may be a sign that your learning guide is helping you.

Increased Curiosity: Feeling an unexpected surge of curiosity or a strong desire to learn something new can indicate your learning guide. They often inspire us to explore new areas of knowledge and skill.

Encouraging Thoughts and Feelings: If you find yourself feeling unusually encouraged or motivated to continue learning despite challenges, this could be your learning guide providing emotional support and encouragement.

Dreams and Visions: Learning guides may also communicate through dreams or meditative visions. You might dream about a wise teacher or mentor offering guidance and insight, which can be a direct connection to your learning guide.

Synchronicities: Pay attention to synchronicities related to your learning journey. For instance, repeatedly encountering books, articles, or people related to a topic you're studying can be a sign from your learning guide.

In my experience, I often recognize my learning guide through moments of sudden insight and the persistent encouragement I feel when tackling new subjects. These signs remind me that I am not alone in my learning journey and that I have a wise and supportive guide by my side.

Connecting with Learning Guides: Techniques and Tips

Building a strong connection with your learning guides can greatly enhance your learning experience. Here are some techniques and tips that have helped me connect with my learning guide:

Set Clear Intentions: Start by setting a clear intention to connect with your learning guide. This can be done through a simple affirmation or prayer. Express your desire for their guidance and support in your learning journey. Here's a specific prayer you can use:

"Dear Learning Guide, I invite you to join me on my journey of knowledge and growth. Please help me to understand, learn, and master new skills. Guide me with your wisdom and support me with your encouragement. Thank you for your presence and guidance."

Meditation: Regular meditation can help you connect with your learning guide. Find a quiet space and focus on your breath to center yourself. Visualize yourself in a serene study environment, such as a beautiful library or a peaceful garden. Invite your learning guide to join you and be open to any messages or insights that come through.

Ask for Guidance: Don't hesitate to ask your learning guide for help with specific questions or challenges. Whether you need clarity on a complex topic or motivation to continue learning, verbalize your request and remain open to their guidance.

Engage in Lifelong Learning: Embrace a mindset of lifelong learning and be open to exploring new subjects and skills. Your learning guide will be more likely to engage with you when you are actively pursuing knowledge and growth.

Keep a Journal: Document your learning experiences and any insights or messages you receive from your learning guide. Journaling can help you recognize patterns and track your progress, strengthening your connection with your guide.

Express Gratitude: Regularly express gratitude to your learning guide for their support and guidance. Thank them for the insights and encouragement they provide, and acknowledge their role in your learning journey.

Historical Significance in Different Cultures

The concept of spirit guides who aid in learning and knowledge is present in many cultures and spiritual traditions. In ancient Greece, the muses were considered divine beings who inspired artists, musicians, and scholars. They were believed to provide the creative spark and wisdom necessary for great works of art and literature. Each muse had a specific domain, such as epic poetry, history, or dance, and they were invoked for inspiration and guidance in their respective fields.

In Eastern traditions, various deities and enlightened beings are invoked for guidance in learning and spiritual growth. Saraswati, the Hindu goddess of knowledge, music, and arts, is often called upon by students and scholars seeking wisdom and creativity. She is depicted with a book and a musical instrument, symbolizing her mastery of knowledge and the arts. Similarly, in Buddhism, Manjushri is the Bodhisattva of wisdom, often depicted wielding a flaming sword that cuts through ignorance.

Indigenous cultures also recognize the presence of spirit guides who help with learning and personal growth. These guides are often seen as wise ancestors or shamans who pass down their knowledge and skills to the living. For example, Native American traditions honor spirit guides and totems embodying the natural world's wisdom, offering lessons and guidance for those who seek it.

In contemporary spiritual practices, the idea of learning guides has evolved to encompass both academic and personal growth. Many people seek the guidance of learning guides to enhance their understanding, develop new skills, and navigate their educational and professional journeys.

Understanding the historical significance of learning guides enriches our appreciation for their role in our lives. These guides connect us to a long tradition of seeking knowledge and wisdom from the spiritual realm. By embracing the presence of our learning guides, we can tap into a wellspring of inspiration and support that transcends time and culture.

Embracing the Journey with Learning Guides

Learning guides are invaluable allies on our journey of knowledge and growth. They provide insights, encouragement, and support, helping us navigate the complexities of learning and personal development. By recognizing their presence and building a strong connection with them, we can enhance our learning experiences and achieve our highest potential. Embracing the historical significance of learning guides further deepens our understanding and appreciation of their role in our lives.

As you continue your learning journey, remember to invite your learning guides to walk with you. Their guidance can illuminate your path, making even the most challenging subjects approachable and enjoyable. Trust in their wisdom, remain curious, and embrace the lifelong adventure of learning and growth.

Chapter 22

Building Relationships with Your Spirit Guides

As the world faces increasing challenges and many struggle to make ends meet, people often seek spiritual answers. They ask me about their spirit guides—who they are, if they have any messages, and so forth. I believe that in times of difficulty, people turn to the spiritual realm when the material world fails them. Yet, when life flows smoothly, they tend to ignore the guidance that the universe and spirit guides offer. This, I feel, is a missed opportunity. Often, there are signs and opportunities presented before things go awry, but these are overlooked. Many times, people tell me, "I had a bad feeling about that," or "I knew I shouldn't have done that," yet they proceed with decisions against their better judgment. One should pause and reflect on the source of these "bad feelings" or intuitive nudges to break this habit.

I often explain that their spirit guides give these warnings or intuitive insights. Building a relationship with your spirit guides is one of the most rewarding aspects of the spiritual journey. These guides provide wisdom, protection, and support. When I began nurturing my relationships with my guides, I noticed a shift in my spiritual practice and overall well-being. The guidance, reassurance, and companionship they offer are invaluable.

A robust relationship with your spirit guides can lead to deeper insights and a clearer understanding of your life's purpose. It helps you navigate challenges with confidence and grace, knowing that you are supported by benevolent beings who have your best interests at heart. Additionally, this connection enhances your intuitive abilities, making it easier to receive and interpret subtle messages from the spiritual realm.

Continuing the Work: Staying Connected with Your Guides

Maintaining a strong connection with your spirit guides requires ongoing effort and attention. In my experience, this relationship flourishes through regular communication and a commitment to continual learning. I make it a habit to talk to my guides throughout the day, sharing my thoughts, feelings, and gratitude. This informal dialogue keeps our connection vibrant and personal.

Staying curious and open to learning more about my guides and the spiritual realm has deepened our bond. I find that reading books, attending workshops, and engaging in practices that expand my understanding are invaluable. These activities keep the relationship dynamic and evolving.

Mindfulness also plays a crucial role in staying connected. By incorporating mindfulness practices into my daily routine, such as mindful breathing or walking, I stay present and aware of the subtle ways my guides communicate with me. This heightened awareness helps me recognize their messages in the small, everyday moments.

Expressing gratitude is another cornerstone of this relationship. Regularly thanking my guides for their presence and guidance strengthens our bond. I make it a point to express gratitude in my prayers, meditations, and daily life. It's a simple yet profound way to honor their support and keep the connection strong.

I also seek their guidance in all areas of my life—personal, professional, and relational. This holistic approach fosters a deeper, more integrated connection with my guides. By involving them in every aspect of my life, I create a relationship that is not only spiritual but also practical and grounded.

The Idea of a Soul Tribe and How Spirit Guides Are Involved

The concept of a soul tribe is deeply enriching and transformative. It embodies the idea that we are part of a larger spiritual family connected by shared purposes and journeys. Our soul tribe includes not only the people in our lives but also our spirit guides. These guides are integral members of our soul tribe, working alongside us to achieve our spiritual goals and fulfill our soul's mission.

In my journey, I've come to see my spirit guides as essential members of my soul tribe. They are my mentors, protectors, and friends, each playing a unique role in my life. This broader perspective helps me appreciate the interconnectedness of all beings and the collaborative nature of our spiritual journey. Understanding that our spirit guides are part of our soul tribe fosters a deeper sense of belonging and support. It reminds us that we are never alone and that we are part of a larger spiritual community dedicated to our growth and well-being.

Our spirit guides are not just external helpers but are woven into the very fabric of our spiritual existence. They share our purpose and are committed to our journey, just as we are to theirs. This mutual dedication creates a bond, enhancing our spiritual path with a sense of shared mission and purpose. They help us connect with others in our soul tribe, facilitate the discovery of our shared goals, and support us in nurturing these relationships. Recognizing our guides as part of our soul tribe enriches our understanding of them and deepens our connection, making it more personal and meaningful.

In conclusion, building and maintaining relationships with your spirit guides is a vital part of the spiritual journey. By fostering daily practices of communication, mindfulness, and gratitude and by embracing the concept of a soul tribe, we can deepen our connection with these benevolent beings. This relationship enriches our lives, providing guidance, support, and a profound sense of companionship as we navigate the complexities of our earthly existence. Embrace your spirit guides, honor their presence, and continue the work of building a strong and lasting bond with these extraordinary allies. Recognize them as integral members of your soul tribe and cherish the unique role they

Alex McCann Johnson

play in your spiritual journey.

Angel Guides

Alex McCann Johnson

Chapter 23

Angelic Guides

In all of my work, I was most surprised when I started to work with angelic beings. Their energy is exceptionally high-vibrational and deeply transformative. The first archangel I connected with was Azrael, who appeared unexpectedly as I was honing my mediumship abilities. Since then, I have developed strong connections with various angels, including my personal guardian angel and other prominent archangels mentioned throughout spiritual traditions.

Angels are often depicted as ethereal beings of light, exuding an otherworldly beauty and a calming presence. Their high vibrational energy can manifest in several ways, such as a sudden sense of peace, warmth, or an inexplicable feeling of being loved and protected. When they enter our space, the atmosphere often shifts, becoming more serene and infused with a divine aura.

Working with angels has been a transformative experience for me. Their presence brings healing, guidance, and protection. They are always ready to help, but they honor our free will and usually await our invitation or request before intervening in our lives. This respectful and non-intrusive nature makes their guidance feel gentle yet profoundly impactful.

History and Cultural Perceptions of Angels

Throughout history, angels have been a cornerstone in the spiritual traditions and myths of many cultures. In ancient times, they were seen as messengers bridging the gap between the divine and humanity, conveying celestial wisdom and guidance.

In Christianity, angels frequently appear in the Bible as messengers from God, protectors, and executors of divine will. Similarly, angels play crucial roles in the lives of prophets and believers in Islam, as seen in the Quran. Judaism also has a rich tradition of angelic beings, described in texts such as the Talmud and Kabbalistic writings, where they perform various tasks and convey divine wisdom.

Beyond the Abrahamic religions, angel-like beings are present in Zoroastrianism, Hinduism, Buddhism, and various indigenous traditions. In Zoroastrianism, Amesha Spentas are akin to archangels, guiding and protecting the faithful. In Hinduism, Devas are divine beings with roles similar to those of angels, overseeing natural elements and moral duties.

Angels also feature prominently in New Age and contemporary spiritual practices. Here, they are viewed as non-denominational beings of light, accessible to anyone regardless of their religious beliefs. This universality reflects their role as loving and supportive guides available to all who seek their presence.

The Non-Religious Perspective on Angels

In modern spirituality, angels are often seen through a non-religious lens, emphasizing their universal and inclusive nature. This perspective views angels as embodiments of divine energy, love, and wisdom, available to everyone, irrespective of religious affiliation.

From this viewpoint, angels are spiritual beings that operate on a high vibrational frequency, assisting in personal growth, healing, and enhancing intuitive abilities. They are not confined to any single doctrine or belief system but are considered benevolent entities supporting humanity's spiritual evolution.

Those who connect with angels from a non-religious perspective often report amazing personal transformations. Angels can help clear negative energy, provide insights during meditation, and offer comfort during times of distress. Through these connections, individuals enhance their spiritual awareness and cultivate a deeper sense of inner peace and purpose.

The Role of Angels in Human Life

Angels play a multifaceted role in human life, offering support, guidance, and protection in various ways:

Guidance and Wisdom: Angels provide insights and guidance, helping us make decisions aligned with our highest good. They can offer clarity during confusing times and inspire us to pursue our true paths.

Healing: Angels, particularly archangels like Raphael, are renowned for their healing abilities. They assist in physical, emotional, and spiritual healing, helping to restore balance and well-being.

Protection: Angels offer protection from harm and negative energies. Archangel Michael, for instance, is famous for his protective presence, shielding us from physical and psychic dangers.

Comfort and Support: During times of grief, stress, or hardship, angels provide comfort and support. Their presence can bring a sense of peace and reassurance, reminding us that we are never alone.

Enhancing Intuition: Working with angels can heighten our intuitive abilities. They help us tune into our inner wisdom, recognize signs and synchronicities, and trust our intuitive nudges.

How to Connect with Angelic Guides

Connecting with angelic guides is a deeply personal and profound experience. Here are some steps to help you begin this journey:

Begin by setting a clear intention to connect with your angelic guides. You can express this through prayer, meditation, or simply by speaking your intention out loud. Creating a sacred space can also enhance this connection. Find a quiet and comfortable place where you can focus on your interaction with the angels. You might want to light a candle, burn incense, or play soothing music to create a serene environment.

During your meditation, invite your angels to join you. Sit in a relaxed position and take several deep breaths to center yourself. You might mentally or verbally ask your angels to be present, saying something like, "I invite my angelic guides to be with me now. Please share your guidance and wisdom with me."

Stay open and receptive during this time. Pay attention to any sensations, thoughts, or images that arise. Angels communicate in various ways, so be open to receiving their messages through feelings, visions, or intuitive knowing. If you're unsure about their presence, ask them to provide you with a sign. This could be something specific, like seeing a particular symbol or number, or something more general, like feeling a sense of warmth or peace.

After your meditation, take a moment to express gratitude for their presence and guidance. Thanking your angels helps strengthen your connection, and we invite continued support. Remember, building a relationship with your angelic guides takes time and practice. Set aside regular moments to connect with them; over time, you will find it easier to recognize their presence and guidance.

Engaging with angelic guides can be an important aspect of your spiritual journey. Their wisdom, healing, and protection offer invaluable support as you navigate life's challenges. By understanding their presence, appreciating their historical and cultural significance, and learning how to connect with them, you can deepen your spiritual awareness and enhance your overall well-being. Embrace your angelic guides with an open heart, honor their presence, and allow their divine energy to guide you toward greater peace, purpose, and spiritual fulfillment.

Chapter 24

The Heirarchy of Angels

The celestial hierarchy is a structured order of angelic beings, each with distinct roles and responsibilities. This hierarchy helps us comprehend the vast and organized nature of the angelic realm, illustrating how these divine beings interact with the human world and the cosmos. Traditionally, the celestial hierarchy is divided into three triads, each containing three orders of angels.

First Triad: Closest to the Divine Presence

Seraphim: Known as the "burning ones," Seraphim are the highest order of angels, closest to the Divine. Their primary role is to praise and worship the Creator continuously, radiating divine love and light. The presence of Seraphim is said to be intensely powerful, often associated with the purest forms of divine energy.

Cherubim: These angels are the guardians of light and stars. Cherubim are celebrated for their knowledge and wisdom, often acting as keepers of the celestial records and secrets of the universe. They hold the sacred duty of preserving the divine light and ensuring the flow of knowledge across the cosmos.

Thrones: Thrones are angels of justice and authority. They serve as divine judges, balancing the scales of karma and ensuring that justice is administered throughout the cosmos. Thrones are seen as the carriers of the divine throne, symbolizing God's justice and authority in the universe.

Second Triad: Govern the Creation

Dominions: These angels oversee the duties of lower angels and ensure that the divine order is maintained. Dominions regulate the activities of guardian angels and other celestial beings, making sure that the cosmos functions according to the divine plan.

Virtues: Virtues are responsible for bestowing divine grace and valor. They bring miracles into the world and inspire humans to acts of goodness and courage. Virtues are often depicted as the bringers of divine energy, empowering humans to overcome challenges and achieve greatness.

Powers: Powers are warrior angels that protect the world from negative forces and spiritual darkness. They act as defenders of the cosmos, battling evil and maintaining order. Powers are seen as angelic soldiers, safeguarding the balance between light and darkness.

Third Triad: Interact with Humanity

Principalities: These angels oversee nations and large groups of people. They are concerned with the collective aspects of humanity, guiding societies and organizations toward the divine will. Principalities play a crucial role in influencing the moral and spiritual direction of communities.

Archangels: Archangels are messengers of the divine and are involved in significant global events and important human affairs. They guide and protect humanity on a larger scale, often delivering crucial messages from the divine. Archangels are seen as the leaders among angels, directing divine missions and assisting in major life transitions.

Angels: The lowest order in the hierarchy, these angels interact most directly with humans. They serve as personal protectors and guides, assisting individuals with everyday matters and spiritual growth. These are the angels we most frequently connect with, providing support and guidance in our daily lives.

The Purpose and Functions of Angels

Angels serve a multitude of purposes and functions, each designed to support and guide humanity while maintaining cosmic order. Their roles are as varied as the beings themselves, ranging from messengers and healers to warriors and protectors.

Messengers: One of the primary roles of angels is to act as messengers between the divine and humans. They deliver important revelations, guidance, and insights that help individuals align with their higher purpose. Throughout history, angels have been known to convey messages that alter the course of human events, often guiding us toward greater understanding and spiritual fulfillment.

Protectors: Angels often serve as guardians, shielding individuals from harm and guiding them away from danger. Guardian angels, in particular, are dedicated to protecting and guiding the people they are assigned to. Their protection can manifest as subtle warnings, feelings of unease, or even miraculous interventions during critical moments.

Healers: Many angels possess healing abilities, offering support for physical, emotional, and spiritual ailments. Archangel Raphael, for example, is known as the healer of the angelic realm, providing restorative energy to those in need. Angels often work behind the scenes to facilitate healing processes, bringing comfort and relief.

Guides: Angels help individuals navigate their spiritual journeys, offering wisdom and insights that promote personal growth and enlightenment. They assist in making important decisions and help individuals stay on their true path. Whether through gentle nudges or revelations, angels provide the guidance needed to align with our highest selves.

Warriors: Some angels are tasked with protecting the cosmos from negative forces and spiritual threats. These warrior angels, such as the Powers, engage in battles against evil to maintain balance and harmony. Their role is crucial in preserving the integrity of the divine plan and ensuring that darkness does not prevail.

Inspiration: Angels inspire acts of goodness, creativity, and courage in humans. They influence positive change and encourage individuals to live in accordance with divine will. By fostering virtues like compassion and bravery, angels help elevate the collective consciousness of humanity.

Cosmic Order: Beyond their interactions with humans, angels play a vital role in maintaining the order of the universe. They ensure that the laws of the cosmos are upheld and that divine justice is administered. Angels oversee the smooth operation of celestial and earthly systems, ensuring that everything aligns with the divine blueprint.

Differences Between Archangels, Guardian Angels, and Other Angelic Beings

Understanding the distinctions between various types of angels can help us better appreciate their unique roles and how they assist us:

Archangels

Archangels are high-ranking angels responsible for overseeing larger aspects of human affairs and global events. They deliver significant messages and provide guidance on a grand scale. Each archangel has specific attributes and areas of expertise, such as healing (Raphael), protection (Michael), and communication (Gabriel). They often work with multiple people simultaneously, guiding and protecting large groups or entire nations. Archangels are invoked during times of significant need or transformation, offering powerful support and intervention.

Guardian Angels

Guardian angels are personal protectors assigned to individuals. Their primary role is to safeguard and guide the person they are entrusted with throughout their life. Guardian angels are deeply attuned to the needs, emotions, and spiritual paths of the individuals they protect, offering personalized guidance and support. They have a close and intimate relationship with their charges, often providing subtle nudges and insights to help them stay on the right path. Guardian angels are accessible at any time and can be called upon for assistance in everyday matters.

Other Angelic Beings

Cherubim: Known for their wisdom and guardianship of light, they are more concerned with cosmic knowledge and protecting sacred spaces. They are less involved in personal affairs and more focused on preserving divine truth and enlightenment.

Seraphim: These high-ranking angels focus on divine worship and the radiance of divine love. Seraphim are less involved in human affairs and more connected to the celestial realms, perpetually immersed in the presence of the Divine.

Thrones, Dominions, Virtues, Powers, Principalities: These orders of angels have more specialized roles, often overseeing broader aspects of the universe and ensuring the proper functioning of divine law and order. They interact less directly with humans but have a significant impact on the spiritual and cosmic framework within which we exist.

The celestial hierarchy and the distinct roles of various angels illustrate the complexity and organization of the angelic realm. By understanding these differences, we can better appreciate how these divine beings support us, protect us, and guide us on our spiritual journeys. Whether through the personal care of guardian angels or the overarching guidance of archangels, angels are integral to our connection with the divine and our path toward spiritual enlightenment. Embracing the wisdom and support of angels allows us to navigate life with greater peace, purpose, and a sense of divine partnership.

Alex McCann Johnson

Chapter 25

Guardian Angels

Among the various types of angelic beings, guardian angels are perhaps the most familiar and comforting. These celestial protectors are with us from the moment of our birth, dedicated to watching over us, offering guidance, and ensuring our well-being. Each of us has at least one guardian angel who is deeply invested in our life's journey, acting as a personal guide and constant companion.

In my experience, connecting with my guardian angel has been a source of immense comfort and support. Whenever I feel lost or in need of reassurance, tuning into the presence of my guardian angel brings a sense of peace and clarity. These angels are always near, ready to assist and protect us in ways both subtle and profound.

Guardian angels are divine beings assigned to us at birth, tasked with the mission of protecting and guiding us throughout our lives. They are embodiments of unconditional love and wisdom, offering their support without judgment or expectation. Unlike other types of spirit guides who may come and go, guardian angels remain with us constantly, providing a steady source of guidance and protection.

From the gentle nudge that steers us away from danger to the comforting presence that soothes our worries, guardian angels are ever-vigilant in their care. They communicate with us through intuitive feelings, dreams, and signs, ensuring we are never alone.

One of my most profound experiences with my guardian angel

occurred when I was earnestly trying to deepen our connection. Despite my repeated attempts, I felt nothing specific, only a pervasive presence that seemed to linger around me. Then, one evening, I awoke to see him standing beside my bed. You'd think I would have been startled, but I felt an overwhelming sense of calm instead. He had dark skin and wore shimmering gold armor that shone brightly, his wings vast and majestic, covering the entire wall behind him. He was there to comfort me and finally let me see the connection I had been seeking. Since that night, he has often appeared to me, always bringing a sense of peace and assurance. Though he never speaks aloud, I intuitively understand the messages he conveys.

Roles and Responsibilities: How Guardian Angels Protect and Guide

Guardian angels play several vital roles in our lives, each aimed at ensuring our safety, well-being, and spiritual growth. Here's how they contribute to our journey:

Protection: The primary role of guardian angels is to protect us from harm. They are constantly vigilant, intervening to shield us from physical danger, negative energies, and spiritual threats. Whether it's a near miss in traffic or a gut feeling to avoid a certain place, our guardian angels are always working behind the scenes to keep us safe.

Guidance: Guardian angels offer gentle guidance to help us navigate life's challenges and make decisions that align with our highest good. They often communicate through intuitive nudges, dreams, and synchronicities, providing insights and clarity. When faced with difficult choices, I often turn to my guardian angel for guidance and find that their wisdom helps me see the path more clearly.

Comfort and Support: During times of grief, stress, or uncertainty, guardian angels provide emotional comfort and support. Their presence can bring a sense of peace and reassurance, reminding us that we are loved and cared for. In my darkest moments, feeling the comforting presence of my guardian angel has been a source of strength and solace.

Spiritual Growth: Beyond their protective and guiding roles, guardian angels also support our spiritual growth. They encourage us to explore our spiritual path, deepen our self-awareness, and connect with our higher purpose. By fostering a relationship with our guardian angels, we can gain insights into our soul's journey and align more closely with our spiritual goals.

Unconditional Love: Above all, guardian angels embody unconditional love. They see us as we truly are—divine beings on a human journey—and offer their support without judgment. This unconditional love helps us to see ourselves with greater compassion and to embrace our true potential.

Recognizing Your Guardian Angel: Signs and Symbols

Recognizing your guardian angel involves tuning into subtle signs and feelings. Here are some common ways to identify their presence:

Sudden Sense of Peace: One of the most telltale signs of your guardian angel's presence is a sudden sense of peace or calm, especially during stressful or challenging times. This comforting energy often envelops you, bringing an immediate sense of relief.

Intuitive Nudges: Guardian angels frequently communicate through intuition. You might feel a strong urge to take a specific action or avoid a particular situation. These intuitive nudges are often your guardian angel's way of guiding you toward safety or wisdom.

Physical Sensations: Many people report physical sensations when their guardian angel is near, such as a warm or tingling feeling. This can manifest as a gentle breeze, a feeling of being lightly touched, or a sense of warmth enveloping your body.

Repeated Symbols: Guardian angels often use symbols to communicate with us. You might notice recurring symbols, such as feathers, specific numbers (like 111 or 444), or coins appearing in your path. These signs typically appear when you need reassurance or guidance.

Dreams and Visions: Guardian angels can also connect with us through dreams or meditative visions. You might dream of a benevolent figure offering comfort or guidance, or you might see symbols associated with angels, such as wings or light, during meditation.

In my own experience, I have recognized my guardian angel through moments of sudden clarity and the comforting sensations that accompany their presence. These signs remind me that my guardian angel is always near, offering their unwavering support and guidance.

Connecting with Guardian Angels: Techniques and Practices

Building a relationship with your guardian angel takes time and intentional effort. Here are some steps that have worked for me:

Set Your Intention: Clearly express your desire to connect with your guardian angel. This can be done through a simple prayer or affirmation. Here's a specific prayer you can use:

"Dear Guardian Angel, I invite you into my life and ask for your loving guidance and protection. Help me to recognize your presence and understand your messages. Thank you for watching over me and guiding me with your divine wisdom. I am open to your support and love."

Create a Sacred Space: Find a quiet place where you can meditate or pray without distractions. This could be a corner of your room dedicated to spiritual practice, adorned with items that hold personal significance, such as candles, crystals, or angel figurines.

Meditate and Invite: Sit quietly, take deep breaths, and invite your guardian angel to join you. Visualize a protective light surrounding you and imagine your guardian angel stepping into this light. Be open to any thoughts, feelings, or images that come to you during this meditation.

Mirror Gazing: A powerful technique to connect with your guardian angel is through mirror gazing. Here's how you can practice it:

- **Find a Quiet Space:** Choose a quiet room where you can

be alone and undisturbed. Place a mirror at eye level and sit comfortably in front of it.

- **Set Your Intention:** Before starting, set a clear intention to see yourself through the eyes of your guardian angel. You might say, "I invite my guardian angel to reveal how they see me, with unconditional love and divine light."

- **Begin Gazing:** Look into your eyes in the mirror. Maintain a soft focus, allowing your gaze to be gentle and relaxed. As you gaze, imagine your guardian angel standing behind you or surrounding you with their presence.

- **Observe Your Feelings:** Pay attention to any feelings, thoughts, or images that come to you. You might feel a sense of warmth, see your reflection soften, or even feel a loving presence beside you.

- **Reflect and Journal:** After your session, take a few moments to reflect on the experience. Write down any insights or messages you received. This can help you integrate the guidance and deepen your connection with your guardian angel.

Be Open and Receptive: Pay attention to any subtle signs or intuitive feelings that arise. Trust in your ability to connect with your guardian angel and be patient with the process. Over time, you will become more attuned to their presence and guidance.

Express Gratitude: Thank your guardian angel for their presence and guidance. Regularly expressing gratitude strengthens your connection and invites more of their support into your life. Acknowledge their role in your journey and show appreciation for their unwavering dedication.

Historical Significance of Guardian Angels

Guardian angels have been a part of human belief systems for centuries, transcending cultural and religious boundaries. In ancient Greece, they were known as personal daemons, spiritual entities assigned to individuals to guide and protect them. These daemons were believed to be intermediaries between the gods and humans, offering wisdom and safeguarding their charges throughout their lives.

In Christianity, the concept of guardian angels is deeply embedded in both doctrine and tradition. Early Christian writings emphasize the role of these celestial protectors, with Church Fathers like St. Jerome and St. Basil asserting that each person has an angel assigned to them at birth. The Bible is replete with references to angels who protect and guide humans, such as the angel who guards Daniel in the lion's den and the angel who guides Peter out of prison. Guardian angels are believed to watch over individuals, guiding them on their spiritual path and protecting them from harm.

Islam also holds a significant belief in guardian angels. According to Islamic teachings, each person has two guardian angels who record their good and bad deeds. These angels, known as Kiraman Katibin, are seen as protectors who guide individuals and keep a record of their actions for the Day of Judgment. The Qur'an mentions angels who guard humans and protect them by the command of Allah, highlighting their role in ensuring the well-being and spiritual growth of believers.

In indigenous traditions, many cultures recognize protective spirits similar to guardian angels. For example, Native American beliefs often include the concept of spirit guides and ancestors who watch over and protect their descendants. These spirits are revered as guardians who offer guidance and protection, helping individuals navigate life's challenges.

Hinduism and Buddhism also feature deities and enlightened beings who provide protection and guidance akin to guardian angels. In Hinduism, deities like Vishnu and Ganesha are often invoked for their protective qualities, while in Buddhism, Bodhisattvas like Avalokiteshvara are seen as compassionate beings who assist others on their path to enlightenment.

These diverse cultural beliefs highlight a universal understanding of personal divine protection and guidance. Throughout history, guardian angels have been revered as compassionate and vigilant beings committed to the well-being of those they protect.

Embracing the Journey with Guardian Angels

Guardian angels are invaluable allies on our life's journey. They provide protection, guidance, and comfort, helping us navigate the complexities of life with greater ease and confidence. By recognizing their presence and building a strong connection with them, we can tap into their divine wisdom and love.

Embracing the historical significance of guardian angels deepens our appreciation for their role in our lives. These celestial beings have been cherished across cultures and religions, embodying a timeless tradition of divine protection and support.

As you continue your journey, remember to invite your guardian angel to walk with you. Their presence can illuminate your path, providing clarity and comfort in times of need. Trust in their unwavering love, and allow their guidance to lead you toward a life filled with peace, purpose, and profound spiritual growth.

Chapter 26

Archangels

When I first began working with angelic beings, the powerful presence and high vibrational energy of archangels struck me offguard. Archangels are a higher order of angels known for their significant roles in guiding and protecting humanity. They act as divine messengers, carrying out important tasks that influence both the spiritual and physical realms.

Each archangel possesses unique attributes and areas of expertise. For example:

- **Archangel Michael:** Known as the protector, Michael wields a mighty sword to shield us from harm and lead us through challenging times. His presence often brings a sense of courage and strength.

- **Archangel Raphael:** Renowned for his healing abilities, Raphael offers comfort and restoration to those in need, whether it be physical, emotional, or spiritual healing.

- **Archangel Gabriel:** As the divine messenger, Gabriel provides clarity, communication, and guidance, often associated with delivering important messages and facilitating clear understanding.

- **Archangel Uriel:** Uriel is considered the light of God, illuminating our paths with wisdom and insight. He helps us to see the bigger picture and understand the deeper truths of our experiences.

Despite their distinct roles, all archangels share common characteristics. They operate on a high vibrational frequency and exude a powerful, loving energy that often brings peace and reassurance. They communicate through various means, including thoughts, visions, and intuitive feelings. The more I work with them, the more I realize how vital their guidance and support are in our lives.

Historical and Mythological Background

The history and mythology surrounding archangels are rich and diverse, spanning various cultures and religious traditions. In Judeo-Christian beliefs, archangels play prominent roles:

- Michael is depicted as a warrior, leading the heavenly armies against the forces of darkness.

- Gabriel is known for delivering pivotal messages, such as the announcement of Jesus' birth to Mary.

- Raphael appears in the Book of Tobit as a healer and guide, assisting Tobias on his journey.

In Islamic tradition, archangels are equally significant:

- Jibril (Gabriel) is the angel who revealed the Quran to the Prophet Muhammad.

- Mikail (Michael) oversees the provision of nourishment to both the body and soul.

- Israfil is believed to have blown the trumpet on the Day of Judgment.

- Azrael is the angel of death, guiding souls to the afterlife.

Beyond these Abrahamic faiths, angelic beings similar to archangels appear in other cultures:

- In Zoroastrianism, Amesha Spentas are comparable to archangels, who guide and protect the faithful.

- In Hinduism, Devas are divine beings with roles akin to those of archangels, overseeing various aspects of the cosmos.

These historical and mythological backgrounds highlight the universal nature of archangels, transcending specific religions and cultures. They are seen as divine messengers and protectors, helping humanity navigate the complexities of life and spiritual growth.

Archangels Across Different Cultures

Archangels appear across different cultures, often with similar attributes and roles, emphasizing their universal significance:

Christianity: Archangels like Michael, Gabriel, and Raphael are revered as powerful and benevolent beings, each associated with specific aspects of divine intervention and support.

Islam: Key archangels include Jibril (Gabriel), Mikail (Michael), Israfil, and Azrael, each fulfilling vital roles such as delivering divine messages, overseeing natural phenomena, and guiding souls.

Hinduism: Divine beings like Indra, Agni, and Varuna oversee various elements and natural forces, maintaining cosmic order and guiding humanity, much like archangels.

Indigenous and Pagan Traditions: Many cultures recognize angelic or spirit beings who act as protectors, healers, and guides, reflecting the universal human experience of seeking divine assistance and connection.

These cultural variations enrich our understanding of archangels, showing that their presence and influence are acknowledged and celebrated worldwide.

Connecting with Archangels

My journey with archangels began unexpectedly but has completely shaped my spiritual practice. Connecting with these powerful beings can be a transformative experience, providing guidance, healing, and protection. Here are some steps that have helped me establish and deepen my connection with archangels:

Set Your Intention: Clearly state your desire to connect with a specific archangel or the archangels in general. Intentions can be spoken out loud, written down, or held in your mind during meditation. For example, you might say, "I invite Archangel Michael to be with me now to provide protection and guidance."

Create a Sacred Space: Find a quiet and comfortable place where you can focus on your connection. Light a candle, burn incense, or play soothing music to create a peaceful environment. This helps raise your vibration and makes it easier to sense the presence of archangels.

Meditate and Invite: Sit comfortably and take several deep breaths to center yourself. Visualize a sphere of divine light surrounding you, inviting the archangels to join you. Use your intuition to feel their presence, which may come as warmth, light, or a sense of peace.

Be Open and Receptive: Pay attention to any thoughts, feelings, or images that come to you. Archangels communicate in various ways, so be open to receiving their messages through different channels. Trust your intuition and the guidance you receive.

Ask for Signs: If you're unsure about the presence of an archangel, ask for a sign. This could be a specific symbol, a repeating number, or an unexpected encounter. Archangels often provide subtle yet clear signs to confirm their presence.

Express Gratitude: After your meditation or prayer, thank the archangels for their guidance and support. Gratitude helps strengthen your connection and invites ongoing assistance.

Practice Regularly: Building a relationship with archangels takes time and practice. Set aside regular moments to connect with them. Over time, you'll find it easier to sense their presence and understand their messages.

In my experience, connecting with archangels has brought immense peace, clarity, and healing into my life. Their guidance has helped me navigate challenges, make important decisions, and deepen my spiritual practice. I encourage you to explore this connection and discover the support and wisdom that archangels can offer.

Chapter 27
Cherubim

Cherubim are among the most revered and mysterious of angelic beings, often depicted as guardians of divine light and profound wisdom. My initial encounter with the concept of cherubim left me in awe of their majestic and multifaceted nature. These high-ranking angels are typically portrayed with multiple wings and eyes, signifying their all-seeing, omniscient presence and their deep connection to the divine mysteries. Their role extends far beyond mere protectors; they are the custodians of sacred spaces and the bearers of divine knowledge.

In my spiritual practice, connecting with the cherubim has opened doors to higher realms of understanding and enlightenment. Their presence feels like a radiant light that illuminates the path to profound truths and divine wisdom. Whenever I seek deeper insight or protection for my spiritual endeavors, I call upon the cherubim to guide and guard me. Their energy is both powerful and serene, offering a sense of safety while gently nudging me toward greater knowledge and enlightenment.

Roles and Responsibilities: Protecting the Sacred and Illuminating the Mind

The cherubim have a crucial role in the celestial hierarchy, tasked with guarding the most sacred aspects of the divine. Here's how their responsibilities manifest in both the spiritual and physical realms:

Guardians of Sacred Spaces: One of the primary roles of the cherubim is to protect sacred places. They are often depicted as standing vigil at the gates of heaven or guarding the throne of God. In the biblical narrative, they are positioned at the entrance to the Garden of Eden to prevent humanity from re-entering and accessing the Tree of Life. This protective role emphasizes their function as gatekeepers of divine mysteries and holy realms. In my experience, invoking the cherubim's presence can create a protected and sanctified space for deep spiritual work.

Bearers of Divine Wisdom: Cherubim are not just protectors but also carriers of profound knowledge. Their multiple eyes symbolize their all-seeing nature, indicating a deep and encompassing understanding of the universe. When seeking enlightenment or answers to complex spiritual questions, cherubim can serve as guides, helping to unveil the mysteries of the cosmos. Their wisdom is both vast and accessible to those who approach with humility and a sincere desire to learn.

Symbols of Omniscience and Divine Authority: The cherubim's appearance—with their many wings and eyes—represents their omnipresence and deep connection to divine truth. This symbolism underscores their role as beings who are privy to all aspects of creation and who possess authority over the sacred. Working with the cherubim has often provided me with insights that feel beyond the ordinary scope of understanding as if they are revealing hidden aspects of the divine plan.

Promoters of Purity and Worthiness: In their role as guardians, the cherubim ensures that only those who are pure and worthy can access the divine and sacred realms. This function serves as a reminder of the importance of spiritual integrity and the pursuit of a higher moral and ethical standard. In my spiritual practice, invoking the cherubim helps me stay aligned with these principles, guiding me to maintain purity in my thoughts, actions, and intentions.

How to Connect with Cherubim: Practical Steps and Techniques

Connecting with the cherubim can be a deeply transformative experience, opening the door to greater wisdom and divine protection. Here are some practical steps and techniques that have helped me establish a connection with these powerful guardians:

Study Sacred Texts: Cherubim are prominently featured in many religious and mystical texts. Delve into scriptures and writings that describe their nature and roles, such as the Bible, the Torah, and mystical Jewish texts like the Kabbalah. Understanding their historical and spiritual significance through these texts can deepen your connection with them.

Meditate on Symbols of Light: Light is a powerful symbol associated with cherubim. During meditation, visualize yourself surrounded by a radiant, protective light that represents their presence. Imagine this light infusing you with wisdom and illuminating the path ahead. This practice can help you attune to the cherubim's energy and open yourself to their guidance.

Create a Sacred Space: Dedicate a space in your home for connecting with the cherubim. Use symbols and objects that evoke their presence, such as images of wings, eyes, or representations of light. This space will serve as a sanctuary for reflection and spiritual growth, allowing you to invite the cherubim into your daily life.

Ask for Guidance and Protection: Directly invite the cherubim to guide and protect you. You might say a specific prayer like:

"Cherubim, Guardians of Light and Wisdom, I invite you into my life and ask for your guidance and protection. Please illuminate my path with your divine wisdom and guard the sacred spaces within and around me. Help me to access the deeper truths and mysteries of the universe. Thank you for your presence and your light."

Engage in Reflective Practices: Spend time in reflection and contemplation, focusing on the qualities and attributes of the cherubim. Consider how their wisdom and protective energy can be integrated into your life. Journaling your thoughts and experiences can also help you deepen your understanding and connection with these powerful beings.

Seek Signs of Their Presence: Cherubim may communicate through symbols and signs in your everyday life. Be attentive to recurring motifs such as wings, eyes, or light. These signs can be a confirmation of their presence and guidance. In my experience, noticing these symbols has often coincided with moments of deep insight or a need for protection.

Historical Significance of Cherubim

Cherubim have a profound and enduring presence in religious and mystical traditions across the world. Their significance is deeply rooted in their roles as protectors and bearers of divine knowledge.

In the Bible, cherubim are first mentioned in the Book of Genesis, where they guard the entrance to the Garden of Eden, preventing humanity from re-entering after the fall. They are also described in the Book of Exodus as adorning the Ark of the Covenant, symbolizing their role as guardians of sacred spaces and divine mysteries. Ezekiel's vision in the Old Testament presents cherubim as creatures with multiple faces and wings, a depiction that emphasizes their all-seeing nature and divine authority.

In Jewish mysticism, particularly within the Kabbalistic tradition, cherubim are considered powerful angels of knowledge and protection. They are seen as intermediaries between God and humanity, ensuring that the sacred remains inaccessible to those who are not prepared. This perspective highlights their role in preserving the sanctity and purity of divine knowledge.

In Christian theology, cherubim are often portrayed as majestic beings who serve directly under God. In religious art and iconography, they are sometimes seen as winged angels who uphold the divine throne. Their presence is invoked in ceremonial contexts to symbolize the protection and sanctity of the sacred.

Although not as prominently featured in Islamic tradition, the concept of angels with attributes similar to cherubim exists. These angels are seen as custodians of divine knowledge and protectors of the heavenly realms, aligning with the cherubim's role in other Abrahamic religions.

Guided by Spirits

The cherubim's consistent portrayal across different cultures and religious traditions underscores their universal role as guardians of divine knowledge and protectors of the sacred. Their historical presence affirms the importance of maintaining spiritual integrity and seeking wisdom with humility and reverence.

Embracing the Journey with Cherubim

Cherubim are powerful and majestic beings who serve as guardians of light, wisdom, and sacred spaces. Their role extends beyond mere protection; they are guides who help us access deeper truths and navigate the mysteries of the universe. By connecting with the cherubim, we can invite their wisdom, protection, and light into our lives, enriching our spiritual journey.

As you continue your path, consider inviting the cherubim to illuminate your understanding and guard your sacred spaces. Allow their presence to inspire you towards greater knowledge, balance, and harmony. Embrace the journey with these divine guardians, and let their light guide you to the deeper truths that lie within and beyond.

Chapter 28

Seraphim

The seraphim are considered the highest and most revered order of angels, existing closest to the Divine Presence. Their name, derived from the Hebrew word "seraph," means "burning ones," reflecting their radiant and fiery nature. Often depicted as beings of pure light and fire, the seraphim embodies the ultimate expression of divine purity and spiritual illumination.

My journey into understanding the seraphim began with a meditation where I visualized these magnificent beings. I was overwhelmed by their intensity and the sheer power of their presence. Their energy was not just light; it was a purifying fire that seemed to cleanse my spirit and elevate my consciousness to new heights. Working with the seraphim has deepened my spiritual practice and connected me to a sense of divine awe and reverence.

Roles and Responsibilities: Maintaining Divine Purity and Perpetual Worship

The seraphim serve several essential roles in the celestial hierarchy, each of which underscores their deep connection to the Divine:

Guardians of Divine Purity: The primary role of the seraphim is to maintain the purity and sanctity of the Divine Presence. They stand as eternal guardians around the throne of God, ensuring that no impurity can come near. Their fiery nature symbolizes their ability to burn away any imperfections, both in the heavenly realm and within our own souls. In my spiritual practice, invoking the seraphim has often felt like undergoing a grand purification, as if their flames were cleansing me from within.

Perpetual Worshipers: Seraphim are known for their continuous praise and worship of the Creator. They sing and chant hymns of adoration, their voices forming a celestial symphony that celebrates the glory of the Divine. This aspect of their existence highlights the importance of devotion and the transformative power of worship. Engaging in practices that elevate our spirit, such as singing or chanting, can help us align with the seraphim's energy and experience a deeper connection to the Divine.

Elevators of Spiritual Vibration: The seraphim's presence helps to raise the vibrational frequency of those they touch. They inspire us to seek higher states of consciousness and spiritual enlightenment. Their light and fire act as catalysts, igniting our inner divine spark and guiding us toward our highest potential. When I meditate on the seraphim, I often feel an uplifting surge of energy that elevates my thoughts and emotions, helping me connect with the highest aspects of my spirituality.

Messengers of Divine Light: Although not typically seen as messengers in the same way as other angels, the seraphim carries the light of divine truth and wisdom. They can illuminate our path and provide insights that lead to profound spiritual awakening. Their presence in my life has often been a source of clarity and understanding, as if their light revealed hidden truths and guided me toward greater wisdom.

How to Connect with Seraphim: Practical Steps and Techniques

Connecting with the seraphim can be a transformative experience, inviting their purifying and elevating energy into your life. Here are some practical steps and techniques that have helped me connect with these highest-order angels:

Engage in Worship: The seraphim are known for their perpetual worship. Participating in spiritual practices that elevate your spirit, such as singing, chanting, or prayer, can help you align with their energy.

Whether through traditional hymns, mantras, or personal expressions of devotion, engaging in worship can create a powerful connection with the seraphim.

Meditate on Fire and Light: Visualize a purifying fire that cleanses your soul. During meditation, imagine yourself surrounded by a brilliant, fiery light that burns away any negativity or impurities. This light represents the presence of the seraphim, purifying and elevating your spirit. Focus on the warmth and brightness of this light, allowing it to fill you with a sense of divine purity and illumination.

Seek Higher Vibration: Aim to raise your vibrational frequency through positive thoughts, actions, and intentions. The seraphim exists at the highest levels of vibration, and aligning yourself with their energy involves striving for purity and positivity in your life. Practice gratitude, compassion, and kindness, and seek to elevate your thoughts and emotions to resonate with the seraphim's divine frequency.

Create a Sacred Space: Dedicate a space in your home for connecting with the seraphim. Use candles, crystals, or other symbols of light and fire to create an environment that reflects their radiant energy. This space can serve as a sanctuary for meditation, worship, and reflection, helping you attune to the seraphim's presence.

Ask for Their Guidance: Directly invite the seraphim into your life. You might say a specific prayer like:

"Seraphim, Guardians of Divine Light and Purity, I invite you into my life. Surround me with your radiant light and purify my soul with your divine fire. Help me to connect with the highest aspects of my spirituality and elevate my spirit to new heights. Thank you for your presence and your endless devotion to the Divine."

Engage with Sacred Texts and Hymns: Reading sacred texts and hymns that praise the Divine can also help you connect with the seraphim. Their voices are often depicted as singing the eternal praises of God, and engaging with these texts can align you with their energy and open your heart to their divine presence.

Historical Significance of Seraphim

The seraphim holds a significant place in various religious and mystical traditions, where they are revered as the highest order of angels and the closest to the Divine. Their presence is most notably mentioned in the Bible, specifically in the Book of Isaiah. Here, Isaiah describes his vision of the seraphim standing above the throne of God, each with six wings, calling out to one another: "Holy, holy, holy is the Lord Almighty; the whole earth is full of his glory" (Isaiah 6:3). This powerful depiction underscores their role as perpetual worshipers and guardians of divine purity.

In Christian mysticism, the seraphim are often seen as embodying the highest state of angelic existence, representing the purest form of love and devotion to God. Their fiery nature and continuous praise are symbolic of their deep, unending connection to the divine source. Throughout history, Christian theologians and mystics have drawn upon the imagery of the seraphim to illustrate the ultimate goal of spiritual ascent and the transformative power of divine love.

In Jewish tradition, the seraphim are similarly revered as exalted beings of light and fire. They are described in various texts as standing in the presence of God, serving as his immediate attendants and the bearers of his divine glory. Their role as protectors of sacred spaces and the divine throne highlights their importance in maintaining the sanctity and purity of the heavenly realm.

In Islamic thought, while not directly named, the concept of angels with attributes similar to the seraphim exists. These angels are seen as beings of immense purity and light, perpetually engaged in the worship and adoration of God. Their presence emphasizes the importance of devotion and the pursuit of spiritual enlightenment.

The seraphim's consistent portrayal across these different traditions underscores their universal role as the highest and most revered of angelic beings. Their historical significance lies in their embodiment of divine purity and their unceasing worship of the Creator, serving as a powerful reminder of the ultimate goal of spiritual ascent and the pursuit

Guided by Spirits
of divine love and light.

Embracing the Journey with Seraphim

The seraphim are the highest order of angels, embodying the ultimate expression of divine purity, love, and light. Their role as perpetual worshipers and guardians of sacred spaces connects them intimately with the Divine Presence. By engaging in practices that elevate our spirit, meditating on symbols of fire and light, and striving to raise our vibrational frequency, we can align ourselves with the seraphim's energy and invite their influence into our lives.

As you continue your spiritual journey, consider inviting the seraphim to illuminate your path with their divine light and purify your soul with their fiery presence. Embrace their role as the highest guardians of divine wisdom and allow their eternal praise and devotion to inspire your own spiritual practice. Let the seraphim guide you toward a deeper connection with the Divine, helping you to achieve a state of purity, enlightenment, and unending love.

Alex McCann Johnson

Chapter 29

Principalities

Principalities are a fascinating and powerful order of angels responsible for the guidance and protection of entire nations, regions, and large communities. Unlike other angels who often focus on individual lives or smaller groups, principalities operate on a grander scale. Their purpose is to oversee the collective actions of societies and influence leaders and decision-makers to promote justice, peace, and divine order.

In my spiritual journey, I have often felt the subtle influence of principalities when contemplating the well-being of larger groups or the state of our world. Their presence is like a steady hand guiding the course of nations toward a path aligned with divine principles. They seem to operate behind the scenes, shaping the moral and ethical frameworks within which societies evolve.

Roles and Responsibilities: Guardians of Collective Welfare

Principalities hold a unique and crucial role within the celestial hierarchy. Their responsibilities extend beyond the individual, focusing on the collective welfare of humanity. Here are some of the key functions they perform:

Guiding Nations and Leaders: One of the primary roles of principalities is to guide those in positions of power and influence. They work to inspire leaders, policymakers, and other decision-makers to act with integrity, wisdom, and compassion. This guidance helps ensure that the actions taken by these individuals promote the welfare of the people and align with divine principles. In times of political turmoil or social unrest, invoking the support of principalities can help bring about wise and just leadership.

Promoting Justice and Peace: Principalities are deeply committed to the promotion of justice and peace on a large scale. They influence the collective consciousness of societies to foster environments where fairness, equality, and harmony can flourish. Their presence can be felt in movements that advocate for human rights, social justice, and the peaceful resolution of conflicts. They help to channel the collective energy of communities towards constructive and positive outcomes.

Ensuring Divine Order: These angels work to maintain divine order within earthly realms. This involves overseeing the implementation of divine laws and ensuring that the moral and ethical standards of societies are upheld. Principalities play a crucial role in balancing the energies within communities, ensuring that chaos and disorder are kept at bay. They act as the architects of societal structures that reflect divine will.

Inspiring Collective Actions: Principalities inspire collective actions that benefit society as a whole. Whether it's community service, charitable initiatives, or grassroots movements, their influence can be seen in efforts that aim to uplift and improve the lives of many. They encourage individuals to think beyond their personal interests and contribute to the greater good.

Protecting Nations and Communities: As guardians of nations and communities, principalities provide protection against forces that threaten collective well-being. This can include shielding societies from conflict, natural disasters, or other large-scale disruptions. They work to preserve the integrity and stability of regions, helping communities to thrive and prosper.

Connecting with Principalities: Practical Steps and Techniques

Building a connection with principalities can enhance our ability to contribute to the collective good and align our actions with divine intentions. Here are some steps and techniques that have helped me connect with these powerful angels:

Pray for Communities and Leaders: One of the most direct ways to connect with principalities is to pray for the well-being of communities and leaders. Send positive energy and prayers to those in positions of power, asking for their guidance and protection. You might say, "Principalities, guardians of nations and communities, please guide our leaders to act with wisdom, justice, and compassion. Help them to make decisions that promote the welfare of all."

Meditate on Global Harmony: During meditation, focus on visualizing peace, justice, and harmony spreading across the world. Imagine a wave of divine light enveloping the planet, bringing balance and healing to all nations. This practice can help you align with the energy of the principalities and support their efforts to promote global harmony.

Act for the Greater Good: Engage in actions that benefit your community and contribute to societal well-being. Whether through volunteer work, advocacy, or simply spreading kindness and positivity, acting for the greater good helps to channel the influence of principalities into the world. Reflect on how you can make a positive impact on your community and take steps to contribute to collective prosperity.

Create Sacred Space for Global Healing: Dedicate a space in your home for prayer and meditation focused on global healing and the well-being of communities. Use symbols of peace, justice, and protection to create an environment that supports your connection with principalities. This space can serve as a sanctuary for focusing your intentions on the collective good.

Study the Teachings of Global Harmony: Engage with spiritual texts and teachings that emphasize the importance of global harmony and collective well-being. This can deepen your understanding of the principles that principalities uphold and help you integrate these values into your own life.

Express Gratitude for Collective Guidance: Regularly express gratitude for the guidance and protection provided by principalities. Thank them for their efforts in maintaining peace and justice in the world and for guiding leaders and communities toward positive outcomes. Gratitude helps to strengthen your connection with these angels and reinforces your alignment with their mission.

Historical Significance of Principalities

The concept of principalities as guardians of nations and communities is embedded in various religious and spiritual traditions. In Christian angelology, principalities are considered the third highest order of angels, often depicted as overseeing the administration of divine law within earthly realms. They are believed to guide and influence leaders and rulers, ensuring that governance aligns with divine will and promotes the welfare of the people.

In Jewish mysticism, principalities are seen as powerful beings who play a crucial role in maintaining the order and balance of creation. They are associated with the oversight of entire nations and cities, reflecting their responsibility for the collective good. This tradition highlights their role in guiding the moral and ethical development of societies.

Islamic teachings also acknowledge the presence of angelic beings who oversee the actions of nations and leaders. These angels are tasked with ensuring that justice and divine order are upheld, mirroring the functions attributed to principalities in other traditions.

In ancient mythology, similar concepts can be found in the form of gods and spirits who were believed to protect and guide entire communities and regions. These deities were often seen as the guardians of societal order and prosperity, influencing the course of events and the actions of rulers.

Throughout history, the idea of principalities has been a powerful reminder of the importance of collective welfare and the need for just and wise leadership. Their presence in religious texts and spiritual traditions shows us their role as divine overseers, guiding humanity toward a path of peace, justice, and harmony. The historical significance of principalities highlights their enduring influence in shaping the moral and ethical frameworks within which societies evolve.

Embracing the Journey with Principalities

Principalities are powerful and benevolent angels dedicated to guiding and protecting nations and communities. Their role in overseeing the collective actions of societies and influencing leaders to act with integrity and wisdom is crucial for promoting justice, peace, and divine order. By connecting with principalities through prayer, meditation, and positive actions, we can align ourselves with their mission and contribute to the greater good of our world.

As you continue your spiritual journey, consider inviting the principalities to guide and protect your community and inspire leaders to govern with justice and compassion. Embrace their presence as guardians of collective welfare and let their influence inspire you to act for the benefit of all. You can help bring about a world that reflects the divine principles of peace, harmony, and justice through your connection with principalities.

Alex McCann Johnson

Chapter 30

Powers

In the angel hierarchy, Powers stands as formidable defenders, often seen as the warrior angels tasked with combating evil forces and maintaining cosmic order. Their primary role is to protect humanity from spiritual and physical threats, ensuring that the balance between good and evil is upheld. Powers are known for their strength, courage, and unwavering commitment to safeguarding the universe from negative entities and energies.

When I first became aware of Powers, I was struck by their fierce yet protective presence. They carry an energy that is both empowering and reassuring, providing a sense of safety and security. Powers are the celestial soldiers in the angelic realm, ever vigilant and ready to defend against any forces that seek to disrupt the divine harmony.

Roles and Responsibilities: Battling Evil and Maintaining Order

Powers are unique among the angelic orders because of their direct involvement in spiritual warfare. Here are some of the key responsibilities they undertake:

Engaging in Spiritual Warfare: Powers are on the front lines of the battle between good and evil. They confront and neutralize negative entities, demonic forces, and malevolent energies that threaten humanity and the divine order. Their presence is a shield against the darkness, ensuring that these forces do not harm the innocent or disrupt the cosmic balance. When facing spiritual challenges or sensing negative influences, calling upon Powers can provide strong and decisive protection.

Protecting Humanity from Harm: These warrior angels are dedicated to safeguarding humanity from both spiritual and physical threats. Whether it's warding off negative influences, protecting against harmful energies, or guiding individuals away from danger, Powers act as guardians who ensure our safety. Their protection is especially valuable during personal crises or when navigating challenging environments.

Maintaining Cosmic Order: Powers play a crucial role in upholding the divine order of the universe. They ensure that the balance between light and darkness is maintained, preventing chaos and disorder from taking hold. This responsibility extends beyond the earthly realm to the entire cosmos, where Powers work to preserve harmony and stability. Their vigilance keeps the forces of chaos in check, allowing the universe to function according to divine law.

Strengthening Spiritual Defenses: In addition to their protective duties, Powers help individuals fortify their own spiritual defenses. They provide guidance on how to strengthen one's aura, enhance personal resilience, and maintain inner peace amidst external turmoil. By connecting with Powers, we can learn to build a strong spiritual foundation that can withstand any challenge.

Promoting Inner Peace: Powers are not only warriors but also advocates of peace. They assist us in finding and maintaining inner peace, even in the midst of conflict. Their guidance helps us navigate through life with a sense of calm and assurance, knowing that we are protected and supported by powerful allies.

Connecting with Powers: Practical Steps and Techniques

Building a connection with Powers can greatly enhance our ability to protect ourselves and maintain inner peace. Here are some steps and techniques that have helped me connect with these warrior angels:

Pray for Protection: One of the most direct ways to connect with Powers is through prayer. During challenging times or when you feel threatened, ask for their protection. You might say, "Powers, mighty protectors, please shield me from harm and guard me against negative forces. Help me to stand strong in the face of adversity and maintain my peace."

Visualize Shields and Armor: Visualization is a powerful tool for invoking the protective energy of Powers. During meditation, imagine yourself surrounded by a shield of light or wearing armor that deflects any negative energy. Visualize Powers standing guard around you, ensuring your safety and fortifying your spiritual defenses.

Engage in Spiritual Cleansing: Perform rituals or practices that cleanse your energy and environment of negativity. This can include cleansing with sage, using salt baths, or setting protective intentions. These practices can help you align with the protective energy of Powers and create a sacred space free from harmful influences.

Meditate on Symbols of Strength: Focus on symbols that represent strength, courage, and protection. This could be imagery of shields, swords, or other warrior symbols. Meditating on these symbols can help you connect with the empowering energy of Powers and reinforce your own inner strength.

Set Boundaries: Powers can assist in establishing and maintaining strong personal boundaries. Reflect on areas of your life where you need to set or reinforce boundaries and ask for their guidance and support. Clear boundaries help protect your energy and maintain your well-being.

Express Gratitude for Protection: Regularly express gratitude for the protection and strength provided by Powers. Thank them for their vigilance and for safeguarding you from harm. Gratitude helps to strengthen your connection and invites ongoing support.

Historical Significance of Powers

Powers have been recognized throughout history as the angels responsible for combating evil and maintaining cosmic order. In Christian angelology, Powers are often depicted as warrior angels who protect humanity from demonic forces and negative influences. They are considered one of the highest orders of angels in the celestial hierarchy, symbolizing their significant role in the divine plan.

In the Bible, Powers are mentioned as the "powers of the heavens," highlighting their role in maintaining the order of the universe. They are seen as defenders of divine justice and protectors of God's creation, ensuring that evil does not prevail.

In Jewish mysticism, Powers are associated with the Sefirot of Geburah on the Tree of Life, representing strength and judgment. They are seen as enforcers of divine law, upholding justice and righteousness within the cosmos.

In Islamic tradition, similar concepts are found in the roles of angels who combat evil and protect believers from harm. These angels are often invoked for protection and guidance, reflecting the universal need for divine guardianship.

Throughout history, Powers have been invoked for protection and strength in the face of adversity. Their presence in various religious and mystical traditions shows their importance as defenders of the cosmic order and protectors of humanity. Powers are seen as the celestial guardians who ensure that good prevails over evil and that the divine balance is maintained.

Embracing the Journey with Powers

Powers are formidable and benevolent angels dedicated to protecting humanity and maintaining cosmic order. Their role as warriors and defenders is crucial in the ongoing battle between light and darkness. By connecting with Powers through prayer, visualization, and spiritual practices, we can fortify our spiritual defenses and find inner peace amidst external challenges.

As you continue your spiritual journey, consider inviting the Powers to guide and protect you. Embrace their presence as warriors of the divine and let their strength and courage inspire you to stand firm in the face of adversity. Through your connection with Powers, you can contribute to the preservation of divine order and the triumph of light over darkness.

Alex McCann Johnson

Chapter 31

Virtues

Virtues, as their name suggests, are angels who embody and bestow grace, valor, and divine virtues upon humanity. These celestial beings are known for their ability to inspire acts of courage, goodness, and miraculous occurrences. When I first encountered the concept of Virtues, I was moved by their influence on our capacity to act with integrity and bravery in the face of life's challenges. Virtues uplift the human spirit, guiding us to embody the highest moral and spiritual principles.

In my experience, Virtues bring a powerful yet gentle presence that encourages us to rise above our limitations and embrace our true potential. They are the silent whispers of encouragement that urge us to act with kindness, courage, and grace, even in difficult times. Their influence helps us recognize and harness the divine power within us to create positive change in our lives and the world around us.

Roles and Responsibilities: Inspiring Miracles and Encouraging Valor

Virtues have a unique and vital role among the angelic orders. They are instrumental in bringing about miracles and encouraging people to act with courage and integrity. Here are some of the key responsibilities they undertake:

Bringing About Miracles: Virtues are known as the angels of miracles. They facilitate divine intervention in our lives, helping to manifest miraculous events that defy ordinary expectations. Whether

173

it's a sudden healing, a serendipitous solution to a problem, or an unexpected act of kindness that transforms a situation, Virtues are often at work behind the scenes. Their presence makes the impossible possible, reminding us of the divine potential that exists in every moment.

Inspiring Courage and Goodness: Virtues inspire us to act with courage and integrity. They encourage us to stand up for what is right, to be brave in the face of adversity, and to lead by example. When we find ourselves in challenging situations that require moral strength, it is often the influence of Virtues that gives us the courage to persevere and the resolve to act in alignment with our highest values.

Uplifting the Human Spirit: One of the most profound roles of Virtues is their ability to uplift the human spirit. They instill a sense of hope, optimism, and positive energy that can lift us out of despair and into a state of grace. Virtues help us see the beauty and goodness in ourselves and others, fostering a sense of compassion and unity.

Promoting Positive Actions: Virtues encourage us to take actions that are aligned with love, kindness, and generosity. They guide us to make choices that benefit not only ourselves but also the greater good. Under their influence, we are inspired to contribute positively to our communities, support those in need, and create a ripple effect of goodness in the world.

How to Recognize Virtues: Identifying Their Presence

Recognizing the presence of Virtues can be a subtle and deeply personal experience. Here are some ways to identify when Virtues are at work in your life:

Sudden Acts of Courage or Kindness: If you find yourself or others around you performing acts of extraordinary courage or kindness, it may be a sign that Virtues are present. These actions often arise spontaneously, driven by a sense of moral duty or compassion that feels divinely inspired.

Miraculous Events: Experiences that seem miraculous or defy ordinary explanation can often be attributed to the influence of Virtues. These events can range from small, everyday miracles to significant, life-changing occurrences that have a profound impact.

A Deep Sense of Grace: Feeling a deep, abiding sense of grace and tranquility in challenging situations can indicate the presence of Virtues. This grace helps us remain calm and centered, even in the midst of turmoil, allowing us to respond with wisdom and compassion.

Inspiration to Act with Integrity: When you feel a strong, inner prompting to act with integrity and align your actions with your highest values, it may be the Virtues guiding you. Their influence encourages us to stay true to our principles and to act in ways that reflect our deepest beliefs.

Elevated States of Joy and Compassion: Virtues often bring an elevated state of joy and compassion that transcends ordinary emotions. This heightened sense of well-being can inspire us to connect with others on a deeper level and to extend kindness and support to those around us.

Connecting with Virtues: Practical Steps and Techniques

Building a connection with Virtues can help you tap into their powerful energy of grace, courage, and miraculous potential. Here are some steps and techniques that have helped me connect with these inspiring angels:

Pray for Miracles: One of the most direct ways to connect with Virtues is through prayer. When you need a miracle or face a challenging situation, ask for the intervention of Virtues. You might say, "Virtues, angels of grace and valor, please bring your divine presence into my life. Help me to experience miracles and to act with courage and integrity."

Meditate on Acts of Valor: Visualization is a powerful tool for connecting with the energy of Virtues. During meditation, focus on images or scenarios that represent acts of valor, kindness, and goodness. Visualize yourself embodying these qualities and feel the presence of Virtues supporting and guiding you.

Embrace Grace: Cultivating grace in your thoughts, words, and actions can help you align with the energy of Virtues. Practice being gentle with yourself and others, and strive to respond to life's challenges with calmness and compassion. Embracing grace in your daily interactions invites the presence of Virtues in your life.

Engage in Acts of Goodness: Take conscious steps to perform acts of kindness and generosity. Whether it's helping a neighbor, volunteering in your community, or simply offering a kind word to someone in need, these actions resonate with the energy of Virtues and strengthen your connection with them.

Focus on Positive Outcomes: When faced with difficulties, try to focus on the positive outcomes and the potential for growth and transformation. Virtues help us see the good in every situation and inspire us to respond with optimism and hope.

Express Gratitude for Miracles: Regularly express gratitude for the miracles and blessings in your life. Thank the Virtues for their guidance and for inspiring you to act with courage and integrity. Gratitude helps to deepen your connection with these angels and invites more positive experiences into your life.

Historical Significance of Virtues

Virtues have been recognized and revered throughout history as powerful agents of divine intervention and moral inspiration. In Christian angelology, Virtues are considered the fifth highest order of angels, tasked with instilling divine virtues in humanity and bringing about miraculous occurrences. They are often depicted as angels who inspire acts of heroism and goodness, guiding individuals to live virtuous lives.

In the Bible, Virtues are mentioned as angels who perform miracles and aid in the divine plan. Their role is to manifest God's grace and power in the world, supporting the faithful in their endeavors and promoting righteousness.

In Jewish mysticism, Virtues are associated with the Sefirot of

Netzach on the Tree of Life, representing victory and endurance. They are seen as the driving force behind actions that lead to moral and spiritual triumph, helping individuals overcome challenges and achieve their highest potential.

In Islamic tradition, the concept of angels who inspire courage and righteousness is also present. These angels are believed to support and protect those who strive to live in accordance with divine principles.

Throughout history, Virtues have been invoked to inspire courage, integrity, and acts of goodness. Their presence in religious and mystical traditions highlights their role as agents of divine intervention and moral guidance. Virtues are seen as the angels who uplift humanity, encouraging us to embody the highest ideals and act gracefully and valorously in all aspects of our lives.

Embracing the Journey with Virtues

Virtues are extraordinary angels who bestow grace and valor upon humanity. They inspire us to act with courage, integrity, and kindness, bringing about miraculous changes and uplifting our spirits. By connecting with Virtues through prayer, meditation, and acts of goodness, we can align ourselves with their powerful energy and invite their influence into our lives.

As you continue your spiritual journey, consider inviting the Virtues to guide and inspire you. Embrace their presence as catalysts for positive change and let their energy help you manifest miracles and act with grace and courage. You can cultivate a life filled with divine grace and boundless potential for good through your connection with Virtues.

Alex McCann Johnson

Chapter 32

Dominions

Dominions, as their name suggests, are the angels of leadership and divine governance. They play a crucial role in maintaining the order of the cosmos and ensuring that the divine will is carried out both in the physical and spiritual realms. My journey with understanding Dominions has deepened my appreciation for their role as celestial administrators who oversee the harmony and functioning of the universe.

Dominions are often seen as the supervisors of other angels, directing their activities and ensuring that everything operates according to the divine plan. They are the bridge between the higher orders of angels and those who directly interact with the earthly realm. This supervisory role makes them integral to the smooth execution of divine commands and the maintenance of universal balance.

In my experiences, whenever I've sought guidance in leadership or felt the need for a higher perspective on complex issues, invoking the presence of Dominions has provided clarity and direction. They offer a broader view, helping us to see beyond immediate concerns and align with a more profound, universal order.

Roles and Responsibilities: Maintaining Divine Order

Dominions have a multifaceted role that encompasses leadership, oversight, and the promotion of divine governance. Here are some key responsibilities they undertake:

Maintaining Divine Order: The primary role of Dominions is to ensure that the divine order is upheld throughout the cosmos. They monitor the execution of the divine will and ensure that every action taken by lower-ranking angels aligns with the overarching plan. This role is vital for maintaining harmony and preventing chaos within the heavenly and earthly realms.

Guiding Leaders: Dominions play a significant role in guiding human leaders, inspiring them to act with wisdom, integrity, and fairness. Whether in positions of power within communities, organizations, or governments, Dominions influence these leaders to make decisions that reflect divine principles. They help leaders understand the impact of their actions and encourage them to lead with justice and compassion.

Overseeing Lower Angels: As overseers, Dominions direct the activities of lower-ranking angels, such as Virtues, Powers, and Principalities. They ensure that these angels fulfill their duties effectively and that their actions contribute to the greater good. This hierarchical structure allows for efficient management of divine tasks and the seamless implementation of divine will.

Promoting Harmony and Balance: Dominions are also responsible for promoting harmony and balance within the universe. They address disruptions and work to restore order when necessary. Their influence helps to maintain a state of equilibrium, ensuring that the cosmos functions smoothly and that the divine plan is realized in every aspect of existence.

In my spiritual practice, I have found that Dominions offer invaluable guidance when faced with leadership challenges or when striving to bring order and balance to chaotic situations. Their presence provides a sense of stability and reassurance, reminding us that we are supported by a higher order of divine governance.

How to Recognize Dominions: Identifying Their Presence

Recognizing the presence of Dominions can be a subtle and profound experience. Here are some ways to identify when Dominions are influencing or guiding you:

Clarity in Leadership: If you find yourself making decisions with exceptional clarity and a deep sense of responsibility, it may be a sign that Dominions are guiding you. They often provide the wisdom needed to navigate complex leadership roles and inspire you to act with integrity and fairness.

Sense of Order and Balance: Feeling a strong need to restore order or balance in your environment can indicate the presence of Dominions. They inspire us to seek harmony and address any disruptions or imbalances in our lives or communities.

Broad Perspective: When you experience a shift in perspective that allows you to see the bigger picture and understand the interconnectedness of events, it may be the influence of Dominions. They help us step back from immediate concerns and view situations from a higher, more comprehensive standpoint.

Inspirations of Justice and Fairness: If you are drawn to advocate for justice, fairness, and the well-being of others, this could be a sign of Dominion's guidance. They inspire actions that reflect divine principles and encourage us to lead with compassion and equity.

Sudden Organizational Skills: An unexpected surge in organizational skills or the ability to bring order to chaotic situations can also be a sign of Dominion at work. They support us in creating structure and efficiency, both in our personal and professional lives.

In my interactions with Dominions, I often feel a sense of responsibility and clarity when making decisions that affect others. Their guidance helps me to lead with a balanced and fair approach, ensuring that my actions align with higher principles and contribute to the greater good.

Connecting with Dominions: Practical Steps and Techniques

Building a connection with Dominions can enhance your leadership skills and help you maintain order and balance in your life. Here are some steps and techniques that have helped me connect with these powerful angels:

Pray for Guidance: One of the most direct ways to connect with Dominions is through prayer. When you find yourself in a leadership role or facing decisions that require wisdom and integrity, ask for the guidance of Dominions. You might say, "Dominions, angels of divine order, please guide me in my leadership roles. Help me to act with wisdom, fairness, and integrity."

Meditate on Divine Order: Visualization is a powerful tool for connecting with the energy of Dominions. During meditation, focus on the harmonious functioning of the cosmos. Visualize a universe in perfect balance, where every element and action aligns with divine will. This practice can help you attune to the orderly and guiding influence of Dominions.

Act with Integrity: Leading with wisdom and fairness in your personal and professional life aligns you with the energy of Dominions. Make a conscious effort to uphold integrity in your actions and decisions. Reflect on how your choices impact others and strive to promote justice and harmony in all your interactions.

Seek Higher Perspective: When faced with challenges or complex situations, try to step back and view them from a broader perspective. Ask yourself how these issues fit into the larger picture and what the most just and balanced approach might be. This practice helps you align with the guidance of Dominions and make decisions that reflect divine order.

Express Gratitude for Order and Guidance: Regularly express gratitude for the order and guidance that Dominions provide. Thank them for their support in maintaining harmony and helping you navigate your leadership roles with clarity and integrity. Gratitude strengthens your connection with these angels and invites their ongoing assistance.

Historical Significance of Dominions

Dominions have been recognized throughout history as the angels responsible for overseeing the divine order and governance of the universe. In Christian angelology, Dominions are considered the fourth highest order of angels, tasked with ensuring that the divine will is enacted across all realms. They are seen as the celestial administrators who direct the activities of lower angels and guide human leaders to act in accordance with divine principles.

In the Bible, Dominions are mentioned as powers that rule over and maintain the order of the heavens and earth. Their role is to uphold the divine structure and ensure that every aspect of creation functions in harmony with God's plan.

In Jewish mysticism, Dominions are associated with the Sefirot of Chesed (kindness) on the Tree of Life, representing divine benevolence and the orderly governance of the cosmos. They are seen as the forces that manage and balance the flow of divine energy, ensuring that it is distributed in a way that promotes justice and compassion.

In Islamic tradition, similar concepts exist where angels are tasked with overseeing the implementation of divine law and order within the universe. These angels, like Dominions, guide and protect leaders, ensuring that their actions reflect the divine will.

Throughout history, Dominions have been invoked for guidance and support in leadership roles. Their presence in religious and mystical traditions highlights their importance in maintaining cosmic harmony and promoting righteous governance. Dominions are seen as the guardians of divine order, ensuring that the universe operates smoothly and that human leaders act with wisdom and integrity.

Embracing the Journey with Dominions

Dominions are remarkable angels who play a crucial role in maintaining divine order and guiding leaders. They provide wisdom, clarity, and support in leadership roles, helping us to act with integrity and promote harmony in our lives and communities. By connecting with Dominions through prayer, meditation, and actions aligned with divine principles, we can benefit from their guidance and ensure that our decisions reflect the highest ideals of justice and fairness.

As you continue your spiritual journey, consider inviting the Dominions to guide you in your leadership roles and to help you maintain order and balance in your life. Embrace their presence as guardians of divine governance and let their influence inspire you to lead with wisdom and compassion. You can align with the divine order and contribute to a more harmonious and just world through your connection with Dominions.

Chapter 33

Thrones

In the celestial hierarchy, Thrones holds a significant and revered position. They are known as the angels of justice and authority, playing a crucial role in maintaining the balance of karma and ensuring that divine justice is served. My understanding of Thrones deepened as I delved into their role as celestial judges, overseeing the intricate workings of justice in both the spiritual and physical realms.

Thrones are often depicted as majestic beings associated with symbols of balance and fairness, such as scales and thrones. Their presence is felt when matters of justice, fairness, and moral dilemmas arise. They guide us in understanding the consequences of our actions and in embracing the karmic balance that governs our lives.

In my spiritual practice, invoking Thrones has been particularly helpful when seeking clarity and resolution in situations that require fairness and impartiality. Their influence helps to illuminate the path of righteousness and ensure that justice prevails.

Roles and Responsibilities: Administering Divine Justice

Thrones are entrusted with the profound responsibility of maintaining cosmic balance and administering divine justice. Here are some key roles they undertake:

Maintaining Karmic Balance: Thrones are the keepers of karma, ensuring that every action is met with an appropriate consequence. They oversee the cosmic ledger of deeds, making sure that positive actions are rewarded and negative actions are met with corrective measures. This role is essential for maintaining the moral and ethical balance of the universe.

Administering Justice: As divine judges, Thrones are responsible for administering justice in both the spiritual and physical realms. They guide individuals and societies in upholding the principles of fairness and righteousness. When faced with legal or moral dilemmas, Thrones provides the wisdom and clarity needed to make just decisions.

Promoting Accountability: Thrones helps us understand and accept the consequences of our actions. They encourage personal responsibility and the acknowledgment of our role in the outcomes we experience. By fostering a sense of accountability, Thrones promotes growth and learning from our experiences.

Guiding Legal and Moral Judgments: Thrones offers guidance in legal matters and moral judgments. They inspire fairness and impartiality, helping leaders, judges, and individuals to act with integrity and uphold justice in their decisions.

Balancing Energies: Beyond human affairs, Thrones also works to balance the energies within the universe. They ensure that the cosmic forces remain in harmony and that any imbalances are addressed promptly. This role is vital for the overall stability and order of creation.

In my own experiences, calling upon Thrones has provided a sense of justice and balance during times of conflict or uncertainty. Their presence brings a calm assurance that fairness will prevail and that every action will be met with the appropriate consequence.

How to Recognize Thrones: Identifying Their Presence

Recognizing the presence of Thrones can be a profound experience, marked by feelings of fairness, justice, and balance. Here are some ways to identify when Thrones are influencing or guiding you:

Sense of Fairness and Balance: If you feel a strong inclination towards fairness and balance in your actions and decisions, it may be a sign that Thrones are guiding you. They inspire a deep commitment to justice and equality.

Resolution of Conflicts: When conflicts are resolved in a fair and just manner, or when you find yourself naturally gravitating towards equitable solutions, this could indicate the influence of Thrones. They help facilitate peaceful and balanced resolutions.

Clarity in Moral and Legal Matters: Experiencing clarity and certainty in moral or legal decisions can be a sign of Thrones' presence. They provide the insight needed to navigate complex ethical dilemmas with integrity.

Symbols of Justice: Encounters with symbols of justice, such as scales, thrones, or images of judges, can signal the presence of Thrones. These symbols often appear when their guidance is needed.

Acceptance of Consequences: Feeling a sense of acceptance and understanding regarding the outcomes of your actions, even when they are challenging, can be a sign of Thrones' influence. They help us embrace the lessons and growth that come from facing the consequences of our deeds.

In my spiritual journey, recognizing Thrones often comes with a deep sense of peace and assurance that justice is being served. Their guidance brings a balanced perspective, helping me navigate life's complexities with fairness and integrity.

Connecting with Thrones: Practical Steps and Techniques

Building a connection with Thrones can enhance your understanding of justice and help you maintain balance in your life. Here are some steps and techniques that have helped me connect with these powerful angels:

Pray for Justice: One of the most direct ways to connect with

Thrones is through prayer. When seeking fairness and clarity in any situation, ask for their guidance. You might say, "Thrones, angels of justice and balance, please guide me in my pursuit of fairness and help me make decisions that uphold divine justice."

Meditate on Scales and Balance: Visualization is a powerful tool for attuning to the energy of Thrones. During meditation, focus on symbols of justice, such as scales or a balanced beam. Visualize these symbols, bringing balance and fairness into your life and decisions.

Act with Integrity: Aligning your actions with the principles of justice and integrity naturally connects you with the energy of Thrones. Strive to be fair and equitable in your dealings with others, and uphold moral and ethical standards in all your interactions.

Accept the consequences: Embracing the outcomes of your actions, whether positive or negative, aligns you with the guidance of Thrones. Reflect on the lessons learned from your experiences and understand how they contribute to your growth and balance.

Seek Balance in All Things: Strive for balance in your personal and professional life. Whether it's balancing work and rest, giving and receiving, or managing emotions, seeking equilibrium connects you with the essence of Thrones.

Express Gratitude for Justice and Balance: Regularly express gratitude for the justice and balance that Thrones provides. Thank them for their role in maintaining cosmic harmony and for guiding you in making just and fair decisions.

Historical Significance of Thrones

Thrones have held a significant place in various religious and mystical traditions throughout history. In Christian angelology, Thrones are considered the third highest order of angels, known for their role in administering divine justice and maintaining the balance of karma. They are depicted as celestial judges who ensure that actions are met with appropriate consequences, reflecting the divine order.

In the Bible, Thrones are mentioned as part of the angelic hierarchy that surrounds the throne of God. They are seen as the enforcers of divine law and order, tasked with upholding the principles of justice and fairness in the heavenly and earthly realms.

In Jewish mysticism, Thrones are associated with the Sefirot of Geburah (strength) on the Tree of Life, representing the power and severity of divine judgment. They are seen as the channels through which divine justice is administered, ensuring that balance and order are maintained within the universe.

In Islamic tradition, similar concepts exist where angels are tasked with maintaining cosmic order and ensuring that divine justice is upheld. These angels, akin to Thrones, oversee the moral and ethical conduct of humanity and guide leaders to act with righteousness.

Throughout history, Thrones have been invoked for guidance in legal matters and moral dilemmas. Their presence in religious texts and mystical traditions show their importance as the arbiters of justice, ensuring that actions align with divine principles and that balance is maintained within the cosmos.

Embracing the Journey with Thrones

Thrones are powerful angels who play a crucial role in maintaining divine justice and balance. They provide guidance in matters of fairness, help us understand the consequences of our actions, and inspire us to act with integrity and righteousness. By connecting with Thrones through prayer, meditation, and actions aligned with justice, we can benefit from their wisdom and ensure that our decisions reflect the highest ideals of fairness and balance.

As you continue your spiritual journey, consider inviting the Thrones to guide you in matters of justice and to help you maintain balance in your life. Embrace their presence as guardians of divine order and let their influence inspire you to live with fairness and integrity. Through your connection with Thrones, you can align with the principles of divine justice and contribute to a more harmonious and just world.

Alex McCann Johnson

Chapter 34
Fallen Angels

As I reflect on the topic of fallen angels, I approach it with a mix of caution and curiosity. Fallen angels are often depicted as those who have turned away from divine light, aligning themselves with forces that oppose the heavenly order. While they are typically associated with negative influences and temptations, it's important to acknowledge that, in some belief systems, they are also seen as complex figures who have had an impact on humanity's journey.

My own spiritual practice does not involve working with fallen angels. I prefer to connect with guides and beings that align with the highest good. However, as someone dedicated to sharing universal wisdom, I recognize that some people do engage with these entities. The reasons for this can vary, from seeking deeper understanding to exploring the darker aspects of spiritual existence.

Fallen angels are intriguing figures in the vast tapestry of spiritual beings. They serve as potent symbols of rebellion, transformation, and the consequences of straying from the divine path. For those who choose to work with them, it's crucial to approach this with discernment and a deep awareness of the potential risks involved.

Historical and Mythological Background

Fallen angels have a significant presence in various religious and mythological traditions. They often embody themes of rebellion, pride, and the struggle between good and evil. Their stories serve as powerful reminders of the importance of humility, obedience, and maintaining a connection to the divine.

In the Bible, one of the most well-known stories is that of Lucifer, an archangel who fell from grace due to his pride and desire to ascend above God. Lucifer's fall is depicted as a consequence of his rebellion against divine authority, and he is often identified with Satan, the adversary who tempts and deceives humanity.

Islamic tradition speaks of Iblis, a being created from smokeless fire who refused to bow to Adam, citing his own superiority. Iblis was cast out of heaven for his disobedience and became a symbol of arrogance and rebellion. He is seen as a tempter who leads people astray, challenging their faith and obedience to God.

Jewish mysticism also touches on the concept of fallen angels. The Book of Enoch, an ancient Jewish text, describes a group of angels known as the Watchers who descended to Earth and intermingled with humans, leading to their fall from grace. These narratives highlight the complex interplay between divine will and individual choice and the repercussions of defying celestial order.

In various mythologies, fallen angels are often associated with themes of transformation and duality. They represent the potential for beings to fall from their original state of grace and the subsequent struggle for redemption or continued rebellion. These stories resonate across cultures, reflecting the universal human experiences of temptation, loss, and the quest for understanding.

Understanding Fallen Angels: Their Role and Influence

Fallen angels are typically seen as entities that influence negative behavior, temptations, and the darker aspects of the human experience. They are believed to exploit weaknesses and amplify fears, leading individuals away from the path of light and toward spiritual discord.

Temptation and Rebellion: Fallen angels are often associated with the act of tempting humans to rebel against divine order. They exploit vulnerabilities, encouraging actions that lead away from spiritual growth and toward moral decay. Understanding their influence helps us recognize and resist temptations that can derail our spiritual journey.

Negative Energies and Entities: These beings are thought to be linked with various forms of negative energy and dark entities. They thrive in environments filled with fear, anger, and despair, feeding off these emotions to strengthen their presence. Recognizing the signs of their influence can help us take steps to protect ourselves and maintain our spiritual integrity.

Complex Figures of Transformation: Despite their association with negative influences, some belief systems view fallen angels as complex figures who contribute to the overall balance of the universe. They can represent aspects of the human condition that need to be acknowledged and integrated rather than completely shunned. For some, working with fallen angels is a way to explore and understand the darker aspects of existence, leading to personal growth and transformation.

Protecting Yourself from Negative Influences

Given the potential risks associated with fallen angels, it's essential to approach any interaction with them with great care. Here are some practices to protect yourself from negative influences and maintain a connection to the light:

Pray for Protection: Invoke the guidance and protection of higher angels and benevolent spiritual beings. You might say, "Archangels of light and guardians of divine order, please surround me with your protective presence and shield me from negative influences."

Engage in Spiritual Cleansing: Regularly cleanse your energy and environment to remove any lingering negative energies. This can be done through practices like cleansing with sage, using protective crystals, or performing energy-clearing rituals.

Maintain High Vibrational Energy: Cultivate positive thoughts, emotions, and actions to raise your vibrational frequency. Engage in activities that bring joy, peace, and fulfillment, and avoid situations or influences that lower your energy.

Set Clear Boundaries: Establish and maintain clear spiritual boundaries. Be mindful of the entities you choose to engage with and ensure that they align with your highest good. Trust your intuition and don't hesitate to distance yourself from any presence that feels harmful or unsettling.

Seek Guidance from Trusted Sources: If you feel drawn to explore the realm of fallen angels, seek guidance from trusted spiritual teachers or practitioners who can provide insights and support. It's important to approach this exploration with knowledge and caution.

Historical Significance of Fallen Angels

Fallen angels hold a prominent place in religious texts and mythologies, serving as cautionary figures that illustrate the consequences of turning away from the divine. Their stories are interwoven with themes of pride, rebellion, and the eternal struggle between good and evil.

In Christianity, the narrative of Lucifer's fall is a powerful symbol of the dangers of pride and the importance of humility. This story has influenced countless works of literature, art, and theology, emphasizing the need for adherence to divine will and the perils of defiance.

In Islam, the account of Iblis highlights the consequences of arrogance and the refusal to submit to divine authority. Iblis's rebellion serves as a reminder of the importance of obedience to God and the spiritual battles that individuals must navigate throughout their lives.

In Jewish mysticism, the tales of the Watchers and their descent to Earth underscore the complexities of interacting with divine and human realms. These stories reflect the tension between celestial beings and their roles, as well as the impact of their actions on humanity.

In various cultural mythologies, fallen angels and similar figures represent the duality of existence and the transformative journey from light to darkness and back again. They serve as symbols of the struggles and challenges inherent in the human condition, offering lessons in resilience, redemption, and the quest for understanding.

Embracing the Journey with Caution

The fallen angels are enigmatic and multifaceted beings that embody themes of rebellion, transformation, and the consequences of straying from the divine path. While they are often associated with negative influences and temptations, they also offer insights into the darker aspects of spiritual existence.

For those who choose to explore the realm of fallen angels, it is crucial to do so with discernment, caution, and a deep awareness of the potential risks involved. By maintaining a connection to higher angels and practicing spiritual protection, we can navigate this exploration safely and thoughtfully.

As you continue your spiritual journey, remember to honor your own path and the guides that resonate most with your highest good. Whether you choose to work with fallen angels or focus on more uplifting spiritual beings, trust in your intuition and remain grounded in your connection to the divine.

Chapter 35

Specific Archangels

Now that we've explored the different types of angels and their roles, I want to dive into the fascinating realm of specific angelic beings, particularly those known as archangels. These archangels are immensely powerful and deeply influential in the spiritual work I do. Learning about them and inviting their presence into your life can profoundly enrich your spiritual journey.

As an angel guide, I took it upon myself to start learning from these celestial beings. Initially, I was drawn to their radiant energy and the way they would subtly, yet unmistakably, influence my surroundings. Each encounter was unique, and over time, I began to distinguish their different energies and roles. Slowly, I started to notice distinct characteristics in each angel that worked with me. As I continued my practice, I learned their names, their specific attributes, and how to engage with them effectively. This journey of discovery has been both enlightening and empowering.

One of the first archangels I connected with was Azrael, who appeared during a particularly intense period of developing my mediumship abilities. Azrael's calming and supportive presence provided me with the reassurance and guidance I needed at the time. Following this encounter, I began to connect with other archangels, each bringing their unique qualities and insights.

Over more time, my understanding deepened, and I became familiar with the archangels' specific roles and how they could assist in various aspects of life and spiritual work. For example, Archangel Michael's protective and courageous energy is unparalleled when facing challenges or fears. His strength and determination are inspiring, and invoking his presence often brings a sense of safety and empowerment.

Archangel Raphael, known for his healing abilities, has been a constant ally in my energy work. Whether it's physical, emotional, or spiritual healing, Raphael's soothing presence and restorative energy have been invaluable. I often call upon him during healing sessions to assist in bringing comfort and balance to those in need.

Archangel Gabriel's role as the messenger of the divine is another aspect I've come to appreciate deeply. Gabriel's clarity and wisdom help in communication and creativity, making his guidance particularly helpful when I'm working on projects or need to convey complex messages with ease and understanding.

Archangel Uriel, with his illuminating wisdom, often provides the insights and clarity needed during times of confusion or indecision. His light helps to shine a path forward, revealing solutions and guiding us toward enlightenment and understanding.

As my practice evolved, I continued to meet more of these magnificent beings. Each archangel has a distinct presence and offers unique support. Working with them has not only enhanced my spiritual practice but also deepened my personal growth and understanding. Their influence has been transformative, leading me to discover my own divinity and how interconnected and loved we all are.

In my early days of angelic work, I was hesitant. I believed that engaging with angels required a devout Christian faith. However, as I delved deeper, I realized that angels transcend religious boundaries. They are universal beings of light and love, available to anyone who seeks their guidance. This revelation broadened my perspective and allowed me to embrace their presence without reservation.

The more I worked with these celestial beings, the more my spirituality grew. They've helped me understand that we are all part of a vast, loving network of divine energy. Realizing this has freed me greatly and strengthened my bond with the universe and the divine.

I'm always in awe when a new angelic presence enters my practice, whether it's during meditation or while working with a client. Sometimes, as a client lies on the massage table, a new angel will appear, bringing with it a fresh wave of energy and insights. Each new encounter is a reminder of the limitless support and love that these beings offer.

In the next part of our exploration of angel guides, I will introduce you to several specific archangels. Each of these magnificent beings has unique qualities and areas of expertise that can greatly assist you on your spiritual path. I encourage you to engage with them, to invite their presence into your life, and to experience the difference they can make. I am genuinely excited to introduce you to these archangels and to share with you the awe-inspiring experiences I've had working with them.

Alex McCann Johnson

Chapter 36

Archangel Ariel

When I first connected with Archangel Ariel, it was an experience that greatly impacted me. I was taking a course by Radleigh Valentine about his Angel Wisdom Tarot deck, and during one of the sessions, I attempted to reach out to Ariel. I was astonished by the intensity of her presence. Ariel came through as fierce and strong, yet her energy was enveloped in a sense of love and protection. This powerful combination of attributes truly embodies her title as the "Lioness of God."

Archangel Ariel is referred to as the "Lioness of God," a title that perfectly captures her dual essence of strength and nurturing care. Ariel is a warrior and protector, particularly of the natural world. Her energy is imbued with the wild and untamed spirit of nature, making her a powerful ally in both personal empowerment and environmental stewardship.

Ariel's connection to the natural world is extensive. She oversees the care and protection of animals and plants and is deeply involved in the healing of the Earth. Those who work with Ariel often find themselves drawn to activities that honor and preserve the environment. Whether it's through conservation efforts, animal rescue, or simply spending time in nature, Ariel encourages us to recognize and respect the interconnectedness of all living things.

In my interactions with her, Ariel has consistently guided me to strengthen my bond with nature and to use my resources and abilities to protect and heal our environment. Her presence is a reminder that each of us has a role to play in the stewardship of the Earth.

Roles and Responsibilities: Archangel Ariel's Connection to Nature

Archangel Ariel's primary role revolves around protecting and healing the natural world. She is often depicted as a fierce guardian of the Earth, with a particular emphasis on environmental balance and conservation. Here are some of the key responsibilities she undertakes:

Protection of Nature: Ariel is the guardian of the natural world. She oversees the well-being of all living creatures, from the smallest insect to the largest mammal. Her influence extends to the elements of earth, water, fire, and air, ensuring that they remain in harmony and balance.

Environmental Healing: Ariel is deeply involved in the healing of environmental damage. She guides us to take actions that support ecological restoration and encourages sustainable practices that protect the Earth's resources. When I feel overwhelmed by the state of the environment, I call upon Ariel for guidance and inspiration to contribute positively.

Empowerment and Courage: Beyond her environmental focus, Ariel also embodies courage and empowerment. She encourages us to face our fears, take bold actions, and stand up for what we believe in. Her energy is both assertive and nurturing, providing the strength we need to pursue our goals and the compassion to care for ourselves and others.

Guidance in Natural Wisdom: Ariel helps us connect deeply with nature and tap into its wisdom. She encourages us to spend time outdoors, meditate in natural settings, and listen to the lessons that the natural world has to offer. This connection fosters a greater appreciation and respect for the environment.

In my own life, Ariel has guided me to make more environmentally conscious choices and seek ways to contribute to preserving our planet. Her guidance often comes as a strong, intuitive push toward actions that support ecological balance and sustainability.

How to Recognize Archangel Ariel: Signs and Symbols

Recognizing the presence of Archangel Ariel can be an enlightening experience. Here are some ways to identify when Ariel is near:

Feeling Drawn to Nature: If you suddenly feel a strong urge to spend time outdoors, visit a park, or engage in activities that connect you with nature, it may be Ariel's influence guiding you. She often encourages us to immerse ourselves in the natural world to restore our energy and gain clarity.

Symbols of Lions or Nature: Ariel is often associated with symbols of lions and other aspects of the natural world. Seeing images or references to lions or noticing an increase in encounters with wildlife can be a sign that Ariel is present.

Sudden Clarity and Courage: Ariel's energy brings a sense of empowerment and fearlessness. If you find yourself feeling unusually courageous or clear-minded about a course of action, it could be Ariel providing the strength and insight you need.

Warmth and Strong Presence: When Ariel is near, you might feel a strong, warm energy surrounding you. Her presence is both commanding and comforting, offering a sense of safety and encouragement.

Increased Environmental Awareness: If you start noticing more about the environment, such as becoming more aware of the beauty of nature or feeling a deep concern for ecological issues, it may be Ariel's way of tuning you into her areas of focus.

From my personal experiences, Ariel's presence often brings a sense of purpose and clarity, especially when I am considering actions related to environmental protection or personal empowerment.

Connecting with Archangel Ariel: Practical Steps and Techniques

Connecting with Archangel Ariel can bring a deeper understanding of our relationship with the natural world and enhance our sense of empowerment. Here are some steps that have helped me connect with Ariel:

Set Your Intention: Begin by clearly stating your desire to connect with Archangel Ariel. You can use a specific prayer to invite her presence. Here's a prayer you can use:

"Dear Archangel Ariel, I invite you into my life and ask for your guidance and protection. Help me to connect with the natural world and to act with courage and strength. Guide my actions to support the healing and preservation of our planet. Thank you for your love and your fierce, protective energy. I am open to your wisdom and support."

Create a Sacred Space: Find a quiet place where you can focus without distractions. Surround yourself with elements of nature, such as plants, stones, or images of animals. This creates a conducive environment for connecting with Ariel's energy.

Meditate and Invite: Sit comfortably and take several deep breaths to center yourself. Visualize a lush, green landscape where you feel safe and connected. Imagine Ariel joining you in this space, her energy powerful yet gentle. Open your heart and mind to any messages or sensations she may bring.

Spend Time in Nature: Ariel's connection to the environment means she often communicates through nature. Spend time outdoors, observe the beauty of the natural world, and listen for her guidance. Whether it's a walk in the park or simply sitting in your garden, being in nature can deepen your connection with Ariel.

Engage in Environmental Activities: Participate in activities that support the environment, such as planting trees, recycling, or volunteering for conservation projects. These actions resonate with Ariel's mission and can strengthen your bond with her.

Practice Mirror Gazing: Just as with other guides, mirror gazing can be a powerful way to connect with Ariel. Stand or sit comfortably in front of a mirror in a quiet room. Focus softly on your reflection and set the intention to see yourself through Ariel's eyes—strong, courageous, and in harmony with nature. Observe any feelings, thoughts, or images that arise.

Ask for Signs: Request specific signs from Ariel to confirm her presence and guidance. This could be anything related to nature or lions. Be open to receiving these signs in unexpected ways.

Express Gratitude: Regularly thank Ariel for her guidance and protection. Acknowledge her role in your life and show appreciation for the support she provides. This strengthens your connection and invites more of her energy into your life.

Historical and Cultural Significance of Archangel Ariel

Archangel Ariel's presence and influence can be traced through various cultural and religious traditions. Her name, meaning "Lioness of God," reflects her fierce and protective nature, particularly in relation to the natural world.

In Jewish mysticism, Ariel is associated with the elements and the animal kingdom, often depicted as a guardian of nature. She is mentioned in texts such as the Apocrypha and is revered for her role in overseeing the Earth's natural processes and the well-being of animals.

In Christian traditions, Ariel is sometimes identified as one of the archangels, albeit less commonly than Michael, Gabriel, or Raphael. She is acknowledged for her protective and nurturing qualities, especially in relation to the environment and the healing of the planet.

In Gnostic beliefs, Ariel is considered a powerful angelic figure involved in the creation and guardianship of the material world. She is seen as a bridge between the physical and spiritual realms, guiding humanity in understanding and respecting the natural world.

These cultural references highlight Ariel's enduring significance as a protector of the Earth and a guide in environmental stewardship.

Her presence is a reminder of humanity's responsibility to care for and preserve the natural world, reflecting a universal appreciation for the interconnectedness of life.

Embracing the Journey with Archangel Ariel

Archangel Ariel is a formidable and loving guide who embodies the spirit of the "Lioness of God." She offers strength, courage, and protection, particularly in our efforts to connect with and protect the natural world. By recognizing her presence and building a relationship with her, we can tap into her powerful energy and guidance.

Embracing Ariel's role in our lives encourages us to become stewards of the environment and to approach life with a sense of fearlessness and purpose. Her guidance helps us see nature's beauty and wisdom and act with conviction and love.

As you continue your journey, invite Archangel Ariel to walk with you. Allow her to inspire you with her strength and to guide you in your efforts to protect and heal the Earth. Trust in her loving support, and let her presence lead you toward a life filled with courage, purpose, and a deep connection to the natural world.

Chapter 37

Archangel Azrael

When I first connected with Archangel Azrael, I was struck by a sense of peace and comfort that enveloped me. Despite his title as the "Angel of Death," Azrael's presence is anything but frightening. He is a compassionate and gentle guide, helping souls transition from the physical realm to the afterlife with grace and serenity. My interactions with him have deepened my understanding of life's final journey and provided solace during times of grief.

Archangel Azrael is often known as the "Angel of Death," a title that reflects his primary role in assisting with the transition of souls from life to the afterlife. However, this designation does not capture the full extent of his comforting and supportive presence. Azrael's energy is incredibly soothing, offering peace and reassurance to both the dying and their loved ones.

Azrael's role is to help souls cross over smoothly and to provide comfort to those left behind. His presence can be felt during times of loss, bringing a sense of calm and understanding to the grieving process. He acts as a bridge between the physical and spiritual realms, ensuring that every soul he guides experiences a gentle and loving transition.

In my experience, Azrael's support has been invaluable during moments of personal loss and in helping others cope with their grief. His presence is like a warm, comforting embrace that reassures us that death is not an end but a continuation of the soul's journey.

Roles and Responsibilities: Helping with Grief and Transition

Archangel Azrael's roles extend beyond merely assisting with the moment of death. Here are the key responsibilities he undertakes:

Assisting with Transition: Azrael's primary role is to guide souls during their transition from the physical world to the afterlife. He gently separates the soul from the body and escorts it to the next phase of its journey. His presence ensures that the process is peaceful and filled with love.

Comforting the Grieving: Azrael provides deep comfort and support to those who are grieving the loss of a loved one. He helps to ease the pain of separation and provides clarity and understanding about the nature of life and death. When I have experienced loss, calling on Azrael has brought both peace and acceptance.

Guiding Souls in the Afterlife: Once a soul has transitioned, Azrael continues to guide it in the afterlife. He helps souls understand their experiences and embrace the lessons they have learned during their earthly lives. This guidance is crucial for the soul's ongoing spiritual growth.

Facilitating Life Purpose and Karmic Understanding: Beyond his role in death, Azrael assists individuals in understanding and embracing their life purposes. He offers insights into past lives and karmic lessons, helping us to navigate our spiritual paths with greater awareness. His guidance can illuminate the reasons behind our challenges and how they contribute to our soul's evolution.

Azrael's gentle and compassionate nature makes him a trusted and comforting guide during life's most challenging transitions. His support can transform our understanding of death and help us find peace in the face of loss.

Recognizing Archangel Azrael: Signs and Symbols

Recognizing the presence of Archangel Azrael can bring a sense of comfort and clarity. Here are some ways to identify when Azrael is near:

Sudden Peace and Calm: If you experience a sudden sense of calm and peace, especially during times of grief or anxiety, it may be Azrael's comforting presence. He often brings a deep, soothing energy that helps to ease emotional pain.

Dreams and Visions: Azrael frequently communicates through dreams and meditative visions. You might dream of a serene, gentle figure guiding you or your loved ones, or you might see symbolic representations of transition and peace.

Feathers and Symbols of Light: Finding feathers or noticing symbols of light and illumination can be a sign of Azrael's presence. These symbols often appear during times of transition or when you are seeking understanding and comfort.

Intuitive Insights: Azrael often provides insights and understanding about the nature of life, death, and the soul's journey. If you suddenly gain clarity or a new perspective on these topics, it could be Azrael guiding you.

Comfort in Solitude: Azrael's presence is deeply comforting, especially in solitude. If you find yourself feeling unusually at peace when alone, it may be Azrael offering his soothing energy.

In my interactions with Azrael, his presence has often been felt as a feeling of comfort, particularly during times of personal loss and transition. His guidance has provided invaluable insights into the nature of life and death, helping me to approach these experiences with greater acceptance and wisdom.

Connecting with Archangel Azrael: Practical Steps and Techniques

Building a connection with Archangel Azrael can provide comfort and guidance during times of grief and transition. Here are some steps that have helped me connect with Azrael:

Set Your Intention: Begin by clearly stating your desire to connect with Archangel Azrael. Use a specific prayer to invite his presence. Here's a prayer you can use:

"Dear Archangel Azrael, I invite you into my life and ask for your gentle guidance and comfort. Help me to navigate the challenges of grief and transition with grace and understanding. Please provide peace to my heart and clarity to my mind. Thank you for your loving presence and your support during these times. I am open to your wisdom and your soothing energy."

Create a Sacred Space: Find a quiet and serene place where you can focus on connecting with Azrael. Light a candle, play soft music, or include items that bring you comfort. Creating a peaceful environment helps facilitate a stronger connection with his energy.

Meditate and Invite: Sit comfortably and take several deep breaths to center yourself. Visualize a gentle, warm light enveloping you, and invite Azrael to join you. Imagine his calming presence surrounding you, offering peace and comfort. Be open to any sensations, thoughts, or images that come through.

Spend Time in Reflection: Reflect on your experiences of loss and transition. Allow yourself to process these emotions and invite Azrael to provide insights and understanding. Journaling your thoughts and feelings can be a helpful way to explore and integrate his guidance.

Engage in Acts of Compassion: Azrael's energy is sincerely compassionate. Engaging in acts of kindness and compassion, whether towards others or yourself, aligns with his presence and can strengthen your connection. This could include offering support to those in grief or simply being gentle with yourself during difficult times.

Practice Mirror Gazing: Mirror gazing can be a powerful technique for connecting with Azrael. Stand or sit comfortably in front of a mirror in a quiet room. Focus softly on your reflection and set the intention to see yourself through Azrael's eyes—full of peace, love, and divine purpose. Observe any feelings, thoughts, or images that arise during this practice.

Ask for Signs: Request specific signs from Azrael to confirm his presence and guidance. These signs could be anything that resonates with peace and transition, such as white feathers, gentle breezes, or moments of unexpected calm.

Express Gratitude: Regularly express gratitude to Azrael for his support and comfort. Acknowledge his role in your life and show appreciation for the peace and understanding he provides. Gratitude helps to strengthen your bond and invites more of his loving energy into your life.

Historical Significance of Archangel Azrael

Archangel Azrael's presence is significant across various religious and cultural traditions. His role as the "Angel of Death" is not limited to a single belief system but spans multiple faiths, each acknowledging his compassionate role in the transition between life and death.

In Islamic tradition, Azrael (also spelled Azra'il) is prominently featured in the Quran as the angel responsible for taking the souls of the deceased. He is depicted as a being of immense compassion, gently separating the soul from the body at the moment of death and guiding it to the afterlife. This portrayal underscores his role as a guide and comforter rather than a harbinger of doom.

In Jewish tradition, Azrael is sometimes identified as the angel who stands at the bedside of the dying, easing their passing. Jewish mystical texts and folklore often depict him as a figure of mercy, helping souls transition smoothly and offering comfort to the living.

Christian tradition also acknowledges Azrael's role, albeit less prominently. In some apocryphal texts, he is seen as a compassionate guide who helps souls understand their life's journey and embrace their transition into the afterlife.

Beyond these Abrahamic faiths, many cultures and spiritual practices recognize a similar figure who assists with death and provides comfort to the grieving. This universal archetype reflects humanity's deep-seated need for assurance and guidance during the profound transition from life to death.

These historical and cultural references highlight Azrael's enduring significance as a compassionate guide and protector. His presence has been a source of comfort and understanding for countless individuals facing the end of life or grieving the loss of loved ones.

Embracing the Journey with Archangel Azrael

Archangel Azrael is a gentle and compassionate guide who plays a vital role in our lives, especially during times of loss and transition. His presence offers peace, comfort, and sincere understanding, helping us navigate the complexities of death and grief with grace and wisdom.

By recognizing Azrael's presence and building a relationship with him, we can find solace in the face of loss and gain deeper insights into the nature of our soul's journey. Embracing his guidance encourages us to approach life and death with acceptance and peace, knowing that we are supported by his loving and gentle energy.

As you continue your spiritual journey, invite Archangel Azrael to walk with you. Allow his comforting presence to bring clarity and peace, and trust in his unwavering support during times of transition. Embrace the wisdom and love that Azrael offers, and let his guidance lead you to a deeper understanding of life's greatest mysteries.

Chapter 38
Archangel Barachiel

When I first connected with Archangel Barachiel, I was enveloped by a profound sense of warmth and joy. Known as the "Angel of Blessings," Barachiel's presence is deeply uplifting and comforting. His role in our lives is to bestow divine blessings and to help us recognize and attract abundance. My experiences with Barachiel have brought immense gratitude and positivity, transforming my perspective on life's daily miracles.

Archangel Barachiel is often referred to as the "Angel of Blessings," a title that perfectly captures his role in bringing divine favor and abundance into our lives. Barachiel's energy is vibrant and joyous, radiating peace and fulfillment. He is a powerful ally in helping us recognize and attract blessings in all areas, from relationships and health to career and spiritual growth.

Barachiel's presence feels like a beacon of light, guiding us to see the beauty and abundance that surround us. He encourages us to adopt a mindset of gratitude and openness, allowing us to receive and appreciate the blessings that the universe offers. Working with Barachiel has shown me that blessings are not just material; they also include moments of joy, love, and growth that enrich our lives every day.

Roles and Responsibilities: Bestowing Blessings and Encouraging Gratitude

Archangel Barachiel's primary role is to facilitate the flow of blessings

213

and abundance into our lives. Here are some of the key responsibilities he undertakes:

Bestowing Divine Blessings: Barachiel helps us attract and recognize the blessings that come our way. Whether it's a new opportunity, a meaningful relationship, or a moment of unexpected joy, Barachiel's presence amplifies these experiences, making them more prominent and fulfilling.

Encouraging a Grateful Mindset: One of Barachiel's most powerful teachings is the importance of gratitude. He guides us to appreciate the blessings we already have and to cultivate a mindset that attracts even more positive experiences. Gratitude, as Barachiel shows us, is the key to unlocking a continuous flow of blessings.

Facilitating Prosperity and Abundance: Barachiel assists in manifesting abundance in all forms. This includes financial prosperity, personal fulfillment, and spiritual growth. His energy helps us align with the vibrational frequency of abundance, allowing us to attract and receive what we desire.

Promoting Peace and Joy: Barachiel's presence brings a deep sense of peace and joy. He helps us find contentment in the present moment and celebrate the simple joys of life. His guidance encourages us to live with a light heart and an open spirit.

Guiding Personal and Spiritual Growth: Beyond material blessings, Barachiel supports our personal and spiritual development. He provides insights and encouragement that help us grow, learn, and evolve on our journey.

In my experience, Barachiel's influence has been a source of continuous joy and gratitude. His guidance has helped me see the abundance in my life and approach each day with a heart full of appreciation and a spirit ready to receive more blessings.

How to Recognize Archangel Barachiel: Signs and Symbols

Guided by Spirits

Recognizing the presence of Archangel Barachiel can bring a heightened sense of joy and gratitude. Here are some ways to identify when Barachiel is near:

Sudden Joy and Warmth: If you experience an unexpected wave of joy and warmth, especially during moments of gratitude or contemplation, it could be Barachiel's presence. His energy is uplifting and filled with light.

Symbols of Abundance: Barachiel often communicates through symbols of abundance, such as coins, overflowing cups, or lush landscapes. These symbols can appear in your environment or in your dreams, signaling his presence and the flow of blessings.

Feelings of Gratitude: A sudden urge to express gratitude or an overwhelming sense of appreciation for your life's blessings can be a sign of Barachiel's influence. He encourages us to focus on the positive aspects of our lives.

Golden Light: Barachiel's energy is often associated with a golden or bright light. If you notice a warm, golden glow during meditation or in your surroundings, it may be a sign that Barachiel is near.

Encounters with Symbols of Prosperity: Repeatedly encountering symbols of prosperity and abundance, such as finding money, seeing rainbows, or receiving gifts, can indicate Barachiel's presence. These experiences remind us of the blessings that are constantly flowing into our lives.

In my interactions with Barachiel, his presence has often been felt as a warm, golden light and an overwhelming sense of joy. His guidance has helped me to embrace a mindset of abundance and recognize the blessings in even the smallest moments of my life.

Connecting with Archangel Barachiel: Practical Steps and Techniques

Building a connection with Archangel Barachiel can enhance your sense of gratitude and attract more blessings into your life. Here are some steps that have helped me connect with Barachiel:

Set Your Intention: Begin by clearly stating your desire to connect with Archangel Barachiel. Use a specific prayer to invite his presence. Here's a prayer you can use:

"Dear Archangel Barachiel, I invite you into my life and ask for your guidance and blessings. Help me to recognize and appreciate the abundance around me. Fill my heart with gratitude and open my spirit to receive your divine gifts. Thank you for your loving presence and the joy you bring. I am open to your wisdom and your light."

Create a Sacred Space: Find a peaceful and comfortable place where you can focus on connecting with Barachiel. Decorate your space with items that represent abundance and prosperity, such as candles, crystals, or flowers. This helps to align your energy with Barachiel's vibrational frequency.

Meditate and Invite: Sit comfortably and take several deep breaths to center yourself. Visualize a golden light surrounding you, radiating warmth and joy. Invite Barachiel to join you in this light and be open to any sensations, thoughts, or images that arise. Feel the light of his blessings envelop you.

Practice Gratitude: Incorporate gratitude practices into your daily routine. This could include keeping a gratitude journal, expressing thanks for the people and experiences in your life, or simply taking a moment each day to appreciate the abundance around you. Barachiel's energy will be drawn to your expressions of gratitude.

Engage in Acts of Generosity: Sharing your blessings with others is a powerful way to connect with Barachiel. Acts of kindness and generosity align with his energy and amplify the flow of blessings in your life. Whether it's helping a friend, donating to a cause, or offering a kind word, these actions attract more positive energy.

Spend Time in Nature: Nature is a reflection of abundance and growth. Spend time outdoors, appreciating the beauty and abundance of the natural world. This connection with nature can help you attune to Barachiel's energy and the flow of blessings in your life.

Practice Mirror Gazing: Mirror gazing can be a powerful technique for connecting with Barachiel. Stand or sit comfortably in front of a mirror in a quiet room. Focus softly on your reflection and set the intention to see yourself through Barachiel's eyes—radiant, abundant, and blessed. Observe any feelings, thoughts, or images that arise.

Ask for Signs: Request specific signs from Barachiel to confirm his presence and guidance. These signs could include symbols of abundance, such as finding coins, seeing butterflies, or experiencing unexpected acts of kindness.

Express Gratitude: Regularly thank Barachiel for his support and blessings. Acknowledge his role in your life and show appreciation for the abundance he helps you recognize and receive. Gratitude strengthens your connection and invites more of his positive energy into your life.

Historical and Cultural Significance of Archangel Barachiel

Archangel Barachiel, though less commonly known than some other archangels, holds a significant place in various spiritual and religious traditions. His name, derived from the Hebrew word for "blessing," reflects his role in bestowing divine favor and abundance.

In Jewish mysticism, Barachiel is revered as a guardian of blessings and prosperity. He is believed to oversee the distribution of divine favor, ensuring that each individual receives the blessings intended for them. Barachiel's role in the Jewish tradition underscores the importance of recognizing and appreciating the gifts we receive.

In Christianity, Barachiel's influence is often associated with the outpouring of God's grace and blessings. He is seen as a conduit for divine favor, helping believers to experience the fullness of God's love and generosity. Barachiel's presence is a reminder of the abundant life that is available to those who live in alignment with divine principles.

In Islamic tradition, although not explicitly named, the concept of angelic beings who distribute God's blessings aligns with the attributes of Barachiel. Angels in Islam are seen as intermediaries who bring God's mercy and favors to humanity, reflecting Barachiel's role as a bearer of blessings.

In various spiritual practices, Barachiel is invoked as a guide for those seeking abundance and fulfillment. His energy is called upon in rituals and meditations aimed at attracting prosperity and recognizing the blessings in one's life.

These cultural and spiritual references highlight Barachiel's enduring significance as a bringer of blessings and abundance. His presence in different traditions reflects a universal recognition of the importance of gratitude and the belief in divine favor.

Embracing the Journey with Archangel Barachiel

Archangel Barachiel is a radiant and loving guide who embodies the essence of blessings and abundance. His presence brings joy, gratitude, and a heightened sense of fulfillment. By recognizing Barachiel's influence and building a relationship with him, we can attract more blessings into our lives and cultivate a mindset of appreciation and abundance.

Embracing the journey with Barachiel means opening our hearts to the infinite possibilities of the universe and trusting in the flow of divine favor. It encourages us to celebrate the beauty and richness of life, to give thanks for the blessings we receive, and to share our abundance with others.

As you continue your spiritual journey, invite Archangel Barachiel to walk with you. Allow his joyful energy to fill your life with blessings and gratitude, and trust in his unwavering support as you embrace the abundance that surrounds you.

Chapter 39
Archangel Chamuel

When I first reached out to Archangel Chamuel, I was seeking guidance during a time of emotional turbulence and conflict. Chamuel, whose name means "He Who Sees God" or "The Eyes of God," is known as the Archangel of Peaceful Relationships. His calming presence and loving energy have helped me foster compassion and understanding in my interactions with others. Chamuel's influence is a beacon of light for those who feel lost or overwhelmed in their relationships, guiding us toward love, harmony, and forgiveness.

Archangel Chamuel is revered for his ability to foster love, compassion, and peaceful relationships. Often depicted as a gentle and serene figure, Chamuel is the archangel to turn to when you seek to heal emotional wounds, resolve conflicts, or strengthen your connections with others. His name, "He Who Sees God," reflects his insight and ability to see the divine potential in every situation and relationship.

Chamuel's energy is soothing and nurturing, helping us to cultivate a sense of peace and understanding both within ourselves and in our interactions with others. He encourages us to approach relationships with an open heart and a spirit of compassion, promoting harmony and mutual respect. When I connect with Chamuel, I feel a deep sense of calm and an enhanced ability to view situations from a place of love and forgiveness.

Alex McCann Johnson

Roles and Responsibilities: Fostering Love, Compassion, and Harmony

Archangel Chamuel's primary role is to promote peaceful relationships and foster love and compassion. Here are some of the key responsibilities he undertakes:

Healing Emotional Wounds: Chamuel helps us heal emotional wounds that may be affecting our relationships. Whether it's a past trauma, a recent conflict, or lingering resentment, Chamuel's loving energy facilitates emotional healing and restoration.

Encouraging Compassion and Forgiveness: Chamuel guides us to approach others with compassion and to practice forgiveness. He helps us understand different perspectives and encourages us to let go of anger and resentment, making room for love and harmony.

Promoting Harmony and Understanding: In times of conflict or misunderstanding, Chamuel's influence fosters a spirit of cooperation and mutual respect. He helps us communicate effectively and find common ground, promoting peaceful resolutions and stronger connections.

Guiding in Relationships: Chamuel assists in strengthening our relationships, whether they are romantic, familial, or friendships. He helps us nurture these bonds with love, patience, and understanding, encouraging us to build deeper and more meaningful connections.

Inspiring Self-Love and Acceptance: Beyond our relationships with others, Chamuel also encourages us to cultivate love and compassion for ourselves. His guidance helps us embrace self-acceptance and develop a healthy, loving relationship with ourselves.

In my journey, Chamuel's guidance has been a source of comforting peace and transformation. His presence has helped me navigate difficult relationships, heal emotional wounds, and cultivate a deeper sense of love and compassion within myself and toward others.

How to Recognize Archangel Chamuel: Signs and Symbols

Recognizing the presence of Archangel Chamuel can bring a deep sense of peace and harmony. Here are some ways to identify when Chamuel is near:

Feelings of Calm and Comfort: Chamuel's presence is often felt as a gentle, calming energy. If you experience a sudden sense of peace and comfort, especially during times of emotional distress or conflict, it may be a sign that Chamuel is with you.

Symbols of Love and Harmony: Chamuel often communicates through symbols associated with love and harmony, such as hearts, doves, or the color pink. These symbols can appear in your environment, dreams, or meditative visions, indicating his nurturing presence.

Heightened Sense of Compassion: If you find yourself feeling unusually compassionate or understanding towards others, especially in challenging situations, it could be Chamuel's influence. He encourages us to approach interactions with empathy and kindness.

Encounters with the Color Pink: Pink is associated with Chamuel's gentle and loving energy. Seeing the color pink repeatedly, whether in nature, clothing, or unexpected places, can be a sign that Chamuel is near and offering his guidance.

Increased Desire for Peace: Feeling a strong desire to resolve conflicts and foster harmony in your relationships can indicate Chamuel's presence. He inspires us to seek peace and understanding in all our interactions.

In my interactions with Chamuel, his presence has often been felt as a soft, comforting energy that brings a sense of peace and clarity. His guidance has helped me view relationships through a lens of compassion and love, fostering deeper connections and more harmonious interactions.

Connecting with Archangel Chamuel: Practical Steps and Techniques

Building a connection with Archangel Chamuel can enhance your sense of love and harmony in relationships. Here are some steps that have helped me connect with Chamuel:

Set Your Intention: Begin by clearly stating your desire to connect with Archangel Chamuel. Use a specific prayer to invite his presence. Here's a prayer you can use:

"Dear Archangel Chamuel, I invite you into my life and ask for your guidance and love. Help me to cultivate compassion and understanding in my relationships. Surround me with your gentle energy and assist me in healing any emotional wounds. Thank you for your nurturing presence and the harmony you bring. I am open to your wisdom and your love."

Focus on Your Heart Chakra: Chamuel is deeply connected to the heart chakra, the center of love and compassion. During meditation, place your hand over your heart and focus on feeling its warmth and energy. Visualize a soft pink light radiating from your heart, inviting Chamuel's loving presence.

Meditate on Pink Light: Pink is the color of love and compassion, associated with Chamuel's energy. During your meditation, visualize yourself surrounded by a beautiful pink light. Imagine this light filling your heart and extending outward, creating a space of peace and harmony. Invite Chamuel to join you in this light and be open to any sensations, thoughts, or images that arise.

Engage in Acts of Kindness: Practicing kindness and compassion towards others aligns with Chamuel's energy. Engage in acts of kindness, whether it's offering a kind word, helping someone in need, or simply listening with empathy. These actions can strengthen your connection with Chamuel and invite more of his loving presence into your life.

Practice Forgiveness: Chamuel encourages us to let go of anger and resentment and to practice forgiveness. Reflect on any relationships or situations where you may be holding onto negative emotions. Set the intention to forgive and release these feelings, allowing Chamuel's energy to facilitate healing and reconciliation.

Spend Time in Nature: Nature is a wonderful way to connect with Chamuel's peaceful energy. Spend time outdoors, appreciating the beauty and harmony of the natural world. This connection with nature can help you attune to Chamuel's guidance and the love and peace he offers.

Ask for Signs: Request specific signs from Chamuel to confirm his presence and guidance. These signs could include symbols of love, such as hearts or doves, or encountering the color pink in meaningful ways.

Express Gratitude: Regularly thank Chamuel for his support and guidance. Acknowledge his role in your life and show appreciation for the love and harmony he helps you cultivate. Gratitude strengthens your connection and invites more of his positive energy into your life.

Historical and Cultural Significance of Archangel Chamuel

Archangel Chamuel holds a significant place in various spiritual and religious traditions. His name, "He Who Sees God," reflects his role as a divine messenger who helps us see the presence of God in our lives and relationships.

In Jewish mysticism, Chamuel is often associated with divine love and compassion. He is considered one of the seraphim, the highest order of angels, who stand in the presence of God and embody His love. Chamuel's role in promoting love and harmony aligns with the Jewish emphasis on community and the importance of peaceful relationships.

In Christianity, Chamuel is viewed as a guardian of divine love and a promoter of peaceful interactions. Although not explicitly named in the Bible, his attributes align closely with those of angels who facilitate love, understanding, and reconciliation. Chamuel's influence in Christian tradition shows us the significance of love and forgiveness in fostering harmonious relationships.

In Islamic tradition, while not directly named, the concept of angels who promote peace and compassion corresponds with Chamuel's attributes. Islamic teachings emphasize the importance of love and mercy in human interactions, resonating with Chamuel's role in guiding peaceful relationships.

In various spiritual and esoteric practices, Chamuel is invoked as a guide for those seeking to heal emotional wounds and cultivate loving relationships. His energy is called upon in rituals and meditations aimed at fostering compassion, understanding, and forgiveness.

These cultural and spiritual references highlight Chamuel's enduring significance as a bringer of love, compassion, and peace. His presence in different traditions reflects a universal recognition of the importance of harmonious relationships and the healing power of love.

Embracing the Journey with Archangel Chamuel

Archangel Chamuel is a loving and gentle guide who embodies the essence of peaceful relationships and divine compassion. His presence brings a deep sense of love, understanding, and harmony into our lives. By recognizing Chamuel's influence and building a relationship with him, we can heal emotional wounds, foster love and compassion, and promote peace in our interactions with others.

Embracing the journey with Chamuel means opening our hearts to the transformative power of love and forgiveness. It encourages us to approach our relationships with empathy and understanding, to let go of anger and resentment, and to cultivate a deep sense of compassion and harmony.

As you continue your spiritual journey, invite Archangel Chamuel to walk with you. Allow his gentle energy to fill your life with love and peace, and trust in his unwavering support as you navigate the complexities of relationships and embrace the beauty of harmonious connections.

Chapter 40
Archangel Daniel

When I first connected with Archangel Daniel, his serene presence struck me, and so did the clarity he brought into my communication. Known as the "Archangel of Eloquence and Diplomacy," Daniel is a powerful guide for those seeking to enhance their ability to communicate with grace, resolve conflicts with wisdom, and foster harmonious relationships. His guidance is invaluable in helping us express our thoughts and feelings effectively, making him the perfect ally in both personal and professional interactions.

Archangel Daniel, whose name means "God is my Judge," embodies the qualities of eloquence, diplomacy, and clear communication. He is often called upon to assist in situations where understanding and harmony are needed. Daniel's presence brings a calming and clarifying energy, helping us articulate our thoughts with precision and sensitivity.

Daniel is particularly beneficial when we are faced with challenging conversations, negotiations, or any situation requiring tact and diplomacy. He aids us in finding the right words and delivering them in a way that is both truthful and compassionate. My experiences with Daniel have been eye-opening, offering guidance that helps me navigate complex interpersonal dynamics with ease and grace.

Roles and Responsibilities: Enhancing Communication and Resolving Conflicts

Archangel Daniel's primary role is to enhance our communication skills and assist in resolving conflicts through diplomacy. Here are some of the key responsibilities he undertakes:

Facilitating Clear Communication: Daniel helps us articulate our thoughts and feelings clearly and effectively. Whether it's in personal relationships, professional settings, or public speaking, Daniel's influence ensures that our messages are conveyed with eloquence and understanding.

Promoting Diplomacy and Peace: Daniel is a master of diplomacy, guiding us to approach conflicts and negotiations with wisdom and fairness. He encourages us to seek peaceful resolutions and find common ground, fostering harmony in our interactions.

Enhancing Listening Skills: Effective communication involves not just speaking but also listening. Daniel helps us become better listeners, encouraging us to understand others' perspectives and respond with empathy and respect.

Encouraging Honest Expression: Daniel supports us in expressing our true selves with authenticity and integrity. He helps us overcome fears of judgment or misunderstanding, allowing us to communicate openly and honestly.

Guiding in Relationships: Daniel aids in fostering clear and loving communication in relationships. He helps us navigate misunderstandings and build stronger, more harmonious connections through effective dialogue and mutual respect.

In my journey, Daniel's guidance has been a source of clarity and peace. His presence has helped me approach conversations with confidence and empathy, ensuring that my communication is both effective and compassionate. As a public speaker, he has been instrumental in my work.

How to Recognize Archangel Daniel: Signs and Symbols

Recognizing the presence of Archangel Daniel can bring a sense of clarity and calm to our communication. Here are some ways to identify when Daniel is near:

Sudden Clarity in Communication: If you experience a sudden sense of clarity or find the right words flowing effortlessly, especially during difficult conversations, it may be a sign that Daniel is assisting you.

Symbols of Writing and Speech: Daniel often communicates through symbols associated with communication, such as pens, books, or speech bubbles. These symbols may appear in your environment or in your dreams, indicating his supportive presence.

Feelings of Calm and Composure: Daniel's presence is often felt as a calming and grounding energy. If you feel unusually composed and centered during stressful interactions, it could be a sign that Daniel is offering his guidance.

Encounters with the Color Blue: Blue, especially a deep or royal blue, is associated with Daniel's energy. Seeing this color repeatedly, whether in your surroundings or in meditation, can indicate his presence and support.

Enhanced Listening Skills: If you notice an increased ability to listen and understand others, it may be Daniel's influence. He helps us become more attentive and empathetic listeners, improving our overall communication.

In my interactions with Daniel, his presence has often been felt as a serene and clarifying force that enhances my ability to communicate effectively and listen deeply. His guidance has been invaluable in fostering harmonious relationships and resolving conflicts with grace.

Connecting with Archangel Daniel: Practical Steps and Techniques

Building a connection with Archangel Daniel can greatly enhance your communication skills and foster diplomacy in your interactions.

Here are some steps that have helped me connect with Daniel:

Set Your Intention: Begin by clearly stating your desire to connect with Archangel Daniel. Use a specific prayer to invite his presence. Here's a prayer you can use:

"Dear Archangel Daniel, I invite you into my life and ask for your guidance and support in my communication. Help me to express my thoughts and feelings with clarity, compassion, and honesty. Guide me in fostering peaceful and harmonious relationships. Thank you for your calming presence and the wisdom you bring. I am open to your guidance and your light."

Focus on the Throat Chakra: Daniel is closely associated with the throat chakra, the center of communication. During meditation, place your hand over your throat and focus on feeling its energy. Visualize a soft blue light radiating from your throat, inviting Daniel's presence and enhancing your ability to communicate clearly.

Meditate on Blue Light: Blue is the color of Daniel's energy, representing clarity and communication. During your meditation, visualize yourself surrounded by a beautiful blue light. Imagine this light filling your entire being, bringing a sense of calm and clarity. Invite Daniel to join you in this light and be open to any sensations, thoughts, or messages that arise.

Practice Active Listening: Engage in practices that improve your listening skills. Pay attention to what others are saying without interrupting or formulating your response. Daniel's energy supports active listening and helps you understand others' perspectives more deeply.

Engage in Honest Dialogue: Make a conscious effort to communicate openly and honestly in your interactions. Express your thoughts and feelings with integrity and encourage others to do the same. Daniel's influence helps create a safe space for authentic dialogue.

Seek Peaceful Resolutions: Approach conflicts and disagreements with a mindset of diplomacy and fairness. Look for ways to find common ground and resolve issues amicably. Daniel's guidance promotes peaceful and harmonious outcomes.

Ask for Signs: Request specific signs from Daniel to confirm his presence and guidance. These signs could include symbols of communication, such as pens or books, or encountering the color blue in significant ways.

Express Gratitude: Regularly thank Daniel for his support and guidance. Acknowledge his role in enhancing your communication and show appreciation for the clarity and diplomacy he helps you cultivate. Gratitude strengthens your connection and invites more of his positive energy into your life.

Historical and Cultural Significance of Archangel Daniel

Archangel Daniel, while not as widely known as some other archangels, holds a significant place in various spiritual and religious traditions. His name, meaning "God is my Judge," reflects his role as a divine arbiter and guide in matters of communication and diplomacy.

In Jewish mysticism, Daniel is often seen as a guide who helps individuals articulate their prayers and communicate effectively with the divine. His role as a mediator and advocate aligns closely with his attributes of clarity and eloquence.

In Christianity, although not explicitly mentioned in the Bible, Daniel's attributes are reflected in the teachings about angels who assist with divine communication and understanding. His influence is seen in the Christian emphasis on clear and truthful communication as a path to spiritual growth and harmonious relationships.

In Islamic tradition, while not directly named, the concept of angels who facilitate communication and understanding corresponds with Daniel's attributes. Islamic teachings emphasize the importance of honesty and clarity in communication, resonating with Daniel's role in promoting eloquence and diplomacy.

In various spiritual and esoteric practices, Daniel is invoked as a guide for those seeking to enhance their communication skills and resolve conflicts peacefully. His energy is called upon in rituals and meditations aimed at fostering clear expression and understanding.

These cultural and spiritual references highlight Daniel's enduring significance as a bringer of eloquence, diplomacy, and clear communication. His presence in different traditions reflects a universal recognition of the importance of effective communication and the role of divine guidance in fostering harmonious relationships.

Embracing the Journey with Archangel Daniel

Archangel Daniel is a powerful and insightful guide who embodies the essence of eloquence, diplomacy, and clear communication. His presence brings a deep sense of clarity and calm to our interactions, helping us express our thoughts with grace and understanding. By recognizing Daniel's influence and building a relationship with him, we can enhance our communication skills, resolve conflicts with wisdom, and foster harmonious relationships.

Embracing the journey with Daniel means opening our hearts to the power of clear and compassionate communication. It encourages us to approach our interactions with empathy and integrity, to listen deeply and respond thoughtfully, and to seek peaceful resolutions in all our dealings.

As you continue your spiritual journey, invite Archangel Daniel to walk with you. Allow his serene energy to fill your life with clarity and grace, and trust in his unwavering support as you navigate the complexities of communication and embrace the beauty of harmonious connections.

Chapter 41
Archangel Gabriel

My first encounter with Archangel Gabriel was during a particularly challenging time when I struggled to articulate my thoughts and emotions. I felt blocked in my creative endeavors and sought clarity in communication. When I reached out to Gabriel, his presence was immediate and powerful, filling me with a sense of calm and focus. Known as the "Messenger Angel," Gabriel assists with all forms of communication, creativity, and the delivery of divine messages. His guidance is invaluable for those seeking to express themselves clearly and connect with their inner creativity.

Archangel Gabriel's name means "God is my strength," reflecting his role as a divine messenger and communicator. Gabriel is often depicted with a trumpet, symbolizing the announcement of important messages and the clear call to action. His energy is pure and vibrant, associated with the colors white and gold, and he is known for his ability to inspire clarity, creativity, and effective communication.

Gabriel's influence extends to various forms of expression, including speaking, writing, and artistic endeavors. He helps us find our voice, articulate our thoughts, and confidently share our ideas. In my experience, Gabriel's guidance has been a beacon of light during times when I needed to convey complex ideas or when I sought inspiration for creative projects. His presence fosters a deep connection with our inner truth, encouraging us to express ourselves authentically and fearlessly.

Roles and Responsibilities: Assisting with Communication and Creativity

Archangel Gabriel plays several vital roles in our lives, focusing on enhancing communication and fostering creativity. Here are some of the key responsibilities he undertakes:

Facilitating Clear Communication: Gabriel helps us communicate with clarity and precision. His guidance ensures that our messages are understood and effectively conveyed, whether we are speaking, writing, or engaging in any form of expression. Gabriel's influence is particularly beneficial during public speaking, negotiations, or any situation where clear communication is crucial.

Inspiring Creativity: Gabriel is a powerful ally for artists, writers, and anyone involved in creative pursuits. He ignites our creative spark and helps us tap into the wellspring of our imagination. When I feel creatively blocked, invoking Gabriel's presence often brings a flood of new ideas and a renewed sense of inspiration.

Delivering Divine Messages: As the messenger angel, Gabriel is responsible for delivering important messages from the divine. He acts as a bridge between the heavenly and earthly realms, ensuring that we receive the guidance and insights needed for our spiritual journey. His messages often come through intuition, dreams, or sudden flashes of understanding.

Supporting New Beginnings: Gabriel's presence is also associated with new beginnings and major life changes. He provides support and encouragement when we embark on new ventures or transitions, helping us approach these changes with confidence and clarity. Gabriel's guidance ensures that we are aligned with our higher purpose and divine timing.

Encouraging Inner Truth and Authenticity: Gabriel inspires us to speak and live our truth. He encourages us to express our authentic selves and to communicate from the heart. His influence helps us overcome fear and self-doubt, empowering us to share our unique perspectives and gifts with the world.

In my journey, Gabriel's guidance has been transformative. His presence has helped me find my voice, articulate my thoughts clearly, and embrace my creative potential. His influence is a reminder to communicate with honesty and integrity and to honor the power of our words and expressions.

How to Recognize Archangel Gabriel: Signs and Symbols

Recognizing the presence of Archangel Gabriel can enhance your communication and creative abilities. Here are some ways to identify when Gabriel is near:

Sudden Clarity in Communication: If you experience a sudden sense of clarity or ease in expressing your thoughts and ideas, it may be a sign that Gabriel is assisting you. His presence helps us articulate our messages with precision and confidence.

Symbols of Communication and Creativity: Gabriel often communicates through symbols associated with communication and creativity, such as trumpets, scrolls, or writing instruments. These symbols may appear in your environment, dreams, or meditative visions, reflecting his influence on your ability to express yourself.

Encounters with the Colors White and Gold: White and gold are colors linked to Gabriel's pure and illuminating energy. Seeing these colors repeatedly, whether in your surroundings or during meditation, can signal his presence and support.

Feelings of Inspiration and Insight: Gabriel's presence often brings a wave of inspiration and insight. If you find yourself feeling unusually creative or receiving sudden flashes of understanding, it could be a sign that Gabriel is guiding you.

Messages in Dreams and Intuition: As the messenger angel, Gabriel frequently communicates through dreams and intuitive insights. Pay attention to any significant dreams or intuitive messages that provide clarity or guidance, as they may be Gabriel's way of reaching out to you.

In my interactions with Gabriel, his presence has often been felt as a bright and uplifting force that enhances my ability to communicate and creates a space for authentic expression. His guidance has helped me articulate complex ideas and tap into my creative potential with ease and confidence.

Connecting with Archangel Gabriel: Practical Steps and Techniques

Building a connection with Archangel Gabriel can enhance your communication skills and ignite your creative spark. Here are some steps that have helped me connect with Gabriel:

Set Your Intention: Begin by clearly stating your desire to connect with Archangel Gabriel. Use a specific prayer to invite his presence. Here's a prayer you can use:

"Dear Archangel Gabriel, I invite you into my life and ask for your guidance and support. It helps me to communicate clearly and express myself creatively. Illuminate my mind with your divine light and inspire me to share my truth with confidence and grace. Surround me with your radiant energy and guide me in my journey of communication and creativity. Thank you for your presence and the clarity you bring. I am open to your wisdom and your light."

Focus on the Throat Chakra: Gabriel is closely associated with the throat chakra, the center of communication and expression. During meditation, place your hand over your throat chakra and focus on feeling its energy. Visualize a bright white or blue light radiating from this area, inviting Gabriel's presence and enhancing your ability to communicate clearly.

Meditate on White Light: Given Gabriel's connection to purity and clarity, meditating on white light can strengthen your connection with him. Visualize yourself surrounded by a radiant white light, feeling its clarity and purity. Invite Gabriel to join you in this space and be open to any messages or insights that come through.

Engage in Creative Activities: Embrace activities that stimulate your creativity, such as writing, painting, or music. Gabriel's influence enhances your creative expression and helps you tap into your inner artist. Allow yourself to immerse in these activities and feel Gabriel's guiding presence.

Pay Attention to Intuition and Dreams: Gabriel often communicates through intuition and dreams. Keep a journal to document any significant dreams or intuitive messages that provide clarity or guidance. Reflecting on these insights can strengthen your connection with Gabriel and help you understand his messages.

Ask for Signs: Request specific signs from Gabriel to confirm his presence and guidance. These signs could include symbols of communication, encounters with the colors white or gold, or moments of unexpected inspiration and clarity.

Express Gratitude: Regularly thank Gabriel for his support and guidance. Acknowledge his role in enhancing your communication and creative abilities and show appreciation for the clarity and inspiration he helps you cultivate. Gratitude strengthens your connection and invites more of his positive energy into your life.

Historical Significance of Archangel Gabriel

Archangel Gabriel holds a significant place in various religious and cultural traditions and is known as the divine messenger and communicator. His name, meaning "God is my strength," reflects his role in delivering important messages and guiding individuals in their communication and creative endeavors.

In Christianity, Gabriel is one of the most prominent archangels, famously known for announcing the birth of Jesus to Mary. This pivotal moment, described in the Gospel of Luke, highlights Gabriel's role in delivering divine messages and facilitating significant events in human history. Gabriel also appeared to the prophet Daniel, explaining visions and offering insights into future events.

In Islam, Gabriel, known as Jibril, plays a crucial role in the revelation of the Quran to the Prophet Muhammad. As the messenger of God, Jibril's revelations form the foundation of the Islamic faith, emphasizing his importance in conveying divine wisdom and guidance. Gabriel's presence in Islam underscores his role as a bridge between the divine and the earthly realms.

In Jewish tradition, Gabriel is one of the four archangels who stand before God, along with Michael, Raphael, and Uriel. He is often depicted as a warrior and a messenger, delivering God's messages and providing protection. Gabriel's influence in Jewish mysticism extends to guiding souls and assisting in the interpretation of dreams and visions.

In various spiritual and esoteric practices, Gabriel is invoked as a guide for those seeking to enhance their communication and creative skills. His energy is called upon in rituals and meditations aimed at fostering clarity, inspiration, and effective expression.

These cultural and religious references highlight Gabriel's significance as a divine messenger and communicator. His presence across different traditions reflects a universal recognition of the importance of clear communication, creative expression, and the delivery of divine messages.

Embracing the Journey with Archangel Gabriel

Archangel Gabriel is a powerful and inspiring guide who embodies the essence of communication, creativity, and divine messaging. His presence brings a deep sense of clarity and inspiration into our lives, helping us express ourselves with confidence and grace. By recognizing Gabriel's influence and building a relationship with him, we can enhance our ability to communicate effectively, ignite our creative potential, and connect with our inner truth.

Embracing the journey with Gabriel means opening our hearts to the transformative power of clear communication and creative expression.

It encourages us to speak our truth, share our ideas, and celebrate the beauty of our unique voices. As you continue your spiritual journey, invite Archangel Gabriel to walk with you. Allow his radiant energy to fill your life with clarity and creativity, and trust in his unwavering support as you navigate the complexities of your communication and embrace the light and truth of your authentic self.

Alex McCann Johnson

Chapter 42
Archangel Haniel

When I first connected with Archangel Haniel, I was drawn to her serene and gentle energy. Known as the "Angel of Joy and Grace," Haniel embodies the beauty and harmony of the divine feminine. Her presence is uplifting and soothing, bringing a sense of calm and balance into our lives. Haniel's guidance helps us embrace our inner beauty, cultivate joy, and navigate life's transitions with grace and poise.

Archangel Haniel's name means "Grace of God" or "Joy of God," reflecting her role in helping us connect with our inner beauty and divine grace. She is often depicted as a radiant, nurturing figure associated with the moon and the harmonious cycles of nature. Haniel's energy is deeply connected to emotions, intuition, and the natural world, guiding us to find joy and balance in our lives.

Haniel is especially known for helping us embrace our feminine qualities, regardless of gender, and encourages us to honor our emotional rhythms and intuitive insights. Her guidance is invaluable during times of emotional turbulence or when we seek to deepen our connection with our true selves.

In my journey, Haniel's presence has been a source of profound comfort and joy. She has helped me navigate life's ups and downs with grace, reminding me to find beauty and harmony in every moment. Her influence encourages us to live authentically and to celebrate the joy and grace that reside within us.

Roles and Responsibilities: Embracing Inner Beauty and Emotional Balance

Archangel Haniel plays several vital roles in our lives, centered around embracing our inner beauty and maintaining emotional balance. Here are some of the key responsibilities she undertakes:

Cultivating Joy and Grace: Haniel inspires us to cultivate joy and grace in our lives. She encourages us to find beauty in the everyday and to approach life's challenges with a sense of poise and elegance. Her influence helps us remain centered and joyful, even in difficult times.

Enhancing Intuition and Emotional Awareness: Haniel is closely connected to our emotions and intuition. She helps us tune into our inner wisdom and understand our emotional cycles. Her guidance enhances our intuitive abilities, allowing us to navigate life's complexities with clarity and insight.

Supporting Emotional Healing: During times of emotional distress or transition, Haniel provides comfort and healing. She helps us process and release negative emotions, fostering a sense of peace and emotional well-being. Her nurturing energy soothes our hearts and supports our emotional recovery.

Connecting with the Divine Feminine: Haniel embodies the qualities of the divine feminine, such as compassion, nurturing, and sensitivity. She encourages us to honor these qualities within ourselves and to embrace our feminine energy. Her presence fosters a deeper connection with our true selves and the natural rhythms of life.

Guiding Through Life's Transitions: Whether we are facing personal changes, career shifts, or spiritual transformations, Haniel's guidance helps us navigate these transitions with grace and confidence. She provides support and clarity, helping us adapt and flourish through life's inevitable changes.

In my experience, Haniel's guidance has been transformative. Her presence has helped me embrace my emotions, trust my intuition, and find joy and balance in my everyday life. Her influence is a reminder to honor our inner beauty and approach life with grace and harmony.

How to Recognize Archangel Haniel: Signs and Symbols

Recognizing the presence of Archangel Haniel can bring a sense of joy and balance into our lives. Here are some ways to identify when Haniel is near:

Feelings of Serenity and Joy: Haniel's presence is often felt as a gentle, soothing energy that brings a deep sense of peace and joy. If you experience an unexpected wave of calm and happiness, especially during emotional turbulence, it may be a sign that Haniel is with you.

Symbols of the Moon and Nature: Haniel is closely associated with the moon and the natural world. Seeing images of the moon, lunar phases, or nature scenes can indicate her presence. These symbols may appear in your environment, dreams, or meditative visions, reflecting her nurturing and harmonious energy.

Encounters with the Color Blue or Silver: Blue and silver are colors associated with Haniel's serene and graceful energy. Repeatedly encountering these colors, whether in your surroundings or during meditation, can signal her presence and support.

Heightened Intuition and Emotional Sensitivity: If you notice an increased sensitivity to your emotions or a stronger intuitive sense, it could be Haniel's influence. She enhances our ability to tune into our inner wisdom and navigate our emotional landscape with grace.

Moments of Beauty and Grace: Haniel often communicates through experiences of beauty and grace. Finding unexpected beauty in everyday moments or feeling a sense of elegance in your actions can be signs that Haniel is guiding you.

In my interactions with Haniel, her presence has often been felt as a calming and uplifting force that enhances my connection with my emotions and intuition. Her guidance has helped me navigate life's transitions with grace and find joy in the simple moments of life.

Connecting with Archangel Haniel: Practical Steps and Techniques

Building a connection with Archangel Haniel can enhance your emotional well-being and foster a sense of joy and grace in your life. Here are some steps that have helped me connect with Haniel:

Set Your Intention: Begin by clearly stating your desire to connect with Archangel Haniel. Use a specific prayer to invite her presence. Here's a prayer you can use:

"Dear Archangel Haniel, I invite you into my life and ask for your guidance and support. Help me to embrace my inner beauty, cultivate joy, and navigate life's transitions with grace. Surround me with your nurturing energy and enhance my connection with my emotions and intuition. Thank you for your gentle presence and the harmony you bring. I am open to your wisdom and your light."

Focus on the Heart and Solar Plexus Chakras: Haniel is deeply connected to the heart and solar plexus chakras, centers of love, joy, and personal power. During meditation, place your hands over these chakras and focus on feeling their energy. Visualize a soft blue or silver light radiating from these areas, inviting Haniel's presence and nurturing your emotional balance.

Meditate with the Moon: Given Haniel's association with the moon, meditating during lunar phases can strengthen your connection with her. Find a quiet space outdoors or by a window where you can see the moon. Focus on its light and energy, and invite Haniel to join you. Visualize her nurturing presence enveloping you and guiding you toward emotional clarity and peace.

Engage in Self-Care and Beauty Rituals: Embrace activities that enhance your sense of joy and grace, such as taking a relaxing bath, practicing yoga, or spending time in nature. These self-care rituals can help you align with Haniel's nurturing energy and foster a deeper connection with her.

Honor Your Emotions: Allow yourself to experience and honor your emotions fully. Whether through journaling, creative expression, or simply sitting with your feelings, acknowledging and embracing your emotions can invite Haniel's supportive presence into your life.

Ask for Signs: Request specific signs from Haniel to confirm her presence and guidance. These signs could include symbols of the moon, encounters with blue or silver colors, or moments of unexpected beauty and joy.

Express Gratitude: Regularly thank Haniel for her support and guidance. Acknowledge her role in enhancing your emotional well-being and show appreciation for the joy and grace she helps you cultivate. Gratitude strengthens your connection and invites more of her positive energy into your life.

Historical and Cultural Significance of Archangel Haniel

Archangel Haniel holds a significant place in various spiritual and religious traditions, embodying the qualities of joy, grace, and emotional balance. Her name, meaning "Grace of God," reflects her role as a divine nurturer and guide in matters of the heart and soul.

In Jewish mysticism, Haniel is often associated with the planet Venus, symbolizing love, beauty, and emotional harmony. She is considered a guardian of the moon's cycles, guiding individuals through their emotional rhythms and intuitive insights.

In Christian tradition, Haniel's attributes align with those of angels who promote love, compassion, and inner peace. Although not explicitly named in the Bible, her influence is seen in the Christian emphasis on grace and the nurturing qualities of the divine feminine.

In Islamic tradition, while not directly named, the concept of angels who foster emotional balance and guide individuals through life's transitions corresponds with Haniel's attributes. Islamic teachings emphasize the importance of maintaining emotional harmony and connecting with the divine through compassion and grace.

In various spiritual and esoteric practices, Haniel is invoked as a guide for those seeking to enhance their emotional well-being and connect with their inner beauty. Her energy is called upon in rituals and meditations aimed at fostering joy, grace, and a deeper connection with the natural world.

These cultural and spiritual references highlight Haniel's enduring significance as a bringer of joy, grace, and emotional balance. Her presence in different traditions reflects a universal recognition of the importance of nurturing our inner selves and embracing the beauty and harmony of life.

Embracing the Journey with Archangel Haniel

Archangel Haniel is a loving and gentle guide who embodies the essence of joy, grace, and emotional balance. Her presence brings a deep sense of peace and harmony into our lives, helping us connect with our inner beauty and navigate life's transitions with elegance and poise. By recognizing Haniel's influence and building a relationship with her, we can enhance our emotional well-being, cultivate joy, and embrace the grace that resides within us.

Embracing the journey with Haniel means opening our hearts to the transformative power of joy and grace. It encourages us to honor our emotions, trust our intuition, and celebrate the beauty and harmony that surround us. As you continue your spiritual journey, invite Archangel Haniel to walk with you. Allow her nurturing energy to fill your life with joy and serenity, and trust in her unwavering support as you navigate the complexities of your emotions and embrace the grace and beauty of your true self.

Chapter 43
Archangel Hamaliel

My first connection with Archangel Hamaliel was during a period of chaotic transition in my life. I felt overwhelmed and needed clarity to sort through the confusion. I learned about him at exactly the perfect time. When I reached out, Hamaliel's presence brought an unexpected sense of calm and order. Known as the "Angel of Logic and Order," Hamaliel specializes in bringing structure, clarity, and analytical insight into our lives. His guidance is invaluable when we are facing complex problems or striving to bring more organization and discipline into our routines.

Archangel Hamaliel's name means "Wrath of God," but don't let the formidable title mislead you. He embodies the divine qualities of logic, order, and disciplined thinking. Hamaliel's presence is deeply grounding and stabilizing, helping us cut through the confusion and see situations with clear, analytical precision.

Hamaliel's guidance is especially beneficial when we need to make sense of complex issues, organize our thoughts, or bring order to chaotic circumstances. His energy is like a gentle yet firm hand guiding us toward clarity and reason. In my experience, Hamaliel has been a steadying force, providing the logical perspective I needed to navigate through life's challenges with a balanced and structured approach.

Roles and Responsibilities: Bringing Structure and Clarity

Archangel Hamaliel plays several essential roles in our lives, focusing on bringing logic and order. Here are some of the key responsibilities he undertakes:

Enhancing Analytical Thinking: Hamaliel sharpens our analytical abilities, helping us break down complex problems into manageable parts. He guides us in evaluating situations logically, allowing us to make well-informed decisions based on clear reasoning.

Promoting Organization and Discipline: Hamaliel's influence encourages us to cultivate order and discipline in our daily routines. Whether it's organizing our workspace, managing our time effectively, or developing structured plans, Hamaliel's guidance helps us maintain a sense of control and efficiency.

Clarifying Confusion: During times of chaos or uncertainty, Hamaliel provides clarity and direction. He helps us see through the fog of confusion and understand the underlying structure of situations. His presence is like a beacon of light, illuminating the path and guiding us toward rational solutions.

Balancing Emotions with Logic: While emotions are essential, they can sometimes cloud our judgment. Hamaliel helps us balance our emotional responses with logical thinking, ensuring that we approach challenges with a calm and clear mind. His guidance fosters a harmonious integration of heart and mind.

Supporting Intellectual Growth: Hamaliel encourages intellectual curiosity and the pursuit of knowledge. He inspires us to explore new ideas, engage in critical thinking, and develop our intellectual capabilities. His presence is a catalyst for learning and personal growth.

In my journey, Hamaliel's guidance has been instrumental in helping me navigate through complex decisions and bring order to my life. His influence has encouraged me to approach challenges with a logical and disciplined mindset, transforming confusion into clarity and chaos into calm.

How to Recognize Archangel Hamaliel: Signs and Symbols

Recognizing the presence of Archangel Hamaliel can bring a sense of clarity and order to our lives. Here are some ways to identify when Hamaliel is near:

Sudden Clarity and Insight: If you experience a sudden sense of clarity or find yourself thinking more analytically, especially during complex situations, it may be a sign that Hamaliel is assisting you.

Symbols of Structure and Order: Hamaliel often communicates through symbols associated with logic and organization. These can include geometric shapes, patterns, or images of scales and balances, reflecting his focus on order and balance.

Encounters with the Color Yellow or Gold: Yellow and gold are colors associated with Hamaliel's bright and clarifying energy. Seeing these colors repeatedly, whether in your environment or during meditation, can signal his presence and support.

Feelings of Calm and Stability: Hamaliel's presence is often felt as a calming and grounding force. If you feel unusually composed and organized during chaotic times, it could be a sign that Hamaliel is offering his guidance.

Enhanced Analytical Abilities: If you notice an increased ability to think logically and analyze situations effectively, it may be Hamaliel's influence. He helps sharpen our intellect and improve our problem-solving skills.

In my interactions with Hamaliel, his presence has often been felt as a steady and clarifying force that enhances my ability to think logically and maintain order. His guidance has helped me approach challenges with a calm and structured perspective.

Connecting with Archangel Hamaliel: Practical Steps and Techniques

Building a connection with Archangel Hamaliel can enhance your ability to bring logic and order into your life. Here are some steps that have helped me connect with Hamaliel:

Set Your Intention: Begin by clearly stating your desire to connect with Archangel Hamaliel. Use a specific prayer to invite his presence. Here's a prayer you can use:

"Dear Archangel Hamaliel, I invite you into my life and ask for your guidance and support. Help me to embrace logic and order in my thoughts and actions. Bring clarity to my mind and assist me in organizing my life with precision and discipline. Surround me with your steadying presence and illuminate my path with your wisdom. Thank you for your guidance and the clarity you bring. I am open to your insights and your light."

Focus on the Solar Plexus Chakra: Hamaliel is closely associated with the solar plexus chakra, the center of personal power and intellectual clarity. During meditation, place your hand over your solar plexus and focus on feeling its energy. Visualize a bright yellow or gold light radiating from this area, inviting Hamaliel's presence and enhancing your logical thinking.

Meditate on Geometric Shapes: Given Hamaliel's connection to structure and order, meditating on geometric shapes can strengthen your connection with him. Visualize yourself surrounded by these shapes, feeling their stability and balance. Invite Hamaliel to join you in this space and be open to any insights or messages that come through.

Organize Your Environment: Embrace activities that promote organization and order, such as decluttering your space, creating schedules, or planning projects. These actions can help align you with Hamaliel's energy and foster a deeper connection with him.

Engage in Critical Thinking: Practice activities that stimulate your analytical abilities, such as solving puzzles, engaging in strategic games, or studying new subjects. Hamaliel's influence supports intellectual growth and enhances your capacity for logical reasoning.

Ask for Signs: Request specific signs from Hamaliel to confirm his presence and guidance. These signs could include symbols of structure, encounters with the colors yellow or gold, or moments of unexpected clarity and insight.

Express Gratitude: Regularly thank Hamaliel for his support and guidance. Acknowledge his role in bringing clarity and order to your life and show appreciation for the insights and stability he helps you cultivate. Gratitude strengthens your connection and invites more of his positive energy into your life.

Historical and Cultural Significance of Archangel Hamaliel

Archangel Hamaliel holds a unique place in various spiritual and esoteric traditions, embodying the qualities of logic, order, and disciplined thinking. Although not as widely recognized as some other archangels, Hamaliel's influence is profound in the realms of intellectual clarity and organizational skills.

In Jewish mysticism, Hamaliel is often associated with the sign of Virgo, symbolizing meticulousness, analytical thinking, and attention to detail. He is seen as a guardian of order and structure, guiding individuals to approach their lives with precision and clarity.

In Christian tradition, while not explicitly named in the Bible, Hamaliel's attributes align with the teachings about angels who assist with understanding and wisdom. His role as an angel of logic and order is reflected in the Christian emphasis on discernment and thoughtful decision-making.

In Islamic tradition, angels who promote clarity and balance in life are seen as divine guides who help individuals navigate through complexity with wisdom and insight. This corresponds with Hamaliel's qualities of enhancing logic and promoting order.

In various spiritual and esoteric practices, Hamaliel is invoked as a guide for those seeking to enhance their analytical abilities and bring more structure into their lives. His energy is called upon in rituals and meditations aimed at fostering intellectual clarity and disciplined thinking.

These cultural and spiritual references highlight Hamaliel's enduring significance as a bringer of logic, order, and clarity. His presence in different traditions reflects a universal recognition of the importance of structured thinking and the role of divine guidance in achieving intellectual and emotional balance.

Embracing the Journey with Archangel Hamaliel

Archangel Hamaliel is a powerful and insightful guide who embodies the essence of logic, order, and disciplined thinking. His presence brings a deep sense of clarity and stability into our lives, helping us navigate complex situations with a calm and analytical mind. By recognizing Hamaliel's influence and building a relationship with him, we can enhance our ability to think logically, organize our lives effectively, and approach challenges with a balanced perspective.

Embracing the journey with Hamaliel means opening our minds to the transformative power of clarity and order. It encourages us to approach our lives with precision and thoughtfulness, to embrace structured thinking, and to find stability in the midst of chaos. As you continue your spiritual journey, invite Archangel Hamaliel to walk with you. Allow his steadying energy to fill your life with clarity and discipline, and trust in his unwavering support as you navigate the complexities of your thoughts and embrace the order and balance of your true self.

Chapter 44
Archangel Hutriel

Archangel Hutriel, often known as "The Rod of God," is an angelic figure associated with divine justice, retribution, and enlightenment. He embodies the qualities of strength, fairness, and illumination, guiding us toward truth and ensuring that justice is served in the spiritual and earthly realms. My journey with Hutriel began when I sought to understand the deeper aspects of divine justice and the balancing of karmic energies. His presence brought clarity and a profound sense of justice, helping me to see situations from a higher perspective.

Hutriel's energy is powerful and unwavering. When I first connected with him, I felt a strong, authoritative presence that commanded respect and evoked a deep sense of fairness. Despite his association with retribution, Hutriel's guidance is compassionate, aiming to restore balance and enlighten those who seek his assistance. His role is not to punish but to bring about a deeper understanding of justice and the natural order.

Roles and Responsibilities: Bringing Justice and Enlightenment

Archangel Hutriel's primary role is to serve as a beacon of divine justice and to enlighten those who are in search of truth and fairness. Here's how he fulfills these responsibilities:

Administering Divine Justice: Hutriel oversees the application of divine justice, ensuring that the spiritual laws of the universe are upheld. When injustices occur, he helps restore balance and order, guiding us

251

toward a fair resolution. I have called upon Hutriel in situations where I felt wronged or when seeking to understand the karmic implications of certain events. His presence provides a sense of reassurance that justice will prevail.

Balancing Karmic Energies: Hutriel assists in balancing karmic energies, helping individuals understand and resolve their karmic debts. He guides us through the lessons that come with our actions, offering insights into how we can restore balance in our lives. In my experiences, Hutriel has helped me navigate complex karmic situations, offering clarity and helping me see the broader spiritual context.

Providing Strength and Guidance: Known for his strong and protective energy, Hutriel provides strength and guidance to those who are facing challenges or injustices. He empowers us to stand up for what is right and to seek truth in all situations. When I've faced difficult decisions or conflicts, invoking Hutriel's presence has given me the courage and clarity to pursue the path of integrity and justice.

Enlightening and Illuminating: Hutriel also plays a role in enlightenment, shedding light on the truth and helping us see beyond illusions. He encourages us to seek knowledge and embrace the light of understanding. His guidance has often illuminated the deeper truths in situations, helping me gain a clearer perspective and make informed decisions.

Protecting the Innocent: Hutriel is a guardian for vulnerable or wronged people. He provides protection and support to those in need, ensuring that they are shielded from further harm. His protective energy is comforting and empowering, particularly in situations where justice needs to be served.

In my journey with Hutriel, his guidance has been invaluable in navigating complex issues of justice and understanding. His presence brings a sense of balance and assurance, reminding me that the universe operates under divine laws of fairness and truth.

How to Recognize Archangel Hutriel: Signs and Symbols

Recognizing the presence of Archangel Hutriel can be a unique and enlightening experience. Here are some ways to identify when Hutriel is near:

Feelings of Strength and Fairness: When Hutriel is present, you may feel an overwhelming sense of strength, fairness, and a desire for justice. This could manifest as a strong urge to address injustices or to seek the truth in a situation.

Symbols of Justice: Hutriel often communicates through symbols associated with justice, such as scales, rods, or beams of light. If you repeatedly encounter these symbols, it could be a sign that Hutriel is guiding you.

Illuminating Insights: Experiencing sudden moments of clarity or understanding, especially related to complex issues or injustices, may indicate Hutriel's influence. His presence often brings enlightenment and helps us see the broader perspective.

Warmth and Authority: You might feel a warm, authoritative presence, similar to the energy of a strong leader or protector. This feeling can be a direct indication of Hutriel's presence, providing reassurance and support.

Dreams of Justice and Light: Hutriel may appear in dreams as a figure of authority or as a source of light, guiding you through situations where justice or truth is needed. These dreams can be powerful affirmations of his role and guidance.

In my experience, Hutriel's presence is unmistakable, bringing a combination of strength, clarity, and a deep sense of justice. I have felt truly amazing in utilizing him during my activism journey. These signs remind me of his unwavering commitment to divine fairness and truth.

Connecting with Archangel Hutriel: Practical Steps and Techniques

Building a connection with Archangel Hutriel can provide much needed guidance and support, especially in matters of justice and truth. Here are some steps and techniques that have helped me connect with Hutriel:

Set Your Intention: Begin by setting a clear intention to connect with Archangel Hutriel. Use a specific prayer to invite his presence. Here's a prayer you can use:

"Dear Archangel Hutriel, I invite you into my life and ask for your guidance in matters of justice and truth. Please help me see clearly and act with integrity and fairness. Protect me from harm and guide me towards balance and enlightenment. I am open to your wisdom and support in restoring divine justice in my life. Thank you for your unwavering strength and clarity."

Visualize Light and Justice: During meditation or quiet reflection, visualize a beam of light or scales of justice. Imagine Hutriel standing beside you, offering his strength and guidance. This visualization can strengthen your connection and invoke his protective energy.

Create a Sacred Space: Dedicate a space in your home to connect with Hutriel. Include symbols of justice, such as scales or rods, and light a candle to represent his illuminating presence. Creating a sacred space can enhance your connection and provide a focused environment for spiritual practice.

Seek Enlightenment: Engage in practices that seek truth and enlightenment. This could include studying spiritual texts, journaling your thoughts and insights, or reflecting on the lessons of your experiences. Hutriel's guidance often comes through moments of deep understanding and clarity.

Ask for Protection and Balance: Whenever you feel vulnerable or in need of justice, ask Hutriel for his protection and guidance. Whether it's during a conflict, a difficult decision, or when seeking balance in your life, verbalize your request and trust in his support.

Express Gratitude: Regularly thank Hutriel for his guidance and protection. Acknowledge his role in your life and express appreciation for the strength and clarity he provides. Showing gratitude can strengthen your connection and invite more of his empowering energy into your life.

Historical Significance of Archangel Hutriel

Archangel Hutriel is a less commonly known figure compared to other archangels, but his role is deeply significant in various spiritual traditions. In mystical and esoteric teachings, Hutriel is often associated with divine justice and the enforcement of spiritual laws. His name, meaning "Rod of God," reflects his role as an instrument of divine authority and retribution.

In Kabbalistic traditions, Hutriel is recognized as a powerful angel who administers divine justice and maintains the balance of spiritual energies. He is seen as a guardian of the truth and an enforcer of cosmic order, ensuring that the principles of justice are upheld in the universe.

Although not prominently featured in mainstream Christian texts, Hutriel's attributes align with the broader Christian understanding of angels who act as protectors and agents of divine justice. His role in restoring balance and fairness resonates with the teachings of justice and righteousness found in Christian doctrine.

Hutriel's influence extends to various other spiritual and mystical practices where he is invoked for protection, clarity, and justice. His presence is often sought in rituals and prayers aimed at resolving conflicts, seeking truth, and restoring balance.

Hutriel's historical significance lies in his role as a guardian of justice and truth, bridging the gap between divine authority and human experience. His presence in different spiritual traditions highlights the universal need for fairness, balance, and enlightenment.

Embracing the Journey with Archangel Hutriel

Archangel Hutriel is a powerful ally who brings justice, strength, and enlightenment into our lives. His presence is deeply reassuring, offering support in navigating complex issues of fairness and truth. By recognizing his influence and building a relationship with him, we can approach life with greater clarity and a commitment to justice.

As you continue your spiritual journey, invite Archangel Hutriel to walk with you. Allow his authoritative and illuminating energy to guide you through life's challenges, and trust in his unwavering support in restoring balance and fairness. Embrace the strength and clarity that Hutriel brings, and know that you are always supported by his divine light.

Chapter 45

Archangel Jeremiel

My first encounter with Archangel Jeremiel was during a period of deep reflection and self-assessment. I felt a strong urge to review my life, understand past decisions, and gain clarity about my future path. When I reached out to Jeremiel, his presence was enlightening. Known as the "Angel of Visions and Dreams," Jeremiel helps us gain insight into our lives, understand our past actions, and envision our future possibilities. His guidance is invaluable for those seeking clarity, introspection, and a deeper understanding of their life's journey.

Archangel Jeremiel's name means "Mercy of God," reflecting his role in helping us review our lives with compassion and understanding. Jeremiel is associated with the violet light of transformation and is often depicted holding a staff or a scroll, symbolizing his role in guiding us through the process of life review and spiritual reflection. His energy is soothing and introspective, encouraging us to look within and understand the deeper meaning behind our experiences.

Jeremiel's influence extends to various aspects of our lives, particularly during times of transition or when we are seeking clarity about our path. He assists us in reviewing our past actions, understanding the lessons we have learned, and envisioning our future with renewed purpose and direction. In my experience, Jeremiel's guidance has been a beacon of light during periods of self-assessment and transformation. His presence fosters a deep connection with our inner wisdom, encouraging us to embrace our experiences with grace and to learn from them with an open heart.

Roles and Responsibilities: Assisting with Life Review and Future Vision

Archangel Jeremiel plays several crucial roles in our lives, focusing on helping us gain insight and clarity through visions and dreams. Here are some of the key responsibilities he undertakes:

Facilitating Life Review: Jeremiel assists us in reviewing our lives, helping us understand our past actions and the lessons we have learned. His guidance allows us to reflect on our experiences with compassion and understanding, encouraging us to grow and evolve. During moments of reflection or meditation, Jeremiel's presence can help us see our life's journey with greater clarity and perspective.

Providing Insight through Visions and Dreams: As the angel of visions and dreams, Jeremiel often communicates through intuitive insights, vivid dreams, and meditative visions. These experiences provide us with valuable guidance and a deeper understanding of our life's purpose and direction. When I have sought Jeremiel's guidance, his messages often come through dreams that offer clarity.

Supporting Spiritual Transformation: Jeremiel's influence is transformative, helping us navigate periods of change and transition. He encourages us to embrace new beginnings and to approach life with a renewed sense of purpose. His energy supports us in releasing old patterns and embracing the opportunities that lie ahead.

Guiding Future Vision: Jeremiel helps us envision our future with hope and optimism. He provides clarity about our goals and aspirations, guiding us toward choices that align with our highest good. His presence inspires us to set positive intentions and to pursue our dreams with confidence and determination.

Encouraging Emotional Healing: Jeremiel's compassionate energy supports us in healing emotional wounds and overcoming regrets. He helps us release feelings of guilt or sorrow associated with past actions, allowing us to move forward with a sense of peace and forgiveness. His guidance fosters emotional resilience and inner strength.

In my journey, Jeremiel's guidance has been instrumental in helping me gain clarity and understanding during times of reflection and transformation. His presence has encouraged me to view my experiences with compassion and to embrace my future with optimism and purpose.

How to Recognize Archangel Jeremiel: Signs and Symbols

Recognizing the presence of Archangel Jeremiel can provide a sense of clarity and direction during periods of introspection and transformation. Here are some ways to identify when Jeremiel is near:

Vivid Dreams and Visions: If you experience vivid dreams or meditative visions that provide insights into your life's journey or future possibilities, it may be a sign that Jeremiel is communicating with you. His messages often come through these intuitive channels, offering guidance and clarity.

Symbols of Reflection and Transformation: Jeremiel often communicates through symbols associated with reflection and transformation, such as mirrors, scrolls, or violet light. These symbols may appear in your environment, dreams, or meditative visions, reflecting his influence on your process of self-assessment and growth.

Encounters with the Color Violet: Violet is a color linked to Jeremiel's transformative and introspective energy. Seeing this color repeatedly, whether in your surroundings or during meditation, can signal his presence and support.

Feelings of Compassion and Understanding: Jeremiel's presence is often felt as a soothing and compassionate force. If you feel an unexpected sense of understanding and forgiveness towards yourself and others, it could be a sign that Jeremiel is guiding you.

Moments of Clarity and Insight: Jeremiel's influence brings clarity and insight, especially during times of reflection or decision-making. If you find yourself gaining a deeper understanding of your past actions or envisioning a clear path forward, it may be Jeremiel's guidance at work.

In my interactions with Jeremiel, his presence has often been felt as a gentle and enlightening force that enhances my ability to reflect on my life and envision my future. His guidance has helped me navigate periods of transition with a sense of purpose and clarity.

Connecting with Archangel Jeremiel: Practical Steps and Techniques

Building a connection with Archangel Jeremiel can enhance your ability to gain insight and clarity through visions and dreams. Here are some steps that have helped me connect with Jeremiel:

Set Your Intention: Begin by clearly stating your desire to connect with Archangel Jeremiel. Use a specific prayer to invite his presence. Here's a prayer you can use:

"Dear Archangel Jeremiel, I invite you into my life and ask for your guidance and support. Help me to review my past with compassion and to gain clarity about my future path. Illuminate my mind with your divine insights and inspire me to embrace my journey with grace and understanding. Surround me with your soothing energy and guide me in my process of reflection and transformation. Thank you for your presence and the wisdom you bring. I am open to your insights and your light."

Focus on the Third Eye Chakra: Jeremiel is closely associated with the third eye chakra, the center of intuition and inner vision. During meditation, place your hand over your third eye chakra and focus on feeling its energy. Visualize a vibrant violet light radiating from this area, inviting Jeremiel's presence and enhancing your ability to gain insights through visions and dreams.

Meditate on Violet Light: Given Jeremiel's connection to the color violet, meditating on violet light can strengthen your connection with him. Visualize yourself surrounded by a radiant violet light, feeling its transformative and introspective energy. Invite Jeremiel to join you in this space and be open to any messages or insights that come through.

Keep a Dream Journal: Document your dreams and any intuitive messages you receive. Keeping a journal can help you recognize patterns and track your progress, strengthening your connection with Jeremiel and helping you understand his messages. Reflecting on your dreams and visions can provide valuable insights into your life's journey and future possibilities.

Engage in Reflection and Self-Assessment: Embrace activities that encourage reflection and self-assessment, such as journaling, meditation, or quiet contemplation. Jeremiel's influence enhances your ability to review your life with compassion and understanding. Allow yourself to explore your past actions and envision your future with a sense of purpose and clarity.

Ask for Signs: Request specific signs from Jeremiel to confirm his presence and guidance. These signs could include symbols of reflection, encounters with the color violet, or moments of unexpected clarity and insight.

Express Gratitude: Regularly thank Jeremiel for his support and guidance. Acknowledge his role in helping you gain insight and clarity, and show appreciation for the compassion and understanding he helps you cultivate. Gratitude strengthens your connection and invites more of his positive energy into your life.

Historical Significance of Archangel Jeremiel

Archangel Jeremiel holds a significant place in various religious and spiritual traditions, known for his role in helping individuals review their lives and gain insights into their past and future. His name, meaning "Mercy of God," reflects his compassionate and understanding nature.

In Judeo-Christian beliefs, Jeremiel is mentioned in the Book of Enoch as one of the archangels who helps souls review their lives after death. He is described as guiding individuals through the process of understanding their actions and preparing for their journey to the afterlife. Jeremiel's presence in these texts underscores his role as a guide and mentor in the realm of introspection and spiritual reflection.

In Christian tradition, Jeremiel is also associated with the end times, helping souls review their lives and understand their deeds in preparation for judgment. His guidance is seen as a source of comfort and clarity during times of transition and transformation.

In various mystical and esoteric practices, Jeremiel is invoked as a guide for those seeking to understand their life's journey and gain insights into their future. His energy is called upon in rituals and meditations aimed at fostering reflection, transformation, and spiritual growth.

These cultural and spiritual references highlight Jeremiel's enduring significance as a bringer of insights and understanding. His presence across different traditions reflects a universal recognition of the importance of introspection, life review, and the guidance of divine wisdom in navigating the complexities of our lives.

Embracing the Journey with Archangel Jeremiel

Archangel Jeremiel is a powerful and insightful guide who embodies the essence of introspection, transformation, and divine insight. His presence brings a deep sense of clarity and understanding into our lives, helping us navigate the complexities of our past and envision our future with renewed purpose and direction. By recognizing Jeremiel's influence and building a relationship with him, we can enhance our ability to gain insights through visions and dreams and connect with our inner wisdom.

Embracing the journey with Jeremiel means opening our hearts to the transformative power of reflection and self-assessment. It encourages us to review our lives with compassion, to learn from our experiences, and to approach our future with hope and optimism. As you continue your spiritual journey, invite Archangel Jeremiel to walk with you. Allow his radiant energy to fill your life with clarity and understanding, and trust in his unwavering support as you navigate the complexities of your life's journey and embrace the light and truth of your authentic self.

Chapter 46

Archangel Jophiel

My journey with Archangel Jophiel began during a time when I struggled with self-image and self-worth. Like many, I often saw myself in a negative light and found it difficult to appreciate my own unique beauty. When I connected with Jophiel, I experienced a subtle shift in how I viewed myself and the world around me. Known as the "Angel of Beauty," Jophiel's presence brought a sense of joy, inspiration, and a deep appreciation for beauty in all forms. Her energy is gentle yet transformative, encouraging us to see the inherent beauty within ourselves and in our surroundings.

Jophiel's name means "Beauty of God," reflecting her role in illuminating the divine beauty that permeates all aspects of life. She helps us cultivate a positive outlook, inspiring creativity and a deep sense of joy. When working with Jophiel, I began to see beauty in everyday moments and, more importantly, within myself. Her guidance was a beacon of light during times of self-doubt, helping me to embrace my unique qualities and to see the world through a lens of beauty and gratitude.

Roles and Responsibilities: Bringing Joy and Inspiration

Archangel Jophiel plays a vital role in fostering beauty, joy, and inspiration in our lives. Her influence extends to various aspects of our personal and spiritual growth. Here are some of the key responsibilities she undertakes:

Promoting Inner and Outer Beauty: Jophiel helps us recognize and appreciate the beauty within ourselves and in the world around us. She encourages us to see beyond superficial appearances and to embrace the deeper, intrinsic beauty that resides in everyone and everything. In my journey, Jophiel's guidance helped me see my own beauty and the unique qualities that make each person special.

Inspiring Creativity: Jophiel is closely associated with artistic expression and creativity. She inspires artists, writers, and musicians to create works that reflect the beauty of the divine. When I felt blocked or uninspired in my creative pursuits, connecting with Jophiel often brought a surge of fresh ideas and renewed enthusiasm.

Cultivating a Positive Outlook: Jophiel's presence fosters a positive and joyful outlook on life. She helps us focus on the good and beautiful aspects of our experiences, encouraging us to maintain an attitude of gratitude and appreciation. Her guidance can transform our perspective, helping us find joy and contentment in even the simplest moments.

Enhancing Environmental Awareness: Jophiel also promotes the appreciation of nature and the environment. She encourages us to see the beauty in the natural world and to take actions that support environmental harmony and conservation. Her influence reminds us of our connection to the Earth and the importance of preserving its beauty.

Supporting Emotional Healing: Jophiel's loving energy helps us heal emotional wounds related to self-worth and self-image. She helps us release negative self-perceptions and embrace our true, beautiful selves. In my experience, her guidance was instrumental in overcoming feelings of inadequacy and fostering a sense of self-acceptance and love.

How to Recognize Archangel Jophiel: Signs and Symbols

Recognizing the presence of Archangel Jophiel can be a delightful and uplifting experience. Here are some ways to identify when Jophiel is near:

Encounters with Yellow Light: Jophiel is often associated with the color yellow, representing light, joy, and inspiration. Seeing this color frequently, especially in moments of contemplation or creativity, may indicate Jophiel's presence.

Feelings of Joy and Upliftment: Jophiel's energy is light and joyful. If you suddenly feel a burst of happiness, inspiration, or a heightened sense of beauty in your surroundings, it could be a sign that Jophiel is with you.

Increased Appreciation of Beauty: When Jophiel is near, you may find yourself noticing and appreciating beauty more acutely. This could be in nature, in art, or in the people around you. Her influence enhances our ability to see and cherish beauty in all forms.

Creative Inspiration: If you experience a surge of creative ideas or a renewed passion for artistic expression, Jophiel's guiding hand might be at play. She often inspires those she touches to create and express their inner beauty through art and other forms of creativity.

Physical Sensations: Some people report feeling a gentle warmth or tingling sensation when Jophiel is present. This comforting physical presence can be a subtle indication of her support and guidance.

In my experiences, I often feel a light and joyful energy that uplifts my spirits and enhances my appreciation for the world's beauty. These signs remind me that Jophiel is always near, ready to inspire and support me in seeing and creating beauty.

Connecting with Archangel Jophiel: Practical Steps and Techniques

Building a connection with Archangel Jophiel can bring immense joy, inspiration, and a deeper appreciation for beauty into your life. Here are some steps that have helped me connect with Jophiel:

Set Your Intention: Begin by clearly stating your desire to connect with Archangel Jophiel. Use a specific prayer to invite her presence. Here's a prayer you can use:

"Dear Archangel Jophiel, I invite you into my life and ask for your guidance and support. Help me to see and appreciate the beauty within myself and in the world around me. Inspire my creativity and fill my heart with joy and gratitude. Surround me with your radiant light and uplift my spirits with your loving energy. Thank you for your presence and the inspiration you bring. I am open to your guidance and your light."

Meditate on Yellow Light: Given Jophiel's connection to the color yellow, meditating on yellow light can strengthen your connection with her. Visualize yourself bathed in a warm, golden-yellow light, feeling its uplifting and joyful energy. Invite Jophiel to join you in this space and be open to any messages or inspirations that come through.

Focus on the Heart Chakra: Jophiel's energy resonates with the heart chakra, the center of love and compassion. During meditation, place your hand over your heart chakra and focus on feeling its energy. Visualize a vibrant yellow light radiating from this area, inviting Jophiel's presence and enhancing your ability to appreciate beauty and cultivate joy.

Engage in Creative Activities: Jophiel inspires creativity and artistic expression. Engage in activities that allow you to express your creativity, such as painting, writing, or playing music. Allow yourself to be open to Jophiel's guidance and inspiration during these activities.

Appreciate Beauty in All Forms: Take time to notice and appreciate the beauty around you. Whether it's a beautiful sunset, a piece of art, or a kind gesture, focus on the moments that bring joy and upliftment. Jophiel's presence can enhance your ability to see and cherish these moments of beauty.

Keep a Gratitude Journal: Document the moments of beauty and joy in your life. Keeping a gratitude journal can help you recognize and appreciate the positive aspects of your experiences, strengthen your connection with Jophiel, and invite more beauty into your life.

Ask for Signs: Request specific signs from Jophiel to confirm her presence and guidance. These signs could include symbols of beauty, encounters with the color yellow, or moments of unexpected joy and inspiration.

Express Gratitude: Regularly thank Jophiel for her support and guidance. Acknowledge her role in helping you see and appreciate the beauty in your life and show appreciation for the joy and inspiration she brings.

Historical Significance of Archangel Jophiel

Archangel Jophiel holds a significant place in various religious and spiritual traditions as the angel of beauty and inspiration. Her name, meaning "Beauty of God," reflects her role in illuminating the divine beauty that exists in all creation.

In Judeo-Christian beliefs, Jophiel is often associated with the promotion of beauty, joy, and creativity. She is believed to have accompanied Adam and Eve during their exile from Eden, providing them with comfort and helping them see the beauty in their new world despite their loss. This story shares Jophiel's role in bringing light and positivity into challenging situations.

In mystical and esoteric traditions, Jophiel is revered as a muse who inspires artists, writers, and musicians to create works that reflect the beauty of the divine. Her influence is seen in the creative expressions that uplift and elevate the human spirit. She is often called upon to provide inspiration and to help individuals see and appreciate the beauty in their surroundings and within themselves.

In contemporary spiritual practices, Jophiel is recognized as a guiding force in fostering self-love, positive self-image, and the appreciation of beauty in all forms. Her presence is sought after for healing emotional wounds related to self-worth and for cultivating a joyful and creative outlook on life.

These historical and cultural references highlight Jophiel's enduring significance as a bringer of beauty and inspiration. Her presence across different traditions reflects a universal recognition of the importance of beauty, joy, and creative expression in elevating the human experience.

Embracing the Journey with Archangel Jophiel

Archangel Jophiel is a powerful and uplifting guide who embodies the essence of beauty, joy, and inspiration. Her presence brings a deep sense of appreciation for the beauty that exists within ourselves and in the world around us. By recognizing Jophiel's influence and building a relationship with her, we can enhance our ability to see and create beauty, cultivate joy, and embrace our unique qualities.

Embracing the journey with Jophiel means opening our hearts to the transformative power of beauty and inspiration. It encourages us to see beyond superficial appearances, to find joy in everyday moments, and to express our creativity with confidence and love. As you continue your spiritual journey, invite Archangel Jophiel to walk with you. Allow her radiant energy to fill your life with light and joy, and trust in her unwavering support as you navigate the complexities of life and discover the beauty that lies within and around you.

Chapter 47

Archangel Kushiel

Archangel Kushiel, often referred to as "The Righteous Punisher," is an angelic figure associated with divine retribution and justice. His name means "Rigid One of God," reflecting his role in dispensing discipline and ensuring that justice is served. When I first connected with Kushiel, I was struck by his stern yet fair presence. Unlike other angels who are often depicted with soft, nurturing energy, Kushiel's presence felt strong and unyielding, like an immovable force of righteousness.

Kushiel's energy is resolute and commanding, and his guidance comes with a sense of authority and finality. Despite his role as a punisher, his actions are not driven by malice but by a deep commitment to uphold divine laws and maintain balance. His influence is felt most strongly when we are in need of clear boundaries and firm guidance. Kushiel helps us understand the consequences of our actions and steers us back toward the path of righteousness and moral integrity.

Roles and Responsibilities: Dispensing Divine Discipline and Upholding Justice

Kushiel's primary role is to administer divine discipline and ensure that justice is upheld in the spiritual and physical realms. Here's how he fulfills these responsibilities:

Enforcing Divine Justice: Kushiel oversees the execution of divine justice, ensuring that those who act unjustly are held accountable. His presence is often felt during times of reckoning when actions must be addressed and lessons learned. In my experiences with Kushiel, he brings a sense of closure and resolution, helping to restore balance and order.

Encouraging Moral Integrity: Kushiel guides us towards living a life of moral integrity and righteousness. He helps us recognize our wrongdoings and encourages us to make amends and live in accordance with higher ethical standards. His influence is especially valuable when we are tempted to stray from the path of truth and integrity.

Providing Firm Guidance: Known for his unwavering stance, Kushiel provides firm guidance and support, particularly in situations where clear boundaries are needed. He empowers us to stand up for what is right and to make decisions that align with our highest values. When I need to make difficult choices or set boundaries, I often call upon Kushiel for his strength and clarity.

Facilitating Accountability: Kushiel helps us understand and accept responsibility for our actions. He teaches us that every action has consequences and that we must be accountable for the choices we make. This aspect of his guidance is crucial for personal growth and spiritual development, as it fosters a deeper understanding of cause and effect.

Restoring Balance and Order: In times of chaos or injustice, Kushiel works to restore balance and order. He intervenes to ensure that divine laws are respected and that fairness prevails. His presence brings a sense of justice and reassurance that the scales will be balanced.

In my journey with Kushiel, his guidance has been instrumental in helping me navigate complex moral dilemmas and understand the importance of living with integrity. His influence is a constant reminder that justice and accountability are essential components of a balanced and harmonious life.

How to Recognize Archangel Kushiel: Signs and Symbols

Recognizing the presence of Archangel Kushiel can be an intense and eye-opening experience. Here are some ways to identify when

Kushiel is near:

Feelings of Strength and Authority: When Kushiel is present, you may feel an overwhelming sense of strength and authority. This could manifest as a strong urge to address injustices or to take firm action in situations that require clear boundaries.

Symbols of Justice and Discipline: Kushiel often communicates through symbols associated with justice and discipline, such as scales, rods, or images of a stern, commanding figure. If you repeatedly encounter these symbols, it could be a sign that Kushiel is guiding you.

Sudden Clarity and Resolution: Experiencing sudden moments of clarity or resolution, especially related to moral or ethical issues, may indicate Kushiel's influence. His presence often brings decisive insights and helps us see the path of righteousness.

Stern Yet Reassuring Presence: You might feel a stern yet reassuring presence, similar to the energy of a strict but fair mentor or guardian. This feeling can be a direct indication of Kushiel's presence, providing support and guidance.

Dreams of Justice and Order: Kushiel may appear in dreams as a figure of authority or as an enforcer of justice, guiding you through situations where accountability or moral integrity is needed. These dreams can be powerful affirmations for his role and guidance.

In my experience, Kushiel's presence is distinct and commanding, bringing a combination of strength, clarity, and a deep sense of justice. These signs remind me of his commitment to divine discipline and moral integrity.

Connecting with Archangel Kushiel: Practical Steps and Techniques

Building a connection with Archangel Kushiel can provide guidance and support, especially in matters of justice and moral integrity. Here are some steps and techniques that have helped me connect with Kushiel:

Set Your Intention: Begin by setting a clear intention to connect with Archangel Kushiel. Use a specific prayer to invite his presence. Here's a prayer you can use:

"Dear Archangel Kushiel, I invite you into my life and ask for your guidance in matters of justice and moral integrity. Please help me to understand the consequences of my actions and to live with accountability and righteousness. Protect me from unjust influences and guide me towards balance and fairness. I am open to your wisdom and strength in restoring divine order in my life. Thank you for your unwavering justice and clarity."

Visualize Justice and Order: During meditation or quiet reflection, visualize symbols of justice and order, such as scales or a rod. Imagine Kushiel standing beside you, offering his strength and guidance. This visualization can strengthen your connection and invoke his protective and authoritative energy.

Create a Sacred Space: Dedicate a space in your home to connect with Kushiel. Include symbols of justice and discipline, such as scales or rods, and light a candle to represent his stern but fair presence. Creating a sacred space can enhance your connection and provide a focused environment for spiritual practice.

Seek Accountability: Engage in practices that encourage accountability and moral integrity. This could include reflecting on your actions, seeking to understand their impact, and making amends where necessary. Kushiel's guidance often comes through moments of deep understanding and the willingness to accept responsibility.

Ask for Protection and Balance: Whenever you feel vulnerable or in need of justice, ask Kushiel for his protection and guidance. Whether it's during a conflict, a tough decision, or when seeking balance in your life, verbalize your request and trust in his support.

Express Gratitude: Regularly thank Kushiel for his guidance and protection. Acknowledge his role in your life and express appreciation for the strength and clarity he provides. Showing gratitude can strengthen your connection and invite more of his empowering energy into your life.

Historical Significance of Archangel Kushiel

Archangel Kushiel is a figure with roots in various spiritual traditions, often associated with divine retribution and justice. His name, meaning "Rigid One of God," reflects his role as an enforcer of divine laws and principles. While less commonly known than other archangels, Kushiel's influence is far-reaching.

Kushiel is recognized as one of the angels who administers divine punishment and justice. In Kabbalistic traditions, he is seen as a guardian of the spiritual laws, ensuring that those who transgress are held accountable. His presence is often invoked in rituals and prayers, seeking justice and balance.

Although not prominently featured in mainstream Christian texts, Kushiel's attributes align with the broader Christian understanding of angels who act as protectors and agents of divine justice. His role in restoring order and enforcing moral integrity resonates with the teachings of righteousness and accountability found in Christian doctrine.

Kushiel's influence extends to various other spiritual and mystical practices where he is invoked for protection, clarity, and justice. His presence is often sought in rituals and prayers aimed at resolving conflicts, seeking truth, and restoring balance.

Kushiel's historical significance lies in his role as a guardian of justice and moral integrity, bridging the gap between divine authority and human experience. His presence in different spiritual traditions highlights the universal need for fairness, balance, and accountability.

Embracing the Journey with Archangel Kushiel.

Archangel Kushiel is a powerful ally who brings justice, strength, and clarity into our lives. His presence is deeply reassuring, offering support in navigating complex issues of fairness and moral integrity. By recognizing his influence and building a relationship with him, we can approach life with greater clarity and a commitment to justice.

As you continue your spiritual journey, invite Archangel Kushiel to walk with you. Allow his authoritative and illuminating energy to guide you through life's challenges, and trust in his unwavering support in restoring balance and fairness. Embrace the strength and clarity that Kushiel brings, and know that you are always supported by his divine light.

Chapter 48
Archangel Matriel

My journey with Archangel Matriel began during a period of deep reflection and spiritual drought. I felt parched for inspiration and spiritual connection, much like a landscape in need of rain. When I first connected with Matriel, known as the "Angel of Divine Rain," I experienced a sense of renewal and revitalization. Matriel's energy is nurturing, symbolizing the life-giving power of rain and the cycles of nourishment that sustain both the physical and spiritual realms.

Matriel is often associated with the elemental force of water, particularly rain, and is revered for her role in bringing physical and spiritual nourishment. Her presence is a reminder that just as rain replenishes the Earth, divine wisdom and guidance can rejuvenate our souls. Working with Matriel has helped me understand the importance of patience and the natural cycles of growth and renewal. She has taught me to embrace periods of stillness and to trust that nourishment and clarity will come in their own time.

Roles and Responsibilities: Nourishing the Soul and Environment

Archangel Matriel plays a multifaceted role in our lives, closely tied to the themes of nourishment, renewal, and the natural cycles of life. Here are some key responsibilities he undertakes:

Providing Spiritual and Emotional Nourishment: Matriel helps us find the spiritual and emotional nourishment we need to thrive. She guides us to sources of inspiration and wisdom that can refresh our spirits and support our personal and spiritual growth. In times when I felt spiritually depleted, Matriel's presence brought a sense of renewal and a reminder that, like the Earth after a drought, my spirit could be replenished.

Facilitating Renewal and Rebirth: Just as rain brings new life to parched lands, Matriel assists in the process of renewal and rebirth. She helps us release old patterns and embrace new beginnings, fostering personal transformation and growth. Her energy is deeply purifying, encouraging us to let go of what no longer serves us and to make space for new experiences and insights.

Supporting Environmental Harmony: Matriel is also associated with the balance and harmony of the natural world. She helps maintain the cycles of rain and water that are essential for sustaining life on Earth. Her guidance can inspire us to take actions that support environmental conservation and to recognize our interconnectedness with the natural world.

Enhancing Patience and Trust: Matriel teaches us the value of patience and trust in the natural cycles of life. She reminds us that just as the Earth goes through seasons, we too, have periods of growth and renewal. Her presence encourages us to trust in the timing of our own journey and to have faith that nourishment and clarity will come when we need them most.

Promoting Emotional Cleansing: Water is a powerful symbol of cleansing, and Matriel's energy is deeply connected to emotional purification. She helps us release pent-up emotions and cleanse our emotional bodies, promoting healing and balance. Working with Matriel can be especially beneficial during times of emotional turmoil or when we need to let go of lingering emotional burdens.

How to Recognize Archangel Matriel: Signs and Symbols

Recognizing the presence of Archangel Matriel can be a deeply calming and nurturing experience. Here are some ways to identify when Matriel is near:

Encounters with Rain or Water: Matriel is closely associated with rain and water. If you find yourself encountering rain unexpectedly or feeling drawn to bodies of water, it could be a sign that Matriel is near. Her presence is often felt during rainstorms or in places where water is a dominant feature.

Feelings of Renewal and Rejuvenation: Matriel's energy brings a sense of renewal and rejuvenation. If you suddenly feel refreshed or revitalized, especially after a period of stagnation or spiritual dryness, it might be Matriel's influence. Her presence can bring a wave of renewed energy and clarity.

Dreams and Visions Involving Water: Matriel may communicate through dreams or visions involving water, such as rain, rivers, or oceans. These dreams often carry messages of cleansing, renewal, and the flow of life. Pay attention to the symbolism of water in your dreams, as it may provide insights into your current spiritual journey.

Physical Sensations: Some people report feeling a gentle, cool sensation or a calming presence when Matriel is near. This can be a sign of her nurturing and soothing energy, providing comfort and reassurance.

Synchronicities Related to Water and Renewal: Look for synchronicities involving water or themes of renewal and growth. These might include hearing songs about rain, reading about water cycles, or encountering symbols of water in your daily life. Such signs can be Matriel's way of communicating her presence and guidance.

In my experiences, I often recognize Matriel's presence through a deep sense of calm and a renewed appreciation for the natural cycles of life. These signs remind me that Matriel is always there to support and nourish me, both physically and spiritually.

Connecting with Archangel Matriel: Practical Steps and Techniques

Building a connection with Archangel Matriel can bring a sense of renewal and nourishment into your life. Here are some steps that have helped me connect with Matriel:

Set Your Intention: Begin by clearly stating your desire to connect with Archangel Matriel. Use a specific prayer to invite her presence. Here's a prayer you can use:

"Dear Archangel Matriel, I invite you into my life and ask for your guidance and support. Help me to find spiritual and emotional nourishment and to embrace the natural cycles of renewal and growth. Surround me with your nurturing energy and assist me in releasing old patterns and embracing new beginnings. Thank you for your presence and the healing rain of wisdom and clarity you bring. I am open to your guidance and your light."

Meditate on Water: Given Matriel's connection to water, meditating on water can strengthen your connection with her. Visualize yourself standing under a gentle rain or by a serene body of water, feeling its cleansing and renewing energy. Invite Matriel to join you in this space and be open to any messages or sensations that come through.

Spend Time in Nature: Matriel's energy is deeply connected to the natural world. Spend time outdoors, particularly near water sources such as rivers, lakes, or the ocean. Allow yourself to feel the soothing and revitalizing energy of nature and invite Matriel to walk with you during these moments.

Engage in Rituals Involving Water: Incorporate water into your spiritual rituals, such as taking a cleansing bath, sprinkling water during meditation, or creating a small altar with water elements. These rituals can help you attune to Matriel's energy and invite her presence into your life.

Practice Emotional Cleansing: Engage in practices that promote emotional cleansing and release. This could include journaling about your feelings, practicing mindfulness, or using techniques such as breathwork or visualization to let go of emotional burdens. Ask Matriel to assist you in this process and to help you find emotional balance and clarity.

Pay Attention to Weather Patterns: Notice the weather, especially changes involving rain or water. These natural occurrences can be reminders of Matriel's presence and her role in bringing renewal and nourishment. Use these moments to connect with Matriel and reflect on the cycles of growth and change in your life.

Express Gratitude: Regularly thank Matriel for her support and guidance. Acknowledge her role in nourishing your spirit and supporting your personal and spiritual growth. Showing appreciation can strengthen your connection and invite more of her nurturing energy into your life.

Historical Significance of Archangel Matriel

Archangel Matriel holds a significant place in various spiritual and religious traditions as the angel associated with rain and nourishment. Her name, often translated as "Rain of God" or "Gift of God," reflects her role in bringing divine sustenance to both the Earth and the human soul.

In Jewish mystical texts, Matriel is recognized as one of the angels who governs natural elements, particularly rain. Her role is to ensure that the cycles of rain and water are maintained, providing the necessary nourishment for life to flourish. This connection to rain underscores her importance in agricultural societies, where rain was seen as a direct blessing from the divine.

In Christian traditions, while Matriel is not explicitly named in the canonical texts, her attributes align with the angelic figures who are believed to oversee the natural elements and ensure the balance and harmony of creation. Her influence is often invoked during prayers for rain and good harvests, reflecting her role as a provider of divine nourishment.

In Eastern spiritual practices, angels like Matriel are often seen as guardians of natural elements. In these traditions, the presence of divine beings who oversee rain and water is essential for maintaining the balance and health of the natural world.

In indigenous cultures, the concept of spirit beings who control rain and weather is prevalent. These beings are revered and called upon during rituals and ceremonies to ensure the prosperity and well-being of the community. Matriel's connection to these practices highlights her universal role as a bringer of nourishment and renewal.

These cultural and historical references highlight Matriel's enduring significance as a guardian of rain and a provider of divine nourishment. Her presence across different traditions reflects a universal recognition of the essential role of water and the cycles of nature in sustaining life and promoting spiritual growth.

Embracing the Journey with Archangel Matriel

Archangel Matriel is a powerful and nurturing guide who embodies the life-giving force of rain and the cycles of renewal and nourishment. Her presence brings a feeling of peace, clarity, and revitalization, helping us navigate the natural rhythms of life and find spiritual and emotional sustenance.

By recognizing Matriel's influence and building a relationship with her, we can enhance our ability to embrace the cycles of growth and renewal, connect with the natural world, and find nourishment for our souls. Embracing the journey with Matriel means opening our hearts to the transformative power of divine nourishment and trusting in the natural flow of life.

As you continue your spiritual journey, invite Archangel Matriel to walk with you. Allow her gentle and revitalizing energy to guide you through periods of growth and change, and trust in her unwavering support as you discover the nourishment and wisdom that lie within and around you.

Chapter 49
Archangel Metatron

My journey with Archangel Metatron began as I delved deeper into energy work and the exploration of sacred geometry. Metatron's presence is both powerful and incredibly enlightening. Known as the "Scribe of God," Metatron serves as a divine record-keeper and a guide to higher spiritual wisdom and understanding. His energy is uniquely connected to sacred geometry, particularly Metatron's Cube, and the transformative power of the violet flame.

Metatron's influence in my life has been transformative, especially in my spiritual practices and the pursuit of deeper knowledge. His guidance helps me access higher realms of consciousness and comprehend complex spiritual concepts. Working with Metatron, I've felt a connection to divine knowledge and a clearer understanding of my spiritual path.

Roles and Responsibilities: Guiding Spiritual Wisdom and Higher Understanding

Archangel Metatron plays a crucial role in guiding us towards spiritual wisdom and understanding. Here are some key responsibilities he undertakes:

Accessing Higher Realms of Consciousness: Metatron helps us elevate our consciousness to connect with higher realms and dimensions. He guides us in expanding our awareness and understanding of the spiritual truths that transcend ordinary human experience. Through meditation and energy work, Metatron facilitates our journey to these higher states of being.

Understanding Sacred Geometry: One of Metatron's primary roles is to help us understand and utilize sacred geometry. Metatron's Cube, a powerful geometric figure, is believed to contain all the shapes that exist within the universe. It serves as a blueprint for creation and a tool for connecting with higher wisdom. Metatron assists us in using these sacred geometries for spiritual growth, healing, and manifesting our intentions.

Recording Divine Knowledge: As the scribe of God, Metatron is responsible for recording all deeds and maintaining the Akashic Records, which are the universal archives of every soul's journey. His role as a divine record-keeper ensures that all actions and experiences are accounted for and accessible for spiritual learning and growth.

Facilitating Personal Transformation: Metatron's energy is transformative, helping us release old patterns and embrace new spiritual insights. The violet flame, often associated with Metatron, is a powerful tool for purification and spiritual transformation. It helps us transmute negative energies and align with our higher purpose.

Guiding Spiritual Learning and Development: Metatron supports our journey of spiritual learning and development. He provides clarity and understanding of complex spiritual concepts, helping us integrate these insights into our daily lives. His guidance encourages continuous growth and the pursuit of higher knowledge.

In my own experience, Metatron's guidance has been instrumental in deepening my spiritual practice and understanding. His presence brings clarity, insight, and a sense of connection to the divine wisdom that shapes our universe.

How to Recognize Archangel Metatron: Signs and Symbols

Recognizing the presence of Archangel Metatron can be a unique experience. Here are some ways to identify when Metatron is near:

Encounters with Sacred Geometry: Metatron is closely associated with sacred geometry, particularly Metatron's Cube. If you find yourself drawn to geometric patterns or symbols, or if you encounter these shapes unexpectedly, it could be a sign of Metatron's presence.

Feelings of Heightened Awareness: Metatron's energy elevates our consciousness and awareness. If you suddenly feel a heightened sense of clarity or understanding, especially regarding spiritual matters, it may be Metatron guiding you.

Experiences of Deep Meditation: During deep meditation or energy work, you might sense a strong, uplifting presence or see visions of vibrant light and geometric patterns. These experiences often indicate Metatron's influence, guiding you to higher realms of consciousness.

Synchronicities Involving Learning and Wisdom: Pay attention to synchronicities related to learning, wisdom, or spiritual development. Encounters with books, articles, or people that lead you to deeper insights can be a sign of Metatron's guidance.

Dreams and Visions of Light: Metatron often communicates through dreams and visions involving brilliant light or intricate geometric patterns. These dreams may carry messages of spiritual wisdom and guidance, encouraging you to explore deeper aspects of your spiritual journey.

In my experiences, Metatron's presence is often felt as a powerful, uplifting energy that brings a sense of clarity and connection to the divine. These signs remind me that Metatron is guiding me toward higher understanding and spiritual growth.

Connecting with Archangel Metatron: Practical Steps and Techniques

Building a connection with Archangel Metatron can open the doors to spiritual wisdom and transformation. Here are some steps that have helped me connect with Metatron:

Set Your Intention: Begin by clearly stating your desire to connect with Archangel Metatron. Use a specific prayer to invite his presence. Here's a prayer you can use:

"Dear Archangel Metatron, I invite you into my life and ask for your guidance and support. Help me to access higher realms of consciousness and understand the sacred wisdom of the universe. Illuminate my path with your divine light and assist me in my quest for spiritual knowledge and growth. Thank you for your presence and the transformative energy you bring. I am open to your guidance and your wisdom."

Meditate on Sacred Geometry: Given Metatron's association with sacred geometry, meditating on these patterns can strengthen your connection with him. Visualize Metatron's Cube or other geometric shapes, allowing their energy to fill your consciousness and open your mind to higher wisdom.

Use the Violet Flame: Incorporate the violet flame into your spiritual practice. Visualize this powerful flame surrounding you, cleansing and transmuting any negative energies. Ask Metatron to guide you in using the violet flame for spiritual purification and transformation.

Spend Time in Quiet Reflection: Find quiet moments for reflection and contemplation. Use this time to focus on your spiritual journey and invite Metatron to provide insights and guidance. Journaling your thoughts and experiences can help you process and integrate the wisdom you receive.

Engage in Energy Work: Practice energy work that aligns with Metatron's transformative energy. This can include Reiki, chakra balancing, or other forms of healing that focus on elevating your spiritual vibration. Invite Metatron to support and enhance your energy work practices.

Create a Sacred Space: Designate a space in your home for connecting with Metatron. Include items that resonate with his energy, such as crystals, symbols of sacred geometry, or images of Metatron's Cube. Creating a sacred space can enhance your connection and provide a focused environment for spiritual practice.

Express Gratitude: Regularly thank Metatron for his support and guidance. Acknowledge his role in helping you access higher wisdom and facilitating your spiritual growth. Showing appreciation can strengthen your connection and invite more of his transformative energy into your life.

Historical Significance of Archangel Metatron

Archangel Metatron holds a unique place in various spiritual and mystical traditions. He is often regarded as one of the highest-ranking angels, known for his role as the "Scribe of God" and the keeper of divine wisdom and knowledge.

Metatron is prominently featured in Jewish mystical texts, such as the Kabbalah. He is believed to have been the prophet Enoch, who was transformed into the angel Metatron after his ascension to heaven. Metatron's responsibilities include recording all deeds in the Book of Life and overseeing the flow of divine energy throughout the cosmos. His association with sacred geometry, particularly the Metatron's Cube, underscores his role in the creation and organization of the universe.

While not explicitly mentioned in the Bible, Metatron's attributes and functions align with those of angelic figures who act as intermediaries between God and humanity. Christian mystics and scholars have recognized Metatron as a powerful guide and teacher, helping believers understand divine truths and access higher states of consciousness.

Although Metatron is not directly named in the Quran, his role as a celestial scribe is echoed in Islamic teachings about angels who record human deeds. His presence is often associated with the archangels who play crucial roles in guiding and protecting souls.

Metatron's significance has been embraced by various esoteric and New Age traditions, where he is seen as a key figure in understanding sacred geometry and accessing the Akashic Records. His influence is sought by those who seek to deepen their spiritual practice and connect with higher realms of knowledge and consciousness.

Metatron's presence in art and literature often symbolizes divine knowledge and the quest for spiritual enlightenment. His imagery is used to represent the interconnectedness of all creation and the pathways to higher understanding.

These historical and cultural perspectives highlight Metatron's enduring role as a bridge between the divine and the human, guiding seekers toward greater spiritual wisdom and understanding.

Embracing the Journey with Archangel Metatron

Archangel Metatron is a powerful guide and teacher who assists us in accessing higher realms of wisdom and understanding. His presence is deeply connected to the transformative power of sacred geometry and the cleansing energy of the violet flame. By recognizing Metatron's influence and building a relationship with him, we can open ourselves to spiritual insights and personal transformation.

As you continue your spiritual journey, invite Archangel Metatron to walk with you. Allow his illuminating energy to guide you towards higher knowledge and deeper understanding. Trust in his unwavering support as you navigate the complexities of life and discover the divine wisdom that lies within and around you.

Chapter 50
Archangel Michael

When I first started working with angelic beings, Archangel Michael was often the one I instinctively called upon. It's almost like a natural response for many people seeking protection and strength. Michael's presence is immediately comforting and empowering, and his energy is unmistakably powerful. Known as the "Protector," Archangel Michael offers strength, courage, and defense against negative energies and harm. Whether facing personal challenges or dealing with negative entities, Michael is the go-to archangel for support and protection.

My initial experiences with Michael involved situations where I felt vulnerable or in need of extra strength. I would visualize his iconic blue light or mighty sword and instantly feel a shield of protection enveloping me. Over time, I realized how versatile and supportive Michael is, not just in moments of fear or danger but in everyday life challenges as well. He is especially effective when working with others, providing a sense of security and empowerment to those who seek his assistance.

Roles and Responsibilities: Offering Strength and Protection

Archangel Michael's primary role is to offer protection, courage, and strength. Here's how he fulfills these responsibilities:

Defending Against Negative Energies: Michael is a powerful defender against negative influences and harmful entities. Whether it's spiritual attacks, toxic environments, or negative thoughts, Michael's presence can dispel these energies and create a safe, protected space around us. I always call on Michael when I need to clear a space of negativity or when facing particularly challenging situations.

Providing Strength and Courage: In times of adversity, Michael offers the strength and courage needed to persevere. He empowers us to face our fears and challenges head-on, reminding us of our inner strength and resilience. When I'm about to take on a difficult task or confront a tough situation, I often ask Michael for his support, and I find myself feeling more confident and courageous.

Guiding and Supporting Others: Michael is exceptional at working with people providing guidance and support. He helps us make wise decisions and navigate through difficult circumstances. His influence can be felt in personal, professional, and spiritual aspects of life, offering clarity and direction when needed.

Removing Negative Entities: One of Michael's well-known roles is assisting in the removal of negative entities or energies. His powerful blue light and sword can cut through any dark or harmful presence, restoring peace and balance. I frequently call upon Michael during energy-clearing sessions to ensure that any lingering negative energies are safely removed.

Encouraging Justice and Integrity: Michael stands for divine justice and righteousness. He encourages us to act with integrity and to stand up for what is right. In situations where fairness and justice are in question, invoking Michael can bring about the strength and clarity needed to address these issues effectively.

In my experience, Michael's guidance has been a beacon of strength and protection. His presence is a constant reminder that I am never alone and that divine support is always available.

How to Recognize Archangel Michael: Signs and Symbols

Recognizing Archangel Michael's presence can be a reassuring and empowering experience. Here are some ways to identify when Michael is near:

Visualizing Blue Light or a Sword: Michael is often associated with a brilliant blue light or a sword of light. If you visualize or see blue light during meditation or in your surroundings, it could be a sign that Michael is with you. Similarly, seeing images or symbols of a sword can indicate his protective presence.

Feelings of Strength and Confidence: Michael's presence brings a sense of strength, confidence, and courage. If you suddenly feel more empowered or capable in the face of challenges, it might be Michael providing you with the support you need.

Encounters with Fire or Heat: Michael is sometimes associated with the element of fire. If you experience sensations of warmth or see flames in visions or dreams, these can be indicators of Michael's influence.

Repetitive Symbols and Messages: Pay attention to recurring symbols, numbers (like 111 or 444), or messages that seem to encourage strength, protection, and courage. These can be subtle signs that Michael is guiding you toward your goals.

Dreams of Protection and Victory: Michael often appears in dreams where he is fighting against darkness or providing protection. Such dreams can be powerful affirmations of his presence and support in your life.

In my own experiences, I've often recognized Michael through the sudden appearance of blue light and an overwhelming sense of courage and determination. These signs always remind me of his unwavering support and protection.

Connecting with Archangel Michael: Practical Steps and Techniques

Building a strong connection with Archangel Michael can provide immense support and protection. Here are some practical steps and techniques that have helped me connect with Michael:

Set Your Intention: Start by setting a clear intention to connect with Archangel Michael. Use a specific prayer to invite his presence. Here's a prayer you can use:

"Dear Archangel Michael, I invite you into my life and ask for your protection and strength. Please shield me from negative energies and guide me with courage and clarity. Help me to face my challenges with confidence and to act with integrity and justice. Thank you for your unwavering support and powerful presence. I am open to your guidance and protection."

Visualize Blue Light or a Sword: During meditation or quiet reflection, visualize a radiant blue light surrounding you. Imagine Michael's sword of light cutting through any negative energies or obstacles in your path. This visualization can strengthen your connection with Michael and invoke his protective energy.

Create a Sacred Space: Designate a space in your home for connecting with Michael. Include items that resonate with his energy, such as blue crystals (like sapphire or lapis lazuli), candles, or images of swords. Creating a sacred space can enhance your connection and provide a focused environment for spiritual practice.

Engage in Protective Rituals: Incorporate rituals that align with Michael's protective role. This can include energy-clearing practices, such as cleansing with sage or using protective symbols and affirmations. Invite Michael to be present during these rituals to amplify their effectiveness.

Ask for Protection and Guidance: Whenever you feel vulnerable or in need of strength, ask Michael for his protection and guidance. Whether it's before a difficult conversation, during a challenging task, or when clearing negative energies, verbalize your request and trust in his support.

Express Gratitude: Regularly thank Michael for his protection and guidance. Acknowledge his role in your life and express appreciation for the strength and courage he provides. Showing gratitude can strengthen your connection and invite more of his protective energy into your life.

Historical Significance of Archangel Michael

Archangel Michael is one of the most revered and venerated figures across various religious and spiritual traditions. His role as a protector and leader against evil is celebrated worldwide.

Michael is prominently featured in Christian texts as the leader of the heavenly armies. He is depicted as a powerful warrior who defends against the forces of darkness. Michael's most famous act in Christian tradition is his defeat of Satan and his angels, as described in the Book of Revelation. He is often called upon for protection and strength, and many churches and shrines are dedicated to his honor.

Known as Mikail in Islam, Michael is recognized as one of the four archangels in Islamic tradition. He is responsible for providing nourishment to human bodies and souls, overseeing natural phenomena, and supporting humanity's spiritual growth. Michael's presence is seen as a source of sustenance and divine support.

Michael is revered in Jewish tradition as a protector of Israel and a defender against the forces of evil. He is mentioned in the Book of Daniel as a great prince who stands guard over the people. Michael's role as a guardian and advocate is deeply rooted in Jewish mystical and liturgical texts.

Beyond the Abrahamic faiths, Michael is acknowledged in various other spiritual and esoteric traditions. He is often invoked in rituals of protection, exorcism, and healing. His influence extends to New Age and contemporary spiritual practices, where he is seen as a powerful guide and protector.

Michael's image as a warrior angel is prevalent in art and literature. He is frequently depicted in armor, wielding a sword, and standing victorious over evil. These portrayals highlight his role as a symbol of divine protection and justice.

Michael's historical significance provides clarity of his enduring role as a protector and defender of humanity. Across different cultures and religions, he remains a powerful figure of strength, courage, and divine support.

Embracing the Journey with Archangel Michael

Archangel Michael is a powerful ally who provides protection, strength, and courage. His presence is deeply comforting and empowering, offering support in both spiritual and everyday challenges. By recognizing his influence and building a relationship with him, we can navigate life with greater confidence and security.

As you continue your spiritual journey, invite Archangel Michael to walk with you. Allow his protective and empowering energy to guide you through life's challenges, and trust in his unwavering support. Embrace the strength and courage that Michael brings, and know that you are always shielded by his divine light.

Chapter 51
Archangel Netzach

Archangel Netzach, often associated with the divine aspect of victory and endurance, represents the eternal and triumphant spirit that guides us through challenges toward success. His name means "Eternity" or "Victory" in Hebrew, embodying both the everlasting nature of the divine and the triumph of perseverance. When I first connected with Netzach, I was struck by the feeling of resilience and optimism he imparted. Unlike other guides who may focus on specific skills or protections, Netzach encourages a broader, more enduring perspective on our life's journey. His presence is a source of motivation and unwavering support, reminding us that true victory comes from persistent effort and faith in the face of adversity.

Netzach's energy is both powerful and uplifting. He encourages us to view challenges as opportunities for growth and to remain steadfast in our pursuits, regardless of the obstacles we encounter. His guidance is invaluable when we find ourselves facing seemingly insurmountable odds, offering the strength and perseverance needed to achieve our goals.

Roles and Responsibilities: Guiding Us Towards Victory and Perseverance

Archangel Netzach plays a crucial role in fostering a spirit of victory and resilience. Here's how he fulfills these responsibilities:

Encouraging Perseverance: Netzach instills in us the determination

293

to keep going, even when the path is difficult. He reminds us that perseverance is key to achieving our goals and that true victory is often achieved through sustained effort and resilience. Whenever I feel like giving up, Netzach's presence serves as a reminder that persistence will lead to success.

Inspiring Optimism and Faith: Netzach helps us maintain a positive outlook and faith in our abilities. He encourages us to believe in ourselves and to trust that we can overcome any challenge. His guidance fosters a sense of hope and confidence, even in the face of uncertainty.

Supporting Personal Growth and Achievement: Beyond the notion of winning or succeeding, Netzach supports our personal growth and self-improvement. He guides us to see every challenge as a stepping stone towards greater wisdom and capability. His influence helps us understand that the journey towards victory is as important as the outcome itself.

Balancing Endurance with Compassion: While Netzach is associated with endurance and persistence, he also teaches the importance of balancing these qualities with compassion and self-care. He reminds us that while it's important to strive for our goals, it's equally crucial to be kind to ourselves and others along the way.

Manifesting Goals and Desires: Netzach aids in the manifestation of our goals and desires by providing the strength and clarity needed to pursue them. He helps us stay focused and aligned with our true intentions, ensuring that our efforts are directed toward meaningful and fulfilling outcomes.

In my own journey, Netzach's guidance has been instrumental in helping me navigate challenges and stay committed to my goals. His influence has taught me the value of perseverance and the importance of maintaining a positive, resilient mindset.

How to Recognize Archangel Netzach: Signs and Symbols

Recognizing the presence of Archangel Netzach can be an empowering experience. Here are some ways to identify when Netzach is near:

Feelings of Motivation and Determination: When Netzach is present, you may feel an unexpected surge of motivation and determination. This could manifest as a strong desire to keep pushing forward, even when faced with significant challenges.

Symbols of Victory and Triumph: Netzach often communicates through symbols associated with victory and endurance, such as laurel wreaths, stars, or images of overcoming obstacles. If you frequently encounter these symbols, it may be a sign that Netzach is guiding you.

Sudden Clarity and Focus: Experiencing sudden moments of clarity and focus, particularly related to your goals and ambitions, can indicate Netzach's influence. His presence often brings a sharp sense of purpose and direction.

Encouraging Thoughts and Emotions: Netzach's guidance is often felt as encouraging thoughts and emotions, urging you to stay positive and resilient. If you find yourself feeling unusually optimistic and driven, it could be a sign that Netzach is supporting you.

Dreams of Triumph and Achievement: Netzach may also appear in dreams or meditative visions, often in contexts related to overcoming challenges or achieving success. These dreams can be powerful affirmations of his role and guidance in your life.

In my experience, Netzach's presence is marked by a profound sense of encouragement and unwavering support. These signs remind me of his commitment to helping us achieve victory through perseverance and faith.

Connecting with Archangel Netzach: Practical Steps and Techniques

Building a connection with Archangel Netzach can provide significant support and inspiration on your journey toward victory and endurance. Here are some steps and techniques that have helped me connect with

Netzach:

Set Your Intention: Begin by setting a clear intention to connect with Archangel Netzach. Use a specific prayer to invite his presence. Here's a prayer you can use:

"Dear Archangel Netzach, I invite you into my life and ask for your guidance in achieving victory and enduring through challenges. Please help me persevere with faith and resilience and maintain a positive outlook even in difficult times. Guide me towards my goals and support me in manifesting my true desires. Thank you for your unwavering strength and encouragement."

Visualize Victory and Endurance: During meditation or quiet reflection, visualize symbols of victory and endurance, such as a laurel wreath or a shining star. Imagine Netzach standing beside you, offering his strength and guidance. This visualization can strengthen your connection and invoke his motivating energy.

Create a Sacred Space: Dedicate a space in your home for connecting with Netzach. Include symbols of victory and resilience, such as images of overcoming obstacles or stars, and light a candle to represent his uplifting and empowering presence. Creating a sacred space can enhance your connection and provide a focused environment for spiritual practice.

Seek Motivation and Clarity: Engage in practices that foster motivation and clarity. This could include setting clear goals, creating vision boards, or journaling about your aspirations and the steps needed to achieve them. Netzach's guidance often comes through moments of deep focus and the pursuit of meaningful goals.

Ask for Guidance and Support: Whenever you face challenges or need motivation, ask Netzach for his guidance and support. Whether it's during a difficult task, a challenging project, or when seeking clarity on your goals, verbalize your request and trust in his assistance.

Express Gratitude: Regularly thank Netzach for his guidance and support. Acknowledge his role in your life and express appreciation for the strength and clarity he provides. Showing gratitude can strengthen your connection and invite more of his empowering energy into your life.

Historical Significance of Archangel Netzach

Archangel Netzach holds a unique and respected place in various spiritual and mystical traditions, often associated with the divine aspects of victory and perseverance. While not as widely recognized as some other archangels, Netzach's influence is important.

Netzach is one of the sephiroth in the Kabbalistic Tree of Life, representing eternity, endurance, and victory. This association highlights Netzach's role in guiding individuals through the challenges of life and toward the ultimate triumph of the soul's journey. In the Kabbalah, Netzach's energy is connected with the eternal struggle and eventual victory over adversity.

Although Netzach is not directly mentioned in mainstream Christian texts, his attributes align with the broader Christian understanding of angels who provide guidance and support through perseverance and faith. Netzach's role in fostering resilience and victory resonates with the teachings of overcoming trials and achieving spiritual success.

Netzach's influence extends to various other spiritual and mystical practices where he is invoked for strength, clarity, and perseverance. His presence is often sought in rituals and prayers aimed at achieving goals, overcoming obstacles, and manifesting desires.

Netzach's historical significance lies in his role as a guardian of victory and endurance, bridging the gap between divine strength and human perseverance. His presence in different spiritual traditions indicate the universal need for resilience, motivation, and the pursuit of meaningful achievements.

Embracing the Journey with Archangel Netzach

Archangel Netzach is a powerful ally who brings resilience, clarity, and the spirit of victory into our lives. His presence is deeply empowering, offering support in navigating challenges and staying committed to our goals. By recognizing his influence and building a relationship with him, we can approach life with greater motivation and perseverance.

As you continue your spiritual journey, invite Archangel Netzach to walk with you. Allow his uplifting and motivating energy to guide you through life's challenges, and trust in his unwavering support in achieving your goals. Embrace the strength and clarity that Netzach brings, and know that you are always supported by his divine light.

Chapter 52
Archangel Raguel

In my spiritual practice, connecting with Archangel Raguel has brought a sense of balance and justice to my life. Known as the "Friend of God," Raguel is the archangel of justice, fairness, and harmony. His name means "Friend of God" in Hebrew, which reflects his role in promoting fairness, resolving conflicts, and restoring harmony in both our personal lives and the larger world.

Raguel's energy is both calm and powerful. He serves as a divine mediator, helping to resolve disputes and ensure that justice is served. When I first called upon Raguel, I was seeking a resolution in a situation that felt overwhelmingly unfair. His presence provided not only clarity but also a sense of peace and understanding that allowed me to approach the issue with a balanced perspective.

Roles and Responsibilities: Bringing Justice and Harmony

Archangel Raguel plays a crucial role in maintaining divine order and promoting harmony. Here's how he fulfills these responsibilities:

Resolving Conflicts: Raguel excels in resolving disputes and misunderstandings. Whether it's a personal conflict or a broader societal issue, Raguel brings clarity and fairness to the situation. His presence helps all parties see the truth and work towards a just resolution.

Promoting Fairness and Justice: Raguel is deeply committed to justice. He ensures that actions align with divine law and that everyone

299

is treated fairly. When you feel that injustice has been done, calling on Raguel can help restore balance and ensure that fairness prevails.

Restoring Harmony: Beyond resolving conflicts, Raguel's role is to restore harmony. He brings peace to chaotic situations and helps reestablish balance. His guidance is invaluable in times of turmoil, offering a path back to harmony and understanding.

Encouraging Fair Play and Ethical Behavior: Raguel promotes ethical behavior and fair play in all aspects of life. He encourages us to act with integrity and respect, fostering environments where justice and kindness prevail.

Balancing Energies: Raguel also assists in balancing our personal energies. He helps us align our actions with our highest values and brings inner harmony by resolving internal conflicts. His influence supports emotional and spiritual equilibrium.

In my own life, Raguel's guidance has been a beacon of fairness and balance. His presence has helped me navigate complex interpersonal dynamics and find peaceful resolutions to conflicts. He has also encouraged me to act with integrity and fairness in all my endeavors.

How to Recognize Archangel Raguel: Signs and Symbols

Recognizing the presence of Archangel Raguel can bring a sense of peace and justice into your life. Here are some ways to identify when Raguel is near:

Feelings of Calm and Fairness: When Raguel is present, you may feel a calming influence that promotes fairness and justice. This sense of tranquility can help you approach conflicts with a balanced and fair perspective.

Symbols of Justice and Balance: Raguel often communicates through symbols associated with justice and balance, such as scales, gavels, or images of peace. Seeing these symbols frequently can be a sign that Raguel is guiding you.

Resolution of Conflicts: Experiencing a sudden resolution to a conflict or misunderstanding can indicate Raguel's influence. His presence often brings clarity and helps facilitate peaceful resolutions.

Encouraging Ethical Decisions: If you find yourself feeling more inclined to act with integrity and fairness, this could be a sign that Raguel is guiding your actions. His influence encourages ethical behavior and fair treatment of others.

Dreams of Peace and Harmony: Raguel may also appear in dreams or meditative visions, often in contexts related to resolving disputes or restoring harmony. These dreams can be affirmations of his role and guidance in your life.

In my experience, Raguel's presence is marked by a sense of peace and fairness. His signs remind me to seek justice and act with integrity in all situations.

Connecting with Archangel Raguel: Practical Steps and Techniques

Building a connection with Archangel Raguel can enhance your sense of justice and harmony. Here are some steps and techniques that have helped me connect with Raguel:

Set Your Intention: Begin by setting a clear intention to connect with Archangel Raguel. Use a specific prayer to invite his presence. Here's a prayer you can use:

"Dear Archangel Raguel, I invite you into my life and ask for your guidance in bringing justice, fairness, and harmony. Please help me resolve conflicts with peace and understanding and encourage me to act with integrity and kindness. Guide me in promoting fairness in all my interactions and decisions. Thank you for your unwavering support and balance."

Visualize Balance and Justice: During meditation or quiet reflection, visualize symbols of balance and justice, such as scales or peaceful landscapes. Imagine Raguel's calming presence bringing harmony to your life. This visualization can strengthen your connection and invoke his harmonious energy.

Create a Harmonious Environment: Dedicate a space in your home to connect with Raguel. Include symbols of peace, balance, and justice, such as calming images or balanced arrangements of objects. Creating a harmonious environment can enhance your connection and provide a focused setting for spiritual practice.

Seek Fairness and Balance: Engage in practices that promote fairness and balance in your life. This could include resolving conflicts with open communication, making ethical decisions, or practicing mindfulness to maintain inner peace. Raguel's guidance often comes through actions that align with justice and harmony.

Ask for Guidance in Resolving Conflicts: Whenever you face disputes or misunderstandings, ask Raguel for his guidance in finding peaceful resolutions. Whether it's a personal conflict or a broader issue, verbalize your request for his support in promoting fairness and understanding.

Express Gratitude: Regularly thank Raguel for his guidance and support. Acknowledge his role in your life and express appreciation for the peace and balance he brings. Showing gratitude can strengthen your connection and invite more of his harmonizing energy into your life.

Historical Significance of Archangel Raguel

Archangel Raguel holds a significant place in various religious and mystical traditions, often associated with divine justice and harmony. Though not as widely recognized as some other archangels, Raguel's influence is profound and far-reaching.

Raguel is mentioned in the Book of Enoch as one of the seven archangels. His role is to oversee the good conduct of other angels and ensure that divine order and harmony are maintained. This association highlights Raguel's role as a guardian of justice and fairness in the heavenly realms.

While Raguel is not explicitly mentioned in the Bible, his presence is acknowledged in apocryphal texts and Christian mystical writings. He is often seen as a mediator and harmonizer, promoting peace and resolving conflicts. Raguel's role aligns with the Christian values of justice, compassion, and reconciliation.

Although Raguel is not a prominent figure in Islamic teachings, the qualities he embodies—justice, fairness, and harmony—are deeply valued in Islamic thought. The concept of angels overseeing justice and promoting peace resonates with Raguel's attributes.

Raguel's influence extends to various other spiritual and mystical practices where he is invoked for justice, harmony, and conflict resolution. His presence is often sought in rituals and prayers aimed at restoring balance and promoting ethical behavior.

Raguel's historical significance lies in his role as a harmonizer and enforcer of divine justice, bridging the gap between divine order and human experiences. His presence in different spiritual traditions underscores the universal need for fairness, peace, and the resolution of conflicts.

Embracing the Journey with Archangel Raguel

Archangel Raguel is a powerful ally who brings justice, fairness, and harmony into our lives. His presence is deeply comforting, offering support in resolving conflicts and promoting ethical behavior. By recognizing his influence and building a relationship with him, we can navigate life's challenges with greater balance and understanding.

As you continue your spiritual journey, invite Archangel Raguel to walk with you. Allow his calming and harmonizing energy to guide you through disputes and challenges, and trust in his unwavering support in promoting fairness and justice. Embrace the peace and balance that Raguel brings, and know that you are always supported by his divine light.

Alex McCann Johnson

Chapter 53
Archangel Raphael

In my spiritual practice, Archangel Raphael is the go-to guide for healing and restoration. Known as the "Healer of God," Raphael is a powerful archangel dedicated to promoting physical, emotional, and spiritual healing. His name means "God heals" in Hebrew, reflecting his divine mission to heal and restore balance in all aspects of life.

Raphael's presence is incredibly comforting and nurturing. Whenever I have called upon him, especially during energy work or when seeking physical healing, I've felt a soothing, green light enveloping me, bringing a sense of peace and well-being. He is not only a healer but also a guide who helps us understand the root causes of our ailments and supports us in our journey to wellness.

Roles and Responsibilities: Assisting with Physical and Emotional Healing

Archangel Raphael's primary role is to assist with healing on all levels—physical, emotional, and spiritual. Here's how he fulfills these responsibilities:

Physical Healing: Raphael is known for his powerful ability to heal physical ailments. Whether it's a minor injury or a serious illness, Raphael's healing energy can aid in the restoration of health. He works with us and through medical professionals to promote recovery and well-being. When I work with Raphael for physical healing, I often visualize his emerald green light surrounding the affected area, bringing relief and rejuvenation.

Emotional Healing: Emotional wounds can be as debilitating as physical ones, and Raphael provides gentle support in healing our emotional scars. He helps us release past traumas, overcome anxiety, and restore emotional balance. In moments of deep emotional distress, calling upon Raphael has brought me immense comfort and helped me navigate my feelings with greater clarity and peace.

Spiritual Healing: Raphael also assists in healing spiritual imbalances. He helps clear negative energies and blockages from our aura and energy field, promoting spiritual growth and harmony. His guidance has been invaluable in helping me align my spiritual practice with my highest good and in restoring my connection to the divine.

Guidance in Health and Wellness: Beyond direct healing, Raphael offers guidance in maintaining a healthy lifestyle. He encourages us to adopt habits and practices that support our physical and emotional well-being. When I seek advice on dietary changes, exercise routines, or holistic health practices, Raphael's insights often provide the direction I need.

How to Recognize Archangel Raphael: Signs and Symbols

Recognizing the presence of Archangel Raphael can be a comforting and uplifting experience. Here are some ways to identify when Raphael is near:

Emerald Green Light: Raphael's energy is often associated with a bright, emerald green light. If you see flashes of green light or feel surrounded by green hues during meditation or healing sessions, it's a strong indication of Raphael's presence.

Feelings of Warmth and Comfort: Raphael's presence is soothing and nurturing. You may feel a sense of warmth, comfort, and peace when he is near. This can manifest as a gentle, reassuring energy that envelops you, especially during times of illness or distress.

Symbols of Healing: Raphael communicates through symbols associated with healing and wellness. You might notice recurring images of the caduceus (a staff with two serpents), healing hands, or even health-related objects like herbs and crystals.

Encounters with Healing Professionals: Experiences where you receive unexpectedly good care from medical professionals or meet people in the healing professions can be signs of Raphael's influence. He often works through doctors, nurses, and healers to provide the care we need.

Dreams and Intuitive Messages: Raphael may also appear in dreams or meditative visions, offering guidance and support. Pay attention to dreams where you receive messages about your health or see symbols of healing. These can be affirmations of Raphael's presence and assistance.

In my own practice, Raphael's signs are often clear and unmistakable. His healing energy brings a sense of peace and renewal, reminding me of the divine support available in my journey to health and balance.

Connecting with Archangel Raphael: Practical Steps and Techniques

Building a connection with Archangel Raphael can enhance your healing process and promote overall well-being. Here are some steps and techniques that have helped me connect with Raphael:

Set Your Intention: Begin by setting a clear intention to connect with Archangel Raphael. Use a specific prayer to invite his healing presence. Here's a prayer you can use:

"Dear Archangel Raphael, I invite you into my life and ask for your healing touch. Please surround me with your emerald green light and help restore balance and wellness to my body, mind, and spirit. Guide me in my journey to health and support me with your nurturing presence. Thank you for your divine healing and comfort."

Visualize Green Light: During meditation or quiet reflection, visualize a vibrant, emerald green light enveloping you. Imagine this light penetrating any areas of pain or discomfort, bringing relief and rejuvenation. This visualization can strengthen your connection with Raphael and enhance his healing influence.

Create a Healing Environment: Dedicate a space in your home for healing and connecting with Raphael. Use green candles, healing crystals (such as malachite or green aventurine), and calming music to create a soothing environment. This space can serve as a sanctuary for receiving Raphael's healing energy.

Focus on Healing Practices: Engage in practices that support your physical and emotional health. This could include yoga, tai chi, Reiki, or other holistic health practices. Raphael's guidance often comes through actions that align with healing and wellness.

Ask for Specific Healing: When you or someone you love needs healing, ask Raphael for specific assistance. Whether it's relief from pain, emotional support, or guidance on health matters, verbalize your request and remain open to his healing touch.

Express Gratitude: Regularly express gratitude to Raphael for his healing and support. Acknowledge his role in your journey to health and well-being, and thank him for the comfort and peace he provides. Showing appreciation can deepen your connection and invite more of his nurturing energy into your life.

Historical Significance of Archangel Raphael

Archangel Raphael holds a prominent place in religious and mystical traditions as the divine healer. His historical significance is reflected in various texts and stories that highlight his role in providing healing and guidance.

Raphael's most well-known appearance is in the Book of Tobit, one of the deuterocanonical books of the Bible. In this story, Raphael, disguised as a human, accompanies Tobias on a journey, providing protection and healing along the way. He heals Tobit's blindness and helps expel a demon tormenting Sarah, showcasing his abilities to heal both physical and spiritual ailments.

Raphael is also revered in Jewish mystical traditions. His name, meaning "God heals," underscores his role as a healer and protector. Jewish texts often describe him as one of the archangels who stand before God, carrying out divine missions of healing and guidance.

Although not explicitly mentioned in the Quran, Raphael is recognized in Islamic tradition as Israfil, the angel who will blow the trumpet on the Day of Judgment. His role is associated with the restoration and rejuvenation of the world, aligning with his healing attributes.

Raphael's influence extends to various esoteric and New Age practices, where he is invoked for healing and spiritual growth. His association with the heart chakra and green light makes him a central figure in energy healing and holistic health practices.

Raphael's historical significance lies in his consistent portrayal as a compassionate and powerful healer. Across different cultures and traditions, he is seen as a divine agent of healing, providing support and comfort in times of illness and distress. His enduring presence in religious and mystical narratives highlights the universal human need for healing and the divine assistance available to us.

Embracing the Journey with Archangel Raphael

Archangel Raphael is a great source of healing and comfort. His presence brings relief from physical and emotional pain, restores balance, and promotes overall well-being. By recognizing his influence and building a relationship with him, we can enhance our healing processes and navigate life's challenges with greater ease and peace.

As you continue your spiritual journey, invite Archangel Raphael to be your companion. Allow his soothing, green light to envelop you and guide you towards health and harmony. Trust in his healing power and embrace the peace and comfort that Raphael brings into your life.

Alex McCann Johnson

Chapter 54
Archangel Raziel

In my journey through spirituality, connecting with Archangel Raziel has been a profoundly enlightening experience. Known as the "Keeper of Secrets," Raziel holds the keys to the mysteries of the universe and divine wisdom. His name means "Secret of God" in Hebrew, reflecting his role as a guide to hidden knowledge and esoteric insights. Raziel's presence is both awe-inspiring and deeply comforting, offering us a glimpse into the vast and intricate workings of the cosmos.

When I first reached out to Raziel, I was seeking answers to complex spiritual questions that had been puzzling me. During a meditation session, I visualized the Book of Secrets, a symbol often associated with Raziel. Suddenly, I felt a powerful yet gentle energy surrounding me, and a sense of clarity and understanding began to unfold. It was as if a veil had been lifted, revealing layers of wisdom I had never perceived before. Since that initial connection, Raziel has been such an interesting guide in my quest for deeper spiritual understanding.

Roles and Responsibilities: Revealing Mystical Knowledge and Insights

Archangel Raziel is revered for his ability to reveal mystical knowledge and insights. His primary role is to guide us in accessing and understanding the deeper truths of the universe. Here's how he assists us:

Unveiling Hidden Knowledge: Raziel helps us tap into hidden or esoteric knowledge that can illuminate our spiritual path. Whether it's understanding the laws of the universe, exploring the mysteries of creation, or delving into the secrets of the soul, Raziel's guidance opens the door to the insights you need.

Deciphering Complex Spiritual Concepts: Spiritual concepts can often be complex and challenging to grasp. Raziel aids in breaking down these intricate ideas into comprehensible and relatable pieces. He acts as a divine teacher, helping us decode the universe's mysteries and integrate them into our understanding.

Enhancing Intuition and Psychic Abilities: Raziel is also known for enhancing our intuitive and psychic abilities. By working with him, we can sharpen our perception and deepen our connection to the divine. His influence can help us become more attuned to subtle energies and spiritual truths that lie beyond our physical senses.

Guiding Spiritual Enlightenment: Beyond revealing secrets, Raziel guides us toward spiritual enlightenment. He encourages us to expand our consciousness and embrace a higher perspective. His teachings foster personal growth and spiritual evolution, helping us align more closely with our true nature and purpose.

In my personal experience, Raziel has been instrumental in guiding me through spiritual discoveries and helping me understand the interconnectedness of all things. His insights have provided clarity during times of confusion and have deepened my appreciation for the mysteries that shape our existence.

How to Invoke Raziel's Guidance: Practical Steps and Techniques

Connecting with Archangel Raziel can be a transformative experience, unlocking the secrets of the universe and enhancing your spiritual journey. Here are some practical steps and techniques to help you invoke Raziel's guidance:

Set Your Intention: Begin by setting a clear intention to connect with Raziel. Use a specific prayer to invite his presence and guidance.

312

Here's a prayer you can use:

"Archangel Raziel, Keeper of Secrets, I invite you into my life and ask for your wisdom and guidance. Please reveal to me the hidden knowledge and insights I need for my spiritual journey. Help me understand the mysteries of the universe and align with my true purpose. Thank you for your divine assistance and enlightenment."

Meditate on Symbols of Wisdom: During meditation, focus on symbols associated with Raziel, such as the Book of Secrets, sacred geometry, or ancient scrolls. Visualize these symbols, opening and revealing their hidden knowledge to you. This practice can help you connect with Raziel's energy and invite his insights into your consciousness.

Create a Sacred Space: Dedicate a space in your home for connecting with Raziel. Use objects that evoke mystery and wisdom, such as crystals, candles, or images of ancient books and scrolls. This space can serve as a sanctuary for receiving Raziel's guidance and exploring esoteric knowledge.

Journal Your Experiences: Keep a journal of your experiences and any insights you receive from Raziel. Writing down your thoughts, dreams, and intuitive hits can help you process and integrate the knowledge he shares. It also provides a valuable record of your spiritual journey and the wisdom you've gained.

Engage in Spiritual Study: Raziel encourages the pursuit of knowledge and spiritual study. Engage with books, courses, and teachings that delve into mystical and esoteric subjects. Your quest for understanding aligns with Raziel's mission to illuminate the mysteries of the universe.

Express Gratitude: Regularly express gratitude to Raziel for his guidance and support. Acknowledge his role in revealing hidden knowledge and enhancing your spiritual journey. Showing appreciation can deepen your connection and invite more of his divine wisdom into your life.

313

Historical Significance of Archangel Raziel

Archangel Raziel holds a prominent place in Jewish mysticism and Kabbalistic traditions. He is often depicted as the author of the Sefer Raziel HaMalach (Book of Raziel the Angel), a mystical text believed to contain the secrets of the universe. According to legend, Raziel wrote this book to guide Adam and Eve after their expulsion from the Garden of Eden, providing them with knowledge to understand the divine mysteries and navigate their new life.

In the Zohar, a foundational work of Kabbalistic literature, Raziel is described as an angel who stands close to God's throne, recording all divine wisdom and secrets. His role as a scribe and keeper of secrets emphasizes his importance in conveying the truths of the cosmos to humanity.

In Islamic tradition, Raziel is associated with the angel who taught Adam the names of all things, granting him knowledge that set him apart from other creatures. This connection emphasizes Raziel's role in bestowing divine knowledge and helping humans understand their place in the universe.

Beyond religious texts, Raziel's influence extends to various esoteric and mystical practices. His association with sacred geometry, symbols of wisdom, and the quest for enlightenment makes him a central figure in many spiritual teachings. Raziel's presence in these traditions highlights the timeless human desire to seek and understand the hidden truths of existence.

Embracing the Journey with Archangel Raziel

Archangel Raziel is a great source of wisdom and insight. His guidance opens doors to the mysteries of the universe and enhances our spiritual understanding. By connecting with Raziel, we can unlock hidden knowledge, deepen our spiritual practice, and embrace the complexities of our existence with greater clarity and confidence.

As you continue your spiritual journey, invite Archangel Raziel to be your guide. Allow his wisdom to illuminate your path and reveal the secrets that lie within and beyond. Trust in his divine knowledge and embrace the transformative power of the mysteries he reveals.

Alex McCann Johnson

Chapter 55
Archangel Samael

When I first started exploring the realm of archangels, I encountered Samael, a figure often surrounded by mystery and complex interpretations. Known as the "Angel of Severity," Samael's role is multifaceted and profound, encompassing both the dispensation of divine justice and the guidance through challenging times. Samael's name means "Venom of God" or "Poison of God" in Hebrew, reflecting his association with both judgment and healing through adversity. Despite the initial intimidating impression, working with Samael has shown me that his purpose is not to bring harm but to guide us through our darker moments with strength and resilience.

My first connection with Samael came during a time when I was facing significant personal challenges. I was seeking clarity and strength to navigate through a period of intense difficulty. As I meditated, I felt a powerful and commanding presence. This was unlike any other angelic presence I had experienced before. Samael's energy was strong and unwavering, providing a sense of direction and fortitude. It was a reminder that even in times of severity, guidance and support are available.

Roles and Responsibilities: Embracing Challenges and Transforming Adversity

Samael is often viewed as a figure who embodies the dual aspects of destruction and healing. His role is to help us confront and overcome obstacles, transforming adversity into strength. Here's how Samael assists us:

Guiding Through Difficult Times: Samael helps us navigate through periods of hardship and struggle. He provides the strength and courage needed to face challenges head-on. His presence is particularly helpful during times of personal crisis, loss, or major life transitions.

Dispensing Divine Justice: As an agent of divine justice, Samael works to restore balance and order. He helps us understand and accept the consequences of our actions, promoting accountability and integrity. This aspect of his role encourages us to align with our highest truth and moral principles.

Facilitating Personal Transformation: Samael guides us through the process of personal transformation. He helps us release old patterns and beliefs that no longer serve us, making way for growth and renewal. His influence is akin to the purifying fire that burns away impurities, leaving us stronger and more refined.

Empowering Strength and Resilience: Samael instills a sense of inner strength and resilience. He encourages us to embrace our power and face challenges with confidence. Under his guidance, we learn to see difficulties as opportunities for growth and self-discovery.

In my experience, Samael's guidance has been invaluable during times of intense transformation. His presence has helped me navigate through my darkest moments, emerging stronger and more resilient. Samael's influence reminds us that even the most severe challenges can be sources of immense growth and empowerment.

How to Invoke Samael's Guidance: Practical Steps and Techniques

Connecting with Archangel Samael can be a powerful and transformative experience. Here are some practical steps and techniques to help you invoke Samael's guidance:

Set Your Intention: Begin by setting a clear intention to connect with Samael. Use a specific prayer to invite his presence and support. Here's a prayer you can use:

"Archangel Samael, Angel of Severity, I invite you into my life and ask for your guidance and strength. Help me navigate through my challenges and transform adversity into growth. Please provide the clarity and courage I need to face my struggles with confidence and resilience. Thank you for your support and protection."

Meditate on Symbols of Strength: During meditation, focus on symbols associated with strength and transformation, such as fire, swords, or the scales of justice. Visualize these symbols surrounding you and feel the powerful, protective energy of Samael.

Create a Sacred Space: Dedicate a space in your home for connecting with Samael. Use objects that resonate with his energy, such as red or black candles, crystals like obsidian or hematite, and images of fire or swords. This space can serve as a sanctuary for receiving Samael's guidance and support.

Ask for Guidance: When you need strength or clarity during difficult times, ask Samael for his guidance. Be specific in your request and remain open to the messages that come through. Trust that Samael will provide the insights and support you need to overcome your challenges.

Embrace the Transformative Process: Samael's guidance often involves facing and transforming challenges. Embrace this process with an open heart and mind, and trust that Samael is guiding you toward greater strength and wisdom.

Express Gratitude: Regularly express gratitude to Samael for his guidance and support. Acknowledge his role in helping you navigate through difficult times and transforming adversity into growth. Showing appreciation can deepen your connection and invite more of his powerful energy into your life.

Historical Significance of Archangel Samael

Archangel Samael holds a significant place in various religious and mystical traditions. In Jewish mysticism and Kabbalah, Samael is often associated with the left-hand path, representing severity, judgment, and the force that purifies through destruction. He is seen as both a punisher and a redeemer, guiding souls through their karmic lessons and helping them achieve purification and spiritual evolution.

In the Zohar, a foundational work of Kabbalistic literature, Samael is described as a powerful archangel who serves as both an accuser and a destroyer, yet his actions ultimately lead to the fulfillment of divine will. His role is complex and multifaceted, reflecting the dual nature of his influence—both as a bringer of justice and a catalyst for transformation.

In Christian tradition, Samael is sometimes equated with the angel of death, guiding souls to the afterlife and overseeing the transition between life and death. This association underscores his role in the processes of endings and new beginnings, aligning with his function as an agent of divine justice and transformation.

Despite his often fearsome reputation, Samael's historical presence highlights the essential role of facing and overcoming adversity. He reminds us that through confronting challenges, we can achieve growth and alignment with our true selves.

Embracing the Journey with Archangel Samael

Archangel Samael is a powerful guide who helps us navigate through the challenges and trials of life. His presence offers strength, clarity, and the courage to face our darkest moments. By connecting with Samael, we can transform adversity into growth, embrace our inner power, and align with our highest truth.

As you continue your spiritual journey, invite Archangel Samael to be your guide. Allow his strength and wisdom to illuminate your path and help you navigate the complexities of life. Trust in his guidance and embrace the transformative power of overcoming adversity.

Chapter 56

Archangel Sandalphon

When I first began exploring the angelic realm, I encountered Archangel Sandalphon, whose energy is deeply intertwined with music, creativity, and harmony. Known as the "Angel of Music," Sandalphon brings a unique blend of inspiration and tranquility through the medium of sound. He is believed to be the bridge between the earthly and the divine, weaving the prayers of humanity into a harmonious symphony that ascends to the heavens. My initial connection with Sandalphon was subtle at first, especially during moments of listening to or creating music. His presence seemed to amplify the beauty and emotional depth of the sound, creating a space where creativity could flourish.

Sandalphon's gentle and nurturing energy helps us find our unique creative voice and express it freely. Whether you are a musician, artist, or simply someone seeking inspiration in daily life, Sandalphon's guidance can open pathways to greater creative expression and inner harmony. His influence encourages us to embrace the joy of creating and to find beauty in every note, every stroke, and every moment of our lives.

Roles and Responsibilities: Bringing Harmony and Creativity

Archangel Sandalphon plays a pivotal role in fostering harmony and creativity. Here's how Sandalphon's presence can influence our lives:

Inspiring Musicians and Artists: Sandalphon is particularly known for guiding musicians and artists. His energy enhances our ability to create and appreciate music, art, and all forms of creative expression. When I seek inspiration for a new project or need to overcome a creative block, calling upon Sandalphon often brings a fresh wave of ideas and a renewed sense of purpose.

Promoting Inner Harmony: Sandalphon's influence extends beyond the realm of music to encompass all aspects of harmony and balance in our lives. He helps us align with the natural rhythms of the universe, fostering a sense of peace and tranquility. In my own practice, meditating with Sandalphon has brought profound inner calm and a deeper connection to the harmonious flow of life.

Encouraging Creative Expression: Sandalphon inspires us to explore our creative potential and express it in meaningful ways. Whether it's through writing, painting, dance, or any other form of art, his guidance helps us tap into our inner wellspring of creativity and bring it into the world. His presence encourages us to embrace our unique gifts and share them with others.

Enhancing Prayer and Meditation: In Jewish tradition, Sandalphon is seen as the angel who delivers the prayers of humans to God. His presence can enhance our spiritual practices, making our prayers and meditations more meaningful and uplifting. When I include music or harmonious sounds in my meditation, I often feel a stronger connection to the divine, as if Sandalphon is helping to carry my intentions and prayers higher.

In my experience, Sandalphon's influence has been transformative. His guidance has not only enhanced my appreciation for music and art but also helped me cultivate a deeper sense of inner peace and balance. Working with Sandalphon, I've learned to view creativity as a sacred act, one that connects us to the divine and expresses the beauty of our souls.

How to Invoke Sandalphon's Guidance: Practical Steps and Techniques

Connecting with Archangel Sandalphon can be a deeply enriching experience, especially if you are seeking to enhance your creativity or find inner harmony. Here are some practical steps and techniques to help you invoke Sandalphon's guidance:

Set Your Intention: Begin by setting a clear intention to connect with Sandalphon. You can use a specific prayer to invite his presence and support. Here's a prayer you might use:

"Archangel Sandalphon, Angel of Music and Harmony, I invite you into my life and ask for your guidance. Please inspire me with your creativity and help me find harmony in all aspects of my life. Assist me in expressing my true self through my art and music, and help me feel your loving presence in my moments of prayer and meditation. Thank you for your support and inspiration."

Meditate on Harmonious Sounds: Find a quiet place and focus on the sounds around you. You can also play soothing music or natural sounds that promote relaxation and inner peace. As you meditate, invite Sandalphon to join you and open yourself to his guidance. Visualize a soft, gentle light surrounding you, filling you with a sense of calm and creative energy.

Create and Listen to Music: Engage in activities that involve music and sound. Whether you're playing an instrument, singing, or simply listening to your favorite music, invite Sandalphon to inspire and guide you. Pay attention to any feelings or insights that arise during these moments, as they may be messages from Sandalphon.

Use Symbolism: Incorporate symbols associated with Sandalphon into your spiritual practice. Musical notes, instruments, or images of a serene, angelic figure can serve as focal points during meditation or as part of your sacred space. These symbols can help strengthen your connection to Sandalphon and remind you of his presence.

Engage in Creative Expression: Explore different forms of creative expression, whether it's painting, writing, dancing, or any other art form that resonates with you. Allow Sandalphon's energy to flow through you, inspiring your work and helping you express your inner beauty and truth.

Express Gratitude: Regularly express gratitude to Sandalphon for his guidance and support. Acknowledge his role in helping you find harmony and creativity, and thank him for the inspiration and joy he brings into your life. Showing appreciation can deepen your connection and invite more of his positive energy.

Historical Significance of Archangel Sandalphon

Archangel Sandalphon holds a unique and significant place in various religious and mystical traditions. In Jewish mysticism, Sandalphon is often described as the angel who weaves the prayers of humans into a harmonious tapestry that ascends to the divine. This role shares his deep connection to music and the sacred nature of sound and vibration. Sandalphon's ability to transform human prayers into celestial music highlights the power of harmonizing the physical and spiritual realms.

In the Kabbalistic tradition, Sandalphon is associated with the Sephirah Malkuth on the Tree of Life, which represents the earthly kingdom. His connection to Malkuth emphasizes his role in grounding divine energies into the material world, creating a bridge between heaven and earth. This aspect of Sandalphon's role reflects his ability to bring spiritual inspiration into our daily lives, helping us manifest our creative and harmonious potential.

In Islamic tradition, although Sandalphon is not directly mentioned in the Quran, there are parallels to his role in the angelic figure of Israfil, who is associated with music and the sound of the trumpet on the Day of Judgment. This connection further illustrates Sandalphon's role as a harbinger of divine sound and music.

Throughout history, musicians, artists, and spiritual seekers have invoked Sandalphon for inspiration and guidance. His presence in various traditions highlights the universal importance of music and creativity as pathways to the divine. Sandalphon's historical significance as the Angel of Music emphasizes his role in helping us find harmony and express our unique creative voices.

Embracing the Journey with Archangel Sandalphon

Archangel Sandalphon is a powerful and gentle guide who brings harmony, creativity, and inspiration into our lives. His presence helps us connect with the divine through music and sound, fostering a deeper appreciation for the beauty and creativity that surround us. By invoking Sandalphon's guidance, we can enhance our creative expression, find inner peace, and align with the harmonious rhythms of the universe.

As you continue your spiritual journey, invite Archangel Sandalphon to be your guide. Allow his harmonious and creative energy to inspire you and bring a deeper sense of joy and balance into your life. Trust in his guidance and embrace the transformative power of music and creativity.

Alex McCann Johnson

Chapter 57
Archangel Uriel

My journey with Archangel Uriel began during a period of deep introspection when I sought clarity and wisdom to navigate life's complexities while also focusing on energy work. Known as the "Light of God," Uriel is a powerful archangel who illuminates our path, providing divine wisdom and insights. His name, derived from the Hebrew meaning "God is my light," perfectly encapsulates his role as a bearer of enlightenment. The first time I invoked Uriel, I was struck by a profound sense of clarity and a warm, illuminating presence that seemed to brighten my thoughts and understanding. Uriel has since become a guiding light in my spiritual practice, helping me see through confusion and find the truth in challenging situations.

Uriel's energy is subtle yet incredibly powerful. He offers guidance that cuts through the fog of uncertainty, helping us discern the right path and make informed decisions. His presence brings a sense of calm and assurance, reminding us that with divine light, we can overcome any darkness. Whether you are seeking answers to life's big questions or need clarity in your everyday decisions, Uriel is the archangel to call upon for wisdom and illumination.

Roles and Responsibilities: Providing Wisdom and Illumination

Archangel Uriel's primary role is to provide wisdom and illumination, guiding us through the complexities of life with divine light. Here's how Uriel's influence can profoundly impact our lives:

Offering Clarity in Confusion: Uriel helps us see clearly when we are faced with confusion or uncertainty. His light cuts through the murkiness, revealing the truth and helping us understand the deeper meaning behind our experiences. When I feel overwhelmed by conflicting emotions or indecision, I call upon Uriel to shine his light on the situation, bringing clarity and understanding.

Illuminating Our Path: Uriel's guidance is like a beacon that lights our way, especially during dark or challenging times. He helps us navigate difficult choices and find the best path forward. In moments of doubt, visualizing Uriel's golden light illuminating my path has provided me with the confidence and direction needed to move forward.

Enhancing Intuition and Insight: Uriel's presence can enhance our intuitive abilities and provide unique insights. He helps us tap into our inner wisdom and see beyond the surface of things. Working with Uriel has sharpened my intuition, allowing me to make decisions that align more closely with my higher self and divine purpose.

Promoting Enlightenment and Spiritual Growth: Uriel's light fosters spiritual growth and enlightenment. He guides us in exploring deeper spiritual truths and understanding the universe's mysteries. Through meditation and contemplation with Uriel, I have gained valuable insights that have significantly contributed to my spiritual development.

Resolving Conflict with Wisdom: Uriel helps resolve conflicts by promoting understanding and wise judgment. His guidance encourages us to approach disagreements with compassion and a clear perspective, finding solutions that bring harmony and peace. In my interactions with others, invoking Uriel has often helped diffuse tensions and foster more constructive and empathetic communication.

In my experience, Uriel's wisdom and illumination are transformative. His guidance has helped me find clarity in confusion, understand complex situations, and navigate life's challenges with greater ease and confidence. Uriel's light has become an invaluable source of support and inspiration on my spiritual journey.

How to Invoke Uriel's Guidance: Practical Steps and Techniques

Connecting with Archangel Uriel can bring clarity and wisdom into your life. Here are some practical steps and techniques to help you invoke Uriel's guidance:

Set Your Intention: Begin by setting a clear intention to connect with Uriel. You can use a specific prayer to invite his presence and support. Here's a prayer you might use:

"Archangel Uriel, Light of God, I invite you into my life and ask for your guidance. Please illuminate my path and provide me with the wisdom and clarity I need to navigate my challenges. Help me see the truth and understand the deeper meaning of my experiences. Thank you for your light and your support."

Visualize Yellow or Gold Light: Find a quiet and comfortable place to sit or lie down. Close your eyes and take several deep breaths to center yourself. Visualize a warm, golden light surrounding you, enveloping you in its glow. Imagine this light filling your mind and heart, bringing clarity and wisdom. This visualization helps attune you to Uriel's energy and opens a channel for his guidance.

Meditate on Symbols of Wisdom: During meditation, focus on symbols that represent wisdom and illumination. These could include a sun, a glowing light, or a shining star. As you meditate, invite Uriel to join you and offer his insights. Be open to any thoughts, feelings, or images that come to you during this time.

Ask for Guidance in Specific Situations: If you need clarity or insight into a particular situation, ask Uriel for his guidance. Clearly state your question or concern and remain open to the answers that come through your intuition or during your meditation. Trust that Uriel's wisdom will provide the clarity you seek.

Pay Attention to Signs and Intuition: Uriel often communicates through subtle signs and intuitive nudges. Pay attention to your thoughts, feelings, and any synchronicities that occur after you've invoked his guidance. These can be messages from Uriel, helping to illuminate your path and provide the answers you need.

Express Gratitude: After your meditation or prayer, thank Uriel for his guidance and support. Acknowledging his role in helping you find clarity and wisdom strengthens your connection and invites more of his illuminating presence into your life.

Historical Significance of Archangel Uriel

Archangel Uriel holds a revered place in various religious and mystical traditions as an angel of wisdom, illumination, and divine light. His name, meaning "God is my light," reflects his role as a bearer of enlightenment and a guide through the complexities of life.

In early Christian traditions, Uriel is often recognized as one of the principal archangels. He is mentioned in apocryphal texts, such as the Book of Enoch, where he serves as a guide and mentor, providing insights into heavenly and earthly mysteries. Uriel's role in these texts underscores his association with divine wisdom and his ability to reveal the hidden truths of the universe.

In Jewish mysticism, Uriel is revered as an angel of light and knowledge. He is often depicted as a guardian of the gates of Eden and a guide to the souls of the righteous. Uriel's light is said to illuminate dark places, bringing understanding and clarity to those where confusion and ignorance exist.

In Islamic tradition, although Uriel is not explicitly named in the Quran, his qualities and roles are reflected in the broader concept of angelic guidance and illumination, emphasizing the universal need for divine light in human lives.

Uriel's influence extends beyond these religious texts into various esoteric and mystical traditions, where he is often called upon for wisdom and guidance. His historical significance highlights his enduring role as a source of enlightenment, helping humanity navigate the spiritual and physical realms with greater clarity and insight.

Embracing the Journey with Archangel Uriel

Archangel Uriel is a powerful and compassionate guide who offers wisdom, clarity, and illumination. His presence helps us see through confusion, understand complex situations, and find the truth in our experiences. By invoking Uriel's guidance, we can navigate life's challenges with greater ease and confidence, embracing a path of light and enlightenment.

As you continue your spiritual journey, invite Archangel Uriel to be your guiding light. Allow his wisdom to illuminate your path and his clarity to reveal the deeper truths of your life. Trust in his guidance and embrace the transformative power of divine light and understanding.

Alex McCann Johnson

Chapter 58
Archangel Zadkiel

My connection with Archangel Zadkiel began during a period in my life when I was struggling with feelings of resentment and the need for forgiveness. I think it is safe to say that we all have these periods at least once in life. Known as the "Angel of Mercy," Zadkiel is a powerful and compassionate guide who helps us release negative emotions and embrace forgiveness. His name, derived from the Hebrew word meaning "Righteousness of God," reflects his divine mission to inspire mercy, compassion, and emotional healing.

Zadkiel's presence is often felt as a soothing, gentle energy that brings a sense of peace and calm. The first time I consciously reached out to Zadkiel, I was enveloped in a warm, violet light that seemed to dissolve my anger and resentment, replacing them with feelings of forgiveness and compassion. Since then, Zadkiel has been a guiding force in my life, helping me to cultivate a more loving and understanding perspective.

Whether you are seeking to forgive someone who has hurt you, release feelings of guilt, or embrace compassion for yourself and others, Zadkiel is the archangel to call upon. His guidance can transform our hearts, helping us to move beyond pain and into a state of love and mercy.

Roles and Responsibilities: Offering Forgiveness and Compassion

Archangel Zadkiel's primary role is to help us cultivate forgiveness and compassion. Here's how his influence can impact our lives:

Releasing Negative Emotions: Zadkiel assists in the release of negative emotions such as anger, resentment, and guilt. His healing energy helps us let go of the emotional burdens that weigh us down and hinder our personal growth. When I work with Zadkiel, I often feel a sense of relief as these heavy emotions are lifted, allowing me to move forward with a lighter heart.

Cultivating Forgiveness: Forgiveness is a key aspect of Zadkiel's guidance. He encourages us to forgive ourselves and others, understanding that holding onto grudges only harms us in the long run. Through his influence, we learn to see situations and people with greater compassion and understanding, making it easier to let go of past hurts. In my journey, embracing Zadkiel's energy has helped me to forgive those who have wronged me and to forgive myself for my own mistakes.

Embracing Compassion: Zadkiel inspires us to develop a deeper sense of compassion for all beings. He teaches us to view others with empathy and kindness, recognizing that everyone is on their own unique path. His presence fosters a loving and compassionate attitude, helping us to connect more deeply with others and to approach life with a more open heart.

Transforming Pain into Love: One of Zadkiel's greatest gifts is his ability to transform pain into love. By working with him, we can alchemize our emotional wounds into sources of strength and compassion. His guidance has shown me that even the most painful experiences can lead to personal growth and deeper connections with others.

Promoting Emotional Healing: Zadkiel's compassionate energy supports us in healing emotional wounds and finding peace. He helps us to process and release past traumas, fostering emotional resilience and well-being. In my experience, invoking Zadkiel during times of emotional turmoil brings a sense of calm and a pathway to healing.

How to Invoke Zadkiel's Guidance: Practical Steps and Techniques

Connecting with Archangel Zadkiel can bring healing and transformation into your life. Here are some practical steps and techniques to help you invoke Zadkiel's guidance:

Set Your Intention: Begin by setting a clear intention to connect with Zadkiel. Use a specific prayer to invite his presence and support. Here's a prayer you might use:

"Archangel Zadkiel, Angel of Mercy, I invite you into my life and ask for your guidance. Please help me to release any negative emotions and to cultivate forgiveness and compassion in my heart. Guide me towards a more loving and understanding perspective. Thank you for your mercy and your healing presence."

Visualize the Violet Flame: Find a quiet and comfortable place to sit or lie down. Close your eyes and take several deep breaths to center yourself. Visualize a violet flame surrounding you, enveloping you in its soothing light. Imagine this flame dissolving any negative emotions and filling you with a sense of peace and compassion. The violet flame is a powerful symbol of transmutation and healing, closely associated with Zadkiel's energy.

Meditate on Symbols of Mercy: During meditation, focus on symbols that represent mercy and compassion, such as a gentle dove or a serene heart. As you meditate, invite Zadkiel to join you and offer his guidance. Be open to any thoughts, feelings, or images that come to you during this time.

Ask for Assistance in Forgiveness: If you are struggling to forgive someone or yourself, ask Zadkiel for his help. Clearly state your desire to release the burden of anger or guilt and to embrace forgiveness. Trust that Zadkiel's healing energy will support you in this process.

Practice Acts of Compassion: Embrace opportunities to show compassion in your daily life. Whether through kind words, thoughtful actions, or simply holding a loving intention for others, practicing compassion invites more of Zadkiel's energy into your life.

Express Gratitude: After your meditation or prayer, thank Zadkiel for his guidance and support. Acknowledging his role in helping you cultivate mercy and compassion strengthens your connection and invites more of his transformative presence into your life.

Historical Significance of Archangel Zadkiel

Archangel Zadkiel has been revered throughout history as a figure of mercy and compassion. In various religious and mystical traditions, he is seen as an angel who promotes forgiveness and emotional healing.

In Jewish mysticism, Zadkiel is often associated with divine justice and mercy. He is believed to have intervened during the binding of Isaac, stopping Abraham from sacrificing his son and thus symbolizing divine mercy and compassion.

In Christianity, Zadkiel is sometimes identified as the angel of mercy and transformation, helping individuals release feelings of guilt and resentment. He is seen as a healer of the heart, guiding believers toward a more compassionate and forgiving way of life.

In esoteric traditions, Zadkiel's presence is invoked during practices involving the violet flame, a powerful symbol of transmutation and healing. His role in these traditions emphasizes the importance of mercy and the transformative power of forgiveness.

Historically, Zadkiel's influence has been significant in guiding individuals toward emotional healing and spiritual growth. His presence in mystical and religious texts highlights the universal need for mercy and compassion, encouraging us to embrace love and understanding in our interactions with others.

Embracing the Journey with Archangel Zadkiel

Archangel Zadkiel is a powerful and compassionate guide who helps us cultivate forgiveness, compassion, and emotional healing. His presence encourages us to release negative emotions and embrace a more loving and understanding perspective. By invoking Zadkiel's guidance, we can transform our hearts and foster deeper connections with ourselves and others.

As you continue your spiritual journey, invite Archangel Zadkiel to guide you toward mercy and compassion. Allow his healing energy to support you in releasing pain and embracing forgiveness. Trust in his guidance and embrace the transformative power of love and understanding in your life.

Alex McCann Johnson

Chapter 59
Archangel Zaphkiel

When I first encountered Archangel Zaphkiel, I was surprised by the sense of stillness and depth that accompanied his presence. Known as the "Angel of Contemplation and Understanding," Zaphkiel is a guide who assists us in accessing deep spiritual insights and connecting with the divine mysteries of the universe. His name, derived from the Hebrew word "Zaphkiel," means "God's Knowledge," reflecting his role in bringing wisdom and understanding to those who seek his guidance.

Zaphkiel's energy is often felt as a serene, introspective force that encourages quiet reflection and deep meditation. My experiences with Zaphkiel have always led me to moments of clarity and insight, especially during times when I sought to understand the deeper meanings and patterns in my life. His guidance has helped me navigate complex spiritual concepts and connect with the higher realms of consciousness.

Whether you are seeking to deepen your spiritual practice, understand the mysteries of the universe, or simply find clarity in your daily life, Zaphkiel is the archangel to call upon. His wisdom and contemplative nature make him a powerful ally in your journey toward greater understanding and enlightenment.

Roles and Responsibilities: Providing Wisdom and Spiritual Insight

Archangel Zaphkiel's primary role is to offer wisdom and spiritual insights. Here's how his influence can significantly enhance your spiritual journey:

Encouraging Deep Reflection: Zaphkiel inspires us to look inward and reflect deeply on our experiences and beliefs. His guidance encourages us to explore our inner worlds, uncovering the truths that lie beneath the surface. When I meditate with Zaphkiel's energy, I often find myself drawn into a state of deep contemplation, where answers and insights flow naturally.

Illuminating Complex Spiritual Concepts: Zaphkiel helps us understand complex spiritual concepts and the divine mysteries of the universe. He acts as a bridge between our earthly understanding and the higher realms of knowledge. His presence can illuminate intricate spiritual teachings, making them accessible and meaningful. In my practice, working with Zaphkiel has clarified many spiritual teachings and concepts that once seemed elusive.

Guiding Spiritual Growth: Zaphkiel supports us in our spiritual growth and development. He encourages us to seek knowledge and wisdom, guiding us towards our highest potential. His influence fosters a deep sense of purpose and direction in our spiritual journeys. Through his guidance, I have found a greater sense of alignment with my spiritual path and a deeper connection to my higher self.

Facilitating Connection with the Divine: Zaphkiel helps us connect with the divine and access the higher realms of consciousness. His energy creates a sacred space for divine communion, allowing us to receive insights and messages from the spiritual realms. When I seek to connect with the divine or receive guidance from higher beings, I know that I can call upon Zaphkiel to facilitate this connection.

Promoting Peace and Understanding: Zaphkiel's serene and contemplative energy promotes inner peace and understanding. He helps us find clarity in confusing or challenging situations, offering a calm and reflective perspective. In times of uncertainty or emotional turmoil, invoking Zaphkiel's presence has brought me a sense of peace and a clearer understanding of my circumstances.

How to Invoke Zaphkiel's Guidance: Practical Steps and Techniques

Connecting with Archangel Zaphkiel can bring wisdom and understanding into your life. Here are some practical steps and techniques to help you invoke Zaphkiel's guidance:

Set Your Intention: Begin by setting a clear intention to connect with Zaphkiel. Use a specific prayer to invite his presence and support. Here's a prayer you might use:

"Archangel Zaphkiel, Angel of Contemplation and Understanding, I invite you into my life and ask for your guidance. Please help me access deeper wisdom and understanding and connect with the divine mysteries of the universe. Thank you for your insights and your calming presence."

Meditate on Symbols of Wisdom: Find a quiet and comfortable place to sit or lie down. Close your eyes and take several deep breaths to center yourself. Visualize symbols of wisdom, such as an open book, a glowing orb, or a serene landscape. Imagine Zaphkiel's presence enveloping you in a calming, contemplative light. Allow yourself to be drawn into a state of deep reflection, open to any thoughts, feelings, or insights that arise.

Engage in Deep Contemplation: Set aside time for deep contemplation and introspection. Choose a topic or question that you seek to understand more deeply, and invite Zaphkiel to guide your thoughts and reflections. Write down your insights and observations, and be open to the subtle messages that Zaphkiel may bring.

Create a Sacred Space for Reflection: Dedicate a space in your home for quiet reflection and meditation. Fill this space with objects that inspire contemplation, such as candles, crystals, or sacred texts. Use this space regularly to connect with Zaphkiel and to seek his guidance.

Seek Knowledge and Understanding: Embrace opportunities to seek knowledge and understanding in your daily life. Read books, attend lectures, and engage in discussions that challenge your thinking and expand your perspective. Invite Zaphkiel to guide you in your quest for wisdom and to help you integrate new insights into your spiritual practice.

Express Gratitude: Regularly express gratitude to Zaphkiel for his guidance and support. Thank him for the wisdom and understanding he brings into your life, and acknowledge his role in helping you navigate your spiritual journey.

Historical Significance of Archangel Zaphkiel

Archangel Zaphkiel has been revered throughout history as a figure of profound wisdom and understanding. In various religious and mystical traditions, he is seen as an angel who promotes deep contemplation and spiritual insight.

In Jewish mysticism, Zaphkiel is often associated with the Sephirah Binah on the Kabbalistic Tree of Life, representing understanding and the deep comprehension of the divine. His role in guiding seekers towards higher knowledge and spiritual enlightenment is central to many mystical teachings.

In Christianity, Zaphkiel is sometimes identified as the angel of contemplation and understanding, helping individuals access the deeper truths of the faith. His presence in Christian mysticism emphasizes his importance in fostering a deeper connection with the divine and promoting spiritual growth.

In esoteric traditions, Zaphkiel is seen as a guardian of secret knowledge and a guide to those who seek to understand the mysteries of the universe. His role in these traditions emphasizes the importance of wisdom and contemplation in the pursuit of spiritual enlightenment.

Historically, Zaphkiel's influence has been significant in guiding individuals toward deeper spiritual understanding and helping them connect with the divine mysteries. His presence in mystical and religious texts highlights the universal need for contemplation and the pursuit of knowledge.

Embracing the Journey with Archangel Zaphkiel

Archangel Zaphkiel is a powerful and contemplative guide who helps us access wisdom and spiritual insights. His presence encourages deep reflection and a greater understanding of the divine mysteries. By invoking Zaphkiel's guidance, we can enhance our spiritual practice and connect with the higher realms of consciousness.

As you continue your spiritual journey, invite Archangel Zaphkiel to guide you toward deeper understanding and contemplation. Allow his calming and insightful energy to support you in your quest for wisdom and to illuminate the deeper truths of your life. Trust in his guidance and embrace the insights that Zaphkiel can bring into your spiritual journey.

Alex McCann Johnson

Chapter 60
Archangel Zuriel

When I first connected with Archangel Zuriel, I was enveloped by a serene and calming presence that brought an immediate sense of peace and balance into my life. Known as the "Angel of Harmony and Balance," Zuriel is a powerful guide who helps us achieve inner equilibrium and align with the natural rhythms of life. His name means "My Rock is God" or "God is my Strength," reflecting his role in providing stability and grounding amidst life's chaos.

Zuriel's energy is like a soothing balm, easing tension and restoring harmony in both our inner and outer worlds. He assists us in finding balance within ourselves and in our relationships, guiding us to live in harmony with the universe. Whenever I call upon Zuriel, I feel a sense of alignment and tranquility, which helps me navigate life's challenges with grace and poise.

Whether you are seeking to balance your emotions, harmonize your relationships, or simply find peace in your daily life, Zuriel is the archangel to call upon. His guidance is invaluable in helping us maintain equilibrium and live harmoniously with ourselves and others.

Roles and Responsibilities: Bringing Harmony and Balance

Archangel Zuriel's primary role is to bring harmony and balance into our lives. Here's how his influence can significantly enhance your sense of equilibrium and peace:

Restoring Inner Balance: Zuriel helps us achieve balance within ourselves, aligning our thoughts, emotions, and actions. His guidance encourages us to find a healthy equilibrium between different aspects of our lives, such as work and leisure, giving and receiving, and activity and rest. When I work with Zuriel, I often feel a gentle reminder to slow down and find harmony in the midst of my busy schedule.

Harmonizing Relationships: Zuriel assists in creating and maintaining harmonious relationships. He helps us communicate effectively, resolve conflicts peacefully, and foster mutual understanding and respect. His presence is particularly beneficial during times of discord or misunderstanding, as he promotes forgiveness and compassion. In my relationships, invoking Zuriel has often led to greater harmony and a deeper connection with others.

Aligning with Natural Rhythms: Zuriel guides us to align with the natural rhythms of life and the universe. He encourages us to live in sync with the cycles of nature, such as the changing seasons and the phases of the moon. This alignment helps us feel more grounded and connected to the world around us. Through my work with Zuriel, I have become more attuned to these natural rhythms and their impact on my well-being.

Promoting Peace and Tranquility: Zuriel's serene energy promotes inner peace and tranquility. He helps us release stress and tension, bringing a sense of calm and stillness into our lives. His guidance is especially helpful during times of upheaval or uncertainty, providing a stabilizing force that helps us navigate challenges with ease. When I meditate with Zuriel, I often feel a deep sense of relaxation and peace that carries through my day.

Encouraging Self-Reflection: Zuriel encourages us to reflect on our lives and make adjustments where needed to achieve greater balance. His insights help us identify areas of imbalance and guide us toward actions that promote harmony and well-being. My work with Zuriel has often led to valuable self-reflections that have significantly improved my sense of balance and fulfillment.

How to Invoke Zuriel's Guidance: Practical Steps and Techniques

Connecting with Archangel Zuriel can bring harmony and balance into your life. Here are some practical steps and techniques to help you invoke Zuriel's guidance:

Set Your Intention: Begin by setting a clear intention to connect with Zuriel. Use a specific prayer to invite his presence and support. Here's a prayer you might use:

"Archangel Zuriel, Angel of Harmony and Balance, I invite you into my life and ask for your guidance. Please help me restore balance and harmony within myself and in my relationships. Thank you for your calming presence and your support in helping me live in alignment with the natural rhythms of life."

Meditate on Symbols of Balance: Find a quiet and comfortable place to sit or lie down. Close your eyes and take several deep breaths to center yourself. Visualize symbols of balance, such as scales, yin, and yang, or a serene landscape. Imagine Zuriel's presence enveloping you in a soothing, balancing light. Allow yourself to be drawn into a state of deep relaxation and equilibrium, open to any thoughts, feelings, or insights that arise.

Create a Sacred Space for Reflection: Dedicate a space in your home for quiet reflection and meditation. Fill this space with objects that inspire balance and harmony, such as crystals, calming colors, or elements of nature. Use this space regularly to connect with Zuriel and to seek his guidance in restoring balance in your life.

Engage in Practices that Promote Balance: Incorporate activities into your daily routine that promote balance and harmony. This could include yoga, tai chi, mindful breathing, or spending time in nature. Invite Zuriel to join you in these practices and to guide you towards a more balanced and harmonious way of living.

Seek Harmony in Relationships: When dealing with conflicts or misunderstandings in your relationships, call upon Zuriel for guidance.

Visualize his calming presence surrounding both you and the other person, fostering a spirit of understanding and compassion. Ask for his help in finding peaceful resolutions and restoring harmony.

Express Gratitude: Regularly express gratitude to Zuriel for his guidance and support. Thank him for the balance and harmony he brings into your life, and acknowledge his role in helping you maintain equilibrium and peace.

Historical Significance of Archangel Zuriel

Archangel Zuriel has been revered throughout history as a figure of harmony and balance. His presence is noted in various religious and mystical traditions, where he is seen as an angel who promotes peace and equilibrium.

In Jewish mysticism, Zuriel is sometimes associated with the angel of the month of September and is linked to the astrological sign of Libra, symbolizing balance and justice. His role in these traditions emphasizes his connection to the natural rhythms of life and his ability to bring harmony to both individuals and the cosmos.

In Christian angelology, Zuriel is recognized as an archangel who assists in maintaining balance and order within the heavenly realms. His presence is called upon to bring peace and tranquility to the faithful, reflecting his role as a stabilizing force in times of turmoil.

In various esoteric teachings, Zuriel is revered as a guide to those seeking to align with the natural cycles and rhythms of the universe. His influence is seen as essential for achieving inner harmony and for living in accordance with the divine order.

Historically, Zuriel's influence has been significant in guiding individuals and communities toward greater balance and harmony. His presence in mystical and religious texts highlights the universal need for equilibrium and the importance of living in harmony with oneself and the world.

Embracing the Journey with Archangel Zuriel

Archangel Zuriel is a powerful and calming guide who helps us achieve balance and harmony in our lives. His presence encourages us to reflect deeply, align with the natural rhythms of life, and foster harmonious relationships. By invoking Zuriel's guidance, we can enhance our sense of equilibrium and navigate life's challenges with grace and peace.

As you continue your spiritual journey, invite Archangel Zuriel to guide you toward deeper harmony and balance. Allow his serene and balanced energy to support you in your quest for inner and outer equilibrium. Trust in his guidance and embrace the sense of peace and harmony that Zuriel can bring into your life.

Alex McCann Johnson

Chapter 61

Continuing Your Journey with Angels

There is so much to gain from working with angels, and I find it fascinating to consider their historical significance. Angels have appeared in various forms and roles throughout history across different cultures and religions. Their universal presence highlights the overall impact they have on humanity.

When I first started working with angels, I was amazed at how their high vibrational energy could profoundly influence my life. My journey began with Archangel Azrael, who suddenly made his presence known as I was working on improving my mediumship abilities. The comfort and clarity Azrael provided were unlike anything I had experienced before, leading me to delve deeper into the world of angelic beings.

Historical Significance of Angels

The historical significance of angels is deeply rooted in many traditions. In the Bible, angels appear as messengers of God, guiding, protecting, and delivering divine messages. Stories of angels are found in both the Old and New Testaments, such as the angel who announced the birth of Jesus to Mary and the angels who protected Daniel in the lion's den. These narratives illustrate the vital roles angels have played in guiding humanity throughout history.

But the presence of angels extends far beyond the Bible. In Islam, angels like Jibril (Gabriel) and Mikail (Michael) are crucial figures, playing significant roles in the lives of prophets and believers. Jibril's revelation of the Quran to Prophet Muhammad is a cornerstone of the Islamic faith, demonstrating the importance of angelic guidance in shaping religious teachings and practices.

In Judaism, angels are also integral, appearing in various texts and traditions. The Talmud and Kabbalistic writings describe numerous angels, each with specific roles and responsibilities. These accounts provide a rich tapestry of angelic activity, emphasizing their involvement in both cosmic and earthly matters.

Even in Zoroastrianism, we find angelic beings known as Amesha Spentas, who are similar to archangels in their roles and functions. These divine entities guide and protect the faithful, ensuring the proper functioning of the natural and spiritual worlds.

Hinduism and Buddhism also feature angel-like beings known as Devas and Bodhisattvas, respectively. These beings oversee various aspects of the cosmos and assist in spiritual growth and protection. Their presence in these traditions further emphasizes the universal nature of angelic beings.

The Universality of Angels

What amazes me is the consistency of angelic presence across different cultures and epochs. This universality suggests that angels are not confined to any one religion or belief system. Instead, they are benevolent beings that transcend cultural boundaries, offering their guidance and support to all who seek it.

In my personal experience, connecting with angels has brought immense benefits. Their guidance has helped me navigate life's challenges, offering comfort during difficult times and clarity when making important decisions. They have also played a crucial role in my spiritual growth, helping me deepen my understanding of the divine and my place within the cosmos.

Practical Steps for Continuing Your Journey

To continue your journey with angels, it's essential to remain open and receptive to their presence. Angels communicate in subtle ways, often through intuition, dreams, signs, and symbols. Paying attention to these forms of communication can enhance your connection with them. Meditation and prayer are powerful tools for inviting angelic guidance. By creating a sacred space and setting your intention to connect with angels, you open yourself up to their wisdom and support.

For instance, building a relationship with your guardian angel can start with setting a clear intention. Begin by finding a quiet place where you can meditate or pray without distractions. Sit quietly, take deep breaths, and invite your guardian angel to join you. Visualize a protective light surrounding you and be open to any thoughts, feelings, or images that come to you. After your meditation, take a moment to express gratitude, thanking your guardian angel for their presence and guidance.

Exploring the various roles and characteristics of different angels can also enrich your journey. Each archangel and angelic being brings unique qualities and areas of expertise, from healing and protection to wisdom and transformation. By understanding these roles, you can more effectively seek the specific guidance and support you need.

Reflecting on the Historical and Cultural Significance

Reflecting on the historical and cultural significance of angels can deepen your appreciation for their role in our lives. Their consistent presence throughout history and across cultures highlights their importance and the impact they have on humanity.

Working with angels offers a wealth of benefits and opportunities for growth. Whether you're seeking guidance, protection, healing, or spiritual insights, angels are always ready to assist. Embrace their presence, remain open to their communication, and express gratitude for their support. As you continue your journey with angels, you will find their wisdom and love enriching your life in countless ways.

Every step I have taken with these divine beings has illuminated my path and brought a deeper understanding of my own spiritual essence. I encourage you to invite angels into your life, to seek their guidance, and to marvel at the transformations they can inspire. Their love and light are boundless, and their support is always available for those who reach out.

Animal Guides

Alex McCann Johnson

Chapter 62

Animal Guides

In my spiritual work, I have been introduced to many amazing and guiding presences, among which animal guides hold a special place. Each of these guides brings unique wisdom and perspective to my journey. For example, my eagle soars high, offering a broad and encompassing view of my life. This majestic bird symbolizes a vision that transcends the mundane, allowing me to see the bigger picture and gain insight into the various aspects of my existence. Similarly, my wolf is a steadfast companion, representing loyalty and community. The ever-growing pack of wolves that accompanies me signifies the dynamic and evolving nature of my spiritual path and the expanding circle of guidance and support I receive.

When I first delved into shamanism, I was astonished at the connection I felt with the animal kingdom. It was as if a new realm of understanding and communication opened up to me. Even in my early encounters with Reiki, I remember vividly a practitioner mentioning the presence of a gorilla in the room. At the time, I thought she was mistaken or perhaps overly imaginative. But now, after countless experiences and deeper exploration, I embrace these encounters with an open heart, welcoming the wisdom and guidance that animal guides offer.

What Are Animal Guides?

Animal guides, often referred to as spirit animals, totem animals, or power animals, are spiritual beings that manifest in the form of animals. They are believed to offer guidance, wisdom, and protection to those who connect with them. These guides are far more than symbolic representations; they embody the deeper aspects of our subconscious and the natural world. They help us navigate life's challenges and opportunities by drawing on their inherent qualities and lessons.

Animal guides serve as mirrors to our inner selves, reflecting our strengths, weaknesses, and potential. They help us uncover hidden aspects of our psyche and provide insights into our personal and spiritual growth. By understanding and working with these guides, we can access a deeper connection with the natural world and gain a richer understanding of our place within it.

Historical and Cultural Significance of Animal Guides

The reverence for animal guides is a universal theme found in spiritual traditions across the globe. In Native American spirituality, totem animals are considered sacred protectors that bestow specific strengths and lessons. Each animal is revered for its unique attributes and the spiritual gifts it imparts. For instance, the eagle is seen as a powerful messenger between the earthly and spiritual realms, embodying vision and freedom. The wolf, on the other hand, symbolizes loyalty, intuition, and the role of the teacher.

In shamanic traditions worldwide, animals play crucial roles in rituals, healing practices, and spiritual journeys. They are often seen as companions and guides who help shamans navigate the spirit world and connect with the divine. The animal's characteristics and behaviors are viewed as lessons that can be applied to the human experience, guiding individuals toward greater understanding and enlightenment.

Ancient Egyptian culture also holds animals in high esteem, with deities such as Anubis and Bastet depicted in animal forms. These gods embody the traits and powers of the animals they represent, such as Anubis's association with the afterlife and protection and Bastet's embodiment of home and fertility. Similarly, in Hinduism, animals like the cow are venerated and considered sacred, representing purity, motherhood, and abundance.

These examples illustrate the universal respect and significance of animals in human spiritual practices. They highlight the role of animals as bridges between the physical and spiritual worlds, offering wisdom and guidance that transcend cultural boundaries.

The Role of Animal Guides in Spiritual Journeys

Animal guides play a multifaceted role in our spiritual journeys. They serve as protectors, ensuring our safety as we explore the unknown realms of our consciousness and the universe. They are also our teachers, imparting lessons through their behaviors, attributes, and the challenges they present to us.

When I began my journey into shamanism, the presence of animal guides was both comforting and enlightening. My eagle guide taught me to elevate my perspective, to rise above the everyday concerns, and to see my life from a higher vantage point. This broader view has been invaluable in navigating the complexities of life, allowing me to approach challenges with a clearer and more detached mindset.

My wolf guide, with his growing pack, has been a constant reminder of the importance of community, loyalty, and leadership. The expanding number of wolves symbolizes the continuous growth and evolution of my spiritual journey and the increasing number of guides and allies that support me. Each encounter with an animal guide brings new lessons and perspectives, deepening my understanding of myself and the world around me.

Animal guides also help us tap into our instincts and intuition. They encourage us to trust our gut feelings and to pay attention to the subtle signs and messages that the universe sends our way. In my practice, I've learned to listen to the whispers of the wind, the rustle of leaves, and the calls of animals, understanding that these are not mere coincidences but messages from my guides.

Animal guides are invaluable allies on our spiritual journeys. They connect us to the natural world, help us navigate our inner landscapes, and offer wisdom and protection along the way. Embracing the presence of animal guides can lead to personal growth, deeper spiritual understanding, and a more harmonious relationship with the world around us. As you continue to explore and connect with these guides, you will discover a rich and supportive network of wisdom and guidance that can greatly enrich your life.

Chapter 63

Humans and Animal Guides

From the earliest days of humanity, there has been an intrinsic bond between humans and animals. This connection goes beyond the physical realm; it delves into the spiritual and emotional depths of our existence. When I first began my journey into shamanism, I was overwhelmed by how intensely I connected with the animal kingdom. It felt as if I had unlocked a part of myself that had always been there, waiting to be discovered.

This deep connection is rooted in the belief that animals possess wisdom and qualities that we, as humans, can learn from. Animals live in harmony with nature, relying on their instincts and the natural rhythms of the earth. By observing and connecting with them, we can gain insights into our own lives and the world around us. For example, my eagle guide teaches me to soar above my problems, to see the bigger picture, and to approach life with a broader perspective. My wolf guide, leading his ever-growing pack, reminds me of the importance of community, loyalty, and leadership.

How Animal Guides Can Help Us Navigate Our Lives

Animal guides serve as spiritual allies, offering guidance, protection, and wisdom. They help us navigate the complexities of life by providing insights and messages that resonate on a deeper level. When faced with difficult decisions or challenging situations, turning to our animal guides can provide clarity and direction.

For instance, during times of uncertainty, I often meditate and visualize my eagle guide. The eagle's keen vision and ability to soar high above the ground helped me gain a clearer perspective on my situation. Similarly, my wolf guide helps me tap into my intuition and instincts, encouraging me to trust myself and my inner wisdom. These guides offer a unique blend of wisdom that bridges the gap between our physical experiences and our spiritual aspirations.

Animal guides also help us connect with our true selves, uncovering hidden strengths and qualities. They remind us to honor our natural instincts and embrace our unique paths. By working with animal guides, we can develop a greater sense of self-awareness and alignment with our life purpose. This connection fosters personal growth and spiritual evolution, enabling us to live more authentically and in harmony with our surroundings.

Examples of Animal Guide Stories from Different Cultures and Myths

Throughout history, various cultures have revered animal guides, incorporating them into their myths, legends, and spiritual practices. These stories highlight the timeless and universal nature of the human-animal connection.

In Native American traditions, animal guides, known as totems, play a central role. Each animal totem carries specific qualities and lessons. For example, the bear symbolizes strength and introspection, teaching individuals to trust their instincts and find inner strength during challenging times. The wolf, often seen as a teacher and guide, emphasizes loyalty, communication, and the importance of family and community. These totems are integral to the spiritual lives of Native Americans, offering protection and wisdom as they navigate their daily lives.

In ancient Egyptian mythology, animals were revered as sacred beings and were often associated with deities. Anubis, the god of mummification and the afterlife was depicted with the head of a jackal. Jackals were believed to guard the dead and guide souls to the afterlife.

Bastet, the goddess of home, fertility, and protection, was depicted as a lioness or a domestic cat, symbolizing grace, power, and nurturing. These animal deities were seen as embodiments of divine qualities, connecting the physical and spiritual realms.

Celtic folklore is rich with stories of animal guides. The stag, for instance, is a powerful symbol of the forest and nature. It represents purity, nobility, and the connection between the physical and spiritual worlds. The salmon, another important animal in Celtic lore, symbolizes wisdom and knowledge. According to legend, eating the Salmon of Knowledge granted one immense wisdom and understanding of the world. These animals were often viewed as guardians and teachers, guiding individuals through the mysteries of life and nature.

In Hindu mythology, animals are often associated with deities, serving as their vahanas (vehicles) and companions. Lord Ganesha, the remover of obstacles, is often depicted riding a mouse, symbolizing the overcoming of fear and the ability to navigate through life's challenges. Hanuman, the monkey god, embodies strength, loyalty, and devotion, inspiring individuals to remain steadfast in their spiritual practices and commitments. These associations underscore the importance of animals in conveying spiritual truths and guiding human behavior.

The Relationship Between Humans and Animal Guides in Practice

When I was studying Norse shamanism, I remember a story about the old nomadic tribes who relied heavily on their connection with animals for survival. These tribes followed the migratory patterns of animals such as reindeer and elk. Losing track of these patterns could mean death due to starvation or exposure. The shamans, deeply connected to nature, would often communicate with animal spirits to guide the tribe on the right path, ensuring they remained aligned with the natural world and its rhythms.

This relationship between humans and animals in Norse shamanism highlights the reliance on animal guides for survival and spiritual guidance. It illustrates how integral these connections were, not just for physical sustenance but for maintaining the spiritual and cultural integrity of the community.

Animal guides are invaluable allies on our spiritual journeys. They connect us to the natural world, help us navigate our inner landscapes, and offer wisdom and protection along the way. Embracing the presence of animal guides can lead to personal growth, deeper spiritual understanding, and a more harmonious relationship with the world around us. As you continue to explore and connect with these guides, you will discover a rich and supportive network of wisdom and guidance that can profoundly enrich your life.

Reflecting on the historical and cultural significance of animal guides enhances our appreciation for their role in our lives. Whether through the eagle's vision, the wolf's loyalty, or the stag's nobility, these guides offer timeless lessons that transcend cultures and eras. By honoring and embracing their presence, we open ourselves to a deeper connection with the universe and the wisdom it holds.

Chapter 64

How Animal Guides Communicate

My journey with animal guides has been nothing short of extraordinary. From dreams and visions to unexpected encounters, the ways in which they communicate with us are as varied as the animals themselves. Understanding these methods of communication has deepened my connection with the animal kingdom and enriched my spiritual practice.

I have learned that animals communicate in unique and sometimes surprising ways, often through their presence and the symbolism they embody. For example, I once saw a cougar come into a session for a woman who was terrified of encountering one on her hikes. This fear always loomed over her. When the cougar appeared, it was not to frighten her but to instill in her the qualities of fierceness, observation, and courage. Over time, she realized that her fear of the cougar symbolized a deeper fear of taking control of her life. Embracing the cougar's energy helped her reclaim her power and approach life with renewed strength.

There are countless stories like this, illustrating how animals show up in my energy healing sessions and later manifest in my clients' lives. One client frequently sees rabbits and associates them with his late wife. Although rabbits are not a common sight for him in the physical world, they seem to appear whenever he is deeply missing her or going through a tough time. These instances remind us that our animal guides are always nearby, offering comfort and messages in both subtle and obvious ways.

Alex McCann Johnson

Methods of Communication

Dreams

One of the most profound ways animal guides communicate with us is through dreams. In the quiet of the night, when our conscious mind is at rest, our guides often come to us with messages and guidance. I vividly remember the first time my eagle guide appeared in a dream. It was soaring high above a vast landscape, its sharp eyes scanning the terrain below. The dream left me with a sense of clarity and purpose, urging me to rise above my daily struggles and view life from a higher perspective.

Dreams are rich with symbolism and meaning. An animal appearing in a dream might not always have a straightforward message; it could represent a quality or lesson the animal embodies. Keeping a dream journal has been invaluable for me. By recording my dreams and reflecting on them, I can decipher the messages and lessons my animal guides are conveying. These nocturnal visits often reveal insights that my waking mind might overlook.

Visions

Visions are another powerful way animal guides communicate. These can occur during meditation, shamanic journeys, or moments of deep introspection. My first vision of my wolf guide happened during a guided meditation. I saw a pack of wolves moving gracefully through a dense forest, with one wolf standing out as the leader. This vision not only introduced me to my wolf guide but also emphasized the importance of leadership, community, and loyalty in my life.

Visions can be spontaneous or intentional. When I seek guidance, I often enter a meditative state, calling upon my animal guides for insight. The images and symbols that arise in these moments often provide the direction I need. Each vision is a doorway into deeper understanding, connecting me more intimately with the wisdom of my guides.

Encounters

Sometimes, animal guides communicate through physical encounters in our waking life. These encounters might seem coincidental, but they carry significant messages. I remember a period when I kept seeing hawks everywhere I went. They would appear in the sky, perched on trees, or even in pictures and symbols around me. Each sighting felt like a nudge from my eagle guide, reminding me to maintain focus and clarity in my endeavors.

These encounters can take various forms. It might be an unusual animal sighting, repeated appearances of an animal in media or conversations, or even a sudden fascination with a particular animal. Paying attention to these patterns can reveal the guidance our animal guides are offering. Each encounter is a reminder that we are always connected to the animal kingdom and that our guides are constantly communicating with us.

Recognizing Signs and Symbols from Animal Guides

Recognizing the signs and symbols from animal guides requires a keen sense of awareness and openness. Our guides communicate in subtle ways, often using symbols and metaphors that resonate with our personal experiences and intuition.

One effective method is to stay present and observant in our daily lives. I make it a habit to notice the animals I encounter, whether in nature, in dreams, or in everyday life. Each animal's appearance prompts me to reflect on its potential message. For example, seeing a butterfly might signify transformation and growth, while a deer could symbolize gentleness and grace.

Another helpful practice is to familiarize oneself with the symbolic meanings of different animals. Many cultures and traditions attribute specific qualities and lessons to various animals. By studying these meanings, we can better interpret the messages our guides are sending us. Understanding the cultural and spiritual significance of different animals enriches our interactions with them and enhances our ability to receive their guidance.

Developing the Sensitivity to Perceive and Interpret Messages

Developing the sensitivity to perceive and interpret messages from animal guides takes practice and patience. It involves honing our intuition and creating a receptive state of mind.

Meditation is a powerful tool for enhancing our sensitivity to spiritual messages. Regular meditation helps quiet the mind, allowing us to tune into the subtle frequencies of our guides. I often begin my meditation sessions by setting an intention to connect with my animal guides, inviting them to share their wisdom with me. This practice creates a sacred space for communication and deepens my connection with the spiritual realm.

Mindfulness practices also play a crucial role. By staying present and fully engaged at the moment, we become more attuned to the signs and symbols around us. Simple practices like mindful breathing, nature walks, or observing animals in their natural habitats can deepen our connection with our guides. These practices foster a heightened awareness that makes it easier to recognize and interpret the subtle messages from our guides.

Journaling our experiences with animal guides can be incredibly insightful. By recording dreams, visions, encounters, and any intuitive messages, we create a valuable resource for reflection and interpretation. Over time, patterns and recurring themes may emerge, providing clarity and understanding of our guides' messages. Journaling not only captures our experiences but also helps us track our spiritual growth and the evolving guidance we receive.

Ultimately, trusting our intuition is key to interpreting messages from our animal guides. Our intuitive sense is a direct line of communication with the spiritual realm. By listening to our gut feelings and inner wisdom, we can accurately understand the guidance we receive. Trusting our intuition requires letting go of doubt and embracing the unknown with confidence. It is through this trust that we can fully embrace the wisdom and support of our animal guides.

In my own journey, I've learned to trust the intuitive nudges and impressions that come to me. Whether it's a sudden thought, a feeling, or a vivid image, I honor these experiences as valuable messages from my guides. Each message, no matter how subtle, is a thread in the intricate tapestry of spiritual communication that connects me to the animal kingdom.

Animal guides communicate with us in diverse and profound ways. By staying open, present, and attuned to their messages, we can navigate our lives with greater clarity, purpose, and wisdom. Embracing the guidance of our animal guides enriches our spiritual journey and deepens our connection with the natural world. As we cultivate sensitivity and trust in our intuitive abilities, we open ourselves to a rich dialogue with these extraordinary beings who offer us unwavering support and insight on our path.

Alex McCann Johnson

Chapter 65

The Spiritual Connection to Animals

Throughout history, humans have revered animals as sacred beings, embodying the spiritual essence and wisdom that guide us on our journeys. My personal encounters with animal guides have deepened my understanding of this ancient and universal connection. Whether through dreams, visions, or encounters, the spiritual presence of animals has been a guiding light in my life, reflecting a rich tapestry of historical perspectives that span ancient civilizations, shamanistic practices, and mythology.

Ancient Civilizations and Their Animal Deities

In ancient civilizations, animals were often seen as embodiments of divine power and wisdom. These cultures believed that animals held the key to understanding the mysteries of the universe and our place within it. This belief is reflected in the numerous animal deities worshiped and revered throughout history.

In ancient Egypt, animals were considered manifestations of the gods, possessing divine qualities and playing crucial roles in spiritual and everyday life. Anubis, the god of mummification and the afterlife was depicted with the head of a jackal. Jackals were closely associated with cemeteries and were believed to protect the dead. This connection to the afterlife made Anubis a pivotal figure in guiding souls through their journey after death. Similarly, Bastet, the goddess of home, fertility, and protection, was depicted as a lioness or a domestic cat. Her dual nature as both fierce lioness and gentle cat symbolized grace, power, and nurturing, embodying the qualities that were essential for both protection and familial harmony.

In ancient Greece, animals were also closely linked with the gods. Zeus, the king of the gods, was often associated with the eagle, symbolizing his power and authority. The eagle, known for its strength and keen sight, represented Zeus's dominion over the sky and his far-reaching influence. Athena, the goddess of wisdom and warfare, was connected to the owl, a symbol of her intelligence and strategic prowess. The owl's ability to see in the dark mirrored Athena's insight and clarity in all matters.

Indigenous cultures around the world have also recognized the spiritual significance of animals. In Native American traditions, animals are seen as messengers and protectors, each carrying specific teachings and qualities. The buffalo, for example, is a symbol of abundance and gratitude, teaching us the importance of honoring and respecting the gifts of the Earth. The eagle, revered across many tribes, represents vision, strength, and a connection to the divine. Its ability to soar high and see from great distances is a metaphor for spiritual insight and enlightenment.

The Role of Animals in Shamanistic Practices

Shamanism, one of the oldest spiritual practices in the world, places a significant emphasis on the connection between humans and animals. Shamans, who serve as intermediaries between the physical and spiritual realms, often work with animal guides to access wisdom, healing, and guidance.

During shamanic journeys, shamans enter altered states of consciousness to communicate with the spirit world. Animal guides play a crucial role in these journeys, acting as protectors and allies. My own experiences with shamanic practices have revealed the natural wisdom that animals can offer. When I journey, I often meet my eagle and wolf guides, who provide me with clarity, protection, and insight. The eagle helps me gain a higher perspective on life's challenges, while the wolf offers guidance on community and personal strength. While these are my two go-to guides on journeys, sometimes others come through.

Animals are also central to shamanic healing practices. Shamans believe that animals possess unique healing energies that can be used to restore balance and harmony within individuals and communities. For instance, the bear is often associated with healing and introspection. In shamanic healing sessions, bear energy might be invoked to help individuals go within, confront their fears, and find inner strength. This process of internal exploration and healing is fundamental to shamanic practice and highlights the power of animal guides.

Ceremonies and rituals in shamanism frequently honor animals. These practices involve calling upon the spirit of a specific animal to lend its power and guidance. In my own practice, I incorporate animal guides into rituals to create a sacred space and invite their wisdom. For example, invoking the elephant during a ceremony can bring qualities of strength, stability, and community to the circle, enriching the collective experience and deepening our connection to the spiritual world.

Animal Symbolism in Mythology and Folklore

Animals have always played a significant role in mythology and folklore, serving as symbols of various qualities and lessons. These stories, passed down through generations, highlight the deep spiritual connection between humans and animals.

In Greek mythology, animals often appear as symbols of the gods and their attributes. The dolphin, for instance, is associated with Apollo, the god of the sun, music, and prophecy. Dolphins were seen as guides for sailors and symbols of harmony and intelligence. They embody Apollo's creative and protective aspects, guiding humans toward enlightenment and safety. The myth of Leda and the Swan tells the story of Zeus transforming into a swan to seduce Leda, showcasing the inventive and mystical nature of animals in myth.

Norse mythology also deeply intertwines animals with the gods and their stories. Odin, the chief god, is accompanied by two ravens, Huginn and Muninn, who fly around the world and bring back information. These ravens symbolize thought and memory, emphasizing the importance of wisdom and knowledge in Odin's domain. The wolf Fenrir, although often seen as a destructive force, represents the raw, untamed power of nature and the cyclical nature of life and death. Fenrir's presence in Norse mythology focuses on the balance between creation and destruction, a fundamental aspect of the natural world.

In Asian folklore, animals often represent virtues and moral lessons. In Chinese mythology, the dragon is a symbol of power, strength, and good fortune. Dragons are revered as wise and benevolent beings that bring prosperity and protection. They embody the harmony and balance that are central to Chinese cosmology. The tale of the White Snake, a story of love and transformation, features a snake spirit who takes human form, highlighting themes of sacrifice and the blending of the human and animal realms. This story emphasizes the deep interconnection between humans and animals and the spiritual lessons they offer.

Embracing the Spiritual Connection to Animals

These historical perspectives illustrate the timeless and universal nature of the spiritual connection between humans and animals. From ancient civilizations and shamanic practices to mythology and folklore, animals have always been seen as powerful spiritual beings, offering guidance, wisdom, and protection. Embracing this connection in my own life has brought me closer to understanding the mysteries of the universe and my place within it.

My personal journey with animal guides has been enriched by this deep historical and cultural context. Whether it's the bison guiding me to see the importance of abundance and resilience or the elephant teaching me about community and strength, these spiritual connections have profoundly influenced my path. They remind me that the natural world is alive with wisdom and that by honoring these connections, we can navigate our lives with greater clarity, purpose, and harmony. As we continue to explore and deepen our relationships with our animal guides, we tap into an ancient well of knowledge that has the power to

Guided by Spirits

transform and illuminate our spiritual journeys.

Alex McCann Johnson

Chapter 66

Modern Views on Animal Spirituality

In recent years, there has been a noticeable resurgence of interest in animal guides within contemporary spirituality. This renewed fascination is part of a broader movement toward reconnecting with nature and exploring alternative spiritual paths. For many, the modern world, with its rapid technological advancements and urbanization, has created a sense of disconnection from the natural world. Animal guides offer a way to bridge this gap, providing a tangible link to the ancient wisdom and harmony found in nature.

This resurgence is evident in various aspects of modern life. Social media platforms are brimming with discussions about animal totems and spirit animals, and there has been a marked increase in workshops, retreats, and online courses dedicated to animal spirituality. Books, podcasts, and educational content on the topic have proliferated, making the wisdom of animal guides more accessible to a wider audience. This growing interest highlights a collective yearning for deeper connections and meaningful experiences, with animal guides offering a pathway to explore spirituality in a grounded and personal way.

In my own work, I have witnessed this growing enthusiasm firsthand. Many individuals who seek my guidance are eager to discover their animal guides and learn how to integrate their teachings into their daily lives. This reflects a broader trend of people seeking to return to a more harmonious and balanced relationship with the natural world.

Alex McCann Johnson

The Integration of Animal Guides in Modern Spiritual Practices

The integration of animal guides into modern spiritual practices is diverse and adaptable, reflecting the unique paths of individuals and communities. Here are some common ways in which animal guides are being incorporated into contemporary spirituality:

Meditation and Visualization

One of the most prevalent methods of connecting with animal guides is through meditation and visualization. By entering a meditative state, individuals can invite their animal guides to reveal themselves and offer guidance. This practice fosters a deep and personal connection, allowing for a sense of presence and attunement to the animal's energy.

In my practice, I often lead guided meditations where participants visualize meeting their animal guides. These meditations provide a safe and nurturing space for individuals to explore their spiritual connections and receive messages from their guides. The feedback I receive is overwhelmingly positive, with many expressing imaginative experiences and newfound insights. For example, a participant might visualize a deer guiding them through a forest, teaching them about gentleness and the importance of moving gracefully through life's challenges.

Shamanic Journeying

Shamanic journeying is another powerful way to connect with animal guides. This ancient practice involves entering an altered state of consciousness, often induced by rhythmic drumming or chanting, to access the spirit world. During these journeys, individuals can meet and interact with their animal guides, receiving healing, wisdom, and guidance.

I vividly remember my first shamanic journey. The rhythmic beat of the drum transported me to a realm where I encountered my eagle and wolf guides. They both came forward in a way that showed me their intentions. These experiences have been transformative, offering deep insights and a sense of connection that transcends the physical world. Shamanic journeying continues to be a cornerstone of my spiritual practice, allowing me to maintain a dynamic relationship with my animal guides.

Rituals and Ceremonies

Incorporating animal guides into rituals and ceremonies is another way to honor their presence and integrate their wisdom into our lives. These practices can range from simple daily rituals to elaborate seasonal ceremonies. For example, one might create an altar dedicated to their animal guide, adorned with symbolic items such as feathers, stones, or images of the animal. Offering prayers, lighting candles, and setting intentions at the altar can strengthen the bond with the animal guide and invite their energy into one's life.

Seasonal ceremonies, such as solstice and equinox celebrations, provide opportunities to honor the cycles of nature and the animal guides that embody these rhythms. During these ceremonies, participants might invoke their animal guides, perform symbolic actions, and reflect on the lessons and guidance they have received. For instance, invoking the spirit of the bear during a winter solstice ceremony might invite introspection and encourage participants to embrace the quiet, reflective energy of winter.

Animal Totems and Symbols

Animal totems and symbols have become popular tools for integrating animal guide wisdom into everyday life. Totem animals, which represent specific qualities and lessons, can be chosen or discovered through personal reflection and spiritual practice. Wearing jewelry, carrying a talisman, or placing artwork depicting one's totem animal in the home are common ways to keep the animal's energy close and present.

I often encourage those I work with to explore the symbolism of their animal guides and find creative ways to incorporate these symbols into their daily routines. For instance, someone who resonates with the qualities of the fox might wear a fox pendant or keep a fox figurine on their desk as a reminder of the fox's cunning and adaptability. These small but meaningful actions help to keep the animal guide's presence and wisdom at the forefront of one's mind.

Dreamwork

Dreamwork is another effective method for connecting with animal guides. Paying attention to dreams and keeping a dream journal can reveal the presence and messages of animal guides. By recording and reflecting on dreams, individuals can gain insights into the guidance their animal guides are offering.

In my experience, dreams are a rich source of communication from the spiritual realm. Many of my own encounters with animal guides have occurred in dreams, providing valuable guidance and reassurance. I encourage others to cultivate this practice, as it can deepen their connection with their guides and enhance their spiritual growth. A recurring dream of a dolphin swimming alongside can signal the need to embrace playfulness and emotional depth in one's life.

Ethical Considerations

Respecting Animal Spirits and Their Significance

In my spiritual journey, I have come to understand the importance of respecting animal spirits and recognizing their significance. These beings are not merely symbolic representations but are considered sacred entities with their own wisdom and power. Treating them with reverence and humility is essential in any spiritual practice involving animal guides.

One of the first lessons I learned from my eagle and wolf guides was the need for deep respect. They are more than just guides; they are wise beings with lessons to teach and messages to convey. This respect extends to all aspects of our interactions with animal spirits. When I call upon my guides, I do so with a sense of gratitude and honor, acknowledging their sacred presence and the profound gift of their guidance.

Ethical Practices in Working with Animal Guides

Working ethically with animal guides involves several key practices:

Consent and Invitation: Always invite animal guides into your spiritual practice rather than summoning them forcefully. This practice acknowledges their autonomy and respects their willingness to assist you. By inviting rather than demanding, we honor their freedom and the sacred nature of their guidance.

Gratitude and Offerings: Show gratitude for the guidance and protection your animal guides provide. This can be done through offerings, prayers, or acts of service. For example, I often leave small offerings such as feathers, stones, or food at natural sites as a way to thank my guides. This practice not only expresses appreciation but also reinforces the connection and respect for their presence.

Responsibility and Integrity: Use the wisdom and power of your animal guides responsibly. Avoid using their guidance for harmful or manipulative purposes. Integrity is crucial in maintaining a positive and respectful relationship with your guides. It's important to approach this relationship with sincerity and a genuine desire for growth and understanding.

Continuous Learning: Commit to ongoing learning about the animals you connect with. Understanding their natural behaviors, habitats, and roles in the ecosystem can deepen your respect and connection with them. This also includes being aware of conservation issues and supporting efforts to protect these animals in the physical world. Knowledge about the animal's real-world existence can enhance our spiritual connection and foster a deeper appreciation for their symbolic roles.

Avoiding Cultural Appropriation and Honoring Traditions

One of the most important ethical considerations in working with animal guides is avoiding cultural appropriation and honoring the traditions from which these practices originate. Spirit has always guided me to learn from different cultures and that no one practice is meant for any specific group of people. However, if you are focusing on a specific culture, it is crucial to honor it and approach it with respect and sensitivity.

Research and Education: Take the time to thoroughly research and understand the cultural context of the practices you are adopting. This includes reading books, attending workshops, and learning from authentic sources within the culture. Educating oneself is the first step towards respectful and meaningful engagement.

Acknowledgment and Attribution: Always acknowledge the cultural origins of the practices you are using. Give credit to the traditions and peoples who have preserved these spiritual practices over generations. This recognition honors the legacy and contributions of these cultures and fosters a respectful approach to their spiritual wisdom.

Respectful Adaptation: While it is natural to adapt spiritual practices to fit your personal journey, do so respectfully. Avoid distorting or oversimplifying the practices. Instead, seek to understand and incorporate the deeper meanings and values inherent in the tradition. Strive to maintain the integrity of the practices while finding ways to integrate them authentically into your own spiritual path.

Support and Reciprocity: Show support for the communities from which these practices originate. This can be done through donations, participating in community events, or supporting initiatives that benefit these communities. Reciprocity is a vital part of many indigenous traditions and reflects a balanced exchange of knowledge and resources. Supporting these communities acknowledges their contributions and helps sustain their cultural heritage.

In my own practice, I have always tried to approach different cultural traditions with an open heart and mind. When I first encountered the concept of animal guides, I was drawn to the shamanic practices of indigenous cultures. I made it a point to learn from respected teachers within those traditions and to honor their teachings with the utmost respect.

Guided by Spirits

I remember feeling initially hesitant when a lady mentioned a gorilla during a Reiki session, thinking she was perhaps overstepping boundaries. However, as I delved deeper into my practice, I realized that the spirit world transcends human-imposed boundaries and that respectful engagement with diverse spiritual traditions can be enriching. The key is to approach these traditions with genuine respect, a willingness to learn, and an intention to honor the wisdom they offer.

The resurgence of interest in animal guides in contemporary spirituality reflects a deep and collective desire to reconnect with nature and explore alternative spiritual paths. The integration of animal guides into modern spiritual practices is diverse and adaptable, offering individuals various ways to connect with and honor these powerful spiritual beings. By embracing the wisdom and guidance of animal guides, we can navigate our lives with greater clarity, purpose, and harmony, fostering a deeper connection with the natural world and our own spiritual essence.

Ethical considerations are fundamental when working with animal guides. Respecting their spirits, practicing ethically, and honoring the cultural traditions from which these practices arise are essential steps in cultivating a deep and respectful relationship with animal guides. By embracing these ethical principles, we ensure that our spiritual practices are rooted in respect, integrity, and a genuine desire to honor the sacred connections we share with the animal kingdom.

Alex McCann Johnson

Chapter 67

Power Animals

During my studies in shamanism, I encountered the concept of power animals—spiritual beings that embody specific strengths and energies unique to each individual. This was made especially clear to me during an exercise where we were asked to discover a power animal for someone else. The lady who identified my power animal found a chimpanzee for me. She explained that the chimpanzee's playful and social nature was intended to balance my perceived "dull and boring" demeanor, infusing my life with joy and connectivity. This experience was both enlightening and transformative, opening my eyes to the unique characteristics and impact of power animals. It also showed me that even animal guides have a sense of humor.

Power animals differ from other spiritual animal guides like totems or spirit animals. They are not necessarily lifelong companions but rather spirits that come into our lives to impart specific lessons, strengths, or energies needed at a particular moment or for a particular phase in our lives. They bring with them qualities and abilities that can help us navigate challenges, inspire us to grow, and empower us to fulfill our potential.

In my experience, connecting with a powerful animal can be a personal journey. These animals offer us the essence of their being, providing guidance, support, and the strength to overcome obstacles. Each power animal carries a unique medicine—a set of attributes or teachings that they share with us to help us grow and evolve.

Roles and Responsibilities: How Power Animals Guide Us

Power animals play several crucial roles in our spiritual and everyday lives, each bringing its own set of strengths and lessons. Here are some of the ways they assist us:

Providing Specific Strengths and Energies: Power animals embody specific qualities that they lend to us. For example, a bear might provide strength and resilience, while a butterfly could bring transformation and renewal. These energies can be particularly helpful during times of challenge or change.

Guiding Us Through Challenges: When faced with difficulties, power animals can offer guidance and support. They help us tap into their innate wisdom and abilities to navigate obstacles and emerge stronger. My chimpanzee power animal, for instance, encourages me to approach life with a sense of play and flexibility, even during tough times.

Enhancing Personal Growth: Power animals inspire us to embrace personal growth and self-discovery. They encourage us to explore new aspects of ourselves and to develop the qualities that they represent. By connecting with our power animals, we can gain insights into our own strengths and potential.

Balancing Our Energies: Just as my chimpanzee balanced my perceived seriousness with playfulness, power animals can help balance our energies. They can counteract tendencies that might be holding us back and promote harmony within ourselves.

Offering Protection and Support: Power animals also act as protectors, offering their strength and presence to shield us from harm. They provide a sense of safety and support, reminding us that we are not alone on our journey.

In my spiritual practice, my power animal has been a source of inspiration and empowerment. The chimpanzee's playful energy helps me approach life with curiosity and joy, encouraging me to embrace new experiences and connect with others more deeply.

How to Recognize Power Animals: Identifying Their Presence

Recognizing the presence of a powerful animal involves tuning into your intuition and being open to the signs and symbols around you. Here are some ways to identify your power animal:

Recurrent Animal Sightings: If you repeatedly encounter a particular animal in your life—whether in dreams, nature, or even in media—it could be a sign that this animal is your power animal. Pay attention to these patterns and consider the qualities of the animal you keep seeing.

Intuitive Feelings: Sometimes, you may feel a strong connection to a specific animal without any apparent reason. This intuitive sense can be a sign that the animal is your power animal, bringing its energy and lessons into your life.

Meditative Visions: During meditation or shamanic journeys, you might see or sense an animal that stands out to you. These visions can provide powerful clues about your power animal and its significance in your life.

Symbolic Encounters: Power animals often communicate through symbols. Look for meaningful animal-related signs in your environment, such as finding feathers, seeing animal images, or frequently hearing references to a specific animal.

Inner Knowing: Sometimes, you just know that a certain animal is your power animal. Trust your inner knowing and be open to exploring the connection further.

In my journey, the discovery of my chimpanzee power animal was confirmed through repeated symbolic encounters and a deep, intuitive connection. This recognition helped me embrace the playful and social aspects of my personality, enhancing my overall well-being and personal growth.

Connecting with Power Animals: Practical Steps and Tips

Establishing a connection with your power animal can be a rewarding and enlightening experience. Here are some steps and tips that can help you connect with your power animal:

Set Clear Intentions: Begin by setting a clear intention to connect with your power animal. You can do this through a simple prayer or affirmation. Express your desire to invite their presence and guidance into your life.

Prayer for Power Animals: "I call upon the power animals, guardian of all life. I ask that you guide and protect me. May I walk in harmony with your wisdom, embrace your gifts with gratitude, and honor your presence in my life."

Meditate and Visualize: Find a quiet and comfortable space where you won't be disturbed. Close your eyes and take a few deep breaths to center yourself. Visualize a serene natural environment, such as a forest or meadow. Imagine yourself meeting your power animal in this space and be open to any images, sensations, or messages that come through.

Engage with Nature: Spend time in nature, observing and appreciating the animals around you. Pay attention to any encounters that feel significant or resonate with you. Nature is a powerful conduit for connecting with powerful animals and understanding their messages.

Learn About the Animal: Research the characteristics, behaviors, and symbolism of the animal you believe to be your power animal. Understanding more about the animal can deepen your connection and provide insights into the lessons it brings.

Create a Sacred Space: Dedicate a space in your home where you can honor and connect with your power animal. This could include images, statues, or objects related to the animal. Use this space for meditation and reflection, inviting your power animal to join you.

Perform a Ritual or Ceremony: Create a personal ritual or ceremony to honor your power animal. This could involve lighting a candle, offering a prayer, or creating an altar with items that represent your power animal. Rituals can help solidify your connection and show your respect for the animal's presence.

Ask for Guidance: Don't hesitate to ask your power animal for guidance in specific situations. Whether you need strength, clarity, or inspiration, invite your power animal to share its wisdom and support with you.

Express Gratitude: Regularly express gratitude to your power animal for its guidance and presence. Thank them for the qualities and lessons they bring into your life, and acknowledge their role in your journey.

In my practice, I have found that regularly connecting with my power animal through meditation and nature walks has strengthened our bond and brought a deeper sense of joy and balance into my life.

Historical Significance of Power Animals

The concept of power animals has roots in various indigenous and shamanic traditions around the world. These cultures recognize the connection between humans and the animal kingdom, viewing animals as spiritual allies and sources of wisdom.

In Native American traditions, power animals are revered as essential guides and protectors. Each person is believed to have a power animal that reflects their inner spirit and strengths. These animals are seen as teachers who provide guidance, protection, and support throughout one's life.

In Siberian shamanism, power animals are considered vital for maintaining spiritual balance and health. Shamans often journey to meet their power animals, seeking their help in healing and navigating the spiritual realm. These animals are seen as companions and protectors, offering their strength and wisdom to aid in the shaman's work.

In Celtic beliefs, animals were seen as powerful symbols of the natural world and its spiritual essence. Power animals, or spirit animals, were believed to provide guidance and protection, embodying the qualities needed to face life's challenges and to connect with the natural and supernatural worlds.

In African traditions, power animals play a crucial role in connecting the human world with the spiritual realm. They are often called upon in rituals and ceremonies to provide strength, protection, and guidance. These animals are seen as bridges between the physical and spiritual worlds, offering their unique energies to support and empower humans.

Understanding the historical significance of power animals deepens our appreciation for their role in our spiritual lives. They connect us to a rich tradition of seeking guidance and strength from the natural world, reminding us of the wisdom and support that animals can offer.

Embracing the Journey with Power Animals

Power animals are invaluable allies on our spiritual journey. They bring unique strengths, wisdom, and guidance that can help us navigate life's challenges and embrace our personal growth. By connecting with these spiritual beings, we tap into the energies and qualities they embody, enriching our lives and expanding our understanding of ourselves.

As you explore your relationship with your power animal, embrace the journey with openness and curiosity. Allow their presence to inspire and empower you and honor the connection that you share. Whether you are seeking strength, clarity, or balance, your power animal is there to support and guide you every step of the way.

Chapter 68

Totem Animals

As I delved deeper into my spiritual journey, the concept of totem animals became a fascinating and integral part of my animal guide experience. Totem animals are spiritual entities that represent a group, clan, or family, embodying the collective qualities and strengths of that group. Unlike power animals, which are personal, totem animals are communal symbols that reflect the identity, values, and spirit of a community.

In my exploration, I discovered that totem animals are more than just symbolic figures; they are revered as spiritual protectors and guides for the entire group they represent. They embody the shared attributes, heritage, and aspirations of their community. My understanding of totem animals deepened through studying various indigenous traditions, where these animals play a central role in both spiritual and social life.

Roles and Responsibilities: How Totem Animals Guide and Protect

Totem animals serve multiple roles and responsibilities within the communities they represent. Here's how they contribute to the well-being and identity of their groups:

Representing Collective Identity: Totem animals symbolize the collective identity and values of a clan, family, or tribe. They encapsulate the traits, strengths, and ethos that define the community. For example, a tiger totem might represent strength and willpower, while a horse totem embodies stamina and freedom.

Providing Guidance and Wisdom: Totem animals offer guidance and wisdom to their community. They are seen as spiritual teachers who provide insights into the collective journey and challenges faced by the group. Their presence encourages members to embody the virtues and strengths associated with their totem.

Offering Protection: Totem animals act as protectors, safeguarding the community from harm and guiding them through difficult times. They are believed to watch over their people, ensuring their safety and well-being.

Strengthening Bonds and Unity: By representing shared attributes and values, totem animals foster a sense of unity and belonging within the community. They remind members of their common heritage and the collective strength they draw from their totem.

Inspiring Rituals and Traditions: Totem animals inspire various rituals and traditions that honor their significance. These practices help reinforce the community's connection to their totem, keeping the spirit and wisdom of the animal alive in their cultural expressions.

In my spiritual practice, I have found that totem animals provide a profound connection to community and heritage. They remind us of the shared values and collective strength that bind us together, offering a deeper understanding of our place within the larger fabric of our group.

How to Recognize Totem Animals: Identifying Their Presence

Recognizing totem animals involves observing both personal and communal symbols that reflect the essence of the group. Here are some ways to identify totem animals:

Community Symbols and Traditions: Look for animals that frequently appear in your community's symbols, stories, and traditions. These animals often hold special significance as totems, representing the collective identity of the group.

Family Heritage: Consider the animals that have been historically important to your family or clan. These could be animals that your ancestors revered or that feature prominently in your family's cultural heritage.

Personal Resonance with Group Symbols: Pay attention to animals that resonate with you personally but also reflect the values and strengths of your community. This dual connection can indicate a deeper link to a totem animal.

Cultural Artifacts and Totem Poles: In many indigenous cultures, totem animals are depicted in cultural artifacts such as totem poles. These artistic representations provide insights into the animals that hold spiritual significance for the community.

Collective Experiences and Symbols: Notice animals that frequently appear in collective experiences, such as community gatherings, rituals, or shared dreams. These recurring appearances can signal the presence of a totem animal guiding and protecting the group.

In my studies, I learned to recognize the presence of totem animals through both personal reflection and communal observation. Understanding their significance in cultural and family contexts has deepened my appreciation for their role in our lives.

Connecting with Totem Animals: Practical Steps and Tips

Establishing a connection with your totem animal can enrich your sense of identity and community. Here are some practical steps and tips to connect with totem animals:

Learn About Your Heritage: Research your family or clan's heritage to discover which animals have historically been important. Understanding your roots can help you identify your totem animal and appreciate its significance.

Engage in Community Rituals: Participate in community rituals and traditions that honor totem animals. These practices can strengthen your connection to your totem and enhance your sense of belonging.

Meditate on Community Symbols: Meditate on symbols and attributes associated with your totem animal. Visualize the animal and contemplate its qualities, reflecting on how they relate to your community and yourself.

Create Art and Symbols: Express your connection to your totem animal through art, such as drawing, painting, or crafting. Creating symbols and representations of your totem can deepen your bond and honor its presence.

Honor Your Totem in Daily Life: Incorporate the qualities and strengths of your totem animal into your daily life. Reflect on how you can embody these traits in your actions and interactions with others.

Connect with Nature: Spend time in nature, observing the behavior and characteristics of your totem animal. This connection can provide insights into its wisdom and deepen your understanding of its role in your life.

Offer Prayers and Gratitude: Regularly offer prayers and expressions of gratitude to your totem animal. Thank them for their guidance and protection, and acknowledge their importance in your community.

Prayer for Totem Animals: "Great Spirit, I honor the presence of my totem animal, who guides and protects our community. May their wisdom and strength inspire us to live in harmony and uphold the values they embody. Thank you for their presence and the collective strength they bring to our lives."

In my practice, connecting with totem animals has been a journey of self-discovery and communal bonding. These animals provide a profound link to our heritage and a source of collective wisdom and strength.

Historical Significance of Totem Animals

Guided by Spirits

Totem animals have deep roots in various indigenous cultures around the world, serving as powerful symbols of community identity and spiritual guidance.

In Native American traditions, totem animals play a central role in the spiritual and social lives of tribes. Each clan or family often has a specific totem animal that represents their lineage, history, and spiritual beliefs. These totems are depicted in intricate totem poles, which are not just artistic expressions but powerful spiritual symbols. The term "totem" itself comes from the Ojibwe word "odoodem," meaning "family mark," highlighting the deep connection between totem animals and the sense of identity and belonging within a community.

In Australian Aboriginal cultures, totems are intertwined with the Dreamtime stories that explain the creation of the world. Each person is connected to a specific totem animal that represents their family, clan, or spiritual lineage. These animals guide and protect the community, providing a sense of continuity and connection to the ancestral spirits.

In African tribal traditions, totem animals are often associated with particular tribes or clans, symbolizing the qualities and strengths of the group. They are revered as spiritual protectors and guides, offering wisdom and guidance to the community.

In Pacific Islander cultures, totem animals are seen as ancestral spirits that protect and guide the tribe. These animals are often depicted in carvings, tattoos, and other cultural artifacts, reflecting their significance in the spiritual and social life of the community.

Understanding the historical significance of totem animals enriches our appreciation for their role in our lives. They connect us to a rich tradition of community and spiritual guidance, reminding us of the collective wisdom and strength that we draw from our totem animals.

Embracing the Journey with Totem Animals

Totem animals are invaluable allies in our spiritual and communal lives. They bring unique strengths, wisdom, and guidance that help us navigate life's challenges and celebrate our shared identity and heritage. By connecting with these spiritual beings, we tap into the profound energies and qualities they embody, enriching our lives and deepening our understanding of ourselves and our communities.

As you explore your relationship with your totem animal, embrace the journey with openness and curiosity. Allow their presence to inspire and empower you, and honor the profound connection that you share with your community. Whether you are seeking strength, clarity, or a deeper sense of belonging, your totem animal is there to support and guide you every step of the way.

Chapter 69

Animal Spirit Guides

Animal spirit guides are unique and powerful beings that stay with us throughout our lives, offering their wisdom, protection, and guidance. Unlike totem animals, which represent collective groups, or power animals, which may come and go as needed, animal spirit guides are personal to each individual. They act as our eyes and ears, helping us navigate life's challenges and learn more about ourselves.

For me, my lifelong animal spirit guides are the wolf and the eagle. The wolf, with its keen sense of loyalty and community, helps me understand the importance of relationships and teamwork. The eagle, soaring high above with sharp vision, teaches me to see the bigger picture and maintain a broad perspective. These guides have been with me in countless situations, providing insights and protection that have shaped my journey.

Animal spirit guides serve as lifelong mentors, offering a needed connection to the natural world and to our deeper selves. They embody the qualities we need to cultivate and the lessons we are here to learn. Through our relationship with them, we can gain a greater understanding of our strengths, challenges, and the path we are meant to walk.

Roles and Responsibilities: Guiding and Protecting Throughout Life

Animal spirit guides take on a range of roles and responsibilities tailored to our personal journey and needs. Here's how they contribute to our lives:

Providing Personal Guidance: Animal spirit guides offer insights and direction specific to our life path. They help us understand our purpose, navigate challenges, and make decisions that align with our highest good. For instance, a bear spirit guide might encourage you to find strength and courage during difficult times, while a dolphin guide might remind you to embrace joy and playfulness.

Offering Protection and Support: These guides are vigilant protectors, safeguarding us from harm and negative influences. They alert us to dangers, both physical and spiritual, and help us maintain our well-being. A lion spirit guide, for example, could provide the fierce protection needed when facing threats, while a rabbit might guide you away from unnecessary risks.

Teaching Life Lessons: Animal spirit guides are dedicated teachers. They help us understand and embody the qualities they represent, whether it's the patience of a turtle, the adaptability of a chameleon, or the independence of a cat. These lessons are not just intellectual but experiential, shaping our character and actions.

Facilitating Personal Growth: Through their guidance, animal spirit guides support our personal and spiritual growth. They encourage us to explore our potential, confront our fears, and evolve into our best selves. A butterfly spirit guide might assist in your transformation during periods of change, while a whale could guide you to deeper emotional and spiritual insights.

Enhancing Connection with Nature: By connecting us with the qualities of specific animals, spirit guides deepen our relationship with the natural world. They remind us of the interconnectedness of all life and inspire us to live in harmony with our environment. A deer spirit guide might help you appreciate the beauty and gentleness of nature, fostering a greater sense of peace and connection.

My wolf and eagle guides have consistently shown me how to balance the dualities of my life – community and independence, ground-level details, and high-level vision. Their presence is a constant reminder of the attributes I need to cultivate and the lessons I am here to learn.

How to Recognize Animal Spirit Guides: Signs and Symbols

Recognizing your animal spirit guide can be a deeply personal and intuitive process. Here are some ways to identify your lifelong animal companions:

Repeated Encounters: Pay attention to animals that frequently appear in your life, whether in dreams, meditations, or real-world encounters. If you repeatedly see an owl or a snake in various contexts, it might be an indication that this animal is your spirit guide.

Personal Resonance: Notice which animals you feel a strong affinity towards or which ones resonate deeply with you. This connection is often a sign that the animal has a special significance in your life. If you have always felt a special bond with wolves or orcas, they might be your spirit guides.

Symbolic Appearances: Look for animals that appear in symbolic forms, such as in art, literature, or even logos and media that catch your attention. These appearances can be subtle nudges from your spirit guides. Seeing images of dragons or peacocks repeatedly might be more than mere coincidence.

Inner Guidance and Intuition: Trust your intuition and inner feelings. Sometimes, you might just "know" which animal is your guide without needing external confirmation. This inner knowing can come through meditation, deep reflection, or a sudden realization.

Synchronicities: Be aware of synchronicities involving specific animals. These can be meaningful coincidences where the animal appears just when you need guidance or support. Encountering a fox in a crucial moment of decision-making could indicate its role as your guide.

In my experience, the wolf and the eagle consistently showed up in my dreams, in meditative visions, and in symbolic forms in my daily life. Their persistent presence and the deep connection I felt with them confirmed their role as my lifelong guides.

Connecting with Animal Spirit Guides: Practical Steps and Tips

Building a strong connection with your animal spirit guides enhances their ability to guide and support you. Here are some practical steps and tips to connect with them:

Meditation and Visualization: Meditate regularly and invite your animal spirit guides to join you. Visualize yourself in a natural setting where your guide appears. Allow yourself to interact with the animal, ask questions, and receive messages.

Nature Walks and Observations: Spend time in nature and observe the animals around you. Pay attention to any particular animals that draw your attention. Nature can be a powerful medium through which your guides communicate with you.

Dream Work: Keep a journal of your dreams, especially those involving animals. Reflect on the messages and themes these dreams present, and consider how they relate to your life.

Art and Symbolism: Create art or collect symbols that represent your animal spirit guides. Drawing, painting, or crafting representations of your guides can deepen your connection and keep their energy present in your daily life.

Rituals and Offerings: Engage in rituals that honor your spirit guides. This can include lighting a candle, offering food, or creating a sacred space in their honor. These practices show respect and gratitude for their presence.

Prayer and Intention Setting: Begin your practice with a prayer or affirmation, expressing your desire to connect with your spirit guides. Clearly state your intention to receive their guidance and support.

Prayer for Animal Spirit Guides: "Spirit, I honor and welcome the presence of my animal spirit guides. Thank you for guiding me with your wisdom, protecting me with your strength, and teaching me with your qualities. I ask for your continued support and guidance on my journey."

In my practice, these steps have helped me cultivate a deep and meaningful connection with my wolf and eagle guides. They provide ongoing support and wisdom, helping me navigate life with greater clarity and confidence.

Historical Significance of Animal Spirit Guides

Animal spirit guides have a rich historical significance, rooted in various cultures and spiritual traditions around the world. They have been revered as sacred entities that offer protection, wisdom, and guidance to individuals and communities.

In Native American traditions, animal spirit guides, often referred to as "spirit animals," play a crucial role in personal and communal spirituality. Each individual is believed to have a personal spirit animal that guides and protects them throughout their life. These animals are seen as powerful allies that embody specific qualities and provide insights into the individual's path and purpose. The significance of spirit animals is celebrated in rituals, storytelling, and art, reflecting their integral role in Native American spiritual practices.

In Celtic mythology, animal guides are revered as messengers from the Otherworld, providing wisdom and guidance. Each animal carries specific meanings and attributes that are significant in the context of Celtic spirituality. For example, the stag is associated with leadership and nobility, while the raven symbolizes transformation and prophecy. These animals are often depicted in Celtic art and legends, highlighting their importance in the spiritual life of the Celts.

In African shamanic traditions, animal spirit guides are considered vital in connecting individuals with the spiritual world. Shamans often work with these guides to gain insights, heal, and communicate with the divine. Animals such as lions, elephants, and leopards are seen as powerful protectors and sources of strength and courage. Their presence in rituals and spiritual practices highlights their role as bridges between the physical and spiritual realms.

In Aboriginal Australian beliefs, animal spirit guides, known as "Dreamtime ancestors," are woven into the spiritual and cultural fabric. These guides are believed to have created the world and continue to guide and protect their descendants. Each individual and community has a unique connection to specific animal ancestors, which is reflected in their stories, rituals, and totems. This connection emphasizes the respect and reverence for animal spirit guides in Aboriginal spirituality.

These historical perspectives illustrate the universal importance of animal spirit guides across cultures. They serve as powerful symbols of wisdom, protection, and guidance, offering a connection to the natural and spiritual worlds.

Embracing the Journey with Animal Spirit Guides

Animal spirit guides are lifelong companions on our spiritual journey. They offer unique insights, protection, and wisdom, helping us navigate the complexities of life and connect with our deeper selves. By recognizing and honoring their presence, we can tap into their natural energies and cultivate a richer, more meaningful connection to the world around us.

As you explore your relationship with your animal spirit guide, approach with openness and gratitude. Allow their guidance to illuminate your path, and honor their presence in your life. Whether you are seeking direction, strength, or a deeper understanding of your purpose, your animal spirit guide is there to support and guide you every step of the way.

Chapter 70

Familiars

Familiars are fascinating and mystical beings that have long been associated with witchcraft and magical practices. Unlike animal spirit guides or totem animals, familiars are believed to be supernatural entities that directly aid witches and magicians in their magical endeavors. While I personally have not experienced a connection with familiars, I have met many individuals who consider their familiars indispensable to their practice. Familiars typically appear in the form of animals, such as cats, dogs, birds, or even less common creatures like toads and spiders. They are thought to possess unique powers and qualities that enhance the magical abilities of their human companions.

The idea of familiars transcends mere companionship; these entities are seen as partners in the magical journey, providing not only support but also an extra layer of protection and power. Whether assisting in spell work, guiding rituals, or simply being present as a source of spiritual comfort, familiars play a vital role in the lives of those who work with them. They are often described as being highly intuitive, able to sense energies and influences that are beyond human perception, and their presence is said to amplify the practitioner's own magical capabilities. For those practitioners who work with familiars, the bond can be incredibly deep and rewarding. It is a relationship built on mutual trust and respect, where the familiar acts not just as a helper but as a loyal and understanding partner in both magical workings and mundane aspects of life.

Roles and Responsibilities: Enhancing Magical Practices

Familiars fulfill a variety of roles in the realm of magic and witchcraft, each tailored to the needs and abilities of their human companions. Here's how they contribute to and enhance magical practices:

Amplifying Magical Energy: Familiars are believed to possess their own magical energies, which can combine with and amplify the practitioner's power. During rituals and spell work, their presence helps to enhance the effectiveness and potency of magical operations. For example, a cat familiar might enhance intuition and psychic abilities, while a raven might assist in communication with the spirit world.

Offering Protection: Familiars serve as guardians, protecting their companions from negative energies and harmful entities. They can sense and ward off potential threats, creating a safe environment for magical practices. A dog familiar might act as a fierce protector against spiritual intrusions, while a serpent could provide a subtle yet powerful defense against unseen dangers.

Guiding and Assisting: Familiars guide their companions through complex magical processes and rituals. They offer insights and assistance, helping to navigate the intricacies of spell casting and energy manipulation. A bird familiar might guide a witch in divination practices, while a toad could assist in understanding and harnessing the power of herbs and natural elements.

Providing Companionship: Beyond their practical roles, familiars offer emotional and spiritual companionship. They provide comfort and support, making the magical journey less solitary and more fulfilling. This companionship can be especially valuable during times of spiritual growth or when facing challenging magical work.

Enhancing Intuition: Familiars are highly attuned to the spiritual and energetic realms, often sensing things that humans cannot. They help to sharpen the practitioner's intuition and awareness, making it easier to detect subtle energies and influences. A cat familiar, known for its keen senses, might help in developing stronger psychic abilities, while a fox could enhance cunning and resourcefulness in magical endeavors.

Acting as Intermediaries: Familiars can also act as intermediaries between their human companions and other spiritual entities or realms. They facilitate communication and interaction with spirits, deities, or elemental forces, making it easier to forge connections and gain insights. A dog familiar might guide a witch in communicating with ancestral spirits, while an owl could help in accessing hidden knowledge and wisdom.

While I may not have a familiar myself, the roles they play in the lives of others are both diverse and profound, offering a unique blend of practical assistance and spiritual enrichment.

How to Recognize Familiars: Signs and Connections

Recognizing a familiar can be a subtle and intuitive process. Here are some ways to identify and confirm the presence of a familiar in your magical practice:

Unusual Bond: A familiar often forms a unique and inexplicable bond with their human companion. This bond goes beyond typical pet-human relationships, characterized by mutual understanding and connection. If you feel an extraordinary closeness to an animal, it may be your familiar.

Spiritual Sensitivity: Familiars display a heightened sensitivity to spiritual and magical energies. They might react strongly to rituals, altars, or other magical activities, indicating their attunement to your practices. For instance, a cat might be drawn to your sacred space during spell work, or a bird might act unusually during divination sessions.

Protective Behavior: Familiars often exhibit protective behaviors, particularly during times of magical or spiritual vulnerability. They might stay close to you during rituals or act as guardians of your sacred space. A dog might position itself at the entrance of your ritual area, or a snake might coil protectively near your altar.

Signs and Symbols: Look for recurring symbols or signs involving a particular animal. This could be through dreams, visions, or repeated encounters in your waking life. These signs can be a confirmation of the familiar's presence. For example, repeatedly dreaming of a hawk or encountering them in unexpected ways could indicate their role as your familiar.

Magical Assistance: If an animal seems to enhance your magical abilities or provide guidance during rituals and spell work, it is likely acting as your familiar. Notice how their presence influences your practice and any enhancements in your magical outcomes. A raven might guide you in understanding complex spell work, while a cat could enhance your divination skills.

Unexplained Presence: Familiars sometimes appear in unexpected places or at times when you need them most. This could be a sudden encounter with a fox during a moment of decision or a feeling of being watched over by an owl at night. Their presence often coincides with moments of significance in your magical practice.

While I may not have a familiar, the experiences shared by others highlight the unique and powerful connection these beings have with their human companions.

Connecting with Familiars: Practical Steps and Tips

Establishing a connection with a familiar involves nurturing the bond and inviting their presence into your magical practice. Here are some practical steps and tips to foster a relationship with your familiar:

Meditate and Invite: Begin with meditation, focusing on opening your mind and spirit to the presence of a familiar. Create a quiet and sacred space, visualize a welcoming environment, and mentally invite a familiar to join you. Allow yourself to feel their energy and be open to any impressions or messages.

Create a Sacred Space: Dedicate a special area in your home for connecting with your familiar. This could be an altar or a specific corner where you keep symbols and offerings that resonate with the animal you believe to be your familiar. Fill this space with objects that represent the qualities and attributes of the familiar you seek to connect with.

Offerings and Rituals: Perform rituals and offer gifts that honor your familiar. This can include food, symbolic items, or acts of kindness that reflect the nature of your familiar. For instance, leave out birdseed for a bird familiar or create a small garden space for a frog.

Study and Learn: Learn about the characteristics and behaviors of the animal you believe to be your familiar. Understanding their natural traits and symbolism can deepen your connection and enhance your interactions. Research their habits, habitat, and spiritual significance to align your practices with their nature.

Daily Interactions: Spend time observing and interacting with animals, especially those you feel a strong connection to. Pay attention to their behaviors and any intuitive responses you feel during these interactions. Engage in activities that allow you to spend time with your familiar, whether it's walking in nature or simply sitting quietly in their presence.

Dream and Vision Work: Keep a journal of your dreams and any visions that involve animals. Reflect on these experiences and consider how they might relate to your familiar. Notice any patterns or recurring themes that might indicate the presence of your familiar in your dreamscape.

Prayer for Familiars: "Spirit of the familiar, I welcome your presence and guidance. Thank you for your protection, wisdom, and companionship in my magical journey. I ask for your continued support and connection, guiding me with your strength and insight."

These practices can help establish and strengthen your bond with your familiar, inviting their unique energy and support into your life.

Historical Significance of Familiars

Familiars have a long and complex history, deeply entwined with the practice of witchcraft and magic across various cultures.

In European folklore, particularly during the witch trials of the early modern period, familiars were often depicted as small animals like cats, dogs, or birds. These animals were believed to be supernatural entities that assisted witches in their magical practices. During these trials, many accused witches were said to have familiars, which were thought to be given to them by the devil. Although these accounts were often rooted in fear and superstition, they highlight the long-standing belief in the spiritual significance of familiars.

In shamanic traditions, familiars are seen as spirit helpers who guide and protect the shaman during their spiritual journeys. These spirit animals or entities assist in navigating the spirit world, providing the shaman with the necessary tools and knowledge to perform their healing and magical work. Familiars in shamanism are revered as powerful allies who enhance the shaman's abilities and ensure their safety during their spiritual endeavors.

In various folklore traditions, familiars are viewed more positively as loyal companions and protectors. They are often portrayed as animals that possess special powers or knowledge, assisting their human partners in their magical work. In some cultures, familiars are considered being ancestral spirits or entities that have chosen to take animal form to assist their human companions.

In modern Wiccan and Pagan practices, familiars are commonly seen as spiritual beings that enhance magical practices and provide protection. They are often viewed as partners in the magical journey, offering insights and assistance in rituals and spell work. Contemporary practitioners have embraced the belief in familiars as powerful allies, and they honor their presence through rituals, offerings, and daily interactions.

These historical perspectives illustrate the enduring belief in the power and significance of familiars across different cultures and traditions. Whether seen as protectors, guides, or magical allies, familiars have played a crucial role in the spiritual and magical practices of many societies throughout history.

Embracing the Journey with Familiars

Familiars are more than just mystical companions; they are partners in our magical journey, offering protection, guidance, and support. By recognizing and honoring their presence, we can tap into their unique energies and enhance our magical practices. Whether you have already connected with a familiar or are seeking to invite one into your life, approach this relationship with openness, respect, and gratitude.

As you explore your connection with your familiar, embrace the lessons and insights they bring. Allow their guidance to illuminate your path and support you in your spiritual and magical endeavors. Whether you are seeking protection, wisdom, or companionship, your familiar is there to walk with you every step of the way.

Alex McCann Johnson

Chapter 71
Mythic Guides

From a young age, I was always mesmerized by mythology. The tales of fantastical beasts and legendary creatures captured my imagination and inspired dreams of epic adventures. I remember visiting the United Kingdom and eagerly searching the waters of Loch Ness for the elusive monster and embarking on expeditions to find Bigfoot or other mysterious beings. This fascination with mythical creatures has oddly shaped my spiritual journey, opening me to the possibility that these beings might serve as guides and allies in our quest for deeper understanding and personal transformation.

Mythical creatures have always captivated the human imagination, appearing in the myths, legends, and folklore of cultures around the world. These beings, often possessing extraordinary powers and qualities, are believed to inhabit realms beyond the ordinary world. As spiritual guides, they offer wisdom, protection, and insight, helping us navigate our spiritual journeys. Whether you are drawn to the majestic dragons, the serene unicorns, or the transformative phoenixes, each mythical guide has something unique to offer.

The Spiritual Significance of Mythic Guides

Mythical creature guides hold imaginative spiritual significance. They serve as powerful symbols of transformation, strength, purity, and wisdom. Unlike more familiar animal guides, these beings transcend the ordinary, representing higher states of consciousness and deeper spiritual truths. They can help us access hidden knowledge, unlock our potential, and connect with the divine.

Transformation and Rebirth: Creatures like the phoenix symbolize the cycle of death and rebirth, guiding us through personal transformation and renewal. When we face significant life changes or seek to overcome challenges, the phoenix can inspire us to rise from the ashes and embrace new beginnings with courage and resilience.

Strength and Power: Dragons, often depicted in both Eastern and Western traditions, embody immense strength and power. They can teach us to harness our inner strength, overcome fears, and stand firm in our convictions. Working with dragon energy can empower us to face life's challenges with confidence and determination.

Purity and Virtue: Unicorns are symbols of purity, grace, and virtue. They encourage us to cultivate these qualities within ourselves and to approach life with an open heart and a clear mind. Unicorns can guide us in maintaining our integrity and following a path of righteousness and truth.

Wisdom and Insight: Many mythical creatures, such as griffins and sphinxes, are considered guardians of sacred knowledge and wisdom. They can help us unlock the mysteries of the universe and gain insights into our lives and spiritual paths. These guides can be invaluable allies in our quest for deeper understanding and enlightenment.

Working with mythical creature guides can be a transformative experience. These guides often appear during times of significant change or spiritual awakening, offering their unique qualities to aid in our growth. Whether through dreams, meditations, or spontaneous encounters, connecting with mythical creatures can provide insights and guidance.

How to Recognize Mythic Guides: Signs and Connections

Recognizing and connecting with mythic guides can be an exhilarating and enriching experience. Here are some ways to identify their presence and establish a connection:

Dreams and Visions: Mythical creatures often appear in vivid dreams or meditative visions, offering guidance or messages. Pay attention to recurring themes or symbols involving mythical beings in your dreamscape. These encounters can be powerful indicators of their presence and guidance.

Symbolic Encounters: You might repeatedly encounter symbols or representations of a particular mythical creature in your daily life. This could be through books, movies, art, or even unexpected sightings of their images. These synchronicities can signal the presence of a mythic guide in your life.

Intuitive Impressions: Feelings of awe, wonder, or a strong connection when thinking about or encountering mythical creatures can be signs of their influence. Trust your intuition and the emotions that arise during these moments, as they often reflect a deeper spiritual connection.

Spontaneous Experiences: Sometimes, mythical guides make their presence known through spontaneous experiences or encounters. This could be a sudden feeling of their energy, an inner knowing, or even a sense of being watched over or guided by a powerful, unseen presence.

Guided Meditations and Rituals: Engage in guided meditations or rituals specifically designed to connect with mythical creatures. Visualize meeting these beings in their natural realms and invite them to share their wisdom and guidance with you. These practices can create a direct and meaningful connection with your mythic guides.

Connecting with Mythic Guides: Practical Steps and Tips

Building a connection with mythic guides involves intentional effort and openness to their unique energies. Here are some practical steps and tips to foster a relationship with these extraordinary beings:

Set the Intention: Begin by setting a clear intention to connect with your chosen mythical guide. This can be done through a simple affirmation or prayer. For example, you might say, "I invite the wisdom

413

and presence of the dragon (or any other mythical creature) into my life. Please guide me with your strength and insight."

Create a Sacred Space: Dedicate a space in your home for connecting with your mythic guides. Decorate this space with symbols, images, or items that resonate with the qualities of your chosen mythical being. This could include figurines, artwork, or objects that evoke their energy.

Meditate on Symbols and Imagery: Meditate regularly while focusing on the symbols or imagery associated with your mythical guide. Visualize yourself in their presence, exploring their realm, and receiving their guidance. For example, if you are connecting with a unicorn, imagine yourself in a serene forest surrounded by their pure and gentle energy.

Engage in Creative Expression: Express your connection with mythical guides through creative activities like drawing, writing, or crafting. This can help deepen your bond and bring their energy into your everyday life. You might write stories inspired by their qualities or create art that reflects their presence and attributes.

Offer Gratitude and Respect: Regularly express gratitude for the guidance and support of your mythic guides. Honor their presence with offerings, rituals, or simple acts of appreciation. This can include lighting candles, placing flowers, or creating altars dedicated to them.

Prayer for Mythic Guides: "Great beings of legend and lore, I call upon your wisdom and strength. Guide me with your timeless insight and protect me with your powerful presence. Help me to embody the qualities you represent and to walk my path with courage and grace."

Historical Significance of Mythic Guides

Mythical creatures have played significant roles in the cultural and spiritual landscapes of various societies throughout history.

In Eastern traditions, dragons are revered as symbols of power, strength, and good fortune. In Chinese mythology, dragons are considered benevolent creatures that bring prosperity and harmony. They are often depicted as guardians of treasures and sacred knowledge, embodying the harmonious balance of yin and yang. The dragon's influence in Eastern culture underscores its role as a protector and benefactor, guiding those who seek its wisdom.

In Western mythology, creatures like unicorns and griffins have been celebrated for their purity and strength. Unicorns, often depicted as symbols of purity and grace, were believed to possess magical healing powers. In medieval Europe, unicorns were also seen as symbols of Christ, representing innocence and the divine. Griffins, with the body of a lion and the wings of an eagle, symbolize the union of earthly and heavenly powers, guarding treasures and sacred sites.

In Native American traditions, mythic beings such as the Thunderbird are revered as powerful spirits connected to the natural world. The Thunderbird is believed to control the elements and bring rain and storms, symbolizing transformation and change. These creatures are seen as messengers of the Great Spirit, guiding and protecting the people with their mighty presence.

In ancient Greek and Roman mythology, creatures like the phoenix and centaur represent themes of rebirth and duality. The phoenix, a bird that regenerates from its ashes, symbolizes eternal life and renewal. Centaurs, with the body of a horse and the torso of a man, embody the struggle between human reason and primal instinct, guiding us to balance these forces within ourselves.

In Celtic folklore, creatures such as the Kelpie, a shape-shifting water spirit, and the Banshee, a harbinger of death, reflect the deep connection between the spiritual and natural worlds. These beings are often seen as guardians of their respective realms, offering guidance and protection to those who honor their presence.

These historical perspectives highlight the enduring significance of mythical creatures in guiding and inspiring humanity. Their presence across different cultures and eras underscores their universal role as symbols of transformation, strength, and wisdom.

Embracing the Journey with Mythic Guides

Mythic guides offer a unique and enriching dimension to our spiritual journey. Their presence invites us to explore the extraordinary, embrace transformation, and connect with the deeper mysteries of the universe. Whether you are drawn to the wisdom of dragons, the purity of unicorns, or the resilience of the phoenix, each mythical guide brings a unique energy and perspective to your life.

As you cultivate your relationship with these legendary beings, allow their qualities to inspire and guide you. Embrace the lessons they offer and integrate their wisdom into your daily practices. With their guidance, you can navigate your spiritual path with greater clarity, courage, and creativity, discovering new depths of understanding and empowerment along the way.

Chapter 72

Dragons

From the moment I first encountered the concept of dragons in mythology, I was captivated by their majesty and mystery. Dragons are iconic mythical creatures that have fascinated humanity for millennia. These powerful beings are revered across various cultures as symbols of strength, wisdom, and transformative power. Their presence in our spiritual journeys can offer insights and guidance.

Dragons, often depicted with wings, scales, and the ability to breathe fire, are known for their immense strength and command over natural elements. They are considered guardians of treasures, both material and spiritual, and embody the balance of cosmic forces. In many traditions, dragons are seen as protectors, guiding seekers on their paths to enlightenment and personal transformation.

The Spiritual Significance of Dragon Guides

Dragon guides hold a special place in the realm of spiritual guidance. They represent a fusion of primal energy and divine wisdom, making them powerful allies in our quest for self-discovery and growth. Here are some of the stronger spiritual aspects they offer:

Transformation and Renewal: Dragons are often associated with transformation and renewal. Their ability to breathe fire symbolizes the power to destroy the old and make way for the new. Working with dragon energy can help us embrace change, release what no longer serves us, and ignite our inner fire for personal growth.

417

Strength and Protection: Dragons are revered for their immense strength and protective nature. They serve as guardians, shielding us from negative influences and empowering us to stand strong in the face of adversity. Calling upon a dragon guide can provide a powerful sense of safety and support during challenging times.

Wisdom and Knowledge: Dragons are considered keepers of ancient wisdom and knowledge. They can guide us in accessing deeper levels of understanding and insight, helping us connect with our inner wisdom and the greater mysteries of the universe. Their guidance can illuminate our spiritual path and enhance our intuitive abilities.

Balance and Harmony: Dragons often embody the balance of opposing forces, such as fire and water or light and dark. They teach us to harmonize these energies within ourselves, promoting a balanced and integrated approach to life. Engaging with dragon energy can help us find equilibrium and align with our true nature.

In my own journey, working with dragon guides has been a source of immense strength and inspiration. Their presence has helped me navigate periods of significant change and growth, offering both protection and insights.

How to Recognize Dragon Guides: Signs and Connections

Connecting with dragon guides can be an exhilarating experience. Here are some ways to recognize their presence and establish a connection:

Dreams and Visions: Dragons often appear in dreams or meditative visions, bringing messages of power and transformation. Pay attention to any recurring dreams involving dragons, as these can be significant indicators of their guidance.

Symbolic Encounters: You might repeatedly encounter dragon imagery in your daily life, such as through artwork, literature, or even tattoos. These synchronicities can signal the presence of a dragon guide and their influence in your life.

Intuitive Feelings: A strong sense of connection or fascination with dragons can be a sign that a dragon guide is reaching out to you. Trust your intuition and the feelings that arise when you think about or encounter dragon symbolism.

Spontaneous Experiences: Dragons may make their presence known through spontaneous experiences, such as a sudden surge of energy or a feeling of being protected. These encounters often occur during times of personal transformation or spiritual awakening.

Guided Meditations and Rituals: Engage in guided meditations or rituals specifically designed to connect with dragon energy. Visualize meeting a dragon in their realm and invite them to share their wisdom and strength with you.

Connecting with Dragon Guides: Practical Steps and Tips

Building a connection with dragon guides involves intentional effort and openness to their powerful energy. Here are some practical steps and tips to foster a relationship with these majestic beings:

Set the Intention: Begin by setting a clear intention to connect with a dragon guide. This can be done through a simple affirmation or prayer. For example, you might say, "I invite the presence and guidance of a dragon guide into my life. Please share your wisdom and strength with me."

Create a Sacred Space: Dedicate a space in your home for connecting with dragon energy. Decorate this space with symbols, images, or items that resonate with dragons, such as candles, crystals, or dragon figurines. This space can serve as a focal point for your interactions with your dragon guide.

Meditate on Dragon Imagery: Meditate regularly while focusing on dragon imagery. Visualize yourself in the presence of a dragon, exploring their realm and receiving their guidance. Imagine the dragon's energy surrounding and empowering you, filling you with strength and wisdom.

Engage in Creative Expression: Express your connection with dragons through creative activities like drawing, writing, or crafting. This can help deepen your bond and bring their energy into your everyday life. You might write stories inspired by their qualities or create art that reflects their presence and attributes.

Offer Gratitude and Respect: Regularly express gratitude for your dragon guide's guidance and support. Honor their presence with offerings, rituals, or simple acts of appreciation. This can include lighting candles, placing symbolic objects, or creating altars dedicated to them.

Prayer for Dragon Guides: "Majestic dragon of wisdom and power, I call upon your guidance and strength. Ignite my inner fire and illuminate my path with your ancient knowledge. Protect me with your fierce energy and help me embrace transformation with courage and grace."

Historical Significance of Dragon Guides

Dragons have played a significant role in the mythologies and spiritual traditions of cultures around the world.

In Chinese culture, dragons are revered as benevolent and powerful beings associated with strength, prosperity, and good fortune. They are seen as protectors of the natural world and symbols of imperial authority. The Chinese dragon is often depicted as a serpent-like creature with a combination of animal features, symbolizing the harmonious balance of various forces.

In European mythology, dragons are often portrayed as fearsome guardians of treasures and sacred sites. They embody the challenges and dangers that heroes must overcome to achieve their goals. These dragons represent both the destructive and protective aspects of nature, and their defeat often symbolizes the triumph of good over evil.

In Norse legends, dragons such as Fafnir and Nidhogg play crucial roles in the sagas of gods and heroes. Fafnir, originally a dwarf, transforms into a dragon to guard his hoard of gold, symbolizing the corrupting influence of greed. Nidhogg, a dragon that gnaws at the roots of Yggdrasil, the World Tree, represents the destructive forces that threaten the cosmos.

In Hindu mythology, the naga, serpent-like beings often associated with dragons, are considered guardians of water and treasures. They symbolize both fertility and the primal forces of nature. Nagas are revered as protectors and are often depicted as having both human and serpentine characteristics.

In indigenous cultures, dragons or dragon-like beings are often seen as powerful spirits connected to the earth and its elements. They are revered as guardians of sacred knowledge and as beings that maintain the balance between the physical and spiritual worlds.

These historical perspectives highlight the enduring significance of dragons in guiding and inspiring humanity. Their presence across different cultures and eras underscores their universal role as symbols of transformation, strength, and wisdom.

Embracing the Journey with Dragon Guides

Dragon guides offer an enriching dimension to our spiritual journey. Their presence invites us to explore the extraordinary, embrace transformation, and connect with the deeper mysteries of the universe. Whether you are drawn to the wisdom of Eastern dragons, the challenge of European dragons, or the mystical nature of serpent-like beings, each dragon guide brings a unique energy and perspective to your life.

As you cultivate your relationship with these legendary beings, allow their qualities to inspire and guide you. Embrace the lessons they offer and integrate their wisdom into your daily practices. With their guidance, you can navigate your spiritual path with greater clarity, courage, and creativity, discovering new depths of understanding and empowerment along the way.

Alex McCann Johnson

Chapter 73

Therianthropic Guides

From childhood tales of centaurs and mermaids to mythical shapeshifters in ancient lore, therianthropic guides—beings that blend human and animal forms—have always fascinated me. These hybrid entities embody a unique dual wisdom, combining the primal instincts and strengths of animals with the intellectual and emotional capacities of humans. They are revered in many cultures and spiritual traditions as powerful symbols of transformation, adaptability, and the harmonious blending of different realms of existence.

Understanding Therianthropic Guides

Therianthropic guides, often depicted in folklore and mythology, serve as intermediaries between the animal and human worlds. They possess both physical and spiritual qualities, making them unique sources of guidance and wisdom. Examples of these guides include centaurs, mermaids, werewolves, and other shapeshifters.

Centaurs, like the wise Chiron from Greek mythology, combine the strength and speed of a horse with the intellect and rationality of a human. They are often portrayed as sages or warriors, embodying the fusion of animalistic power and human wisdom.

Mermaids, with their enchanting songs and dual existence in both water and land, symbolize emotional depth and adaptability. These beings, part human and part fish, are often associated with the mysteries of the subconscious and the ebb and flow of emotions.

Shapeshifters in various cultures are beings that can change their form at will, often taking on both human and animal shapes. They represent the ultimate adaptability and the fluidity of identity, teaching us about the transformative power within us.

These guides help us connect with both our primal instincts and our higher intellectual and emotional faculties, offering a balanced perspective on life's challenges and opportunities.

The Spiritual Significance of Therianthropic Guides

Therianthropic guides hold such spiritual significance due to their dual nature. Here's how they can influence and enhance our spiritual journey:

Embracing Duality: These guides teach us to embrace the dual aspects of our nature—the instinctual and the rational, the wild and the civilized. They remind us that balance and integration of these facets are crucial for a harmonious and fulfilling life.

Transformation and Adaptability: Therianthropic guides, especially shapeshifters, symbolize the power of transformation and adaptability. They inspire us to be flexible and resilient, capable of changing our form or perspective to navigate life's challenges.

Connection to Nature and the Subconscious: Guides like mermaids and centaurs connect us deeply with nature and our subconscious mind. They help us understand our emotions, instincts, and the hidden depths of our psyche, promoting a deeper self-awareness and emotional intelligence.

Wisdom and Strength: The combination of human intellect and animal strength in these guides provides a unique blend of wisdom and power. They encourage us to harness our inner strengths and apply them wisely in our spiritual and everyday lives.

My journey with therianthropic guides has been transformative, teaching me to appreciate and integrate all aspects of my being.

Their presence in my life has helped me navigate complex emotional landscapes and adapt to changing circumstances with grace and strength.

Recognizing Therianthropic Guides: Signs and Connections

Connecting with therianthropic guides involves recognizing their unique signs and symbols. Here's how you might identify their presence in your life:

Dreams and Visions: These guides often appear in dreams or meditative visions, showing their dual forms or shapeshifting abilities. Pay attention to dreams where you encounter beings that are part human and part animal, as these are likely signs of the therianthropic guides reaching out.

Symbolic Encounters: You might repeatedly encounter imagery or symbols associated with these hybrid beings in your daily life. This could be through art, literature, or even random sightings of related symbols that catch your attention.

Intuitive Feelings: A strong sense of connection or fascination with beings that blend human and animal forms can indicate the presence of a therianthropic guide. Trust your intuition and the emotions that arise when you think about or encounter these entities.

Spontaneous Experiences: Moments where you feel unusually attuned to both your rational mind and your instinctual, animalistic side can be signs of a therianthropic guide's influence. These experiences often occur during periods of personal growth or transformation.

Guided Meditations and Rituals: Engaging in guided meditations or rituals that focus on connecting with hybrid beings can help you establish a deeper bond with your therianthropic guides. Visualize meeting these guides in their realms and inviting them to share their wisdom and energy with you.

Connecting with Therianthropic Guides: Practical Steps and Tips

Building a connection with therianthropic guides requires openness and a willingness to explore the integration of different aspects of your being. Here are some steps and tips to help you connect with these powerful guides:

Set the Intention: Start by setting a clear intention to connect with a therianthropic guide. This can be done through a simple affirmation or prayer. For example, you might say, "I invite the presence and guidance of a therianthropic guide into my life. Please share your dual wisdom and strength with me."

Create a Sacred Space: Dedicate a space in your home for connecting with hybrid beings. Decorate this space with symbols, images, or items that resonate with therianthropic energy, such as artwork of centaurs, mermaids, or shapeshifters. This space can serve as a focal point for your interactions with your guide.

Meditate on Duality: Meditate regularly while focusing on the dual aspects of your nature. Visualize yourself meeting a therianthropic guide, exploring their realm, and receiving their guidance. Imagine blending your rational and instinctual sides, finding balance and harmony within yourself.

Engage in Creative Expression: Express your connection with these guides through creative activities like drawing, writing, or crafting. Create art that reflects their presence and attributes or write stories inspired by their qualities. This can help deepen your bond and bring their energy into your everyday life.

Offer Gratitude and Respect: Regularly express gratitude for the guidance and support of your therianthropic guide. Honor their presence with offerings, rituals, or simple acts of appreciation. This can include lighting candles, placing symbolic objects, or creating altars dedicated to them.

Prayer for Therianthropic Guides: "Wise and powerful therianthropic guide, I call upon your dual wisdom and strength. Help me embrace both my rational mind and my instinctual spirit. Guide me in finding balance and harmony within myself and navigating the complexities of life with your insight."

Historical Significance of Therianthropic Guides

Therianthropic guides have played significant roles in the mythologies and spiritual traditions of cultures around the world.

In Greek mythology, centaurs like Chiron are prominent figures. Chiron, known as the "wounded healer," was a wise and compassionate being who used his dual nature to teach and heal. His knowledge of medicine and healing arts made him a revered guide, symbolizing the integration of human intellect and animal strength.

In various Native American traditions, therianthropic beings often appear in creation myths and spiritual stories. These entities, such as the Skinwalkers of Navajo lore, are seen as powerful and sometimes dangerous beings capable of transforming their shape to influence the world around them. They embody the deep connection between humans and animals and the transformative power of this relationship.

In Celtic mythology, creatures like the Púca are shapeshifters that can take on both human and animal forms. These beings are often mischievous but also wise, teaching lessons about adaptability and the fluid nature of identity. The Púca's ability to change shape reflects the Celtic understanding of the interconnectedness and fluidity of life.

In Norse mythology, beings like the Fenrir wolf and Jormungandr, the World Serpent, blend animalistic and mythical elements. These creatures are central to the cosmology and symbolize the primal forces of nature that influence human fate. They represent the power and chaos that come from integrating animalistic and human aspects.

In modern fantasy and literature, therianthropic beings continue to captivate our imagination. Characters like werewolves and shapeshifters explore themes of duality, transformation, and the struggle between different aspects of identity. These modern depictions draw on ancient traditions, highlighting the enduring fascination with beings that embody both human and animal qualities.

These historical perspectives highlight the universal appeal and significance of therianthropic guides. Their presence across different cultures and eras underscores their role as symbols of integration, transformation, and the blending of diverse aspects of existence.

Embracing the Journey with Therianthropic Guides

Therianthropic guides offer a unique and enriching dimension to our spiritual journey. Their dual nature invites us to explore the integration of our human and animalistic sides, fostering a deeper understanding of ourselves and the world around us. Whether you are drawn to the wisdom of centaurs, the adaptability of shapeshifters, or the emotional depth of mermaids, each therianthropic guide brings a distinct perspective and energy to your life.

As you cultivate your relationship with these remarkable beings, allow their qualities to inspire and guide you. Embrace the lessons they offer and integrate their wisdom into your daily practices. With their guidance, you can navigate your spiritual path with greater balance, adaptability, and insight, discovering new depths of understanding and empowerment along the way.

Chapter 74

Integrating Animal Wisdom

Spirit animals are universal. They transcend cultural boundaries and have been a part of human spirituality for millennia. Their presence in our lives is a reminder of the interconnectedness of all beings and the shared wisdom of the natural world. As we deepen our connection with spirit animals, we become more attuned to the rhythms of nature and the subtle energies that guide our existence.

In today's fast-paced and technology-driven world, reconnecting with spirit animals offers a way to realign ourselves with the natural world. This resurgence of interest in spirit animals reflects a broader movement towards finding balance and meaning by drawing upon the ancient wisdom that these guides embody. Spirit animals serve as reminders of our innate connection to nature and the insights it holds for our spiritual journeys.

Daily Practices for Connection

Integrating the wisdom of spirit animals into our daily lives requires regular and intentional practices. These routines help maintain a strong bond and keep the communication channels open between us and our guides.

Morning Rituals: Begin each day by acknowledging the presence of your spirit animals. This can be a simple prayer, a moment of silence, or a brief meditation. Setting this intention helps to create a sacred space for your spirit animals to communicate with you throughout the day. For example, you might start your day with a quiet moment reflecting on the qualities of your spirit animal, setting an intention to embody those traits as you go about your day.

Mindful Observation: Pay attention to the animals you encounter in your daily life. Whether it's a bird flying overhead, a cat crossing your path, or a dream about a specific animal, these encounters often carry messages and insights from your spirit guides. Observing these moments with mindfulness can reveal significant guidance. If you repeatedly notice a particular animal, take time to reflect on its possible symbolic meanings and how they relate to your current life circumstances.

Meditation and Visualization: Regularly meditate and visualize your spirit animals. See yourself interacting with them, receiving their guidance, and integrating their lessons into your life. This practice strengthens your bond and keeps the connection vibrant. For instance, during meditation, you might visualize walking through a forest and encountering your spirit animal, feeling its presence, and receiving its wisdom.

Journaling: Keep a journal of your experiences with spirit animals. Record your dreams, meditative visions, and any significant encounters. Reflecting on these entries can reveal patterns and deeper meanings, enhancing your understanding of your guides' messages. Over time, you may notice recurring themes or insights that provide clarity and direction.

Rituals and Ceremonies

Rituals and ceremonies are powerful tools for honoring and deepening our connection with spirit animals. These practices create sacred spaces where we can celebrate and connect with our guides.

Seasonal Ceremonies: Perform ceremonies during significant times of the year, such as solstices and equinoxes, to honor your spirit animals. These ceremonies can include offerings, drumming, and storytelling, creating a sacred space to celebrate and connect with your guides. For example, during the autumn equinox, you might gather with others to share stories of your spirit animals and offer thanks for the guidance they have provided over the past season.

Offerings and Altars: Create an altar dedicated to your spirit animals. Place symbolic items such as feathers, stones, and images of your guides on the altar. Offerings of food, water, or other meaningful items can be made to honor their presence and guidance. This physical representation serves as a focal point for your connection and a place to express gratitude and reverence.

Creative Expression: Use art, music, dance, and writing as ways to honor and connect with your spirit animals. Expressing your experiences and visions through creative outlets can deepen your relationship and provide new insights. You might paint a picture of your spirit animal, compose a song inspired by its energy, or write a poem that captures the essence of your encounters.

Interpreting Messages and Lessons

Understanding the messages from spirit animals involves reflection, intuition, and a willingness to explore their symbolic meanings.

Symbolism: Reflect on the symbolic meanings of your spirit animals. What qualities do they embody, and how do these qualities relate to your life? Understanding their symbolism can provide valuable insights into the guidance they offer. For instance, if your spirit animal is a fox, consider how its traits of cunning and adaptability might apply to your current challenges or opportunities.

Intuition: Trust your intuition and the feelings that arise during your interactions with spirit animals. These intuitive insights are often the key to understanding their messages. Sometimes, a particular feeling or thought will stand out during an encounter with your spirit animal, providing a clue to the message it is trying to convey.

Patterns and Consistency: Look for patterns and recurring themes in your encounters with spirit animals. Consistent messages and symbols can help clarify their guidance and reveal deeper meanings.

For example, if you frequently dream of a certain animal, its repeated presence could indicate a significant lesson or area of focus in your life.

Clarity Requests: If you are unsure about the messages you receive, ask your spirit animals for clarity. During meditation or rituals, request further insights or specific guidance on how to proceed. This open communication invites deeper understanding and helps you navigate any uncertainties.

Overcoming Challenges

Working with spirit animals can sometimes present challenges, such as doubts or the complexity of having multiple guides.

Doubts and Skepticism: It is natural to encounter doubts and skepticism when working with spirit animals, especially if this is a new practice for you. Trust your experiences and the intuitive feelings that arise. Seek support from spiritual communities or groups where others share their experiences with spirit animals. Sharing and hearing about others' journeys can validate your experiences and provide encouragement.

Multiple Spirit Animals: Sometimes, you may find yourself connected to more than one spirit animal. Recognize that each guide may play a different role in your life. During meditative sessions, ask each spirit animal for specific messages and guidance. Balance their energies by dedicating time to each guide and integrating their lessons harmoniously. For instance, you might work with a bear for strength and resilience while also engaging with a hummingbird for joy and lightness.

The Future of Spiritual Guidance

As we continue to evolve on our spiritual journeys, the role of spirit animals in our lives may change and expand. These guides are dynamic and responsive to our growth, offering new lessons and insights as we progress. Embracing this evolution allows us to remain open to the ever-present wisdom of the natural world and the spiritual realm.

Evolving with Your Spirit Guides: Spirit animals are not static; they evolve with us, reflecting our spiritual growth and changing needs. Embrace this dynamic relationship by remaining open to new guides and lessons. As you grow, new spirit animals may enter your life, bringing fresh insights and perspectives. Honor these changes and continue to cultivate your connection with the spiritual realm. For example, as you move through different life stages, you might find that different spirit animals come forward to guide you through specific transitions and challenges.

Spirit animals are spiritual allies that offer guidance, protection, and wisdom. By integrating their teachings into our daily lives, performing rituals to honor their presence, and interpreting their messages with intuition and reflection, we can deepen our spiritual practice and navigate our journeys with greater clarity, purpose, and harmony. Embracing the wisdom of our spirit animals enriches our lives, opening us to the vast and magical possibilities of the spiritual realm. As we continue to evolve, may we always remain connected to the sacred guidance of our spirit animals, honoring their presence and the timeless wisdom they offer?

Alex McCann Johnson

Nature and Elemental Guides

Alex McCann Johnson

Chapter 75
Nature and Elemental Guides

Nature and elemental spirits are entities believed to inhabit the natural world and embody the essence of the elements. These spirits exist in various forms and possess unique characteristics tied to their specific element or natural domain. Nature spirits, also known as nature devas or nature beings, are often associated with living aspects of the environment, such as trees, plants, rivers, and mountains. Elemental spirits, on the other hand, represent the four classical elements: earth, water, air, and fire. Each type of spirit has its own distinct personality, purpose, and way of interacting with humans.

Nature and elemental spirits are considered guardians and keepers of the natural world. They are often depicted as protectors who maintain the balance and harmony of their respective domains. While some cultures view these spirits as benevolent and helpful, others may see them as mischievous or even malevolent, depending on their behavior and the context of their interactions with humans. Regardless of their nature, these spirits play crucial roles in the ecosystems they inhabit, and their presence is integral to the health and vitality of the natural world.

The Belief in Nature and Elemental Spirits

The belief in nature and elemental spirits has deep roots in various cultures and traditions around the world. Although their manifestations and the specifics of their roles vary across different belief systems, the fundamental idea of spirits inhabiting and influencing the natural world is a common thread.

Ancient Greek Philosophy: The concept of elementals was introduced by the philosopher Empedocles, who proposed that everything in the universe is composed of four elements: earth, water, air, and fire. These elements were later personified as elemental spirits by Paracelsus, a Swiss alchemist and physician, who described them as gnomes (earth), undines (water), sylphs (air), and salamanders (fire). These spirits were believed to not only embody the physical properties of their respective elements but also to possess consciousness and purpose, interacting with the natural world and humanity.

Indigenous Cultures: Many indigenous cultures honor the spirits of animals, plants, and natural features such as rivers and mountains. For example, Native American tribes often hold ceremonies and rituals to communicate with and appease these spirits, viewing them as integral to the health and well-being of the community. These spirits are seen as part of a larger spiritual ecosystem, working together to maintain the balance of nature and the welfare of the people who live within it.

Celtic Mythology: In Celtic mythology, faeries are a well-known example of nature spirits. Faeries are believed to inhabit forests, meadows, and other natural settings, where they protect and nurture the land. They are often depicted as playful and elusive beings who can be both helpful and trickster-like in their interactions with humans. The faeries' role in Celtic culture underscores the importance of living in harmony with nature and respecting the unseen forces that govern the natural world.

Asian Traditions: In Japanese Shintoism, kami are spirits or deities that reside in natural objects and phenomena such as trees, rocks, rivers, and mountains. These spirits are worshipped in shrines and are believed to influence various aspects of life and nature. The reverence for kami in Shintoism highlights the deep connection between the spiritual and natural worlds and the belief that all aspects of nature are imbued with spiritual significance.

The Role of These Spirits in Modern Spiritual Practices

In contemporary spirituality, the connection with nature and elemental spirits has seen a resurgence, reflecting a broader movement towards environmental awareness and spiritual connection with the natural world. These spirits are seen as allies and teachers who offer guidance, healing, and insight.

Meditation and Visualization: One common practice for connecting with nature and elemental spirits is through meditation and visualization. By entering a meditative state, individuals can invite these spirits to reveal themselves and communicate. For instance, during meditation, one might visualize a forest spirit emerging from the trees, offering wisdom and guidance related to personal growth or environmental stewardship.

Shamanic Practices: Shamanic journeying remains a powerful method for interacting with nature and elemental spirits. Shamans enter altered states of consciousness to commune with these spirits, seeking their assistance in healing and divination. Through rhythmic drumming or chanting, practitioners can travel to the spirit world, where they may encounter earth spirits like gnomes, who provide grounding and stability, or water spirits like undines, who offer emotional healing and insight.

Rituals and Ceremonies: Rituals and ceremonies play a significant role in honoring and connecting with nature and elemental spirits. These practices can range from simple daily offerings to elaborate seasonal ceremonies. For example, creating an altar with symbolic items such as stones, leaves, and water to honor earth and water spirits can be a daily ritual that fosters a deeper connection with these elements. During the winter solstice, a ceremony might include lighting candles to invoke the presence of fire spirits, inviting their warmth and transformative power into the season.

Creative Expression: Engaging in creative activities like painting, music, and dance can also be a powerful way to connect with nature and elemental spirits. By expressing the energies and characteristics of these spirits through art, individuals can deepen their relationship with them and gain new insights. For example, painting a landscape infused with the vibrant energy of fire spirits can evoke their dynamic and passionate qualities, offering a visual and emotional connection to their essence.

The Importance of Connecting with Nature and Elemental Guides

Personal and Spiritual Growth: Connecting with nature and elemental spirits can significantly enhance personal and spiritual growth. These spirits serve as guides and teachers, offering wisdom and insights that help individuals navigate their spiritual journeys. By attuning to the energies of nature and the elements, people can develop a deeper understanding of themselves and their place in the world. For example, working with an air spirit might inspire a person to embrace freedom and creativity, leading to a more expansive and liberated approach to life.

Healing and Guidance: Nature and elemental spirits are often called upon for their healing abilities. They possess powerful energies that can aid in physical, emotional, and spiritual healing. Earth spirits, such as gnomes, are associated with grounding and stability, making them valuable allies in healing practices focused on restoring balance and strength. Water spirits, like undines, are linked to emotions and intuition, offering support in healing emotional wounds and enhancing intuitive abilities. For instance, during a period of emotional turmoil, calling upon water spirits can provide soothing and nurturing energy, helping to navigate and heal from intense feelings.

Enhancing Environmental Awareness and Responsibility: Connecting with nature and elemental spirits fosters a deep sense of environmental awareness and responsibility. As individuals develop relationships with these spirits, they become more attuned to the needs and well-being of the natural world. This heightened awareness often leads to a greater commitment to environmental stewardship and sustainable living. Nature and elemental spirits teach us the importance of living in harmony with the earth and respecting its resources. They remind us that we are part of a larger web of life and that our actions have a direct impact on the environment. By honoring these spirits and working to protect their domains, individuals contribute to the preservation and healing of the planet. This can manifest in simple actions like reducing waste and conserving water or in more significant efforts like participating in conservation projects and advocating for environmental policies.

Nature and elemental spirits play a vital role in our spiritual and cultural lives. By connecting with these guides, we can experience personal and spiritual growth, receive healing and guidance, and enhance our awareness and responsibility towards the environment. Embracing these relationships enriches our lives and fosters a deeper connection with the natural world and its many wonders. As we cultivate our bonds with these spirits, we not only benefit from their wisdom and support but also contribute to the broader effort of living in harmony with the earth. In a world increasingly disconnected from nature, these connections offer a pathway back to balance, respect, and reverence for the living world around us.

Alex McCann Johnson

Chapter 76

Connecting with Nature Spirits

When I first started working with spirit, I noticed a spark when working with the directions. This realization led me to explore the concept of the Medicine Wheel and seasonal spirits based on elements. The Medicine Wheel is a sacred symbol used by various indigenous cultures to represent the interconnectedness of life and the cycles of nature. It serves as a tool for understanding the spiritual aspects of the world and oneself. In this context, the Medicine Wheel is closely tied to the elements, directions, and seasonal spirits, each offering unique wisdom and guidance.

The Medicine Wheel and Seasonal Spirits Based on Elements

The Four Directions and Their Spirits

Great Spirit of the East

The East is associated with the element of air, new beginnings, and the dawn. It represents the start of new cycles and is often seen as a place of inspiration and enlightenment. In Native American traditions, the East is revered as the direction of the rising sun, symbolizing birth, rebirth, and renewal. The Great Spirit of the East brings clarity, vision, and the breath of life, helping individuals to see things from a higher perspective and encouraging openness and the pursuit of knowledge.

In the Incan Medicine Wheel, the East is linked with the Condor, a majestic bird that soars high above the Andes, symbolizing vision and spiritual enlightenment. The Condor teaches us to rise above our challenges and view our lives from a broader perspective.

Great Spirit of the South

The South corresponds to the element of fire and the energy of growth and vitality. It is associated with the summer season, a time of abundance and flourishing life. For Native Americans, the South is a place of warmth, trust, and innocence. The Great Spirit of the South encourages growth, passion, and the nurturing of the self and community, often associated with youth and the exuberance of life, reminding us to embrace joy and creativity.

In the Incan tradition, the South is connected to the Serpent, representing transformation and the shedding of old ways. The Serpent guides us in letting go of what no longer serves us, allowing for growth and renewal.

Great Spirit of the West

The West is aligned with the element of water and the setting sun, symbolizing introspection, intuition, and the end of cycles. It represents the autumn season, a time of harvesting and reflection. The Great Spirit of the West in Native American culture is seen as a source of deep wisdom and emotional insight. This spirit helps us to delve into our inner world, confront our shadows, and find balance through understanding and acceptance.

The Incan Medicine Wheel associates the West with the Jaguar, an animal known for its strength and solitary nature. The Jaguar teaches us to navigate the darkness within and to emerge with greater personal power and clarity.

Great Spirit of the North

The North corresponds to the element of earth and the winter season, symbolizing wisdom, stability, and introspection. It represents the time of rest and the culmination of life cycles. In Native American traditions, the North is revered as a place of elders and ancestral wisdom. The Great Spirit of the North offers guidance, protection, and the grounding energy needed to withstand challenges, encouraging us to honor our ancestors and the lessons they impart.

In the Incan tradition, the North is associated with the Hummingbird, a creature that defies the odds with its remarkable endurance and agility. The Hummingbird symbolizes perseverance and the pursuit of joy and beauty, even in difficult times.

The Shamanic Medicine Wheel

In shamanic practices, the Medicine Wheel serves as a map for spiritual journeys and healing. It represents the cyclical nature of life and the continuous flow of energy through the four directions. Each direction is a doorway to specific spiritual energies and guides that assist in personal and communal healing.

The East (Air): In shamanic practices, the East is the realm of the eagle, symbolizing vision, clarity, and spiritual awakening. It is a place of new beginnings and inspiration, where one seeks guidance for the journey ahead.

The South (Fire): The South is represented by the coyote or the serpent in shamanic traditions, symbolizing growth, passion, and transformation. It is a place of learning and developing one's strengths and abilities.

The West (Water): The West is often associated with the bear, representing introspection, healing, and the emotional body. It is a place to face one's fears and heal past wounds, fostering emotional resilience and wisdom.

The North (Earth): The North is represented by the buffalo or the deer, symbolizing wisdom, endurance, and grounding. It is a place of stillness and reflection where one connects with ancestral knowledge and the cycles of life.

Seasonal Spirits Based on Elements

The Medicine Wheel also connects to the seasons, each embodying the spirit of its corresponding element and direction. Recognizing these spirits helps to harmonize with the natural rhythms and energies throughout the year.

Spring (East/Air): Spring is a time of renewal and new beginnings, aligned with the East and the element of air. The spirit of spring encourages fresh starts, creativity, and the blossoming of new ideas and projects.

Summer (South/Fire): Summer embodies the spirit of growth and vitality, aligned with the South and the element of fire. This season's spirit encourages us to embrace our passions, nurture our relationships, and enjoy the fullness of life.

Autumn (West/Water): Autumn is a time of reflection and harvest, aligned with the West and the element of water. The spirit of autumn guides us to gather the fruits of our labor, reflect on our experiences, and prepare for the inward journey of winter.

Winter (North/Earth): Winter represents rest and introspection, aligned with the North and the element of earth. The spirit of winter encourages us to slow down, seek inner wisdom, and connect with our roots and traditions.

The Medicine Wheel is a tool for connecting with the spiritual energies of the natural world. By understanding and honoring the spirits of the four directions and their associated elements and seasons, we can align ourselves with the rhythms of nature and gain deeper insights into our spiritual journeys. Whether through Native American, Incan, or shamanic traditions, the Medicine Wheel offers a timeless framework for healing, growth, and transformation, guiding us toward greater harmony and balance in our lives.

Chapter 77
Nature and Elements

Nature and the elements are fundamental to our understanding of the world and our place within it. They represent the basic building blocks of life and the forces that shape our environment and our experiences. Throughout history, various cultures have revered these elements—earth, water, air, and fire—not only as physical substances but as profound spiritual entities. These elements are integral to the cycles of nature and the flow of energy within the universe. My journey into understanding nature and the elements began with recognizing their presence in the world around me and exploring their deeper spiritual significance.

The Four Classical Elements

The concept of the four classical elements—earth, water, air, and fire—has been a cornerstone of many philosophical and spiritual systems. Each element embodies specific qualities and energies that influence both the physical and spiritual realms.

Earth

The element of earth is the foundation of stability, grounding, and physicality. It represents the material world and the tangible aspects of life. Earth is the soil beneath our feet, the mountains that rise towards the sky, and the trees that root deeply into the ground. It is the element that gives us a sense of stability and connection to the physical plane.

Spiritually, earth is associated with qualities such as patience, endurance, and reliability. It teaches us to be grounded and to find strength and resilience in our roots. When I connect with the earth element, I feel a deep sense of calm and stability. Walking barefoot on the ground or spending time in nature helps me to center myself and reconnect with the solid foundation that supports my life.

Water

Water is the element of emotion, intuition, and flow. It is the rivers that carve through the land, the oceans that cover vast expanses, and the rain that nourishes the earth. Water's fluid and adaptable nature embodies the essence of change and transformation.

In the spiritual realm, water is linked to emotions and the subconscious mind. It encourages us to be in touch with our feelings and to flow with the currents of life. Water teaches us to embrace change and to trust our intuition. For me, connecting with the water element often involves spending time near lakes, rivers, or the ocean. The rhythmic sound of water and its ever-changing nature remind me to stay adaptable and open to the ebb and flow of life's experiences.

Air

The element of air represents intellect, communication, and freedom. It is the wind that moves across the landscape, the breath that sustains life, and the invisible currents that connect us all. Air is the force that inspires thoughts, ideas, and the exchange of knowledge.

Spiritually, air is associated with clarity, creativity, and insight. It encourages us to explore new ideas, communicate openly, and seek a higher perspective. When I work with the air element, I often engage in practices that enhance mental clarity and creativity. Breathing exercises, spending time in open spaces, and meditating on the movement of the wind help me to harness the uplifting and expansive qualities of air.

Fire

Fire is the element of energy, transformation, and passion. It is the flame that brings warmth and light, the sun that fuels life on earth, and the force that drives change and growth. Fire is dynamic and powerful, capable of both creation and destruction.

In the spiritual context, fire represents the drive and motivation that propel us forward. It is associated with passion, courage, and the transformative power of change. Connecting with the fire element involves embracing its energy and using it to ignite creativity and personal growth. For me, lighting candles, sitting by a bonfire, or simply basking in the sun are ways to connect with the invigorating and transformative qualities of fire.

Nature Spirits and Elemental Beings

Beyond their physical and energetic qualities, the elements are often personified as spirits or beings in various cultural and spiritual traditions. These elemental beings are seen as guardians and embodiments of their respective elements, each with distinct personalities and roles.

Earth Spirits

Earth spirits, also known as gnomes or nature devas, are believed to inhabit the physical world, particularly within the soil, rocks, and plants. They are the keepers of the earth's treasures and the guardians of its stability and abundance. In my experience, connecting with earth spirits brings a sense of grounding and nurturing. When I sit quietly in a forest or garden, I can feel the presence of these beings, supporting and sustaining the life around me.

Water Spirits

Water spirits, such as undines or naiads, dwell in rivers, lakes, and oceans. They are the essence of the fluid and emotional qualities of water. These spirits are often seen as healers and guides, helping to cleanse and purify both the physical and emotional realms. When I connect with water spirits, I find clarity and emotional healing. Listening to the gentle flow of a stream or the crashing waves of the sea helps me to release emotional burdens and gain deeper insights into my inner world.

Air Spirits

Air spirits, often referred to as sylphs, are associated with the skies, winds, and all things ethereal. They embody the qualities of movement, inspiration, and communication. Air spirits are said to inspire creativity and to carry messages from the spiritual realm. My interactions with air spirits often occur during moments of stillness when I can feel the subtle movements of the wind. These encounters bring fresh ideas and a sense of liberation and perspective.

Fire Spirits

Fire spirits, including salamanders or fire elementals, are seen as the living embodiment of fire's transformative and energetic nature. They are the catalysts of change and the bearers of light and warmth. Fire spirits inspire passion and action, driving us to pursue our goals and dreams. Connecting with fire spirits energizes and motivates me, especially when I engage in activities that involve heat and light, like sitting by a fire or enjoying the warmth of the sun.

Integrating the Elements into Daily Life

Integrating the elements into daily life can enhance our spiritual practice and deepen our connection with the natural world. Here are some ways to work with each element:

Earth:

- Spend time in nature, gardening, hiking, or simply walking barefoot on the ground.

- Create a sacred space with stones, crystals, and plants to invite grounding energy.

- Practice mindfulness and grounding techniques to stay connected to the present moment.

Water:

- Visit bodies of water such as rivers, lakes, or the ocean to connect with water's fluid energy.

- Incorporate water into your rituals, such as cleansing baths or setting intentions by a stream.

- Allow your emotions to flow and embrace change with the adaptability of water.

Air:

- Spend time outdoors in open spaces, enjoying the breeze and the movement of the wind.

- Practice deep breathing exercises to connect with the air element and enhance mental clarity.

- Engage in creative activities like writing, painting, or singing to harness the inspiration of air.

Fire:

- Light candles or sit by a fire to connect with the transformative energy of fire.

- Embrace your passions and take bold actions towards your goals, fueled by fire's motivation.

- Practice rituals that involve light and heat, such as sunbathing or fire ceremonies.

Nature and the elements are not just physical forces but spiritual entities that influence our lives and our environment. By understanding and connecting with these elements, we can tap into their unique qualities and energies, enriching our spiritual practice and deepening our connection with the natural world. Whether through the grounding presence of earth, the fluid adaptability of water, the inspiring freedom of air, or the transformative power of fire, working with the elements offers a pathway to greater harmony, balance, and spiritual growth. Embracing the wisdom of the elements helps us to navigate our lives with clarity and purpose, fostering a deep sense of interconnectedness with all of creation.

Chapter 78

Guardians of the Earth

The element of earth is foundational, embodying stability, grounding, and nourishment. It represents the physical world and the material aspects of life, providing the foundation upon which everything else is built. Earth is associated with fertility, growth, and the cycles of nature, reflecting the rhythms of birth, death, and renewal.

In many spiritual traditions, the earth is revered as a nurturing mother, offering sustenance and support. Connected to the direction of the north, earth symbolizes solidity and endurance. Its energy is slow, steady, and grounding, helping to anchor us in the present moment and connect us deeply to the physical realm.

The element of earth also links closely to our body and senses, encouraging us to be fully present and experience life through touch, taste, and smell. By attuning to the earth's energy, we cultivate a deeper sense of stability, security, and well-being, which is essential for our overall balance and harmony.

Earth Elementals and Spirits

Earth elementals and spirits are believed to inhabit natural landscapes such as forests, mountains, and caves. These beings embody the essence of the earth, each with unique characteristics and roles that contribute to the health and vitality of the natural world.

Types of Earth Spirits

Gnomes: Gnomes are perhaps the most well-known earth elementals. Often depicted as small, humanoid beings who live underground, they tend to the roots of trees and plants. Gnomes are guardians of the earth's treasures, such as minerals and gemstones, and are known for their wisdom and practical knowledge.

Trolls: In Scandinavian folklore, trolls are earth spirits that inhabit caves, mountains, and forests. They are often depicted as large, rugged beings with a deep connection to the land. Trolls are seen as both protectors and tricksters, embodying the raw, untamed aspects of nature.

Dwarves: In various mythologies, dwarves are skilled craftsmen and miners who live underground. They are celebrated for their expertise in metalwork and their ability to uncover hidden treasures within the earth. Dwarves symbolize industriousness and the transformative power of the earth's resources.

Dryads: Dryads are tree spirits from Greek mythology associated with specific trees, particularly oaks. They are seen as the living essence of the tree, nurturing and protecting it. Dryads symbolize the deep bond between the earth and the flora it sustains.

Giants: In many mythologies, giants are earth spirits that embody the power and majesty of the natural world. They are often associated with mountains and large rock formations, representing the strength and endurance of the earth.

Their Roles and Characteristics

Earth spirits play various roles in folklore and spiritual traditions, acting as guardians, nurturers, and protectors of the natural world. They are deeply connected to the physical realm, ensuring the health and vitality of the land and its resources.

Gnomes, for example, are seen as custodians of the earth's treasures, protecting the minerals and gemstones hidden underground. Their wisdom and practical skills are valued in many traditions, and they are often called upon for guidance in matters related to the earth and material wealth.

Trolls and giants, with their formidable presence, embody the raw power of the earth. They are protectors of the land, ensuring that it remains wild and untamed. While they can be intimidating, their role is to maintain the balance and integrity of the natural world.

Dryads and other plant spirits nurture the flora of the earth, fostering growth and vitality. They are deeply connected to the cycles of nature, symbolizing the interconnectedness of all life.

Connecting with Earth Spirits: Earth-Based Rituals and Practices

Connecting with earth spirits can be a grounding and enriching experience, fostering a deeper relationship with the natural world. Here are some earth-based rituals and practices to attune to the energy of these beings and invite their presence into your life:

Spending Time in Nature: One of the simplest and most powerful ways to connect with earth spirits is to spend time in natural landscapes. Walk barefoot on the earth, feeling the soil and grass beneath your feet. Sit quietly against a tree or on a rock, focusing on your breath and the sensations of the earth. Allow yourself to enter a meditative state, attuning to the grounding energy of the earth.

Creating a Sacred Space: Incorporate elements of the earth into your meditation or sacred space. Use stones, crystals, and plants as focal points for grounding and connection. These elements serve as physical representations of the earth's energy, helping to anchor your intentions and foster a deeper connection with earth spirits.

Grounding Meditation: Perform a grounding meditation by visualizing roots extending from your body into the earth, anchoring you firmly to the ground. Imagine drawing up the earth's energy through these roots, filling your body with a sense of stability and strength. This practice helps you feel more centered and connected to the physical realm.

Prayer for Connecting with Earth Spirits: "Guardians of the Earth, I honor your presence and the wisdom you hold. Help me connect deeply with the earth and its nurturing energy. Guide me to walk in harmony with nature and to appreciate the gifts of the physical world. Thank you for your protection and guidance."

Understanding Earth Symbolism

The element of earth holds symbolism in many spiritual traditions, representing stability, grounding, and nourishment. By understanding this symbolism, we can deepen our connection with earth spirits and the element of earth itself.

Stability: Earth's association with stability reflects its solid and enduring nature. Just as the earth provides a foundation for all life, grounding us in the physical realm, earth spirits teach us to cultivate stability and security in our own lives. They remind us of the importance of being present and fully experiencing the physical world.

Nurturing: The nurturing aspect of the earth is linked to its role in sustaining life. The earth provides food, shelter, and resources, supporting all living beings. Earth spirits, as guardians and nurturers, embody this nurturing energy, encouraging us to care for ourselves and the environment.

Growth and Renewal: Earth symbolizes growth and renewal. Just as plants grow and thrive in the soil, we too, can cultivate our own growth and transformation. Earth spirits guide us in understanding the cycles of nature, helping us to align with these rhythms and embrace change.

In my own journey, I've found that earth spirits often communicate through sensations of grounding and stability. Their presence is calming and reassuring, helping me to feel more connected to the physical world. By honoring and connecting with these spirits, I've gained a deeper appreciation for the earth and its many gifts.

Historical Significance of Earth Spirits

Gnomes: Gnomes have been a part of European folklore for centuries, particularly in Germanic and Scandinavian traditions. They are believed to dwell underground, guarding the earth's treasures and working to maintain the health of the soil. Their presence in tales and myths emphasizes their role as protectors of the natural world and custodians of hidden knowledge.

Trolls: Trolls feature prominently in Norse mythology and Scandinavian folklore. They are often depicted as formidable beings with a strong connection to the earth, living in caves and mountains. Trolls embody the untamed aspects of nature and are frequently portrayed as both protectors and challenges to humanity, reflecting the complex relationship between people and the natural world.

Dwarves: Dwarves appear in many mythologies, including Norse and Germanic traditions. Known for their craftsmanship and mining skills, dwarves are often associated with the earth's hidden riches and the transformative power of its resources. Their expertise in working with metals and stones highlights the importance of industry and the creative potential of the earth.

Dryads: Dryads, or tree nymphs, originate from Greek mythology. These spirits are intimately connected to individual trees, particularly oaks. They are seen as guardians of the forests, nurturing and protecting their trees. Dryads symbolize the deep bond between the earth and plant life, representing the interconnectedness and mutual support within the natural world.

Giants: Giants are a staple in various mythological traditions, from the Jotunn in Norse mythology to the Titans in Greek myths. These colossal beings are often linked to the earth and its mighty landscapes, such as mountains and rock formations. Giants represent the immense power and endurance of the earth, standing as symbols of strength and stability. They are seen in cultures throughout the world, from Annunaki in Sumerian and Babylonian myths to the Sarnake people in the Navajo stories.

Embracing Earth Spirits on Your Journey

The guardians of the earth element are powerful and nurturing beings that embody the essence of the earth. Through rituals, practices, and an understanding of earth symbolism, we can connect with these spirits and invite their grounding and nurturing energy into our lives. Whether through personal experiences or the rich tapestry of myths and legends, earth spirits continue to inspire and guide us, reminding us of the stability and nourishment that lies within the element of earth.

By embracing the teachings and presence of earth spirits, we can cultivate a deeper connection with the natural world and foster a greater sense of stability, security, and well-being in our lives. As you explore these connections, allow yourself to be open to the wisdom and guidance that these ancient and powerful beings have to offer.

Chapter 79

Guardians of the Water

Water is one of the fundamental elements in many spiritual and philosophical traditions, embodying fluidity, emotion, intuition, and transformation. It is a vital life force, essential for all living beings, and it holds a deep, mystical connection to the subconscious and the soul.

In various cultures, water is seen as a purifying and healing element, often used in rituals to cleanse and renew. The flowing nature of water symbolizes the continuous movement and change inherent in life. Its ability to shape landscapes, whether through gentle streams or powerful floods, reflects the transformative power of emotions and the subconscious mind.

The element of water is associated with the west in many traditions and is connected to the moon, which influences tides and governs the cycles of emotion and intuition. Water's depth and mystery make it a powerful symbol for exploring the hidden aspects of ourselves and the world around us.

Water Elementals and Spirits

Water elementals and spirits are believed to inhabit bodies of water, from oceans and rivers to lakes and springs. These beings are thought to embody the essence of water, each type with its unique characteristics and roles. They play crucial roles in maintaining the balance and vitality of the natural world and offer profound spiritual insights.

Types of Water Spirits

Undines: Undines are water elementals that personify the spirit of fresh water. They are often depicted as beautiful, graceful beings resembling humans who live in rivers, streams, and ponds. Undines are known for their nurturing and healing qualities, representing purity and emotional depth. They are believed to govern the flow and quality of freshwater and assist in emotional healing and clarity.

Naiads: Naiads are freshwater nymphs from Greek mythology, associated with springs, wells, and brooks. They are guardians of these water sources, ensuring their purity and vitality. Naiads are often portrayed as youthful and enchanting, with an intimate connection to the life-giving properties of water. They inspire creativity and help individuals connect with the natural cycles of life.

Nereids: In Greek mythology, Nereids are sea nymphs, daughters of the sea god Nereus. They inhabit the Mediterranean Sea and are known to assist sailors in distress. Nereids symbolize the nurturing and protective aspects of the ocean, guiding those who venture into the depths and offering solace and support during turbulent times.

Merrows: In Irish folklore, merrows are mermaid-like beings who live in the sea. They are said to be able to come ashore and take human form, often interacting with humans. Merrows are believed to bring messages from the ocean depths and have a dual nature of both charm and danger. They bridge the gap between the human world and the mysteries of the sea.

Rusalka: In Slavic mythology, rusalki are water nymphs associated with rivers and lakes. They are often depicted as beautiful but sometimes dangerous, luring young men to their watery realms. Rusalki embody the mysterious and sometimes perilous nature of water, reminding us of the need to respect and understand the powerful forces of nature.

Their Roles and Characteristics

Water spirits play various roles in folklore and spiritual traditions.

They are often seen as guardians and protectors of their aquatic realms, maintaining the balance and health of water bodies. They are also associated with emotional healing, intuition, and transformation.

Nurturing and Healing: The nurturing aspect of water spirits is reflected in their ability to heal and purify. They assist in emotional cleansing, helping individuals release negative emotions and find inner peace. Their presence is calming and soothing, guiding us to embrace our emotions and process our experiences in a healthy way.

Intuitive Guidance: Water spirits are known for their intuitive nature. They help us access the depths of our subconscious, encouraging us to trust our instincts and explore hidden aspects of ourselves. Their guidance often comes through dreams and intuitive insights, leading us to astonishing realizations and understanding.

Transformative Power: Water spirits embody the transformative power of water. Just as water can change form—from liquid to solid to vapor—these spirits facilitate personal and spiritual transformation. They help us navigate the ebb and flow of life, supporting us through periods of change and growth.

Connecting with Water Spirits

Water Rituals and Practices

Connecting with water spirits can be a deeply enriching experience, fostering a sense of harmony and insight. Water rituals and practices are effective ways to attune to the energy of these beings and invite their presence into your life.

Spending Time Near Water: One simple yet powerful ritual involves spending time near a natural body of water. Whether it's a river, lake, or ocean, immersing yourself in the sights, sounds, and sensations of water can help you attune to its spirit. Sitting quietly by the water, I focus on my breath and the rhythmic flow of the waves or current, allowing myself to enter a meditative state. This practice connects me with the soothing and transformative energy of water.

Water Offering: Another practice is to perform a water offering. Collect pure, natural water and pour it as an offering to the water spirits, expressing gratitude and asking for their guidance and protection. This act of giving honors the spirits and establishes a reciprocal relationship. It's a way to show respect for the life-giving properties of water and the spirits that dwell within it.

Creating a Sacred Space with Water Elements: Incorporating water elements into your meditation space can also invite water spirits. I often include fountains, bowls of water, or even images of water bodies in my sacred space. These elements serve as focal points for connecting with the energy of water, helping to foster a serene and reflective environment.

Water Meditation: Performing a water meditation is another effective way to connect with water spirits. Imagine yourself floating in a gentle stream or being enveloped by the waves of the ocean. Visualize the water cleansing and purifying your energy, washing away stress and negativity. This practice helps to align your energy with the fluid and nurturing qualities of water.

Prayer for Connecting with Water Spirits: "Guardians of the Water, I honor your presence and the wisdom you hold. Help me to connect deeply with the flow and purity of the water element. Guide me to navigate my emotions and intuition with grace and understanding. Thank you for your nurturing and transformative energy."

Understanding Water Symbolism

Water holds symbolism in many spiritual traditions, representing emotions, intuition, and the subconscious. By understanding this symbolism, we can deepen our connection with water spirits and the element of water itself.

Emotional Fluidity: Water's association with emotions reflects its fluid and ever-changing nature. Just as water can be calm or turbulent, our emotions can vary widely. Water spirits teach us to navigate these emotional currents with grace and understanding, encouraging us to embrace our feelings rather than suppress them. They remind us that our emotions are a vital part of our human experience.

Intuitive Depth: The intuitive aspect of water is linked to its depth and mystery. Like the hidden depths of the ocean, our intuition often lies beneath the surface of conscious awareness. Water spirits guide us in accessing this inner wisdom, helping us to trust our instincts and follow our inner guidance. They encourage us to explore the unknown and uncover the truths hidden within us.

Purification and Renewal: Water symbolizes purification and renewal. Just as water cleanses the body, it can also cleanse the spirit. Engaging in water rituals and connecting with water spirits can help release emotional and energetic blockages, leading to a sense of renewal and clarity. Water spirits assist us in letting go of the past and embracing new beginnings.

In my own journey, I've found that water spirits often communicate through dreams and intuitive insights. Their subtle yet profound messages guide me to explore the depths of my emotions and inner world. By honoring and connecting with these spirits, I've gained a deeper understanding of myself and the transformative power of water.

Historical Significance of Water Spirits

Water spirits have held significant roles in various cultures throughout history, embodying the essence of water and its profound influence on life and spirituality.

Undines: Undines are deeply rooted in Western esoteric traditions, particularly within Paracelsian alchemy, where they are described as elemental beings of water. They are seen as guardians of freshwater bodies and are often invoked in magical practices for their healing and purifying properties. Their historical presence underscores their role in maintaining the balance and vitality of freshwater ecosystems.

Naiads: Naiads are prominent figures in Greek mythology, where they are revered as the protectors of freshwater sources. They were believed to inhabit springs, wells, and brooks, playing a crucial role in ensuring the purity and life-giving properties of these waters. Naiads were often honored in local rituals and considered essential to the prosperity and health of communities.

Nereids: The Nereids, as sea nymphs of Greek mythology, are known for their nurturing and protective roles in the Mediterranean Sea. They were worshipped by sailors and coastal communities, who believed the Nereids could provide safe passage and rescue from sea dangers. Their historical significance lies in their association with the ocean's life-sustaining and protective qualities.

Merrows: In Irish folklore, merrows are magical beings that embody the allure and mystery of the sea. They are often depicted as benevolent, bringing messages from the ocean's depths, but also possessing a dual nature that can be both charming and perilous. Merrows have been part of Ireland's rich maritime culture, symbolizing the deep connection between the Irish people and the sea.

Rusalka: Rusalki are water spirits from Slavic mythology, associated with rivers and lakes. They are often depicted as beautiful but sometimes dangerous, embodying the enchantment and potential peril of water. Historically, rusalki have been part of Slavic folklore and are believed to influence the fertility of the land and the health of crops, reflecting the integral role of water in sustaining life.

Embracing Water Spirits on Your Journey

The guardians of the water element are powerful and nurturing beings that embody the essence of water. Through rituals, practices, and an understanding of water symbolism, we can connect with these spirits and invite their healing and transformative energy into our lives. Whether through personal experiences or the rich tapestry of myths and legends, water spirits continue to inspire and guide us, reminding us of the wisdom and mystery that lies within the element of water.

By embracing the teachings and presence of water spirits, we can cultivate a deeper connection with the element of water and foster a greater sense of emotional balance, intuitive insight, and spiritual renewal. As you explore these connections, allow yourself to be open to the wisdom and guidance that these ancient and powerful beings have to offer.

Alex McCann Johnson

Chapter 80

Guardians of the Air

The element of air is associated with the mind, intellect, communication, and the breath of life. It represents freedom, movement, and the invisible forces that connect all things. Air is essential for life, carrying oxygen to our lungs and facilitating the flow of energy and ideas.

In many spiritual traditions, air is seen as a messenger, conveying thoughts, prayers, and intentions across great distances. It is connected to the east, symbolizing new beginnings, clarity, and vision. The energy of air is light, expansive, and ever-changing, reflecting the qualities of adaptability and inspiration.

Air's association with the mind and intellect encourages us to think clearly, communicate effectively, and remain open to new ideas and perspectives. By tuning into the element of air, we can cultivate a sense of mental clarity, freedom, and connection.

Air Elementals and Spirits

Air elementals and spirits are believed to inhabit the skies, winds, and breezes, embodying the essence of air. These beings are thought to be ethereal and elusive, each type with its unique characteristics and roles.

Types of Air Spirits

Sylphs: Sylphs are air elementals that personify the spirit of the air. They are often depicted as graceful, winged beings who move effortlessly through the sky. Sylphs are known for their association with clarity of thought, inspiration, and the flow of ideas. They are considered the guardians of intellectual pursuits and creativity, often assisting in the mental processes that lead to insight and innovation.

Sprites: Sprites are small, playful spirits often seen as guardians of the air. They are depicted as light, fluttering beings that resemble fairies or tiny glowing orbs. Sprites are known for their joyfulness and quick movements, symbolizing the playful and dynamic nature of the air. They bring light-heartedness and spontaneity, encouraging us to embrace the lighter side of life.

Zephyrs: In Greek mythology, Zephyrus is the god of the west wind, bringing gentle and beneficial breezes. Zephyrs are spirits associated with gentle winds and breezes, symbolizing calmness, peace, and subtle influences. They are the bringers of mild weather and are often invoked to foster peace and tranquility in our surroundings.

Aerials: Aerials are spirits that inhabit the upper atmosphere, often associated with storms and powerful winds. They are seen as both majestic and formidable, embodying the raw power of the air element. Aerials can represent the chaotic and transformative forces of nature, reminding us of the power of change and the necessity of adaptability in our lives.

Their Roles and Characteristics

Air spirits play various roles in folklore and spiritual traditions, acting as messengers, inspirers, and guides. They are deeply connected to the mental and communicative aspects of life, ensuring the flow of ideas and energy.

Inspiration and Clarity: Sylphs, for example, are seen as beings of inspiration and clarity. Their presence is associated with mental sharpness and the ability to think clearly and creatively. They are often called upon for guidance in intellectual pursuits and creative endeavors, helping us to unlock new ideas and solutions.

Joy and Playfulness: Sprites, with their playful nature, bring joy and lightness to the air. They symbolize the importance of playfulness and spontaneity, reminding us to embrace the lighter side of life and the freedom of expression. Sprites encourage us to find joy in our daily lives and to remain open to new experiences.

Calmness and Peace: Zephyrs, associated with gentle breezes, bring calmness and peace. They are seen as subtle influencers, gently guiding thoughts and emotions toward harmony and balance. Zephyrs help us to remain calm and centered, even in the midst of life's challenges.

The Power of Change: Aerials, on the other hand, embody the power and majesty of the air element. They are associated with storms and strong winds, symbolizing the transformative and sometimes chaotic forces of the air. Their role is to remind us of the power of change and the importance of adaptability. Aerials teach us to embrace the storms of life and to harness their energy for growth and transformation.

Connecting with Air Spirits

Air-Based Rituals and Practices

Connecting with air spirits can be a liberating and enlightening experience, fostering a deeper relationship with the mental and communicative aspects of life. Air-based rituals and practices are effective ways to attune to the energy of these beings and invite their presence into your life.

Spending Time in Open, Airy Spaces: One simple yet powerful ritual involves spending time in open, airy spaces such as hilltops, meadows, or by the sea. Feeling the wind on your skin, breathing deeply, and observing the movement of the air can help you attune to its energy. Standing with your arms outstretched, I focus on the sensations of the wind, allowing myself to feel its presence and invite the spirits of the air to connect with me.

Creating a Sacred Space with Air Elements: Another practice is to create a sacred space with elements of air. I could incorporate feathers, wind chimes, and incense into my meditation space, using them as focal points for connection and inspiration. These elements serve as physical representations of the air's energy, helping to enhance my intentions and foster a deeper connection with air spirits.

Breathing Meditation: Performing a breathing meditation is another effective way to connect with air spirits. During this meditation, I focus on my breath, imagining it as a flow of air moving in and out of my body. I visualize each breath cleansing and energizing me, connecting me to the element of air and the spirits that inhabit it. This practice helps me to feel more mentally clear and connected to the flow of ideas and inspiration.

Prayer for Connecting with Air Spirits: "Guardians of the Air, I honor your presence and the wisdom you hold. Help me to connect deeply with the clarity and inspiration of the air element. Guide me to think clearly, communicate effectively, and embrace the flow of ideas. Thank you for your uplifting and enlightening energy."

Understanding Air Symbolism

The element of air holds symbolism in many spiritual traditions, representing the mind, intellect, communication, and freedom. By understanding this symbolism, we can deepen our connection with air spirits and the element of air itself.

Clarity of Thought and Communication: Air's association with the mind and intellect reflects its role in clarity of thought and communication. Just as air carries sounds and ideas, air spirits teach us to cultivate clear and effective communication, both with ourselves and with others. They remind us of the importance of expressing our thoughts and ideas with honesty and clarity.

Freedom and Expansiveness: The freedom and expansiveness of air symbolize the limitless potential of the mind and spirit. Air spirits encourage us to embrace new perspectives, think creatively, and remain open to the flow of inspiration. They remind us that, like the wind, we can move freely and adapt to changing circumstances.

Movement and Change: Air also symbolizes movement and change. Just as air is constantly in motion, bringing fresh energy and new beginnings, air spirits guide us in embracing change and transformation. They teach us to let go of stagnation and remain flexible, allowing us to flow with the currents of life.

In my own journey, I've found that air spirits often communicate through sudden insights and flashes of inspiration. Their presence is invigorating and uplifting, helping me to feel more connected to the flow of ideas and the breath of life. By honoring and connecting with these spirits, I've gained a deeper appreciation for the element of air and its many gifts.

Historical Significance of Air Spirits

Air spirits have held significant roles in various cultures throughout history, embodying the essence of air and its influence on life and spirituality.

Sylphs: Sylphs are deeply rooted in Western esoteric traditions, particularly within Paracelsian alchemy, where they are described as elemental beings of air. They are seen as the guardians of the skies and are often invoked for their ability to bring clarity and insight. Sylphs' historical significance highlights their role in inspiring intellectual pursuits and creative endeavors.

Sprites: Sprites, with their joyful and playful nature, are commonly found in European folklore. They are seen as protectors of the air, often interacting with humans in ways that bring delight and wonder. Historically, sprites have been associated with the playful aspects of nature and the importance of maintaining a light-hearted approach to life.

Zephyrs: Zephyrs, as the gentle west wind, have been celebrated in Greek mythology and art for their calming and beneficial influence. They were believed to bring mild weather and favorable conditions for growth. The historical significance of Zephyrs emphasizes the importance of gentle guidance and the positive impact of subtle influences.

Aerials: Aerials, as spirits of the upper atmosphere, are often depicted in myths and legends as powerful beings associated with storms and strong winds. They symbolize the raw power and majesty of the air, reminding us of the importance of respecting nature's forces. Historically, aerials have been invoked to harness the energy of storms and to navigate the transformative power of change.

Embracing Air Spirits on Your Journey

The guardians of the air element are powerful and inspiring beings that embody the essence of air. Through rituals, practices, and an understanding of air symbolism, we can connect with these spirits and invite their clarity and inspiration into our lives. Whether through personal experiences or the rich tapestry of myths and legends, air spirits continue to inspire and guide us, reminding us of the clarity and freedom that lies within the element of air.

By embracing the teachings and presence of air spirits, we can cultivate a deeper connection with the element of air and foster a greater sense of mental clarity, freedom, and spiritual insight. As you explore these connections, allow yourself to be open to the wisdom and guidance that these ancient and powerful beings have to offer.

Chapter 81
Guardians of the Fire

The element of fire is dynamic and transformative, representing energy, passion, and willpower. Fire embodies both creation and destruction, symbolizing the cycle of birth, death, and renewal. It is associated with warmth, light, and the life-giving energy of the sun, as well as the fierce, consuming power of flames.

In many spiritual traditions, fire is seen as a purifying force capable of burning away impurities and facilitating transformation. It is connected to the south, symbolizing vitality, courage, and action. The energy of fire is intense and radiant, driving creativity, ambition, and personal growth.

Fire's association with the heart and spirit encourages us to tap into our inner passion and drive. By tuning into the element of fire, we can cultivate a sense of empowerment, motivation, and the courage to pursue our goals.

Fire Elementals and Spirits

Fire elementals and spirits are believed to inhabit flames, heat, and light, embodying the essence of fire. These beings are thought to be powerful and radiant, each type with its unique characteristics and roles.

Types of Fire Spirits

Salamanders: Salamanders are the most well-known fire elementals. They are often depicted as lizard-like creatures that thrive in flames.

Salamanders are known for their association with transformation and renewal, symbolizing the purifying and life-giving aspects of fire. Their presence is said to bring warmth and inspire action, helping us harness our inner fire to achieve our goals.

Phoenix: In many mythologies, the phoenix is a legendary bird that cyclically regenerates or is reborn from its ashes. The phoenix embodies the themes of resurrection, immortality, and the transformative power of fire. This majestic creature inspires us to embrace change and renewal, showing that from the ashes of destruction can arise new life and possibilities.

Djinn: In Middle Eastern folklore, djinn (or genies) are spirits made of smokeless fire. They are often depicted as powerful beings capable of great feats and transformations. Djinn symbolizes the unpredictable and formidable nature of fire, reminding us of its dual potential to both create and destroy. They are seen as protectors and guides, helping to illuminate our paths and ignite our passions.

Will-o'-the-Wisp: These ghostly lights seen by travelers at night, especially over bogs, swamps, or marshes, are often associated with mischievous spirits that lead people astray. Will-o'-the-Wisps represent the mysterious and elusive nature of fire, guiding us through the darkness but also challenging us to stay true to our path and intentions.

Their Roles and Characteristics

Fire spirits play various roles in folklore and spiritual traditions, acting as agents of transformation, inspiration, and protection. They are deeply connected to the energizing and purifying aspects of life.

Purifying Flames: Salamanders, for example, are seen as beings of transformation and renewal. Their presence is associated with the purifying power of fire, burning away the old to make way for the new. They are often called upon for guidance in matters of personal growth and transformation, helping us to embrace change and rise from our own ashes.

Cleansing and Renewal: The phoenix, with its cycle of death and rebirth, symbolizes the power of renewal and immortality. Its story inspires us to embrace change and trust in the process of transformation, knowing that new beginnings follow endings. The phoenix teaches us resilience and the ability to regenerate, no matter how challenging the circumstances.

Unpredictable and Creative: Djinn, embodying the raw power of fire, are both revered and feared for its formidable abilities. They symbolize the unpredictable and sometimes dangerous nature of fire, reminding us of its potential for both creation and destruction. Djinn are powerful allies in manifesting our desires and protecting us from negative influences.

The Elusive Guiding Light: Will-o'-the-Wisps, with their mysterious and elusive nature, represent the guiding light of the fire. They remind us of the importance of staying true to our path and being cautious of distractions that might lead us astray. These spirits challenge us to discern the true light of guidance from the deceptive glimmers that could mislead us.

Connecting with Fire Spirits

Fire-Based Rituals and Practices

Connecting with fire spirits can be a powerful and transformative experience, fostering a deeper relationship with the energizing and purifying aspects of life. Fire-based rituals and practices are effective ways to attune to the energy of these beings and invite their presence into your life.

Spending Time Around Fire: One simple yet powerful ritual involves spending time around a fire, such as a bonfire, campfire, or even a lit candle. Observing the flames, feeling their warmth, and listening to the crackling sounds can help you attune to the energy of fire. Sitting quietly by the fire, I focus on the movement and light of the flames, allowing myself to enter a meditative state and invite the spirits of fire to connect with me.

Fire Offering: Another practice is to perform a fire offering. I write down my intentions, desires, or things I wish to release on a piece of paper and then burn it in the fire. This act symbolizes transformation and renewal, using the fire's energy to manifest or let go of what is written. As I watch the paper burn, I visualize the fire spirits assisting in this process, guiding my intentions to fruition or helping me release what no longer serves me.

Creating a Sacred Space with Fire Elements: Creating a sacred space with fire elements can also invite fire spirits. I often incorporate candles, incense, and images of flames into my meditation space, using them as focal points for connection and transformation. These elements are physical representations of the fire's energy, helping amplify my intentions and foster a deeper connection with fire spirits.

Prayer for Connecting with Fire Spirits: "Guardians of the Fire, I honor your presence and the power you hold. Help me to connect deeply with the transformative and purifying energy of the fire element. Guide me to embrace change, ignite my passions, and burn away all that no longer serves me. Thank you for your invigorating and empowering energy."

Understanding Fire Symbolism

The element of fire holds symbolism in many spiritual traditions, representing energy, passion, transformation, and purification. By understanding this symbolism, we can deepen our connection with fire spirits and the element of fire itself.

Energy and Passion: Fire's association with energy and passion reflects its dynamic and radiant nature. Just as fire provides warmth and light, fire spirits teach us to cultivate our inner energy and passion. They remind us of the importance of pursuing our goals with determination and enthusiasm, fueling our actions with the fire of our spirit.

Transformation and Renewal: The transformative aspect of fire is linked to its ability to burn away the old and make way for the new. Fire spirits guide us in embracing change and transformation, helping us to let go of what no longer serves us and to trust in the process of renewal. They inspire us to rise from the ashes of our past and forge a new path with courage and conviction.

Purification and Clarity: Fire also symbolizes purification and clarity. Just as fire can cleanse and purify, it can also bring clarity and insight. Fire spirits encourage us to confront our fears and obstacles, using their purifying energy to gain a deeper understanding of ourselves and our path. They help us to see clearly through the smoke and find the light within.

In my own journey, I've found that fire spirits often communicate through feelings of warmth and inspiration. Their presence is invigorating and empowering, helping me to feel more connected to my inner strength and passion. By honoring and connecting with these spirits, I've gained a deeper appreciation for the element of fire and its many gifts.

Historical Significance of Fire Spirits

Fire spirits have held significant roles in various cultures throughout history, embodying the essence of fire and its profound influence on life and spirituality.

Salamanders: In Western esoteric traditions, particularly within alchemy, salamanders are described as elemental beings of fire. They are seen as the guardians of the flames and are often invoked for their ability to bring transformation and renewal. Salamanders' historical significance highlights their role in the purifying and life-giving aspects of fire.

Phoenix: The phoenix is a universal symbol of rebirth and renewal, found in many cultures, including ancient Egyptian, Greek, and Chinese mythology. Its ability to rise from its own ashes symbolizes the cycle of death and rebirth, making it a powerful emblem of immortality and transformation. The phoenix's historical significance underscores its role as a guide through periods of change and regeneration.

Djinn: In Middle Eastern folklore, djinn are spirits of fire with immense power and influence. They are both revered and feared for their ability to shape reality and transform situations. Historically, djinn have been seen as intermediaries between the human and the divine, embodying the dual nature of fire as both a creative and destructive force.

Will-o'-the-Wisp: In European folklore, Will-o'-the-Wisps are mysterious lights that appear at night, often leading travelers astray. These spirits are linked to the enigmatic and unpredictable nature of fire. Their historical presence highlights the allure and danger of following the unknown, teaching us the importance of discernment and staying true to our path.

Embracing Fire Spirits on Your Journey

The guardians of the fire element are powerful and transformative beings that embody the essence of fire. Through rituals, practices, and an understanding of fire symbolism, we can connect with these spirits and invite their energizing and purifying energy into our lives. Whether through personal experiences or the rich tapestry of myths and legends, fire spirits continue to inspire and guide us, reminding us of the profound energy and transformation that lies within the element of fire.

By embracing the teachings and presence of fire spirits, we can cultivate a deeper connection with the element of fire and foster a greater sense of empowerment, motivation, and spiritual growth. As you explore these connections, allow yourself to be open to the wisdom and guidance that these ancient and powerful beings have to offer.

Chapter 82

Plant Spirits

From an early age, I was drawn to the world of plants, enchanted by their beauty and the sense of calm they bring. You'll find I even have plants scattered all over my home now. Plants have been humanity's companions since the dawn of time, providing us with food, shelter, medicine, and even spiritual insight. In the realm of spirituality, plant spirits are considered powerful guides that offer healing, wisdom, and a connection to the natural world.

When I first delved into shamanism, I learned about the profound connection between plants and the spirit world. Although I did not partake in sacred plant medicine ceremonies, my teacher emphasized that we do not need to rely solely on these plants to connect with their spirit. This teaching resonated with me. I've come to understand that plant spirits can guide us in countless ways, whether through their presence in our environment, their use in herbal remedies, or their spiritual teachings.

Understanding Plant Spirits: What They Are and Their Role

Plant spirits are the ethereal essence of the plants we see around us. They embody the life force and unique characteristics of each plant species, offering their gifts to those who seek their wisdom and healing. In various spiritual traditions, plants are seen not just as physical entities but as conscious beings with their own spirits and energies.

Each plant has its own spirit, which can be connected with and honored. Some plants are known for their healing properties, while others are revered for their ability to facilitate spiritual journeys or protect against negative energies. By building a relationship with these spirits, we can access a wealth of knowledge and support.

In my experience, connecting with plant spirits has been a journey of discovering the subtle yet profound energies that plants hold. Whether it's the calming presence of lavender or the protective aura of sage, each plant spirit has a unique way of interacting with us and enhancing our lives.

Roles and Responsibilities: How Plant Spirits Assist Us

Plant spirits play a multifaceted role in our lives, contributing to our physical, emotional, and spiritual well-being. Here are some of the ways they assist us:

Healing: Many plants have medicinal properties that have been used for centuries to treat various ailments. Plant spirits amplify these healing qualities, offering not just physical relief but also emotional and spiritual healing. For example, the spirit of chamomile is known for its soothing and calming effects, helping to alleviate anxiety and promote relaxation.

Guidance: Plant spirits often serve as guides, offering wisdom and insights during meditation, dreams, or rituals. They can help us understand the deeper aspects of our lives and provide clarity on our spiritual path. The spirit of mugwort, for example, is known to enhance intuition and facilitate vivid dreams, guiding us through the realms of the subconscious.

Protection: Some plants are revered for their protective qualities, creating a shield against negative energies and influences. The spirit of rosemary, traditionally used for protection and purification, can help cleanse our space and energy, keeping us safe from harm.

Transformation: Certain plants are associated with transformation and spiritual growth, aiding us in shedding old patterns and embracing new beginnings. The spirit of basil, known for its purifying and rejuvenating properties, can support us in times of change and renewal.

Connection: Plant spirits deepen our connection to nature and the earth, reminding us of our interdependence with the natural world. They help us cultivate a sense of grounding and rootedness, enhancing our overall sense of well-being. With its strong and enduring presence, the spirit of oak symbolizes stability and strength, fostering a deep connection to the earth.

In my own practice, I have found that plant spirits often offer subtle yet powerful guidance. Whether it's through the aroma of essential oils, the act of drinking herbal tea, or simply spending time in nature, the presence of plant spirits enriches my spiritual journey and supports my overall health and well-being.

How to Connect with Plant Spirits: Techniques and Tips

Connecting with plant spirits can be a deeply enriching experience, opening us up to the wisdom and healing of the natural world. Here are some techniques and tips that have helped me build a strong connection with plant spirits:

Set Clear Intentions: Begin by setting a clear intention to connect with a specific plant spirit or the plant spirits in general. You can express this intention through a simple prayer or affirmation. For example, you might say, "I invite the spirit of lavender to guide and heal me," or "I seek to connect with the wisdom of the plant kingdom."

Spend Time in Nature: Immersing yourself in nature is one of the most effective ways to connect with plant spirits. Spend time in gardens, forests, or any natural setting where plants thrive. Observe their shapes, colors, and movements, and pay attention to any feelings or insights that arise. Sit quietly by a tree or in a garden, and open yourself to the presence of the plant spirits around you.

Meditate with Plants: Meditation can be a powerful tool for connecting with plant spirits. Sit quietly with a plant or a piece of its foliage, such as a leaf or flower. Focus on your breath and the plant's presence, allowing its energy to merge with yours. Visualize the plant's spirit and ask for its guidance or healing. Be open to any messages or sensations that come through.

Use Plant Medicine: Herbal remedies, essential oils, and flower essences are all ways to work with plant spirits on a physical level. Choose plants that resonate with your needs and intentions, and incorporate them into your daily routine. When using these remedies, take a moment to acknowledge and honor the plant spirit, inviting its healing and support.

Create a Sacred Space: Dedicate a space in your home for connecting with plant spirits. Include plants, flowers, or herbal arrangements that you feel drawn to. Use this space for meditation, reflection, or ritual work, and invite the plant spirits to join you in this sacred environment.

Ask for Guidance: Don't hesitate to ask the plant spirits for guidance or support. Whether you're seeking healing, clarity, or inspiration, plant spirits are always willing to assist. Speak to them as you would to a wise friend, and trust in their wisdom and generosity.

Offer Gratitude: Regularly express gratitude to the plant spirits for their presence and support. Thank them for their healing, guidance, and the beauty they bring into your life. This practice of gratitude helps to strengthen your connection and invites more blessings from the plant kingdom.

Prayer for Connecting with Plant Spirits: "Spirit of the plants, I honor your presence and the gifts you bring. Help me to connect deeply with your wisdom and healing energy. Guide me to the plants that can support my journey and teach me to listen to your subtle messages. Thank you for your nurturing and transformative power."

Historical Significance of Plant Spirits

Plant spirits have played a significant role in human culture and spirituality for millennia. Across various traditions, they have been revered as powerful allies in healing, protection, and spiritual growth.

Guided by Spirits

In many indigenous cultures, plants are seen as sacred beings with their own spirits and consciousness. Shamans and healers often communicate with plant spirits to gain knowledge and perform healing rituals. For example, in the Amazonian tradition, the plant spirit of Ayahuasca is considered a powerful teacher and healer, guiding individuals on profound spiritual journeys.

The ancient Egyptians held plants in high regard, using them in medicine, magic, and rituals. They believed that certain plants, such as the lotus and papyrus, were imbued with divine energy. The lotus, in particular, was a symbol of creation and rebirth, representing the journey of the soul.

Traditional Chinese Medicine (TCM) is deeply connected to the wisdom of plant spirits. Chinese herbalism uses a wide variety of plants to restore balance and harmony within the body. Each plant is believed to carry a unique energetic signature that can influence the body's qi (vital energy) and overall health.

During the Middle Ages, European herbalists and alchemists revered plant spirits for their healing and magical properties. Plants like mandrake, mistletoe, and sage were believed to have powerful spiritual energies that could protect, heal, and transform. Herbalism was a common practice among healers and wise women who often communicated with plant spirits to enhance their remedies and potions.

In Hinduism, plants are seen as manifestations of the divine, each with its own spiritual significance. The Tulsi plant, for example, is considered sacred and is worshiped as a goddess. In Ayurveda, the ancient Indian system of medicine, plant-based treatments are used to balance the body's doshas and promote holistic health.

Embracing Plant Spirits on Your Journey

Plant spirits are powerful and nurturing allies that offer healing, wisdom, and a deep connection to the natural world. By building a relationship with these spirits, we can tap into their energy and support, enhancing our physical, emotional, and spiritual well-being.

Whether through personal experiences or the rich traditions of various cultures, plant spirits continue to inspire and guide us. By honoring their presence and inviting their energy into our lives, we can cultivate a deeper appreciation for the natural world and the many gifts it provides.

As you explore your connection with plant spirits, allow yourself to be open to their wisdom and healing. Embrace their guidance and let their nurturing energy support you on your journey of growth and transformation.

Chapter 83

Tree Spirits

From a young age, I've always been enchanted by trees. Perhaps growing up in North Dakota where there are not very many trees has influenced my love for them. Their towering presence and serene energy have a way of grounding and comforting me. Trees are not just majestic elements of the landscape; they are ancient beings that have witnessed the passage of time and hold a deep well of wisdom. In many spiritual traditions, trees are seen as powerful spirits that connect the heavens and the earth, offering guidance, protection, and a sense of stability.

While studying various spiritual paths, I came to understand the significance of tree spirits. These spirits embody the essence of the trees they inhabit, each with unique characteristics and gifts to share. Connecting with tree spirits has been a transformative experience, allowing me to tap into their deep-rooted wisdom and draw strength from their enduring presence.

Understanding Tree Spirits: What They Are and Their Role

Tree spirits are the ethereal essence or soul of the trees. They are believed to inhabit every tree, imbuing it with life and unique energy. These spirits serve as guardians of their natural realms, protectors of the forests, and keepers of ancient wisdom. Each type of tree has its own spirit, which embodies its distinct characteristics and energies.

Tree spirits play a vital role in connecting us to nature and the earth. They act as bridges between the physical and spiritual worlds, offering insights into the cycles of life, growth, and renewal. By building a relationship with tree spirits, we can access their healing energy, learn their teachings, and feel more grounded and connected to the natural world.

In my experience, tree spirits have a gentle yet powerful presence. Whether sitting beneath a towering oak or leaning against a whispering willow, I feel a deep sense of calm and wisdom emanating from these ancient beings. Each tree spirit I connect with offers unique guidance and support, reflecting the tree's inherent qualities and strengths.

Roles and Responsibilities: How Tree Spirits Assist Us

Tree spirits provide a range of benefits, contributing to our physical, emotional, and spiritual well-being. Here are some of the ways they assist us:

Grounding and Stability: Trees are symbols of strength and endurance, deeply rooted in the earth. Their spirits help us cultivate a sense of grounding and stability, providing support during times of uncertainty and change. Connecting with tree spirits can help anchor our energy and bring us back to a state of balance and centeredness.

Healing and Renewal: Many trees are known for their healing properties, and their spirits amplify these qualities. Tree spirits can aid in physical healing, emotional release, and spiritual renewal. For example, the spirit of a birch tree is associated with new beginnings and purification, offering support for those seeking to start anew or cleanse old energies.

Wisdom and Insight: Trees have witnessed countless cycles of growth and change, accumulating a wealth of wisdom over time. Tree spirits are carriers of this ancient knowledge, offering insights into the rhythms of life and the interconnectedness of all things. They can guide us in understanding our own life cycles and finding our place within the larger tapestry of existence.

Protection and Guardianship: Trees stand as sentinels of their environment, providing shelter and protection to countless creatures. Tree spirits extend this protective energy to us, offering a sense of safety and security. For instance, the spirit of a cedar tree is known for its strong protective qualities, creating a shield against negative influences.

Connection and Community: Trees are often central to the ecosystems they inhabit, fostering connections and supporting a diverse community of life. Tree spirits teach us about the importance of connection and community, encouraging us to nurture our relationships and support one another. The spirit of a maple tree, with its expansive branches and sweet sap, symbolizes generosity and interconnectedness.

In my own journey, I've found that tree spirits often provide guidance through subtle impressions and feelings of reassurance. Whether seeking clarity on a difficult decision or simply needing to feel more grounded, I've learned to turn to the wisdom of tree spirits for support and insight.

How to Connect with Tree Spirits: Techniques and Tips

Connecting with tree spirits can be a deeply rewarding experience, fostering a deeper relationship with nature and the wisdom of the earth. Here are some techniques and tips that have helped me build a strong connection with tree spirits:

Set Clear Intentions: Begin by setting a clear intention to connect with a specific tree spirit or the spirits of trees in general. You can express this intention through a simple prayer or affirmation. For example, you might say, "I invite the spirit of the oak tree to share its wisdom and strength with me," or "I seek to connect with the spirits of the trees for guidance and grounding."

Spend Time with Trees: Immersing yourself in the presence of trees is one of the most effective ways to connect with their spirits. Spend time in forests, parks, or any natural setting where trees thrive. Sit quietly at the base of a tree, lean against its trunk, or walk among the trees, paying attention to their energy and presence.

Meditate with Trees: Meditation can be a powerful tool for connecting with tree spirits. Find a comfortable spot near a tree or visualize yourself surrounded by trees. Focus on your breath and the presence of the tree, allowing its energy to merge with yours. Visualize the roots of the tree extending deep into the earth, grounding you and connecting you to the earth's energy.

Create a Sacred Space with Tree Elements: Incorporate elements of trees into your meditation or sacred space. This could include branches, leaves, bark, or even images of trees. These elements serve as physical representations of the tree's energy, helping to enhance your connection and focus.

Listen and Observe: Pay attention to the subtle ways in which tree spirits communicate. This might include sensations, thoughts, or feelings that arise when you are near trees or messages received in dreams or meditations. Trust your intuition and be open to the guidance and insights that tree spirits offer.

Offer Gratitude and Respect: Show appreciation for the presence and guidance of tree spirits. This can be done through simple acts of respect, such as offering water to a tree, leaving a small gift, or simply expressing your gratitude. Honoring the spirits in this way helps to strengthen your connection and invite more of their energy into your life.

Prayer for Connecting with Tree Spirits: "Spirit of the trees, I honor your presence and the wisdom you share. Help me to connect deeply with your energy and to learn from your strength and stability. Guide me in grounding and growing, and show me the way to balance and harmony. Thank you for your nurturing and transformative power."

Historical Significance of Tree Spirits

Tree spirits have been revered in many cultures and spiritual traditions throughout history. Their presence is often seen as a source of wisdom, protection, and connection to the divine.

In Celtic spirituality, trees are considered sacred beings, each with its own spirit and energy. The Celts believed that trees were the homes of spirits and deities and served as gateways to other realms. The oak tree, in particular, was revered as a symbol of strength and wisdom, often associated with the Druids, who sought guidance and inspiration from the spirits of the trees.

In Shinto, the indigenous spirituality of Japan, trees are seen as sacred dwellings for kami (spirits or gods). Trees, especially ancient or unique ones, are often honored with shrines and offerings. These tree spirits are believed to protect the land and bring blessings to the people. The practice of venerating tree spirits reflects a deep respect for nature and the interconnectedness of all life.

Many Native American tribes hold trees in high regard, viewing them as living beings with their own spirits. Trees are often seen as teachers and protectors, offering guidance and support. The Iroquois, for example, have a deep reverence for the Great Tree of Peace, a symbol of unity and strength that plays a central role in their cultural and spiritual life.

In Norse mythology, the world tree Yggdrasil is a central figure connecting the various realms of existence. This immense ash tree is home to many beings and is a source of all wisdom and stability. The spirits of Yggdrasil's branches and roots embody the interconnectedness of all life and the cyclical nature of the cosmos.

Trees are often associated with spiritual enlightenment and divine presence in Buddhism. The Bodhi tree, under which the Buddha attained enlightenment, is revered as a symbol of spiritual awakening and wisdom. Many other trees are also considered sacred, providing shelter and inspiration for meditation and reflection.

Embracing Tree Spirits on Your Journey

Tree spirits are powerful and nurturing allies that offer wisdom, healing, and a deep connection to the earth. By building a relationship with these spirits, we can tap into their energy, enhancing our physical, emotional, and spiritual well-being.

Whether through personal experiences or the rich traditions of various cultures, tree spirits continue to inspire and guide us. By honoring their presence and inviting their energy into our lives, we can cultivate a deeper appreciation for the natural world and the many gifts it provides.

As you explore your connection with tree spirits, allow yourself to be open to their wisdom and healing. Embrace their guidance and let their nurturing energy support you on your journey of growth and transformation.

Chapter 84

Weather Spirits

From a young age, I've always been fascinated by the power and beauty of weather. Storms, rainbows, and the gentle breeze have all captivated my imagination. This fascination has only deepened as I have explored the spiritual realm, discovering the powerful beings known as weather spirits. These spirits embody the forces of nature, guiding and influencing the weather patterns that shape our world. Weather spirits are dynamic and powerful entities, each associated with specific weather phenomena, offering guidance, protection, and insight into the natural world.

Understanding Weather Spirits: What They Are and Their Role

Weather spirits are the ethereal beings or energies that govern and influence the various weather patterns and elements. They are believed to control the wind, rain, storms, sunshine, and other meteorological phenomena. Each type of weather spirit embodies the essence of its particular element, reflecting its unique characteristics and powers.

The role of weather spirits is multifaceted. They not only influence the physical weather but also symbolize the emotional and spiritual climates of our lives. By connecting with these spirits, we can gain insight into our own inner weather patterns, learn to navigate the storms, and bask in the sunlight of our personal journeys.

In my experience, weather spirits are powerful yet subtle guides. Their presence can be felt in the gentle caress of the wind, the soothing sound

491

of rain, or the awe-inspiring power of a thunderstorm. Each weather spirit I connect with offers unique guidance and support, mirroring the dynamic and ever-changing nature of the weather itself.

Roles and Responsibilities: How Weather Spirits Assist Us

Weather spirits provide a range of benefits, contributing to our physical, emotional, and spiritual well-being. Here are some of the ways they assist us:

Balance and Harmony: Weather spirits help maintain the balance and harmony of the natural world. Just as they ensure the proper distribution of rain, sunlight, and wind, they also help us find balance and harmony in our own lives. By attuning to the energy of weather spirits, we can align ourselves with the natural rhythms and cycles of life.

Transformation and Renewal: Weather spirits are agents of transformation and renewal. Storms, for example, clear away old and stagnant energies, making way for new growth and possibilities. Similarly, weather spirits can help us release old patterns and embrace change, fostering personal and spiritual growth.

Emotional Release and Cleansing: Rain and storms are often associated with emotional release and cleansing. Weather spirits can assist us in letting go of suppressed emotions and finding emotional clarity and healing. By connecting with these spirits, we can experience a sense of purification and renewal.

Inspiration and Creativity: The ever-changing nature of the weather can be a source of inspiration and creativity. Weather spirits, particularly those associated with sunlight and gentle breezes, can ignite our creative spark and help us see the world with fresh eyes. Their energy encourages us to embrace new ideas and express ourselves freely.

Protection and Guidance: Just as weather spirits protect the natural world, they can also offer protection and guidance to us. During challenging times, the strength and resilience of weather spirits, such as those of thunder and lightning, can provide us with the courage and clarity to navigate difficult situations.

In my own journey, I've found that weather spirits often provide guidance through the symbolism of weather patterns and phenomena. Whether seeking balance, transformation, or inspiration, I've learned to turn to the wisdom of weather spirits for support and insight.

How to Connect with Weather Spirits: Techniques and Tips

Connecting with weather spirits can be a deeply enriching experience, fostering a deeper relationship with nature and the elements. Here are some techniques and tips that have helped me build a strong connection with weather spirits:

Set Clear Intentions: Begin by setting a clear intention to connect with a specific weather spirit or the spirits of weather in general. You can express this intention through a simple prayer or affirmation. For example, you might say, "I invite the spirit of the wind to share its wisdom and guidance with me," or "I seek to connect with the spirits of the weather for balance and inspiration."

Spend Time in Nature: Immersing yourself in the natural elements is one of the most effective ways to connect with weather spirits. Spend time outdoors, observing and experiencing different weather conditions. Whether it's feeling the wind on your face, walking in the rain, or basking in the sunlight, allow yourself to engage with the elements fully.

Meditate with Weather Elements: Meditation can be a powerful tool for connecting with weather spirits. Find a comfortable spot in nature or visualize yourself surrounded by the elements. Focus on your breath and the sensations of the weather, allowing its energy to merge with yours. Visualize the spirit of the weather element you wish to connect with, inviting it to share its guidance and energy.

Create a Sacred Space with Weather Symbols: Incorporate elements of weather into your meditation or sacred space. This could include symbols such as feathers for wind, bowls of water for rain,

493

candles for sunlight, or even recorded sounds of weather phenomena. These elements serve as physical representations of the weather's energy, helping to enhance your connection and focus.

Listen and Observe: Pay attention to the subtle ways in which weather spirits communicate. This might include sensations, thoughts, or feelings that arise during different weather conditions or messages received in dreams or meditations. Trust your intuition and be open to the guidance and insights that weather spirits offer.

Offer Gratitude and Respect: Show appreciation for the presence and guidance of weather spirits. This can be done through simple acts of respect, such as making offerings of natural elements or expressing your gratitude. Honoring the spirits in this way helps to strengthen your connection and invite more of their energy into your life.

Prayer for Connecting with Weather Spirits: "Spirits of the weather, I honor your presence and the dynamic energy you share. Help me to connect deeply with your essence and to learn from your balance and transformation. Guide me in navigating the storms and embracing the sunshine, and show me the way to harmony and inspiration. Thank you for your nurturing and powerful energy."

Historical Significance of Weather Spirits

Weather spirits have been revered in many cultures and spiritual traditions throughout history. Their presence is often seen as a source of wisdom, protection, and connection to the natural world.

In Greek mythology, various gods and spirits were associated with different weather phenomena. Zeus, the king of the gods, wielded thunder and lightning as symbols of his power. Boreas, the god of the north wind, was seen as a powerful and often harsh figure. The Greeks believed that these deities controlled the weather and could be invoked for favorable conditions.

Many Native American tribes hold deep reverence for the spirits of the weather. The Hopi, for example, perform intricate ceremonies to honor and invoke rain spirits, known as Kachinas, to bring much-needed rain to their arid lands. These rituals reflect a deep understanding of the interconnectedness of life and the importance of harmony with the natural world.

In Celtic spirituality, weather spirits were often personified as powerful deities. The Morrigan, a goddess associated with war and fate, was also linked to storms and the tumultuous forces of nature. The Celts performed rituals to honor these spirits, seeking their protection and guidance.

In Hinduism, various deities are associated with weather and natural elements. Indra, the god of rain and thunderstorms, is one of the most prominent. He is often invoked during times of drought to bring rain and ensure the fertility of the land. These deities are seen as vital forces that sustain life and maintain balance in the world.

In Shinto, the indigenous spirituality of Japan, weather spirits, known as kami, are revered and honored. The Japanese believe that these spirits inhabit natural phenomena such as rain, wind, and storms. Shrines and rituals are dedicated to these kami, reflecting a deep respect for the natural world and its forces.

Embracing Weather Spirits on Your Journey

Weather spirits are powerful and dynamic allies that offer wisdom, protection, and a deep connection to the natural elements. By building a relationship with these spirits, we can tap into their energy and support, enhancing our physical, emotional, and spiritual well-being.

Whether through personal experiences or the rich traditions of various cultures, weather spirits continue to inspire and guide us. By honoring their presence and inviting their energy into our lives, we can cultivate a deeper appreciation for the natural world and the many gifts it provides.

As you explore your connection with weather spirits, allow yourself to be open to their wisdom and energy. Embrace their guidance and let their dynamic presence support you on your journey of growth and

Alex McCann Johnson
transformation.

Chapter 85
Faeries

From a young age, stories of faeries have always captivated my imagination. These enchanting beings, often depicted in folklore and fairy tales, possess a magical allure that bridges the realms of the natural and the supernatural. Faeries, or "fair folk," are believed to be guardians of nature, embodying the spirit of the earth, plants, and animals. My fascination with faeries has led me to explore their deeper significance in the spiritual world, where they are seen not just as mythical creatures but as powerful protectors and guides.

Understanding Faeries: What They Are and Their Role

Faeries are often described as small, ethereal beings with a deep connection to the natural world. They are considered to be intermediaries between humans and the natural elements, each type of faerie having its own unique role and characteristics. While popular culture often portrays them as whimsical and playful, faeries are much more complex, embodying both benevolent and mischievous traits.

Faeries play a crucial role in maintaining the balance and harmony of nature. They are believed to nurture the growth of plants, protect animals, and oversee the health of ecosystems. In many spiritual traditions, faeries are also seen as guardians of hidden wisdom and ancient knowledge, capable of bestowing blessings and insights upon those who honor and respect them.

In my exploration of faerie lore, I've found that these beings are not to be taken lightly. Their presence demands respect and reverence, and their guidance, while often subtle, can be transformative. Faeries invites us to reconnect with the natural world's magic, reminding us of the wonder and beauty surrounding us.

Roles and Responsibilities: How Faeries Assist Us

Faeries provide a range of benefits, contributing to our physical, emotional, and spiritual well-being. Here are some of the ways they assist us:

Guardians of Nature: Faeries are deeply connected to the natural world, protecting and nurturing. They ensure the health and vitality of plants, animals, and ecosystems. By attuning to the energy of faeries, we can develop a deeper appreciation for nature and a commitment to its preservation.

Bringers of Magic and Wonder: Faeries embody the magic and wonder of the natural world. Their presence can inspire us to see the world through a lens of enchantment and possibility. They encourage us to embrace our inner child, fostering a sense of curiosity, creativity, and joy.

Guides to Hidden Wisdom: Faeries are keepers of ancient knowledge and hidden wisdom. They can guide us in accessing deeper insights and understanding about ourselves and the world. Through their connection to the earth's secrets, faeries help us uncover our own inner truths and spiritual gifts.

Facilitators of Healing and Transformation: Faeries are often associated with healing and transformation. They use their magical abilities to heal the land and its inhabitants, and they can assist us in our own healing journeys. Whether it's emotional, physical, or spiritual healing, faeries offer their gentle and powerful support.

Protectors Against Negative Energies: In many traditions, faeries are seen as protectors who guard against negative influences and energies. They can help shield us from harm and provide a safe and nurturing environment for growth and exploration.

In my own journey, I've experienced the guidance of faeries through moments of clarity and unexpected encounters with nature's beauty. Their presence has brought a sense of magic and wonder into my life, encouraging me to embrace the mysteries of the natural world and my own inner landscape.

How to Connect with Faeries: Techniques and Tips

Connecting with faeries can be a magical and enriching experience, fostering a deeper relationship with nature and the unseen realms. Here are some techniques and tips that have helped me build a strong connection with faeries:

Set Clear Intentions: Begin by setting a clear intention to connect with faeries. You can express this intention through a simple prayer or affirmation. For example, you might say, "I invite the faeries to share their magic and wisdom with me," or "I seek to connect with the faeries for guidance and inspiration."

Spend Time in Nature: Faeries are deeply connected to the natural world, so spending time outdoors is one of the most effective ways to connect with them. Visit forests, meadows, gardens, or any natural setting where you feel drawn. Pay attention to the sights, sounds, and sensations around you, and remain open to the subtle presence of faeries.

Create a Faerie Garden: Creating a dedicated space for faeries in your garden or home can invite their energy. Incorporate plants, flowers, and natural elements that faeries are believed to love, such as ferns, moss, and wildflowers. Adding small decorations like tiny houses, crystals, and water features can also attract faerie energy.

Meditate with Faerie Imagery: Meditation can help you attune to the presence of faeries. Visualize yourself in a magical forest or a meadow filled with light and color. Imagine the faeries appearing and surrounding you with their energy. Allow yourself to feel their presence and invite their guidance and support.

Listen to Nature's Whispers: Faeries often communicate through the subtle sounds and movements of nature. Pay attention to the rustling of leaves, the song of birds, or the gentle breeze. These whispers can carry the messages and presence of faeries, guiding you to deeper insights and connections.

Offerings and Gratitude: Show appreciation for the presence and guidance of faeries. You can make simple offerings such as flowers, shiny objects, or sweet treats. Expressing gratitude through words or actions helps to strengthen your connection and invite more of their magical energy into your life.

Prayer for Connecting with Faeries: "Dear Faeries, guardians of nature and bearers of magic, I invite you into my life with an open heart and a joyful spirit. Please guide me with your wisdom and surround me with your enchanting presence. I was hoping you could help me to see the beauty and wonder of the world through your eyes, and teach me to honor and protect the magic of nature. Thank you for your blessings and your light."

Historical Significance of Faeries

Faeries have been a part of human folklore and spiritual traditions for centuries, with their presence documented in various cultures around the world. Their roles and characteristics often reflect the values and beliefs of the societies they inhabit.

In Celtic mythology, faeries are known as the "Tuatha Dé Danann," a race of supernatural beings who inhabited Ireland before the arrival of humans. They are often associated with the Sidhe, the ancient mounds or hills believed to be entrances to the faerie realm. The Celts believed that faeries were powerful protectors of nature and could bestow blessings or curses.

In medieval Europe, faeries were seen as both benevolent and mischievous spirits. They were thought to inhabit the wilderness and were often associated with specific natural features such as springs, trees, or flowers. European faerie tales often depict them as granting wishes or providing aid to those who respected them while tricking or punishing those who offended them.

In many Asian cultures, faerie-like beings are also prevalent. In Japanese folklore, the "Yokai" are spirits and supernatural entities that include faerie-like beings such as Tengu (bird-like spirits) and Kitsune (fox spirits). These beings often possess magical powers and are seen as guardians of nature and sacred places.

Among various indigenous cultures, faerie-like spirits are seen as protectors and nurturers of the natural world. For example, the Aboriginal Australians have the concept of "Mimis," spirits that inhabit rock formations and are guardians of the land. These spirits are deeply respected and are believed to hold the wisdom of the earth.

Embracing Faeries on Your Journey

Faeries are enchanting and powerful allies that offer magic, protection, and a deep connection to the natural world. By building a relationship with these spirits, we can tap into their energy, enhancing our physical, emotional, and spiritual well-being.

Whether through personal experiences or the rich traditions of various cultures, faeries continue to inspire and guide us. By honoring their presence and inviting their energy into our lives, we can cultivate a deeper appreciation for the magic and wonder of nature.

As you explore your connection with faeries, allow yourself to be open to their wisdom and enchantment. Embrace their guidance and let their presence bring joy, inspiration, and a sense of wonder into your journey.

Alex McCann Johnson

Chapter 86

Continuing with Nature and Elemental Guides

The journey of connecting with nature and elemental guides is not a destination but an ongoing, evolving experience that deeply enriches our lives. By weaving the wisdom and energy of these spirits into our daily routines, we cultivate a relationship that offers continuous growth, guidance, and inspiration.

One simple yet profound way to integrate these practices is by incorporating small, mindful rituals into our everyday lives. These rituals don't need to be elaborate; they can be as simple as starting the day with a moment of gratitude for the elements. For instance, you might begin your morning by acknowledging the grounding energy of the earth, the cleansing flow of water, the invigorating breath of air, and the transformative warmth of fire. This practice sets a positive tone for the day, aligning you with the natural rhythms and energies around you.

Creating sacred spaces in our homes can also help keep us connected to these elemental forces. Consider setting up a small altar that includes representations of each element: crystals or stones for earth, a bowl of water for water, a feather for air, and a candle for fire. This altar can serve as a focal point for meditation, reflection, or simply a reminder of your connection to the natural world. I find that having such a space not only grounds me but also brings a sense of peace and balance to my daily life.

Regular meditation or visualization practices focusing on the elements and their associated spirits can deepen our connection and awareness. For example, a meditation where you visualize yourself walking through a forest, feeling the earth beneath your feet, hearing the rustling leaves (air), seeing a stream (water), and feeling the warmth of the sun (fire) can create a sense of alignment with the natural world. These practices help us to embody the qualities of the elements, fostering inner balance and clarity.

Paying attention to the signs and messages from nature in our surroundings is another practical way to stay attuned to these energies. Whether it's the sudden appearance of a particular flower, a change in weather patterns, or the growth of trees around us, these observations can provide insights and guidance from nature spirits. For instance, noticing sunflowers repeatedly crossing your path might symbolize positivity and the need to embrace joy. These natural encounters often carry meaningful messages if we take the time to reflect on them.

The Evolving Relationship with Nature and Elemental Spirits

Our relationship with nature and elemental spirits is dynamic and evolves over time, much like any meaningful relationship. As we spend more time attuning to these energies, we become more receptive to their presence and more adept at interpreting their messages. This relationship is built on mutual respect and reciprocity, where we honor the spirits, and in return, they offer their wisdom and support.

Over time, you may find that your sensitivity to the subtle energies of nature increases, allowing you to perceive and interact with the spirits more clearly. This evolving connection can lead to personal and spiritual growth, guiding you toward greater self-awareness, balance, and harmony with the natural world. For example, you might start to feel a deeper connection to the earth when gardening or a sense of clarity and calm when near water, indicating a growing rapport with these elemental energies.

The more we engage with these practices, the more integrated they become into our lives, shifting from conscious effort to an intuitive, natural part of our existence. This deepening relationship enhances our ability to navigate life's challenges and embrace its beauty with a sense of wonder and gratitude. You might find that practices like walking in nature or meditating on the elements become second nature, offering comfort and insight during times of uncertainty.

Encouragement for Continued Exploration and Learning

The journey with nature and elemental spirits is never truly complete; there is always more to explore and learn. Each encounter with these spirits offers new insights and deepens our understanding of the interconnectedness of all life.

I encourage you to continue your exploration with curiosity and an open heart. Seek out new experiences in nature, learn about different cultures' perspectives on nature spirits, and experiment with various rituals and practices to see what resonates with you. For example, you might explore Celtic traditions of working with faeries or delve into shamanic practices that honor elemental beings.

Keeping a journal of your experiences, dreams, and insights can be valuable for reflection and growth. This practice helps track your journey and reveals patterns and themes in your interactions with nature spirits. Over time, you might notice recurring symbols or messages that provide deeper understanding and guidance.

Sharing your journey with others who have similar interests can also be enriching. Whether through community groups, online forums, or simply with friends, discussing your experiences can offer support and deepen your collective understanding. It can be incredibly validating to hear others' stories and recognize the shared journey of connecting with the natural world.

Remember, the spirits of nature and the elements are always present, ready to guide and inspire you. By remaining open, respectful, and curious, you can cultivate a rich and rewarding relationship with these powerful allies, leading to a life filled with wonder, wisdom, and connection. Whether you're drawn to the grounding presence of the earth, the emotional depths of water, the clarity of air, or the transformative power of fire, each element and spirit offers unique gifts and insights to explore.

Integrating the practices of connecting with nature and elemental spirits into our everyday lives enriches our experience and fosters an evolving relationship that supports continuous growth and learning. Embrace this journey with an open heart, and let the spirits of nature and the elements guide you toward a deeper connection with the world around you and within you. As you continue to explore these relationships, may you find a sense of peace, purpose, and joy in the intricate dance of life's elemental forces.

Ancestor Guides

Alex McCann Johnson

Chapter 87

Ancestor Guides

I have done ancestral work with clients, and it is always remarkable to witness the changes in familial patterns that arise from these connections. Engaging with our ancestors can bring about shifts and healing within a family's lineage. This process highlights the significant role and importance of ancestor guides in our lives.

Ancestor guides are spiritual entities that originate from our lineage. They encompass direct family members, extended relatives, and even beings from past lives or ancient civilizations. These guides are believed to offer wisdom, guidance, and support, assisting us as we navigate both our spiritual and daily lives. They are ever-present, ready to help us understand our purpose, overcome challenges, and honor our heritage. In my experiences with clients, I have seen how acknowledging and working with ancestor guides can lead to deep personal insights and transformative healing.

Understanding the Role and Importance of Ancestor Guides

Understanding the role and importance of ancestor guides is essential to appreciating how they influence and shape our lives. Ancestor guides serve as bridges between the past and present, offering insights that can help us make better decisions and understand our place in the world. They remind us that we are part of a larger tapestry of human experience, connected by the threads of our lineage. This connection can be a source of great strength and wisdom, providing context and continuity to our lives.

Types of Ancestor Guides:

- **Direct Ancestors:** These are immediate family members such as parents, grandparents, and great-grandparents. They are often the most accessible and relatable guides, providing insights that are directly tied to our personal and familial experiences. For example, a grandmother who was known for her wisdom and nurturing nature might continue to offer guidance and support from the spiritual realm.

- **Indirect Ancestors:** These include extended relatives like stepmothers, brother-in-laws, and any other not directly related person. While they may not have been as biologically connected to us in life, their experiences and insights still contribute to our family's collective wisdom. A dear family friend who was a skilled craftsman might inspire us to develop our talents and passions.

- **Past Life Ancestors:** These guides are connected to our past lives, bringing wisdom and lessons from those experiences. They can help us understand patterns and relationships that transcend our current lifetime. For instance, a past life mother that was a healer might influence our current desire to help and nurture others.

- **Ancient Civilization Ancestors:** These beings hail from long-lost civilizations, carrying ancient knowledge and cultural wisdom. Their guidance often relates to broader, more universal themes, such as the cycles of nature, spiritual practices, and societal roles. An ancestor from an ancient culture might provide insights into traditional healing practices or spiritual rituals that can enrich our current life.

- **Star Seed Ancestors:** These are believed to be extraterrestrial beings linked to our soul's cosmic origin. They offer perspectives that extend beyond the earthly realm, often focusing on higher consciousness, universal love, and the interconnectedness of all life. Connecting with star seed ancestors can help us explore our spiritual identity on a cosmic scale and understand our place in the larger universe.

Connecting with Ancestor Guides

Incorporating the guidance of ancestor guides into our spiritual practice enriches our journey and deepens our connection to our heritage. Here are some ways to connect with and honor your ancestor guides:

Ancestral Altars: Creating an ancestral altar is a powerful way to honor and connect with your ancestors. This sacred space can include photographs, heirlooms, candles, and offerings such as food, flowers, or incense. Spending time at the altar, offering prayers, and meditating can help you feel their presence and receive their guidance. This daily practice becomes a bridge to the spiritual realm, keeping the connection alive and active. For example, I have seen how setting up an altar with family photos and cherished mementos brings a sense of comfort and continuity, fostering a deeper sense of belonging and connection to one's roots.

Meditation and Visualization: Meditation can be a direct way to connect with your ancestor guides. Sit quietly, close your eyes, and visualize a place where you feel safe and connected to your lineage. Invite your ancestors to join you in this space, and remain open to any messages or feelings that arise. This practice can be incredibly grounding and insightful, providing a space where you can receive wisdom and support from your ancestors. Through meditation, many people report feeling a palpable presence or receiving intuitive insights that guide them in their daily lives.

Dreamwork: Dreams are a common way for ancestors to communicate. Before going to sleep, set an intention to connect with your ancestor guides. Keep a journal by your bed to record any dreams or impressions you receive. Over time, patterns and messages may become clearer. I have often found that dreams can provide insights into ancestral influences and unresolved issues, offering a unique window into the subconscious mind and the spirit world. For instance, a recurring dream about a family home might be an invitation to explore one's heritage or address unresolved family dynamics.

Rituals and Ceremonies: Performing rituals and ceremonies to honor your ancestors can strengthen your connection. These can include lighting candles, offering food and drink, or performing traditional practices that honor your cultural heritage. Such rituals create a sacred space where the presence of your ancestors can be felt, and their guidance can be more readily received. Engaging in these practices helps to maintain a living relationship with your ancestors, honoring their legacy and integrating their wisdom into your life.

Genealogy Research: Learning about your family history can deepen your connection to your ancestors. Researching your genealogy and understanding the lives and experiences of your ancestors can bring you closer to them and provide context for their guidance. This exploration can reveal hidden strengths, challenges, and patterns within your lineage, offering valuable insights into your own life. For example, discovering a lineage of resilient and resourceful ancestors can inspire you to tap into those same qualities in your current challenges.

Listening and Intuition: Pay attention to the subtle ways your ancestors may communicate with you throughout your day. This could be through signs, synchronicities, or a sudden feeling of their presence. Trust your intuition and inner knowing when it comes to interpreting these messages. Whether it's a song that suddenly plays on the radio, a significant date that keeps appearing, or a sense of being watched over, these signs can be powerful indicators of your ancestors' ongoing presence and support.

Embracing Ancestor Guides on Your Journey

Ancestor guides are powerful and nurturing beings that provide wisdom, guidance, and support. Understanding their role and incorporating practices to connect with them can enrich our spiritual journey and deepen our connection to our heritage. Whether through personal experiences or the collective wisdom of our lineage, ancestor guides continue to inspire and guide us, reminding us of the connections we share with our past and the valuable lessons they offer for our present and future.

Embracing the presence of our ancestor guides not only honors their memory but also empowers us to carry their wisdom forward, enriching our lives and the lives of future generations. Through these connections, we become stewards of our heritage, weaving the lessons and strengths of our ancestors into the fabric of our own lives. As we navigate our journey with their guidance, we are reminded that we are never truly alone; we are part of a vast and interconnected tapestry of life, supported by the enduring love and wisdom of those who came before us.

Alex McCann Johnson

Chapter 88

The Wisdom of Ancestors

As an energy worker, I've found that ancestral healing is so important. You'd be surprised by the patterns that emerge with each generation. The wisdom of our ancestors is a source of guidance and support woven into the very fabric of our existence. This ancestral knowledge, accumulated over generations, offers us insights that can help us navigate the complexities of modern life with greater understanding and clarity.

Ancestral wisdom encompasses the collective experiences, lessons, and knowledge of those who came before us. It is the essence of their lived experiences, their triumphs and failures, their joys and sorrows. This wisdom is invaluable because it provides us with a rich tapestry of insights that can help us make informed decisions, avoid pitfalls, and embrace opportunities with a deeper sense of purpose and confidence.

How Ancestral Knowledge Can Guide and Support Us

Understanding Our Roots: Ancestral wisdom helps us understand where we come from. It grounds us in our heritage and provides a sense of belonging and identity. Knowing the stories and struggles of our ancestors can give us a greater appreciation for the sacrifices they made and the paths they paved for us. This understanding can instill a sense of pride and responsibility to honor their legacy.

Learning from the Past: By tapping into ancestral wisdom, we can learn valuable lessons from the past. Our ancestors faced many of the same challenges we encounter today, and their experiences can offer practical solutions and cautionary tales. For instance, understanding how previous generations dealt with hardships, conflicts, and changes can provide us with strategies to handle similar situations more effectively.

Emotional and Spiritual Support: Ancestral guides offer emotional and spiritual support. They remind us that we are never truly alone; we are part of a continuum that stretches back through time. This connection can be a source of comfort and strength during difficult times. By feeling their presence and drawing on their wisdom, we can find solace and encouragement to persevere.

Guidance in Decision-Making: When faced with important decisions, ancestral wisdom can provide clarity and direction. Our ancestors' experiences can serve as a compass, helping us weigh options and foresee potential outcomes. By reflecting on their choices and the consequences they faced, we can make more informed decisions that align with our values and long-term goals.

Healing and Growth: Ancestral wisdom plays a crucial role in healing and personal growth. Many of the issues we face, such as recurring patterns or emotional wounds, have roots in our ancestral lineage. By acknowledging and understanding these connections, we can address unresolved issues and break harmful cycles. This healing process not only benefits us but also helps future generations.

Cultural Preservation: Embracing ancestral wisdom helps preserve cultural heritage and traditions. It ensures that the knowledge and practices of our ancestors are passed down to future generations. This preservation fosters a sense of continuity and respect for the diversity of human experiences. It also enriches our lives by keeping alive the customs, rituals, and values that define our cultural identity.

The Immensity of Our Ancestral Network

The sheer number of our ancestors is staggering. If we consider that each person has two parents, four grandparents, eight great-grandparents, and so on, the number of direct ancestors doubles with each generation we go back. This exponential growth means that just ten generations back, we each have 1,024 ancestors and twenty generations back, the number reaches over a million. This immense network of individuals forms a vast reservoir of collective wisdom and experience.

Embracing Ancestral Wisdom

By embracing the wisdom of this extensive lineage, we open ourselves to a deeper understanding of who we are and where we come from. We gain valuable insights that can guide us through life's journey, providing support, healing, and a sense of connection that transcends time.

Ancestral Healing Work

Identifying Ancestral Patterns: The first step in ancestral healing work is to identify the patterns and behaviors that have been passed down through generations. These could include recurring emotional issues, health problems, relationship dynamics, or behavioral patterns. By recognizing these patterns, we can begin to understand their origins and how they impact our lives.

Connecting with Ancestors: Establishing a connection with our ancestors is crucial for healing. This can be done through meditation, visualization, or rituals that invite the presence of our ancestors. Creating a sacred space or altar with photographs, heirlooms, and offerings can facilitate this connection. During these sessions, ask your ancestors for their guidance and support in healing the family lineage.

Healing Ceremonies and Rituals: Performing ceremonies and rituals specifically designed for ancestral healing can be powerful. These might include lighting candles, offering food and drink, and reciting prayers or affirmations that focus on releasing negative patterns and inviting positive energy. Traditional practices from your cultural heritage can be especially meaningful.

Energy Healing Techniques: Utilizing energy healing techniques, such as Reiki, can help to clear ancestral blockages and heal emotional wounds. During an energy healing session, focus on the intention of releasing ancestral trauma and inviting healing energy into the family lineage. Visualize this energy flowing through you and extending back through your ancestors, bringing peace and resolution.

Therapeutic Practices: Engaging in therapeutic practices like family constellations can also be effective. This method involves exploring family dynamics and relationships through role-playing, helping to reveal hidden patterns and unresolved issues. Working with a skilled therapist or facilitator can provide deeper insights and facilitate healing.

Forgiveness and Reconciliation: Forgiveness is a powerful tool in ancestral healing. Holding onto anger or resentment towards past generations can perpetuate negative patterns. By practicing forgiveness and seeking reconciliation, we can release these burdens and promote healing. This might involve writing letters to deceased ancestors expressing forgiveness and gratitude or performing rituals that symbolize letting go of past hurts.

Dreamwork: Setting an intention before sleep to connect with ancestors through dreams can provide valuable insights. Keep a journal by your bed to record any dreams or impressions. Over time, patterns and messages may become clearer, guiding the healing process.

Ongoing Communication: Maintaining an ongoing dialogue with your ancestors is essential. Regularly spend time at your ancestral altar, meditate, or engage in rituals that honor their presence. This continuous connection helps to reinforce the healing work and ensures that you remain open to their guidance and support.

Sharing the Healing: As you progress in your ancestral healing work, consider sharing your experiences and insights with family members. This can help to foster a collective healing process and strengthen the bonds within your family. Encouraging others to explore their connections with ancestors can lead to a deeper understanding and greater harmony within the family.

The wisdom of our ancestors is a treasure trove of knowledge and guidance. By honoring and integrating this wisdom into our lives, we not only enrich our own experiences but also continue the legacy of those who came before us. In doing so, we create a bridge between the past and the present, ensuring that the lessons and insights of our ancestors continue to illuminate our path forward.

Engaging in ancestral healing work allows us to identify and address the patterns and issues that have been passed down through generations. By connecting with our ancestors, performing healing ceremonies, utilizing energy healing techniques, and practicing forgiveness, we can promote healing and growth for ourselves and future generations. Embracing this process helps us to understand our roots, learn from the past, and preserve our cultural heritage, fostering a deeper sense of connection and continuity with our ancestral lineage. Through these connections, we become stewards of our heritage, weaving the lessons and strengths of our ancestors into the fabric of our own lives. As we navigate our journey with their guidance, we are reminded that we are never truly alone; we are part of a vast and interconnected tapestry of life, supported by the enduring love and wisdom of those who came before us.

Alex McCann Johnson

Chapter 89

Direct Ancestors

Having detailed knowledge about my ancestry has been a gift that has impacted my spiritual journey. Knowing that I have Scandinavian roots and bearing the clan name McCann has given me a deep sense of connection to my heritage. Visiting homesteads where my family took root has enriched my understanding of who I am and where I come from. This connection to my direct ancestors has been a source of strength and wisdom, guiding me in both everyday life and spiritual practices.

Direct ancestors are those from our family lineage, including parents, grandparents, and so on. They are the individuals who have come before us, directly contributing to our existence and shaping our family history. Connecting with direct ancestors goes beyond understanding genealogy; it involves acknowledging and honoring the spiritual and emotional legacy they have left behind.

In my experience, direct ancestors can offer insight. They carry the stories, wisdom, and experiences of our family line, and connecting with them can provide a deep sense of belonging and purpose. Whether through dreams, meditations, or rituals, acknowledging the presence and influence of our direct ancestors can be a powerful source of guidance and healing.

The Spiritual Significance of Direct Ancestors

Direct ancestors play a significant role in our spiritual journey. They provide a link to our past, helping us understand our identity and purpose. Here's how connecting with direct ancestors can influence our spiritual lives:

Sense of Identity and Belonging: Knowing and honoring our direct ancestors gives us a deeper understanding of our roots and heritage. It helps us see ourselves as part of a larger continuum, contributing to a sense of belonging and identity.

Wisdom and Guidance: Ancestors often possess valuable knowledge and life lessons that can guide us in our own lives. They have experienced the trials and triumphs of life and can offer insights and perspectives that we might not find elsewhere.

Emotional and Spiritual Healing: Connecting with ancestors can help heal family wounds and patterns that have been passed down through generations. Understanding their struggles and triumphs allows us to address unresolved issues and find peace within our family lineage.

Strength and Resilience: The stories of our ancestors often reflect incredible strength and resilience. By connecting with their legacy, we can draw upon their fortitude to face our own challenges with courage and perseverance.

Honoring Heritage and Traditions: Recognizing and celebrating the customs, traditions, and values of our ancestors keeps their memory alive and enriches our own lives. It fosters a deeper appreciation for our cultural and familial heritage.

In my journey, connecting with my Scandinavian roots and the McCann clan has provided a sense of identity and strength. It has helped me understand the resilience and values that have been passed down through generations, guiding me in both personal and spiritual growth.

Recognizing and Connecting with Direct Ancestors

Building a connection with direct ancestors involves acknowledging their presence and honoring their legacy. Here are some ways to recognize and connect with your direct ancestors:

Family Stories and Genealogy: Start by exploring your family history. Talk to relatives, research genealogical records, and gather stories about your ancestors. Understanding their lives and experiences provides a foundation for connecting with their spirit.

Dreams and Visions: Direct ancestors often communicate through dreams or meditative visions. Pay attention to recurring themes, symbols, or messages in your dreams that might be related to your family history. These encounters are invitations to explore their energy and wisdom further.

Intuitive Feelings: Trust your intuition when it comes to ancestors. If you feel a strong connection to a particular ancestor or experience a sense of their presence, it's likely that they are reaching out to you.

Rituals and Offerings: Engage in rituals or make offerings to honor your ancestors. This might include setting up an ancestral altar with photos and mementos, lighting candles, or preparing food that they enjoyed. These acts of remembrance strengthen your connection to their spirit.

Guided Meditations: Use guided meditations focused on connecting with your ancestors. Visualize meeting them in a serene setting, such as a family home or a place significant to your heritage. Invite them to share their wisdom and energy with you.

Cultural Traditions: Participate in cultural practices and traditions that honor your heritage. This might include celebrating festivals, performing traditional rituals, or learning about your cultural customs. Engaging in these activities fosters a deeper connection to your ancestral roots.

Practical Steps to Work with Direct Ancestors

Honoring and connecting with direct ancestors involves respect, intention, and mindful practices. Here are some steps and tips to help you build a meaningful relationship with your ancestors:

Set the Intention: Start by setting a clear intention to connect with your direct ancestors. This can be done through a simple affirmation or prayer. You might say, "I invite the presence and wisdom of my ancestors into my life. Please guide me and share your insights with me."

Create an Ancestral Altar: Dedicate a space in your home to honor your ancestors. Fill this space with photos, heirlooms, and objects that remind you of your family heritage. This altar serves as a focal point for your interactions and offerings.

Research Your Family History: Delve into your genealogy and learn about your ancestors' lives. Understanding their stories, challenges, and accomplishments provides a deeper connection to their spirit.

Perform Ancestral Rituals: Engage in rituals to honor your ancestors. This might include lighting candles, offering prayers, or performing acts of kindness in their name. These rituals help keep their memory alive and strengthen your bond.

Meditate with Ancestral Energy: During meditation, focus on connecting with your ancestors. Visualize their presence and invite their guidance. Pay attention to any sensations, thoughts, or images that arise during the meditation.

Offer Gratitude and Respect: Regularly express gratitude for the guidance and support of your ancestors. Thank them for their presence and acknowledge the sacrifices they made to pave the way for you.

Prayer for Direct Ancestors: "Beloved ancestors, I honor your presence and your legacy. Please guide me with your wisdom and help me connect deeply with our family heritage. Share your stories and strength with me, and help me honor your memory with respect and gratitude."

Historical Significance of Direct Ancestors

The reverence for direct ancestors is deeply rooted in various cultural and spiritual traditions:

Guided by Spirits

In African and Indigenous cultures, ancestors are seen as powerful spiritual beings who continue to influence the lives of their descendants. Practices such as ancestor veneration involve rituals, offerings, and prayers to honor and seek guidance from ancestors. These traditions emphasize the ongoing connection between the living and the dead, highlighting the role of ancestors in providing protection, wisdom, and support.

In East Asian cultures, particularly in China and Japan, ancestor worship is an integral part of family life. Ancestors are honored through rituals, altars, and offerings, with the belief that they provide guidance and blessings to their descendants. These practices reflect a deep respect for family lineage and the importance of maintaining a harmonious relationship with one's ancestors.

In European traditions, particularly among the Celts and Scandinavians, ancestors were revered as guardians of the family and the land. Ancestor veneration included rituals to honor the dead, celebrate their memory, and seek their protection. These practices fostered a sense of continuity and connection across generations, reinforcing the bond between the living and their forebears.

In Latin American cultures, the Day of the Dead (Día de los Muertos) is a prominent celebration that honors deceased loved ones. Families create altars, known as ofrendas, decorated with photos, food, and mementos to welcome the spirits of the departed. This vibrant tradition reflects the belief that the dead continue to be an integral part of the family and community.

In modern spiritual practices, the concept of ancestor reverence has been embraced by many seeking to reconnect with their roots and gain guidance from their lineage. Ancestral healing and connection practices have gained popularity, emphasizing the importance of honoring one's heritage and integrating ancestral wisdom into contemporary life.

These historical perspectives highlight the universal reverence for direct ancestors and their role as guides, protectors, and sources of wisdom. Across cultures and eras, ancestors have been seen as integral to the spiritual and familial fabric, offering their support and guidance to those who honor their memory.

Embracing the Journey with Direct Ancestors

Connecting with direct ancestors offers a link to our past and a source of strength and wisdom for our present and future. Their stories, sacrifices, and triumphs are part of our own journey, shaping who we are and guiding us in our path.

As you build your relationship with your ancestors, honor their legacy and learn from their experiences. Whether through family stories, rituals, or personal reflection, the connection to your direct ancestors can enrich your life and deepen your understanding of your heritage. Embrace their presence with respect and gratitude, and allow their wisdom to guide you on your spiritual journey.

Chapter 90

Indirect Ancestors

In exploring my family tree and heritage, I've come to realize the impact not only of my direct ancestors but also of those who are part of the broader lineage. Indirect ancestors are those who are not directly in your bloodline but still play a significant role in your ancestral heritage. These might include extended family members, influential figures within your cultural or spiritual community, or even those who have contributed to the collective legacy of your people. Connecting with indirect ancestors can enrich our understanding of our heritage and provide additional layers of support and wisdom.

Understanding Indirect Ancestors

Indirect ancestors encompass a wider scope of influence and connection beyond our immediate family. They may include:

- **Extended Family Members:** This can include aunts, uncles, cousins, and other relatives who have shaped the family's history and contributed to its collective story.

- **Cultural and Community Figures:** Influential individuals within your cultural or spiritual community who have left a significant legacy, even if they are not directly related to you.

- **Historical and Legendary Figures:** People from your cultural or national history who have made significant contributions and are revered as part of the collective heritage.

For me, understanding the role of indirect ancestors has broadened my perspective on my heritage. Visiting the homesteads of distant relatives and learning about their lives has deepened my appreciation for the collective journey of my family. These connections remind us that our identity is woven from a rich tapestry of influences and experiences.

The Spiritual Significance of Indirect Ancestors

Indirect ancestors play a crucial role in our spiritual development. Here's how they can influence and support us:

Expanding Our Sense of Belonging: By acknowledging the contributions of indirect ancestors, we broaden our sense of community and belonging. We recognize that we are part of a larger narrative that extends beyond our immediate family.

Enhancing Cultural and Spiritual Connection: Indirect ancestors often embody the values, traditions, and wisdom of our culture. Connecting with them deepens our understanding of these aspects and helps us integrate them into our lives.

Providing Broader Perspectives and Lessons: Indirect ancestors bring diverse experiences and lessons that can offer new insights and guidance. Their stories can inspire us to explore different aspects of our heritage and personal growth.

Strengthening Collective Identity: Honoring indirect ancestors strengthens our connection to the collective identity of our community or culture. It fosters a sense of unity and shared purpose, reinforcing the bonds that hold us together.

Offering Protection and Guidance: Just like direct ancestors, indirect ancestors can provide spiritual protection and guidance. Their presence can be a source of strength and support, helping us navigate challenges and uncertainties.

In my journey, recognizing the influence of indirect ancestors has enriched my spiritual practice. It has allowed me to draw from a broader pool of wisdom and experience, deepening my connection to my heritage and community.

Recognizing and Connecting with Indirect Ancestors

Building a connection with indirect ancestors involves recognizing their presence and honoring their contributions. Here are some ways to connect with your indirect ancestors:

Explore Extended Family Stories: Research and learn about the lives of extended family members and their contributions to your family history. Their stories can provide valuable insights and strengthen your connection to your broader lineage.

Honor Cultural and Community Figures: Acknowledge and celebrate the influential figures within your cultural or spiritual community. Participate in cultural events, read about their lives, and incorporate their teachings into your practice.

Study Historical and Legendary Figures: Delve into the history and legends of your culture. Learn about the heroes, leaders, and visionaries who have shaped your heritage. Their stories can inspire and guide you.

Create a Collective Ancestral Altar: Dedicate a space in your home to honor not just your direct ancestors but also the broader lineage. Include symbols, photos, and items representing the influential figures and cultural heritage of your community.

Engage in Cultural Practices and Traditions: Participate in rituals, ceremonies, and traditions that honor your cultural heritage. These practices can deepen your connection to your indirect ancestors and their legacy.

Meditate on Community and Legacy: During meditation, focus on the broader community and collective legacy you are part of. Visualize the support and guidance of indirect ancestors, and invite their wisdom into your life.

Practical Steps to Work with Indirect Ancestors

Honoring and connecting with indirect ancestors involves intentional practices and a broader perspective. Here are some steps and tips to help you build a meaningful relationship with your indirect ancestors:

Set the Intention: Begin by setting a clear intention to connect with your indirect ancestors. This can be done through a simple affirmation or prayer. You might say, "I invite the presence and wisdom of my indirect ancestors into my life. Please guide me and share your insights with me."

Create a Collective Altar: Dedicate a space in your home to honor your broader lineage. Include symbols, photos, and items representing your extended family, cultural figures, and historical heroes. This altar serves as a focal point for your interactions and offerings.

Research and Learn: Explore the stories and contributions of extended family members and influential figures within your culture. Understanding their lives and experiences provides a deeper connection to their spirit.

Perform Rituals and Ceremonies: Engage in rituals or ceremonies that honor your indirect ancestors. This might include lighting candles, offering prayers, or participating in cultural traditions. These acts of remembrance strengthen your connection to their legacy.

Offer Gratitude and Respect: Regularly express gratitude for the guidance and support of your indirect ancestors. Thank them for their presence and acknowledge the impact they have had on your community and heritage.

Prayer for Indirect Ancestors: "Beloved indirect ancestors, I honor your presence and your legacy. Please guide me with your wisdom and help me connect deeply with our collective heritage. Share your stories and strength with me, and help me honor your memory with respect and gratitude."

Historical Significance of Indirect Ancestors

The reverence for indirect ancestors is evident in various cultural and spiritual traditions around the world:

In Filipino culture, the concept of "Kapwa" emphasizes interconnectedness and community. Ancestors are not just immediate family members but include the extended network of kin and community members who have shaped the collective identity. Festivals such as "Undas" (All Saints' Day) and "Araw ng mga Patay" (Day of the Dead) are celebrated to honor both direct and indirect ancestors, reflecting a deep respect for the broader ancestral heritage.

In Hawaiian culture, the practice of "Ohana" extends beyond blood relations to include extended family and community. The Hawaiian tradition of "Ho'oponopono," a practice of reconciliation and forgiveness, often involves acknowledging and honoring the influence of both direct and indirect ancestors. This cultural emphasis on collective unity and respect for all ancestors underscores the importance of community and shared lineage.

In Mongolian culture, the reverence for ancestors includes honoring historical figures and leaders who have contributed to the nation's legacy. Festivals such as "Tsagaan Sar" (Lunar New Year) and "Naadam" celebrate the cultural heritage and achievements of both direct ancestors and legendary figures. Mongolians believe in the spiritual guidance and protection of their ancestors, reflecting a deep respect for the broader ancestral influence on their lives.

In modern spiritual practices, the concept of indirect ancestors has been embraced as part of a holistic approach to ancestral reverence. People recognize the importance of acknowledging not just immediate family members but also the broader network of influential figures and community members who have shaped their heritage. This broader perspective fosters a deeper connection to the collective legacy and spiritual guidance of their community.

These historical perspectives highlight the universal reverence for indirect ancestors and their role as guides, protectors, and sources of wisdom. Across cultures and eras, indirect ancestors have been seen as integral to the spiritual and communal fabric, offering their support and guidance to those who honor their memory.

Embracing the Journey with Indirect Ancestors

Connecting with indirect ancestors offers a link to our broader heritage and community. Their stories, contributions, and legacy are part of our collective journey, shaping who we are and guiding us in our path.

As you build your relationship with your indirect ancestors, honor their legacy and learn from their experiences. Whether through family stories, cultural traditions, or personal reflection, the connection to your indirect ancestors can enrich your life and deepen your understanding of your heritage. Embrace their presence with respect and gratitude, and allow their wisdom to guide you on your spiritual journey.

Chapter 91

Past Life Ancestors

From a young age, the concept of past lives and reincarnation fascinated me. I would often dream of different eras and places, feeling a strange familiarity with them. These experiences led me to explore the idea of past life ancestors—those we have been connected with in previous lifetimes. Unlike our current lineage, past life ancestors are souls with whom we have shared bonds in other lifetimes. Connecting with them can provide insights into our spiritual journey and help us understand recurring patterns, relationships, and experiences in our present life.

Past life ancestors are souls that have had significant connections with us in previous incarnations. These connections might have been as family members, friends, mentors, or even adversaries. The relationships we formed with these souls continue to influence our present life, often bringing unresolved issues or valuable lessons that we need to address.

Key aspects of past life ancestors include:

Deep Soul Connections: These ancestors are often souls with whom we have shared strong, meaningful relationships in past lives. Their influence can manifest in our current relationships and life experiences, providing clues to unresolved issues or lessons.

Recurring Patterns and Lessons: Patterns in our present life, such as recurring challenges or attractions to certain cultures or periods, may be linked to our connections with past life ancestors. Understanding these patterns can offer insights into our soul's journey and growth.

Guidance and Support: Past life ancestors can serve as spiritual guides, offering wisdom and support based on the experiences and lessons they shared with us in previous lifetimes. They can help us navigate current challenges and deepen our understanding of our soul's path.

Healing and Resolution: Connecting with past life ancestors can facilitate the healing of old wounds and the resolution of unfinished business from previous incarnations. This process can bring a sense of closure and balance to our current life.

For me, exploring connections with past life ancestors has been a transformative journey. It has helped me understand my deep affinity for certain cultures and historical periods, as well as recurring themes in my life. These connections have provided insights into my spiritual growth and personal development.

The Spiritual Significance of Past Life Ancestors

Past life ancestors play a crucial role in our spiritual evolution. Here's how they can influence and support us:

Deepening Self-Awareness: By exploring our connections with past life ancestors, we gain a deeper understanding of ourselves and our soul's journey across lifetimes. This awareness helps us recognize and address recurring patterns and lessons.

Enhancing Spiritual Growth: Past life ancestors offer insights that can accelerate our spiritual growth. Their experiences and wisdom provide valuable guidance as we navigate our current life and work through karmic issues.

Facilitating Healing and Resolution: Connecting with past life ancestors can help heal unresolved issues from previous lifetimes. This healing process brings a sense of closure and balance, allowing us to move forward with greater clarity and purpose.

Strengthening Soul Connections: Recognizing and honoring our past life ancestors strengthens our connection to the broader tapestry of our soul's journey. It helps us appreciate the intricate web of relationships and experiences that shape our spiritual path.

Providing Spiritual Guidance: Past life ancestors often serve as spiritual guides, offering support and insights that are relevant to our current challenges and goals. Their guidance can help us make sense of our present experiences and align with our higher purpose.

In my journey, connecting with past life ancestors has enriched my spiritual practice. It has provided me with a deeper sense of continuity and purpose, linking my present life with the broader narrative of my soul's journey.

Recognizing and Connecting with Past Life Ancestors

Building a connection with past life ancestors involves recognizing their presence and exploring the lessons they bring. Here are some ways to connect with your past life ancestors:

Explore Recurring Patterns: Reflect on recurring themes, challenges, or attractions in your life. These patterns may be linked to past life connections. Journaling about these experiences can provide valuable insights into your relationships with past life ancestors.

Engage in Past Life Regression: Past life regression therapy can help you access memories and experiences from previous lifetimes. This process can reveal significant connections with past life ancestors and the lessons they bring.

Meditate on Soul Connections: During meditation, focus on connecting with souls from your past lives. Visualize yourself in a peaceful, timeless space where you can invite your past life ancestors to join you. Be open to any images, feelings, or messages that arise.

Create a Past Life Altar: Dedicate a space in your home to honor your past life ancestors. Include symbols, artifacts, or items that represent different eras, cultures, or significant experiences from your past lives. This altar serves as a focal point for your interactions and offerings.

Seek Spiritual Guidance: Work with a spiritual counselor or guide who specializes in past life exploration. They can help you uncover and understand connections with past life ancestors and their impact on your current life.

Perform Rituals and Ceremonies: Engage in rituals or ceremonies that honor your past life ancestors. This might include lighting candles, offering prayers, or participating in traditions from your past lives. These acts of remembrance strengthen your connection to their legacy.

Prayer for Past Life Ancestors: "Beloved past life ancestors, I honor your presence and the connections we share across lifetimes. Please guide me with your wisdom and help me understand the lessons and patterns of our past. Share your stories and strength with me, and help me embrace our shared journey with respect and gratitude."

Historical Significance of Past Life Ancestors

The reverence for past life ancestors is evident in various cultural and spiritual traditions around the world:

In Indian culture, the concept of reincarnation is deeply embedded in Hindu philosophy. The belief in past lives and the impact of past life connections is a central tenet. Rituals such as "Shraddha," performed to honor ancestors, reflect the enduring significance of past life relationships and their influence on present life.

In Tibetan Buddhism, the practice of recognizing past life connections is integral to understanding one's spiritual path. Tibetan Buddhists believe in the concept of "Tulku," where enlightened beings reincarnate to continue their spiritual work. Rituals and ceremonies often involve honoring past lives and seeking guidance from past life connections.

In ancient Egyptian culture, the belief in the afterlife and the continuity of the soul was a core aspect of their spiritual practices. The

Egyptians believed that the soul could return in different forms, and they performed elaborate rituals to honor and connect with their ancestors, both directly and from past lives.

In contemporary spiritual practices, the exploration of past lives has become a significant aspect of personal and spiritual growth. Practices such as past life regression therapy, meditation, and ancestral rituals are used to uncover and honor past life connections. These practices reflect the ongoing importance of understanding and integrating past life experiences into our present lives.

These historical perspectives highlight the universal reverence for past life ancestors and their role as guides, protectors, and sources of wisdom. Across cultures and eras, past life ancestors have been seen as integral to the spiritual and communal fabric, offering their support and guidance to those who honor their memory.

Embracing the Journey with Past Life Ancestors

Connecting with past life ancestors offers a link to our broader spiritual heritage. Their stories, contributions, and legacy are part of our collective journey, shaping who we are and guiding us in our path.

As you build your relationship with your past life ancestors, honor their legacy and learn from their experiences. Whether through past life exploration, cultural traditions, or personal reflection, the connection to your past life ancestors can enrich your life and deepen your understanding of your spiritual journey. Embrace their presence with respect and gratitude, and allow their wisdom to guide you on your path.

Alex McCann Johnson

Chapter 92
Lost Civilization Ancestors

Throughout my journey into past life exploration and spiritual discovery, I've uncovered connections to lost civilizations like Lemuria. These connections have opened my eyes to the rich and mystical legacies of these ancient societies. Civilizations such as Atlantis, Lemuria, and Mu have long fascinated humanity with their tales of advanced knowledge, deep spiritual wisdom, and mysterious disappearances. Exploring these lost civilizations as part of our ancestral lineage can provide insights and a deeper understanding of our spiritual heritage.

Lost civilization ancestors refer to the souls and beings that were part of ancient, often mythical societies that existed long before recorded history. These civilizations, such as Atlantis, Lemuria, and Mu, are believed to have possessed advanced knowledge and spiritual insights that are still relevant today. While evidence of their physical existence remains a topic of debate, their spiritual and cultural legacies continue to resonate with many people across the world.

Key aspects of lost civilization ancestors include:

Advanced Knowledge and Wisdom: These ancestors are often credited with possessing understanding in areas such as technology, spirituality, healing, and connection with nature. They are seen as keepers of ancient wisdom that can guide us in modern times.

Deep Spiritual Connections: Lost civilizations are frequently depicted as having a harmonious relationship with the natural world and the spiritual realms. Their ancestors are believed to offer guidance on how to live in balance and harmony with all life.

Mystical and Mysterious Qualities: The mysterious nature of these civilizations adds a layer of intrigue and allure. They represent a bridge to realms of knowledge and existence that go beyond our current understanding.

Guides in Transformation: These ancestors can help us navigate significant changes and personal transformations. They provide insights into how to integrate ancient wisdom into our contemporary lives and use it to foster growth and evolution.

Connecting with lost civilization's ancestors has been an enlightening experience for me. It has allowed me to tap into ancient wisdom and insights that have significantly influenced my spiritual path and understanding of the world.

The Spiritual Significance of Lost Civilization Ancestors

Lost civilization ancestors play a unique and transformative role in our spiritual journey. Here's how they can influence and support us:

Accessing Ancient Wisdom: These ancestors are seen as custodians of ancient knowledge. They offer insights that can help us understand complex spiritual concepts and apply timeless principles to our modern lives.

Fostering Spiritual Growth: The advanced spiritual practices and philosophies of these civilizations can inspire and guide us towards higher levels of consciousness and deeper spiritual awareness.

Guiding Personal Transformation: Lost civilization ancestors often appear during times of significant change or spiritual awakening. Their guidance can help us navigate these transitions with grace and wisdom, drawing on their experiences of transformation.

Enhancing Connection with Nature and the Cosmos: Many of these civilizations are believed to have had a deep connection with nature and the cosmos. Their ancestors can teach us how to reconnect with the natural world and understand our place within the larger universe.

Inspiring Innovation and Creativity: The advanced technologies and creative achievements of these civilizations can inspire us to think beyond conventional limits and explore new possibilities in our own lives and endeavors.

In my explorations, connecting with lost civilization ancestors has provided me with valuable perspectives on how to integrate ancient wisdom into contemporary life. Their guidance has been instrumental in deepening my spiritual practice and fostering personal growth.

Recognizing and Connecting with Lost Civilization Ancestors

Building a connection with lost civilization's ancestors involves recognizing their presence and exploring their teachings. Here are some ways to connect with these ancient guides:

Explore Your Fascinations: Reflect on your attractions to certain ancient cultures or civilizations. Your interest in specific myths, legends, or historical periods might be linked to past life connections with these lost societies. Journaling about these attractions can provide insights into your relationships with lost civilization ancestors.

Engage in Past Life Regression: Past life regression therapy can help you access memories and experiences from lifetimes in ancient civilizations. This process can reveal significant connections with lost civilization ancestors and the wisdom they bring.

Meditate on Ancient Symbols: During meditation, focus on symbols and imagery associated with lost civilizations, such as the Atlantean trident, Lemurian crystals, or Mu's sacred geometry. Visualize yourself in these ancient societies and invite your ancestors to join you. Be open to any images, sensations, or messages that arise.

Create a Sacred Space: Dedicate a space in your home to honor your connections with lost civilizations. Include artifacts, symbols, or items that represent these ancient cultures. This altar serves as a focal point for your interactions and offerings to your lost civilization ancestors.

Seek Spiritual Guidance: Work with a spiritual counselor or guide who specializes in past life exploration and ancient wisdom. They can help you uncover and understand connections with lost civilization ancestors and their impact on your current life.

Perform Rituals and Ceremonies: Engage in rituals or ceremonies that honor your lost civilization ancestors. This might include lighting candles, offering prayers, or participating in traditions from these ancient cultures. These acts of remembrance strengthen your connection to their legacy.

Offer Gratitude and Respect: Regularly express gratitude for the guidance and support of your lost civilization ancestors. Thank them for their presence and acknowledge the impact they have had on your soul's journey.

Prayer for Lost Civilization Ancestors: "Beloved ancestors of ancient civilizations, I honor your presence and the wisdom you bring from times long past. Please guide me with your ancient knowledge and help me understand the mysteries of the universe. Share your stories and strength with me, and help me embrace our shared journey with respect and gratitude."

Historical Significance of Lost Civilization Ancestors

The reverence for lost civilization ancestors is evident in various cultural and spiritual traditions around the world:

In Atlantean mythology, Atlantis is often depicted as an advanced civilization with exceptional spiritual and technological knowledge. The story of Atlantis, as told by Plato, has inspired countless explorations into the potential wisdom and insights that Atlantean ancestors might offer. These ancestors are believed to have mastered the balance between technological advancement and spiritual enlightenment, providing a blueprint for harmonizing progress with inner growth.

Guided by Spirits

In Lemurian traditions, Lemuria is portrayed as a paradise-like land where inhabitants lived in perfect harmony with nature and the spiritual realms. Lemurian ancestors are often associated with deep spiritual wisdom, healing abilities, and a strong connection to the natural world. They are believed to guide us in nurturing our connection to the Earth and embracing a more holistic way of living.

In the lore of Mu, Mu is described as an ancient continent in the Pacific Ocean, home to a highly advanced and spiritually evolved civilization. The ancestors from Mu are seen as keepers of esoteric knowledge and sacred geometry, offering insights into the nature of reality and the cosmos. Their teachings emphasize the importance of unity and the interconnectedness of all life.

These historical perspectives highlight the universal reverence for lost civilization ancestors and their role as guides, protectors, and sources of wisdom. Across cultures and eras, these ancestors have been seen as integral to the spiritual and communal fabric, offering their support and guidance to those who honor their memory.

Embracing the Journey with Lost Civilization Ancestors

Connecting with lost civilization ancestors offers a link to our broader spiritual heritage. Their stories, contributions, and legacy are part of our collective journey, shaping who we are and guiding us in our path.

As you build your relationship with your lost civilization ancestors, honor their legacy and learn from their experiences. Whether through past life exploration, cultural traditions, or personal reflection, the connection to your lost civilization ancestors can enrich your life and deepen your understanding of your spiritual journey. Embrace their presence with respect and gratitude, and allow their wisdom to guide you on your path.

Alex McCann Johnson

Chapter 93

Starseed Ancestors

From a young age, I was fascinated by the stars and the vastness of the universe. This curiosity eventually led me to explore the concept of Starseed ancestors. Unlike our terrestrial ancestors, Starseed ancestors are believed to be advanced, benevolent beings from other star systems and galaxies. These cosmic ancestors have influenced our spiritual evolution and continue to guide us on our journey.

Starseed ancestors come from various extraterrestrial civilizations, each with its unique qualities, wisdom, and energies. They are often seen as our spiritual forebears, having seeded the Earth with their knowledge and genetic material to aid humanity's development. Understanding and connecting with these cosmic ancestors can provide insights into our spiritual path and our place in the universe.

Starseed ancestors are beings from other star systems who have a deep connection to Earth and its inhabitants. They are often described as highly evolved and spiritually advanced, possessing wisdom and knowledge far beyond our current understanding. These ancestors are believed to have played a crucial role in the development of human civilization, both in ancient times and continuing into the present.

Starseed ancestors come from various star systems, each known for specific traits and contributions to human evolution. For example, the Pleiadians are known for their compassion and healing abilities, the Arcturians for their technological and spiritual advancements, and the Sirians for their wisdom and connection to the divine feminine. These beings are often seen as our spiritual guides and mentors, helping us to awaken our true potential and align with our higher purpose.

In my journey, connecting with Starseed ancestors has been a source of universal guidance. Their presence offers a broader perspective on our existence, reminding us that we are part of a much larger cosmic family. By tapping into their wisdom, we can gain a deeper understanding of our soul's mission and the greater plan for humanity.

Roles and Responsibilities: How Starseed Ancestors Assist Us

Starseed ancestors provide a range of benefits, contributing to our spiritual growth and the evolution of humanity as a whole. Here are some of the ways they assist us:

Guiding Spiritual Evolution: Starseed ancestors offer guidance and support in our spiritual development. They help us to awaken to our true nature and expand our consciousness. Their teachings often emphasize the importance of love, unity, and living in harmony with the universe.

Imparting Advanced Knowledge: These ancestors are known for their advanced knowledge in various fields, including science, technology, and spirituality. They share this wisdom with us to help accelerate our progress and solve complex challenges. Their insights can inspire new ideas and innovations that benefit humanity.

Facilitating Healing and Transformation: Many Starseed ancestors are skilled in healing and energy work. They assist us in releasing old patterns, healing past traumas, and transforming our lives. Their energy can help raise our vibration and align us with our highest potential.

Promoting Unity and Cooperation: Starseed ancestors encourage us to embrace our interconnectedness and work together for the greater good. They inspire us to move beyond divisions and conflicts, fostering a sense of unity and cooperation among all beings.

Protecting and Supporting Earth's Ascension: These ancestors are deeply invested in the well-being of our planet. They support Earth's ascension process and help humanity navigate the shifts and changes occurring at this time. Their guidance can provide stability and clarity during periods of upheaval.

In my own experience, Starseed ancestors have provided invaluable wisdom. Their presence has helped me to see beyond the limitations of the physical world and connect with my higher self. By aligning with their energy, I have gained greater clarity and purpose in my spiritual journey.

How to Connect with Starseed Ancestors: Techniques and Practices

Connecting with Starseed ancestors can be a transformative experience, offering galactic insights. Here are some techniques and practices that have helped me establish a strong connection with these cosmic beings:

Set Clear Intentions: Begin by setting a clear intention to connect with your Starseed ancestors. You can express this intention through a simple prayer or affirmation. For example, you might say, "I invite my Starseed ancestors to connect with me and share their wisdom and guidance."

Meditate on Cosmic Imagery: Meditation is a powerful tool for connecting with Starseed ancestors. Visualize yourself traveling through the stars, surrounded by cosmic light and energy. Imagine meeting your Starseed ancestors and feeling their presence. Allow any images, thoughts, or sensations to come through, and be open to their messages.

Use Star-Based Symbols and Tools: Incorporate symbols and tools related to the stars and galaxies into your practice. This could include star-shaped crystals, images of constellations, or artifacts that resonate with specific star systems. These items can serve as focal points for your connection and amplify your intentions.

Study Starseed Lineages: Learn about the different Starseed lineages and their characteristics. Understanding the qualities and contributions of various star systems can help you identify and connect with your own Starseed ancestry. Books, courses, and online resources can provide valuable insights into these cosmic lineages.

Perform Galactic Activations: Engage in practices that activate your connection to Starseed energies. This could include energy work, light language, or sound healing sessions that focus on awakening your Starseed DNA and aligning you with higher frequencies. These activations can deepen your connection and enhance your awareness of Starseed guidance.

Maintain a Journal: Keep a journal to document your experiences and insights when connecting with Starseed ancestors. Writing down your thoughts, dreams, and any messages you receive can help you recognize patterns and understand their guidance more clearly.

Prayer for Connecting with Starseed Ancestors: "Dear Starseed ancestors, guardians of cosmic wisdom and light, I invite you to connect with me and share your guidance and knowledge. Help me to awaken to my true nature and align with my highest purpose. Surround me with your loving energy and assist me in my spiritual journey. Thank you for your presence and your support."

Historical Significance of Starseed Ancestors

Starseed ancestors have been a part of human belief systems and spiritual traditions for millennia, with their influence documented in various cultures around the world.

The ancient Egyptians believed in beings from the star system Sirius, whom they revered as gods and divine guides. The connection to Sirius was central to their mythology and spiritual practices, with the star playing a significant role in their calendar and the alignment of their monuments. The Great Pyramid of Giza, for example, is aligned with the Orion constellation, reflecting the Egyptians' deep connection to their Starseed ancestors.

The Mayans also held a connection to the stars, particularly the

Pleiades constellation. They believed that their ancestors came from the Pleiades and that their calendar was based on the cycles of these stars. The Mayan pyramids and temples are aligned with celestial bodies, highlighting their advanced astronomical knowledge and reverence for their Starseed lineage.

Many indigenous cultures around the world have stories and legends of star beings who came to Earth and interacted with their ancestors. For example, the Dogon people of West Africa have detailed knowledge of the Sirius star system, which they attribute to teachings from beings who visited them from Sirius. Similarly, Aboriginal Australians speak of the Wandjina spirits, who are believed to be ancestral beings from the stars.

In contemporary times, the concept of Starseed ancestors has gained popularity in various spiritual movements. Channelers and mediums often communicate with beings from other star systems, sharing their messages of love, unity, and ascension. Books, workshops, and online communities dedicated to Starseed wisdom continue to explore and expand our understanding of these cosmic ancestors.

Embracing Starseed Ancestors on Your Journey

Starseed ancestors are powerful and wise guides that offer a deep connection to the cosmos and our spiritual heritage. By building a relationship with these beings, we can tap into their vast knowledge and support, enhancing our understanding of ourselves and our place in the universe.

Whether through personal experiences or the rich traditions of various cultures, Starseed ancestors continue to inspire and guide us. By honoring their presence and inviting their energy into our lives, we can cultivate a deeper appreciation for our cosmic lineage and the infinite possibilities of our spiritual journey.

As you explore your connection with Starseed ancestors, allow yourself to be open to their wisdom and guidance. Embrace their support and let their presence bring clarity, inspiration, and a sense of cosmic

Alex McCann Johnson

wonder into your life.

Chapter 94

Integrating Ancestral Wisdom

Incorporating the wisdom of my ancestors into my daily life has been a transformative journey. The guidance and support from these ancestral guides have enriched my understanding of myself and the world around me. Here are some ways I've found to integrate their wisdom into everyday practices, reflections on my journey, and encouragement for anyone seeking to deepen their connection with their ancestors.

Ways to Incorporate Guidance from Ancestor Guides into Daily Life

Daily Rituals and Practices: Every morning, I take a few moments to honor my ancestors. Lighting a candle and spending a few minutes in silent reflection or prayer helps me start the day with a sense of connection and gratitude. These simple rituals ground me and set a positive tone for the day ahead. It's in these quiet moments that I often feel the presence of my ancestors most strongly, providing a sense of peace and continuity.

Creating a Sacred Space: I've dedicated a small space in my home as an ancestral altar. It's adorned with photographs, heirlooms, and items that remind me of my family lineage. This space serves as a daily reminder of my roots and a focal point for meditation and reflection. Spending time here allows me to feel connected to my past and to draw strength and inspiration from those who came before me.

Mindful Living: Incorporating ancestral wisdom into my daily life means living mindfully and intentionally. I strive to make decisions that honor the values and lessons passed down through generations, whether it's through sustainable living practices, showing kindness to others, or pursuing personal growth and learning. By living in a way that reflects the values of my ancestors, I feel more aligned with my true self and more connected to the larger human experience.

Listening to Intuition: My ancestors often communicate through intuition—those subtle nudges and feelings that guide me. By paying attention to my inner voice and trusting these instincts, I feel more aligned with their guidance and support. This intuitive connection often manifests in moments of clarity or sudden inspiration, which I've learned to recognize as messages from my ancestral guides.

Storytelling and Sharing: Sharing family stories and traditions with loved ones helps keep the wisdom of my ancestors alive. Whether it's during family gatherings or casual conversations, these stories create a sense of continuity and belonging, reminding us of the legacy we carry forward. Through storytelling, I've discovered not only the resilience and courage of my ancestors but also the humor and joy that were part of their lives.

Engaging in Ancestral Arts and Crafts: Engaging in traditional arts, crafts, or culinary practices that my ancestors cherished is another way I honor their legacy. Cooking a family recipe, practicing a traditional craft, or learning a cultural dance connects me to my heritage in a tangible and meaningful way. These activities are not just hobbies but sacred practices that deepen my bond with my ancestors and keep their traditions alive.

Reflecting on the Journey of Connecting with Ancestor Guides

Reflecting on my journey of connecting with ancestor guides, I realize how far I've come and the impact this connection has had on my life. Initially, I approached this journey with curiosity and a bit of skepticism. However, as I delved deeper, the presence of my ancestors became undeniable, offering insights and guidance that resonated deeply with me.

Moments of Clarity and Comfort: I've experienced moments of profound clarity and comfort, especially during challenging times. Knowing that I have the support and wisdom of my ancestors behind me has given me strength and resilience. For example, during difficult decisions or times of stress, I often meditate and seek their guidance, finding peace and direction in their subtle messages.

Navigating Doubts and Difficulties: The journey hasn't always been easy—there have been moments of doubt and difficulty—but the rewards have been immense. Doubts about whether I was truly connecting or just imagining things were common initially. However, through persistent practice and reflection, I've learned to trust in the process and in the presence of my ancestors.

Personal Growth and Understanding: Through meditation, dream work, and intentional practices, I've developed a deeper understanding of myself and my purpose. My ancestors have taught me about resilience, love, and the importance of honoring our roots while embracing growth and change. This journey has also helped me break free from limiting patterns and beliefs, allowing me to live more authentically and fully.

Encouragement for Continued Exploration

To anyone seeking to connect with their ancestor guides, I encourage you to continue exploring this rewarding journey. Here are some thoughts to inspire you:

Be Open and Patient: Building a connection with your ancestors takes time and openness. Be patient with yourself and the process. Trust that your ancestors are present and ready to support you, even if the connection doesn't feel immediate. Each step you take towards them is a step towards greater understanding and closeness.

Stay Curious: Let your curiosity guide you. Explore different methods of connecting, whether it's through meditation, journaling, rituals, or learning about your family history. Each step brings you closer to your ancestors. Don't be afraid to try new practices or seek out new sources of wisdom; your journey is uniquely yours.

Embrace Your Unique Path: Everyone's journey with their ancestors is unique. Embrace what feels right for you and trust your instincts. There's no one-size-fits-all approach to connecting with ancestor guides. Follow what resonates with you and allow your relationship with your ancestors to develop naturally.

Reflect and Integrate: Take time to reflect on the insights and guidance you receive. Integrate these lessons into your daily life, allowing them to shape your actions and decisions. This ongoing practice will deepen your connection and enrich your life. By continually reflecting on and applying their wisdom, you honor your ancestors and strengthen the bond you share with them.

Final Thoughts on the Importance of Honoring and Learning from Ancestors

Honoring and learning from our ancestors is a sacred and transformative practice. It reminds us that we are part of a larger tapestry woven together by the threads of those who came before us. Their experiences, wisdom, and love are a source of generational support.

By connecting with our ancestors, we honor their legacy and ensure that their wisdom continues to illuminate our path. This practice fosters a sense of belonging, continuity, and purpose, enriching our lives and the lives of future generations. In embracing our ancestral connections, we not only heal and grow but also contribute to a greater collective consciousness.

Our ancestors' stories and lessons become part of our story, guiding us toward a more mindful, compassionate, and enlightened existence. So, take the time to honor your ancestors, listen to their wisdom, and integrate their guidance into your daily life. Their presence is a gift, offering us the strength, insight, and inspiration to navigate our journeys with grace and purpose.

Deities

Alex McCann Johnson

Chapter 95

Deities

From a young age, I was always fascinated by the stories of gods and goddesses from various cultures. These stories, filled with wonder and mystery, made me feel connected to something greater than myself. As I delved deeper into my curiosity, I began to understand that deities are not just characters in ancient myths but powerful spiritual guides who can offer wisdom, support, and guidance.

Deities serve as intermediaries between the human and divine realms. They are manifestations of the universal energies that shape our world and our lives. Each deity embodies specific attributes, virtues, and aspects of life, making them relatable and accessible to us in different ways. By connecting with these divine entities, I discovered that I could tap into their unique energies to aid my spiritual growth and personal development.

I have found that building a relationship with a deity requires patience, respect, and an open heart. It is a deeply personal and transformative experience that can provide insights into the universal workings of cosmic forces. Whether through meditation, rituals, or simply invoking their presence in daily life, these spiritual guides have become an integral part of my journey, offering guidance and support when I need it most.

Historical and Cultural Significance

The reverence for deities spans across cultures and centuries, illustrating the universal human need to understand and connect with the divine. Each culture has its own pantheon of gods and goddesses, each with distinct characteristics and stories that reflect the values, beliefs, and experiences of the people who worship them.

For example, the ancient Greeks saw their gods as larger-than-life figures who embodied human traits and emotions. The stories of Zeus, Athena, and Apollo are not just mythological tales but reflections of the Greek understanding of the world and their place within it. Similarly, the Hindu pantheon, with its rich tapestry of deities like Brahma, Vishnu, and Shiva, represents the diverse and multifaceted nature of the divine in the Hindu worldview.

In Norse mythology, deities such as Odin, Thor, and Freyja play crucial roles, embodying wisdom, strength, and love. These deities were central to the spiritual and daily lives of the Norse people, guiding them through both war and peace. The Egyptian pantheon, with gods like Ra, Isis, and Anubis, provided the ancient Egyptians with a structured understanding of life, death, and the cosmos.

Throughout history, these deities have been worshipped, venerated, and called upon for guidance, protection, and blessings. Temples, rituals, and festivals dedicated to them have been central to communal and individual spiritual practices. These traditions have been passed down through generations, keeping the connection to the divine alive and evolving.

In my exploration of various spiritual traditions, I have come to appreciate the depth and richness of these cultural narratives. They provide a framework for understanding the divine and offer a way to engage with the spiritual realm that is both meaningful and accessible. By studying and connecting with deities from different cultures, I have gained a broader perspective on spirituality and a deeper appreciation for the universal quest for the divine.

Methods to Connect with Deities

Connecting with deities involves practices that open us to their energies and guidance. Here are some methods I used to establish and nurture these connections:

Meditation and Visualization: Regular meditation focused on a specific deity can help create a deep spiritual bond. Visualize the deity, their attributes, and symbols, inviting their presence and guidance into your life. During meditation, I often visualize a serene setting where I meet the deity, allowing their energy to merge with mine.

Rituals and Offerings: Performing rituals and making offerings to deities is a way to honor and connect with them. This can include lighting candles, offering flowers, food, or other items that are meaningful to the deity. These acts of devotion create a reciprocal relationship, where I give something in exchange for their guidance and support.

Sacred Spaces: Creating an altar or sacred space dedicated to a deity can provide a focal point for your devotions. Adorn the space with images, statues, and symbols associated with the deity. This space becomes a sanctuary where I can focus my thoughts and connect with the divine presence.

Mantras and Prayers: Reciting mantras and prayers specific to a deity can invoke their energy and presence. These practices help attune your mind and spirit to the frequency of the deity. Chanting their names or reciting prayers allows me to feel their vibrational energy and bring their attributes into my life.

Study and Reflection: Learning about the myths, stories, and teachings of a deity can deepen your understanding and connection. Reflecting on their attributes and how they relate to your life can provide insights and inspiration. Reading ancient texts or modern interpretations helps me to grasp the deeper meanings behind their stories and how they can guide me today.

Benefits of Connecting with Deities

The benefits of connecting with deities are manifold, enriching both your spiritual and daily life:

Guidance and Wisdom: Deities offer timeless wisdom and guidance that can help you navigate life's challenges and make informed decisions. For instance, consulting Athena, the goddess of wisdom, can provide clarity and strategic insight during complex situations.

Emotional and Spiritual Support: Feeling the presence of a deity can provide comfort and support, especially during difficult times. Their energy can help you feel grounded and protected. In times of sorrow, invoking the compassionate Kuan Yin can bring a sense of peace and solace.

Personal and Spiritual Growth: The teachings and attributes of deities can inspire personal and spiritual growth, encouraging you to embody their virtues and qualities. Learning from Ganesh's ability to remove obstacles or from the transformative power of Kali can empower you to overcome personal challenges and embrace change.

Enhanced Spiritual Practice: Regular interaction with deities through meditation, rituals, and prayer can deepen your spiritual practice and bring a sense of sacredness to your daily routine. Incorporating the discipline of Mars or the nurturing essence of Demeter into my daily practices helps to bring balance and purpose to my life.

Connection to the Divine: Building a relationship with a deity fosters a direct connection to the divine, enriching your sense of spirituality and purpose. This connection creates a bridge to higher realms of consciousness and deepens my understanding of the universal energies at play in my life.

By integrating the wisdom and guidance of deities into your life, you can create a rich, supportive, and transformative spiritual practice. These divine connections offer insights and help you navigate your journey with greater clarity, strength, and compassion.

As you explore the world of deities, remember that this journey is deeply personal and unique. Each deity brings its own energy and lessons, and by embracing these connections, you open yourself to a broader and more enriched spiritual experience. Whether through the structured practices of established traditions or your own intuitive methods, the guidance of deities can illuminate your path and enhance your life in profound ways.

Alex McCann Johnson

Chapter 96

Serving the Universal Plan

As I continue to explore and deepen my understanding of spirituality, I have come to see deities as integral parts of the universe's grand design. Each deity plays a unique role, embodying specific aspects of the cosmos and the forces that shape our reality. Whether they govern natural phenomena, human virtues, or cosmic principles, deities serve as the building blocks of the spiritual framework that underpins the universe.

In many traditions, deities are seen as the architects and caretakers of the world. They are responsible for the creation, preservation, and transformation of life and the cosmos. For instance, in Hinduism, the trinity of Brahma, Vishnu, and Shiva represents the cyclical nature of creation, maintenance, and destruction, illustrating how deities work together to maintain the balance of the universe. This concept is not just limited to Hinduism. In Egyptian mythology, the goddess Ma'at embodies truth and cosmic order, maintaining the balance and harmony of the universe through her divine principles.

The Norse pantheon also demonstrates this dynamic interplay. Odin, the Allfather, represents wisdom and knowledge, constantly seeking to understand the mysteries of the cosmos. Thor, the god of thunder, protects humanity and the divine realms, ensuring stability and order through his might. Freyja, the goddess of love and fertility, oversees growth and prosperity, nurturing life in all its forms.

These deities are more than mythological figures; they symbolize the fundamental forces and energies that govern existence. Their stories and attributes reflect the natural laws and principles that operate within the universe, providing a framework for understanding how the world functions and evolves.

How Deities Interact with Humanity

One of the most fascinating aspects of deities is their interaction with humanity. Deities are not distant, unattainable beings; they are deeply involved in our lives, guiding us, protecting us, and helping us grow spiritually. Through various means, such as dreams, signs, synchronicities, and direct communication, deities reach out to us, offering their wisdom and support.

In my own spiritual practice, I have experienced this interaction firsthand. When I invoke a deity, whether through prayer, meditation, or ritual, I feel their presence in my life. They communicate in subtle ways, often through symbols or intuitive insights, helping me navigate challenges and make decisions aligned with my higher purpose. For instance, during a difficult time, I once meditated on the guidance of Athena, the Greek goddess of wisdom and strategy. I received a sudden clarity and a solution to my problem, which felt like a direct insight from her.

Each culture has its own unique ways of connecting with deities. In ancient Greece, people would visit oracles and temples to seek divine guidance. These sacred sites, like the Oracle of Delphi, were believed to be the dwelling places of gods, where divine messages could be received through the priestesses. Similarly, in Shinto, the Japanese honor their deities, or kami, through rituals and offerings at shrines. These practices create a sacred space for interaction, fostering a deep and personal relationship between humans and the divine.

In modern spiritual practices, people often connect with deities through personalized rituals and meditative practices. For example, in Wicca, practitioners might create altars and cast circles to invite the presence of deities during their rituals. In Hinduism, daily puja (worship) involves offering food, flowers, and prayers to the deities, inviting their blessings and guidance into the home and life.

These interactions highlight the accessibility of deities in our lives. They are not confined to the realms of myth and legend but are active participants in our spiritual journeys. By building relationships with these divine entities, we can draw on their strengths and wisdom to enhance our lives and spiritual growth.

The Universal Plan and Spiritual Evolution

Deities are not only concerned with individual lives but also with the broader evolution of humanity and the universe. They serve a universal plan, a divine blueprint that guides the spiritual evolution of all beings. This plan is dynamic and ever-evolving, aiming to bring about higher levels of consciousness, harmony, and balance in the cosmos.

As I reflect on my spiritual journey, I realize that the guidance I receive from deities is part of this larger plan. They help me align with my soul's purpose and contribute to the collective evolution of humanity. By following their guidance, I am not only growing spiritually but also playing a part in the unfolding of the universal plan.

This understanding has given me a great sense of purpose and connection. It reminds me that we are all interconnected and that our spiritual growth contributes to the greater good. Deities, as divine entities, are here to assist us in this journey, helping us navigate the complexities of life and evolve toward greater wisdom and enlightenment.

In many traditions, the concept of a universal plan is intertwined with the roles of deities. In Buddhism, the Bodhisattvas are seen as enlightened beings who have chosen to remain in the cycle of birth and death to help others achieve enlightenment. They are integral to the spiritual evolution of humanity, guiding individuals towards compassion and wisdom.

Similarly, in the Yoruba religion, the Orishas are deities who act as intermediaries between humans and the supreme god, Olodumare. They guide the spiritual and moral development of their followers, helping them align with their destinies and the universal plan.

The idea of a universal plan is also present in the stories of gods and goddesses from various other cultures. These narratives often reflect the ongoing battle between order and chaos, light and darkness, and the role of deities in maintaining balance and harmony in the universe.

Understanding the role of deities in the universal plan encourages us to see our own lives as part of a larger, interconnected tapestry. Our actions, growth, and decisions contribute to the broader cosmic order. Deities, with their timeless wisdom and insight, offer us the guidance we need to navigate our paths and fulfill our roles within this grand design.

Deities play an integral role in the universe's grand design, embodying the forces that shape our reality and guiding us toward spiritual growth and enlightenment. They interact with humanity in ways, offering guidance, protection, and support as we navigate our journeys.

By understanding and connecting with these divine entities, we align ourselves with the universal plan and contribute to the broader evolution of humanity and the cosmos. The presence of deities in our lives enriches our spiritual experiences and deepens our connection to the divine forces that govern the universe. As we continue to explore and honor these connections, we find ourselves part of a dynamic, ever-evolving tapestry of life guided by the wisdom and love of the deities who serve the universal plan.

Chapter 97

Hindu

Hinduism, one of the world's oldest and most diverse religions, offers a rich tapestry of beliefs, practices, and deities. Unlike many other religions, Hinduism does not have a single founder or a unified set of doctrines. Instead, it encompasses a wide range of philosophies, rituals, and traditions that have evolved over thousands of years. This pluralistic nature of Hinduism allows for a deep and multifaceted approach to understanding the divine.

At the heart of Hinduism is the concept of Brahman, the ultimate, unchanging reality that pervades everything in the universe. Brahman is often described as an abstract, formless, and limitless entity. To make this vast concept more accessible to human understanding, Brahman is personified in various forms and deities, each representing different aspects of the cosmic order and human experience. These deities are central to Hindu worship and spirituality, and they are venerated through a variety of rituals, prayers, and festivals.

Main Gods and Goddesses of the Hindu Pantheon

Brahma - The Creator: Brahma is the god of creation and one of the Trimurti, the Hindu trinity that includes Vishnu and Shiva. He is depicted with four heads, each facing a different direction, symbolizing his all-encompassing knowledge and the creation of the four Vedas, the sacred texts of Hinduism. Brahma's role is to create the universe and all living beings. However, he is less worshiped in contemporary Hinduism compared to other deities, with only a few temples dedicated to him.

Vishnu - The Preserver: Vishnu is the preserver and protector of the universe. He maintains cosmic order and dharma (moral law). Vishnu is often depicted with a serene expression, holding a conch shell, a discus, a mace, and a lotus. He is known for his ten avatars (incarnations), including Rama and Krishna, who descend to earth to restore balance and righteousness. Festivals like Diwali, celebrating his return as Rama, and Krishna Janmashtami, marking Krishna's birth, are significant in Hindu worship.

Shiva - The Destroyer: Shiva, the destroyer or transformer, completes the Trimurti. He represents the cycle of destruction and rebirth necessary for the universe's renewal. Shiva is often depicted in deep meditation, with a third eye representing higher consciousness and a cobra around his neck, symbolizing his mastery over death and time. He is also shown dancing the Tandava, a cosmic dance that symbolizes the cycle of creation, preservation, and destruction. Maha Shivaratri, a festival dedicated to Shiva, involves fasting, night vigils, and chanting to honor his transformative power.

Lakshmi - The Goddess of Wealth: Lakshmi is the goddess of wealth, prosperity, and fortune. She is often depicted sitting or standing on a lotus flower, symbolizing purity and spiritual power and holding lotus blossoms in her hands. Lakshmi is the consort of Vishnu and is worshipped for bringing material and spiritual wealth. During Diwali, homes are decorated with lights and rangoli to welcome Lakshmi and seek her blessings for prosperity and happiness.

Saraswati - The Goddess of Knowledge: Saraswati, the goddess of knowledge, music, and the arts, is usually depicted playing a veena (a musical instrument) and sitting on a white lotus, signifying wisdom and purity. She is the consort of Brahma and is revered by students, musicians, and artists. The festival of Vasant Panchami, marking the arrival of spring, is dedicated to Saraswati, with people wearing yellow, the goddess's favorite color, and engaging in music and learning activities.

Parvati - The Divine Mother: Parvati, also known as Shakti, is the goddess of power, love, and fertility. She is the wife of Shiva and the mother of Ganesha and Kartikeya. Parvati is depicted in various forms, from the gentle Annapurna to the fierce Durga and Kali, each representing different aspects of the feminine divine. Navaratri, a festival celebrated over nine nights, honors her different forms and their roles in the cosmic balance.

Ganesha - The Remover of Obstacles: Ganesha, the elephant-headed god, is one of the most beloved deities in Hinduism. He is worshipped as the remover of obstacles and the patron of arts and sciences. Ganesha is depicted with a large belly, symbolizing generosity and acceptance, and he often holds a modak, representing the rewards of a disciplined life. Ganesh Chaturthi, a ten-day festival celebrating his birth, involves elaborate processions and immersions of Ganesha idols in water.

Durga - The Warrior Goddess: Durga is a powerful warrior goddess who combats evil and protects the righteous. She is depicted riding a lion or tiger, with multiple arms each holding a weapon, symbolizing her ability to protect her devotees from all directions. Durga Puja, particularly celebrated in West Bengal, involves worship, music, dance, and the immersion of Durga idols in water after a period of intense festivities.

Kali - The Goddess of Time and Death: Kali, a fierce aspect of Parvati, is the goddess of time, change, and destruction. She is depicted with a dark complexion, wild hair, and a garland of skulls, embodying the power of time to devour all things. Kali represents the destruction of ego and the illusory nature of the material world. Despite her terrifying appearance, she is also seen as a benevolent mother who protects her devotees from negative influences. Kali Puja, celebrated during Diwali in Bengal, honors her fierce but protective nature.

Hanuman - The Devotee and Protector: Hanuman, the monkey god, is revered for his unwavering devotion to Rama and his immense strength and courage. He is a central figure in the epic Ramayana, where he plays a pivotal role in the battle against the demon king Ravana.

Hanuman is often depicted with a mace and a heart showing the image of Rama and Sita, symbolizing his loyalty and love. Hanuman Jayanti, his birthday, is celebrated with fasting, prayer, and reading of the Ramayana.

The Creation Story of the Hindu Pantheon

The Hindu creation story is a rich and complex narrative that explains the origin of the universe and the role of deities in its formation and maintenance. According to Hindu cosmology, the universe goes through endless cycles of creation, preservation, and destruction.

In the beginning, there was only the primordial, unmanifested Brahman. From this infinite source, a cosmic egg, or Hiranyagarbha, emerged, containing the seeds of all life. As the egg opened, it gave birth to Brahma, the creator god, who began the process of shaping the cosmos and all living beings.

Brahma, with his four heads and creative power, initiated the cycle of creation. He created the rishis (sages) and the various forms of life that populate the earth. However, Brahma's role in creation is not solitary. The preservation of this creation is overseen by Vishnu, who incarnates in different forms (avatars) to restore order and protect the universe from chaos and evil.

Shiva, the destroyer, plays an equally crucial role. His dance of destruction, the Tandava, signifies the end of one cycle and the beginning of another, ensuring the continuous renewal and regeneration of the cosmos. Shiva's role is not merely destructive; it is essential for the balance and sustainability of the universe.

This trinity of Brahma, Vishnu, and Shiva, known as the Trimurti, represents the cyclical nature of existence and the dynamic interplay between creation, preservation, and destruction. Each of these deities is supported by their consorts—Saraswati, Lakshmi, and Parvati—who provide the necessary energies and attributes to sustain their divine partners' roles.

Honoring the Hindu Pantheon

Hindu deities are honored through various texts, rituals, and festivals, each reflecting the rich diversity of Hindu worship practices.

Sacred Texts: The Vedas, Upanishads, Puranas, and epics like the Mahabharata and Ramayana are the foundational texts that narrate the stories and teachings of the Hindu deities. These texts provide the theological and philosophical framework for understanding the roles and attributes of the gods and goddesses.

Festivals: Hindu festivals are vibrant expressions of devotion and celebration. Diwali, the festival of lights, honors Lakshmi and the return of Rama. Holi, the festival of colors, celebrates the playful spirit of Krishna. Navaratri is a nine-night festival dedicated to the various forms of Durga. Each festival involves elaborate rituals, prayers, music, dance, and community gatherings, creating a deep connection between the devotees and the divine.

Daily Worship and Rituals: Daily worship, or puja, involves offering prayers, flowers, food, and incense to the deities. Temples and home altars serve as sacred spaces where devotees connect with their chosen deities, seek blessings, and express their gratitude. Regular recitation of mantras, like the Gayatri Mantra for Saraswati or the Vishnu Sahasranama (a thousand names of Vishnu), enhances the spiritual bond with the divine.

Pilgrimages: Pilgrimages to sacred sites, such as Varanasi for Shiva or Vrindavan for Krishna, are an important aspect of honoring Hindu deities. These journeys are seen as acts of devotion and opportunities for spiritual renewal.

By engaging in these practices, devotees not only honor the deities but also align themselves with the divine energies that these gods and goddesses represent. This alignment fosters spiritual growth, inner peace, and a deeper understanding of the universe and our place within it.

Alex McCann Johnson

Chapter 98

Greek

Greek mythology has always fascinated me with its rich tapestry of stories, gods, and goddesses. It offers a glimpse into the ancient Greek worldview, where deities played a central role in explaining natural phenomena, human behavior, and the mysteries of life. These myths are more than just stories; they are reflections of the values, fears, and aspirations of the people who created them.

The Greek pantheon is composed of a multitude of gods and goddesses, each with their own distinct personalities, domains, and attributes. From the mighty Zeus to the wise Athena, these deities are woven into the fabric of Greek culture and spirituality. They reside on Mount Olympus, the highest mountain in Greece, where they govern various aspects of the world and human life. These gods and goddesses are not distant, ethereal beings but very much involved in the everyday lives of humans, often exhibiting emotions and behaviors that mirror those of their worshippers.

Main Gods and Goddesses of the Greek Pantheon

Zeus - King of the Gods: Zeus is the ruler of Mount Olympus and the king of all the gods. He governs the sky and wields thunderbolts as his weapon, symbolizing his power and authority. Zeus is also associated with law, order, and justice, often depicted sitting on his throne with a lightning bolt in hand. His many myths portray him as a powerful yet sometimes capricious figure who maintains the balance of the cosmos. Despite his supreme status, Zeus is known for his numerous love affairs

573

with goddesses and mortal women alike, which often lead to the birth of other important deities and heroes.

Hera - Goddess of Marriage and Family: Hera is the queen of the gods and the wife of Zeus. She is the goddess of marriage, women, and family, often depicted wearing a crown and holding a scepter or a pomegranate, symbolizing fertility. Despite her powerful position, Hera is frequently portrayed as a jealous and vengeful wife, especially towards Zeus's lovers and their offspring. Her commitment to marriage and family, however, makes her a protector of these institutions. In art and mythology, she represents the ideal of marital fidelity and the sanctity of the family unit.

Poseidon - God of the Sea: Poseidon, brother of Zeus, is the god of the sea, earthquakes, and horses. He wields a trident and is often depicted riding a chariot pulled by magnificent sea creatures. Poseidon is known for his tempestuous nature, capable of both creating and calming storms. He is worshipped by sailors and those who depend on the sea, and he plays a crucial role in many myths, including the story of Atlantis and his conflict with Odysseus in Homer's Odyssey. Poseidon's control over the ocean's vast and unpredictable forces symbolizes the Greeks' respect and fear of the sea's power.

Demeter - Goddess of Agriculture: Demeter is the goddess of agriculture, grain, and fertility. She is often shown with sheaves of wheat or a cornucopia, symbolizing abundance and the bounty of the earth. Demeter's most famous myth involves her daughter Persephone's abduction by Hades, which explains the changing seasons. Her grief during Persephone's absence causes winter, while her joy at her daughter's return brings about spring and summer. Demeter's connection to the earth and the cycle of life and death underscores the importance of agriculture and the seasons in ancient Greek life.

Athena - Goddess of Wisdom and War: Athena, born from the forehead of Zeus, is the goddess of wisdom, war, and crafts. She is depicted wearing armor, with a helmet, shield, and spear, and accompanied by an owl, a symbol of wisdom. Athena is a virgin goddess who represents strategic warfare and rational thought, contrasting with the brute force of Ares, the god of war. She is also the patroness of Athens, the city named in her honor after she gifted its people the olive tree. Athena's blend of intellect and military prowess makes her a revered figure in Greek mythology, embodying the values of knowledge and strategic warfare.

Apollo - God of the Sun, Music, and Prophecy: Apollo is the god of the sun, music, poetry, and prophecy. He is often shown with a lyre, symbolizing his association with the arts, and a bow and arrows. Apollo is the twin brother of Artemis and a key figure in many myths, including his role as the slayer of the Python and his unfortunate love affairs. As the god of prophecy, he is linked to the Oracle of Delphi, where priests and priestesses would interpret his will and deliver prophecies. Apollo's diverse domains reflect the Greeks' appreciation for the balance between intellectual, artistic, and physical pursuits.

Artemis - Goddess of the Hunt and the Moon: Artemis, Apollo's twin sister, is the goddess of the hunt, wilderness, and the moon. She is depicted with a bow and arrows, often accompanied by a stag or hunting dogs. Artemis is a virgin goddess who protects young women and is associated with childbirth despite her own chastity. Her connection to the moon and the natural world makes her a symbol of the untamed and independent spirit. Artemis's dual role as both a huntress and a protector highlights the Greek appreciation for the balance between nurturing and wildness in the natural world.

Ares - God of War: Ares is the god of war, representing the brutal and chaotic aspects of conflict. Unlike Athena, who symbolizes strategic warfare, Ares embodies the violence and bloodshed of battle. He is often depicted in full armor, with a spear and shield, and accompanied by figures representing fear and panic. Despite his important role, Ares is not widely revered in Greek mythology, often portrayed as rash and impulsive. His tumultuous relationships, including his affair with Aphrodite, and his frequent defeats in myth reflect the Greeks' ambivalent view of war's destructive nature.

Aphrodite - Goddess of Love and Beauty: Aphrodite, born from the sea foam, is the goddess of love, beauty, and desire. She is depicted as an enchanting figure, often with a dove or a mirror. Aphrodite's influence extends beyond romantic love to encompass attraction, pleasure, and procreation. She is central to many myths, including her role in the Trojan War and her numerous liaisons with gods and mortals. Aphrodite's presence in Greek mythology highlights the powerful and sometimes tumultuous nature of love and beauty, influencing both divine and mortal realms.

Hephaestus - God of Fire and Craftsmanship: Hephaestus is the god of fire, metalworking, and craftsmanship. He is depicted with a hammer and anvil, symbolizing his skills as a blacksmith and artisan. Despite his physical imperfections and being thrown from Mount Olympus by his mother Hera, Hephaestus is revered for his ingenuity and creativity. He is the creator of many divine weapons and artifacts, including Zeus's thunderbolts and Achilles' armor. Hephaestus's story illustrates the value of skill and perseverance, as well as the power of fire and creativity.

Hades - God of the Underworld: Hades is the god of the underworld and the ruler of the dead. Often depicted with his three-headed dog, Cerberus, he governs the realm of the afterlife. Despite his dark domain, Hades is not considered evil but rather a stern and just overseer of the dead. He is also associated with wealth and the riches that come from the earth. The myth of his abduction of Persephone and their subsequent marriage underscores his role in the cycles of death and rebirth. Hades's domain is a reminder of the Greeks' belief in the afterlife and the inevitability of death.

Dionysus - God of Wine and Festivity: Dionysus is the god of wine, festivity, and ecstasy. He is often shown holding a grapevine or a cup of wine, surrounded by revelers. Dionysus represents the liberating and intoxicating aspects of life, encouraging both joy and madness. His worship involved ecstatic rituals and celebrations, known as Dionysian mysteries, which sought to break down societal norms and connect with the divine through ecstatic experiences. Dionysus's dual nature as both a bringer of joy and a harbinger of chaos reflects the Greeks' understanding of the balance between order and excess.

The Creation Story of the Greek Pantheon

The Greek creation story is a compelling narrative that begins with the primordial void, Chaos. From Chaos emerged Gaia (Earth), Tartarus (the Underworld), and Eros (Love). Gaia, personifying the Earth, gave birth to Uranus (the Sky), and together, they produced the Titans, the Cyclopes, and the Hecatoncheires (giants with a hundred hands).

Uranus, fearing the power of his offspring, imprisoned them within Gaia. In retaliation, Gaia conspired with her youngest Titan son, Cronus, who overthrew Uranus by castrating him with a sickle provided by Gaia. From the blood of Uranus, the Furies, and the Giants were born, and from his severed genitals, Aphrodite emerged from the sea foam.

Cronus then took control and became the ruler of the cosmos. However, he too, feared the prophecy that he would be overthrown by his own children. To prevent this, he swallowed each of his offspring at birth. Rhea, his wife, saved their youngest child, Zeus, by hiding him in a cave on the island of Crete and giving Cronus a stone wrapped in swaddling clothes to swallow instead.

Zeus grew up in secret and, once strong enough, waged war against Cronus and the Titans. With the help of his siblings, whom he freed from Cronus's stomach, and other allies like the Cyclopes and the Hecatoncheires, Zeus defeated the Titans in a great battle known as the Titanomachy. The Titans were subsequently imprisoned in Tartarus, and Zeus became the supreme ruler of the gods.

Zeus and his siblings—Poseidon, Hades, Hera, Demeter, and Hestia—divided the realms among themselves. Zeus took the sky, Poseidon the sea, and Hades the underworld. Hera became the queen of the gods, overseeing marriage and family, while Demeter and Hestia took charge of agriculture and the hearth, respectively. This division of power established the rule of the Olympian gods, who then set about ordering the cosmos and overseeing human affairs.

Alex McCann Johnson

Honoring the Greek Pantheon

Sacred Texts: The ancient Greeks honored their gods through epic poems and hymns, with texts like Homer's "Iliad" and "Odyssey," and Hesiod's "Theogony" and "Works and Days" being central to understanding the divine narratives. These texts not only recount the myths but also illustrate the moral and ethical frameworks of the time.

Temples and Sacred Sites: The Greeks built magnificent temples to honor their gods, such as the Parthenon for Athena in Athens and the Temple of Zeus in Olympia. These sacred sites were places of worship, sacrifice, and festivals, serving as focal points for communal worship and individual devotion.

Festivals: Numerous festivals were held to honor the gods, often involving processions, sacrifices, and games. For example, the Olympic Games were held in honor of Zeus, and the Panathenaic Festival celebrated Athena. Dionysus was honored with theatrical performances during the Dionysia, reflecting his connection to drama and festivity.

Daily Worship and Rituals: Daily life in ancient Greece was infused with the worship of gods. Offerings, prayers, and libations were made to household deities and at public altars. The Greeks believed in maintaining a reciprocal relationship with the gods, seeking their favor, and expressing gratitude through these practices.

Oracles and Divination: Oracles, such as the Oracle of Delphi dedicated to Apollo, were important centers for seeking divine guidance. People from all over Greece and beyond would come to these sites to receive prophecies and advice from the gods, interpreted by the priests and priestesses.

By engaging in these practices, ancient Greeks maintained a close and personal relationship with their deities. Today, these myths and traditions continue to inspire and inform modern spiritual practices, reflecting the enduring legacy of the Greek pantheon.

Chapter 99

Roman

Roman mythology, much like its Greek counterpart, is a rich tapestry of gods, goddesses, and mythic narratives that were deeply woven into the fabric of Roman society. The Romans were heavily influenced by Greek mythology, adopting and adapting many of the Greek gods and stories to fit their own cultural and religious practices. However, Roman mythology also developed its own unique deities and traditions, reflecting the values, governance, and daily life of ancient Rome.

The Roman pantheon is characterized by a pantheon of deities who governed various aspects of the natural world and human life. These gods and goddesses were integral to the Roman state religion, and their worship was essential to maintaining the favor of the divine and the prosperity of the empire. Unlike the more personal and anthropomorphic Greek deities, Roman gods were often seen as more austere and function-driven, embodying the principles of Roman order and duty.

Main Gods and Goddesses of the Roman Pantheon

Jupiter - King of the Gods: Jupiter, known as Jove, is the Roman equivalent of the Greek god Zeus. He is the supreme deity of the Roman pantheon and the god of the sky, thunder, and lightning. Jupiter is often depicted with a thunderbolt in hand and an eagle at his side, symbolizing his authority and connection to the heavens. As the chief protector of the Roman state and its laws, he was worshipped in grand temples, such as the Temple of Jupiter Optimus Maximus on the Capitoline Hill. Jupiter's role extended to overseeing the welfare of the Roman people and the governance of justice and social order.

Juno - Goddess of Marriage and the State: Juno is the queen of the gods and the wife of Jupiter, mirroring the role of Hera in Greek mythology. She is the goddess of marriage and childbirth and the protector of the Roman state. Juno is often depicted with a diadem and a peacock, her sacred animal. She was worshipped as Juno Moneta, the protector of funds, and Juno Regina, the queen of the gods. Juno's festivals, such as Matronalia, celebrated marriage and the feminine virtues of Roman women. Her guidance and protection were considered vital to the success and stability of the state and family life.

Neptune - God of the Sea: Neptune, the Roman counterpart to the Greek Poseidon, is the god of the sea, freshwater, and horses. He is depicted holding a trident, often accompanied by sea creatures. Neptune was revered by sailors and those engaged in maritime activities. His festivals, such as Neptunalia, celebrated his power over the waters and included rituals for securing safe passage and favorable conditions at sea. Neptune's influence extended to freshwater sources, essential for Roman agriculture and daily life, making his worship crucial to the survival and prosperity of the Romans.

Minerva - Goddess of Wisdom and Strategic Warfare: Minerva, similar to the Greek Athena, is the goddess of wisdom, strategic warfare, and the arts. She is depicted wearing armor, with a helmet and spear, and is often accompanied by an owl, symbolizing wisdom. Minerva was also the patroness of crafts, particularly weaving and metalworking, and was venerated by artisans and scholars. The festival of Quinquatria was celebrated in her honor, marked the beginning of the campaign season, and included various forms of artistic and intellectual competitions. Minerva's influence on learning and strategic planning made her a key deity in both the intellectual and military spheres of Roman life.

Venus - Goddess of Love and Beauty: Venus, the Roman equivalent of Aphrodite, is the goddess of love, beauty, and fertility. She is often depicted as a beautiful woman emerging from the sea or surrounded by doves. Venus played a crucial role in Roman mythology as the mother of Aeneas, the Trojan hero who founded the lineage leading to the establishment of Rome. As a result, Venus was also seen as a protector of the Roman people and the divine ancestor of Julius Caesar and his successors. Her festival, Veneralia, celebrated love and beauty with rituals seeking her favor in matters of romance and prosperity.

Mars - God of War: Mars, originally an agricultural deity, evolved into the primary god of war and one of the most important deities in the Roman pantheon. Unlike the Greek Ares, Mars was revered not only for his martial prowess but also as a father of the Roman people. He is often depicted in full battle armor, with a spear and shield. Mars was considered the father of Romulus and Remus, the legendary founders of Rome, and his festivals, such as the March and October Horse, were integral to the Roman military calendar. Mars's dual role as a god of agriculture and war reflects the Roman values of discipline and the readiness to protect and expand their territory.

Vesta - Goddess of the Hearth and Home: Vesta is the goddess of the hearth, home, and family, embodying the stability and sanctity of the Roman household. She is depicted as a modest woman holding a flame, symbolizing the eternal fire that burned in her temples. The Vestal Virgins, her priestesses, were tasked with maintaining the sacred fire in the Temple of Vesta in Rome. Vesta's festival, Vestalia, was a time when householders honored the goddess with rituals and offerings to ensure the protection and prosperity of their homes. Vesta's presence in Roman religion underscored the importance of domestic harmony and the continuity of the state through the well-being of the family unit.

Apollo - God of the Sun, Music, and Prophecy: Apollo is one of the few gods whose name and attributes were directly borrowed from Greek mythology. He is the god of the sun, music, poetry, and prophecy. Depicted with a lyre and a laurel wreath, Apollo was revered for his beauty and artistic skills. He played a significant role in Roman religion as the god who could heal and bring plagues, and his oracles were sought for guidance in times of crisis. The Roman festival of Ludi Apollinares honored Apollo with games and theatrical performances, celebrating his influence over the arts and his power to protect and enlighten humanity.

Diana - Goddess of the Hunt and the Moon: Diana, the Roman counterpart of Artemis, is the goddess of the hunt, wilderness, and the moon. She is often depicted with a bow and arrows, accompanied by a stag or hunting dogs. Diana was also revered as a protector of women and children, especially during childbirth. Her sanctuary at Lake Nemi, known as Diana Nemorensis, was a significant cult center, and her festival, Nemoralia, involved rituals by moonlight and offerings at the sacred lake. Diana's connection to the natural world and the cycles of the moon made her a powerful symbol of the untamed and protective aspects of the divine.

Vulcan - God of Fire and Forge: Vulcan, the Roman equivalent of Hephaestus, is the god of fire, metalworking, and craftsmanship. He is depicted with a blacksmith's hammer and anvil, often shown at his forge. Vulcan was revered as the maker of weapons and tools for the gods and heroes. His festival, Vulcanalia, was held in August to protect against destructive fires during the hot, dry season. Offerings were made to Vulcan by throwing small animals into a fire, symbolizing a plea for protection and the beneficial use of fire. Vulcan's role in creating both practical and divine artifacts underscores the Romans' appreciation for skill and ingenuity.

Mercury - God of Commerce and Communication: Mercury, known as Hermes in Greek mythology, is the god of commerce, communication, and travel. He is depicted with winged sandals and a caduceus, a staff with two snakes entwined, symbolizing his role as a messenger. Mercury was also the patron of merchants, travelers, and thieves. His ability to move freely between the mortal and divine worlds made him a guide for souls to the afterlife. The festival of Mercuralia was celebrated by merchants who sprinkled water from a sacred well on their goods and ships, seeking Mercury's blessing for prosperity and safe travels.

Ceres - Goddess of Agriculture and Grain: Ceres, similar to the Greek Demeter, is the goddess of agriculture, grain, and the fertility of the land. She is depicted with sheaves of wheat or a cornucopia, symbolizing the bounty of the earth. Ceres was central to Roman agricultural practices and rituals, particularly those associated with the growth and harvest of crops. The festival of Cerealia celebrated the sowing and reaping of crops, with games and processions dedicated to her. Ceres's importance in Roman religion reflects the critical role of agriculture in sustaining Roman society and the emphasis on fertility and abundance in daily life.

The Creation Story of the Roman Pantheon

The Roman creation myth shares similarities with Greek mythology but also incorporates distinct Roman elements and deities. The story begins with Chaos, a formless void from which the primordial deities emerge. From Chaos came Terra (Earth) and Caelus (Sky), who gave birth to the Titans, the Cyclopes, and the Giants.

Terra and Caelus's union produced Saturn, the Roman counterpart of Cronus. Saturn, fearing a prophecy that he would be overthrown by his children, swallowed each one at birth. However, his wife, Ops (Rhea), saved their youngest child, Jupiter, by hiding him and giving Saturn a stone to swallow instead. Jupiter grew up in secret and eventually led a rebellion against Saturn and the Titans, similar to the Greek Titanomachy.

With the help of his siblings, whom he freed from Saturn's stomach, and other allies like the Cyclopes, Jupiter defeated the Titans and imprisoned them in Tartarus. Jupiter, along with his brothers Neptune and Pluto, then divided the cosmos among themselves. Jupiter took the sky, Neptune the sea, and Pluto the underworld.

This division established the rule of the Olympian gods, who were responsible for various aspects of the world and human life. Jupiter became the supreme ruler, overseeing the other gods and maintaining the order of the cosmos. The Roman pantheon thus reflects a structured and hierarchical universe governed by divine principles and the interplay of various deities.

Honoring the Roman Pantheon

Sacred Texts: The Romans did not have a single sacred text equivalent to the Greek "Iliad" or "Odyssey," but they recorded their myths and religious practices in works like Ovid's "Metamorphoses" and Virgil's "Aeneid." These texts provide a rich source of Roman mythology and the stories of their gods.

Temples and Sacred Sites: Romans built grand temples to honor their gods, such as the Pantheon, which was dedicated to all the gods, and the Temple of Jupiter Optimus Maximus. These temples were centers of worship and public rituals, where citizens could seek the favor of the gods and participate in communal religious life.

Festivals: The Roman calendar was filled with festivals dedicated to various deities. Saturnalia, in honor of Saturn, was one of the most famous, featuring feasting, gift-giving, and a temporary reversal of social roles. Lupercalia, associated with fertility and purification, involved rituals to promote health and protect against evil spirits. These festivals were integral to Roman social and religious life, reinforcing the community's connection to the divine.

Daily Worship and Rituals: Daily life in Rome involved numerous rituals and practices to honor the gods. Romans would make offerings at household altars, participate in public sacrifices, and invoke the gods in prayers for protection, success, and guidance. The concept of "numen," or divine presence, was central to Roman religion, emphasizing the belief that the gods' favor was essential for personal and communal well-being.

Oracles and Divination: The Romans practiced various forms of divination to seek guidance from the gods, including augury, the interpretation of the flight patterns of birds, and haruspicy, the examination of animal entrails. These practices were used to make decisions and seek approval from the divine for public and private actions.

The Roman pantheon and its associated practices illustrate the deep connection between the Romans and their gods. This relationship was built on mutual respect, reverence, and the belief in the gods' active involvement in human affairs. Today, the legacy of the Roman gods continues to influence modern culture, language, and spiritual practices, reflecting their enduring impact on human history.

Alex McCann Johnson

Chapter 100

Norse

Norse mythology is a rich and complex tapestry of gods, goddesses, giants, and mythical creatures. It originates from the ancient Scandinavian and Germanic peoples, who passed down these tales through oral tradition. The myths capture the Norse worldview, their understanding of nature, and the cyclical nature of life and death.

The Norse gods, known as the Aesir and Vanir, inhabit Asgard, one of the Nine Worlds connected by the cosmic tree Yggdrasil. These deities are deeply woven into the fabric of Norse culture and spirituality, governing various aspects of the natural world and human life. The stories of their adventures, conflicts, and relationships reflect the values and beliefs of the Norse people, offering insights into their approach to life, honor, and the cosmos.

Main Gods and Goddesses of the Norse Pantheon

Odin - The All-Father, God of Wisdom and War: Odin is the chief of the Aesir, the king of the gods, and one of the most complex deities in the Norse pantheon. He is the god of wisdom, war, poetry, and death. Odin is often depicted as a one-eyed, bearded old man, wearing a cloak and a wide-brimmed hat, and accompanied by his ravens, Huginn (thought) and Muninn (memory), who fly across the world to bring him news. He sacrificed his eye for wisdom at Mimir's well and hung himself on Yggdrasil to gain knowledge of the runes. Odin's relentless pursuit of knowledge and his role as the god of the slain warriors who join him in Valhalla, highlight his deep connection to both wisdom and warfare.

Frigg - Goddess of Marriage and Motherhood: Frigg, Odin's wife, is the queen of the Aesir and the goddess of marriage, motherhood, and domestic affairs. She is known for her wisdom and foresight, although she seldom reveals her knowledge. Frigg is often associated with the earth and fertility and is depicted spinning clouds on her spindle. She is also linked with prophecy and weaving the fates, reflecting her role as a nurturing yet powerful figure. Frigg's deep concern for her family and her protective nature are central themes in many myths, such as her attempts to prevent the death of her son Baldr.

Thor - God of Thunder and Protector of Mankind: Thor, one of the most popular gods in the Norse pantheon, is the god of thunder, lightning, storms, and strength. He is depicted as a mighty warrior with a red beard, wielding his enchanted hammer Mjölnir, which is capable of leveling mountains and destroying giants. Thor rides a chariot pulled by two goats, Tanngrisnir and Tanngnjóstr, and his adventures often involve battling giants and other monstrous beings. As the protector of Midgard (the world of humans), Thor is revered for his courage and his role in maintaining the balance between order and chaos. His character embodies the virtues of strength, bravery, and loyalty.

Loki - The Trickster God: Loki is the enigmatic and controversial trickster god known for his cunning, shape-shifting abilities and often disruptive behavior. Although not originally part of the Aesir, Loki becomes Odin's blood brother and takes part in many adventures with the gods. He is responsible for both causing and solving problems among the gods, such as engineering the death of Baldr and later aiding in the construction of Asgard's walls. Loki's dual nature as both a helper and a hindrance reflects the complex interplay of chaos and order in Norse mythology. Eventually, his betrayals lead to his imprisonment and his crucial role in the events of Ragnarök, the end of the world.

Baldr - God of Light and Purity: Baldr, the son of Odin and Frigg, is the god of light, purity, and beauty. He is loved by all the gods and considered the best among them. Baldr's dreams of his own death lead to his mother, Frigg, extracting oaths from all things to not harm him, except for the mistletoe, which was deemed too insignificant. Loki exploits this loophole, causing Baldr's death by tricking the blind god Höðr into killing him with a mistletoe dart. Baldr's death marks a significant event in Norse mythology, foreshadowing the doom of the gods at Ragnarök. His eventual resurrection after Ragnarök symbolizes hope and renewal.

Freyja - Goddess of Love, Beauty, and Fertility: Freyja is one of the most prominent goddesses in Norse mythology, associated with love, beauty, fertility, and war. She is a member of the Vanir, a group of gods associated with nature and fertility, who joined the Aesir after a truce. Freyja rides a chariot pulled by cats and is often depicted wearing her magical necklace, Brísingamen. She possesses a cloak of falcon feathers that allows her to fly between worlds. Freyja's dual role as a goddess of fertility and a chooser of the slain warriors who go to her hall, Fólkvangr, highlights her connection to both life and death.

Freyr - God of Fertility and Prosperity: Freyr, Freyja's brother and a prominent Vanir god, is the god of fertility, prosperity, and kingship. He is associated with sunshine, rain, and the bountiful harvests that ensure the survival of the community. Freyr is often depicted with his magical boar, Gullinbursti, and his ship, Skidbladnir, which can sail on land, sea, or air. He is also linked to peace and happiness, making him a central figure in ensuring the well-being of the land and its people. Freyr's marriage to the giantess Gerd symbolizes the union of opposing forces and the harmony of nature.

Tyr - God of War and Justice: Tyr is the god of war, justice, and law. He is known for his courage and honor, exemplified by his willingness to sacrifice his hand to bind the monstrous wolf Fenrir. Tyr's role as a god of war is distinct from that of Odin and Thor; he represents the more honorable and lawful aspects of conflict, focusing on justice and fair combat. His association with legal proceedings and the maintenance of social order reflects the Norse emphasis on law and oaths. Tyr's sacrifice to bind Fenrir highlights his dedication to the greater good and the protection of the gods.

Heimdall - The Watchman of the Gods: Heimdall is the vigilant guardian of the Bifrost, the rainbow bridge that connects Asgard to Midgard. He is depicted with keen senses, able to hear grass grow and see for hundreds of miles, making him an unparalleled watchman. Heimdall is also known as the "shining god" and is often associated with light and the dawn. He possesses a horn, Gjallarhorn, which he will blow to signal the beginning of Ragnarök. Heimdall's role as the eternal watchman and his eventual confrontation with Loki during Ragnarök underscore his importance in maintaining the safety and order of the cosmos.

Njord - God of the Sea and Wealth: Njord, the father of Freyja and Freyr, is the god of the sea, wind, and wealth. He is one of the Vanir gods who joined the Aesir after the war between the two groups. Njord is associated with seafaring, fishing, and prosperity, making him an important deity for coastal communities and those who rely on the sea for their livelihood. His marriage to the giantess Skadi represents the union of the sea and the mountains, though their different affinities lead to an eventual separation. Njord's blessings are sought for safe voyages and bountiful catches, reflecting his role in providing wealth and stability.

Hel - Goddess of the Underworld: Hel is the ruler of the realm of the dead that bears her name, where she oversees those who did not die gloriously in battle. She is the daughter of Loki and the giantess Angrboda, and her domain, Niflheim, is a cold and shadowy place. She is depicted as a figure with a half-living, half-dead appearance, symbolizing her connection to both life and death. Despite her somber role, Hel's realm is a place of rest and reflection for the souls who reside there. Her presence in Norse mythology highlights the inevitability of death and the importance of the afterlife in the Norse belief system.

Skadi - Goddess of Winter and Hunting: Skadi, a giantess, is the goddess of winter, hunting, and skiing. After the death of her father, the giant Thiazi, she sought compensation from the gods and chose to marry Njord as part of her recompense. Skadi prefers the cold mountains to Njord's coastal home, leading to their separation. She is often depicted with a bow and arrows, ready for the hunt. Skadi's association with the harsh, wintery landscapes and her fierce independence make her a symbol of strength and resilience. Her marriage to Njord represents the difficult balance between contrasting elements and the quest for harmony.

The Creation Story of the Norse Pantheon

The Norse creation story begins with the primordial void, Ginnungagap, lying between the realms of fire (Muspelheim) and ice (Niflheim). The interaction of these elemental forces gave rise to the first living being, Ymir, the ancestor of the giants. From Ymir's body, the first man and woman were born.

As the ice melted, a cow named Audhumla emerged, whose milk nourished Ymir. Audhumla also licked the salty ice, eventually revealing Buri, the first of the gods. Buri's descendants, including Odin, Vili, and Ve, grew strong and wise. They eventually overthrew Ymir, creating the world from his body. Ymir's flesh became the earth, his blood the seas, his bones the mountains, and his skull the sky.

The gods then created the first humans, Ask and Embla, from two trees, gifting them with life, intelligence, and senses. Odin and his brothers established Asgard, the realm of the gods, and organized the cosmos into Nine Worlds, connected by Yggdrasil, the World Tree.

This creation story sets the stage for the ongoing interactions between gods, giants, and humans, encapsulating the Norse understanding of the world's origins and its inherent cycles of creation and destruction.

Honoring the Norse Pantheon

Sacred Texts: The Poetic Edda and the Prose Edda are central texts that provide a rich collection of Norse myths and stories. These works, compiled in medieval Iceland, preserve the ancient lore and offer insights into the cosmology, deities, and heroes of the Norse tradition.

Temples and Sacred Sites: Although many physical temples to the Norse gods have been lost to history, sacred sites such as groves, mountains, and rivers were often dedicated to their worship. Today, places like the Temple at Uppsala in Sweden and the Gamla Uppsala site are known for their historical significance in Norse religious practices.

Festivals: Norse festivals were tied to the agricultural calendar and significant events in the myths. Blóts, sacrificial feasts, were held to honor the gods and spirits. Important festivals include Yule, celebrating the winter solstice and rebirth, and Althing, an assembly with both legal and religious significance.

Daily Worship and Rituals: Daily life for the Norse included rituals to honor the gods and seek their favor. These could range from offerings of food and drink at home altars to more elaborate communal ceremonies. Respecting the natural world and the cycles of life was integral to their spirituality.

Modern Revival and Practices: Today, there is a resurgence of interest in Norse mythology and spirituality. Modern practitioners, often known as Heathens or Asatru, revive ancient rituals, celebrate traditional festivals, and honor the gods through various contemporary practices. This revival reflects a deep respect for the heritage and enduring wisdom of the Norse pantheon.

The Norse pantheon, with its rich array of deities and stories, offers timeless lessons about strength, resilience, and the intricate balance of life. By exploring and honoring these ancient gods, we connect with the enduring spirit of the Norse people and the mysteries of the cosmos they sought to understand.

Chapter 101

Celtic

Celtic mythology encompasses the spiritual beliefs, gods, and legends of the ancient Celtic people, who once inhabited large parts of Europe, including present-day Ireland, Scotland, Wales, and France. This mythology is deeply rooted in nature and the landscape, reflecting the Celts' close relationship with the natural world. The Celts did not leave a single, unified body of mythology; rather, their stories and deities vary widely across regions and tribes, making Celtic mythology a rich and diverse tapestry.

The Celtic gods and goddesses are often connected to natural features such as rivers, mountains, and forests, and they embody various aspects of life, war, fertility, and the underworld. These deities are celebrated in a multitude of tales that have been passed down through oral tradition and later recorded in medieval texts. The myths and legends of the Celts are filled with heroic feats, magical transformations, and deep spiritual insights, offering a window into their worldview and values.

Main Gods and Goddesses of the Celtic Pantheon

Dagda - The Good God: Dagda is one of the most powerful and revered gods in the Celtic pantheon. Known as the "Good God," he is associated with fertility, agriculture, strength, and abundance. The Dagda is often depicted as a large, bearded man carrying a massive club capable of killing and resurrecting. He also possesses a magic cauldron that provides endless sustenance and a harp that controls the seasons. As a chief of the Tuatha Dé Danann, a mythical race of divine beings, the Dagda plays a crucial role in ensuring the prosperity and protection of his people. His attributes of wisdom and resourcefulness make him a central figure in Celtic mythology.

Brigid - Goddess of Fire and Inspiration: Brigid, also known as Brigit or Brigantia, is one of the most beloved deities in Celtic mythology. She is the goddess of fire, healing, poetry, and smithcraft. Brigid is often depicted as a radiant woman associated with both the hearth and the forge. She is also a goddess of fertility and childbirth, revered as a protector of mothers and infants. Brigid's festival, Imbolc, celebrated on February 1st, marks the beginning of spring and is a time of purification and renewal. Her dual aspects as a healer and inspirer of creativity highlight her nurturing and transformative powers.

Lugh - God of Light and Skill: Lugh, often called Lugh Lámhfhada ("Lugh of the Long Arm"), is a multifaceted god associated with light, crafts, and warfare. He is known for his mastery of many skills, earning him the title of Samildánach ("the many-skilled"). Lugh is often depicted with a spear or sling and is celebrated as a warrior, king, and savior of the Tuatha Dé Danann. His festival, Lughnasadh, held on August 1st, marks the harvest season and is a time of feasting and games. Lugh's role as a bringer of light and his prowess in various arts reflect his importance as a deity of excellence and inspiration.

Morrigan - Goddess of War and Fate: The Morrigan, or Morrígu, is a complex and enigmatic goddess associated with war, fate, and sovereignty. She is often depicted as a trio of sisters or as a single goddess with multiple aspects. The Morrigan is known for her ability to shape-shift into a raven or crow, symbolizing death and transformation. She appears on battlefields to influence the outcome of conflicts and guide the souls of the fallen. The Morrigan's role as a harbinger of doom and her connection to the land's sovereignty highlight her power over life and death. Her presence in mythology underscores themes of fate, prophecy, and the cyclical nature of life.

Danu - Mother Goddess of the Tuatha Dé Danann: Danu, or Anu, is revered as the mother goddess of the Tuatha Dé Danann, the supernatural race of beings in Celtic mythology. She embodies the earth's fertility and abundance, nurturing the land and its people. Danu is often associated with rivers and water, symbolizing life-giving forces and the flow of time. Although direct myths about Danu are scarce, her presence is deeply felt as the progenitor and protector of the Tuatha Dé Danann. Her role as a mother figure connects her to themes of creation, nurturing, and the continuity of life.

Cernunnos - The Horned God of Nature: Cernunnos is a prominent deity in Celtic mythology, often depicted with the antlers of a stag and associated with nature, animals, fertility, and the underworld. He is seen as a guardian of the forest and a symbol of the wild, untamed aspects of nature. Cernunnos is often shown seated in a meditative pose, surrounded by animals, and holding a torch, a symbol of power and authority. His connection to the cycle of life and death and his role as a mediator between the physical and spiritual realms highlight his significance as a deity of nature and transformation.

Aengus - God of Love and Youth: Aengus, also known as Aonghus or Angus Óg ("Aengus the Young"), is the god of love, youth, and poetic inspiration. He is the son of the Dagda and Boann, the river goddess. Aengus is often depicted as a handsome young man with birds circling his head, representing love and passion. His most famous myth involves his search for his beloved, Caer, whom he finds transformed into a swan. Aengus's tales emphasize themes of love, transformation, and the pursuit of happiness. His youthful and charismatic nature makes him a symbol of beauty and poetic inspiration.

Manannán mac Lir - God of the Sea and Magic: Manannán mac Lir is the god of the sea, weather, and magic. He is the son of Lir, a sea deity, and is often depicted as a powerful figure wielding a spear or trident. Manannán is known for his magical abilities and his role as a guide for souls traveling to the Otherworld. He possesses a ship that can sail without wind and a cloak that grants invisibility. Manannán's connection to the sea and his role as a guardian of the afterlife reflect his influence over both the physical and spiritual realms. His presence in mythology underscores the importance of the sea and its mysteries in Celtic culture.

Arawn - King of the Underworld: Arawn is the ruler of Annwn, the Otherworld in Welsh mythology, associated with death, the afterlife, and the mysteries beyond the mortal realm. He is often depicted as a fair and just king, guiding the souls of the dead and overseeing a realm of beauty and abundance. Arawn is known for his role in the tale of Pwyll, where he exchanges places with the human hero to defeat a common enemy. This story highlights themes of trust, honor, and the thin veil between life and death. Arawn's connection to the Otherworld underscores the Celtic belief in an afterlife that is both a place of rest and a continuation of the soul's journey.

Macha - Goddess of Sovereignty and War: Macha is one of the aspects of the Morrigan and is associated with sovereignty, war, and horses. She is a powerful figure in Irish mythology, often depicted as a warrior queen. Macha's most famous myth involves her race against the king's horses while heavily pregnant, demonstrating her strength and determination. She curses the men of Ulster with the pains of childbirth as a result of their mistreatment. Macha's connection to the land and her role in bestowing and protecting sovereignty reflect her importance as a goddess of power and justice.

Belenus - God of the Sun and Healing: Belenus, also known as Bel or Beli, is a god associated with the sun, healing, and light. He is often depicted with a radiant face or surrounded by flames, symbolizing his connection to the life-giving energy of the sun. Belenus is celebrated during the festival of Beltane, which marks the beginning of the summer season and is a time of purification and renewal. His role as a healer and his association with warmth and vitality make him a significant figure in the Celtic pantheon, representing the power of light to nurture and transform.

The Creation Story of the Celtic Pantheon

Celtic mythology does not have a single, unified creation story but rather a collection of myths that describe the origins of the world and the gods. One of the most prominent narratives involves the Tuatha Dé Danann, a divine race of beings who descended from the sky and settled in Ireland.

The Tuatha Dé Danann arrived in Ireland from four mythical cities—Falias, Gorias, Finias, and Murias—each of which provided them with magical treasures, such as the Stone of Destiny, the Spear of Lugh, the Sword of Nuada, and the Cauldron of the Dagda. These treasures symbolized their divine power and wisdom.

Upon their arrival, the Tuatha Dé Danann encountered the Fir Bolg, the previous inhabitants of Ireland, and a series of battles ensued. After defeating the Fir Bolg, the Tuatha Dé Danann established their rule over the land, bringing prosperity and harmony. However, their reign was challenged by the Fomorians, a race of chaotic and destructive beings.

The pivotal battle between the Tuatha Dé Danann and the Fomorians, known as the Battle of Mag Tuired, resulted in the triumph of the Tuatha Dé Danann, securing their dominance and establishing order in the land. This victory marked the beginning of their golden age, where they governed with wisdom and fairness.

This creation story highlights themes of conflict and resolution, the balance between order and chaos, and the importance of divine guidance in maintaining harmony. The Tuatha Dé Danann's descent from the sky and their interactions with other races reflect the Celtic belief in a dynamic and interconnected world where gods and humans coexist and influence each other's destinies.

Honoring the Celtic Pantheon

Sacred Texts: The myths and legends of the Celtic gods are primarily preserved in medieval manuscripts such as the "Lebor Gabála Érenn" (The Book of Invasions), the "Mabinogion," and the "Táin Bó Cúailnge" (The Cattle Raid of Cooley). These texts offer rich narratives that provide insights into the deities, heroes, and cultural practices of the ancient Celts.

Sacred Sites: Sacred sites like stone circles, wells, and groves are deeply significant in Celtic spirituality. Sites such as Newgrange in Ireland, believed to be aligned with the winter solstice, and the Isle of Anglesey in Wales, a center for Druidic worship, are important places for connecting with the Celtic gods. These locations were often places of pilgrimage and ritual, where the Celts honored their deities and sought their blessings.

Festivals: The Celtic calendar is marked by significant festivals that honor the deities and the changing seasons. Samhain, celebrated on October 31st, marks the end of the harvest and the beginning of winter, a time when the veil between worlds is thin. Imbolc, on February 1st, honors Brigid and heralds the coming of spring. Beltane, on May 1st, celebrates fertility and the blooming of life, while Lughnasadh, on August 1st, is a festival of abundance and the first harvest. These festivals are times of celebration, reflection, and connection with the divine.

Daily Practices: Daily life in Celtic society involved numerous rituals and practices to honor the gods and spirits. Offerings of food, drink, and other gifts were made at household altars and in nature. The Celts also observed auspicious days and performed rites to ensure the well-being of their families and communities. The concept of "geis," or sacred obligations, guided personal conduct and reflected the deep respect for divine will and order.

Modern Practices: Today, there is a resurgence of interest in Celtic spirituality, with many people seeking to reconnect with the ancient traditions and honor the gods through contemporary practices. Modern Druids and Pagans celebrate the festivals, perform rituals in nature, and incorporate Celtic symbols and stories into their spiritual lives. This revival reflects a desire to preserve and adapt the wisdom of the Celtic pantheon for modern times.

The Celtic pantheon, with its diverse and vibrant array of deities, offers insights into the natural world, human experience, and the divine. By exploring and honoring these ancient gods and goddesses, we can connect with the enduring spirit of the Celts and the timeless wisdom they sought to understand and celebrate.

Chapter 102
Egyptian

Egyptian mythology is one of the most ancient and complex systems of belief in human history, with roots that stretch back over 5,000 years. It encompasses a rich tapestry of gods, goddesses, and mythological stories that explain the creation of the world, the workings of nature, and the afterlife. These myths were deeply intertwined with the daily lives and spiritual practices of the ancient Egyptians.

The deities of the Egyptian pantheon were seen as powerful, multifaceted beings who played crucial roles in maintaining the order and balance of the universe. They were associated with various aspects of life, from the forces of nature to human activities, and were worshipped in temples, through rituals, and in personal devotion. The gods and goddesses of Egypt were often depicted with unique and iconic symbols and attributes, reflecting their roles and powers.

Main Gods and Goddesses of the Egyptian Pantheon

Ra (Re) - The Sun God: Ra, the god of the sun, is one of the most important deities in Egyptian mythology. He is often depicted as a man with the head of a falcon crowned with a solar disk encircled by a serpent. Ra is the embodiment of the sun's life-giving and destructive power. As the supreme ruler of the gods, he travels across the sky each day in his solar barque, bringing light and warmth to the world. At night, he journeys through the underworld, battling the forces of chaos, including the serpent Apophis, to ensure the sun rises again each morning. Ra's role as the creator god and his daily cycle of death and rebirth symbolize the eternal nature of life and the universe.

Osiris - God of the Afterlife and Resurrection: Osiris, one of the most revered gods in Egyptian mythology, is the god of the afterlife, resurrection, and fertility. He is depicted as a mummified king with green skin, symbolizing rebirth and regeneration. Osiris presides over the judgment of the dead, determining the fate of souls in the afterlife. According to myth, he was killed and dismembered by his brother Set, only to be resurrected by his wife, Isis, and his sister, Nephthys. This story of death and rebirth made Osiris a symbol of eternal life and the cycle of nature. He is also associated with the fertility of the land and the annual flooding of the Nile, which brings new life to the crops.

Isis - Goddess of Magic and Motherhood: Isis, the wife of Osiris and mother of Horus is one of the most beloved goddesses in the Egyptian pantheon. She is known for her magical prowess, her role as a healer, and her deep maternal love. Often depicted with a throne-shaped crown or as a woman nursing her child, Isis symbolizes the power of motherhood and the protection of children. Her tireless search for the pieces of Osiris's body and her ability to resurrect him demonstrate her magical abilities and her dedication to her family. Isis's worship spread far beyond Egypt, and she became a universal goddess of magic, healing, and protection.

Horus - God of the Sky and Kingship: Horus, the son of Osiris and Isis, is the god of the sky and kingship. He is depicted as a falcon or a man with a falcon's head, often wearing the double crown of Upper and Lower Egypt. Horus avenged his father, Osiris by defeating Set, the god of chaos, in a series of epic battles. This victory established Horus as the rightful ruler of Egypt and the embodiment of divine kingship. Each pharaoh was considered the living incarnation of Horus, ruling with his authority and protection. Horus's eyes, representing the sun and the moon, symbolize his vigilance and his role as a guardian of the kingdom.

Anubis - God of Mummification and the Afterlife: Anubis, the god of mummification and the afterlife, is depicted as a man with the head of a jackal. He is the guardian of the dead and the overseer of the embalming process, ensuring that the bodies of the deceased are properly prepared for their journey to the afterlife. Anubis also presides over the weighing of the heart ceremony, where the deceased's heart is weighed against the feather of Ma'at to determine their fate in the afterlife. His role as a protector and guide in the realm of the dead underscores his importance in the funerary rites and beliefs of the ancient Egyptians.

Thoth - God of Wisdom and Writing: Thoth, the god of wisdom, writing, and knowledge, is often depicted as an ibis or a man with the head of an ibis, holding a writing palette. He is credited with inventing writing and the hieroglyphs, making him the patron of scribes and scholars. Thoth is also associated with the moon and timekeeping, and he plays a crucial role in maintaining the cosmic order. As the divine scribe, he records the judgments of the dead and the deeds of the gods. Thoth's wisdom and his role in the creation and preservation of knowledge highlight his significance in Egyptian culture and mythology.

Hathor - Goddess of Love and Joy: Hathor, the goddess of love, beauty, music, and joy, is often depicted as a woman with cow horns and a solar disk or as a cow. She is associated with motherhood, fertility, and the nurturing aspects of femininity. Hathor is also known as the "Mistress of Dendera," where her temple stands as a testament to her worship. She embodies the joy of life and the pleasures of the senses, and she is a protector of women and children. Hathor's role as a goddess of celebration and her connection to the afterlife, where she welcomes souls into the next world, reflect her multifaceted nature.

Set - God of Chaos and the Desert: Set, the god of chaos, storms, and the desert, is often depicted as a man with the head of a mysterious animal known as the Set animal. He represents the destructive forces of nature and the challenges that disrupt order and harmony. Set is both a villain and a necessary force in Egyptian mythology. While he is the antagonist who kills his brother Osiris, he is also a protector who defends the sun god Ra during his nightly journey through the underworld. Set's complex nature symbolizes the duality of destruction and protection, chaos and stability.

Nephthys - Goddess of Mourning and Protection: Nephthys, the

601

sister of Isis and Osiris, is the goddess of mourning, protection, and the afterlife. She is often depicted as a woman with hieroglyphic symbols on her head, representing her name. Nephthys plays a supportive role in the myths of Osiris, aiding Isis in the resurrection of Osiris and protecting Horus during his infancy. She is associated with the funerary rites and the preparation of the dead for the afterlife. Nephthys's role as a mourner and her protective nature emphasize her importance in the context of death and the transition to the afterlife.

Ma'at - Goddess of Truth and Justice: Ma'at, the goddess of truth, justice, and cosmic order, is depicted as a woman with an ostrich feather on her head. She embodies the principles of balance and harmony that are essential to the universe and society. Ma'at's feather is used in the weighing of the heart ceremony to judge the souls of the deceased. Her presence ensures that truth and righteousness prevail, and her principles guide the actions of gods and humans alike. Ma'at's significance in maintaining the order of the cosmos underscores her central role in Egyptian spirituality and ethics.

Sekhmet - Goddess of War and Healing: Sekhmet, the lioness-headed goddess, is associated with war, destruction, and healing. She is depicted as a fierce warrior who can bring plagues upon her enemies or provide protection and healing to her followers. Sekhmet's dual nature as a bringer of both destruction and healing reflects the balance between chaos and order. In times of peace, she transforms into Hathor, symbolizing the nurturing aspects of femininity. Sekhmet's role as a powerful protector and healer underscores her importance in the Egyptian pantheon.

Ptah - God of Creation and Craftsmen: Ptah, the god of creation and craftsmanship, is often depicted as a mummified man holding a staff that combines symbols of power, life, and stability. He is the patron of artisans, builders, and architects. Ptah is associated with the creative processes, and the spoken word is believed to have brought the universe into existence through his divine speech. His role as a creator god and his connection to the arts highlight his significance in the cultural and spiritual life of ancient Egypt.

The Creation Story of the Egyptian Pantheon

The Egyptian creation myth varies across different regions, but a prominent version is the Heliopolitan creation story, centered around the god Atum.

According to this myth, in the beginning, there were only the primordial waters of chaos called Nun. From these waters emerged Atum, the first god, who created himself through the power of his will. Atum stood on the first land, a mound rising from the waters, symbolizing the emergence of order from chaos.

Atum, desiring companionship, produced the first divine couple through his actions. He created Shu, the god of air, and Tefnut, the goddess of moisture, by either spitting them out or through self-fertilization. Shu and Tefnut represented the principles of life and separation, establishing the framework for creation.

Shu and Tefnut gave birth to Geb, the god of the earth, and Nut, the goddess of the sky. Shu separated Geb and Nut, creating space for life to flourish. Geb and Nut's union produced four children: Osiris, Isis, Set, and Nephthys, who formed the core family of the Egyptian pantheon.

Osiris and Isis became the rulers of the earth, representing fertility and harmony. Set, jealous and chaotic, opposed Osiris, leading to the dramatic myths of Osiris's death and resurrection. These stories encapsulate the themes of life, death, and rebirth central to Egyptian belief.

This creation story emphasizes the themes of emergence from chaos, the establishment of order, and the ongoing cycles of life and death. It reflects the Egyptians' understanding of the cosmos as a balance between opposing forces maintained by the gods' continuous efforts.

Honoring the Egyptian Pantheon

Sacred Texts: The Pyramid Texts, Coffin Texts, and the Book of the Dead are crucial sources of Egyptian religious and mythological knowledge. These texts, inscribed on tombs and burial objects, guide the dead through the afterlife and offer prayers and spells to honor the gods.

Temples and Sacred Sites: Ancient Egyptian temples, such as those at Karnak, Luxor, and Abu Simbel, were dedicated to the gods and served as centers of worship and ritual. These magnificent structures were built to honor the gods and to serve as places where priests performed daily rituals and ceremonies.

Festivals: Egyptian festivals were vibrant celebrations that honored the gods and marked important agricultural and cosmic events. The Opet Festival celebrated the god Amun and the rejuvenation of the pharaoh's power. The Feast of Wagy was a commemoration of Osiris's death and resurrection. These festivals were times of communal joy, offering, and renewal.

Daily Worship and Rituals: Daily life in ancient Egypt was infused with rituals to honor the gods. Offerings of food, drink, and incense were made at household altars and in temples. The practice of wearing amulets and reciting prayers ensured the gods' protection and favor.

Modern Revival and Practices: Today, there is a growing interest in Egyptian spirituality and mythology. Modern practitioners, often known as Kemetic Pagans, revive ancient rituals, celebrate traditional festivals, and honor the gods through contemporary practices. This revival reflects a deep respect for the heritage and enduring wisdom of the Egyptian pantheon.

The Egyptian pantheon, with its rich array of deities and profound myths, offers timeless lessons about creation, balance, and the cycles of life. By exploring and honoring these ancient gods and goddesses, we connect with the enduring spirit of ancient Egypt and the profound mysteries of the cosmos they sought to understand and celebrate.

Chapter 103

Babylonian

Babylonian mythology, a rich and complex tapestry of deities, myths, and cosmological beliefs, emerged from the ancient Mesopotamian region encompassing modern-day Iraq. As part of the broader Mesopotamian mythological tradition, Babylonian myths share roots with Sumerian and Akkadian beliefs, reflecting the cultural and religious heritage of one of the world's earliest civilizations.

Babylon, a city-state that rose to prominence in the 18th century BCE under King Hammurabi, became a center for worship and cultural development. Its mythology is characterized by a pantheon of gods and goddesses who embody natural forces, aspects of life, and cosmic principles. These deities played crucial roles in the daily lives of the Babylonians, guiding their understanding of the world, their practices, and their relationships with the divine.

The Babylonian gods and goddesses were revered in grand temples and through elaborate rituals. Their stories, recorded in cuneiform on clay tablets, reveal insights into the creation of the world, the nature of humanity, and the eternal struggle between order and chaos.

Main Gods and Goddesses of the Babylonian Pantheon

Marduk - Supreme God and Hero: Marduk, the chief deity of Babylon, is a god of creation, justice, and healing. He is often depicted with a serpent dragon or a spade, symbols of his authority and power. Marduk's rise to supremacy is detailed in the "Enuma Elish," the

Babylonian creation epic, where he defeats Tiamat, the primordial goddess of chaos, to become the king of the gods. As the protector of Babylon, Marduk embodies the principles of order and justice, ensuring the stability and prosperity of the cosmos and the city.

Ishtar (Inanna) - Goddess of Love and War: Ishtar, known as Inanna in Sumerian mythology, is the goddess of love, beauty, fertility, and warfare. She is often depicted as a powerful and assertive figure adorned with symbols of lions, stars, and a celestial disc. Ishtar's dual nature as a goddess of both love and war reflects the complexities of human emotions and the balance between creation and destruction. Her most famous myth involves her descent into the Underworld to rescue her lover, Tammuz, showcasing her bravery and the transformative power of love.

Ea (Enki) - God of Wisdom and Water: Ea, also known as Enki in Sumerian mythology, is the god of wisdom, water, and creation. He is depicted as a bearded man surrounded by flowing water and fish, symbols of his dominion over the freshwater and knowledge. Ea is a master of magic and crafts, often acting as a mediator and problem-solver among the gods. His role in the creation of humanity and his assistance in various myths highlight his wisdom and benevolence. Ea's association with water symbolizes life, purification, and the hidden depths of knowledge.

Anu - God of the Sky and the Heavens: Anu is the god of the sky and the supreme deity in the early Sumerian and later Babylonian pantheon. He is often depicted as an enthroned figure representing the overarching power of the heavens. Anu is the father of many gods, including Enlil and Ishtar, and his authority is paramount in the cosmic hierarchy. Although his direct involvement in myths is limited, his presence as the highest god underscores the structure and order of the divine realm.

Enlil - God of Air and Storms: Enlil is the god of air, storms, and agriculture. He is depicted as a powerful and unpredictable deity, capable of bringing both blessings and destruction. Enlil's role as a god of storms and the atmosphere reflects the Mesopotamians' dependence on and fear of the natural elements. He is a central figure in the creation and ordering of the world, as seen in myths like the "Atrahasis," where he decrees the Great Flood. Enlil's authority over the elements underscores his importance in maintaining the balance and fertility of the earth.

Ninhursag (Ki) - Mother Goddess and Earth Mother: Ninhursag, also known as Ki, is the mother goddess and the personification of the fertile earth. She is often depicted as a nurturing figure associated with mountains and the nourishing aspects of the earth. Ninhursag is a creator goddess who plays a crucial role in the formation of humanity and the animal kingdom. Her nurturing nature and connection to the earth make her a central figure in the Mesopotamian understanding of life and sustenance.

Shamash - God of the Sun and Justice: Shamash, the god of the sun and justice, is depicted as a radiant figure often shown with rays emanating from his shoulders. As the sun god, Shamash travels across the sky, illuminating the world and overseeing all human actions. He is also the arbiter of justice, presiding over legal matters and ensuring fairness. Shamash's role in upholding justice and truth is central to the Babylonian concept of law and morality, and he is often invoked in prayers for justice and protection.

Sin (Nanna) - God of the Moon and Time: Sin, also known as Nanna in Sumerian mythology, is the god of the moon and time. He is depicted as an elderly man with a flowing beard, often shown with the crescent moon. Sin's regular phases symbolize the passage of time and the cyclical nature of life. He is associated with wisdom and the divine order of the universe. Sin's influence extends to agriculture and navigation, guiding the rhythms of planting and the tides. His serene and constant presence in the night sky reflects the stability and continuity of the cosmos.

Nergal - God of the Underworld and War: Nergal is the god of the underworld, war, and plague. He is depicted as a fierce warrior, often accompanied by lions or carrying a weapon. Nergal's domain is the underworld, where he rules over the dead and presides over the darker aspects of existence. His association with war and disease reflects the destructive forces of nature and the inevitable cycle of death and rebirth. Despite his fearsome attributes, Nergal also plays a role in the balance of life, embodying the duality of destruction and renewal.

Tiamat - Primordial Goddess of Chaos: Tiamat is the primordial goddess of the salt sea and chaos, depicted as a fearsome dragon or serpent. In the "Enuma Elish," she represents the chaotic forces that existed before creation. Tiamat's battle with Marduk symbolizes the struggle between order and chaos, with her eventual defeat leading to the creation of the world. Her body forms the heavens and the earth, and her legacy as a symbol of chaos remains central to the Babylonian understanding of the universe's origins and the ongoing battle to maintain order.

The Creation Story of the Babylonian Pantheon

The "Enuma Elish," the Babylonian creation epic, is one of the most significant texts in Mesopotamian mythology. It describes the creation of the world and the rise of Marduk as the supreme god.

In the beginning, there was only primordial chaos, represented by the mingling of the saltwater goddess Tiamat and the freshwater god Apsu. From their union, the first gods were born, including Anu, Enlil, and Ea. As the younger gods became noisy and disruptive, Apsu decided to destroy them, but Ea, the god of wisdom, learned of his plan and killed Apsu.

Tiamat, enraged by Apsu's death, gathered an army of monsters and waged war against the younger gods. She appointed Kingu, her consort, to lead her forces. In response, the gods chose Marduk to be their champion. Marduk accepted the challenge on the condition that he would become the supreme ruler of the gods if he succeeded.

Armed with powerful weapons, Marduk confronted Tiamat in a fierce battle. He defeated her by trapping her in a net and splitting her body in two. From her divided form, Marduk created the heavens and the earth. He used her blood to fashion rivers and her eyes to create the sources of the Tigris and Euphrates. Marduk then established the order of the cosmos, setting the sun, moon, and stars in their places.

To further solidify his rule, Marduk used the blood of Kingu, Tiamat's consort, to create humanity. Humans were made to serve the gods and to uphold the cosmic order established by Marduk. This creation story underscores the themes of conflict, order, and the divine mandate to maintain balance in the universe.

Honoring the Babylonian Pantheon

Sacred Texts: The "Enuma Elish" and the "Epic of Gilgamesh" are foundational texts that provide insights into Babylonian mythology and cosmology. These epics, written in cuneiform on clay tablets, preserve the stories of the gods and their interactions with the world.

Temples and Sacred Sites: The ziggurats of ancient Mesopotamia, such as the Etemenanki in Babylon, served as monumental temples dedicated to the gods. These towering structures were centers of worship and ritual, where priests conducted ceremonies to honor the deities and seek their favor.

Festivals: The Akitu festival, celebrated during the spring equinox, was a major event in Babylonian religion. This festival marked the New Year and involved rituals to reaffirm the king's divine mandate and the cosmic order established by the gods. It included processions, sacrifices, and the recitation of the "Enuma Elish."

Daily Worship and Rituals: Daily life in Babylon was filled with rituals to honor the gods. Offerings of food, drink, and incense were made at household altars and in temples. Prayers and hymns were recited to invoke the gods' protection and blessings.

Modern Practices: Today, there is a growing interest in ancient Mesopotamian spirituality. Modern practitioners explore the myths, conduct rituals inspired by ancient practices, and seek to connect with the gods of the Babylonian pantheon. This revival reflects a fascination with the rich cultural heritage and enduring wisdom of the Babylonians.

The Babylonian pantheon, with its diverse and powerful deities, offers timeless insights into the nature of the cosmos and humanity's place within it. By honoring and exploring these ancient gods and goddesses, we connect with a profound legacy that continues to inspire and illuminate the path of spiritual discovery.

Chapter 104
Yoruba

The Yoruba religion, one of the oldest and most influential spiritual traditions in Africa, originates from the Yoruba people of southwestern Nigeria and the Benin region. Known as Ifá or Orisha worship, this rich religious system encompasses a profound cosmology, vibrant rituals, and a deep connection to the natural and spiritual worlds. Yoruba mythology centers on a pantheon of deities called Orishas, each representing different aspects of nature, humanity, and the cosmos.

Yoruba beliefs and practices have had a lasting impact beyond Africa, particularly through the transatlantic slave trade, leading to the development of related religions such as Santería in Cuba, Candomblé in Brazil, and Vodou in Haiti. These diasporic faiths retain the core elements of Yoruba spirituality, emphasizing the worship of Orishas and the importance of ancestral reverence.

Main Orishas of the Yoruba Pantheon

Olodumare - The Supreme God: Olodumare, also known as Olorun or Eledumare, is the supreme deity in the Yoruba pantheon. As the creator of the universe and the source of all life, Olodumare embodies the ultimate authority and the highest spiritual realm. Although not directly worshipped, Olodumare is revered as the origin of all Orishas and the force that sustains the cosmos. In Yoruba cosmology, Olodumare is considered omnipotent, omniscient, and omnipresent, representing the unity and interconnectedness of all things.

Orunmila - God of Wisdom and Divination: Orunmila is the Orisha of wisdom, knowledge, and divination. He is regarded as the chief advisor to Olodumare and the guardian of the Ifá divination system, a sacred practice used to seek guidance and understand the will of the divine. Orunmila is often depicted as an elderly, wise figure embodying patience and foresight. He is invoked by diviners, known as Babalawos or Iyalawos, who interpret the messages of the divine through the Ifá oracle. Orunmila's role as the custodian of wisdom makes him a crucial figure in guiding individuals and communities.

Obatala - God of Purity and Creation: Obatala, the Orisha of purity, wisdom, and creation, is considered the father of all Orishas. He is depicted as a serene and dignified figure, often dressed in white, symbolizing purity and peace. According to Yoruba mythology, Obatala was tasked by Olodumare with creating humanity. He is associated with clarity, truth, and justice, and he is revered as a protector of those with physical disabilities, as he is believed to have created them while intoxicated. Obatala's gentle and nurturing nature makes him a source of compassion and guidance.

Ogun - God of Iron and War: Ogun is the Orisha of iron, war, and labor. He is depicted as a powerful and fierce warrior, wielding weapons made of iron. Ogun is the patron of blacksmiths, soldiers, and all those who work with metal. He embodies strength, determination, and resilience. Ogun's role in forging tools and weapons underscores his importance in industry and warfare, making him a symbol of both protection and destruction. Rituals honoring Ogun often involve offerings of iron objects, palm wine, and roosters.

Shango - God of Thunder and Lightning: Shango, the Orisha of thunder, lightning, and fire, is one of the most popular and dynamic deities in the Yoruba pantheon. He is often depicted with a double-headed axe and surrounded by flames, symbolizing his power and authority. Shango is associated with masculinity, virility, and leadership. His fiery nature represents both the destructive and regenerative forces of fire. Shango's followers invoke him for strength, courage, and success, and he is honored with energetic drumming, dancing, and offerings of red foods and animals.

Yemoja (Yemaya) - Goddess of the Sea and Motherhood: Yemoja, also known as Yemaya, is the Orisha of the sea, motherhood, and fertility. She is often depicted as a nurturing and protective mother, embodying the essence of the ocean. Yemoja is the mother of all Orishas, and her waters are believed to cleanse and heal. She is associated with the moon and the rhythms of the tides, reflecting her influence over fertility and the feminine principle. Yemoja is honored through rituals involving water, seashells, and offerings of fish and fruits.

Oshun - Goddess of Love and Fresh Water: Oshun is the Orisha of love, beauty, fertility, and fresh water. She is depicted as a radiant and enchanting woman, often adorned with jewelry and golden clothing. Oshun is the goddess of rivers and streams, symbolizing abundance, sensuality, and the flow of life. She is also a healer and a protector of women and children. Oshun's devotees seek her blessings for love, prosperity, and artistic inspiration. Offerings to Oshun typically include honey, oranges, and peacock feathers.

Esu (Elegba) - Trickster God and Messenger: Esu, also known as Elegba or Eshu, is the Orisha of communication, crossroads, and change. He is depicted as a cunning and playful trickster who governs the exchange between the spiritual and material worlds. Esu is the messenger of the gods and the mediator between humans and the divine. He opens and closes the paths of life, making him a crucial figure in rituals and decision-making processes. Esu's unpredictable nature reflects the complexity of fate and the importance of adaptability. Offerings to Esu often include candy, rum, and red and black items.

Oya - Goddess of Winds and Storms: Oya is the Orisha of winds, storms, and transformation. She is depicted as a fierce and powerful woman, often wielding a sword and associated with the buffalo. Oya governs the forces of change and the passage between life and death. She is the guardian of cemeteries and a guide for the spirits of the dead. Oya's energy is dynamic and electrifying, symbolizing the sudden shifts and upheavals that lead to new beginnings. Rituals honoring Oya involve offerings of dark foods, red wine, and copper items.

Alex McCann Johnson

The Creation Story of the Yoruba Pantheon

In Yoruba mythology, the creation of the world is a collaborative effort involving Olodumare, Orunmila, and several other Orishas. The story begins with Olodumare, the supreme god, who decides to create the earth. He calls upon Orunmila, the god of wisdom and divination, to oversee the project.

Olodumare provides Orunmila with a chain of gold to descend from the heavens and a calabash containing sacred materials, including soil, a rooster, and a chameleon. Orunmila is also given a shell filled with water and a palm nut.

As Orunmila descends from the heavens, he pours the soil from the calabash onto the primordial waters. He then releases the rooster, which scratches the soil, spreading it across the surface and creating land. The chameleon is sent to test the stability of the new earth, moving cautiously and ensuring that it is solid and ready for habitation.

After confirming the earth's stability, Orunmila plants the palm nut, which grows into a mighty tree, symbolizing life and abundance. This tree becomes the axis mundi, connecting the heavens and the earth.

Obatala, another significant Orisha, is tasked with the creation of human beings. He molds the first humans from clay, giving them form and shape. However, before he can complete his work, Obatala becomes intoxicated from palm wine and falls asleep. In his absence, Olodumare breathes life into the clay figures, giving them spirit and consciousness.

When Obatala awakens, he sees his creations and feels remorse for their imperfections resulting from his inebriation. Nevertheless, Olodumare reassures him, and Obatala accepts his role as the father of humanity, vowing to protect and guide them.

This creation story emphasizes themes of cooperation, the interplay between order and chaos, and the divine origins of humanity. It reflects the Yoruba belief in the interconnectedness of the spiritual and material worlds and the continuous involvement of the Orishas in the lives of humans.

Honoring the Yoruba Pantheon

Sacred Texts: The Yoruba religion does not have a singular holy book like many other religions. Instead, its teachings and myths are passed down orally through a rich tradition of storytelling, chants, and songs. The "Odù Ifá," a collection of verses used in the Ifá divination system, contains much of the spiritual wisdom and guidance of the Yoruba faith.

Temples and Sacred Sites: Yoruba temples, known as "shrines," are sacred spaces dedicated to the worship of specific Orishas. These shrines are often adorned with symbols, statues, and offerings that honor the deities. Each Orisha has specific sacred sites, such as rivers, mountains, and trees, where they are believed to dwell and where devotees can connect with their energy.

Festivals: The Yoruba calendar is filled with vibrant festivals that celebrate the Orishas and the cycles of nature. Festivals like the "Odun Ifá," dedicated to Orunmila, and the "Odun Egungun," honoring the ancestors, are times of communal celebration, ritual performances, and offerings. These festivals reinforce the connection between the community, the Orishas, and the ancestors.

Daily Worship and Rituals: Daily worship in the Yoruba tradition involves making offerings of food, drink, and other items to the Orishas and ancestors. These offerings are placed on altars or in sacred spaces within the home or community. Prayers and songs are also an integral part of daily worship, invoking the presence and blessings of the Orishas.

Modern Practices: Yoruba spirituality continues to thrive both in Africa and among the diaspora. Modern practitioners honor the Orishas through rituals, music, dance, and art. They often participate in ceremonies led by priests and priestesses and engage in practices that keep the traditions alive and relevant in contemporary life.

The Yoruba pantheon, with its rich array of Orishas and creation myths, offers timeless wisdom and guidance. By honoring and exploring these deities, we can connect with a deep and enduring spiritual heritage that continues to inspire and guide us in our journey of self-discovery and spiritual growth.

Chapter 105
Shinto

Shinto, often described as the indigenous spirituality of Japan, is a unique and ancient tradition deeply rooted in the natural world and the veneration of kami, the sacred spirits or deities. Unlike many organized religions, Shinto does not have a single founder, a sacred scripture, or a set of dogmatic beliefs. Instead, it is a collection of practices, rituals, and beliefs that have evolved over centuries, reflecting the Japanese people's deep connection to nature and their ancestors.

The term "Shinto" means "the way of the gods," and it encompasses a rich tapestry of mythology, rituals, and festivals that celebrate the presence of kami in all aspects of life. Kami can be deities, spirits of natural phenomena, ancestral spirits, or even revered historical figures. These kami are believed to inhabit everything from the tallest mountains and ancient forests to the smallest streams and household shrines.

Main Kami of the Shinto Pantheon

Amaterasu - Goddess of the Sun and the Universe: Amaterasu, the sun goddess, is one of the most important and revered kami in Shinto. She is considered the ruler of the heavens and the universe, embodying the light, warmth, and life-giving energy of the sun. Amaterasu is often depicted as a radiant and benevolent figure, bringing light and order to the world. According to Shinto mythology, she is the ancestor of the Japanese imperial family, making her a central figure in both religious and cultural traditions. The Grand Shrine of Ise, one of Japan's most sacred sites, is dedicated to Amaterasu and is a major pilgrimage destination.

Susanoo - God of Storms and the Sea: Susanoo, the storm god and brother of Amaterasu, is known for his tempestuous and unpredictable nature. He governs the seas and storms, embodying the raw and powerful forces of nature. Susanoo's myths often depict his rebellious and chaotic actions, which lead to both conflict and eventual redemption. Despite his wild nature, Susanoo is also celebrated as a hero who protects humanity from evil forces. He is associated with bravery and the power to overcome obstacles. His worship includes rituals to appease his fierce temper and to seek protection from natural disasters.

Tsukuyomi - God of the Moon: Tsukuyomi, the moon god, is the serene and contemplative counterpart to his siblings, Amaterasu and Susanoo. He governs the night and the moon, representing the calm, reflective, and orderly aspects of nature. Tsukuyomi's mythology often portrays him as a more distant and less active figure compared to his siblings, emphasizing his role in maintaining balance and harmony. His worship is less prominent than that of Amaterasu and Susanoo, but he remains an important part of the celestial trinity in Shinto belief.

Inari - God of Rice, Fertility, and Prosperity: Inari is a widely revered kami associated with rice, agriculture, fertility, and prosperity. This deity is often depicted with foxes, which are considered Inari's messengers and are believed to bring good fortune and protection. Inari is one of the most popular and versatile deities in Shinto, worshipped by farmers for bountiful harvests, by merchants for prosperity, and by individuals seeking success and protection. The Fushimi Inari Shrine in Kyoto, with its thousands of vermilion torii gates, is dedicated to Inari and attracts millions of pilgrims and visitors each year.

Tenjin - Deified Spirit of Scholarship and Learning: Tenjin, originally known as Sugawara no Michizane, is a deified spirit revered as the patron of scholarship and learning. A historical figure renowned for his intellect and poetic talents, Tenjin was posthumously elevated to kami status after his death. Students and scholars pray to Tenjin for success in their academic endeavors, and his shrines are especially popular during exam seasons. Tenjin's influence extends to arts and literature, making him a beloved figure among those pursuing knowledge and cultural achievements.

Hachiman - God of War and Archery: Hachiman is the kami of war archery, and the protector of warriors. He is revered as a divine protector of Japan and the Japanese people, embodying the virtues of courage, honor, and strength. Hachiman is often depicted as a warrior or a sacred bird, symbolizing vigilance and martial prowess. His worship extends beyond military aspects, as he is also considered a guardian of agriculture and the nation's wellbeing. The Hachiman shrines, found throughout Japan, are sites where people seek his protection and blessings for success in their endeavors.

Ebisu - God of Fishermen and Luck: Ebisu is the god of fishermen, commerce, and good fortune. He is one of the "Seven Lucky Gods" and is often depicted as a jovial figure carrying a large fish, symbolizing abundance and prosperity. Ebisu's cheerful and approachable nature makes him a popular deity among merchants and those seeking happiness and success. His festivals, celebrated with joy and feasting, highlight his role as a bringer of good fortune and protector of livelihoods. The Ebisu Shrine in Kyoto is a notable site where people gather to honor him and seek his blessings.

Raijin and Fujin - Gods of Thunder and Wind: Raijin and Fujin are the twin gods of thunder and wind, respectively. Raijin, the thunder god, is often depicted with drums, which he uses to create thunder and lightning. He embodies the fierce and powerful forces of nature, often seen as both a protector and a destroyer. Fujin, the wind god, carries a large bag of winds and is depicted as a wild, tempestuous figure. Together, they represent the dynamic and uncontrollable elements of the natural world. Their worship includes rituals to appease their tempers and to seek protection from storms and natural disasters.

Izumo no Okuni - Goddess of Dance and Theater: Izumo no Okuni is a legendary figure and a kami associated with dance and theater, particularly the traditional Japanese performing art of Kabuki. While not a deity in the traditional sense, she is venerated as a cultural hero who contributed to the development of Japanese performing arts.

Okuni's influence is celebrated in various festivals and performances, and she is honored as a patron of creativity and artistic expression.

The Creation Story of the Shinto Pantheon

The Shinto creation myth, known as the "Kojiki" or "Records of Ancient Matters," begins with the birth of the first deities from the primordial chaos. The divine couple Izanagi and Izanami were tasked with creating the islands of Japan and populating them with life.

Izanagi and Izanami stood on the floating bridge of heaven and stirred the chaotic waters below with a jeweled spear. As they lifted the spear, drops of brine fell and formed the first island, Onogoro. Descending to this newly created land, Izanagi and Izanami performed a sacred marriage ritual and began their task of creation.

Together, they gave birth to the various islands of Japan and numerous kami, representing natural elements and forces. However, tragedy struck when Izanami died while giving birth to the fire god, Kagutsuchi. Overcome with grief, Izanagi journeyed to the underworld, Yomi, to retrieve her.

In Yomi, Izanagi found Izanami transformed into a decayed and terrifying figure. Horrified, he fled back to the world of the living, pursued by the vengeful spirits of the underworld. Upon escaping, Izanagi performed a purification ritual to cleanse himself of Yomi's impurities.

During this purification, three significant deities were born from Izanagi: Amaterasu from his left eye, Tsukuyomi from his right eye, and Susanoo from his nose. These deities, representing the sun, moon, and storms, respectively, became central figures in the Shinto pantheon.

This creation story underscores themes of birth, death, purification, and the cyclical nature of life and the universe. It highlights the Shinto belief in the sacredness of nature and the importance of maintaining harmony and balance in the world.

Honoring the Shinto Pantheon

Sacred Texts: The "Kojiki" (Records of Ancient Matters) and the "Nihon Shoki" (Chronicles of Japan) are two of the most important texts in Shinto. These ancient writings provide the foundational myths and historical accounts of the kami and the early Japanese emperors. While Shinto lacks a single sacred scripture, these texts are revered as essential sources of spiritual and cultural wisdom.

Shrines and Sacred Sites: Shinto shrines, or "jinja," are the focal points of worship and the dwelling places of the kami. These shrines, often nestled in natural settings, range from grand structures like the Ise Grand Shrine dedicated to Amaterasu to smaller, local shrines honoring regional kami. Each shrine has a torii gate, which marks the transition from the mundane to the sacred. Visitors perform purification rituals and offer prayers and offerings to the kami.

Festivals: Shinto festivals, or "matsuri," are vibrant celebrations that honor the kami and mark important seasonal and agricultural events. Festivals such as the "New Year" (Shogatsu), "Obon" (Festival of the Dead), and the "Gion Matsuri" in Kyoto involve processions, dances, music, and offerings. These festivals are times of communal joy and gratitude, reinforcing the connection between the people and the divine.

Daily Worship and Rituals: Daily worship in Shinto includes simple practices such as bowing and clapping at a shrine to attract the attention of the kami. Offerings of food, sake, and symbolic items are made to express gratitude and seek blessings. Personal shrines, known as "kamidana," are also common in homes, where families honor their ancestral spirits and protective kami.

Modern Practices: Shinto continues to thrive in modern Japan, with its principles of nature reverence and purity resonating deeply in contemporary life. Many Japanese people visit shrines during significant life events such as births, marriages, and the New Year. Shinto rituals and festivals remain integral to Japanese culture, reflecting a harmonious blend of ancient tradition and modern practice.

Alex McCann Johnson

The Shinto pantheon, with its diverse and powerful kami, offers insights into the sacredness of nature and the interconnectedness of all life. By honoring and exploring these ancient spirits, we can connect with a deep and enduring spiritual heritage that continues to inspire and guide us in our journey of self-discovery and spiritual growth.

Chapter 106
Chinese

Chinese mythology and religion encompass a vast and diverse collection of beliefs, practices, and deities that have evolved over thousands of years. This rich spiritual tradition blends ancient mythological tales, Taoist philosophies, Confucian teachings, and Buddhist influences, creating a complex and interconnected worldview. At the heart of Chinese spirituality is the belief in a harmonious balance between heaven, earth, and humanity, known as the "Three Realms."

Central to Chinese religion is the veneration of deities who embody various aspects of nature, human virtues, and cosmic principles. These deities are revered for their wisdom, power, and ability to influence both the physical and spiritual realms. They are honored through rituals, prayers, festivals, and daily practices, reflecting the deep-rooted respect for the divine and the interconnectedness of all life.

Main Deities of the Chinese Pantheon

Jade Emperor - Supreme Ruler of Heaven: The Jade Emperor, or Yu Huang, is the supreme ruler of heaven and the highest deity in the Chinese pantheon. He presides over all other gods, spirits, and humans, maintaining order and justice throughout the cosmos. The Jade Emperor is often depicted as a majestic figure seated on a throne, wearing imperial robes and a crown, symbolizing his authority and divine power. He is celebrated during the Chinese New Year with grand ceremonies and offerings, as he is believed to oversee the destiny and wellbeing of all beings.

Guanyin - Goddess of Mercy and Compassion: Guanyin, also known as the "Bodhisattva of Compassion," is one of the most beloved and widely venerated deities in Chinese spirituality. She embodies infinite compassion, mercy, and kindness, offering solace and aid to those in distress. Guanyin is often depicted as a serene and graceful figure, holding a vase of pure water and a willow branch, symbols of her healing and nurturing powers. Her name means "Observer of Sounds," referring to her ability to hear and respond to the cries of suffering in the world. Devotees pray to Guanyin for protection, guidance, and relief from pain and hardship.

Nezha - Protector of the Innocent: Nezha is a youthful and dynamic deity known for his courage, rebellious spirit, and protective nature. Originally a mortal hero, he was deified after performing extraordinary feats and defeating powerful demons. Nezha is often depicted as a fierce young warrior, riding on flaming wheels and wielding magical weapons. He is revered as the protector of children and the innocent, defending them from harm and injustice. Nezha's story emphasizes themes of resilience, redemption, and the triumph of good over evil.

Fuxi and Nüwa - Creator Deities: Fuxi and Nüwa are the twin deities credited with the creation of humanity and the establishment of civilization. Fuxi, often depicted with a human upper body and a serpent's lower body, is known as the god of writing, fishing, and hunting. He is believed to have taught humans essential skills such as weaving nets and taming animals. Nüwa, also depicted with a serpentine lower body, is the goddess of marriage and fertility. She is revered for molding the first humans from clay and repairing the pillars of heaven after a great catastrophe. Together, Fuxi and Nüwa symbolize the union of yin and yang, creation, and the nurturing of life.

Shangdi - Supreme God and Ruler of the Cosmos: Shangdi, also known as the "Supreme Deity," is one of the oldest and most revered gods in Chinese spirituality. He is regarded as the sovereign ruler of the cosmos, overseeing the natural order, justice, and the welfare of humanity. Shangdi is often associated with the North Star, symbolizing his role as the guiding force of the universe. In ancient times, he was worshipped through elaborate state rituals and sacrifices conducted by emperors, who sought his blessings for peace, prosperity, and divine favor.

Zhong Kui - God of Ghosts and Demon Queller: Zhong Kui is the formidable god of ghosts and exorcism, known for his ability to vanquish evil spirits and protect the living from malevolent forces. According to legend, Zhong Kui was a scholar who, after being unjustly treated, committed suicide. In death, he was transformed into a deity by the Jade Emperor, tasked with controlling and expelling harmful spirits. Zhong Kui is often depicted as a fierce, bearded figure wielding a sword, and his image is commonly displayed in homes and temples to ward off evil and bring good fortune.

Zao Jun - Kitchen God and Protector of the Household: Zao Jun, also known as the Kitchen God or Stove God, is the deity of the hearth and the protector of the home and family. He is believed to oversee the moral conduct of households and report back to the Jade Emperor at the end of the lunar year. Zao Jun is traditionally honored with offerings of food and incense, particularly during the Chinese New Year. His role underscores the importance of family harmony, morality, and domestic well-being in Chinese culture.

Chang'e - Goddess of the Moon: Chang'e is the enchanting goddess of the moon, known for her grace and beauty. According to legend, she was a mortal who ascended to the moon after consuming an elixir of immortality. Chang'e's story is deeply intertwined with the Mid-Autumn Festival, where people celebrate her with mooncakes and lanterns. She is often depicted with a jade rabbit, her companion on the moon, symbolizing purity, longevity, and the cyclical nature of life. Devotees honor Chang'e for blessings of love, fertility, and enlightenment.

Guan Yu - God of War and Loyalty: Guan Yu, also known as the "God of War," is celebrated for his martial prowess, loyalty, and unwavering sense of justice. Originally a historical figure and warrior during the late Eastern Han dynasty, Guan Yu was deified for his heroic deeds and integrity. He is often depicted with a red face and a long, flowing beard, wielding a massive green dragon crescent blade. Guan

Yu is revered by soldiers, police officers, and those seeking protection and righteousness. His temples are popular throughout China and the diaspora, where he is honored as a symbol of courage and virtue.

Huangdi (Yellow Emperor) - Legendary Ruler and Cultural Hero: Huangdi, the Yellow Emperor, is a legendary figure in Chinese mythology, credited with founding Chinese civilization and introducing many cultural innovations. He is often depicted as a wise and benevolent ruler associated with the invention of the compass, medicine, and the arts. Huangdi's reign is considered a golden age of peace and prosperity. As a cultural hero, he symbolizes the unity and enduring spirit of the Chinese people, and his legacy is celebrated in various festivals and rituals honoring his contributions to society.

The Creation Story of the Chinese Pantheon

Chinese creation myths are rich with symbolism and insights into the origins of the universe and humanity. One of the most well-known creation stories involves the primordial giant Pangu.

According to the myth, the universe was once a formless chaos contained within a cosmic egg. After 18,000 years, Pangu emerged from the egg, bringing order to the chaos. As he grew, he separated the sky from the earth, holding them apart with his immense strength. Pangu's body became the foundation of the world; his breath formed the wind and clouds, his voice created thunder, and his eyes became the sun and moon. When Pangu finally died, his body transformed into the mountains, rivers, and forests, giving life and form to the world.

In another creation myth, Nüwa, the goddess of creation, played a crucial role in shaping humanity. After the heavens and earth were established, Nüwa, moved by loneliness and compassion, fashioned the first humans from yellow clay. She breathed life into them, creating the ancestors of humanity. To populate the world, she dipped a rope into the mud and flicked it, causing droplets to form and come to life. These beings became the common people, while the ones she crafted by hand became the nobility.

Nüwa is also credited with repairing the broken pillars of heaven after a great catastrophe. Using five-colored stones, she mended the sky and restored balance to the world, demonstrating her role as a protector and nurturer of life.

These creation stories illustrate the themes of order emerging from chaos, the interconnectedness of all life, and the nurturing power of the divine. They reflect the Chinese belief in a harmonious and balanced universe where humans, nature, and the cosmos are intricately linked.

Honoring the Chinese Pantheon

Sacred Texts: The "Shangshu" (Book of Documents), the "Shiji" (Records of the Grand Historian), and the "Daodejing" (Tao Te Ching) are among the most revered texts in Chinese spiritual traditions. These works contain historical records, philosophical teachings, and mythological accounts that provide profound insights into the nature of the cosmos and the divine.

Temples and Sacred Sites: Chinese temples are dedicated to various deities and serve as places of worship, community gathering, and cultural heritage. Major temples, such as the Temple of Heaven in Beijing and the Jade Emperor Pagoda in Shanghai, are significant centers of worship. These sites are adorned with intricate statues, altars, and offerings that honor the deities and invite their blessings.

Festivals: Chinese festivals are vibrant celebrations that honor the deities and the cycles of nature. The Chinese New Year, the Mid-Autumn Festival, and the Dragon Boat Festival are among the most widely celebrated. These festivals involve elaborate rituals, family gatherings, feasting, and the exchange of blessings. They reinforce the connection between the people, the deities, and the rhythms of the natural world.

Daily Worship and Rituals: Daily practices in Chinese spirituality often include lighting incense, offering food and drink, and performing prayers at home altars or temple shrines. These rituals express gratitude, seek protection, and invite the deities' guidance. The presence of ancestral tablets and images of deities in homes underscores the deep integration of spiritual and familial reverence in daily life.

Modern Practices: In contemporary China and among the global Chinese diaspora, traditional practices continue to evolve and adapt. Many people still honor the deities through rituals, festivals, and personal devotion. The integration of modern life with ancient traditions reflects the enduring relevance and vitality of the Chinese spiritual heritage.

The Chinese pantheon, with its vast array of deities and rich creation myths, offers timeless wisdom and guidance. By honoring and exploring these divine beings, we connect with an enduring spiritual heritage that continues to inspire and guide us on our journey of self-discovery and spiritual growth.

Chapter 107
Aboriginal

Australian Aboriginal spirituality is one of the oldest continuous spiritual traditions in the world, deeply rooted in the land, the Dreamtime, and the stories of creation. For Aboriginal Australians, the connection to the land is sacred and intrinsic to their identity and culture. The Dreamtime, or Dreaming, refers to the time of creation when ancestral beings formed the world and established the laws of nature and society.

The Dreamtime stories and their associated spiritual beings form the core of Aboriginal cosmology. These ancestral spirits are believed to still inhabit the land, guiding and influencing the lives of the people. The spiritual practices, rituals, and ceremonies of Aboriginal Australians are centered around maintaining harmony with these spirits and the natural world.

Main Spiritual Beings in Aboriginal Australian Mythology

Baiame - The Sky Father and Creator: Baiame, often referred to as the Sky Father, is a prominent creator spirit in many Aboriginal Australian cultures, particularly among the Wiradjuri, Kamilaroi, and Wonnarua peoples. Baiame is believed to have descended from the sky to shape the earth and give life to its inhabitants. He established the laws and customs that govern the natural and social order. Baiame is often depicted as a tall, imposing figure, embodying wisdom, authority, and the paternal care of his people. Sacred sites, known as Baiame's caves, feature ancient rock paintings and are places of reverence and pilgrimage.

Daramulum - The Son of **Baiame and the God of the Moon:** Daramulum is the son of Baiame and a powerful figure in the Aboriginal pantheon, particularly among the Eora and Dharug peoples. Known as the god of the moon and a protector of men, Daramulum is often associated with initiation ceremonies and the teaching of sacred knowledge. He is depicted as a figure with one leg, symbolizing his connection to the moon and its cycles. Daramulum's role includes overseeing rituals and ensuring that the laws of Baiame are upheld, particularly in matters of male rites of passage and spiritual practices.

Bunjil - The **Eaglehawk Creator:** Bunjil, the Eaglehawk, is a significant creator spirit among the Aboriginal peoples of southeastern Australia, including the Kulin Nation and the Wurundjeri people. Bunjil is revered as the creator of the land, the animals, and the people. He is often depicted as a majestic eagle soaring above the landscape, symbolizing his role as a guardian and protector. According to legend, Bunjil shaped the rivers, mountains, and forests, and he continues to watch over his creation from the sky. Bunjil's sacred places are important cultural sites, and his spirit is honored in ceremonies and storytelling.

Mamaragan - The Lightning Spirit: Mamaragan, also known as Namarrkun, is the lightning spirit and weather god of the Yolngu people in northern Australia. Mamaragan is depicted as a powerful, imposing figure who controls the thunder and lightning. He is said to travel across the sky in storm clouds, wielding a lightning bolt in each hand. Mamaragan's presence is a reminder of the raw and unpredictable forces of nature, and he is revered as both a bringer of life-giving rain and a symbol of nature's destructive power. Ceremonies and songs are performed to honor Mamaragan and to seek his protection and favor.

Yhi - The Sun Goddess and Bringer of Light: Yhi is the sun goddess and a central figure in the creation stories of the Aboriginal peoples of southeastern Australia. As the bringer of light, warmth, and life, Yhi is celebrated for awakening the earth and nurturing all living things. According to legend, Yhi emerged from the Dreamtime, bringing light to the darkness and causing plants to grow and animals to awaken. Her journey across the sky each day is a symbol of renewal and the continuous cycle of life. Yhi is often depicted as a radiant, benevolent figure whose presence ensures the fertility and vitality of the land.

Tiddalik - The Giant Frog and the Flood: Tiddalik is a well-known figure in Aboriginal mythology, particularly among the Kurnai and Gunai peoples. According to the legend, Tiddalik was a giant frog who drank all the water in the world, causing a severe drought. The other animals, desperate for water, devised a plan to make Tiddalik laugh and release the water. Eventually, Tiddalik laughed so hard that he spilled the water, refilling the rivers and lakes and restoring balance to the land. The story of Tiddalik highlights themes of greed, cooperation, and the importance of maintaining harmony with the natural world.

Wagyl - The Rainbow Serpent and the Creator of Rivers: The Rainbow Serpent, known as Wagyl in the Noongar culture of southwestern Australia, is one of the most revered and widely recognized deities in Aboriginal spirituality. Wagyl is a powerful and transformative spirit believed to have shaped the landscape and created the rivers and waterways. The Rainbow Serpent's movements carved out the valleys and formed the mountains, bringing life and water to the land. The Rainbow Serpent is often depicted as a large, colorful snake, symbolizing fertility, creation, and the cyclical nature of life. Ceremonies and rituals honoring the Rainbow Serpent are integral to maintaining the health and balance of the environment.

The Dreamtime: Creation Stories of the Australian Pantheon

Dreamtime, or dreaming, is the foundational concept of Aboriginal spirituality, encompassing creation stories and the spiritual essence of the land and its people. It is a timeless realm where ancestral beings shaped the world and established the laws that govern life.

In one of the most well-known Dreamtime stories, the Rainbow Serpent emerged from the earth and began to move across the land, creating mountains, valleys, and rivers with its sinuous body. As it traveled, it brought life to the land, awakening plants, animals, and humans. The Rainbow Serpent's movements created the physical features of the landscape and established the flow of water, essential for life. The story of the Rainbow Serpent underscores the interconnectedness of all living things and the importance of water and fertility in sustaining life.

Another prominent creation story involves Bunjil, the Eaglehawk, who is credited with creating the land, the people, and the laws of the Kulin Nation. Bunjil and his helpers, often depicted as other animals, traveled across the land, shaping its features and imparting knowledge and customs to the people. Bunjil's actions ensured the prosperity and harmony of the land, and his spirit continued to watch over the Kulin Nation from the sky. The story of Bunjil highlights the themes of guardianship, law, and the sacred connection between the people and their land.

In the mythology of the Eora and Dharug peoples, Daramulum, the son of Baiame, played a crucial role in shaping the world. After creating the land and its inhabitants, Daramulum ascended to the sky, becoming the moon. His presence in the night sky serves as a reminder of the cycles of life and the passage of time. Daramulum's story emphasizes the importance of celestial bodies in Aboriginal spirituality and their influence on the natural and social order.

The story of Yhi, the sun goddess, tells of her emergence from the Dreamtime to bring light and life to a dark and dormant world. As she traveled across the sky, her radiant light caused plants to grow and animals to awaken. Yhi's journey across the sky each day symbolizes the renewal and sustenance of life. Her story celebrates the vital role of the sun and the cyclical nature of time and existence.

Honoring the Australian Pantheon

Sacred Sites: Aboriginal Australians honor their deities and ancestral spirits through sacred sites scattered across the landscape. These sites, often marked by rock art, carvings, or natural formations, are places of deep spiritual significance. They serve as reminders of the creation stories and the ongoing presence of the ancestral beings. Visiting and caring for these sites is an essential part of maintaining spiritual and cultural connections.

Ceremonies and Rituals: Ceremonies and rituals are central to Aboriginal spiritual practice. These include dance, music, storytelling, and the use of sacred objects. Ceremonies such as the Corroboree are communal gatherings where stories of the Dreamtime are performed, reinforcing cultural identity and spiritual bonds. These rituals often involve offerings, songs, and dances that honor the ancestral beings and celebrate the cycles of nature.

Art and Storytelling: Aboriginal art and storytelling are powerful ways of honoring the deities and preserving their stories. Dot paintings, bark paintings, and rock art depict the ancestral beings and their journeys across the land. These artworks are not only expressions of cultural heritage but also serve as visual connections to the spiritual world. Storytelling, passed down through generations, keeps the Dreamtime narratives alive and ensures that the wisdom of the ancestors continues to guide the community.

Daily Practices: Daily life in Aboriginal communities is infused with spirituality. Activities such as hunting, gathering, and caring for the land are performed with a deep sense of respect for the ancestral spirits. Practices such as smoking ceremonies, where smoke is used to cleanse and protect, are common in daily rituals. These practices reflect the ongoing relationship with the spiritual world and the commitment to living in harmony with nature.

Modern Adaptations: In contemporary Australia, Aboriginal spirituality continues to thrive, adapting to modern contexts while preserving its ancient roots. Many Aboriginal people integrate traditional beliefs with Christianity or other religions, creating a unique and evolving spiritual landscape. The revival of language, art, and cultural practices, along with the recognition of sacred sites and traditional land rights, highlights the enduring significance of Aboriginal spirituality in modern Australia.

The Australian pantheon, with its rich tapestry of deities and creation stories, offers insights into the sacredness of the land and the interconnectedness of all life. By honoring and exploring these ancient spirits, we connect with a deep and enduring spiritual heritage that

Alex McCann Johnson

continues to inspire and guide us in our journey of self-discovery and spiritual growth.

Chapter 108
Philippine

Philippine mythology is a rich and diverse collection of beliefs, stories, and deities that reflect the cultural and spiritual heritage of the Filipino people. Before the arrival of Spanish colonizers in the 16th century, the various indigenous groups of the Philippines practiced animism, ancestor worship, and veneration of a multitude of gods and spirits. These traditions have been passed down through generations, blending with later influences to form a unique spiritual landscape.

The deities and spirits in Philippine mythology are deeply connected to nature and the elements, embodying the forces of creation, fertility, war, and the afterlife. They are revered in rituals, ceremonies, and everyday practices, reflecting the deep respect and connection the Filipino people have for their environment and ancestral heritage.

Main Deities of the Philippine Pantheon

Bathala - The Supreme God and Creator: Bathala, also known as Bathalang Maykapal, is the supreme deity in Tagalog mythology, often seen as the creator of the universe and the principal god. Bathala is considered the source of life and the ruler of the heavens, earth, and the underworld. He is revered as a benevolent and wise god who oversees the balance and order of the cosmos. Bathala's worship includes rituals and offerings to seek his blessings for prosperity, protection, and guidance.

Apo Laki - God of the Sun and War: Apo Laki, sometimes simply known as Laki, is a prominent deity in the pantheon, revered as the god of the sun and war. He is celebrated for his strength, bravery, and protective qualities. Apo Laki is often depicted as a powerful warrior with a radiant presence, symbolizing the vital energy of the sun. In times of conflict, warriors would invoke Apo Laki for courage and victory. Festivals and rituals honoring the sun are part of the worship practices dedicated to him.

Mayari - Goddess of the Moon and Combat: Mayari is the beautiful and fierce goddess of the moon in Kapampangan mythology. She is often portrayed as the sister of Apo Laki and is associated with combat and strength. According to legend, Mayari lost one of her eyes during a battle with her brother over who would rule the world. As a result, she became the goddess of the moon, her light softer and gentler compared to the sun. Mayari is revered for her resilience and her role in guiding and protecting the night.

Amihan - Goddess of Wind and Birds: Amihan is the deity of wind and birds in Tagalog mythology. She is often depicted as a bird or a gentle breeze, embodying the spirit of freedom and the natural flow of life. Amihan's presence is felt in the soft winds that bring rain and in the flight of birds across the sky. She is honored in rituals that seek to ensure favorable winds for travel and agriculture. Her gentle nature and association with the cycles of the seasons make her a beloved figure in Filipino folklore.

Tala - Goddess of the Morning and Evening Star: Tala is the goddess of the morning and evening stars, often seen as a guiding light in the darkness. She is considered a protector of travelers and those who seek guidance and direction. Tala's brilliance and clarity symbolize hope and the promise of a new beginning. In some traditions, she is believed to be the daughter of Bathala, shining brightly in the sky as a beacon of divine presence and support. Worshippers honor Tala with prayers and offerings to seek her guidance and protection.

Kaptan - God of the Sky and Father of Gods: Kaptan is the god of the sky and a central figure in Visayan mythology. He is often regarded as the father of gods and the ruler of the heavens. Kaptan's power extends over the celestial realms, where he governs the weather and the elements. He is revered as a wise and just deity who ensures the harmony and balance of the universe. Rituals dedicated to Kaptan often involve prayers and offerings for good weather, successful harvests, and protection from natural disasters.

Amanikable - God of the Sea and Fishermen: Amanikable is the god of the sea and a significant deity for coastal and fishing communities. He is known for his sometimes tempestuous nature, reflecting the unpredictable and powerful forces of the ocean. Amanikable is both feared and revered, as he controls the tides, storms, and bounty of the sea. Fishermen and sailors offer sacrifices and prayers to Amanikable to seek safe voyages, abundant catches, and calm waters. His worship highlights the deep respect for the ocean and its vital role in the lives of the people.

Hanan - Goddess of Morning and Time: Hanan is the goddess of the morning and the passage of time in Tagalog mythology. She is associated with the dawn, representing renewal, hope, and the beginning of new cycles. Hanan's presence marks the transition from night to day, bringing light and the promise of a new start. She is honored in rituals that celebrate new beginnings, such as the start of a new year or a significant life event. Worshippers seek Hanan's blessings for clarity, direction, and the successful unfolding of time's journey.

Ikapati - Goddess of Fertility and Agriculture: Ikapati, also known as Lakapati, is the goddess of fertility and agriculture, revered for her nurturing and life-giving qualities. She is often depicted with bountiful harvests and is invoked to ensure the fertility of the land and the prosperity of crops. Ikapati's blessings are sought by farmers and those involved in agriculture to guarantee abundance and sustenance. Rituals and offerings to Ikapati include the first fruits of the harvest and ceremonies that honor the cycles of planting and growth.

Sidapa - God of Death and the Afterlife: Sidapa is the god of death and the afterlife in Visayan mythology. He is a mysterious and often feared figure who determines the fate of souls after death. Sidapa is believed to reside on Mount Madia-as, where he measures the lives of individuals and guides their souls to the afterlife. Despite his association with death, Sidapa is not seen as malevolent but as a necessary force that oversees the transition between life and the spiritual realms. His worship involves rituals and prayers for honoring the deceased and ensuring their safe passage to the afterlife.

The Creation Story of the Philippine Pantheon

The creation stories of the Philippine pantheon are rich with symbolism and reflect the deep connection between the people, the land, and the divine. One of the most prominent creation myths involves Bathala, the supreme god, and his role in shaping the world and its inhabitants.

In the beginning, there was nothing but a vast and empty void. Bathala, the supreme god, emerged from this void and began to create the universe. He first shaped the heavens, then the earth, filling it with mountains, rivers, and valleys. Bathala breathed life into the land, bringing forth plants, animals, and, finally, humans.

Bathala loved his creations and sought to protect and nurture them. He established the natural laws that govern the world and assigned various deities to oversee different aspects of life and nature. Apo Laki was given the sun, bringing warmth and light to the earth, while Mayari, with her resilience and grace, became the goddess of the moon, guiding the night.

To ensure harmony and balance, Bathala created the winds, personified by Amihan, to carry the rains and pollinate the plants. Tala, the goddess of the stars, was placed in the sky to guide travelers and illuminate the night. The seas were entrusted to Amanikable, whose temperamental nature mirrored the ocean's unpredictable power.

Over time, these deities worked together to maintain the balance and order of the world. They nurtured the land, protected its inhabitants, and ensured the continuity of life. Bathala's creation story emphasizes the interconnectedness of all beings and the divine guardianship that sustains the cosmos.

Honoring the Philippine Pantheon

Rituals and Offerings: In traditional Filipino culture, rituals and offerings play a crucial role in honoring the deities. These practices include prayers, songs, dances, and the presentation of food, flowers, and other symbolic items. Each deity is honored according to their domain and attributes. For example, offerings to Amanikable often involve seafood and items related to the sea, while rituals for Ikapati focus on agricultural produce and the blessings of fertility.

Festivals: Many Filipino festivals have roots in pre-colonial traditions and continue to honor the deities of the Philippine pantheon. The Ati-Atihan Festival, held in Aklan, celebrates the god Anito with vibrant dances, music, and costumes. The Pahiyas Festival in Lucban, Quezon, honors the agricultural goddess Ikapati, showcasing bountiful harvests and elaborate decorations made from fruits and vegetables. These festivals reflect the enduring influence of indigenous spirituality in Filipino culture.

Sacred Sites: Numerous sacred sites across the Philippines are associated with the deities and their myths. Mount Banahaw, for example, is considered a holy mountain and a place of pilgrimage for those seeking spiritual healing and connection. The caves of Mount Madia-as are believed to be the dwelling place of Sidapa, the god of death. Visiting these sites and performing rituals there is a way to honor the deities and connect with their sacred presence.

Daily Practices: In modern Filipino households, ancestral and deity worship continues through daily practices such as lighting candles, offering prayers, and maintaining altars. These altars often feature images or symbols of the deities, alongside photographs and mementos of ancestors. This integration of deity and ancestor worship reflects the holistic approach to spirituality that characterizes Filipino culture.

Modern Adaptations: Today, many Filipinos blend traditional practices with Christian beliefs, creating a unique and evolving spiritual landscape. The reverence for deities and ancestral spirits persists, adapting to contemporary contexts while preserving its deep roots. This synthesis of ancient and modern practices highlights the resilience and adaptability of Filipino spirituality.

The Philippine pantheon, with its rich array of deities and creation stories, offers profound insights into the spiritual and cultural heritage of the Filipino people. By honoring and exploring these divine beings, we connect with a deep and enduring tradition that continues to inspire and guide us on our journey of self-discovery and spiritual growth.

Chapter 109

Mayan

Mayan mythology is an intricate tapestry of stories, deities, and rituals that reflect the deep spirituality and cosmology of the ancient Maya civilization. The Maya, who flourished in Mesoamerica for millennia, developed a complex system of beliefs that intertwined their understanding of the cosmos, natural phenomena, and human existence. At the heart of these beliefs is a pantheon of gods and goddesses who oversee various aspects of life, the natural world, and the cycles of time.

The Maya saw their gods as integral parts of the universe, each playing specific roles in maintaining the balance and harmony of creation. These deities were honored through elaborate ceremonies, intricate calendars, and monumental architecture, all designed to align human activities with the divine order.

Main Deities of the Mayan Pantheon

Itzamná - God of Creation and Wisdom: Itzamná is one of the most significant gods in the Mayan pantheon, revered as the god of creation, wisdom, and the sky. He is often depicted as an old man with a kindly demeanor, symbolizing his role as a wise teacher and creator. Itzamná is associated with writing, medicine, and the arts, making him a patron of knowledge and culture. As the creator god, he is believed to have shaped the world and established the laws that govern the universe. Temples dedicated to Itzamná were centers of learning and healing, where priests and scholars sought his guidance and blessings.

Kukulkan - The Feathered Serpent: Kukulkan, also known as Quetzalcoatl in Aztec mythology, is the powerful feathered serpent god who represents the sky, wind, and rain. Kukulkan is depicted as a serpent covered in feathers, embodying the union of earth and sky and symbolizing transformation and renewal. He is revered as a bringer of knowledge and civilization, credited with teaching the Maya about agriculture, architecture, and the calendar. Kukulkan's presence is most famously represented in the Temple of Kukulkan at Chichen Itza, where the serpent's shadow appears to descend the pyramid during the equinoxes, symbolizing his descent from the heavens.

Chac - The God of Rain and Storms: Chac is the god of rain, storms, and agriculture, playing a crucial role in ensuring the fertility of the land and the success of crops. He is often depicted with a serpent-like nose and large fangs, symbolizing his control over the weather and his ability to bring both nourishing rain and destructive storms. Chac was worshipped with ceremonies and offerings designed to appease him and secure his favor for abundant rainfall. His importance is evident in the numerous rain-related rituals and the presence of his imagery in temples and other sacred sites.

Ix Chel - The Goddess of the Moon and Fertility: Ix Chel is the revered goddess of the moon, fertility, childbirth, and medicine. She is often depicted as an old woman with a serpent crown, representing her wisdom and connection to the cycles of life and death. Ix Chel is also associated with weaving and the arts, reflecting her role as a creator and nurturer. She is honored as a protector of women and children, and her temples were places of pilgrimage for those seeking blessings for childbirth and healing. Her lunar influence made her a central figure in the Mayan calendar and rituals related to time and the natural cycles.

Hun Hunahpu - The Maize God: Hun Hunahpu, the god of maize, is a central figure in Mayan mythology, representing the vital importance of corn as the staple food and a symbol of life and renewal. He is often depicted with green foliage and maize sprouting from his body, embodying the cycle of growth, death, and rebirth. Hun Hunahpu's story is closely linked to the Hero Twins, his sons, who play a crucial role in the Mayan creation narrative and their journey through the underworld. Ceremonies honoring Hun Hunahpu were integral to the agricultural calendar, ensuring the fertility of the crops and the well-being of the community.

Kinich Ahau - The Sun God: Kinich Ahau is the radiant sun god responsible for bringing light, warmth, and life to the world. He is often depicted as a powerful figure with the symbol of the sun on his forehead. Kinich Ahau's daily journey across the sky symbolizes the cycles of time and the balance between day and night. He is also associated with the rulers of the Maya, who are believed to be his earthly representatives. Temples dedicated to Kinich Ahau were constructed to align with solar movements, and rituals honoring him sought to ensure the continued vitality and prosperity of the land.

Yum Kaax - The God of the Forest and Wildlife: Yum Kaax is the god of the forest, wildlife, and agriculture, revered as a protector of the natural world and a provider of sustenance. He is often depicted surrounded by plants and animals, symbolizing his role as the guardian of the wilderness and the crops. Yum Kaax was especially important to hunters and farmers who relied on his blessings for successful hunts and bountiful harvests. Offerings and rituals were performed in his honor to maintain harmony between humans and nature, ensuring the health and balance of the ecosystems upon which the Maya depended.

Xbalanque and Hunahpu - The Hero Twins: Xbalanque and Hunahpu are the legendary Hero Twins, central figures in the Mayan epic known as the Popol Vuh. They are renowned for their adventures in the underworld, where they defeated the lords of Xibalba and restored balance to the world. The Hero Twins symbolize duality, resilience, and the triumph of light over darkness. Their story is a narrative of courage, cunning, and the quest for justice, resonating deeply with the values and beliefs of the Maya. Temples and ball courts were often dedicated to their memory, and their feats were celebrated in rituals and performances that reflected the ongoing struggle between good and evil.

Ek Chuaj - The God of Commerce and War: Ek Chuaj is the god of commerce, war, and cacao, representing the dual aspects of trade and conflict. He is often depicted as a warrior with a distinctive black body and carrying a sack of goods, symbolizing his role in facilitating trade and prosperity. Ek Chuaj was revered by merchants and warriors alike, who sought his protection and favor in their endeavors. Cacao, a sacred commodity, was closely associated with Ek Chuaj, and rituals involving cacao were conducted to honor his influence and ensure success in both trade and warfare.

The Creation Story of the Mayan Pantheon

The creation story of the Mayan pantheon is vividly captured in the Popol Vuh, the sacred text that recounts the origins of the world, the gods, and humanity. According to the Popol Vuh, the universe was created through the collaborative efforts of several deities who sought to bring order to chaos and light to darkness.

In the beginning, there was only the void and the primordial sea. From this emptiness emerged the creators, Heart of Sky (Huracán) and Heart of Earth, along with other divine beings. Together, they envisioned the world and brought it into existence. They created the land, the mountains, and the forests, filling the world with life and beauty.

To illuminate their creation, the gods created the sun, moon, and stars, giving light and order to the cosmos. They then sought to create beings who could honor and worship them. Their first attempts included the creation of animals and beings made from mud and wood, but these creatures failed to possess the intelligence and spirit necessary to venerate the gods.

Undeterred, the gods tried again, fashioning humans from maize dough, a sacred substance that embodies life and sustenance. This time, their creation was successful. The humans were given the gift of knowledge and the ability to worship, fulfilling the gods' desire for beings who could appreciate and honor their creation.

The Popol Vuh also tells the story of the Hero Twins, Hunahpu and Xbalanque, who embarked on a perilous journey to the underworld, Xibalba. Through their courage and wit, they defeated the lords of

Xibalba and restored balance to the world. Their victory symbolized the triumph of life over death and light over darkness, reinforcing the themes of duality and renewal in Mayan cosmology.

Honoring the Mayan Pantheon

Rituals and Offerings: Rituals and offerings are central to Mayan spirituality, performed to honor the gods and ensure their favor. These practices often include the offering of food, drink, incense, and flowers at altars and sacred sites. Priests and community members conduct ceremonies that involve prayers, chants, and the burning of copal, a sacred resin, to invoke the presence of the gods and seek their blessings for fertility, protection, and prosperity.

Festivals: The Maya celebrate various festivals throughout the year, each dedicated to different gods and aspects of life. These festivals are marked by processions, dances, and rituals that reflect the agricultural cycles, celestial events, and mythological narratives. For example, the Haab calendar, which tracks the solar year, includes significant festivals such as Wayeb, a period of introspection and preparation for the new year, and K'atun, commemorating the 20-year cycle of the calendar.

Sacred Sites: Sacred sites known as cenotes, temples, and pyramids play a crucial role in Mayan religious practices. These sites are believed to be portals to the divine and the underworld. Pilgrimages to these locations involve offerings and rituals to honor the gods and seek their guidance. Notable sites include Chichen Itza, home to the Temple of Kukulkan, and Tikal, with its towering pyramids and temples dedicated to various deities.

Daily Practices: Daily life for the Maya is imbued with spiritual observances and rituals. These include offerings made at household altars, prayers for guidance and protection, and the observance of auspicious days according to the Mayan calendar. The practice of milpa, a traditional agricultural system, is also seen as a way to honor the gods and maintain harmony with the land.

Modern Adaptations: Today, many descendants of the Maya continue to honor their traditional gods and practices, blending them with contemporary spirituality. Festivals and rituals that celebrate the Mayan pantheon are still observed, and the teachings of the Popol Vuh remain an integral part of cultural and spiritual identity. Efforts to preserve and revive the language, traditions, and religious practices of the Maya are ongoing, reflecting a deep respect for their heritage and a desire to keep the connection to the divine alive.

The Mayan pantheon, with its rich array of deities and creation stories, offers profound insights into the spiritual and cultural heritage of the Maya. By honoring and exploring these divine beings, we connect with a deep and enduring tradition that continues to inspire and guide us on our journey of self-discovery and spiritual growth.

Chapter 110

Incan

Incan mythology is a rich and complex tapestry of beliefs that reflect the values, environment, and cosmology of the Inca civilization, which flourished in the Andes region of South America. The Inca were deeply connected to their natural surroundings, seeing the mountains, rivers, and celestial bodies as living entities imbued with spiritual significance. This connection is evident in their pantheon of gods and goddesses, each representing different aspects of the natural world and human experience.

Central to Incan spirituality is the concept of reciprocity and harmony with nature, known as ayni. The Inca believed that maintaining a balanced relationship with the gods and nature was crucial for the prosperity and well-being of their society. Rituals, offerings, and ceremonies were integral to their daily lives, ensuring that the deities were honored and their favor secured.

Main Deities of the Incan Pantheon

Viracocha - The Creator God: Viracocha, also known as Wiraqocha, is the supreme creator god in Incan mythology. He is considered the source of all life and the creator of the universe, including the sun, moon, stars, and the earth. Viracocha is often depicted as a benevolent figure who brought order to chaos and gave shape to the cosmos. According to legend, he emerged from Lake Titicaca and traveled across the land, teaching humanity and spreading knowledge before disappearing into the ocean. Viracocha's worship involved offerings and ceremonies

647

aimed at maintaining cosmic order and harmony.

Inti - The Sun God: Inti, the sun god, is one of the most revered deities in the Incan pantheon. He is considered the ancestor of the Inca people and the father of their rulers. Inti is often depicted as a golden disc with rays emanating from it, symbolizing his role as the life-giving force that nourishes the earth and its inhabitants. The Inca held Inti in high regard, believing that he provided warmth, light, and agricultural fertility. The grand Temple of the Sun in Cusco was dedicated to Inti, and the annual Inti Raymi festival celebrated his power and presence with elaborate rituals, dances, and offerings.

Mama Killa - The Moon Goddess: Mama Killa, also known as Mama Quilla, is the goddess of the moon, time, and fertility. She is revered as the protector of women and children, governing the menstrual cycle and the tides. Mama Killa is often depicted as a beautiful woman holding a silver disc, representing the moon's phases and its influence on the natural world. The Inca believed that Mama Killa controlled the passage of time, marking the months and seasons. Hero worship included rituals to ensure successful harvests, fertility, and protection for families. Temples dedicated to Mama Killa often featured intricate silverwork to honor her luminous presence.

Pachamama - The Earth Mother: Pachamama, or Pacha Mama, is the goddess of the earth, fertility, and agriculture. She is considered the nurturing mother who sustains all life and provides for the needs of her children. Pachamama is deeply connected to the cycles of planting and harvesting, and her favor is sought to ensure bountiful crops and healthy livestock. The Inca honored Pachamama through offerings of food, drink, and coca leaves, as well as rituals performed at sacred sites like mountains and springs. Even today, many Andean communities continue to venerate Pachamama, reflecting the enduring reverence for the earth and its resources.

Illapa - The God of Thunder and War: Illapa, also known as Illapaq, is the god of thunder, rain, and war. He is often depicted as a warrior wielding a club and a sling, representing his control over the elements and his role as a protector of the people. Illapa's thunder and lightning were believed to bring rain, essential for agriculture and the survival of the Inca. The Inca prayed to Illapa during times of drought and conflict, seeking his intervention and support. Temples dedicated to Illapa were strategically placed in highland regions, where his power over weather and war was especially revered.

Mama Cocha - The Goddess of the Sea: Mama Cocha, also known as Mama Qocha, is the goddess of the sea, lakes, and rivers. She is considered the provider of water and sustenance, crucial for the survival of the Incan civilization. Mama Cocha is often depicted as a serene figure, embodying the gentle and nourishing aspects of water. Her worship involved rituals to ensure safe voyages, abundant fish, and the purification of water sources. The Inca offered sacrifices and performed ceremonies near bodies of water to honor Mama Cocha and seek her blessings for prosperity and protection.

Supay - The God of Death and the Underworld: Supay is the god of death and the ruler of the underworld, known as Ukhu Pacha. He is often associated with the darker aspects of life and the afterlife, governing the spirits of the deceased and the realm below the earth. Supay is depicted as a fearsome figure, yet he is also a guardian of the balance between life and death. The Inca performed rituals to appease Supay and ensure the safe passage of souls to the afterlife. Offerings and sacrifices were made to honor him and to protect the living from his potentially malevolent influence.

Apu - The Spirit of the Mountains: Apu refers to the sacred spirits of the mountains, revered as powerful deities that protect and provide for the people. Each major mountain in the Andes is considered an Apu, embodying the spirit and essence of the landscape. The Inca believed that the Apus controlled the weather, the fertility of the land, and the well-being of the community. Offerings and ceremonies were conducted at the base of these mountains to honor the Apus and seek their favor. Pilgrimages to sacred peaks were common, reflecting the deep spiritual connection between the Inca and their mountainous homeland.

Mama Sara - The Goddess of Grain: Mama Sara, also known as Saramama, is the goddess of grain and agriculture, particularly revered for her connection to maize (corn), a staple crop for the Inca. She is often depicted with corn cobs or ears of grain, symbolizing abundance and fertility. The Inca celebrated Mama Sara with rituals and offerings during planting and harvest seasons, seeking her blessings for successful crops and sustenance. Her worship highlights the importance of maize in Incan culture and the deep respect for the cycles of agriculture.

The Creation Story of the Incan Pantheon

The creation story of the Incan pantheon begins with Viracocha, the great creator god, emerging from the primordial waters of Lake Titicaca. According to legend, Viracocha brought light into the darkness and formed the sun, moon, and stars to illuminate the world. He then created the earth, shaping its mountains, rivers, and valleys.

Viracocha fashioned the first beings from stone, imbuing them with life and knowledge. However, these early creations did not honor him, leading Viracocha to send a great flood to cleanse the world. After the floodwaters receded, he created humanity anew, this time endowing them with a deep sense of respect and reverence for the divine.

The sun god, Inti, and the moon goddess, Mama Killa, were among Viracocha's creations, assigned to watch over the heavens and guide the cycles of day and night. Inti was given the responsibility of nurturing the earth with his light, while Mama Killa governed the passage of time and the rhythms of the natural world.

Pachamama, the earth mother, emerged to care for the land and its creatures, ensuring the fertility and abundance of the soil. Illapa, the thunder god, was tasked with controlling the weather bringing rain to sustain crops and protect the people. These deities, along with others like Mama Cocha and Supay, worked together to maintain the balance and harmony of the cosmos.

As the Inca civilization grew, they established a deep connection with these gods, building temples and sacred sites to honor their presence. The stories of creation and the deeds of the gods were passed down through generations, preserving the spiritual heritage and guiding the lives of the Incan people.

Honoring the Incan Pantheon

Rituals and Offerings: Rituals and offerings were central to Incan religious practices, performed to honor the gods and ensure their favor. These rituals included the sacrifice of llamas, the offering of coca leaves, and the pouring of chicha (corn beer) as libations. Ceremonies were conducted at sacred sites such as temples, mountain peaks, and springs, where priests and community members gathered to pray, chant, and present gifts to the deities.

Festivals: The Inca celebrated numerous festivals throughout the year, each dedicated to different gods and natural cycles. One of the most significant was Inti Raymi, the Festival of the Sun, held in June to honor Inti. This grand festival marked the winter solstice and included elaborate rituals, dances, and feasts to celebrate the sun's return and the renewal of life. Other important festivals included Qoyllur Rit'i, celebrating the start of the agricultural season, and the Capac Raymi, a royal festival dedicated to the sun and the ancestors.

Sacred Sites: Sacred sites known as huacas were integral to Incan spirituality. These included natural features like mountains, rivers, and caves, as well as man-made structures like temples and shrines. The Temple of the Sun in Cusco was one of the most revered sites, dedicated to Inti and housing gold-plated altars and ceremonial spaces. Pilgrimages to these sacred sites were common, and offerings were made to honor the gods and seek their blessings.

Daily Practices: Daily life in Incan society was imbued with religious observances and rituals. People offered prayers and thanks to the gods before meals, during agricultural work, and in moments of personal or communal significance. The practice of ayni—reciprocal exchange and mutual support—was a reflection of the spiritual principle of maintaining harmony with the gods, the community, and the natural world.

Modern Adaptations: Today, many descendants of the Inca continue to honor the traditional gods and practices, blending them with modern spirituality. Festivals like Inti Raymi are still celebrated in Peru and across the Andes, attracting thousands of participants and visitors. The connection to the land and the reverence for the natural world remain strong as people continue to seek the guidance and blessings of the Incan gods.

The Incan pantheon, with its rich array of deities and creation stories, offers insights into the spiritual and cultural heritage of the Andean people. By honoring and exploring these divine beings, we connect with a deep and enduring tradition that continues to inspire and guide us on our journey of self-discovery and spiritual growth.

Chapter 111

Hawaiian

Hawaiian mythology is deeply intertwined with the natural world and the rich cultural heritage of the Hawaiian people. The Hawaiian pantheon is a vibrant collection of gods, goddesses, and spirits that reflect the islands' unique environment and the values of its inhabitants. These deities embody the forces of nature, elements of the earth, and human qualities, guiding and influencing the lives of the Hawaiian people.

The Hawaiian spiritual worldview is rooted in a profound respect for the ʻāina (land) and the interconnectedness of all living things. This belief system, known as Hawaiian animism, emphasizes that everything in the natural world has a spirit or mana (spiritual energy). The deities of the Hawaiian pantheon are revered as powerful beings who embody this mana and play crucial roles in maintaining the balance and harmony of the cosmos.

Main Deities of the Hawaiian Pantheon

Kāne - God of Creation and Light: Kāne is one of the most important gods in Hawaiian mythology, revered as the god of creation, light, and life. He is considered the father of all living things and the creator of the world. Kāne's name means "man" or "male," and he embodies the life-giving forces of nature, including sunlight, fresh water, and the earth itself. In Hawaiian cosmology, Kāne is often associated with the rising sun and the eastern direction, symbolizing new beginnings and the dawn of life. Rituals and prayers to Kāne seek his blessings for prosperity, fertility, and the sustenance of life.

Lono - God of Fertility, Peace, and Agriculture: Lono is the god of fertility, peace, and agriculture, playing a vital role in ensuring the abundance of crops and the well-being of the people. He is associated with rain, growth, and the cycles of nature. Lono's influence is celebrated during the Makahiki season, a period of rest, renewal, and thanksgiving that coincides with the harvest and the beginning of the new year. During Makahiki, war and labor cease, and people honor Lono with feasts, games, and rituals that express gratitude for the land's bounty and seek continued blessings for the coming year.

Pele - Goddess of Volcanoes and Fire: Pele is the powerful and dynamic goddess of volcanoes and fire, known for her fierce and unpredictable nature. She is considered the creator of the Hawaiian Islands, forming them through her volcanic activities. Pele's presence is most strongly felt on the island of Hawaiʻi, particularly at Kīlauea, one of the world's most active volcanoes. She is both revered and feared, symbolizing the destructive and creative forces of nature. Pele's worship involves offerings of food, flowers, and chants to honor her fiery spirit and seek protection from her wrath. Her legend reminds us of the raw power of the earth and the cycles of destruction and renewal.

Kanaloa - God of the Ocean and Healing: Kanaloa is the god of the ocean, healing, and the underworld. He is often associated with Kāne as his complementary counterpart, representing the dark, mysterious, and transformative aspects of the universe. Kanaloa's domain includes the vast expanse of the ocean, tides, and marine life. He is revered by sailors, fishermen, and those who seek his healing powers. Kanaloa's worship involves rituals and offerings made at the ocean's edge, seeking his guidance and protection for safe voyages and abundant catches. His connection to healing also makes him an important figure in traditional Hawaiian medicine and spiritual practices.

Hiʻiaka - Goddess of Hula and Healing: Hiʻiaka is the beloved goddess of hula, healing, and the arts. She is the younger sister of Pele and is known for her gentle and nurturing nature. Hiʻiaka is celebrated for her role in bringing life, health, and joy to the people. She is the patroness of hula dancers, who honor her through their performances and rituals. Hiʻiaka's stories are deeply intertwined with the practice of hula, which is not only a dance but a form of storytelling that preserves Hawaiian culture and history. Her worship includes the chanting of mele (songs) and the performance of hula to invoke her blessings for health, creativity, and spiritual connection.

Ku - God of War, Politics, and Prosperity: Ku is the formidable god of war, politics, and prosperity. He is one of the four major deities in Hawaiian mythology and is often associated with strength, power, and authority. Ku's worship includes rituals that invoke his support in battles, governance, and the pursuit of wealth and success. He is also revered as a protector of the land and its people, ensuring their safety and well-being. Ku's presence is honored in ceremonies that involve offerings of food, kapa (bark cloth), and traditional chants that seek his favor in times of conflict and his blessings for prosperity and stability.

Hina - Goddess of the Moon and Creativity: Hina is the goddess of the moon, femininity, and creativity. She is often depicted as a beautiful and nurturing figure who embodies the gentle and cyclical nature of the moon. Hina's influence extends to various aspects of life, including art, weaving, and storytelling. She is revered for her wisdom and her ability to inspire creativity and introspection. In Hawaiian mythology, Hina is also associated with the tides and the rhythms of the natural world. Her worship involves rituals that honor the phases of the moon and seek her guidance for creative endeavors and emotional balance.

Kamapuaʻa - The Pig God and Shape-Shifter: Kamapuaʻa is the mischievous and complex pig god, known for his ability to shape-shift into various forms, including a pig, a fish, and a man. He is celebrated for his dual nature, embodying both the nurturing and wild aspects of the natural world. Kamapuaʻa's stories often involve his adventures and conflicts with other deities, including his tumultuous relationship with Pele. He is revered as a protector of agriculture and a symbol of fertility and abundance. Kamapuaʻa's worship includes offerings of food and chants that honor his playful and transformative spirit.

Laka - Goddess of Hula and Forests: Laka is the goddess of hula, forests, and fertility. She is revered as the originator of hula, the sacred dance that preserves Hawaiian culture and connects people to their ancestors and the land. Laka is also associated with the lush and vibrant growth of the forests, symbolizing the fertility and life-giving power of nature. Her worship involves the creation of lei (garlands) and the gathering of sacred plants and flowers used in hula performances. Laka's blessings are sought by dancers and those who work with the land to ensure prosperity, health, and spiritual connection.

Haumea - Goddess of Childbirth and Fertility: Haumea is the goddess of childbirth, fertility, and the earth. She is revered as a powerful mother figure who oversees the cycles of life and the processes of birth and creation. Haumea's influence extends to the fertility of the land and the health and well-being of women and children. Her worship includes rituals and offerings that honor her role in bringing new life into the world and sustaining the abundance of the earth. Haumea's stories emphasize the importance of nurturing, family, and the interconnectedness of all living things.

The Creation Story of the Hawaiian Pantheon

The creation stories of the Hawaiian pantheon are deeply rooted in the concept of the Kumulipo, the Hawaiian creation chant. The Kumulipo describes the origin of the universe and the genealogies of the gods, humans, and all living beings. It is a poetic and spiritual narrative that reflects the interconnectedness and sacredness of all life.

The Kumulipo begins in a time of darkness, a primordial state before the existence of light and life. From this darkness emerged the first deities and the seeds of creation. Kāne, the god of creation, and his counterpart Kanaloa, the god of the ocean, brought forth the elements of the universe and the foundation of life.

As the chant progresses, it describes the birth of the land, the sea, and the sky. The islands of Hawai'i were formed by the volcanic activities of Pele, the goddess of fire. Her powerful eruptions and flows of lava created the mountains, valleys, and fertile plains.

Guided by Spirits

With the land taking shape, the gods and goddesses of the Hawaiian pantheon worked together to bring life and balance to the world. Lono, the god of fertility, ensured the abundance of crops and the harmony of nature. Hina, the goddess of the moon, guided the cycles of time and the rhythms of life.

The Kumulipo also tells of the creation of humans, who were born from the union of the gods and the earth. They were given the gifts of intelligence, creativity, and spirituality, enabling them to live in harmony with the natural world and honor the deities who shaped their existence.

Honoring the Hawaiian Pantheon

Rituals and Offerings: In Hawaiian culture, rituals and offerings are essential practices for honoring the deities. These rituals often include the chanting of prayers, the offering of food and flowers, and the performance of hula. Each deity is honored in a manner that reflects their unique attributes and the aspects of life they govern. For example, offerings to Pele might include items such as ʻawa (kava), a traditional Hawaiian plant used in ceremonies, while rituals for Lono involve offerings of fruits and vegetables to celebrate the harvest.

Festivals: Hawaiian festivals are vibrant celebrations that honor the deities and the cycles of nature. The Makahiki season, dedicated to Lono, is a time of thanksgiving, rest, and renewal, marked by feasts, games, and rituals. The Merrie Monarch Festival, named after King David Kalākaua, is a modern celebration that honors Hawaiian culture and the art of hula, which pays tribute to deities like Laka and Hiʻiaka.

Sacred Sites: Sacred sites across the Hawaiian Islands are revered as places where the presence of the deities is strongly felt. These sites include volcanoes, mountains, waterfalls, and heiau (temples). Visiting these sacred places and performing rituals there is a way to connect with the deities and honor their power and presence. For instance, the summit of Mauna Kea is considered sacred to many Hawaiian deities and is a site for traditional ceremonies and offerings.

Daily Practices: In contemporary Hawaiian life, many people maintain daily practices that honor the deities and their ancestors. These practices include the chanting of mele (songs), the recitation of prayers, and the creation of lei as offerings. These daily acts of devotion reflect a deep respect for the spiritual heritage and the ongoing relationship with the Hawaiian pantheon.

Modern Adaptations: Today, Hawaiian spirituality continues to evolve, blending traditional practices with modern influences. Many Hawaiians incorporate the worship of deities into their personal and communal lives, celebrating their heritage while embracing contemporary spirituality. This fusion of old and new practices highlights the resilience and adaptability of Hawaiian culture and its deep-rooted connection to the divine.

The Hawaiian pantheon, with its rich array of deities and creation stories, offers insights into the spiritual and cultural heritage of the Hawaiian people. By honoring and exploring these divine beings, we connect with a deep and enduring tradition that continues to inspire and guide us on our journey of self-discovery and spiritual growth.

Chapter 112

Aztec

Aztec mythology is a vibrant and complex system of beliefs that reflect the rich cultural heritage of the Aztec civilization, which thrived in central Mexico before the Spanish conquest. At the heart of Aztec spirituality is a reverence for the gods and the natural forces they control. The Aztecs believed that the gods were deeply involved in every aspect of life, from the daily cycles of the sun and rain to the fate of empires and individuals.

The Aztec pantheon is diverse, comprising gods and goddesses who govern various domains such as agriculture, war, love, and the underworld. These deities are celebrated in intricate rituals, grand ceremonies, and monumental architecture that highlight the Aztecs' devotion and their desire to maintain harmony between the celestial and earthly realms.

Main Deities of the Aztec Pantheon

Huitzilopochtli - God of the Sun and War: Huitzilopochtli, meaning "Hummingbird of the South," is one of the most important deities in the Aztec pantheon. He is the god of the sun and war, revered as the protector and patron of the Aztec people. Huitzilopochtli is often depicted as a fierce warrior adorned with hummingbird feathers, symbolizing his swift and powerful nature. He is associated with the sun's daily journey across the sky and the relentless struggle to maintain cosmic order. The Great Temple (Templo Mayor) in Tenochtitlán, the Aztec capital, was dedicated to Huitzilopochtli, where human sacrifices were performed to nourish the sun and ensure its rise each day.

Quetzalcoatl - The Feathered Serpent: Quetzalcoatl, also known as the "Feathered Serpent," is a major god associated with wind, air, and learning. He is a deity of creation, wisdom, and the arts, often depicted as a serpent adorned with feathers, symbolizing his dual nature as both a sky and earth entity. Quetzalcoatl is believed to have taught the Aztecs important aspects of their culture, including writing, agriculture, and the calendar. He is also seen as a god of mercy and resurrection who sacrificed himself to create humanity. Temples dedicated to Quetzalcoatl were centers of learning and cultural development, reflecting his role as a benefactor of civilization.

Tlaloc - The God of Rain and Fertility: Tlaloc is the powerful god of rain, water, and fertility, essential for agricultural prosperity and survival. He is depicted with goggle-like eyes and fangs, often holding lightning bolts, symbolizing his control over storms and precipitation. Tlaloc's influence is crucial for ensuring bountiful crops and the well-being of the people. The Aztecs believed that he resided in Tlalocan, a paradise associated with eternal spring and abundance. Rituals and sacrifices were performed to appease Tlaloc and secure his favor, especially during times of drought or agricultural need. The Templo Mayor also featured a shrine dedicated to Tlaloc, emphasizing his importance alongside Huitzilopochtli.

Tezcatlipoca - The God of Night and Sorcery: Tezcatlipoca, known as the "Smoking Mirror," is a complex and multifaceted god associated with night, sorcery, and destiny. He is depicted with a black obsidian mirror, which he uses to see into the future and control the fates of gods and humans alike. Tezcatlipoca embodies both creation and destruction, embodying the dual nature of life and death. He is often portrayed as a trickster and a shape-shifter, testing the moral character and resolve of individuals. The Aztecs honored Tezcatlipoca through elaborate ceremonies and rituals, seeking his guidance and protection while acknowledging his potential for chaos and upheaval.

Chalchiuhtlicue - The Goddess of Water and Rivers: Chalchiuhtlicue, meaning "She of the Jade Skirt," is the goddess of water, rivers, and lakes. She is also associated with fertility and childbirth, often depicted with flowing water and adorned with jade, symbolizing purity and life-giving properties. Chalchiuhtlicue is considered a nurturing deity who sustains all living things through her waters. She is the wife or consort of Tlaloc, further linking her to the essential elements of rain and fertility. Rituals in her honor included offerings and prayers to ensure the abundance of water and successful agricultural cycles.

Tonatiuh - The Sun God: Tonatiuh is the sun god who reigns over the current era, known as the Fifth Sun in Aztec cosmology. He is depicted as a radiant figure with a disc surrounded by flames, representing the life-giving and destructive power of the sun. Tonatiuh is believed to require regular nourishment through human sacrifices to maintain his strength and ensure the continuation of the world. The Aztecs conducted elaborate ceremonies, including the ritual of tonalpohualli (sacred calendar), to honor Tonatiuh and secure his favor for the prosperity and survival of their society.

Coyolxauhqui - The Moon Goddess**:** Coyolxauhqui, meaning "Golden Bells," is the moon goddess and sister of Huitzilopochtli. She is depicted as a dismembered figure, symbolizing her defeat and the ongoing cosmic struggle between the sun and the moon. According to Aztec mythology, Coyolxauhqui led an attack against her mother, Coatlicue, but was defeated and dismembered by her brother Huitzilopochtli. Her image, carved into the Coyolxauhqui Stone, was found at the base of the Templo Mayor, illustrating her role in the celestial dynamics and the perpetual cycle of conflict and balance in the cosmos.

Mictlantecuhtli - The God of Death and the Underworld: Mictlantecuhtli is the fearsome god of death and the ruler of Mictlan, the underworld. He is depicted as a skeletal figure adorned with bones and skulls, embodying the inevitable fate of all living beings. Mictlantecuhtli governs the souls of the deceased and oversees their journey through the afterlife. The Aztecs believed that after death, souls would traverse the nine levels of Mictlan to reach their final resting place. Rituals and offerings were made to Mictlantecuhtli to ensure a safe passage for the deceased and to honor the cycle of life and death.

Xipe Totec - The God of Fertility and Renewal: Xipe Totec, known as the "Flayed One," is the god of fertility, agriculture, and renewal. He is depicted wearing the flayed skin of a human, symbolizing the renewal of life through death and sacrifice. Xipe Totec's imagery is associated with the shedding of old skin and the rebirth of the natural world. The Aztecs celebrated him with the festival of Tlacaxipehualiztli, which included ritual dances, ceremonies, and offerings to ensure the renewal of crops and the prosperity of the community. His worship emphasized the interconnectedness of life, death, and regeneration.

The Creation Story of the Aztec Pantheon

The Aztec creation story is a rich narrative that explains the origins of the world and the cycles of time through the deeds of the gods. Central to this story is the concept of the Five Suns, each representing an era of creation and destruction.

According to Aztec mythology, the universe was created and destroyed four times before the current era. Each era, or Sun, was ruled by a different god and ended in cataclysmic events that brought about the demise of that world.

1. **First Sun - Jaguar Sun (Nahui Ocelotl):** The first Sun was ruled by Tezcatlipoca. During this era, the inhabitants were giants, but they were eventually devoured by jaguars when Tezcatlipoca was overthrown.

2. **Second Sun - Wind Sun (Nahui Ehecatl):** The second Sun was ruled by Quetzalcoatl. In this period, the world was populated by people who were transformed into monkeys by powerful winds when Quetzalcoatl lost control.

3. **Third Sun - Rain Sun (Nahui Quiahuitl):** Tlaloc governed the third Sun. This era ended when fiery rain fell from the sky, turning the people into turkeys as the world was consumed by flames.

4. **Fourth Sun - Water Sun (Nahui Atl):** Chalchiuhtlicue ruled the

fourth Sun. During this time, the world was submerged in a great flood, and the people were turned into fish.

5. **Fifth Sun - Earthquake Sun (Nahui Ollin):** The current and fifth Sun is ruled by Tonatiuh. It is believed that this era will end in earthquakes and cataclysms. The Aztecs saw themselves living in this final epoch under the vigilant eye of Tonatiuh, the sun god.

The creation of humanity in the Fifth Sun involved the sacrifice of the gods. To set the sun and moon in motion, the gods gathered at Teotihuacan, where two gods, Nanahuatzin and Tecciztecatl, sacrificed themselves by leaping into a great fire, becoming the sun and moon. However, the sun remained motionless until the other gods sacrificed themselves, shedding their blood to give it the energy to move across the sky.

This story emphasizes the themes of sacrifice and renewal that are central to Aztec spirituality. The gods' willingness to sacrifice themselves for the continuation of the world reflects the Aztec belief in the necessity of offerings and ceremonies to sustain the balance and harmony of the cosmos.

Honoring the Aztec Pantheon

Rituals and Offerings: The Aztecs were known for their elaborate rituals and ceremonies dedicated to their gods. Offerings, including food, incense, flowers, and even human sacrifices WHICH WE DO NOT DO ANYMORE, were made to honor the deities and seek their favor. Temples and pyramids served as the focal points for these rituals, where priests conducted ceremonies to ensure the continued support of the gods.

Festivals: The Aztec calendar was filled with festivals, each dedicated to different gods and aspects of life. These festivals included dances, music, feasts, and processions, reflecting the importance of communal celebration and religious observance. Notable festivals include the Feast of the Dead to honor Mictlantecuhtli and the Festival of Flaying for

Xipe Totec.

Sacred Sites: The Aztecs built monumental structures to honor their gods, such as the Templo Mayor in Tenochtitlán, which was dedicated to Huitzilopochtli and Tlaloc. These sacred sites were centers of worship, pilgrimage, and community life, where people gathered to connect with the divine and participate in religious activities.

Daily Practices: Daily life for the Aztecs was infused with spiritual observances. People offered prayers and thanks to the gods before meals, during work, and in times of need. Personal altars in homes were used for private devotions and offerings, maintaining a constant connection with the divine.

Modern Adaptations: Today, the legacy of the Aztec pantheon continues to inspire spiritual practices and cultural heritage. Descendants of the Aztecs and people interested in Mesoamerican spirituality honor these gods through modern rituals, festivals, and educational efforts. Celebrations like the Day of the Dead reflect the enduring influence of Aztec beliefs and the importance of honoring the ancestors and the divine.

The Aztec pantheon, with its diverse array of gods and creation stories, offers an understanding of the Aztec worldview and spirituality. By exploring and honoring these deities, we gain insights into their rich cultural heritage and connect with timeless themes of sacrifice, renewal, and the intricate balance of life.

Chapter 113
Sumerian

Sumerian mythology is among the oldest known spiritual traditions in the world, originating from the ancient civilization of Sumer in Mesopotamia, around 4500 to 1900 BCE. The Sumerians are often credited with developing one of the first complex societies and pioneering many aspects of culture and technology, including writing, which has preserved their rich mythological heritage.

Sumerian myths and deities provide insights into the values, beliefs, and understanding of the cosmos held by one of humanity's earliest urban civilizations. These myths were recorded on clay tablets in cuneiform script, and they reveal a pantheon of gods and goddesses who were deeply integrated into every aspect of Sumerian life, from the natural world to societal structure.

Main Deities of the Sumerian Pantheon

An (Anu) - The Sky Father and King of the Gods: An, also known as Anu, is the supreme god of the Sumerian pantheon, representing the sky and the overarching cosmic order. As the father of the gods and the ruler of the heavens, An embodies authority, justice, and the power of creation. He is often depicted as a distant yet omnipotent deity who delegates the administration of the cosmos to other gods. An's primary role is to maintain the divine order and ensure the stability of the universe. Temples dedicated to An were the centers of political and religious power, reflecting his status as the ultimate arbiter among the gods.

Enlil - God of Air, Storms, and Kingship: Enlil, the god of air, storms, and kingship, is one of the most influential deities in the Sumerian pantheon. He is seen as the god who separates heaven and earth, thus making the creation of life possible. Enlil is a powerful and sometimes wrathful god who oversees the fate of nations and rulers. He is also associated with the granting of divine authority to kings, reinforcing their legitimacy and right to rule. Enlil's sanctuary, the Ekur temple in Nippur, was one of the most important religious sites in ancient Mesopotamia, where he was worshipped as the god who controls the elements and the destiny of the world.

Inanna (Ishtar) - Goddess of Love, War, and Fertility: Inanna, known as Ishtar in later Mesopotamian cultures, is the goddess of love, war, and fertility. She is one of the most complex and celebrated deities in Sumerian mythology, embodying both creative and destructive forces. Inanna is often depicted as a fierce warrior and a passionate lover, reflecting her dual nature as a goddess who can bring both life and death. Her myths include her descent into the underworld, where she confronts the forces of death and returns, symbolizing the cycles of life, death, and rebirth. Temples dedicated to Inanna were centers of worship and cultural activities, emphasizing her role as a protector of cities and a bringer of prosperity and victory.

Enki (Ea) - God of Wisdom, Water, and Creation: Enki, also known as Ea in Akkadian mythology, is the god of wisdom, water, and creation. He is a benevolent deity associated with the gifts of intelligence, craftsmanship, and the nourishing powers of fresh water. Enki is often depicted with flowing streams of water and fish, symbolizing his role as the provider of life-sustaining resources. He is known for his wisdom and cunning, often intervening in myths to help humanity or other gods. Enki's sanctuary, the Abzu in Eridu, was a significant religious center where he was venerated as the god who brings balance and harmony through his knowledge and creative abilities.

Ninhursag (Ki) - Goddess of the Earth and Fertility: Ninhursag, also known as Ki, is the goddess of the earth and fertility. She is a nurturing mother figure who embodies the life-giving and sustaining powers of the earth. Ninhursag is revered as the protector of life and the bringer of fertility, ensuring the growth and prosperity of crops and livestock. She is often depicted with mountains or plants, symbolizing her connection to the natural world and her role as a provider. Ninhursag's worship involved rituals and offerings that honored the cycles of nature and sought her blessings for bountiful harvests and the well-being of communities.

Nanna (Sin) - God of the Moon and Time: Nanna, also known as Sin in Akkadian, is the god of the moon and the passage of time. He is associated with the cycles of the moon and the measurement of time, playing a crucial role in the Sumerian calendar and agricultural planning. Nanna is often depicted as a wise and serene deity, guiding the night with his gentle light. His primary sanctuary was the ziggurat of Ur, one of the most significant religious structures in ancient Mesopotamia. Nanna's influence extended to the regulation of time and the seasons, making him a key figure in the organization of both celestial and terrestrial order.

Utu (Shamash) - God of the Sun and Justice: Utu, known as Shamash in Akkadian, is the god of the sun and justice. He is depicted as a radiant figure who brings light and truth to the world, exposing hidden wrongs and ensuring fairness. Utu is revered as the arbiter of justice, overseeing laws and social order. His daily journey across the sky symbolizes the constant vigilance of the sun, illuminating the world and maintaining the balance between good and evil. Utu's temples were places where justice was sought, and his influence was invoked in legal matters and the pursuit of truth and integrity.

Ereshkigal - Goddess of the Underworld: Ereshkigal is the formidable goddess of the underworld, ruling over the land of the dead. She is depicted as a powerful and somber figure who governs the spirits of the deceased and maintains the order of the afterlife. Ereshkigal's realm, known as Kur or Irkalla, is a place where souls are judged and reside after death. Her role in Sumerian mythology is crucial in maintaining the balance between life and death, and she is often involved in myths that explore the journey to and from the underworld. Ereshkigal's stories highlight the inevitability of death and the importance of respecting the natural cycles of life.

Ninurta - God of War, Agriculture, and Healing: Ninurta is a multifaceted deity associated with war, agriculture, and healing. He is depicted as a fierce warrior who protects the land from chaos and evil forces. Ninurta's prowess in battle is matched by his role as a patron of farmers and healers, symbolizing the balance between destruction and cultivation. He is often portrayed with agricultural tools or weapons, reflecting his dual nature. Ninurta's worship included rituals that honored his protective and nurturing aspects, seeking his favor in both conflict and the fertility of the land.

The Creation Story of the Sumerian Pantheon

The Sumerian creation myth, often found in texts like the Enuma Elish, describes the origins of the universe and the roles of the gods in shaping the world. According to Sumerian mythology, the universe began as a primordial sea, an endless expanse of water known as the Apsu, which represented the primeval chaos.

From this chaotic sea emerged the first gods, including An (the sky) and Ki (the earth). These primordial deities gave birth to Enlil, who separated the sky from the earth, creating the space necessary for life to exist. Enlil's act of separation brought order to the cosmos, allowing the earth to become fertile and life to flourish.

Enki, the god of wisdom and water, played a pivotal role in further shaping the world and bestowing knowledge and skills upon humanity. He created the rivers, streams, and canals that irrigated the land, bringing forth life and prosperity. Enki's wisdom and creativity were crucial in the development of civilization, as he taught humans the arts of agriculture, writing, and craftsmanship.

The Sumerians believed that the gods continued to shape and govern the world through their interactions and conflicts. Myths such as the epic of Gilgamesh and the tale of Inanna's descent into the underworld illustrate the dynamic relationships among the gods and their influence

Guided by Spirits
on the mortal realm.

Honoring the Sumerian Pantheon

Rituals and Offerings: The Sumerians practiced elaborate rituals and offerings to honor their gods and seek their favor. These practices included sacrifices of animals, food, and precious items, as well as prayers and hymns recited at temples and sacred sites. Rituals were often conducted to ensure agricultural fertility, successful harvests, and protection from natural disasters and enemies.

Festivals: The Sumerians celebrated numerous festivals throughout the year, each dedicated to different gods and aspects of life. These festivals were marked by processions, feasts, and communal activities that reflected the agricultural cycles, celestial events, and mythological narratives. Notable festivals included the Akitu festival, celebrating the New Year and the renewal of the king's divine mandate.

Sacred Sites: Temples and ziggurats were the focal points of Sumerian religious life, serving as the dwelling places of the gods on earth. These monumental structures were centers of worship, pilgrimage, and administrative activities. The ziggurat of Ur, dedicated to the moon god Nanna, and the Ekur temple in Nippur, dedicated to Enlil, were among the most significant religious sites in ancient Sumer.

Daily Practices: Daily life for the Sumerians was deeply intertwined with their spirituality. They offered prayers and thanks to the gods before meals, during work, and in times of need. Personal altars in homes were used for private devotions and offerings, maintaining a constant connection with the divine.

Modern Adaptations: Today, the legacy of the Sumerian pantheon continues to inspire spiritual practices and cultural heritage. Scholars, enthusiasts, and practitioners explore and revive Sumerian myths, rituals, and philosophies, seeking to understand and honor one of the earliest and most influential civilizations in human history.

The Sumerian pantheon, with its array of powerful gods and rich creation stories, provides an understanding of the Sumerian worldview and spirituality. By exploring and honoring these deities, we connect with the ancient wisdom and traditions that have shaped human consciousness and continue to inspire our search for meaning and connection in the cosmos.

Chapter 114

Native American

Native American spirituality is deeply rooted in a profound connection with nature, community, and the cosmos. It encompasses a rich diversity of beliefs, practices, and deities across numerous tribes and nations. Each tribe has its own unique cosmology and pantheon of spiritual beings, reflecting the landscapes they inhabit and the life experiences they share. Central to Native American spirituality is the belief that everything in the universe is alive and interconnected, imbued with spirit and meaning.

Native American mythology includes a vast array of stories that explain the origins of the world, the forces of nature, and the moral principles that guide human behavior. These stories are often passed down orally through generations, serving as both educational tools and expressions of cultural identity. The deities and spirits in these myths play crucial roles in maintaining the balance and harmony of the natural world, guiding the people in their daily lives and spiritual practices.

Main Deities and Spirits in Native American Traditions

Given the diversity among Native American tribes, there is no single unified pantheon. However, many tribes share common themes and types of spiritual beings. Here are some significant deities and spirits from various Native American traditions:

Great Spirit (Wakan Tanka, Gitche Manitou) - The Supreme Being: The Great Spirit, known by different names among various tribes (such as Wakan Tanka among the Lakota or Gitche Manitou among the Algonquian peoples), is often considered the supreme being and creator of the universe. The Great Spirit is viewed as an all-encompassing force that governs the natural world and all living beings within it. This deity embodies the essence of life and is honored as the source of wisdom, power, and harmony. The Great Spirit is central too many Native American spiritual practices, emphasizing the interconnectedness and sacredness of all creation.

Coyote - The Trickster and Teacher: Coyote is a prominent figure in many Native American mythologies, particularly among tribes in the Southwestern United States. As a trickster god, Coyote is known for his cunning, playful, and sometimes foolish behavior. He often disrupts the natural order with his antics, but through his mischief, he also teaches valuable lessons about human nature and the complexities of life. Coyote's stories illustrate themes of transformation, resilience, and the importance of adaptability. While he can be mischievous, Coyote is also a revered figure who embodies the duality of creation and destruction, reflecting the unpredictable aspects of existence.

Raven - The Creator and Trickster: Raven is a central figure in the spiritual traditions of the Pacific Northwest Coast tribes, such as the Haida, Tlingit, and Tsimshian. He is both a creator and a trickster, known for his intelligence, wit, and transformative powers. Raven is credited with shaping the world and bringing light to humanity by stealing the sun, moon, and stars from a powerful chief. Through his cleverness and curiosity, Raven often finds himself in humorous and challenging situations, teaching people about the balance between light and darkness, order and chaos. Raven's tales highlight the importance of creativity, resourcefulness, and the pursuit of knowledge.

Thunderbird - The Powerful Protector: The Thunderbird is a powerful spirit in the traditions of many tribes across North America, including the Plains, Great Lakes, and Northwest Coast regions. This majestic bird is believed to control the forces of weather, particularly thunder and lightning. The Thunderbird is often depicted as a massive bird with wings that create thunder when they flap and eyes that shoot lightning. It is revered as a protector of the people, capable of warding off evil spirits and bringing rain to nourish the land. The Thunderbird symbolizes strength, power, and divine intervention, playing a crucial role in maintaining balance and harmony in the natural world.

Spider Grandmother - The Wise and Nurturing Guide: Spider Grandmother is a revered figure in the mythologies of Southwestern tribes, such as the Hopi and Navajo. She is known as a wise and nurturing guide who weaves the web of life, connecting all living beings. Spider Grandmother is a creator and protector, often providing guidance and assistance to humanity in times of need. In Hopi tradition, she taught the people how to grow crops, make pottery, and understand the interconnectedness of all things. Her stories emphasize the importance of wisdom, patience, and the intricate patterns that connect life's many threads.

White Buffalo Woman - The Bringer of Peace and Prosperity: White Buffalo Woman is a sacred figure in the Lakota Sioux tradition. She is revered as a messenger of the Great Spirit and the bringer of peace, harmony, and prosperity. According to Lakota legend, White Buffalo Woman appeared to the people during a time of great need, bringing with her the sacred pipe (chanunpa) and teaching them important spiritual rituals and ways of living in balance with nature. She promised to return in times of need to help the people once more. White Buffalo Woman's teachings continue to guide the Lakota in their spiritual practices and their relationship with the natural world.

Glooskap - The Hero and Protector: Glooskap is a cultural hero and protector in the mythologies of the Wabanaki Confederacy, which includes tribes such as the Abenaki, Penobscot, and Passamaquoddy. He is often depicted as a powerful figure who shapes the landscape, battles monsters, and brings order to the world. Glooskap's stories reflect his role as a teacher and protector, guiding the people in their daily lives and helping them overcome challenges. He embodies the virtues of courage, wisdom, and compassion, and his legends emphasize the importance of living in harmony with nature and respecting the forces that govern the world.

Alex McCann Johnson

Creation Stories in Native American Mythology

One common creation story among many Native American tribes is the Earth Diver myth. This narrative often begins with a vast, primordial ocean and a sky realm inhabited by deities. The story typically involves a god or cultural hero who dives into the ocean to retrieve earth or mud from the depths, which then expands to form the land.

For example, in the Seneca tradition, the Sky Woman falls from the sky and is caught by animals in the water below. The creatures, including a turtle, muskrat, and beaver, work together to bring up mud from the ocean floor to create an island on the turtle's back, where Sky Woman can live. This tale emphasizes themes of cooperation, the sacredness of animals, and the interconnectedness of all life.

The Emergence myth is another prevalent creation story, particularly among tribes in the Southwestern United States. In these myths, the first people or ancestors emerge from an underworld or a series of lower worlds to reach the surface, where they establish the current world.

In the Hopi tradition, the people emerged from the depths of the earth through a sipapu, a small hole or portal, guided by the spiritual beings who oversee the different levels of existence. This emergence represents a journey of growth, purification, and the transition from chaos to order. The Hopi believe that their ancestors emerged into this world with the help of Spider Grandmother and other spiritual guides, who taught them how to live in harmony with nature and maintain balance in the world.

Many Native American creation stories involve a trickster figure who plays a crucial role in shaping the world. These tricksters, such as Coyote or Raven, often use their wit and cunning to bring light, land, or other essential elements into existence.

In the Pacific Northwest, the Raven is a central figure in myth creation. According to the Haida people, Raven found the world in darkness and stole the sun, moon, and stars from a powerful chief to bring light to the world. Through his cleverness and determination, Raven transformed the chaotic, dark world into a place filled with light and life. These stories highlight the themes of transformation, the balance between order and chaos, and the idea that even seemingly mischievous actions can have profound and positive outcomes.

Honoring the Native American Pantheon

Rituals and Ceremonies: Native American spiritual practices are deeply intertwined with rituals and ceremonies that honor the deities and spirits. These practices often include offerings, dances, songs, and the use of sacred objects such as the peace pipe or the drum. Ceremonies like the Sun Dance, Sweat Lodge, and Vision Quest are central to many tribes, providing a means to connect with the divine and seek spiritual guidance and healing.

Sacred Sites: Many Native American tribes have sacred sites that are revered as places of spiritual power and connection. These sites, such as mountains, rivers, and caves, are often seen as the dwelling places of deities and spirits. Visiting these sacred sites, making offerings, and participating in ceremonies there are ways to honor the spiritual beings associated with these places.

Seasonal Festivals: Seasonal festivals mark important times of the year and the cycles of nature. These festivals often involve communal gatherings, feasts, and rituals that celebrate the changing seasons and honor the deities and spirits who govern the natural world. Festivals like the Green Corn Ceremony and the Powwow are examples of these communal celebrations.

Daily Practices: Daily life for many Native Americans includes practices that maintain a connection with the spiritual world. This can involve offering prayers, using smudging herbs like sage for purification, and acknowledging the presence of spirit in all aspects of life. These practices help keep the balance between the physical and spiritual realms and ensure the continued favor and guidance of the gods and spirits.

Modern Adaptations: Today, Native American spiritual practices continue to evolve, blending traditional beliefs with contemporary life. Many tribes are actively preserving and revitalizing their cultural heritage through education, storytelling, and the practice of rituals and ceremonies. The resurgence of interest in Native American spirituality among both indigenous and non-indigenous people reflects a growing appreciation for the wisdom and depth of these traditions.

The Native American pantheons, with their rich array of deities and creation stories, offers an understanding of the natural world and the spiritual dimensions of life. By exploring and honoring these gods and spirits, we gain insights into the values and beliefs that have shaped Native American cultures for millennia. Embracing these traditions allows us to connect with the timeless themes of harmony, respect, and the sacredness of all life.

Chapter 115
Slavic

Slavic mythology is a rich tapestry of deities, spirits, and legends that have evolved over centuries among the Slavic peoples of Eastern Europe. Before the widespread adoption of Christianity, the Slavs practiced a form of paganism deeply connected to nature, the seasons, and the cycles of life. This ancient belief system was characterized by a pantheon of gods and goddesses who governed various aspects of the natural world and human existence.

The Slavic pantheon is diverse, reflecting the vast geography and cultural variations among the Slavic tribes. These deities were worshipped in sacred groves, on hilltops, and by rivers, where rituals and festivals were conducted to honor their presence and seek their favor. Although much of the original Slavic mythology was not written down until later, it has been preserved through folklore, songs, and oral traditions passed down through generations.

Main Deities of the Slavic Pantheon

Perun - God of Thunder and War: Perun is the supreme god of the Slavic pantheon, ruling over the skies, thunder, and lightning. Often compared to the Norse god Thor or the Greek god Zeus, Perun is a powerful deity associated with war, justice, and the protection of the people. He is depicted as a strong warrior wielding a mighty axe or hammer, symbols of his ability to strike down enemies and maintain order. Perun's name is invoked for protection in battle and during storms, and he is honored as the king of the gods and the enforcer of moral law.

677

His sacred symbols include the oak tree, the eagle, and the axe, which are often used in rituals to call upon his strength and guidance.

Veles - God of the Underworld, Cattle, and Wealth: Veles is a complex deity who governs the underworld, cattle, and wealth. As the counterpart to Perun, Veles represents the earthly and malevolent aspects of life, including the cycles of death and rebirth. He is often depicted as a serpent or dragon, symbolizing his connection to the earth and his role as a guardian of the underworld. Veles is also the protector of livestock and agricultural prosperity, making him a vital deity for the agrarian Slavs. His dual nature as both a god of the underworld and a bringer of wealth highlights the balance between the seen and unseen worlds and the interplay of life and death.

Mokosh - Goddess of Fertility, Women, and the Earth: Mokosh is the great mother goddess of the Slavic pantheon, associated with fertility, women, and the earth. She is revered as the protector of women's work, especially in spinning, weaving, and childbirth. Mokosh embodies the nurturing and life-giving aspects of nature, and her presence is seen in the fertile fields and the nurturing soil. She is often depicted with symbols of the earth and water, such as wells and spinning wheels, reflecting her role as a provider and sustainer of life. Mokosh is honored with offerings of grain and cloth, and rituals dedicated to her seek her blessings for fertility and the protection of the home and family.

Svarog - God of Fire and Blacksmithing: Svarog is the god of fire and blacksmithing, often regarded as the creator of the universe and the father of other important deities. He is associated with the sun, celestial fire, and the forge, embodying the transformative power of fire. Svarog is credited with creating the first humans and bestowing upon them the skills of metalworking and craftsmanship. His sacred flames represent both the destructive and creative forces of fire, and he is revered as the bringer of civilization and technology. Svarog's worship involves the maintenance of sacred fires and rituals that honor the creative and purifying aspects of fire.

Dazhbog - God of the Sun and Prosperity: Dazhbog is the god of the sun and prosperity, often depicted as a radiant and generous deity who bestows light and wealth upon the world. He is seen as the giver of life and the provider of warmth and abundance. Dazhbog's journey across the sky each day symbolizes the eternal cycle of day and night, and his influence is essential for the growth of crops and the sustenance of life. He is honored with prayers and rituals that seek his blessings for a bountiful harvest and the well-being of the community. Dazhbog's festivals celebrate the sun's power and its role in bringing prosperity and joy.

Svetovid - God of War, Fertility, and Abundance: Svetovid is a multifaceted god associated with war, fertility, and abundance. He is often depicted with four heads, each facing a different direction, symbolizing his all-seeing and all-knowing nature. Svetovid is a protector and warrior deity, invoked for victory in battle and the protection of the land. He is also a god of fertility and abundance, ensuring the prosperity and growth of the people and their resources. Svetovid's worship involves elaborate rituals and sacrifices, often conducted at his sacred shrines, where his four-headed idols are prominently displayed. His festivals celebrate his power and his ability to bring success and prosperity.

Morana (Marzanna) - Goddess of Winter and Death: Morana, also known as Marzanna, is the goddess of winter and death, representing the end of the life cycle and the coming of the cold, barren season. She is depicted as a dark and somber figure who ushers in the winter and the inevitability of death. Morana's role in the pantheon is to remind the people of the natural cycles of life and death and the importance of accepting and honoring these transitions. Rituals dedicated to Morana often involve symbolic acts of death and rebirth, such as the burning or drowning of effigies to mark the end of winter and the return of spring. Her stories and ceremonies reflect the themes of transformation and renewal.

Lada - Goddess of Love, Beauty, and Harmony: Lada is the goddess of love, beauty, and harmony, often associated with the warmth and vibrancy of spring and summer. She embodies the nurturing and joyful aspects of life, promoting peace, fertility, and the blossoming of nature. Lada is celebrated for her role in fostering relationships, love, and community bonds. She is depicted as a beautiful and radiant figure, often surrounded by flowers and symbols of growth. Festivals in her honor are filled with music, dancing, and rituals that celebrate love, the beauty of nature, and the renewal of life. Lada's presence is invoked to bring harmony and joy to both individuals and communities.

Rod - The Primal God of Creation and Fate: Rod is considered the primal god of creation and fate in Slavic mythology. He is believed to be the origin of all life and the cosmos, holding the power over birth and destiny. Rod's influence extends to the cycles of life and the weaving of fate, determining the paths of gods and humans alike. He is often associated with the ancestral spirits and the continuity of the family line. Rituals honoring Rod focus on the themes of creation, protection, and the preservation of lineage and heritage. His presence is revered as the foundation of existence and the guiding force behind the unfolding of life's events.

Creation Stories of the Slavic Pantheon

The creation myths of the Slavic people are varied and often intertwined with their deities and the natural world. One common theme is the emergence of the world from chaos and the role of the gods in shaping the cosmos.

One Slavic creation myth speaks of the world emerging from a cosmic egg. In this myth, the universe began as a great cosmic egg floating in the primordial waters. Inside the egg, the forces of creation were contained. When the egg hatched, it gave birth to the earth, the sky, and all living beings. The shell of the egg became the firmament of the heavens, and the yolk and white formed the land and seas. The gods and goddesses, including Perun and Veles, emerged from this cosmic birth, taking their places to govern the elements and the natural order.

Another creation story revolves around the eternal conflict between Perun and Veles. According to this myth, Perun, the god of thunder and the sky, and Veles, the god of the earth and the underworld, were once allies. However, a great dispute arose between them, leading to a cosmic battle. Veles, often depicted as a serpent or dragon, would steal from

Perun's domain, causing chaos and disorder. Perun, in response, would strike Veles with his thunderbolts, driving him back into the underworld. This battle symbolizes the ongoing struggle between order and chaos, light and darkness, and the cycles of nature. Through their conflict, the world is continually renewed and maintained.

In another myth, Svarog, the god of fire and blacksmithing, is depicted as the divine craftsman who forged the world. Using his celestial forge, Svarog shaped the land, the mountains, and the seas, imbuing them with the power of fire and creation. He crafted the first humans from clay and breathed life into them, teaching them the arts of metalworking and civilization. Svarog's act of creation established the foundations of the world and the principles of craftsmanship and knowledge.

Honoring the Slavic Pantheon

Rituals and Offerings: Slavic rituals and offerings often involve fire, water, and natural elements. Sacred groves, rivers, and mountains serve as sites for these rituals, where people gather to make offerings of food, drink, and symbolic items to the gods. Fire plays a central role, symbolizing purification, transformation, and the presence of the divine.

Seasonal Festivals: Seasonal festivals mark important times of the year and celebrate the cycles of nature. These festivals, such as Kupala Night, dedicated to the summer solstice, and Maslenitsa, celebrating the end of winter, involve communal feasting, dancing, and ceremonies that honor the gods and the changing seasons.

Daily Practices: Daily life for those who honor the Slavic gods includes small acts of devotion and recognition. This can involve lighting candles, saying prayers, and making small offerings at household altars. These practices help maintain a continuous connection with the deities and the natural world.

Modern Adaptations: Today, there is a growing interest in reviving and adapting Slavic pagan traditions. People explore their cultural heritage through festivals, educational events, and the practice of rituals that honor the ancient gods and spirits. This revival reflects a desire to reconnect with the wisdom and spirituality of the past, integrating it into contemporary life.

The Slavic pantheon, with its diverse deities and rich creation myths, offers an understanding of the natural world and the spiritual dimensions of life. By exploring and honoring these gods and goddesses, we gain insights into the values and beliefs that have shaped Slavic cultures for centuries. Embracing these traditions allows us to connect with the timeless themes of harmony, respect, and the sacredness of all life.

Chapter 116
Māori

Māori mythology is the rich and vibrant spiritual tradition of the Māori people, the indigenous inhabitants of Aotearoa (New Zealand). This tradition is deeply rooted in the natural world and encompasses a wide range of gods and spirits who govern the forces of nature, life, and the cosmos. Māori spirituality emphasizes the interconnectedness of all things and the sacredness of the land (whenua), the sky (rangi), and the sea (moana).

The Māori worldview, or Te Ao Māori, is holistic, viewing the spiritual and physical realms as interconnected and interdependent. This perspective is reflected in their stories, rituals, and everyday practices. Māori mythology is passed down through whakapapa (genealogy), waiata (songs), karakia (prayers), and pūrākau (stories), which preserve the wisdom and knowledge of their ancestors.

Main Deities and Spirits of the Māori Pantheon

Ranginui (Rangi) - Sky Father: Ranginui, commonly known as Rangi, is the Sky Father and a principal deity in Māori mythology. Together with his wife Papatūānuku, the Earth Mother, Rangi represents the celestial realm. According to Māori creation myths, Rangi and Papa were once tightly embraced, and their children lived in the darkness between them. The separation of Rangi and Papa by their children brought light into the world and created the sky and the earth as distinct entities. Rangi's tears are said to be the rain, reflecting his eternal longing for Papatūānuku. He is honored in rituals that seek to connect the human realm with the divine and celestial.

Papatūānuku (Papa) - Earth Mother: Papatūānuku, often referred to as Papa, is the Earth Mother and the nurturing force of life. She is the foundation of all living things, providing sustenance and shelter. In Māori mythology, Papa and Rangi's separation allowed the creation of the world, with Papa remaining as the fertile earth that supports all life. She is revered in practices that emphasize the sacredness of the land and the importance of living in harmony with nature. Rituals involving planting, harvesting, and caring for the land often invoke Papatūānuku's blessings and protection.

Tāne Mahuta - God of Forests and Birds: Tāne Mahuta is the god of forests and birds and one of the most significant deities in Māori mythology. He is credited with separating his parents, Rangi and Papa, bringing light into the world. Tāne is also known for creating humans and many forms of life. He crafted the first woman, Hineahuone, from the sacred red earth and breathed life into her. Tāne's domain encompasses all trees and birds, and he is honored in rituals that seek to preserve the forests and maintain ecological balance. His influence is seen in the lush, verdant landscapes of New Zealand, and he is invoked for wisdom, strength, and growth.

Tangaroa - God of the Sea: Tangaroa is the god of the sea and all its creatures, including fish and marine life. He is a powerful and revered deity, reflecting the Māori's deep connection to the ocean. Tangaroa's domain extends to all waters, and he is considered the ancestor of many sea-dwelling creatures. His stories often emphasize the respect and care that must be shown to the sea and its inhabitants. Fishermen and those who rely on the ocean for sustenance offer prayers and rituals to Tangaroa, seeking his favor and protection. Tangaroa's influence underscores the importance of the sea in Māori life and the need to live in harmony with this vital resource.

Tūmatauenga (Tū) - God of War and Humanity: Tūmatauenga, or Tū, is the god of war, conflict, and humanity. He embodies the warrior spirit and the principles of courage, strength, and strategic thinking. Tūmatauenga is one of the sons of Rangi and Papa, and he played a key role in the separation of his parents, advocating for decisive action. Tūmatauenga is also the ancestor of all humans, and his name is invoked in matters of conflict, justice, and human endeavor. Warriors and those seeking strength and determination honor Tūmatauenga through rituals and ceremonies that emphasize the values of bravery and resilience.

Rongo - God of Peace and Cultivation: Rongo is the god of peace, agriculture, and cultivated plants. He is associated with the prosperity and well-being that comes from the earth's bounty. Rongo's influence extends to the harmonious relationships and the nurturing aspects of life. As the deity responsible for crops and food, Rongo is honored during planting and harvest times, with rituals seeking his blessings for abundant and successful yields. His stories and attributes highlight the importance of peace, cooperation, and the fruitful rewards of working with the land. Rongo represents the balance and tranquility that come from living in harmony with nature and each other.

Hine-nui-te-pō - Goddess of Death and the Underworld: Hine-nui-te-pō is the goddess of death and the ruler of the underworld. She plays a crucial role in the Māori understanding of life and death, guiding souls to the afterlife. Hine-nui-te-pō was originally Hine-tītama, the dawn maiden, created by Tāne Mahuta. Upon discovering that Tāne was her father, she fled to the underworld, transforming into Hine-nui-te-pō. Her realm is a place of rest and transition for departed souls, and she is revered in funeral rites and ceremonies that honor the dead. Hine-nui-te-pō's stories teach about the cycles of life and death and the enduring connection between the living and the deceased.

Māui - Demigod and Trickster: Māui is one of the most beloved figures in Polynesian mythology, known for his daring exploits and trickster qualities. In Māori tradition, Māui is a cultural hero who accomplished many great feats, including fishing up the North Island of New Zealand from the sea and slowing down the sun to extend the length of the day. Māui's adventures often involve cleverness, bravery, and a bit of mischief, making him a symbol of ingenuity and resilience. His stories inspire people to overcome challenges, think creatively, and push the boundaries of what is possible. Māui's legacy continues to influence

Māori culture, reminding us of the power of wit and determination.

Creation Stories of the Māori Pantheon

One of the most important creation stories in Māori mythology is the separation of Ranginui (Rangi) and Papatūānuku (Papa). In the beginning, Rangi, the Sky Father, and Papa, the Earth Mother, were locked in a tight embrace, with their children confined in the darkness between them. The children, who were gods of various elements and aspects of nature, felt constrained and yearned for light and space. After much deliberation, Tāne Mahuta, the god of forests, decided to push his parents apart. With great effort, he placed his feet against Papa and lifted Rangi upwards, creating the sky and the earth as separate entities. This act brought light into the world and allowed life to flourish. The separation of Rangi and Papa is seen as the moment of creation, where order emerged from chaos, and the physical world as we know it was formed.

Another significant creation story involves Māui and his fishing expedition. Māui, known for his curiosity and boldness, often sought to prove his capabilities. One day, he fashioned a fishhook from his grandmother's jawbone and set out on a fishing trip with his brothers. Using his magical fishhook, Māui caught a giant fish from the depths of the ocean. This fish, known as Te Ika-a-Māui, became the North Island of New Zealand. Māui's brothers, eager to claim the fish for themselves, began to carve it up, creating the mountains and valleys. This story explains the geographical features of the North Island and emphasizes Māui's role as a creator and cultural hero. It also highlights the themes of exploration, ingenuity, and the transformative power of human actions.

Honoring the Māori Pantheon

Rituals and Ceremonies: Māori spirituality involves numerous rituals and ceremonies that honor the gods and spirits. These practices include karakia (prayers), hāngī (earth-cooked feasts), and pōwhiri (welcome ceremonies). Ceremonies often take place on marae, communal sacred spaces that serve as the heart of Māori community life. These rituals are integral to maintaining the connection between the people, their ancestors, and the gods.

Seasonal Festivals: The Māori calendar is marked by several important festivals that celebrate the cycles of nature and honor the deities. Matariki, the Māori New Year, is one of the most significant festivals. It occurs in late June or early July when the Pleiades star cluster rises in the sky. Matariki is a time for remembering the dead, celebrating new life, and planning for the future. It involves feasting, storytelling, and rituals that connect the community with the gods and the natural world.

Daily Practices: Daily life for Māori includes practices that reflect their spiritual beliefs and connection to the gods. This can involve offering prayers and thanks to the deities, caring for the land and environment, and maintaining the customs and traditions that honor their ancestors and spiritual heritage.

Modern Adaptations: Today, Māori spirituality continues to thrive and evolve. There is a strong emphasis on preserving and revitalizing traditional practices, language, and cultural knowledge. Many Māori actively engage in cultural education, ceremonies, and festivals that honor their gods and heritage. This modern adaptation ensures that the rich legacy of Māori mythology and spirituality remains vibrant and relevant in contemporary life.

The Māori pantheon, with its array of powerful gods and rich creation myths, offers a deep and meaningful connection to the natural world and the spiritual dimensions of life. By exploring and honoring these deities, we gain insights into the values, beliefs, and cultural heritage of the Māori people. Embracing these traditions allows us to appreciate the timeless themes of creation, transformation, and the sacredness of the land, sea, and sky, fostering a deeper connection with the spiritual essence of the world.

Alex McCann Johnson

Chapter 117

Mongolian

Mongolian mythology and spirituality are deeply intertwined with the vast landscapes and nomadic lifestyle of the Mongolian people. The spiritual beliefs of the Mongols are shaped by their intimate relationship with the natural world, where the sky, land, and animals play pivotal roles. This connection is reflected in their reverence for Tengriism, an ancient spiritual tradition that honors the sky god Tengri and a host of nature spirits and deities.

Tengriism, often referred to as the "Sky Religion," is one of the oldest known religions, dating back to the early nomadic cultures of Central Asia. It is a shamanistic and animistic belief system that sees the world as animated by spirits and governed by the cosmic power of Tengri, the eternal blue sky. Tengriism emphasizes living in harmony with nature, respecting the land and its creatures, and maintaining a balanced relationship between the physical and spiritual realms.

Main Deities and Spirits of the Mongolian Pantheon

Tengri - Sky God: Tengri, the supreme deity in Mongolian mythology, is often referred to as the Eternal Blue Sky. He is the primary god in Tengriism and is considered the creator and ruler of the universe. Tengri is associated with the vast, open skies of Mongolia, symbolizing infinity, eternity, and the source of life and destiny. The Mongols believe that Tengri watches over them, granting favor and guidance to those who live in harmony with the natural world and the cosmic order. In everyday life, Tengri is honored through rituals and offerings that seek

689

his blessings for protection, prosperity, and success. Shamans often invoke Tengri during ceremonies to align with his powerful energy and to gain insights into the will of the heavens.

Etügen (Etügen Eke) - Earth Mother: Etügen, also known as Etügen Eke, is the Earth Mother goddess in Mongolian spirituality. She represents the fertile and nurturing aspects of the earth, embodying the life-giving forces of nature. As the goddess of the land, Etügen is deeply revered by the Mongols, who depend on the earth for sustenance and survival. Etügen is often depicted as a maternal figure who provides for her children and ensures the abundance of crops and livestock. In traditional Mongolian rituals, offerings of milk, grains, and other food items are made to Etügen to express gratitude for her bounty and to seek her continued blessings for a prosperous life.

Erlik Khan - God of the Underworld: Erlik Khan is the god of the underworld and the ruler of the spirits of the dead in Mongolian mythology. He is a complex figure, often portrayed as a powerful and somewhat fearsome deity who governs the afterlife and the souls of the deceased. Erlik Khan's domain is a place of judgment and transition, where souls are evaluated and prepared for their next journey. Despite his association with death and the underworld, Erlik Khan is also seen as a necessary part of the cosmic balance, ensuring that the cycle of life and death continues. In shamanic practices, ceremonies are performed to honor Erlik Khan and to seek his protection for the souls of the departed.

Ülgen - Creator God: Ülgen is a prominent creator god in Mongolian mythology, associated with light, goodness, and the creative forces of the universe. He is often seen as a benevolent deity who shapes the world and brings order to chaos. Ülgen is revered as a powerful force for creation and growth, guiding the development of life and the progression of the cosmos. In the spiritual practices of the Mongols, Ülgen is honored through rituals that celebrate the creative and transformative aspects of life. His influence is invoked in times of new beginnings, growth, and the pursuit of positive change.

Gesar - Hero and Protector: Gesar is a legendary hero and cultural icon in Mongolian mythology, often depicted as a warrior king and protector of his people. The epic of King Gesar, one of the longest epic poems in the world, tells the story of his battles against evil forces and his quest to bring peace and justice to the land. Gesar's tales are filled with adventure, bravery, and the triumph of good over evil, reflecting the values and aspirations of the Mongolian people. Gesar is honored in rituals and storytelling traditions that celebrate his heroic deeds and his role as a protector. His legend serves as a source of inspiration and a symbol of resilience and courage in the face of adversity.

Böködei Mergen - God of Hunting: Böködei Mergen is the god of hunting and a significant deity for the nomadic Mongolian people, who traditionally relied on hunting for their livelihood. He is depicted as a skilled archer and hunter, embodying the qualities of precision, strength, and respect for the natural world. Böködei Mergen is honored by hunters seeking success and safety in their endeavors, and his favor is sought through rituals that emphasize harmony with nature and the responsible stewardship of wildlife.

Khan Tengri - Spirit of the Sacred Mountain: Khan Tengri is the spirit of one of the highest peaks in the Tien Shan mountain range, revered as a sacred mountain in Mongolian spirituality. The name "Khan Tengri" means "King Heaven," reflecting the mountain's towering presence and spiritual significance. It is believed to be the abode of powerful spirits and a place where the earthly and divine realms intersect. Pilgrimages and offerings are made to Khan Tengri to seek blessings, protection, and the favor of the mountain spirits.

Creation Stories of the Mongolian Pantheon

In Mongolian creation mythology, Tengri, the Eternal Blue Sky, is the supreme force that brought the universe into existence. According to the myth, in the beginning, there was only the endless sky and the vast, empty earth. Tengri, as the creator deity, looked upon the world and decided to fill it with life and order.

Tengri breathed life into the earth, creating the land, rivers, mountains, and all living beings. He appointed Etügen as the Earth Mother to nurture and sustain the life he had created. Tengri also created the sun, moon,

691

and stars, establishing the rhythms of day and night and the cycles of the seasons. This act of creation set the stage for the ongoing dance of life, growth, and renewal that characterizes the natural world.

Tengri's creation of the world is seen as an ongoing process, with the sky god continually overseeing and guiding the balance of nature and the destiny of all beings. This story underscores the central role of Tengri in Mongolian spirituality as the source of life and the guardian of cosmic harmony.

Another significant creation myth involves Erlik Khan and his role as the ruler of the underworld. According to this story, Erlik Khan was originally a god who assisted in the creation of the world. However, he eventually became associated with the underworld and the spirits of the dead, taking on the role of the judge and guardian of the afterlife.

Erlik Khan's domain is depicted as a dark and mysterious place where souls are judged and prepared for their journey to the next world. He ensures that the souls of the dead find their rightful place and that the balance between the living and the dead is maintained. This story highlights the importance of respecting the cycle of life and death and the necessity of Erlik Khan's role in the cosmic order.

Honoring the Mongolian Pantheon

Shamanic Rituals and Ceremonies: Shamanic practices are central to Mongolian spirituality. Shamans serve as intermediaries between the human and spirit worlds, conducting rituals to communicate with deities and spirits, seek guidance, and perform healing. These ceremonies often involve drumming, chanting, and offerings, creating a sacred space for spiritual connection.

Seasonal Festivals: The Mongolian calendar is marked by various festivals that celebrate the cycles of nature and honor the deities. Tsagaan Sar, the Lunar New Year, is one of the most important festivals, celebrating the coming of spring and the renewal of life. Naadam, the national festival, includes traditional sports such as wrestling, horse racing, and archery, reflecting the nomadic heritage and the connection to nature.

Offerings and Altars: Offerings and altars are common ways to honor the gods and spirits. People often make offerings of food, milk, and incense to seek the favor and blessings of the deities. Altars can be set up in homes or at sacred sites, adorned with symbols and items that represent the divine forces.

Respect for Nature: Living in harmony with nature is a fundamental aspect of Mongolian spirituality. Respect for the land, animals, and natural resources is expressed through sustainable practices, conservation efforts, and rituals that honor the spirits of the earth and the sky.

The Mongolian pantheon, with its rich array of deities and creation myths, provides a connection to the natural world and the spiritual dimensions of life. By exploring and honoring these gods and spirits, we gain insights into the values, beliefs, and cultural heritage of the Mongolian people. Embracing these traditions allows us to appreciate the timeless themes of creation, transformation, and the sacredness of nature, fostering a deeper connection with the spiritual essence of the world.

Alex McCann Johnson

Chapter 118

Wiccan

Wicca is a modern pagan witchcraft religion that draws upon a diverse array of ancient and contemporary spiritual practices. It was developed in the mid-20th century and has since become one of the most prominent and widely practiced forms of modern paganism. Wicca is often seen as a nature-based religion, celebrating the cycles of the moon, the seasons, and the interconnectedness of all life.

Central to Wiccan belief is the reverence for the divine in both its feminine and masculine forms. Wiccans typically honor a Goddess and a God, recognizing them as dual aspects of the divine that embody the balance of nature. These deities are often seen as immanent, meaning they are present within the world and all its inhabitants. This belief fosters a deep respect for the natural world and the sacredness of life.

Wiccan practices are highly individualistic and eclectic, allowing practitioners to draw from various traditions and pantheons. This flexibility means that Wiccans may honor deities from a wide range of cultures, integrating them into their personal spiritual practices. Wicca's rituals and celebrations are designed to align with the natural rhythms of the earth, honoring the cycles of the moon and the changing seasons through the Wheel of the Year.

Main Deities in Modern Wicca

The Goddess: The Goddess in Wicca is a representation of the divine feminine. She is often seen as the embodiment of nature, fertility, and the cycles of birth, life, death, and rebirth. The Goddess is typically associated with the moon and its phases, which reflect her changing aspects as the Maiden, Mother, and Crone.

- **Maiden:** The Maiden represents youth, new beginnings, and the waxing phase of the moon. She is associated with spring and the renewal of life, embodying purity, independence, and potential.

- **Mother:** The Mother symbolizes fertility, growth, and the full moon. She is the nurturing aspect of the Goddess, connected to the summer and the abundance of nature. She represents love, creativity, and the power to sustain life.

- **Crone:** The Crone embodies wisdom, transformation, and the waning phase of the moon. She is linked to autumn and winter, the time of harvest and rest. The Crone is the keeper of secrets and mysteries, offering guidance through change and endings.

The Goddess can also be represented through various other cultural deities such as Diana (Roman), Isis (Egyptian), or Brigid (Celtic). In rituals, she is often invoked through the symbol of the moon or with items like a chalice, cauldron, or flowers.

The God: The God in Wicca is the counterpart to the Goddess, embodying the divine masculine. He is associated with the sun, representing the cycles of light and darkness, growth and decay. The God is typically seen in his aspects as the Horned God and the Green Man, reflecting his connection to nature, fertility, and the wilderness.

- **Horned God:** The Horned God is a symbol of virility, strength, and the wild. He is often depicted with antlers or horns, representing his role as the lord of animals and the forests. He embodies the untamed forces of nature and the cycle of life and death.

- **Green Man:** The Green Man represents the vegetative and regenerative aspects of God. He is connected to the earth and the growth of plants, symbolizing the vitality and renewal of nature.

The Green Man is often depicted as a face surrounded by leaves or emerging from foliage.

The God's energy complements that of the Goddess, together forming the dynamic balance of male and female, light and dark, life and death. In rituals, he is invoked through symbols like the sun, a blade, or a wand.

Additional Deities in Wiccan Practice

While the Goddess and the God are central figures in Wicca, many Wiccans also honor other deities from various traditions. This eclectic approach allows practitioners to connect with specific deities that resonate with their personal spiritual journeys. Some commonly revered deities in Wiccan practice include:

- **Hecate:** Often invoked as a goddess of magic, the moon, and the underworld, Hecate is associated with crossroads, thresholds, and transitions. She is a powerful figure in Wiccan rituals focused on transformation and protection.

- **Cernunnos:** Known as the Celtic Horned God, Cernunnos is associated with nature, fertility, and the wild. He embodies the primal, untamed energy of the forest and is honored in rituals celebrating the natural world and the cycles of life.

- **Aphrodite:** As the Greek goddess of love and beauty, Aphrodite is often invoked in Wiccan practices related to love, desire, and self-esteem. She represents the power of attraction and the celebration of sensuality.

- **Freya:** A Norse goddess of love, fertility, and battle, Freya is honored for her strength, beauty, and magical prowess. She is called upon in rituals seeking empowerment, love, and protection.

- **Thor:** Known for his strength and thunderous power, the Norse god Thor is revered in Wiccan practices for his role as a protector and warrior. He is invoked in rituals seeking courage and defense against harm.

Creation Stories and Theological Concepts in Wicca

Wicca does not have a single, universally accepted creation story. Instead, it embraces a variety of myths and theological concepts from different traditions. This pluralistic approach allows Wiccans to explore multiple perspectives on creation and the origins of the universe.

One common Wiccan theological concept is the idea of the divine dance between the Goddess and the God. This dance represents the ongoing cycle of creation, growth, death, and rebirth. The interplay between the Goddess and the God symbolizes the dynamic balance of opposites and the eternal flow of energy that sustains life. Through their union and separation, the universe is constantly renewed, reflecting the cycles of nature and the rhythms of the seasons.

Another metaphor often used in Wicca is the spiral, which represents the continuous, ever-expanding cycle of life. The spiral reflects the idea that life is not linear but cyclical, with each turn of the spiral bringing new experiences, growth, and learning. This concept emphasizes the importance of embracing change and transformation as integral parts of the spiritual journey.

The Wheel of the Year

The Wheel of the Year is a central concept in Wicca, representing the annual cycle of seasons and the sacred festivals that mark the turning points of the year. The Wheel of the Year includes eight Sabbats, each corresponding to a significant solar event or seasonal transition:

- **Samhain:** Celebrated on October 31st, Samhain marks the end of the harvest and the beginning of the dark half of the year. It is a time for honoring ancestors and the spirits of the dead.

- **Yule:** Celebrated on the Winter Solstice, Yule marks the rebirth of the sun and the return of light. It is a time for celebrating the triumph of light over darkness and the promise of renewal.

- **Imbolc:** Celebrated on February 1st or 2nd, Imbolc marks the midpoint between winter and spring. It is a time for purification and preparing for new growth.

- **Ostara:** Celebrated on the Spring Equinox, Ostara marks the balance between light and dark. It is a time for celebrating fertility, renewal, and the awakening of nature.

- **Beltane:** Celebrated on May 1st, Beltane marks the beginning of the light half of the year. It is a time for celebrating life, love, and the blossoming of nature.

- **Litha:** Celebrated on the Summer Solstice, Litha marks the peak of the sun's power and the longest day of the year. It is a time for celebrating abundance, strength, and the fullness of life.

- **Lammas (Lughnasadh):** Celebrated on August 1st, Lammas marks the beginning of the harvest season. It is a time to give thanks for the earth's bounty and share the fruits of the harvest.

- **Mabon:** Celebrated on the Autumn Equinox, Mabon marks the balance between light and dark and the second harvest. It is a time for giving thanks, reflecting on the year, and preparing for the coming winter.

Honoring the Wiccan Pantheon

Rituals and Ceremonies: Wiccan rituals and ceremonies are designed to honor the Goddess, the God, and other deities. These practices often include casting a circle to create sacred space, invoking the deities, and performing magical workings. Rituals are conducted to align with the cycles of the moon (Esbats) and the seasonal festivals (Sabbats).

Altars and Sacred Spaces: Creating an altar is a common practice in Wicca. Altars are adorned with symbols, statues, and offerings for the deities. They serve as focal points for meditation, ritual, and connection with the divine. Sacred spaces, whether indoors or in nature, provide a dedicated area for spiritual practice and honoring the deities.

Offerings and Devotions: Offerings and devotions are ways to express gratitude and honor the deities. These can include candles, flowers, food, or incense. Regular devotions and prayers help maintain a personal connection with the deities and invite their presence into daily life.

Magic and Spellwork: Magic and spellwork are integral aspects of Wiccan practice. Wiccans use rituals, symbols, and intentions to work in harmony with natural forces and the deities. Spellwork is often done in alignment with the phases of the moon and the cycles of the seasons, reflecting the interconnectedness of all things.

The Wiccan pantheon, with its emphasis on the Goddess and the God, offers a rich and flexible framework for modern spiritual practice. By honoring these deities and embracing the diverse traditions within Wicca, practitioners can create a meaningful and personal connection with the divine. The celebration of the Wheel of the Year, the integration of rituals and offerings, and the reverence for nature and the cycles of life all contribute to a vibrant and evolving spiritual path. Wicca's inclusive and adaptive nature allows individuals to explore and connect with the divine in ways that resonate deeply with their own experiences and beliefs.

Chapter 119

Integrating Knowledge of Deities

Exploring the vast world of deities has been a transformative part of my spiritual journey. Whether it's Pele's fiery presence in Hawaii, the ancient wisdom of Egyptian gods, or the timeless strength of Greek deities, each encounter has enriched my understanding of the divine. I've also met people deeply connected to Norse paganism, further expanding my appreciation for how these ancient gods and goddesses shape and reflect our cultural and spiritual identities.

As we journey through the diverse pantheons and spiritual traditions of the world, we uncover universal themes that connect us all: creation, transformation, harmony, and the quest for wisdom. Integrating the knowledge of these deities into your spiritual practice can enrich your life, providing guidance and support.

Choosing a Deity or Pantheon

Selecting a deity or pantheon to work with is often an intuitive process guided by personal resonance and curiosity. Each deity embodies specific energies and qualities that can impact your spiritual journey.

Listen to Your Intuition: Start by tuning into your inner self. Which cultures, stories, or divine attributes resonate with you? Perhaps you've always been fascinated by the Norse god Thor's unyielding strength, or you feel a deep connection to the nurturing and protective energy of the

Egyptian goddess Isis. Trust these intuitive nudges as they often point toward deities that can offer meaningful guidance.

Research and Reflect: Dive into the myths, attributes, and cultural contexts of the deities that call to you. Understanding their stories, symbols, and roles can provide valuable insights into how their energies can align with your life's journey. Reflect on how their virtues and challenges mirror your own experiences and aspirations.

Feel the Connection: As you explore, notice which deities evoke a strong emotional or spiritual response. This connection might manifest as a sense of comfort, empowerment, or curiosity. For example, during my travels, Pele's fiery energy in Hawaii felt like a powerful force of transformation, igniting a personal sense of renewal and strength.

Creating Rituals and Practices

Integrating deities into your spiritual practice involves creating rituals and daily habits that honor their presence and invite their guidance into your life.

Setting Up Altars: Design a sacred space in your home dedicated to the deities you wish to connect with. Your altar can include statues, symbols, or offerings that reflect their attributes. For instance, my possible altar dedicated to Pele could include volcanic stones and red candles, symbolizing her fiery nature.

Offering Prayers and Gifts: Regularly offer prayers and gifts to your deities. This practice establishes a relationship and invites their presence into your life. Incense, flowers, and food are traditional offerings, but you can also offer personal items or acts of kindness that you feel would honor the deity.

Celebrating Festivals: Engage in celebrations or rituals during festivals associated with the deities. These times are ideal for deepening your connection and reflecting on the lessons and gifts of the divine. Participating in the vibrant celebrations of Beltane can connect you with the fertility and abundance of the Earth, honoring deities of growth and renewal.

Meditation and Visualization: Use meditation to focus on the deity's attributes and visualize their presence. This practice helps internalize their qualities and opens channels for receiving their guidance. I sometimes meditate on Athena's wisdom, visualizing her owl as a guide, leading me through challenges with clarity and insight.

Encouragement for Further Exploration and Connection

The journey of connecting with deities is continuous and ever-evolving. Embrace it with curiosity, openness, and a willingness to explore beyond familiar boundaries.

Stay Curious: Let your curiosity lead you to new deities and traditions. Read myths, study ancient texts, and immerse yourself in the cultural contexts that shape these spiritual beings. Discovering the stories of deities like the Hawaiian goddess Hina or the Mayan god Itzamna can provide fresh perspectives and deepen your spiritual insights.

Trust Your Intuition: Your spiritual practice is deeply personal. Trust your intuition to guide you toward the deities and practices that resonate most with you at any given time. Your connection might change as you grow and evolve, guiding you to different deities whose energies align with your current path.

Share Your Journey: Engage with a community of like-minded seekers. Sharing experiences and insights can foster deeper connections and mutual support. Joining a local or online group dedicated to Norse mythology, for example, can provide valuable insights and a sense of camaraderie as you explore the mysteries of gods like Odin and Freyja.

Adapt and Grow: Allow your connection with deities and your spiritual practices to evolve over time. As your understanding deepens and your spiritual path unfolds, your relationship with the divine will naturally change and grow. Embrace this evolution and let it enrich your journey.

Integrating the knowledge of deities into your spiritual practice offers a source of wisdom, guidance, and inspiration. By choosing deities that resonate with you, creating meaningful rituals, and continuously exploring new spiritual dimensions, you invite the divine presence of these ancient gods and goddesses into your life. Embrace this journey with an open heart and mind, and let the wisdom of these deities illuminate your path, enriching your spiritual journey with their timeless energy and guidance.

Ascended Masters

Alex McCann Johnson

Chapter 120
Ascended Masters

When I first embarked on my spiritual journey, the concept of Ascended Masters was a mystery to me. During a meditation session, I felt a powerful presence, a guiding force from a higher realm. This encounter sparked my curiosity and led me to explore who these beings were. Ascended Masters, as I came to understand, are enlightened souls who have transcended the cycle of reincarnation and attained a state of spiritual perfection. They have mastered the lessons of earthly existence and now serve as guides and teachers from higher dimensions.

The significance of Ascended Masters lies in their unwavering dedication to aiding humanity's spiritual evolution. They offer wisdom, healing, and guidance to those seeking enlightenment and higher consciousness. Their teachings transcend religious boundaries, resonating with universal truths found in various spiritual traditions. Connecting with Ascended Masters can accelerate our spiritual growth, helping us navigate life's challenges with grace and insight.

Historical Context and Origins

The origins of Ascended Masters are as diverse as the cultures that revere them. Throughout history, different civilizations have recognized and honored these enlightened beings. In ancient Egypt, the mystery schools taught about the ascended wisdom of Thoth and Isis. These deities, often regarded as Ascended Masters, were believed to hold the keys to spiritual knowledge and transformation.

707

In Eastern traditions, figures like Buddha and Quan Yin embody the qualities of Ascended Masters. The Buddha, having achieved enlightenment under the Bodhi tree, dedicated his life to teaching the path to liberation from suffering. Quan Yin, known as the Goddess of Mercy, offers compassion and healing to all who seek her aid. These figures exemplify the journey from human limitations to divine consciousness.

In more recent history, the Theosophical Society, founded in the late 19th century, played a pivotal role in bringing the concept of Ascended Masters to the Western world. Helena Blavatsky, one of the society's founders, introduced the idea of these enlightened beings through her writings and teachings. She described Ascended Masters as a group of advanced spiritual beings who oversee the evolution of humanity, offering their wisdom to guide us through the complexities of the physical and spiritual realms.

Role in Spiritual Traditions and Practices

Ascended Masters are revered across various spiritual traditions for their impact on humanity's spiritual development. In my own practice, I have found their guidance to be invaluable, often providing clarity and support during times of uncertainty. They are seen as the keepers of divine knowledge, accessible to those who seek with an open heart and a sincere desire for growth.

In many spiritual practices, invoking the presence of Ascended Masters is a common ritual. Whether through meditation, prayer, or ceremonial offerings, practitioners connect with these higher beings to receive guidance, healing, and protection. For example, during meditation, I often call upon the Ascended Master Saint Germain, known for his transformative violet flame, which purifies and transmutes negative energies. This practice has become a cornerstone of my spiritual routine, helping me to release old patterns and embrace a higher state of being.

Ascended Masters also play a crucial role in channeling sessions, where individuals serve as conduits for their messages. These sessions can provide insights and directions for personal and collective spiritual growth. The messages from Ascended Masters often emphasize the importance of love, compassion, and unity, encouraging us to transcend our egoic limitations and embrace our divine nature.

How to Connect with Ascended Masters

Connecting with Ascended Masters involves developing a spiritual practice that aligns with their energies and guidance. Here are some ways to establish and nurture these connections:

Meditation and Visualization: Regular meditation focused on a specific Ascended Master can help create a deep spiritual bond. Visualize the Master, their attributes, and symbols, inviting their presence and guidance into your life.

Prayer and Invocation: Simple prayers or invocations directed to Ascended Masters can open channels of communication. Speak from the heart, expressing your needs and desires for guidance.

Rituals and Offerings: Perform rituals and make offerings that honor the Ascended Masters. This can include lighting candles, offering flowers, or other meaningful items that resonate with the Master's energy.

Study and Reflection: Learning about the lives, teachings, and symbols of Ascended Masters can deepen your understanding and connection. Reflect on their messages and how they relate to your life.

Benefits of Connecting with Ascended Masters

The benefits of connecting with Ascended Masters are manifold, enriching both your spiritual and daily life:

Guidance and Wisdom: Ascended Masters offer timeless wisdom and guidance that can help you navigate life's challenges and make informed decisions.

Emotional and Spiritual Support: Feeling the presence of an Ascended Master can provide comfort and support, especially during difficult times. Their energy can help you feel grounded and protected.

Personal and Spiritual Growth: The teachings and attributes of Ascended Masters can inspire personal and spiritual growth, encouraging you to embody their virtues and qualities.

Enhanced Spiritual Practice: Regular interaction with Ascended Masters through meditation, rituals, and prayer can deepen your spiritual practice and bring a sense of sacredness to your daily routine.

Connection to the Divine: Building a relationship with Ascended Masters fosters a direct connection to the divine, enriching your sense of spirituality and purpose.

Ascended Masters are the torchbearers of spiritual evolution. Their teachings and guidance illuminate the path to enlightenment, offering a beacon of hope and wisdom in our journey toward higher consciousness. As I continue to deepen my connection with these enlightened beings, I am constantly reminded of their enduring presence and the limitless potential for transformation that they bring into our lives. By integrating their knowledge and wisdom into your spiritual practice, you can tap into a profound source of guidance, support, and inspiration, helping you navigate the journey of life with greater clarity and purpose.

Chapter 121

The Path to Ascension

The concept of ascension has fascinated and inspired spiritual seekers throughout the ages. It represents a profound transformation, a shift from the limitations of the physical world to the boundless realms of higher consciousness. When I first encountered the idea of ascension, it felt like a distant, almost unattainable goal. However, as I delved deeper into my spiritual practice, I realized that ascension is not about escaping the human experience but about transcending its limitations and embodying our highest potential.

Ascension can be understood as the process of raising one's vibrational frequency and expanding one's awareness to higher states of being. It involves the integration of body, mind, and spirit, leading to a harmonious existence aligned with divine principles. This journey is marked by a gradual shedding of old patterns, beliefs, and attachments that no longer serve our highest good. Through this process, we awaken to our true nature as spiritual beings having a human experience.

In essence, ascension is the journey of returning to our divine essence. It is the recognition that we are not separate from the Source but intrinsically connected to it. As we ascend, we move closer to this divine unity, experiencing greater love, wisdom, and peace. This path requires dedication, patience, and a willingness to confront and heal our deepest wounds.

Alex McCann Johnson

Spiritual Growth and Enlightenment

The path to ascension is inherently linked to spiritual growth and enlightenment. Spiritual growth is the continuous expansion of our consciousness and the deepening of our understanding of ourselves and the universe. It involves cultivating virtues such as compassion, forgiveness, and humility and integrating them into our daily lives.

Enlightenment, on the other hand, is often seen as the pinnacle of spiritual growth. It is the state of being fully awake, where one perceives reality without the distortions of ego and illusion. Enlightenment is not a distant goal reserved for saints and mystics but a natural progression on the path of ascension. It is the realization of our true nature and the embodiment of divine wisdom.

My journey of spiritual growth began with small steps—meditation, reading spiritual texts, and seeking guidance from teachers. Each practice brought me closer to a deeper understanding of myself and the world around me. I began to notice shifts in my perception, feeling more connected to the present moment and less entangled in the drama of daily life. This gradual awakening was not without its challenges. I had to confront my fears, insecurities, and limiting beliefs. However, each obstacle served as a catalyst for deeper healing and growth.

Ascension is not a linear path but a spiraling journey where we revisit old wounds and patterns at deeper levels of awareness. Each cycle brings us closer to our true essence, shedding layers of conditioning and illusion. This process requires perseverance and self-compassion. It is important to honor our progress and trust that each step, no matter how small, contributes to our overall growth.

Journey of the Soul and the Role of Ascended Masters

The journey of the soul is a timeless odyssey that spans lifetimes. It is the soul's quest to experience, learn, and evolve through various incarnations. Each lifetime offers unique lessons and opportunities for growth. The path to ascension is a significant milestone in this journey, marking the soul's readiness to transcend the limitations of the physical

712

realm and embrace its divine nature.

Ascended Masters play a crucial role in this journey. These enlightened beings have walked the path before us and have attained a state of spiritual mastery. They serve as guides, mentors, and protectors, offering their wisdom and support to those on the path of ascension. When I first connected with an Ascended Master, it was through meditation that I felt the presence of a loving, compassionate energy. This presence provided clarity and guidance, helping me navigate the challenges of my spiritual journey.

Ascended Masters are like beacons of light, illuminating the path ahead. They offer teachings and insights that help us understand the deeper aspects of our existence. Through their guidance, we learn to navigate the complexities of the human experience with grace and wisdom. They remind us that we are never alone on this journey and that their support is always available to us.

One of the most important lessons I have learned from Ascended Masters is the importance of self-love and acceptance. They teach us that we are worthy of love and that our true nature is divine. This realization has been transformative for me, helping me to release self-judgment and embrace my authentic self. The guidance of Ascended Masters has also helped me develop a deeper connection with my intuition and inner wisdom.

As we progress on the path of ascension, we may encounter periods of intense transformation and awakening. These moments can be challenging but are also opportunities for growth. Ascended Masters provide the support and encouragement needed to navigate these transitions. Their presence is a reminder of the infinite potential within us and the divine purpose that guides our journey.

Integrating Ascension into Daily Life

Integrating the concept of ascension into daily life involves aligning our actions, thoughts, and intentions with our highest spiritual ideals. This can be achieved through various practices and commitments that foster personal and spiritual growth.

Daily Spiritual Practices: Regular meditation, prayer, and reflection help to center our consciousness and attune our energy to higher frequencies. These practices create a foundation for spiritual growth and a deeper connection with the divine.

Mindful Living: Living mindfully means being present in each moment and making choices that reflect our values and spiritual goals. It involves cultivating awareness and compassion in our interactions and decisions.

Healing and Transformation: Embracing the process of healing and transformation is crucial for ascension. This includes working through emotional wounds, releasing limiting beliefs, and embracing new perspectives that support our growth.

Seeking Guidance and Support: Connecting with spiritual guides, mentors, and communities can provide invaluable support and wisdom on the path to ascension. Sharing our journey with others fosters a sense of belonging and collective growth.

The path to ascension is a sacred journey of spiritual growth and enlightenment. It is the process of awakening to our true nature and embodying our highest potential. Ascended Masters play an integral role in this journey, offering their wisdom and guidance to support our evolution. As we embrace this path, we move closer to our divine essence, experiencing greater love, wisdom, and peace. This journey is a testament to the resilience and potential of the human spirit, and it is an honor to walk this path alongside the guidance of the Ascended Masters. By integrating the principles of ascension into our daily lives, we align ourselves with the divine, fostering a life of profound purpose and connection.

Chapter 122

Why Connect with Ascended Masters?

When I first began exploring the realm of Ascended Masters, it felt like discovering an ancient, hidden library filled with wisdom and timeless truths. The more I learned about these enlightened beings, the more I realized how much their guidance could illuminate my spiritual path. Connecting with Ascended Masters has been one of the most transformative experiences in my spiritual journey, bringing countless benefits to my life.

The primary benefit of connecting with Ascended Masters is the spiritual guidance they provide. When I first started working with these beings, I was in a period of deep personal confusion. I felt lost and uncertain about my direction in life. Seeking answers, I turned to meditation and prayer, hoping to find some clarity. It was during these practices that I first sensed the presence of an Ascended Master named Saint Germaine. The experience was subtle yet profound—a feeling of warmth and reassurance that seemed to envelop me.

As I continued to deepen my connection with Ascended Masters, I found that their guidance came through in various ways: intuitive insights during meditation, symbols and messages in dreams, and even through the words of others. This guidance helped me navigate difficult decisions and provided a sense of peace and direction that I had previously lacked. The wisdom of Ascended Masters is not just theoretical; it is deeply practical and applicable to everyday life. They offer perspectives that help us see beyond our immediate concerns, encouraging us to embrace a higher understanding of our experiences.

For instance, there was a time when I struggled with forgiveness. Holding onto resentment was weighing heavily on my spirit. In a meditation session, I called upon an Ascended Master known for his compassion and wisdom. The message I received was simple yet transformative: "Forgiveness is not about condoning the actions of others but about freeing yourself from the burden of anger." This insight shifted my perspective entirely, enabling me to let go of my resentment and find inner peace.

Enhancing Personal and Collective Consciousness

One of the most remarkable aspects of working with Ascended Masters is their ability to enhance both personal and collective consciousness. On a personal level, their teachings encourage us to expand our awareness and elevate our thoughts, emotions, and actions. As I integrated their wisdom into my daily life, I noticed a profound shift in my consciousness. I became more mindful, compassionate, and aligned with my higher self.

Ascended Masters also play a significant role in raising humanity's collective consciousness. Their teachings often emphasize the interconnectedness of all beings and the importance of living in harmony with one another and with the planet. By working with these enlightened beings, we not only uplift ourselves but also contribute to the greater good of all. This collective upliftment is crucial in times of global challenges, where unity and higher consciousness are needed more than ever.

An example of this collective enhancement occurred during a group meditation I attended. We collectively invoked the presence of the Buddha known for his work in global peace and harmony. The energy in the room became palpable, and many of us felt a sense of unity and shared purpose. This experience reinforced the idea that when we come together with a common intention, we can create powerful waves of positive change.

Developing Deeper Spiritual Awareness

Working with Ascended Masters has significantly deepened my spiritual awareness. Before I connected with them, my spiritual practice was largely intellectual—I read books, attended workshops, and engaged in discussions. While these activities were valuable, they did not fully satisfy my yearning for a direct, experiential understanding of the divine. The Ascended Masters provided that missing piece.

Their teachings encourage us to go beyond intellectual understanding and to experience spirituality directly. This experiential approach has opened my awareness to the subtle energies and higher dimensions that exist beyond our physical reality. Through practices such as meditation, visualization, and energy healing, I have learned to tune into these higher frequencies and connect with the presence of Ascended Masters.

One particularly transformative experience occurred during a meditation where I focused on connecting with the Ascended Master Saint Germain. As I visualized his presence, I felt a surge of violet flame envelop me. It was as if I was being bathed in a light that cleansed and uplifted my entire being. This experience opened my awareness even more to the subtle energies that surround us and strengthened my connection to the spiritual realm.

These connections have also enhanced my intuition and inner guidance. By regularly seeking the counsel of Ascended Masters, I have learned to trust my inner knowing more deeply. This trust has been instrumental in making decisions and navigating life's uncertainties. The Ascended Masters often remind us that we have innate wisdom and that by quieting the mind and tuning into our inner guidance, we can access this wisdom.

Moreover, the teachings of Ascended Masters have encouraged me to cultivate virtues such as compassion, patience, and humility. These virtues are not only essential for personal growth but also for building harmonious relationships and communities. By embodying these qualities, we contribute to a more compassionate and enlightened world.

Their guidance has provided clarity and direction, helping me navigate life's challenges with greater ease. By enhancing personal and collective consciousness, they inspire us to live in harmony with ourselves, each other, and the planet. Through deepening our spiritual awareness, they help us access higher states of being and experience the divine directly. The path of working with Ascended Masters is a transformative journey that leads to greater wisdom, peace, and enlightenment. As I continue to walk this path, I am constantly reminded of the boundless love and support that these enlightened beings offer, guiding us toward our highest potential.

Chapter 123

Jesus Christ

Jesus Christ is revered as one of the most profound and influential spiritual figures in human history. Known for his teachings on love, compassion, forgiveness, and the path to spiritual awakening, Jesus has guided millions of souls toward a deeper understanding of divine love and truth. In my spiritual journey, the teachings and presence of Jesus have been a source of inspiration and guidance, helping me navigate the complexities of life with a sense of grace and purpose.

Jesus Christ, also referred to as Yeshua, is the central figure of Christianity, believed to be the incarnation of God on Earth. Born in Bethlehem over 2,000 years ago, his life and teachings have had an unparalleled impact on the world. Jesus is known for his miracles, his parables, and his message of unconditional love and redemption.

He is often depicted as a compassionate healer, a wise teacher, and a selfless savior who sacrificed his life for the salvation of humanity. In Christian belief, Jesus' resurrection signifies the triumph over sin and death, offering the promise of eternal life to all who follow his teachings.

The Spiritual Significance of Jesus Christ

Jesus Christ's spiritual significance transcends religious boundaries, offering timeless wisdom and guidance that can enrich the lives of individuals from all walks of life. Here are some key aspects of his spiritual significance:

Unconditional Love and Compassion: Jesus' teachings emphasize the power of love and compassion as fundamental forces for transformation. He encouraged people to love their neighbors as themselves and to extend kindness and forgiveness to others, even to their enemies. This message of love is a cornerstone of his teachings and continues to inspire countless individuals to live more compassionate and loving lives.

Forgiveness and Redemption: Central to Jesus' message is the concept of forgiveness and the possibility of redemption. He taught that no matter one's past mistakes or sins, there is always a path to forgiveness and spiritual renewal. This principle offers hope and healing, encouraging individuals to seek forgiveness and to forgive others, fostering a sense of inner peace and reconciliation.

Spiritual Awakening and Transformation: Jesus' life and teachings serve as a guide for spiritual awakening and personal transformation. He called people to look beyond material concerns and to seek the kingdom of God within. His teachings challenge us to awaken to our true divine nature and to align our lives with higher spiritual values.

Faith and Trust in Divine Providence: Jesus exemplified faith and trust in God's will. He taught that faith can move mountains and that trusting in divine providence brings peace and strength in times of uncertainty. His life serves as a testament to the power of faith and the importance of surrendering to a higher divine plan.

Service and Sacrifice: Jesus' ultimate act of sacrifice—laying down his life for others—embodies the highest form of service and selflessness. He taught that true greatness comes from serving others and that love is best expressed through selfless acts of kindness and generosity.

Recognizing and Connecting with Jesus Christ

Connecting with Jesus Christ involves opening your heart to his teachings and presence. Here are some ways to recognize and connect with Jesus:

Feelings of Deep Compassion and Love: When you feel an overwhelming sense of compassion and love, it can be a sign of Jesus' presence. These feelings often inspire acts of kindness and a desire to help others.

Guidance Through Intuition and Prayer: Jesus often communicates through intuitive insights and responses to prayers. Pay attention to moments of clarity, peace, and guidance that come during or after prayer and meditation.

Symbols of Peace and Light: Seeing or visualizing symbols such as the cross, light, or a dove can be indications of Jesus' presence. These symbols often bring a sense of peace and comfort.

Inspirational Teachings: Reading and reflecting on Jesus' teachings in the Bible or other spiritual texts can deepen your connection with him. His words offer timeless wisdom and guidance for personal and spiritual growth.

Acts of Service and Kindness: Engaging in selfless acts of service and kindness can help you embody the spirit of Jesus and feel closer to his teachings. Serving others in need is a powerful way to connect with his message of love and compassion.

Prayer for Connection with Jesus Christ: "Dear Jesus, I open my heart to your presence. Guide me with your love and wisdom. Help me to live in compassion, to forgive, and to serve others selflessly. Walk with me on my journey, and let your light illuminate my path. Amen."

Historical Significance of Jesus Christ

The historical significance of Jesus Christ is vast and multifaceted, encompassing his impact on religion, culture, and history.

Jesus' life and teachings are the foundation of Christianity, one of the world's major religions. His message of love, forgiveness, and salvation has shaped the beliefs and practices of millions of Christians around the globe. The spread of Christianity has had a monumental influence on Western civilization and beyond, affecting art, philosophy, law, and social values.

Throughout history, Jesus has been a central figure in art, literature, and music. His image and stories have inspired countless works of art, from Renaissance paintings to contemporary literature and films. The portrayal of Jesus in culture has helped to convey his message and maintain his presence in the collective consciousness.

Jesus' teachings on love, compassion, and justice have influenced moral and ethical thought for centuries. His Sermon on the Mount, which includes the Beatitudes, has been a source of inspiration for ethical teachings and social justice movements. Leaders such as Mahatma Gandhi and Martin Luther King Jr. have drawn upon Jesus' principles of nonviolence and love in their struggles for social change.

For many, Jesus symbolizes hope, redemption, and the possibility of transformation. His story of sacrifice and resurrection provides a powerful narrative of overcoming adversity and the promise of new beginnings. This message has offered comfort and inspiration to people facing challenges and seeking spiritual renewal.

While Jesus is primarily associated with Christianity, his influence extends to other faith traditions as well. In Islam, Jesus (known as Isa) is revered as a prophet and a significant figure in the Quran. His teachings and example continue to resonate with people of various religious and spiritual backgrounds, promoting values of compassion, forgiveness, and love.

Embracing the Journey with Jesus Christ

Embracing a relationship with Jesus Christ invites us to live with greater love, compassion, and spiritual awareness. His teachings and presence provide a guide for navigating life's challenges and seeking deeper meaning and purpose.

As you explore your connection with Jesus, approach with an open heart and a willingness to learn and grow. Whether through prayer, meditation, study, or acts of service, allow his teachings to guide and inspire you. Embrace the wisdom and love that Jesus offers, and let his example of compassion and selflessness illuminate your path.

Alex McCann Johnson

Chapter 124
The Buddha

The Buddha, known as Siddhartha Gautama, is one of the most revered spiritual figures in history. His teachings on enlightenment, compassion, and the nature of suffering have influenced countless individuals across the world. As a guide, the Buddha offers a path to inner peace, wisdom, and spiritual awakening. My journey with the Buddha has been transformative, providing insights into the nature of the mind and the path to liberation.

Siddhartha Gautama, known as the Buddha, was a prince born in ancient India around 563 BCE. Despite his luxurious upbringing, he was deeply troubled by the suffering he observed in the world. This led him to renounce his royal life in search of a deeper understanding of existence. After years of ascetic practice and meditation, he attained enlightenment under the Bodhi tree and became the Buddha, which means "the awakened one."

The Buddha's teachings, known as the Dharma, offer a deep understanding of the nature of suffering and the path to its cessation. The Four Noble Truths and the Eightfold Path are central to his teachings, which provide a practical framework for achieving enlightenment and living a life of wisdom, ethical conduct, and mental discipline.

The Spiritual Significance of Buddha

The Buddha's teachings offer timeless wisdom and practical guidance for anyone seeking spiritual growth and liberation. Here are some key aspects of his spiritual significance:

Understanding and Overcoming Suffering: The Buddha's insights into the nature of suffering, or "dukkha," are foundational to his teachings. He explained that suffering arises from attachment and desire and that by understanding and relinquishing these, one can achieve freedom from suffering. This principle provides a powerful framework for personal transformation and spiritual growth.

The Path to Enlightenment: The Buddha's life and teachings illuminate the path to enlightenment, which involves cultivating wisdom, ethical conduct, and mental discipline. The Eightfold Path outlines practical steps for developing the right understanding, intention, speech, action, livelihood, effort, mindfulness, and concentration. Following this path leads to inner peace and ultimate liberation.

Compassion and Loving-Kindness: Central to the Buddha's teachings is the cultivation of compassion ("karuna") and loving-kindness ("metta"). He emphasized the importance of developing a compassionate heart towards all beings, and his teachings provide practical methods for fostering these qualities in our daily lives.

Mindfulness and Meditation: The Buddha taught that mindfulness and meditation are essential practices for developing awareness and understanding the nature of the mind. By cultivating mindfulness, we can observe our thoughts and emotions without attachment, leading to greater clarity and insight.

Impermanence and Non-Attachment: The Buddha's teachings highlight the impermanent nature of all phenomena. Understanding impermanence helps us let go of attachment and live more fully in the present moment. This insight is a cornerstone of the path to spiritual freedom.

Recognizing and Connecting with Buddha

Connecting with the Buddha involves embracing his teachings and incorporating his principles into your life. Here are some ways to recognize and connect with the Buddha:

Feelings of Inner Peace and Clarity: The presence of the Buddha can be felt as a deep sense of peace and clarity. When you experience moments of tranquility and insight, it can be a sign of his influence.

Guidance Through Mindfulness and Meditation: The Buddha's teachings are best experienced through the practice of mindfulness and meditation. Regular meditation practice can help you connect with his wisdom and cultivate the qualities he taught.

Symbols of Enlightenment and Compassion: The Buddha is often associated with symbols such as the Bodhi tree, the lotus flower, and the Dharma wheel. These symbols can serve as reminders of his teachings and presence.

Inspirational Teachings: Reading and reflecting on the Buddha's teachings can deepen your connection with him. His words offer insights into the nature of the mind and the path to spiritual awakening.

Acts of Compassion and Kindness: Engaging in acts of compassion and loving kindness can help you embody the spirit of the Buddha and feel closer to his teachings. Helping others and promoting peace and understanding in your community are powerful ways to honor his legacy.

Prayer for Connection with Buddha: "Dear Buddha, I open my heart to your wisdom and compassion. Guide me on the path to enlightenment, help me cultivate mindfulness and loving-kindness, and illuminate my mind with your teachings. May I live with awareness, compassion, and peace. Amen."

Historical Significance of Buddha

The historical significance of the Buddha is vast, spanning over two millennia and impacting various cultures and societies around the world.

The Buddha's enlightenment and subsequent teachings laid the foundation for Buddhism, a major world religion that has influenced millions of people. His teachings provide a comprehensive path to spiritual awakening and ethical living, and they continue to be practiced and revered across many cultures.

Beyond its religious significance, Buddhism has profoundly influenced various aspects of culture and philosophy. In countries like India, China, Japan, Tibet, and Thailand, Buddhist teachings have shaped art, literature, ethics, and social practices. The concepts of mindfulness, compassion, and non-attachment have permeated many aspects of daily life and thought.

Over centuries, Buddhism has spread from its origins in India too many parts of the world, adapting to different cultures and societies. This adaptability has allowed it to flourish globally, with diverse traditions such as Theravada, Mahayana, and Vajrayana Buddhism emerging, each offering unique interpretations of the Buddha's teachings.

In contemporary times, the Buddha's teachings on mindfulness and meditation have found widespread acceptance beyond traditional religious contexts. These practices are now integral too many modern wellness and self-improvement programs, reflecting the enduring relevance of the Buddha's insights into the nature of mind and well-being.

The Buddha's image and teachings have become universal symbols of peace, wisdom, and enlightenment. His serene depiction in art and sculpture inspires a sense of calm and reverence, serving as a reminder of the potential for spiritual awakening and the pursuit of inner peace.

Embracing the Journey with Buddha

Embracing a relationship with the Buddha involves integrating his teachings into your daily life and seeking to embody the qualities he exemplified. His path to enlightenment offers a timeless guide for overcoming suffering, cultivating compassion, and achieving spiritual awakening.

As you explore your connection with the Buddha, approach with an open heart and a commitment to personal growth. Whether through mindfulness, meditation, study, or acts of compassion, let his teachings guide and inspire you. Embrace the wisdom and peace that the Buddha offers, and allow his example of enlightenment and loving-kindness to illuminate your path.

Alex McCann Johnson

Chapter 125

El Morya

In my spiritual journey, I have found the guidance of El Morya to be both empowering and transformative. Known as the Chohan of the First Ray of Divine Will and Power, El Morya embodies the strength, courage, and steadfastness of the divine will. His teachings emphasize the importance of aligning our personal will with the higher will of the Divine, guiding us to live with purpose, integrity, and unwavering determination.

El Morya is one of the Ascended Masters, a group of enlightened beings who have transcended the limitations of physical existence and now serve as spiritual guides. He is particularly known for his work with the First Ray, which is associated with the color blue and represents the attributes of divine will, leadership, and power.

El Morya is believed to have incarnated several times throughout history in roles that required strong leadership and unwavering commitment to divine principles. Some of his notable incarnations include King Arthur of Britain, Melchior (one of the three wise men who visited the infant Jesus), and Thomas More, a counselor to King Henry VIII of England. Each of these lives exemplified his dedication to truth, integrity, and the higher will of the Divine.

As an Ascended Master, El Morya works closely with individuals who are striving to develop their inner strength, leadership abilities, and commitment to their spiritual path. His guidance is particularly valuable for those who seek to live in alignment with divine will and to serve the greater good with courage and determination.

The Spiritual Significance of El Morya

El Morya's teachings offer insights into the nature of divine will and the importance of aligning our personal will with it. Here are some key aspects of his spiritual significance:

Alignment with Divine Will: El Morya emphasizes the importance of aligning our actions, thoughts, and intentions with the higher will of the Divine. This alignment helps us to live with greater purpose and integrity and to act as instruments of divine will in the world. By surrendering our ego-driven desires and embracing the guidance of our higher self, we can achieve a deeper sense of fulfillment and spiritual growth.

Strength and Courage: One of El Morya's most significant attributes is his embodiment of strength and courage. He encourages us to face challenges and adversities with unwavering resolve and to stand firm in our commitment to truth and righteousness. His guidance can help us develop the inner fortitude needed to overcome obstacles and pursue our spiritual goals with determination.

Leadership and Service: El Morya's teachings also highlight the importance of leadership and service to others. He inspires us to take on roles of responsibility and to use our talents and abilities for the benefit of humanity. Whether in our personal lives or in broader societal roles, El Morya encourages us to lead with integrity and to serve as examples of divine will and power.

Transformation and Growth: Working with El Morya can be a catalyst for personal transformation and growth. His energy helps us to release old patterns and beliefs that no longer serve us and to embrace new ways of thinking and being that are aligned with our higher purpose. By following his guidance, we can achieve greater clarity, focus, and spiritual evolution.

Recognizing and Connecting with El Morya

Connecting with El Morya involves tuning into his powerful and transformative energy. Here are some ways to recognize and connect with him:

Feelings of Strength and Determination: The presence of El Morya can often be felt as a surge of strength and determination. When you feel a strong sense of resolve or a renewed commitment to your goals, it may be a sign of his influence.

Guidance in Leadership and Service: El Morya often works with those who are called to leadership roles or who seek to serve others. If you find yourself drawn to positions of responsibility or to helping others, this could be an indication of his guidance.

Symbols of the First Ray: El Morya is associated with the First Ray of Divine Will and Power, which is often represented by the color blue. You may notice an increased presence of this color in your surroundings or feel drawn to blue objects and symbols.

Inspirational Teachings: Studying the teachings and writings of El Morya can deepen your connection with him. His messages often focus on the principles of divine will, strength, and leadership, offering valuable insights and guidance.

Prayer and Meditation: One of the most direct ways to connect with El Morya is through prayer and meditation. By focusing on his energy and inviting his presence into your life, you can receive his guidance and support in your spiritual journey.

Prayer for Connection with El Morya: "Beloved El Morya, Chohan of the First Ray, I call upon your strength and wisdom. Guide me in aligning my will with the divine will and help me to act with courage, integrity, and purpose. Illuminate my path and empower me to serve others with love and determination. Amen."

Historical Significance of El Morya

The historical significance of El Morya is highlighted by his various incarnations and his role in guiding humanity toward higher principles of leadership and divine will.

As King Arthur, El Morya embodied the ideals of noble leadership, justice, and the pursuit of truth. His reign is often depicted as a golden age of chivalry and honor, where he led with wisdom and a deep commitment to the welfare of his people.

In his incarnation as Melchior, one of the three wise men who visited the infant Jesus, El Morya demonstrated his role as a seeker of divine truth and a bearer of gifts that symbolize spiritual wisdom and enlightenment.

As Thomas More, El Morya exemplified the principles of integrity and moral courage. He stood firm in his beliefs and values, even in the face of great personal risk, and is remembered as a martyr for his steadfast commitment to truth and righteousness.

In contemporary spiritual teachings, El Morya is recognized as a powerful guide and mentor. His messages continue to inspire individuals to live in alignment with divine will and to serve as leaders and examples of higher principles in their communities.

El Morya's influence throughout history underscores his role as a beacon of strength, integrity, and divine will. His teachings and guidance remain relevant today, offering a path to personal and spiritual empowerment for those who seek to align their lives with the higher purpose of the Divine.

Embracing the Journey with El Morya

Embracing a relationship with El Morya involves aligning with his principles of strength, courage, and divine will. By integrating his teachings into your daily life, you can cultivate a deeper sense of purpose and commitment to your spiritual path.

Guided by Spirits

As you explore your connection with El Morya, approach with a spirit of dedication and openness. Whether through meditation, study, or acts of leadership and service, let his guidance inspire you to live with integrity and to pursue your goals with unwavering resolve. Embrace the strength and clarity that El Morya offers, and allow his presence to empower you on your journey of spiritual growth and transformation.

Alex McCann Johnson

Chapter 126
Kuthumi

In my journey through spiritual exploration, encountering the teachings of Kuthumi has been enlightening. Known as the Master of Wisdom and Compassion, Kuthumi guides us toward deeper understanding and empathy, helping us integrate spiritual wisdom into our daily lives. His presence is gentle yet powerful, encouraging a life filled with love, learning, and self-discovery.

Kuthumi is one of the revered Ascended Masters, recognized for his embodiment of wisdom, compassion, and universal love. He is often associated with the Second Ray, which is connected to the attributes of love, wisdom, and understanding. Kuthumi's energy inspires us to seek knowledge, cultivate compassion, and live harmoniously with ourselves and others.

Kuthumi is believed to have had several significant incarnations that reflect his dedication to wisdom and spiritual growth. Among these, he is often identified with figures such as Saint Francis of Assisi, a beacon of humility and love for all creatures, and Pythagoras, the Greek philosopher known for his contributions to mathematics and spiritual teachings. These lives highlight Kuthumi's commitment to the pursuit of truth and the practice of compassion.

As an Ascended Master, Kuthumi works closely with those who seek to deepen their understanding of spiritual principles and develop a compassionate heart. His guidance is invaluable for those on the path of learning, self-improvement, and spiritual enlightenment.

Alex McCann Johnson

The Spiritual Significance of Kuthumi

Kuthumi's teachings offer insights into the nature of wisdom, compassion, and the interconnectedness of all life. Here are some key aspects of his spiritual significance:

Wisdom and Knowledge: Kuthumi encourages the pursuit of knowledge and the application of wisdom in our lives. He teaches that true wisdom goes beyond intellectual understanding and involves a deep comprehension of spiritual truths. By seeking knowledge and cultivating an open mind, we can navigate life's challenges with greater clarity and insight.

Compassion and Empathy: One of Kuthumi's most significant attributes is his embodiment of compassion and empathy. He inspires us to develop a kind and understanding heart, to see the divine in all beings, and to act with love and consideration. His teachings emphasize the importance of compassion as a foundation for personal growth and harmonious relationships.

Integration of Spiritual Principles: Kuthumi guides us in integrating spiritual principles into our daily lives. He encourages us to live with integrity, to act in alignment with our values, and to apply spiritual wisdom in our interactions and decisions. By living in harmony with these principles, we can create a more fulfilling and balanced life.

Harmonious Living: Kuthumi's energy fosters a sense of peace and harmony. He helps us cultivate inner tranquility and to extend that peace into our external environment. His guidance can assist us in resolving conflicts, finding balance, and creating a harmonious life.

Recognizing and Connecting with Kuthumi

Connecting with Kuthumi involves attuning to his gentle energy. Here are some ways to recognize and connect with him:

Feelings of Peace and Harmony: Kuthumi's presence is often felt as a deep sense of peace and harmony. When you experience a sudden calmness or a resolution of conflict, it may be a sign of his influence.

Guidance in Learning and Understanding: Kuthumi frequently assists those who are dedicated to learning and expanding their knowledge. If you find yourself drawn to studying new subjects or gaining deeper insights, this could be his way of guiding you.

Symbols of Compassion and Wisdom: Kuthumi is associated with symbols of wisdom and compassion, such as the color yellow or golden light, which represents the Second Ray. You may notice these symbols appearing in your life as indicators of his presence.

Inspirational Teachings: Studying the teachings and writings attributed to Kuthumi can deepen your connection with him. His messages often focus on love, wisdom, and the importance of living a balanced and harmonious life.

Prayer and Meditation: One of the most direct ways to connect with Kuthumi is through prayer and meditation. By inviting his presence and focusing on his qualities, you can receive his guidance and support.

Prayer for Connection with Kuthumi: "Beloved Kuthumi, Master of Wisdom and Compassion, I call upon your guidance. Help me to cultivate wisdom and understanding, to live with compassion and empathy, and to integrate spiritual principles into my daily life. Fill my heart with peace and harmony, and guide me on my path of learning and growth. Amen."

Historical Significance of Kuthumi

Kuthumi's historical significance is highlighted by his various incarnations and his role in guiding humanity towards wisdom and compassion.

In his incarnation as Saint Francis of Assisi, Kuthumi exemplified the principles of humility, love for all creatures, and devotion to a simple and compassionate life. Saint Francis is remembered for his deep connection with nature and his dedication to serving others, reflecting

Kuthumi's commitment to universal love and understanding.

As Pythagoras, Kuthumi contributed to the fields of mathematics, philosophy, and spirituality. Pythagoras is known for his teachings on the harmony of the universe and the interconnectedness of all things. His work laid the foundation for the integration of scientific and spiritual knowledge, embodying Kuthumi's emphasis on the pursuit of wisdom and truth.

In contemporary spiritual teachings, Kuthumi is recognized as a powerful guide and mentor. His messages continue to inspire individuals to seek knowledge, cultivate compassion, and live in harmony with themselves and others. Kuthumi's influence throughout history underscores his role as a beacon of wisdom and compassion, guiding humanity toward a deeper understanding of spiritual truths.

Kuthumi's historical presence highlights his enduring impact on the pursuit of wisdom and the practice of compassion. His teachings and guidance remain relevant today, offering a path to personal and spiritual fulfillment for those who seek to live a life of love, learning, and harmonious living.

Embracing the Journey with Kuthumi

Embracing a relationship with Kuthumi involves aligning with his principles of wisdom, compassion, and harmonious living. By integrating his teachings into your daily life, you can cultivate a deeper sense of purpose and a more compassionate heart.

As you explore your connection with Kuthumi, approach with a spirit of openness and dedication. Whether through meditation, study, or acts of kindness and understanding, let his guidance inspire you to live with integrity and to pursue your goals with wisdom and compassion. Embrace the peace and clarity that Kuthumi offers, and allow his presence to support you on your journey of spiritual growth and enlightenment.

Chapter 127
Paul the Venetian

My introduction to Paul the Venetian came during a meditation session focused on tapping into creativity and artistic expression. Known as the Master of Artistic Expression and Love, Paul the Venetian inspires us to see beauty in all things and to express that beauty through our creative endeavors. His influence helps us tap into our artistic potential and cultivate a deeper appreciation for the aesthetic and emotional aspects of life.

Paul the Venetian is an Ascended Master associated with the Third Ray of Divine Love. This ray is characterized by attributes of love, beauty, and creativity. Paul the Venetian embodies these qualities, guiding those who seek to enhance their creative abilities and live a life infused with love and beauty.

He is believed to have been incarnated as Paolo Veronese, a renowned Renaissance painter known for his grand, vibrant works that often depicted historical and religious scenes. His art was celebrated for its color, composition, and emotional depth. Through his life as Veronese, Paul the Venetian demonstrated the impact that artistic expression can have on humanity, inspiring us to appreciate and create beauty in our own lives.

As an Ascended Master, Paul the Venetian continues to inspire and guide artists, musicians, writers, and anyone seeking to express their inner beauty and creativity. His presence encourages us to embrace our creative passions and to see the divine love and beauty in everything around us.

The Spiritual Significance of Paul the Venetian

Paul the Venetian's teachings offer insights into the nature of creativity, love, and beauty. Here are some key aspects of his spiritual significance:

Artistic Expression: Paul the Venetian inspires us to explore and develop our artistic talents. He teaches that creativity is a divine gift that allows us to express our innermost thoughts, feelings, and visions. Whether through painting, music, writing, or any other form of art, he encourages us to share our unique perspectives with the world.

Love and Beauty: As a master of the Third Ray, Paul the Venetian embodies divine love and beauty. He helps us recognize and appreciate the beauty in all things, from the natural world to human relationships and creative works. His guidance fosters a deeper connection to the love and beauty that surround us, encouraging us to cultivate these qualities in our lives.

Harmonious Living: Paul the Venetian promotes the idea that living in harmony with our surroundings and expressing our inner beauty through creativity can lead to a more fulfilling and balanced life. His teachings emphasize the importance of integrating love and beauty into every aspect of our lives, from our thoughts and actions to our homes and communities.

Compassion and Understanding: Paul the Venetian encourages us to approach others with compassion and understanding. By seeing the beauty in each person and embracing their unique qualities, we can build deeper and more meaningful relationships. His influence helps us develop a loving and accepting attitude towards ourselves and others.

Recognizing and Connecting with Paul the Venetian

Connecting with Paul the Venetian involves attuning to his gentle and inspiring energy. Here are some ways to recognize and connect with him:

Feelings of Creative Inspiration: If you experience sudden bursts of creative inspiration or feel drawn to artistic activities, it may be a sign that Paul the Venetian is guiding you. His presence often manifests as a desire to create and express yourself through various forms of art.

Appreciation of Beauty: A heightened awareness of beauty in your surroundings and a deep appreciation for art and nature can indicate Paul the Venetian's influence. You may find yourself more attuned to the colors, shapes, and emotions in the world around you.

Symbols of Love and Beauty: Paul the Venetian is associated with symbols of love and beauty, such as roses, vibrant colors, and elegant forms. Seeing these symbols repeatedly in your life can be a sign of his presence.

Inspirational Messages: Messages of encouragement to pursue your creative passions or to embrace love and beauty in your life are often attributed to Paul the Venetian. These messages can come through dreams, meditations, or intuitive insights.

Prayer and Meditation: One of the most direct ways to connect with Paul the Venetian is through prayer and meditation. By inviting his presence and focusing on his qualities, you can receive his guidance and support.

Prayer for Connection with Paul the Venetian: "Beloved Paul the Venetian, Master of Artistic Expression and Love, I invite your presence into my life. Help me to see and appreciate the beauty around me and to express my inner creativity with love and passion. Guide me in cultivating compassion and understanding towards myself and others. Fill my heart with your divine love and inspire me to live a life infused with beauty and harmony. Amen."

Historical Significance of Paul the Venetian

Paul the Venetian's historical significance is deeply intertwined with his incarnation as Paolo Veronese and his role as an Ascended Master.

As Paolo Veronese, Paul the Venetian was a masterful artist of the Renaissance era, known for his vivid and grandiose paintings. His works are celebrated for their rich color palettes, intricate compositions, and emotional depth. Veronese's art captured the beauty and complexity of human experiences and historical narratives, leaving a lasting impact on the world of art. His ability to convey beauty and emotion through his paintings exemplifies the qualities that Paul the Venetian embodies as an Ascended Master.

As a master of the Third Ray, Paul the Venetian's influence extends beyond his life as Veronese. He represents the divine qualities of love, beauty, and creativity that inspire humanity to seek and appreciate the aesthetic and emotional aspects of life. Throughout history, his teachings have encouraged individuals to explore their creative potential and to infuse their lives with love and beauty.

Paul the Venetian continues to be a source of inspiration for artists, musicians, writers, and creatives of all kinds. His guidance helps individuals tap into their artistic abilities and express their unique perspectives with grace and passion. Historical accounts and spiritual teachings reflect his enduring influence on the pursuit of beauty and the expression of divine love through art.

Paul the Venetian's historical significance lies in his role as a beacon of artistic expression and his embodiment of love and beauty. His teachings and guidance inspire us to see the world through a lens of creativity and compassion, encouraging us to live a life filled with artistic expression and appreciation for the beauty that surrounds us.

Embracing the Journey with Paul the Venetian

Embracing a relationship with Paul the Venetian involves opening yourself to the flow of creativity and the presence of beauty in your life. By integrating his teachings into your daily routine, you can cultivate a deeper appreciation for art and develop your unique creative voice.

Guided by Spirits

As you explore your connection with Paul the Venetian, approach with a spirit of openness and dedication. Whether through artistic practice, meditation, or acts of kindness, let his guidance inspire you to express your inner beauty and to appreciate the love and aesthetics that enrich our world. Embrace the joy and inspiration that Paul the Venetian offers, and allow his presence to illuminate your path of creative and spiritual growth.

Alex McCann Johnson

Chapter 128
Serapis Bey

In my exploration of spiritual teachings, I encountered Serapis Bey, a revered Ascended Master known as the Master of Ascension and Discipline. His guidance is integral for those seeking to elevate their spiritual consciousness and align with the divine path of self-mastery and ascension.

Serapis Bey is often depicted as a stern yet benevolent guide, deeply committed to helping souls achieve spiritual ascension and mastery over their lower selves. He is the Chohan of the Fourth Ray, which is the Ray of Purity, Discipline, and Ascension. This ray embodies qualities of purity, clarity, and unwavering focus on spiritual goals.

Historically, Serapis Bey is believed to have lived as a high priest in Atlantis, where he was dedicated to maintaining the spiritual integrity and discipline of the society. Later, he is said to have incarnated as the Egyptian Pharaoh Amenhotep III, known for his deep commitment to spiritual practices and his role as a bridge between the divine and human realms. His connection to the great pyramid of Giza, often called the Ascension Temple, highlights his enduring association with the principles of ascension and higher learning.

As an Ascended Master, Serapis Bey's mission is to assist humanity in purifying their souls and ascending to higher states of consciousness. He helps us cultivate discipline, overcome obstacles, and maintain a steadfast commitment to our spiritual paths. His teachings emphasize the importance of rigorous self-discipline and the pursuit of purity in all

Alex McCann Johnson

aspects of life.

The Spiritual Significance of Serapis Bey

Serapis Bey's teachings provide insights into the nature of discipline, purity, and spiritual ascension. Here are some key aspects of his spiritual significance:

Ascension and Self-Mastery: Serapis Bey is the Master of Ascension, guiding souls through the process of raising their vibrations and aligning with their higher selves. He teaches that ascension is a journey of self-mastery, requiring dedication, discipline, and a commitment to spiritual growth. His guidance helps us navigate the challenges of this journey and achieve a state of spiritual purity.

Purity and Clarity: The Fourth Ray, governed by Serapis Bey, embodies the qualities of purity and clarity. He assists us in purifying our thoughts, emotions, and actions, helping us release any lower energies that hinder our spiritual progress. His influence encourages us to seek clarity in our intentions and actions, aligning ourselves with the highest aspects of our being.

Discipline and Focus: Serapis Bey's teachings emphasize the importance of discipline and focus on the spiritual path. He guides us in developing the self-discipline needed to overcome distractions and remain committed to our spiritual goals. His presence instills a sense of inner strength and determination, helping us stay on course even in the face of challenges.

Sacred Geometry and Ascension: Serapis Bey is closely associated with the principles of sacred geometry, particularly the pyramid, which symbolizes ascension and the integration of spiritual and physical realms. His teachings often involve the use of sacred symbols and structures to facilitate spiritual growth and transformation.

Healing and Transformation: Through his guidance, Serapis Bey offers healing and transformation. He helps us release old patterns and energies that no longer serve us, paving the way for spiritual renewal and growth. His influence is particularly powerful during times of significant change and personal transformation.

Recognizing and Connecting with Serapis Bey

Connecting with Serapis Bey involves aligning with his disciplined and ascension-focused energy. Here are some ways to recognize and connect with him:

Feelings of Discipline and Commitment: If you feel a strong sense of discipline and commitment to your spiritual path, it may be a sign that Serapis Bey is guiding you. His presence often instills a renewed focus and determination to pursue your spiritual goals.

Experiences of Purification: Moments of deep purification and release of old energies can indicate Serapis Bey's influence. You may find yourself drawn to practices that cleanse your body, mind, and spirit, such as fasting, detoxing, or engaging in energy healing.

Symbols of Sacred Geometry: Serapis Bey is closely associated with sacred geometry, especially the pyramid. Seeing or meditating on these symbols can help you connect with his energy and align with his teachings on ascension and transformation.

Guidance During Transformation: During periods of significant change or transformation, Serapis Bey's presence can provide support and guidance. If you find yourself navigating major life changes or spiritual shifts, his influence may be helping you through the process.

Prayer and Meditation: One of the most direct ways to connect with Serapis Bey is through prayer and meditation. By inviting his presence and focusing on his qualities, you can receive his guidance and support in your journey of ascension and self-mastery.

Prayer for Connection with Serapis Bey: "Beloved Serapis Bey, Master of Ascension and Discipline, I invite your presence into my life. Help me to cultivate purity, clarity, and unwavering discipline on my spiritual path. Guide me in my journey of self-mastery and ascension, and assist me in releasing any energies that no longer serve me. Fill my heart with your divine strength and determination, and inspire me to rise to higher states of consciousness. Amen."

Historical Significance of Serapis Bey

Serapis Bey's historical significance is deeply rooted in his association with the principles of ascension, discipline, and sacred geometry.

Serapis Bey is believed to have been a high priest in Atlantis, a civilization renowned for its advanced spiritual practices and knowledge. His role in Atlantis was to maintain the spiritual purity and discipline of the society, guiding souls in their ascension process. Later, as Pharaoh Amenhotep III, he continued to uphold these principles, bridging the human and divine realms and fostering a culture of spiritual enlightenment in ancient Egypt. His connection to the Ascension Temple in the Great Pyramid of Giza symbolizes his enduring influence on the path of ascension and higher learning.

Serapis Bey's association with sacred geometry, particularly the pyramid, highlights his role in teaching the principles of spiritual alignment and transformation. The pyramid, a symbol of ascension and the integration of the physical and spiritual realms embodies the essence of his teachings. Throughout history, sacred geometry has been used in spiritual practices to facilitate alignment with divine energies and to support the process of ascension. Serapis Bey's influence in this area underscores his role as a guardian of these ancient and powerful principles.

As the Chohan of the Fourth Ray, Serapis Bey oversees the ray of purity, discipline, and ascension. His teachings on this ray emphasize the importance of maintaining spiritual purity and clarity and the necessity of self-discipline in achieving spiritual mastery. Historically, the Fourth Ray has been associated with the transformative power of light and the purification of the soul, aligning with Serapis Bey's mission to guide souls on their path to ascension.

Serapis Bey's teachings have influenced various mystical traditions and spiritual practices throughout history. His emphasis on discipline, purity, and ascension resonates with the core principles of many spiritual paths, including esoteric Christianity, Theosophy, and modern New Age movements. His role as a guide and teacher in these traditions highlights his enduring significance in the quest for spiritual enlightenment and mastery.

Serapis Bey's historical significance lies in his role as a master of ascension and a guardian of sacred principles. His teachings and influence have guided souls throughout history in their journey of self-mastery and spiritual growth, fostering a deeper understanding of the path to ascension and the importance of discipline and purity.

Embracing the Journey with Serapis Bey

Embracing a relationship with Serapis Bey involves committing to a path of discipline, purity, and ascension. By integrating his teachings into your daily life, you can cultivate a deeper connection to your higher self and align with the divine principles of the Fourth Ray.

As you explore your connection with Serapis Bey, approach with a spirit of dedication and openness. Whether through meditation, sacred geometry, or practices of purification, let his guidance inspire you to pursue self-mastery and spiritual growth. Embrace the clarity and discipline that Serapis Bey offers, and allow his presence to illuminate your path of ascension and transformation.

Alex McCann Johnson

Chapter 129
Hilarion

In my journey of exploring the vast realm of spiritual guides, I encountered Hilarion, an Ascended Master known for his profound connection to healing, truth, and scientific wisdom. His teachings have deeply influenced my understanding of these concepts and continue to guide me in integrating them into my life.

Hilarion is revered as the Chohan of the Fifth Ray, which is associated with healing, truth, and scientific knowledge. His energy is often described as bright green, symbolizing the healing and restorative powers he embodies. Historically, Hilarion is believed to have lived as Saint Hilarion in the fourth century, where he was known for his ascetic life and miraculous healing abilities.

As an Ascended Master, Hilarion's mission is to assist humanity in aligning with truth and understanding the deep connections between spirituality and science. He encourages a balance between intellect and intuition, guiding us to seek knowledge that aligns with higher truths and promotes healing on all levels—physical, emotional, mental, and spiritual.

The Spiritual Significance of Hilarion

Hilarion's teachings offer insights into the nature of healing and the pursuit of truth. Here are some key aspects of his spiritual significance:

Healing and Restoration: Hilarion is a powerful guide for those

753

seeking healing. He works with the green ray of healing energy, helping to restore balance and harmony within the body and mind. His guidance can be especially valuable for healers and those in the medical field, as he assists in understanding the deeper causes of illness and the path to true healing.

Pursuit of Truth: As the Chohan of the Fifth Ray, Hilarion emphasizes the importance of truth in all aspects of life. He helps us discern truth from illusion, encouraging us to seek knowledge that aligns with our highest good. His teachings inspire us to live authentically and to embrace honesty and integrity in our thoughts, words, and actions.

Integration of Science and Spirituality: Hilarion bridges the gap between scientific inquiry and spiritual wisdom. He supports the integration of these fields, guiding us to see the divine order in the natural world and to understand the spiritual principles underlying scientific discoveries. His influence fosters a deeper appreciation for the harmony between science and spirituality.

Clarity and Focus: Hilarion's energy brings clarity and focus, helping us to see situations and challenges from a higher perspective. He assists in clearing mental confusion and aligns us with our true purpose, making it easier to navigate the complexities of life with a clear and focused mind.

Spiritual Guidance for Healers and Scientists: Hilarion is a mentor for those in the fields of healing and science. He offers guidance and support in their endeavors, helping them to advance their understanding and application of healing techniques and scientific principles. His influence encourages a holistic health and well-being approach, integrating scientific and spiritual insights.

Recognizing and Connecting with Hilarion

Connecting with Hilarion can be a transformative experience, especially for those seeking healing, clarity, and truth. Here are some ways to recognize and connect with him:

Feelings of Healing and Restoration: If you experience a deep sense of healing and renewal, it may be a sign that Hilarion is present. His energy is often felt as a soothing, restorative force that brings balance and harmony to the body and mind.

Moments of Clarity and Insight: Hilarion's influence often brings moments of clear understanding and insight. If you find yourself gaining new perspectives or understanding complex issues with ease, it could be Hilarion's guidance at work.

Attraction to Green Light and Symbols: The green ray is closely associated with Hilarion. If you are drawn to green light or symbols of healing, such as the caduceus (a staff entwined with two serpents), it might indicate his presence.

Interest in the Integration of Science and Spirituality: Those who feel a strong interest in combining scientific knowledge with spiritual wisdom may be under Hilarion's guidance. He inspires the exploration of how these fields complement and enhance each other.

Prayer and Meditation: To connect with Hilarion, you can engage in prayer or meditation focused on healing and truth. Visualize a vibrant green light surrounding you and invite Hilarion's presence into your space. Open your mind and heart to his guidance and be receptive to the insights and healing energy he offers.

Prayer for Connection with Hilarion: "Beloved Hilarion, Master of Healing and Truth, I invite your presence into my life. Guide me in aligning with truth and understanding the deeper causes of healing. Help me integrate scientific knowledge with spiritual wisdom and seek clarity and focus in all that I do. Surround me with your healing light and restore balance and harmony to my body, mind, and spirit. Amen."

Historical Significance of Hilarion

Hilarion's historical significance is deeply rooted in his association with healing, truth, and scientific and spiritual wisdom integration.

Alex McCann Johnson

Hilarion is historically linked to Saint Hilarion, a monk and ascetic who lived in the fourth century. Known for his miraculous healing abilities and deep spiritual insights, Saint Hilarion's life exemplified the principles of healing and ascension. He performed numerous healings and was revered for his ability to bring about physical and spiritual restoration. His legacy as a healer continues to influence those who seek to understand and apply the principles of true healing.

As the Chohan of the Fifth Ray, Hilarion oversees the ray of healing, truth, and scientific knowledge. His teachings emphasize the importance of aligning with higher truths and pursuing knowledge that promotes healing and well-being. Historically, the Fifth Ray has been associated with the advancement of medical and scientific understanding, reflecting Hilarion's influence in these fields.

Hilarion's role as a bridge between science and spirituality is significant in the context of historical advancements in both fields. Throughout history, many of the greatest scientific discoveries have been guided by a deep sense of spiritual purpose and insight. Hilarion's teachings encourage a holistic approach to understanding the world, integrating scientific knowledge with spiritual wisdom to foster a deeper appreciation for the divine order in the natural world.

In contemporary times, Hilarion's influence extends to various healing practices and modalities. His teachings inspire healers and practitioners to adopt a holistic approach to health and wellness, combining traditional medical knowledge with spiritual insights and energy healing techniques. Hilarion's guidance continues to support the evolution of healing practices that honor the interconnectedness of body, mind, and spirit.

Hilarion's historical significance lies in his role as a master of healing and truth, guiding humanity toward a deeper understanding of the principles of health and well-being. His teachings on the integration of science and spirituality and his influence on the advancement of healing practices highlight his enduring impact on the pursuit of knowledge and the quest for true healing.

Embracing the Journey with Hilarion

Embracing a relationship with Hilarion involves committing to a path of healing, truth, and the integration of knowledge. By aligning with his teachings and energy, you can cultivate a deeper connection to your true self and the principles of the Fifth Ray.

As you explore your connection with Hilarion, approach with a spirit of openness and dedication. Whether through meditation, healing practices, or the pursuit of knowledge, let his guidance inspire you to seek truth and foster healing in all aspects of your life. Embrace the clarity and wisdom that Hilarion offers, and allow his presence to illuminate your path of healing and spiritual growth.

Alex McCann Johnson

Chapter 130
Lady Master Nada

In my spiritual journey into the Ascended Masters, I encountered Lady Master Nada, known for her connection to love, compassion, and selfless service. Her teachings and energy have deeply influenced my understanding of these principles and continue to guide me in embodying them in my life.

Lady Master Nada is revered as a master of love, compassion, and selfless service. She is often depicted with a serene and gentle presence, embodying the qualities of divine love and nurturing. Nada's name means "nothing" in Spanish, symbolizing the ego's dissolution and the focus on serving others with pure, unconditional love.

Historically, Nada is believed to have lived several lifetimes dedicated to service and spiritual growth. In one notable incarnation, she served in the courts of Atlantis as a judge, bringing fairness and love into her decisions. In her ascended state, she continues to work tirelessly to promote peace, harmony, and healing on Earth.

As an Ascended Master, Nada's mission is to assist humanity in opening their hearts to unconditional love, healing emotional wounds, and embracing the path of service. She encourages us to cultivate compassion and kindness, both towards ourselves and others, and to live in alignment with our higher purpose.

The Spiritual Significance of Lady Master Nada

Lady Master Nada's teachings offer insights into the nature of love, compassion, and service. Here are some key aspects of her spiritual significance:

Unconditional Love and Compassion: Nada embodies the essence of unconditional love and compassion. She helps us heal our hearts and release any barriers to giving and receiving love. Her guidance encourages us to cultivate a loving and compassionate attitude towards ourselves and others, fostering deeper connections and harmonious relationships.

Healing Emotional Wounds: Nada is a powerful guide for emotional healing. She assists in releasing past traumas, forgiving ourselves and others, and restoring emotional balance. Her energy provides comfort and support during times of emotional distress, helping us navigate and heal from our wounds.

Selfless Service and Altruism: Nada inspires us to live a life of selfless service and altruism. She encourages us to focus on how we can contribute to the well-being of others and the greater good. Her teachings highlight the importance of serving with a pure heart, without attachment to outcomes or recognition.

Balance and Harmony: Nada's presence brings balance and harmony into our lives. She helps us find equilibrium in our emotions, relationships, and life paths. Her guidance supports us in creating a harmonious environment where love and peace can flourish.

Spiritual Growth and Ascension: As a master of the Sixth Ray, which represents peace, service, and ministration, Nada supports our spiritual growth and ascension. She guides us in aligning with our soul's purpose and living a life of higher consciousness and divine service.

Recognizing and Connecting with Lady Master Nada

Connecting with Lady Master Nada can be a deeply transformative experience, especially for those seeking to cultivate love, compassion, and service in their lives. Here are some ways to recognize and connect with her:

Feelings of Love and Comfort: If you experience a deep sense of love and comfort, it may be a sign that Nada is present. Her energy is often felt as a warm, nurturing force that brings peace and reassurance.

Moments of Compassion and Altruism: Nada's influence often brings moments of compassion and a desire to help others. If you find yourself feeling an urge to serve or acts of kindness come naturally, it could be her guidance at work.

Attraction to Pink Light and Symbols: The pink ray is closely associated with Nada. If you are drawn to pink light or symbols of love and service, such as hearts or roses, it might indicate her presence.

Interest in Service and Healing: Those who feel a strong interest in helping others and promoting healing may be under Nada's guidance. She inspires a commitment to service and the healing of emotional wounds.

Prayer and Meditation: To connect with Nada, you can engage in prayer or meditation focused on love, compassion, and service. Visualize a soft pink light surrounding you and invite Nada's presence into your space. Open your heart to her guidance and be receptive to the healing and nurturing energy she offers.

Prayer for Connection with Lady Master Nada: "Beloved Lady Master Nada, I invite your presence into my life. Guide me in opening my heart to unconditional love and compassion. Help me heal my emotional wounds and embrace a path of selfless service. Surround me with your nurturing light and support me in creating balance and harmony in my life. Amen."

Historical Significance of Lady Master Nada

Lady Master Nada's historical significance is deeply rooted in her association with love, compassion, and service.

In her Atlantean incarnation, Nada served as a judge in the courts of Atlantis. She was known for her fairness, wisdom, and deep compassion. Her decisions were guided by a strong sense of justice and love, reflecting her commitment to serving the greater good. This role highlights her historical significance in promoting peace and harmony through selfless service.

As the Chohan of the Sixth Ray, Nada oversees the ray of peace, service, and ministration. Historically, the Sixth Ray has been associated with the nurturing of humanity and promoting the principles of love, compassion, and selfless service. Nada's teachings emphasize the importance of living a life dedicated to the well-being of others, encouraging us to serve with humility and grace.

In contemporary times, Nada's influence extends to various spiritual and healing practices. Her teachings inspire individuals to cultivate compassion and engage in service-oriented activities. Nada's guidance supports the healing of emotional wounds and the fostering of harmonious relationships. Her presence in modern spiritual practices highlights her enduring impact on promoting love and service in the world.

Lady Master Nada's historical significance lies in her role as a master of love and service, guiding humanity towards a deeper understanding of these principles. Her teachings on unconditional love, emotional healing, and selfless service continue to inspire and uplift those who seek to live in alignment with their higher purpose.

Embracing the Journey with Lady Master Nada

Embracing a relationship with Lady Master Nada involves committing to a path of love, compassion, and service. By aligning with her teachings and energy, you can cultivate a deeper connection to your true self and the principles of the Sixth Ray.

As you explore your connection with Nada, approach with an open heart and a spirit of service. Whether through meditation, healing practices, or acts of kindness, let her guidance inspire you to embody love and serve others. Embrace the nurturing and compassionate energy that Nada offers, and allow her presence to illuminate your path of spiritual growth and selfless service.

Alex McCann Johnson

Chapter 131

Saint Germain

From the moment I first heard about Saint Germain, I was captivated by his connection to transformation, alchemy, and the Violet Flame. As an Ascended Master, Saint Germain has guided countless individuals in their spiritual journeys, helping them embrace their divine potential and manifest positive change in their lives.

Saint Germain, also known as the Master of the Violet Flame, is revered for his deep wisdom and transformative power. He is considered the master of alchemy, teaching the principles of transmutation and transformation. Historically, Saint Germain is associated with the legendary figure, the Comte de Saint Germain, who was known for his remarkable longevity and mysterious presence in European history.

Saint Germain's teachings focus on the power of the Violet Flame, a spiritual energy that purifies and transforms negative energies into positive ones. This flame is a symbol of forgiveness, transmutation, and spiritual freedom, helping individuals release karmic burdens and embrace their higher selves.

As the Chohan of the Seventh Ray, which represents freedom, mercy, and ceremonial order, Saint Germain encourages us to break free from limitations and embrace our divine potential. He offers guidance in mastering the art of alchemy—both in the physical and spiritual realms—enabling us to create positive change and manifest our highest aspirations.

The Spiritual Significance of Saint Germain

Saint Germain's teachings offer insights into the nature of transformation, freedom, and spiritual alchemy. Here are some key aspects of his spiritual significance:

Transformation and Alchemy: Saint Germain is the master of transformation and alchemy, guiding us in transmuting negative energies into positive ones. His teachings on the Violet Flame provide powerful tools for purifying our thoughts, emotions, and actions, enabling us to transform our lives and embrace our divine potential.

Freedom and Personal Liberation: As the Chohan of the Seventh Ray, Saint Germain promotes the principles of freedom and personal liberation. He encourages us to break free from limiting beliefs, habits, and karmic patterns that hold us back. His guidance supports us in reclaiming our sovereignty and living authentically.

Mastery of the Violet Flame: The Violet Flame is central to Saint Germain's teachings. This spiritual energy helps us release past traumas, forgive ourselves and others, and purify our beings. Working with the Violet Flame can lead to profound healing and spiritual growth, transforming our lives on multiple levels.

Divine Alchemy and Manifestation: Saint Germain teaches the art of divine alchemy, empowering us to manifest our desires and create positive change. By mastering the principles of alchemy, we can align our intentions with the divine will and bring forth our highest aspirations.

Ceremonial Magic and Rituals: As the master of ceremonial order, Saint Germain emphasizes the importance of rituals and ceremonies in spiritual practice. These practices help us connect with higher energies, align with divine intentions, and create sacred spaces for transformation.

Recognizing and Connecting with Saint Germain

Connecting with Saint Germain can be a transformative and empowering experience. Here are some ways to recognize and connect with his energy:

Feelings of Transformation and Liberation: If you experience a strong desire for transformation and personal liberation, it may be a sign that Saint Germain is present. His energy inspires us to embrace change and pursue our highest potential.

Attraction to the Violet Flame: Being drawn to the Violet Flame or symbols of transmutation and alchemy can indicate Saint Germain's influence. The flame's purifying and transformative qualities are closely associated with his teachings.

Moments of Insight and Creative Inspiration: Saint Germain often brings moments of deep insight and creative inspiration. If you find yourself receiving sudden ideas or feeling a surge of creative energy, it could be his guidance at work.

Synchronicities and Symbolic Encounters: Pay attention to synchronicities and encounters with symbols of alchemy, transformation, or freedom. These could be signs of Saint Germain's presence and support.

Prayer and Meditation: To connect with Saint Germain, you can engage in prayer or meditation focused on transformation, freedom, and the Violet Flame. Visualize the Violet Flame surrounding you and invite Saint Germain's presence into your space. Be open to the guidance and insights he offers.

Prayer for Connection with Saint Germain: "Beloved Saint Germain, Master of Transformation and Alchemy, I invite your presence into my life. Guide me in embracing the power of the Violet Flame and help me release all that no longer serves my highest good. Support me in breaking free from limitations and manifesting my divine potential. Surround me with your transformative light and lead me on the path of freedom and spiritual mastery. Amen."

Historical Significance of Saint Germain

Saint Germain's historical significance is rooted in his association with transformation, alchemy, and the pursuit of spiritual freedom.

Saint Germain is often identified with the Comte de Saint Germain, a mysterious figure in 18th-century Europe known for his remarkable longevity and alchemical prowess. The Count was reputed to be a master of many languages, a gifted musician, and an alchemist who possessed secrets of eternal youth. His enigmatic presence and rumored immortality have made him a legendary figure in European history.

In spiritual traditions, Saint Germain is revered as the master of the Violet Flame. This flame is a powerful tool for transmutation and purification, capable of transforming negative energies into positive ones. Historically, the Violet Flame has been used in various spiritual practices to facilitate healing, forgiveness, and spiritual liberation.

Saint Germain's teachings have had a clear impact on the Theosophical Society and the New Age movement. He is often regarded as an Ascended Master who guides humanity towards enlightenment and spiritual freedom. His influence is evident in the widespread use of the Violet Flame and the emphasis on personal transformation and liberation in modern spiritual practices.

Saint Germain is a central figure in the I AM Activity and the Ascended Master Teachings, spiritual movements that emphasize the power of the spoken word and the presence of the divine within each individual. These teachings highlight Saint Germain's role in helping humanity realize their inherent divinity and embrace their potential for transformation and mastery.

Saint Germain's historical significance lies in his role as a master of alchemy, transformation, and spiritual freedom. His teachings on the Violet Flame and divine alchemy continue to inspire and empower those on the path of spiritual growth and liberation.

Embracing the Journey with Saint Germain

Embracing a relationship with Saint Germain involves committing to a path of transformation, freedom, and mastery. By aligning with his teachings and energy, you can cultivate a deeper connection to your true self and the principles of the Seventh Ray.

As you explore your connection with Saint Germain, approach with an open heart and a willingness to embrace change. Whether through meditation, rituals, or working with the Violet Flame, let his guidance inspire you to transform your life and manifest your highest potential. Embrace the powerful and liberating energy that Saint Germain offers, and allow his presence to illuminate your path of spiritual mastery and divine alchemy.

Alex McCann Johnson

Chapter 132

Quan Yin

More recently in my spiritual journey, I was drawn to the serene and loving presence of Quan Yin. Her energy is gentle yet immensely powerful, offering a sanctuary of compassion and mercy. Known as the Goddess of Compassion, Quan Yin is revered across various spiritual traditions for her boundless love and her commitment to alleviating suffering.

Quan Yin, also spelled Kuan Yin or Guanyin, is one of the most beloved figures in East Asian spiritual traditions. She is often depicted as a beautiful woman holding a vase of pure water or a willow branch, symbols of her nurturing and healing qualities. Quan Yin's name translates to "She Who Hears the Cries of the World," highlighting her role as a compassionate listener and a savior to those in need.

In Buddhism, Quan Yin is considered an embodiment of the Bodhisattva Avalokiteshvara, who chose to remain in the earthly realm to assist all beings in achieving enlightenment. Her commitment to compassion and mercy transcends individual needs, embracing the suffering of all beings with the intention of bringing relief and peace.

Quan Yin is not only a symbol of compassion but also a guide for those seeking to cultivate these qualities within themselves. Her teachings emphasize the importance of empathy, forgiveness, and loving-kindness in our interactions with others and in our own self-care.

The Spiritual Significance of Quan Yin

Quan Yin's presence in spiritual practice offers lessons in compassion, mercy, and forgiveness. Here are some key aspects of her spiritual significance:

Embodiment of Compassion: Quan Yin embodies the highest form of compassion. Her energy encourages us to open our hearts to the suffering of others and to respond with kindness and empathy. By aligning with Quan Yin, we can learn to approach life with a more compassionate and loving attitude.

Healing and Mercy: Quan Yin is often called upon for healing and protection. Her mercy extends to all beings, offering solace and relief from pain and suffering. Working with Quan Yin can help us find emotional and spiritual healing, fostering a sense of peace and well-being.

Guide for Forgiveness: One of Quan Yin's core teachings is the power of forgiveness. She helps us release feelings of anger, resentment, and guilt, guiding us toward a state of inner harmony and reconciliation. Her presence can be a powerful catalyst for letting go of past wounds and embracing forgiveness.

Alleviating Suffering: Quan Yin's mission is to alleviate the suffering of all beings. She teaches us to be aware of the pain around us and to take compassionate action to alleviate it. This extends not only to others but also to ourselves as we learn to treat our own struggles with kindness and understanding.

Role as a Protector: In addition to her compassionate qualities, Quan Yin is also seen as a protector. She is often invoked for safety and guidance, especially in difficult times. Her protective energy offers a sense of security and reassurance, helping us navigate challenges with grace and resilience.

Recognizing and Connecting with Quan Yin

Connecting with Quan Yin can bring peace and compassion into your life. Here are some ways to recognize and deepen your connection with her:

Feelings of Deep Compassion and Empathy: If you find yourself experiencing heightened feelings of compassion and empathy, it may be a sign that Quan Yin is present. Her energy often inspires us to care deeply for others and to seek ways to alleviate suffering.

Attraction to Symbols of Water and Lotus: Quan Yin is frequently associated with water and the lotus flower. Being drawn to these symbols can indicate her influence. The lotus, which rises from the mud to bloom beautifully, symbolizes purity and spiritual awakening, much like Quan Yin's teachings.

Experiences of Healing and Comfort: Quan Yin's presence is often felt as a soothing and healing energy. If you experience a sense of comfort and relief during challenging times, it maybe her compassionate touch guiding you toward peace.

Dreams and Visions: Quan Yin may appear in dreams or meditative visions as a gentle, nurturing figure. These encounters can offer insights and guidance, reflecting her role as a compassionate protector and healer.

Prayer and Meditation: To connect with Quan Yin, you can engage in prayer or meditation focused on compassion and mercy. Visualize her serene form and invite her presence into your heart. Be open to the feelings and messages that arise during these practices.

Prayer for Connection with Quan Yin: "Beloved Quan Yin, Goddess of Compassion and Mercy, I invite your presence into my life. Fill my heart with your boundless love and guide me in showing compassion to myself and others. Help me to forgive and release past wounds, and offer me your healing and protection. Surround me with your nurturing energy and lead me on the path of peace and mercy. Amen."

Historical Significance of Quan Yin

Quan Yin's historical significance is deeply rooted in East Asian religious and cultural traditions. Her influence spans across Buddhism, Taoism, and various folk religions, making her one of the most universally revered figures.

In Buddhist traditions, Quan Yin is seen as an incarnation of the Bodhisattva Avalokiteshvara. Her compassionate mission is to listen to the cries of suffering beings and to assist them in finding relief and enlightenment. Throughout history, she has been worshipped as a deity who embodies the ideal of selfless compassion, and her image is found in countless temples and shrines across Asia.

In Taoism, Quan Yin is also recognized as a divine figure associated with mercy and healing. She is often invoked in rituals and prayers for protection and health. In Chinese folk religion, she is considered a motherly figure who provides guidance and support, often depicted holding a child, symbolizing her role as a protector of children and families.

Quan Yin's influence extends beyond religious contexts, becoming a cultural symbol of compassion and benevolence. Festivals and ceremonies dedicated to her honor are celebrated throughout East Asia, reflecting her enduring presence in the collective consciousness of these cultures.

Throughout history, Quan Yin has inspired countless works of art and literature. She is often depicted in paintings, sculptures, and poetry, embodying the ideals of beauty, grace, and compassion. These artistic representations celebrate her role as a beacon of hope and a source of spiritual inspiration.

In modern times, Quan Yin's appeal has transcended cultural boundaries, and she is revered by spiritual seekers worldwide. Her teachings on compassion and mercy resonate with universal human values, making her a beloved figure in the global spiritual community.

Embracing the Journey with Quan Yin

Embracing a relationship with Quan Yin involves opening your heart to her teachings of compassion, mercy, and forgiveness. By inviting her presence into your life, you can cultivate a deeper sense of empathy and a more profound connection to the divine.

As you explore your connection with Quan Yin, approach with an open heart and a willingness to embody her qualities. Whether through meditation, rituals, or acts of kindness, let her guidance inspire you to live with greater compassion and understanding. Embrace the nurturing and healing energy that Quan Yin offers, and allow her presence to illuminate your path of love and mercy.

Alex McCann Johnson

Chapter 133

Lao Tzu

In my exploration of spiritual teachings, the wisdom of Lao Tzu has had a huge impact on my understanding of the natural flow of life and the importance of simplicity and humility. As the founder of Taoism, Lao Tzu's insights into the nature of existence and the way of living harmoniously with the Tao (the Way) continue to inspire and guide countless individuals on their spiritual journeys.

Lao Tzu, also spelled Laozi, is a legendary figure in Chinese philosophy and is considered the father of Taoism. His name translates to "Old Master" or "Old Sage," reflecting his enduring wisdom and timeless teachings. Lao Tzu is traditionally credited with writing the "Tao Te Ching," a foundational text that offers insights into the nature of the Tao and how to live in accordance with its principles.

The "Tao Te Ching" is a guide to living a life of balance, simplicity, and alignment with the natural order. Lao Tzu's teachings emphasize the importance of humility, non-action (wu wei), and the inherent interconnectedness of all things. His work encourages us to let go of rigid control, to trust the flow of life, and to embrace the inherent wisdom of simplicity and stillness.

Despite the mystery surrounding his life, Lao Tzu's influence is undeniable. Whether he was a historical figure or a symbolic representation of ancient wisdom, his teachings have shaped Chinese culture and continue to resonate with spiritual seekers worldwide.

The Spiritual Significance of Lao Tzu

Lao Tzu's teachings offer a path to inner peace, balance, and a deep understanding of the natural world. Here are some key aspects of his spiritual significance:

Embracing Simplicity and Humility: Lao Tzu teaches that true wisdom lies in simplicity and humility. He encourages us to live modestly, to value contentment over material wealth, and to cultivate a sense of humility in our interactions with others and the world.

Living in Harmony with the Tao: Central to Lao Tzu's philosophy is the concept of the Tao, the underlying principle that governs all existence. By aligning ourselves with the Tao, we can live in harmony with the natural flow of life, experiencing a sense of ease and fulfillment.

The Power of Non-Action (Wu Wei): One of Lao Tzu's most important teachings is the principle of wu wei, or effortless action. This concept advocates for a way of living that is free from force and struggle, where actions arise naturally and in harmony with the flow of the universe.

Interconnectedness and Balance: Lao Tzu emphasizes the interconnectedness of all things and the importance of maintaining balance in our lives. He teaches that by recognizing and respecting the cycles of nature, we can find harmony and peace within ourselves and in our relationships with others.

The Value of Inner Stillness: Lao Tzu's writings often highlight the importance of inner stillness and contemplation. By cultivating a quiet mind and a calm heart, we can connect more deeply with the Tao and access the wisdom that lies within us.

Recognizing and Connecting with Lao Tzu

Connecting with Lao Tzu and his teachings can bring clarity and peace into your life. Here are some ways to recognize and deepen your connection with him:

Feelings of Calm and Peace: If you find yourself experiencing a deep sense of calm and peace, it may be a sign that you are aligning with the teachings of Lao Tzu. His wisdom often brings a sense of tranquility and acceptance of life's natural flow.

Attraction to Simplicity and Nature: Being drawn to simplicity, minimalism, and a deep appreciation for nature can indicate Lao Tzu's influence. His teachings encourage us to find beauty and wisdom in the natural world and in the simplicity of everyday life.

Experiences of Effortless Action: When you find yourself acting effortlessly and in harmony with your surroundings, it may be a reflection of the principle of wu wei. This alignment with the natural flow of life is a core aspect of Lao Tzu's philosophy.

Dreams and Visions of Ancient Wisdom: Lao Tzu may appear in dreams or meditative visions as an old sage or as symbols related to ancient Chinese wisdom. These encounters can offer insights and guidance, reflecting his role as a teacher of timeless truths.

Engagement with Taoist Practices: Practicing Tai Chi, Qigong, or other Taoist arts can help you connect with the essence of Lao Tzu's teachings. These practices embody the principles of balance, flow, and harmony that are central to his philosophy.

Prayer for Connection with Lao Tzu: "Wise Lao Tzu, guide me with your ancient wisdom. Help me to embrace simplicity and humility, to live in harmony with the Tao, and to cultivate inner stillness and peace. Show me the way of effortless action and help me to find balance and contentment in all that I do. Amen."

Historical Significance of Lao Tzu

Lao Tzu's historical significance is deeply rooted in the development of Taoism and Chinese philosophy. Although little is known about his life, his legacy as a spiritual teacher is evident in the enduring influence of the "Tao Te Ching" and the principles it espouses.

Lao Tzu is traditionally regarded as the founder of Taoism, one of the major philosophical and religious traditions in China. His teachings laid the foundation for Taoist thought, which emphasizes living in harmony with the Tao, the natural order of the universe.

Lao Tzu's philosophy has shaped Chinese culture, influencing art, literature, politics, and everyday life. The values of simplicity, humility, and non-action advocated in the "Tao Te Ching" have permeated Chinese society for centuries.

Lao Tzu's wisdom transcends cultural and temporal boundaries. The "Tao Te Ching" has been translated into numerous languages and remains a cornerstone of spiritual literature worldwide. Its teachings continue to resonate with those seeking a path of peace, simplicity, and alignment with the natural flow of life.

The principles of Taoism, as articulated by Lao Tzu, have inspired a wide range of spiritual practices, including Tai Chi, Qigong, and various forms of meditation. These practices emphasize balance, flow, and the cultivation of inner peace, reflecting the core tenets of Lao Tzu's philosophy.

Lao Tzu's image as the "Old Master" represents the timeless nature of his teachings. His insights into the nature of existence and the path to harmonious living continue to inspire and guide individuals on their spiritual journeys, making him a revered figure in the pantheon of spiritual sages.

Embracing the Journey with Lao Tzu

Embracing a relationship with Lao Tzu involves opening yourself to his teachings of simplicity, humility, and harmony with the Tao. By inviting his wisdom into your life, you can cultivate a deeper sense of peace and alignment with the natural world.

As you explore your connection with Lao Tzu, approach with an open heart and a willingness to embody his principles. Whether through meditation, contemplation, or daily practices, let his guidance inspire you to live with greater ease and grace. Embrace the simplicity and wisdom that Lao Tzu offers, and allow his presence to illuminate your path to peace and fulfillment.

Alex McCann Johnson

Chapter 134
White Tara

From the moment I began exploring the depths of Buddhist teachings and practices, I was drawn to the serene and nurturing presence of White Tara. Known as the goddess of compassion, healing, and longevity, White Tara embodies the divine feminine energy that comforts, protects, and nurtures. Her calm and loving nature offers solace and guidance to those who seek her blessings, making her a revered figure in Tibetan Buddhism and beyond.

White Tara, also known as Sita Tara, is one of the most beloved and venerated deities in the Tibetan Buddhist pantheon. She is often depicted with a white, luminous body, symbolizing purity, wisdom, and the radiant light of compassion. White Tara is typically portrayed with seven eyes—one on each palm, one on each sole of her feet, and three on her face—representing her ability to see and respond to the suffering of all beings.

As a manifestation of the goddess Tara, White Tara is considered the embodiment of enlightened activity and the mother of all Buddhas. She is often invoked for healing, protection, and the extension of life. Her gentle and peaceful demeanor invites practitioners to cultivate inner peace, compassion, and resilience in the face of life's challenges.

In my own spiritual practice, connecting with White Tara has brought a sense of comfort and healing. Her presence is a reminder of the boundless compassion and support that is available to us, even in the most difficult times.

The Spiritual Significance of White Tara

White Tara's significance extends beyond her role as a compassionate goddess. She embodies several key spiritual principles that can guide and inspire us on our journey:

Healing and Longevity: White Tara is often invoked for her healing powers. She is believed to bring relief from physical and emotional suffering and to promote long life and well-being. Her energy is especially beneficial for those who are ill or facing significant health challenges.

Compassion and Wisdom: As a manifestation of the Bodhisattva of Compassion, White Tara teaches us the importance of cultivating compassion and empathy for ourselves and others. Her wisdom helps us see beyond our immediate struggles, offering a broader perspective and deeper understanding of life's experiences.

Protection and Guidance: White Tara is known for her protective qualities. She shields us from negative influences and guides us through difficult situations with her gentle yet powerful presence. Her seven eyes symbolize her vigilance and ability to see all aspects of reality, ensuring that no cry for help goes unheard.

Purity and Enlightenment: The white color of Tara signifies purity and the aspiration for enlightenment. She encourages us to purify our thoughts, emotions, and actions, aligning ourselves with our highest potential and spiritual truth.

In my journey with White Tara, I have found her guidance to be a source of strength and clarity. She has helped me navigate personal challenges with grace and has inspired me to cultivate a deeper sense of compassion and purpose in my life.

Recognizing and Connecting with White Tara

Connecting with White Tara can bring immense healing and peace into your life. Here are some ways to recognize and deepen your connection with her:

Feelings of Peace and Comfort: When White Tara is near, you may experience a deep sense of calm and reassurance. Her presence often brings a soothing energy that envelope you in warmth and tranquility.

Attraction to White or Luminous Light: Being drawn to white light or feeling a comforting, luminous presence may indicate White Tara's influence. Her radiant light is a symbol of purity and compassion that guides and protects.

Symbols of Compassion and Healing: Encountering symbols associated with compassion, healing, or longevity, such as lotus flowers or images of Tara, can be a sign of her presence. These symbols remind us of her nurturing and supportive energy.

Dreams and Visions: White Tara may appear in dreams or meditative visions, offering guidance and comfort. Her image often brings messages of hope and healing, encouraging you to trust in her support.

Engagement with Buddhist Practices: Practicing Buddhist meditation, chanting Tara mantras, or studying texts related to Tara can help you connect more deeply with White Tara. These practices align you with her compassionate energy and invite her blessings into your life.

Prayer for Connection with White Tara: "White Tara, compassionate goddess of healing and protection, I invite your presence into my life. Surround me with your radiant light and guide me with your boundless compassion. Help me to find healing, peace, and wisdom in all that I do. May your gentle strength inspire me to live with love and grace. Amen."

Historical Significance of White Tara

White Tara's historical significance is deeply rooted in Tibetan Buddhism, where she is revered as a powerful and compassionate deity. Her origins trace back to the Indian Buddhist tradition, where she emerged as a female Bodhisattva embodying the virtues of compassion and protection.

White Tara is believed to have originated in India, where she was venerated as a goddess who could grant health, longevity, and wisdom. Her worship spread to Tibet and other regions, where she became an integral part of Buddhist practice and devotion.

In Tibetan Buddhism, White Tara holds a prominent place as a protector and healer. She is often invoked in prayers and rituals for her ability to alleviate suffering and extend life. Monasteries and practitioners throughout Tibet honor her with statues, thangkas (sacred paintings), and dedicated ceremonies.

White Tara's teachings and practices have significantly influenced Buddhist meditation and healing traditions. Her mantras and visualizations are used to cultivate compassion, promote healing, and connect with the divine feminine energy.

White Tara has been a subject of artistic and literary expression for centuries. Her serene and luminous depictions in Buddhist art reflect her role as a symbol of purity and compassion. Buddhist texts and teachings often highlight her wisdom and protective qualities, emphasizing her importance in spiritual practice.

White Tara embodies the divine feminine aspect of enlightenment, representing the nurturing and protective qualities of a mother. Her historical presence underscores the value of feminine wisdom and compassion in spiritual traditions, offering a balanced perspective that honors both masculine and feminine energies.

Embracing the Journey with White Tara

Embracing a relationship with White Tara involves opening yourself to her healing, protective, and compassionate energy. By inviting her presence into your life, you can experience peace, healing, and spiritual growth.

As you explore your connection with White Tara, approach with an open heart and a willingness to embody her principles of compassion and wisdom. Whether through meditation, prayer, or daily acts of kindness, let her guidance inspire you to live with greater love and understanding. Embrace the nurturing and supportive energy that White Tara offers, and allow her presence to illuminate your path to healing and enlightenment.

Alex McCann Johnson

Chapter 135
Lady Portia

In my journey of personal growth, I encountered the majestic and compassionate presence of Lady Portia. Known as the Goddess of Justice and Opportunity, Lady Portia embodies fairness, balance, and the transformative power of choices. Her energy is deeply aligned with the principles of karma and the law of cause and effect, guiding us to make decisions that align with our highest good.

Lady Portia is an Ascended Master and a member of the Karmic Board, a group of enlightened beings responsible for overseeing the karmic consequences of human actions. As the twin flame of Saint Germain, she works closely with the Violet Flame, a powerful tool for transmutation and spiritual purification. Her role is to bring balance, justice, and opportunity into our lives, helping us navigate the complexities of karma and make empowered choices.

Often depicted holding the scales of justice, Lady Portia's presence is both serene and powerful. She encourages us to embrace fairness and integrity in all our actions and to seek opportunities for growth and transformation. In my experience, connecting with Lady Portia has brought a sense of balance and clarity, especially when facing difficult decisions or seeking to resolve conflicts.

The Spiritual Significance of Lady Portia

Lady Portia's influence extends beyond her role as a divine arbiter of justice. She embodies several key spiritual principles that can guide and inspire us on our journey:

Justice and Fairness: Lady Portia teaches us the importance of fairness and equity in our interactions with others. She encourages us to consider the consequences of our actions and to strive for justice in all aspects of life. Her energy helps us see beyond personal biases and make decisions that honor the greater good.

Opportunities and Choices: As the Goddess of Opportunity, Lady Portia opens doors to new possibilities and paths. She guides us to recognize and seize opportunities that align with our soul's purpose and highest potential. Her presence reminds us that every moment is an opportunity to choose growth, love, and transformation.

Karma and Balance: Lady Portia's deep connection to the principles of karma and balance helps us understand the impact of our actions on our spiritual journey. She assists us in balancing our karmic debts and using the lessons of our past to create a harmonious and fulfilling future.

Empowerment and Integrity: Lady Portia inspires us to act with integrity and to stand in our power. She encourages us to make choices that reflect our true values and to take responsibility for our actions. Her guidance empowers us to live authentically and to align our decisions with our highest ideals.

In my work with Lady Portia, I have found her guidance to be a source of wisdom and empowerment. She has helped me navigate the complexities of karma, embrace growth opportunities, and act with greater fairness and integrity in my life.

Recognizing and Connecting with Lady Portia

Connecting with Lady Portia can bring balance, justice, and new opportunities into your life. Here are some ways to recognize and deepen your connection with her:

Feelings of Fairness and Balance: When Lady Portia is near, you may experience a heightened sense of fairness and a desire to bring balance to situations. Her presence often encourages a deeper reflection on justice and the impact of your actions.

Attraction to Scales or Symbols of Justice: Being drawn to symbols of justice, such as scales or images of Lady Portia, may indicate her influence. These symbols remind us of the importance of fairness and balance in our lives.

Opportunities and Synchronicities: Encountering unexpected opportunities or noticing synchronicities that guide you toward positive outcomes can be a sign of Lady Portia's presence. She often works through the unfolding of new possibilities and the alignment of events.

Dreams and Visions: Lady Portia may appear in dreams or meditative visions, offering guidance and insights related to justice, balance, and opportunities. Her messages often inspire a deeper understanding of your path and the choices you face.

Engagement with Spiritual Practices: Practicing meditation, working with the Violet Flame, or studying texts related to karma and justice can help you connect more deeply with Lady Portia. These practices align you with her energy and invite her guidance into your life.

Prayer for Connection with Lady Portia: "Lady Portia, Goddess of Justice and Opportunity, I invite your presence into my life. Surround me with your wisdom and guide me to act fairly and honestly. Help me to recognize and seize the opportunities that align with my highest good. May your balance and justice inspire me to make choices that honor the greater good. Amen."

Historical Significance of Lady Portia

Lady Portia's historical significance is deeply rooted in the esoteric and spiritual traditions that recognize the role of the Karmic Board and the Ascended Masters. Her influence spans across various spiritual teachings, where she is revered as a guardian of justice and a guide to karmic balance.

As a member of the Karmic Board, Lady Portia oversees the karmic consequences of human actions, helping to ensure that justice and balance are maintained. This role highlights her deep connection to the principles of karma and her responsibility for guiding humanity towards fairness and integrity.

Lady Portia's work with the Violet Flame, alongside her twin flame Saint Germain, underscores her role in spiritual transmutation and purification. The Violet Flame is a powerful tool for releasing negative energies and transforming karma, reflecting Lady Portia's mission to bring healing and balance to the soul.

Throughout history, Lady Portia has been invoked in spiritual teachings and practices that emphasize justice, balance, and empowerment. Her presence is recognized in various mystical traditions, where she is seen as a source of wisdom and a guide to righteous action.

Lady Portia is often depicted in spiritual art and literature as a figure of serene authority, holding the scales of justice. These representations highlight her role as a divine arbiter and her commitment to promoting fairness and equity in all things.

Embracing the Journey with Lady Portia

Embracing a relationship with Lady Portia involves opening yourself to her guidance on justice, opportunities, and karmic balance. By inviting her presence into your life, you can experience wisdom, fairness, and empowerment.

As you explore your connection with Lady Portia, approach with an open heart and a willingness to embrace her principles of justice and opportunity. Whether through meditation, prayer, or daily acts of fairness, let her guidance inspire you to live with greater balance and integrity. Embrace the opportunities that Lady Portia brings, and allow her presence to illuminate your path to a more just and fulfilling life.

Chapter 136
Commander Ashtar

One of the most fascinating encounters was with Commander Ashtar, the leader of the Ashtar Command. This experience has deeply enriched my understanding of extraterrestrial intelligence and cosmic guidance. Commander Ashtar is a prominent figure in the Galactic Federation, overseeing a collective of beings dedicated to the protection and spiritual upliftment of humanity. His presence exudes a sense of calm authority and wisdom, guiding us toward higher consciousness and universal peace.

Commander Ashtar is often described as a benevolent extraterrestrial being of great wisdom and compassion, hailing from the star system of Sirius. He leads the Ashtar Command, a group of advanced extraterrestrial beings and lightworkers who assist in the spiritual evolution of Earth and its inhabitants. Ashtar's mission is to foster peace, protect humanity from negative influences, and guide us in our journey toward higher consciousness.

In my own experiences with Commander Ashtar, I have felt his reassuring presence during times of uncertainty and spiritual seeking. He offers practical guidance, helping me navigate the complexities of life with a greater sense of purpose and alignment. His energy feels like a beacon of light, providing clarity and direction in my spiritual path.

The Spiritual Significance of Commander Ashtar

Commander Ashtar's influence extends far beyond his role as a cosmic protector. He embodies several key spiritual principles that resonate deeply with our journey toward enlightenment:

Protection and Guidance: As the leader of the Ashtar Command, Commander Ashtar is dedicated to the protection of Earth and its inhabitants. He shields us from negative extraterrestrial influences and guides us through the challenges of our spiritual awakening. His presence offers a sense of security and assurance as we navigate the unknown.

Higher Consciousness: Ashtar's mission is deeply aligned with the elevation of human consciousness. He encourages us to expand our awareness, embrace our spiritual potential, and align with the higher frequencies of love and light. His guidance helps us transcend the limitations of our physical reality and connect with our cosmic heritage.

Universal Peace: Commander Ashtar advocates for universal peace and harmony. He inspires us to cultivate peace within ourselves and extend it to the world around us. His teachings emphasize the importance of unity, cooperation, and the recognition of our interconnectedness with all beings in the universe.

Spiritual Evolution: Ashtar's presence is a catalyst for spiritual growth and transformation. He supports our personal and collective evolution, guiding us to align with the divine plan and fulfill our highest purpose. His wisdom helps us understand our role in the grand tapestry of the universe and inspires us to live with greater authenticity and purpose.

In my journey with Commander Ashtar, I have found his guidance to be a source of enlightenment and empowerment. His messages often come through as insights during meditation, dreams, or moments of deep reflection, offering clarity and direction in my spiritual path.

Recognizing and Connecting with Commander Ashtar

Connecting with Commander Ashtar can bring insights and cosmic wisdom into your life. Here are some ways to recognize and deepen your connection with him:

Sense of Cosmic Presence: When Commander Ashtar is near, you may feel a strong sense of cosmic awareness or a deep connection to the universe. His presence often feels expansive, as if you are tuning into a broader perspective of existence.

Attraction to Stars and Space: Being drawn to the stars, space, or the idea of extraterrestrial life can be a sign of Ashtar's influence. This attraction often signifies a deeper connection to the cosmos and the higher dimensions that Ashtar represents.

Messages and Synchronicities: Pay attention to messages or synchronicities related to cosmic themes, such as references to the Galactic Federation, space missions, or star beings. These signs can be subtle indications of Ashtar's guidance.

Dreams and Visions: Ashtar may appear in dreams or meditative visions, offering guidance and insights related to your spiritual journey. His presence in these experiences often brings a sense of peace, clarity, and cosmic connection.

Engagement with Cosmic Themes: Explore books, articles, or teachings related to extraterrestrial intelligence, the Galactic Federation, and cosmic spirituality. Engaging with these themes can enhance your connection with Commander Ashtar and align you with his mission.

Prayer for Connection with Commander Ashtar: "Commander Ashtar, leader of the Ashtar Command, I invite your presence into my life. Surround me with your light and wisdom, and guide me in my journey towards higher consciousness and universal peace. Help me align with the divine plan and fulfill my highest purpose. Amen."

Historical Significance of Commander Ashtar

Commander Ashtar's historical significance is rooted in various spiritual and metaphysical teachings that emerged in the mid-20th century. His name and presence have been channeled by numerous individuals, contributing to a rich tapestry of messages and guidance that span decades.

Commander Ashtar first gained prominence in the 1950s through channeling sessions. He was introduced as a benevolent extraterrestrial leader committed to helping humanity through times of crisis and spiritual awakening. His messages often focused on themes of peace, protection, and the elevation of human consciousness.

The Ashtar Command, under his leadership, is described as a vast network of star beings and lightworkers dedicated to safeguarding Earth and assisting in its ascension process. This concept has been explored in various spiritual texts and channelings, highlighting Ashtar's role as a cosmic protector and guide.

Over the years, Commander Ashtar's influence has extended to various spiritual communities and practices. His messages continue to inspire individuals seeking to connect with their cosmic origins and align with higher dimensions of consciousness. Ashtar's presence in modern spirituality underscores the growing interest in extraterrestrial guidance and the exploration of our place in the universe.

Commander Ashtar is often depicted in spiritual art and literature as a tall, radiant being with a commanding presence. These representations capture his role as a leader and protector, offering a visual anchor for those who connect with his energy.

Embracing the Journey with Commander Ashtar

Embracing a relationship with Commander Ashtar involves opening yourself to his guidance on cosmic consciousness, protection, and spiritual evolution. By inviting his presence into your life, you can gain cosmic insights and align with the higher frequencies of the universe.

As you explore your connection with Commander Ashtar, approach with an open heart and a willingness to expand your awareness. Whether through meditation, prayer, or cosmic exploration, let his guidance inspire you to live with greater purpose and alignment. Embrace the cosmic wisdom and protection that Commander Ashtar offers, and allow his presence to illuminate your path to a more enlightened and connected existence.

Alex McCann Johnson

Chapter 137
Ascended Masters in Modern Spirituality

The New Age movement, which gained momentum in the late 20th century, has been significantly influenced by the teachings of Ascended Masters. These enlightened beings offer timeless wisdom that resonates deeply with the ideals of spiritual growth, personal transformation, and global harmony that define the New Age ethos. Their teachings encompass a broad spectrum of spiritual principles, including the unity of all life, the power of thought and intention, and the importance of living in alignment with higher consciousness.

Ascended Masters like Saint Germain, Kuthumi, and El Morya have become central figures within the New Age community. Their messages often emphasize the need for personal responsibility, the importance of spiritual discipline, and the transformative power of love and compassion. By embodying these teachings, individuals are encouraged to elevate their own consciousness and contribute to the collective awakening of humanity.

The influence of Ascended Masters in the New Age movement can also be seen in the widespread adoption of practices such as meditation, energy healing, and the use of affirmations. These practices, inspired by the teachings of Ascended Masters, help individuals to connect with their higher selves, heal past traumas, and manifest their desires.

Integrating Ancient Wisdom with Contemporary Practices

One of the remarkable aspects of Ascended Masters is their ability to bridge ancient wisdom with contemporary practices. Their teachings provide a framework for integrating timeless spiritual principles into modern life, making divine insights accessible and applicable to today's challenges.

For instance, the practice of meditation, which has roots in ancient traditions, has been revitalized and popularized in the New Age movement through the guidance of Ascended Masters. Techniques such as the Violet Flame meditation, associated with Saint Germain, offer powerful spiritual purification and transformation tools. These practices help individuals to cleanse their energy fields, release negative patterns, and align with their higher purpose.

Ascended Masters also emphasize the importance of using modern tools such as affirmations and visualization to harness the power of the mind. Individuals can co-create their reality and attract experiences that align with their spiritual goals by focusing on positive thoughts and intentions. This integration of ancient wisdom with contemporary practices empowers individuals to navigate the complexities of modern life while remaining connected to their spiritual essence.

Channeled Messages and Teachings

Channeling, the practice of receiving and transmitting messages from non-physical entities, has become a significant aspect of the New Age movement. Several prominent channels have brought forth the teachings of Ascended Masters, providing valuable insights and guidance to spiritual seekers.

One of the most influential channels is Alice Bailey, who channeled the teachings of the Ascended Master Djwhal Khul. Her extensive body of work, including titles such as "The Externalization of the Hierarchy" and "Esoteric Healing," offers profound insights into the nature of the soul, the dynamics of spiritual healing, and the unfolding of the divine plan. Bailey's contributions have shaped the foundation of modern esoteric thought and continue to inspire contemporary spiritual practices.

Another notable channel is Elizabeth Clare Prophet, founder of The Summit Lighthouse and the Church Universal and Triumphant. She channeled messages from a variety of Ascended Masters, including Saint Germain, El Morya, and Kuthumi. Her teachings emphasize the importance of personal transformation, the use of decrees and affirmations, and the pursuit of spiritual mastery. Prophet's work has played a crucial role in popularizing the concept of Ascended Masters and their teachings within the New Age community.

Evaluating the Authenticity of Channeled Information

While channeled messages from Ascended Masters can offer truly fantastic insights and guidance, it is important to approach them with discernment. Evaluating the authenticity of channeled information involves several key considerations:

- **Consistency and Coherence:** Authentic messages from Ascended Masters typically exhibit a high degree of consistency and coherence with established spiritual principles. They align with the core teachings of love, compassion, and unity and offer practical guidance for spiritual growth.

- **Vibration and Energy**: The energy and vibration of authentic channeled messages often carry a sense of clarity, purity, and upliftment. These messages resonate deeply with the heart and soul, inspiring feelings of peace, empowerment, and higher awareness.

- **Discernment and Inner Guidance**: It is essential to use personal discernment and inner guidance when evaluating channeled information. Trusting one's intuition and seeking confirmation through meditation, prayer, or contemplation can help validate the authenticity of the messages received.

- **Ethical Integrity**: Authentic channeled messages typically emphasize ethical integrity, personal responsibility, and the importance of aligning with higher spiritual values. They encourage individuals to act with compassion, honesty, and respect for all beings.

Ascended Masters and Global Transformation

Ascended Masters play a pivotal role in the current global spiritual awakening, guiding humanity through a period of transformation and evolution. Their teachings and presence help to raise the collective consciousness, inspiring individuals to awaken to their true nature and embrace their spiritual potential.

In this time of significant change, Ascended Masters offers guidance on how to navigate the challenges and opportunities that arise. They emphasize the importance of inner work, self-awareness, and the cultivation of virtues such as love, compassion, and forgiveness. By aligning with these higher principles, individuals can contribute to the creation of a more harmonious and enlightened world.

Ascended Masters also support the activation and expansion of spiritual gifts and abilities. They encourage individuals to explore their intuitive, healing, and creative potentials, empowering them to play an active role in the spiritual evolution of humanity. Through their guidance, individuals are inspired to step into their roles as lightworkers, healers, and conscious co-creators.

Collective Consciousness and Planetary Healing

The influence of Ascended Masters extends beyond individual transformation to encompass collective consciousness and planetary healing. Their teachings emphasize the interconnectedness of all life and the importance of working together to heal and uplift the planet.

Ascended Masters often highlight the significance of collective intention and meditation in creating positive change. Group meditations, global healing events, and synchronized prayers are powerful tools for amplifying positive energy and raising the vibration of the collective consciousness. By coming together with a shared intention, individuals can create a ripple effect that influences the entire planet.

Ascended Masters guide us in healing our relationship with the Earth. They teach us to honor and respect the natural world, to engage in sustainable practices, and to cultivate a sense of stewardship for the planet. Their guidance inspires us to take conscious actions that support the well-being of all living beings and the Earth itself.

Ascended Masters play a crucial role in modern spirituality, offering timeless wisdom and guidance that inspire personal and collective transformation. Through their influence in the New Age movement, channeled messages, and teachings on global transformation, they helped to raise the collective consciousness and promote planetary healing. By connecting with these enlightened beings and integrating their teachings into our lives, we can contribute to the ongoing spiritual awakening and the creation of a more harmonious and enlightened world.

Alex McCann Johnson

Galactic Guides

Alex McCann Johnson

Chapter 138
Galactic Guides

When I first embarked on my journey to connect with spiritual guides, I had no idea that my path would lead me to the stars. The concept of galactic guides might seem far-fetched to some, but these celestial beings offer wisdom and guidance for many who seek a deeper connection with the universe. Galactic guides are extraterrestrial entities that transcend our earthly existence, bringing insights from advanced civilizations across the cosmos. They are here to assist us in our spiritual growth, offering perspectives that are often beyond our immediate comprehension but deeply transformative.

Understanding galactic guides begins with opening our minds to the vastness of the universe and the possibility that we are not alone. These guides can come from various star systems, each with its own unique wisdom and energy. Some of the most commonly known galactic guides include the Arcturians, Pleiadians, Sirians, and Andromedans, among others. Each group brings a different kind of guidance tailored to help us navigate our spiritual paths and the challenges we face in our lives.

History and Cultural Perspectives

Throughout history, different cultures have perceived and interacted with extraterrestrial beings in various ways. Ancient civilizations like the Egyptians, Sumerians, and Mayans have left artifacts and writings suggesting contact with beings from other worlds. For example, the Dogon tribe of Mali has intricate knowledge of the Sirius star system, which they attribute to visitors from Sirius B. This knowledge was passed down through generations long before modern astronomy confirmed the existence of the star.

In Eastern traditions, the concept of celestial beings is not uncommon. Hindu mythology speaks of gods and goddesses who travel between realms, often depicted in flying chariots. Similarly, Buddhist texts describe enlightened beings from other worlds who come to assist humanity. While often cloaked in the language of myth and religion, these stories may very well point to encounters with advanced extraterrestrial beings.

In more recent history, the rise of ufology and the widespread reports of UFO sightings have brought the idea of extraterrestrial contact into the public consciousness. While some dismiss these accounts as mere fantasies or misinterpretations, others see them as evidence of ongoing interactions with galactic beings. Personally, I believe that many of these encounters are genuine, offering glimpses into the broader universe and the beings who inhabit it.

Purpose and Benefits

The role of galactic guides in our spiritual development cannot be overstated. These beings operate from a higher vibrational frequency, bringing a level of wisdom and understanding that can help us transcend our earthly limitations. Their purpose is to assist us in our evolution, both individually and collectively. By connecting with galactic guides, we can gain insights that lead to personal growth and a deeper understanding of our place in the universe.

One of the primary benefits of working with galactic guides is the expansion of our consciousness. These guides help us see beyond the confines of our everyday reality, opening our minds to new possibilities and ways of thinking. They often bring messages of unity, love, and cooperation, encouraging us to embrace these principles in our own lives.

Galactic guides also assist us in healing. Their advanced knowledge of energy and frequency can help us release old patterns and traumas that no longer serve us. Through their guidance, we can learn to balance our energies, align our chakras, and raise our vibrational frequency. This healing process not only benefits us personally but also contributes to the collective healing of humanity and the Earth.

Moreover, galactic guides can provide practical guidance on navigating our lives. Whether it's offering insights into our life purpose, helping us make important decisions, or supporting us through challenging times, these guides are always available to offer their wisdom. Their perspective, coming from a place of higher consciousness, can often provide clarity and direction that we might not be able to see on our own.

Connecting with galactic guides requires an open heart and mind. It involves meditation, intention, and a willingness to receive. In my experience, the more we attune ourselves to higher frequencies and set the intention to connect, the more these beings make their presence known. They may come through in dreams, during meditation, or even in everyday moments when we least expect it.

How to Connect with Galactic Guides

Meditation and Intention: One of the most effective ways to connect with galactic guides is through meditation. Setting a clear intention to connect with these beings can create a powerful link. Begin by finding a quiet space where you can relax and focus. Close your eyes and take several deep breaths, allowing your mind to quiet and your body to relax. Visualize a beam of light connecting you to the universe and invite your galactic guides to join you. Be open to any impressions, feelings, or images that come through during this time.

Dream Work: Galactic guides often communicate through dreams, offering insights and guidance while we sleep. Before going to bed, set the intention to connect with your galactic guides. Keep a dream journal by your bed to record any dreams or impressions you receive. Over time, you may notice patterns or recurring themes that offer valuable insights into your spiritual journey.

Signs and Synchronicities: Pay attention to signs and synchronicities in your daily life. Galactic guides often use these subtle hints to communicate their presence and guidance. This could be in the form of repeating numbers, sudden inspirations, or encounters with certain animals. Trust your intuition and be open to the messages these signs bring.

Visualization and Astral Travel: Visualization techniques and astral travel can also facilitate connections with galactic guides. During a quiet moment, visualize traveling to a distant star system and meeting your guides. Imagine their appearance, the energy they emit, and any messages they might have for you. This practice can deepen your connection and make their presence more tangible.

Channeled Communication: Some individuals find that they can communicate with galactic guides through channeling. This involves allowing the guides to speak or write through you, offering their wisdom directly. If you feel drawn to this method, it's important to create a safe and protected space and to approach channeling with respect and an open heart.

Galactic guides are invaluable allies on our spiritual journey. They bring a wealth of knowledge and wisdom that can help us grow, heal, and evolve. By opening ourselves to their guidance, we can experience transformations and gain a deeper understanding of our place in the cosmos. As we continue to explore and connect with these celestial beings, we step into a greater awareness of the interconnectedness of all life, both on Earth and beyond. Embracing their presence enriches our spiritual practice and illuminates the path toward our highest potential.

Chapter 139
A Multidimensional Perspective

The concept of galactic guides often evokes images of extraterrestrial beings with advanced technology and knowledge. However, their work transcends our conventional understanding of guidance. These celestial entities are involved in a wide array of activities aimed at assisting humanity and the planet in its evolutionary journey. Their contributions are multifaceted and profound, from fostering spiritual awakening to aiding in technological advancements.

Spiritual Awakening and Growth

One of the primary roles of galactic guides is to facilitate our spiritual awakening and growth. They do this by offering wisdom that helps us expand our consciousness and understand our place in the universe. Galactic guides, such as the Pleiadians and Arcturians, are often involved in teaching us about the nature of reality, the importance of unity, and the power of love and light.

Guidance on the Path to Enlightenment: The Pleiadians, known for their deep connection to the heart chakra, often guide us to embrace love and compassion. Their teachings emphasize the importance of healing old wounds and opening our hearts to higher vibrations. They encourage us to see beyond the illusions of separation and recognize the interconnectedness of all beings.

The Arcturians, on the other hand, are renowned for their focus on the development of higher consciousness. They provide tools and techniques for expanding our awareness, such as advanced meditation practices and energy healing methods. Their guidance often involves helping us navigate through the complexities of our emotions and thoughts, leading us toward greater clarity and inner peace.

Facilitating Ascension: Galactic guides also play a crucial role in the process of ascension. This journey involves raising our vibrational frequency and aligning with higher states of consciousness. The Andromedans, for example, are known for their work in assisting individuals and the planet in ascending to higher dimensions. They offer insights into the nature of multidimensional reality and guide us in integrating these higher frequencies into our daily lives.

During my own meditative journeys, I have felt the presence of Andromedan guides, who have provided me with insights into the nature of time and space. Their teachings have helped me understand that our physical existence is just one aspect of a much larger, interconnected reality.

Healing and Energy Work

Galactic guides are also deeply involved in the healing and balancing of our energies. They possess advanced knowledge of how energy flows through the universe and within our bodies. By working with these guides, we can experience advanced healing on physical, emotional, and spiritual levels.

Energy Balancing and Chakra Alignment: Sirians are often called upon for their expertise in energy healing and chakra alignment. They help us clear blockages in our energy fields and restore the natural flow of energy throughout our bodies. This can significantly improve our physical health, emotional well-being, and spiritual clarity.

In one of my healing sessions, I connected with a Sirian guide who assisted in balancing my energy field. I felt a warm, soothing energy enveloping me, and afterward, I experienced a sense of lightness and clarity that I hadn't felt in a long time. The work that was done allowed me to notice that the person had little energy running into the palm chakras, thus creating a blockage and ultimately causing carpal tunnel. Luckily, I was able to clear that blockage and get that flow of energy moving. This encounter reinforced my belief in the healing capabilities of these celestial beings.

Cellular and DNA Healing: Some galactic guides, such as the Lyrans, are known for their work in cellular and DNA healing. They assist in activating dormant aspects of our DNA, which can enhance our physical and psychic abilities. This activation process is often associated with the awakening of our latent potential and the expansion of our consciousness.

The Lyrans' teachings have helped me understand the importance of aligning our physical and energetic bodies. By working with them, I have been able to tap into deeper levels of my own potential and enhance my intuitive abilities.

Technological Advancements and Knowledge Sharing

Galactic guides are also instrumental in sharing advanced knowledge and technology with humanity. They often provide insights and innovations that can help us address some of the most pressing challenges we face today.

Inspiration for Scientific and Technological Breakthroughs: The Sirians and Arcturians, in particular, are known for their contributions to technological advancements. They have been credited with inspiring many of the breakthroughs in science and technology that we are witnessing today. From renewable energy solutions to advancements in medical technology, their influence is seen in various fields.

During periods of deep meditation and reflection, I have received insights that seemed to come from beyond my own understanding. These moments have often led to creative solutions and ideas that I later realized were aligned with the teachings of galactic guides.

Environmental Sustainability: Galactic guides are also deeply concerned with the health and sustainability of our planet. The

Pleiadians, for example, emphasize the importance of living in harmony with nature and adopting sustainable practices. They offer guidance on how we can reduce our ecological footprint and create a more balanced relationship with the Earth.

In my interactions with Pleiadian guides, I have been inspired to make changes in my own lifestyle to align more closely with sustainable practices. Their teachings have encouraged me to be more mindful of my impact on the environment and to seek ways to contribute to the healing of our planet.

Supporting Global and Cosmic Transformation

Beyond individual guidance, galactic guides are actively involved in supporting global and cosmic transformation. They work behind the scenes to assist in the evolution of human consciousness and the stabilization of planetary energies.

Assisting in Collective Awakening: Galactic guides play a vital role in the collective awakening of humanity. They help to elevate the collective consciousness and support the transition from old paradigms to new, more enlightened ways of being. This involves guiding humanity through periods of upheaval and transformation, helping us to embrace the changes necessary for our evolution.

Maintaining Cosmic Balance: In the broader cosmic context, galactic guides also work to maintain balance and harmony within the universe. They are involved in various interstellar councils and alliances that oversee the welfare of different star systems and galaxies. Their efforts ensure that the energies and dynamics of the cosmos remain in alignment with the higher principles of love and unity.

Personal Experiences and Reflections

Throughout my journey, connecting with galactic guides has been a transformative experience. Their guidance has helped me expand my consciousness, heal on multiple levels, and gain a deeper understanding of the universe. Each encounter has reinforced my belief in the interconnectedness of all life and the limitless potential for growth and evolution.

I encourage anyone who feels drawn to explore this realm to approach it with an open heart and mind. Whether through meditation, energy work, or simply setting the intention to connect, the presence of galactic guides can bring insights and support to your spiritual journey.

The work of galactic guides is vast and multifaceted, encompassing spiritual growth, healing, technological advancements, and global transformation. They offer a higher perspective that helps us navigate our challenges and embrace our potential as beings of light. By opening ourselves to their guidance, we can tap into the infinite wisdom of the cosmos and contribute to the creation of a more enlightened and harmonious world.

Alex McCann Johnson

Chapter 140

Arcturians

In my journey with energy work, I stumbled upon a practice called Arcturian Reiki. This discovery opened up a new perspective on energy healing, allowing me to amplify my ability to channel healing energies and connect with higher dimensions. Arcturian Reiki introduced me to the Arcturians, advanced beings from the star system Arcturus, who are known for their deep wisdom and powerful healing abilities. Working with Arcturian energies has been transformative, providing energetic insights and enhancing my spiritual growth and healing practices.

The Arcturians are highly evolved, benevolent beings from the Arcturus star system, one of the brightest stars in the night sky. They are often described as having a deep connection to the divine and possess advanced spiritual and technological knowledge. Arcturians are considered to be among the most spiritually advanced civilizations in our galaxy. They are here to assist humanity in its evolutionary journey, offering guidance, healing, and wisdom.

Key characteristics of the Arcturians include:

Advanced Healing Abilities: Arcturians are renowned for their exceptional healing abilities. They use their advanced understanding of energy and frequency to promote deep healing on physical, emotional, and spiritual levels. In my experience with Arcturian Reiki, their energy is incredibly powerful yet gentle, capable of facilitating profound transformations.

817

Deep Spiritual Wisdom: Arcturians possess a vast reservoir of spiritual wisdom. They help us understand complex spiritual concepts and assist in accessing higher states of consciousness. Their teachings often focus on personal and planetary ascension, guiding us to align with our highest potential.

Technological Mastery: Alongside their spiritual expertise, Arcturians are known for their advanced technological abilities. They often use these technologies to enhance healing and facilitate communication across dimensions.

Compassion and Guidance: Arcturians are deeply compassionate and are dedicated to supporting humanity. They provide guidance and protection, helping us navigate challenges and align with our soul's purpose.

Connecting with the Arcturians through Arcturian Reiki has been an enlightening experience for me. Their presence is nurturing and uplifting, guiding me to deeper levels of understanding and healing.

The Spiritual Significance of Arcturians

The Arcturians play a crucial role in supporting humanity's spiritual evolution. Here's how they can impact and support our spiritual journey:

Facilitating Deep Healing: Arcturians use their advanced healing techniques to promote deep, holistic healing. They help us release energetic blockages, heal past traumas, and restore balance within our energy systems. Their healing abilities extend beyond the physical, addressing emotional and spiritual imbalances as well.

Expanding Consciousness: Through their teachings and energy transmissions, Arcturians assist us in expanding our consciousness. They guide us to explore higher dimensions and connect with our higher selves, facilitating a deeper understanding of our place in the universe.

Supporting Personal and Planetary Ascension: Arcturians are committed to aiding in the ascension process of both individuals and the planet. They provide insights and tools to help us align with higher frequencies and navigate the shifts occurring on Earth.

Promoting Unity and Cooperation: The Arcturians emphasize the importance of unity and cooperation among all beings. They inspire us to work together for the collective good and to recognize our interconnectedness with all of creation.

Enhancing Spiritual Practices: Whether through meditation, energy healing, or other spiritual practices, the Arcturians can enhance and deepen our experiences. Their presence elevates our practice, helping us to access higher states of awareness and spiritual insight.

My work with the Arcturians has impacted my spiritual journey. Their guidance and healing have helped me to navigate personal challenges and expand my understanding of energy and consciousness.

Recognizing and Connecting with Arcturians

Building a connection with the Arcturians involves recognizing their presence and inviting their guidance into your life. Here are some steps to help you connect with these enlightened beings:

Engage in Energy Healing Practices: Practices like Arcturian Reiki or other forms of energy healing can help you connect with Arcturian energies. These practices align you with their frequency and facilitate a deeper connection.

Meditate on Arcturian Energy: During meditation, focus on the energy of the Arcturus star system. Visualize a bright, radiant light emanating from Arcturus, enveloping you in its healing and wisdom. Invite the Arcturians to connect with you and be open to any sensations, thoughts, or images that arise.

Study Arcturian Teachings: Explore books, channels, and resources that offer insights into Arcturian wisdom and guidance. Understanding their teachings can deepen your connection and enhance your ability to receive their messages.

Visualize Arcturian Presence: Imagine yourself in the presence of Arcturian beings. Visualize their calming, luminous energy surrounding you, offering support and guidance.

Seek Guidance in Dreams and Meditations: Pay attention to dreams and meditative experiences where Arcturians may appear. They often communicate through subtle impressions or intuitive feelings during these states. Keep a journal to document and reflect on these encounters.

Practice Heart-Centered Awareness: Arcturian energy is deeply connected to the heart. Engage in practices that open and align your heart chakra, such as heart-focused meditation, gratitude practices, and acts of kindness.

Prayer for Arcturian Guidance: "Beloved Arcturians, I invite your presence and wisdom into my life. Guide me in expanding my consciousness, healing my energy, and embracing my true purpose. Help me to connect with the light and wisdom within me and to live in harmony with all beings. Thank you for your gentle guidance and support."

Historical Significance of Arcturians

The concept of Arcturians and their influence has been present in various spiritual and metaphysical teachings for centuries. Ancient civilizations, such as the Egyptians and Sumerians, had deep connections with the stars and often referenced beings from other worlds in their mythology and spiritual practices. These early cultures recognized the wisdom and advanced knowledge of beings like the Arcturians.

In modern times, the Arcturians have become prominent in the works of many spiritual channelers and authors. Notable figures like Edgar Cayce, the "Sleeping Prophet," spoke of advanced beings from Arcturus who possessed great knowledge and compassion. In his readings, Cayce described Arcturus as a gateway to higher realms and a source of advanced spiritual knowledge.

Guided by Spirits

Books and teachings from spiritual channels such as David K. Miller and Patricia Pereira have further explored the role of Arcturians as guides and healers. These works often describe the Arcturians as being deeply involved in humanity's spiritual evolution, offering their wisdom and support during times of transformation and change.

Astrologically, the star Arcturus has been revered as a point of cosmic connection and spiritual significance. It is often associated with leadership, protection, and the pursuit of higher knowledge. For many, Arcturus represents a beacon of light and guidance in the vastness of the universe.

These historical perspectives highlight the enduring belief in the Arcturians as enlightened beings who guide and assist humanity. Their presence in ancient mythology, modern channelings, and astrological teachings underscores their role as spiritual guides and protectors, bridging the gap between the celestial and the earthly.

Embracing the Journey with Arcturians

Connecting with the Arcturians offers a link to a reservoir of cosmic wisdom and support. Their teachings and guidance can enrich your life and deepen your understanding of your spiritual path.

As you build your relationship with these enlightened beings, honor their legacy and learn from their experiences. Whether through meditation, energy healing, or personal reflection, the connection to the Arcturians can provide invaluable insights and guidance. Embrace their presence with respect and gratitude, and allow their wisdom to illuminate your path.

Alex McCann Johnson

Chapter 141

Pleiadians

I was introduced to the Pleiadians through the book *Bringers of the Dawn* by Barbara Marciniak. Initially, the teachings in the book felt abstract and elusive, but as my journey progressed, the wisdom it offered began to resonate deeply with me. This introduction to the Pleiadians opened my eyes to a new realm of spiritual understanding and connection.

The Pleiadians are believed to be a highly evolved extraterrestrial race from the Pleiades star cluster, often referred to as the Seven Sisters. These beings are said to be our spiritual ancestors, with a connection to humanity and a vested interest in our evolution and enlightenment. Pleiadians are described as benevolent and deeply compassionate beings who offer guidance, healing, and wisdom to assist us in our spiritual growth.

Key characteristics of the Pleiadians include:

Deep Compassion and Empathy: Pleiadians are known for their profound sense of compassion and empathy. They understand the challenges we face on Earth and offer gentle, loving support to help us navigate these difficulties.

Advanced Spiritual Wisdom: The Pleiadians possess deep spiritual knowledge and understanding. They often guide us in exploring higher dimensions of consciousness and unlocking our potential for spiritual growth.

Focus on Healing and Transformation: Pleiadian teachings often emphasize healing, both on a personal and planetary level. They provide tools and insights to help us heal from past traumas, release negative patterns, and embrace our true selves.

Commitment to Human Evolution: Pleiadians are dedicated to assisting humanity in its evolutionary journey. They encourage us to awaken to our divine nature, recognize our interconnectedness, and live in harmony with all beings.

In my interactions with the Pleiadians, I have experienced their guidance as incredibly nurturing and supportive. Their teachings have helped me to open up to new perspectives and embrace the journey of spiritual awakening with greater clarity and courage.

The Spiritual Significance of Pleiadians

The Pleiadians play a crucial role in guiding humanity towards greater awareness and spiritual enlightenment. Here's how they can impact and support our spiritual journey:

Awakening Higher Consciousness: The Pleiadians assist us in expanding our consciousness and accessing higher dimensions of existence. They help us to perceive beyond the physical realm and connect with our higher selves and the divine.

Promoting Healing and Wholeness: Through their teachings and energy, the Pleiadians guide us in healing emotional wounds, releasing limiting beliefs, and integrating all aspects of our being. They support us in achieving wholeness and balance.

Encouraging Unity and Cooperation: The Pleiadians emphasize the importance of unity and cooperation among all beings. They remind us of our interconnectedness and inspire us to work together for the greater good of humanity and the planet.

Guiding Personal and Planetary Transformation: The Pleiadians provide insights and tools for both personal and planetary transformation.

They encourage us to align with our true purpose, embrace positive change, and contribute to the healing and evolution of the Earth.

Offering Spiritual Protection: The Pleiadians also offer protection and support during challenging times. They help us to navigate spiritual obstacles and maintain our alignment with higher frequencies of love and light.

Working with the Pleiadians has been transformative for me. Their gentle guidance and profound wisdom have helped me to navigate my spiritual journey with greater ease and confidence and to embrace the opportunities for growth and transformation that life presents.

Recognizing and Connecting with Pleiadians

Building a connection with the Pleiadians involves recognizing their presence and inviting their guidance into your life. Here are some steps to help you connect with these enlightened beings:

Meditate on Pleiadian Light: During meditation, focus on the light and energy associated with the Pleiades. Visualize a bright, loving light surrounding you, and invite the Pleiadians to connect with you. Be open to any sensations, thoughts, or images that arise.

Read Pleiadian Teachings: Explore books and resources that offer insights into Pleiadian wisdom and guidance, such as *Bringers of the Dawn*. Understanding their teachings can deepen your connection and enhance your ability to receive their messages.

Visualize Pleiadian Presence: Imagine yourself in the presence of Pleiadian beings. Visualize their gentle, compassionate energy enveloping you, offering love, support, and guidance.

Seek Guidance in Dreams and Meditations: Pay attention to dreams and meditative experiences where Pleiadians may appear. They often communicate through subtle impressions or intuitive feelings during these states. Keep a journal to document and reflect on these encounters.

Prayer for Pleiadian Guidance: "Beloved Pleiadians, I invite your presence and wisdom into my life. Guide me in awakening to my higher consciousness, healing my heart, and embracing my true purpose. Help me to connect with the love and light within me and to live in harmony with all beings. Thank you for your gentle guidance and support."

Historical Significance of Pleiadians

The concept of Pleiadians and their influence has deep roots in various spiritual and metaphysical teachings. Many ancient cultures, such as the Greeks, Egyptians, and Native Americans, have stories and myths associated with the Pleiades star cluster. For example, the Greek myth of the Pleiades describes them as the seven daughters of Atlas and Pleione, who were transformed into stars. This myth speaks to their celestial and spiritual significance, often seen as guides or protectors in the sky.

In the modern era, the idea of Pleiadians gained prominence through the work of channelers who claim to receive messages from these beings. Authors like Barbara Marciniak have shared Pleiadian teachings that emphasize spiritual awakening and transformation. These teachings often focus on personal and planetary evolution, encouraging humanity to embrace higher states of consciousness and unity.

The Pleiadians are also frequently mentioned in discussions about extraterrestrial contact and UFO sightings. Some believe that the Pleiadians have been visiting Earth for centuries, guiding and assisting humanity in its spiritual evolution. This perspective aligns with various accounts of encounters and experiences reported by individuals around the world.

Astrologically, the Pleiades star cluster has held significance in numerous traditions. It is often seen as a point of cosmic connection and a source of spiritual energy. For instance, in astrology, the Pleiades are associated with the zodiac sign Taurus and are considered a powerful influence in both individual and collective transformations.

These historical perspectives highlight the enduring belief in the

Pleiadians as enlightened beings who guide and assist humanity. Their presence in ancient myths, modern channelings, and cosmic teachings underscores their role as spiritual guides and protectors, bridging the gap between the celestial and the earthly.

Embracing the Journey with Pleiadians

Connecting with the Pleiadians offers a link to a reservoir of cosmic wisdom and support. Their teachings and guidance can enrich your life and deepen your understanding of your spiritual path.

As you build your relationship with these enlightened beings, honor their legacy and learn from their experiences. Whether through meditation, study, or personal reflection, the connection to the Pleiadians can provide invaluable insights and guidance. Embrace their presence with respect and gratitude, and allow their wisdom to illuminate your path.

Alex McCann Johnson

Chapter 142

Sirians

My first encounter with the concept of Sirians came through a fascinating connection between whales and the star system Sirius. This connection intrigued me, as it suggested that these magnificent creatures, which have always held a deep spiritual significance, might be linked to advanced beings from Sirius. As I delved deeper, I discovered that the Sirius star system, comprising Sirius A, Sirius B, and Sirius C, holds spiritual alignments and connections to various aspects of cosmic wisdom and divine consciousness.

Sirians are highly evolved, benevolent beings from the Sirius star system, located in the constellation Canis Major. Sirius is often referred to as the "Dog Star" and is one of the brightest stars visible from Earth. The Sirians are known for their deep spiritual wisdom, advanced technological knowledge, and their strong connection to Earth and its inhabitants.

The Sirians are traditionally aligned with three stars within the Sirius system, each with unique attributes and influences:

- **Sirius A:** Known for its alignment with Christ's consciousness or logos, Sirius A is connected with the Ascended Masters of the Light and the Councils of Light. These beings offer guidance and wisdom, helping to elevate human consciousness and promote spiritual enlightenment.

- **Sirius B:** This star is deeply connected with whales and dolphins, revered for their intelligence and spiritual depth. The beings from Sirius B are believed to have a strong affinity with these aquatic mammals, embodying the wisdom and grace of the sea.

- **Sirius C:** Aligned with the Divine Feminine, Sirius C is associated with total empowerment and the healing of the Universe. The energies from Sirius C support the integration of divine feminine qualities, fostering balance and nurturing in the cosmic and earthly realms.

In my exploration, the Sirians have provided a deep well of spiritual insights and connections. Their energies are often described as uplifting and illuminating, guiding humanity towards higher levels of understanding and consciousness.

The Spiritual Significance of Sirians

The Sirians play a crucial role in aiding humanity's spiritual development and evolution. Their influence spans various aspects of spiritual growth, healing, and cosmic alignment:

Elevating Consciousness: Sirians, particularly those aligned with Sirius A, help in raising human consciousness. They offer guidance that aligns with Christ's consciousness, promoting love, compassion, and unity. Their teachings help individuals and the collective move towards a more enlightened state of being.

Wisdom and Connection: The beings from Sirius B bring forth the wisdom of whales and dolphins, symbols of intelligence and emotional depth. They guide us in understanding our connections to these ancient creatures and the greater ocean of consciousness. This connection enhances our appreciation of the natural world and its intricate relationships.

Divine Feminine Energy: Sirius C's alignment with the Divine Feminine fosters empowerment and healing. The energies from this star support the integration of nurturing, intuitive, and compassionate qualities. This balance is crucial for personal and planetary healing, promoting harmony and wholeness.

Technological and Spiritual Advancements: Sirians are known for their advanced technological capabilities, often used to support spiritual growth and healing. Their knowledge helps humanity explore and integrate new technologies in a way that aligns with spiritual principles and cosmic harmony.

Working with Sirians can provide transformative insights and support, guiding individuals through their spiritual journeys and helping them align with their higher purpose.

Recognizing and Connecting with Sirians

Connecting with the Sirians involves tuning into their specific energies and inviting their guidance into your life. Here are some steps to help you recognize and establish a connection with these advanced beings:

Meditate on the Sirius Star System: During meditation, focus on the bright light of Sirius in the night sky. Visualize the energies of Sirius A, B, and C, each with their unique attributes. Invite the Sirians to connect with you and be open to any sensations, thoughts, or images that arise.

Explore Marine Life Wisdom: Spend time near water or engage with whales and dolphins, either physically or through visualization and contemplation. Reflect on the qualities these creatures embody and how they might relate to Sirian energies.

Align with Christ Consciousness: Practice meditations and affirmations that align with love, unity, and higher consciousness. This alignment can help you connect with the wisdom of Sirius A and the Ascended Masters of Light.

Embrace Divine Feminine Qualities: Focus on nurturing, intuitive, and compassionate practices. Engage in activities that promote healing and balance, both personally and in your interactions with others.

Study Sirian Teachings: Read books and explore resources that discuss Sirian wisdom and guidance. Understanding their teachings can deepen your connection and enhance your ability to receive their messages.

Prayer for Sirian Guidance: "Beloved beings of Sirius, I invite your presence and wisdom into my life. Guide me in raising my consciousness, connecting deeply with nature, and embracing the divine qualities within. Help me to align with the energies of Sirius A, B, and C and to integrate your teachings into my spiritual journey. Thank you for your light and guidance."

Historical Significance of Sirians

The concept of Sirians and their influence has been acknowledged in various spiritual and metaphysical traditions for centuries. The star Sirius has been revered by ancient civilizations as a source of wisdom and spiritual power.

Sirius held significant importance in ancient Egyptian culture. It was associated with the goddess Isis and considered a celestial beacon of spiritual knowledge and rebirth. The heliacal rising of Sirius marked the annual flooding of the Nile, a vital event for agriculture and prosperity. This alignment was seen as a divine synchronization between the heavens and Earth.

The Dogon people of Mali have long revered Sirius and have intricate knowledge of the star system, which they attribute to ancient contacts with beings from Sirius. Their legends describe detailed astronomical knowledge, including the existence of Sirius B, a star invisible to the naked eye but known to modern science only since the 20th century. This knowledge suggests a deep, ancient connection with the star and its inhabitants.

In contemporary spiritual and channeling communities, Sirians are often portrayed as highly evolved beings aiding humanity's spiritual evolution. Notable channelers and authors, such as Patricia Cori and Barbara Marciniak, have shared messages from the Sirians, emphasizing their role in guiding Earth through significant transformations and ascension processes.

These historical perspectives highlight the enduring reverence for Sirius and its beings, underscoring their influence and significance in guiding humanity toward higher wisdom and spiritual alignment.

Embracing the Journey with Sirians

Working with the Sirians offers a unique opportunity to connect with advanced beings dedicated to supporting humanity's spiritual journey. Their wisdom, healing, and guidance can impact your life, helping you navigate the complexities of spiritual growth and align with your highest potential.

As you explore this connection, honor the deep history and teachings of the Sirians. Whether through meditation, contemplation of nature, or study, allow their energies to guide and inspire you. Embrace their presence with respect and openness, and let their light illuminate your path toward greater wisdom and understanding.

Alex McCann Johnson

Chapter 143

Vegans

In my galactic exploration, I encountered the concept of beings from the star system Vega. Their energy was immediately captivating, characterized by a sense of clarity and enlightenment. Vegans, as they are commonly referred to, are advanced beings from Vega, the brightest star in the constellation Lyra. Known for their wisdom and deep understanding of the cosmic order, Vegans offer guidance in intellectual pursuits, spiritual growth, and the alignment of body, mind, and spirit.

Vegans are highly evolved entities originating from Vega, a star located approximately 25 light-years from Earth. Vega holds significant prominence in the night sky, often serving as a guiding star in navigation due to its brightness and position. The beings from Vega are reputed for their intellectual and spiritual advancements, embodying a deep connection to the universal consciousness.

The Vegans are often described as having a serene and calm demeanor, reflective of their advanced state of spiritual and intellectual evolution. They are associated with the integration of intellect and spirituality, helping us harmonize our mental capacities with our higher spiritual understanding. Their guidance is particularly beneficial in areas of intellectual exploration, technological innovation, and deep spiritual insight.

The Spiritual Significance of Vegans

Vegans play a crucial role in helping humanity evolve intellectually and spiritually. Their influence is pivotal in several key areas:

Intellectual Advancement: Vegans are known for their understanding of the universe and the intricate workings of the mind. They assist us in enhancing our cognitive abilities, fostering intellectual growth, and encouraging the pursuit of knowledge. Their guidance can lead to breakthroughs in scientific and technological fields, promoting innovations that benefit humanity.

Spiritual Integration: Beyond their intellectual prowess, Vegans are deeply spiritual beings. They help us bridge the gap between the mind and spirit, teaching us how to integrate intellectual understanding with spiritual wisdom. This integration fosters a holistic approach to personal and collective growth, aligning our mental faculties with our spiritual aspirations.

Harmonizing Energies: Vegans are adept at balancing and harmonizing energies. They guide us in aligning our physical, mental, and spiritual selves, promoting overall well-being and a sense of inner peace. Their energy is calming and centering, helping us navigate the complexities of life with clarity and poise.

Cosmic Connection: As beings from Vega, Vegans have a connection to the cosmic order. They help us understand our place in the universe and align with the larger cosmic flow. This connection enhances our ability to perceive the interconnections between all aspects of existence, fostering a sense of unity and purpose.

In my experience, working with Vegans has provided insights into the nature of consciousness and the integration of intellect and spirituality. Their presence is a guiding light in my journey towards greater understanding and alignment.

Recognizing and Connecting with Vegans

Connecting with the Vegans involves tuning into their specific energies and inviting their guidance into your life. Here are some steps to help you recognize and establish a connection with these advanced beings:

Meditate on the Star Vega: During meditation, focus on the bright light of Vega in the night sky. Visualize its energy reaching out to you, inviting you to connect with the wisdom of the Vegans. Be open to any sensations, thoughts, or images that arise as you meditate on this star.

Seek Intellectual and Spiritual Balance: Engage in practices that harmonize your intellectual pursuits with your spiritual growth. This could include studying spiritual texts, exploring new areas of knowledge, or contemplating the interconnectedness of all things. The Vegans are likely to engage with you when you seek to balance these aspects of yourself.

Pay Attention to Signs of Clarity and Insight: Vegans often communicate through moments of sudden clarity or deep insights. If you experience these "aha" moments, particularly in intellectual or spiritual contexts, it may be a sign that the Vegans are guiding you.

Engage in Harmonizing Practices: Participate in activities that promote balance and alignment, such as yoga, tai chi, or energy work. These practices can help you attune to the harmonious energies of the Vegans and facilitate a deeper connection.

Study Cosmic and Intellectual Concepts: Delve into subjects related to cosmology, advanced technologies, or spiritual philosophy. Exploring these areas can open channels of communication with the Vegans and align you with their energies.

Prayer for Vegan Guidance: "Beings of Vega, I invite your presence and wisdom into my life. Guide me in harmonizing my intellect with my spirit and help me to align with the cosmic flow. Please assist me in my pursuit of knowledge and spiritual understanding and illuminate my path with your clarity and insight. Thank you for your guidance and light."

Historical Significance of Vegans

The historical significance of Vegans is intertwined with ancient cosmology and modern spiritual thought. In various cultural myths and legends, Vega has been revered as a significant star with profound spiritual implications.

Vega's prominence in the sky has made it a focal point in the astronomy and mythology of many ancient cultures. In Chinese mythology, Vega is known as "Zhi Nu," part of the legend of the weaver girl and the cowherd, symbolizing love and perseverance. The star's bright and stable light was often associated with guidance and cosmic order, making it a key figure in celestial navigation and timekeeping.

In contemporary spiritual and metaphysical communities, Vegans are often described as highly advanced beings with a deep connection to Earth and humanity. Books and channeled messages from figures like Patricia Cori and others have brought attention to the spiritual guidance offered by the Vegans. Their influence is seen as pivotal in helping humanity transition into higher states of consciousness and integrating new paradigms of thought.

Vega has also captured the interest of astronomers and scientists. Its brightness and proximity to Earth have made it a subject of extensive study. The star's prominence in the study of stellar evolution and its role in marking the northern pole star in the distant future highlight its ongoing significance in both scientific and spiritual contexts.

These historical perspectives underscore the enduring relevance of Vega and its beings, offering a bridge between ancient wisdom and modern exploration.

Embracing the Journey with Vegans

Working with the Vegans offers a unique opportunity to align with beings who embody the integration of intellect and spirituality. Their guidance can lead to personal growth and a deeper understanding of the cosmos.

Guided by Spirits

As you explore this connection, honor the wisdom and teachings of the Vegans. Whether through meditation, intellectual exploration, or harmonizing practices, allow their energies to guide and inspire you. Embrace their presence with respect and curiosity, and let their light illuminate your path toward greater clarity and understanding.

Alex McCann Johnson

Chapter 144

Andromedans

My first encounter with Andromedans came during a deep meditation session focused on exploring higher dimensions. Their energy felt incredibly expansive, embodying freedom and wisdom. Andromedans are beings from the Andromeda Galaxy, known for their advanced consciousness and dedication to promoting universal freedom and enlightenment. They are often described as benevolent guides who help us expand our awareness and break free from limiting beliefs and structures.

Andromedans originate from the Andromeda Galaxy, our closest galactic neighbor, situated over 2.5 million light-years from Earth. This galaxy, with its vast spiral arms and stunning beauty, mirrors the expansive nature of its inhabitants. Andromedans are believed to be highly evolved beings who possess a deep understanding of the universe and the principles of freedom and higher consciousness.

Characterized by their advanced spiritual and technological prowess, Andromedans are often depicted as tall, graceful beings with a light, ethereal presence. Their primary mission is to assist other civilizations, including humanity, in their spiritual evolution and to foster a sense of universal connectedness and freedom.

The Spiritual Significance of Andromedans

Andromedans play a crucial role in guiding us towards higher states of consciousness and promoting the principles of freedom and expansion. Here's how they contribute to our spiritual journey:

Promoting Higher Consciousness: Andromedans help us elevate our consciousness to understand deeper spiritual truths and universal laws. They guide us in expanding our awareness beyond the physical realm and into the higher dimensions of existence. Their insights often lead to realizations about our purpose and the nature of reality.

Encouraging Freedom and Sovereignty: A core message from the Andromedans is the importance of personal and collective freedom. They inspire us to break free from limiting beliefs, societal constraints, and outdated structures that no longer serve our highest good. Their energy supports the pursuit of autonomy and the realization of our true potential.

Fostering Unity and Universal Connection: Andromedans emphasize the interconnectedness of all beings and the importance of unity in diversity. They teach us to see beyond our differences and to recognize the shared essence that binds us all. This perspective fosters a sense of universal love and cooperation.

Guiding Technological and Spiritual Advancement: With their advanced knowledge, Andromedans assist in harmonizing technological progress with spiritual evolution. They guide us in using technology ethically and wisely, ensuring that it serves the greater good and supports our spiritual growth.

In my experience, working with Andromedans has opened new vistas of understanding and freedom. Their guidance has helped me navigate complex spiritual concepts and embrace a more expansive view of life.

Recognizing and Connecting with Andromedans

Connecting with Andromedans involves tuning into their specific frequencies and inviting their expansive, liberating energy into your life. Here are some steps to help you recognize and establish a connection with these advanced beings:

Meditate on the Andromeda Galaxy: During meditation, visualize the Andromeda Galaxy in its vast and beautiful form. Imagine its light reaching out to you, inviting you to connect with the Andromedans. Feel their expansive and freeing energy as you meditate.

Seek Personal and Collective Freedom: Engage in practices and make choices that promote freedom and autonomy, both for yourself and others. The Andromedans are likely to connect with you when you align with their values of freedom and expansion.

Pay Attention to Signs of Expansion and Liberation: Andromedans often communicate through experiences and insights that encourage you to expand your horizons and break free from limitations. Notice any sudden feelings of liberation or new perspectives that open up to you.

Engage in Practices That Elevate Consciousness: Participate in activities that raise your vibration and expand your awareness, such as advanced meditation techniques, energy work, or studying higher-dimensional concepts. These practices can help you attune to the Andromedan energy.

Prayer for Andromedan Guidance: "Beings of Andromeda, I invite your expansive and liberating presence into my life. Guide me in elevating my consciousness and embracing the freedom and unity of the universe. Help me to break free from limitations and to realize my true potential. Thank you for your wisdom and guidance."

Historical Significance of Andromedans

The Andromedans have a significant place in various spiritual and metaphysical traditions, often seen as messengers of higher wisdom and freedom.

While direct references to the Andromedans are rare in ancient texts, many cultures speak of star beings and celestial guides that resemble the descriptions of Andromedans. These beings were often seen as teachers and helpers who brought knowledge and enlightenment from the stars. The expansive and liberating nature attributed to the Andromedans can be paralleled with the myths of gods and heroes who sought to uplift humanity.

In contemporary spiritual literature, Andromedans are frequently mentioned in the context of extraterrestrial guides who are here to assist humanity's transition to higher states of consciousness. Books and channelings from authors like Alex Collier and others have brought attention to the Andromedans' role in guiding our spiritual evolution and promoting universal freedom.

The Andromeda Galaxy itself has been a subject of fascination for astronomers and scientists. Its proximity and similarity to our Milky Way make it an object of study for understanding galactic formation and evolution. This scientific interest reflects humanity's broader curiosity about our cosmic neighbors and the potential for intelligent life beyond our galaxy.

These historical perspectives highlight the enduring relevance of Andromedans and their influence on our understanding of freedom, consciousness, and cosmic connection.

Embracing the Journey with Andromedans

Working with the Andromedans offers a unique opportunity to align with beings who embody the principles of higher consciousness and universal freedom. Their guidance can lead to personal liberation and a deeper connection to the cosmos.

As you explore this connection, honor the wisdom and teachings of the Andromedans. Whether through meditation, seeking personal freedom, or engaging in practices that elevate your consciousness, allow their energy to guide and inspire you. Embrace their presence with respect and curiosity, and let their expansive light illuminate your path toward greater understanding and freedom.

Chapter 145

Orions

My first introduction to Orions came through my fascination with the Orion constellation, particularly the famous Orion's Belt. The alignment and brightness of these stars have always drawn me, sparking curiosity about their deeper spiritual significance. Orions, as spiritual guides, are known for their dedication to truth, balance, and order. They are often seen as guardians of cosmic knowledge and arbiters of justice, helping us navigate our spiritual paths with clarity and integrity.

Orions originate from the star system associated with the Orion constellation, one of the most recognizable patterns in the night sky. This constellation is steeped in myth and lore, often depicted as a mighty hunter in various cultures. The beings from this star system are believed to possess advanced wisdom and a strong sense of justice, mirroring the constellation's prominent and powerful presence in the sky.

Orions are typically characterized by their commitment to truth and balance. They are seen as impartial and discerning, often guiding those who seek to uncover deeper truths and align with higher principles. Their energy is often described as sharp and focused, cutting through confusion and deception to reveal clarity and order.

The Spiritual Significance of Orions

Orions play a crucial role in guiding us towards truth and balance in our spiritual journeys. Here's how they contribute to our growth and understanding:

Promoting Truth and Integrity: Orions are dedicated to the pursuit of truth and the maintenance of integrity. They encourage us to seek and speak the truth in all aspects of our lives. Their guidance helps us align with our authentic selves and live in accordance with our highest values.

Fostering Balance and Harmony: These guides are deeply attuned to the principles of balance and order. They assist us in finding harmony within ourselves and in our interactions with the world. Whether it's balancing our emotions, relationships, or spiritual practices, Orions help us achieve equilibrium and stability.

Illuminating Cosmic Knowledge: Orions are keepers of cosmic knowledge. They help us access and understand universal truths, expanding our awareness beyond the mundane and into the mysteries of the cosmos. Their insights often lead to deeper spiritual revelations and a greater understanding of the interconnectedness of all things.

Guiding Justice and Fairness: With their strong sense of justice, Orions guide us in making fair and just decisions. They support us in standing up for what is right and ensuring that our actions align with ethical and moral standards. Their influence encourages us to act with integrity and uphold the principles of fairness.

In my experiences with Orions, I have found their guidance to be unwavering and precise. They have helped me cut through confusion and find clarity in moments of uncertainty, always steering me toward truth and balance.

Recognizing and Connecting with Orions

Connecting with Orions involves tuning into their distinctive energy and inviting their guidance into your life. Here are some ways to recognize and establish a connection with these wise and discerning beings:

Meditate on Orion's Belt: During meditation, focus on the three bright stars of Orion's Belt. Visualize their alignment and brightness, and invite the energy of the Orions to connect with you. Feel their sharp and clear presence as you meditate.

Seek Truth and Clarity: Engage in practices that promote honesty and transparency in your life. Orions are likely to connect with you when you are committed to seeking and living your truth. Reflect on areas where you can be more authentic and align with your true self.

Pay Attention to Signs of Balance and Order: Orions often communicate through experiences that encourage balance and harmony. Notice any situations that call for fairness or reveal deeper truths. These moments can be a sign of Orion guidance.

Engage in Ethical and Fair Practices: Strive to make decisions that are fair and just, both for yourself and others. Orions support actions that uphold integrity and justice, and aligning with these values can help you connect with their energy.

Prayer for Orion Guidance: "Beings of Orion, I invite your wisdom and clarity into my life. Guide me towards truth and balance, and help me align with my highest principles. Illuminate my path with your discernment and support me in making fair and just decisions. Thank you for your unwavering guidance and integrity."

Historical Significance of Orions

The Orions have significant historical and cultural relevance, often symbolizing wisdom, strength, and guidance in various traditions.

In ancient Egyptian mythology, the stars of the Orion constellation were associated with Osiris, the god of the afterlife, and were believed to be a gateway to the heavens. The alignment of the pyramids at Giza with Orion's Belt underscores the constellation's importance in connecting the earthly realm with the divine.

Many indigenous cultures around the world, including the Aboriginal Australians and Native Americans, have stories and legends about the Orion constellation. These tales often depict Orion as a hunter or warrior, symbolizing strength, leadership, and the pursuit of truth.

Alex McCann Johnson

In contemporary spiritual circles, Orions are often seen as advanced beings who guide humanity toward greater wisdom and understanding. Channelers and spiritual practitioners frequently describe encounters with Orions as enlightening and transformative, offering deep insights into the nature of reality and the cosmos.

These historical perspectives highlight the enduring significance of Orions as symbols of truth, balance, and cosmic knowledge. Their influence spans across time and cultures, reflecting their universal role in guiding humanity toward higher understanding.

Embracing the Journey with Orions

Working with Orions offers a unique opportunity to align with beings who embody the principles of truth and balance. Their guidance can lead to a deeper connection to universal wisdom.

As you explore this connection, honor the integrity and discernment of the Orions. Whether through meditation, seeking truth, or engaging in practices that promote balance and fairness, allow their energy to guide and inspire you. Embrace their presence with respect and curiosity, and let their sharp light illuminate your path toward greater truth and harmony.

Chapter 146

Lyrans

In my explorations of galactic guides, the Lyrans stood out as beings of ancient wisdom with adventurous spirit. My initial fascination with the Lyrans was sparked by their reputation as the original explorers of the cosmos, seeding knowledge and civilization across various star systems. The Lyrans are believed to come from the star system of Lyra, and their energy is often described as pioneering, wise, and deeply connected to the origins of many galactic civilizations.

The Lyrans are thought to be some of the oldest and most advanced beings in the galaxy. Their civilization is often considered the root race from which many other star races have descended, including the Pleiadians and the Sirians. Lyrans are depicted as having a regal and feline-like appearance, reflecting their agility, strength, and nobility.

Lyrans are known for their deep connection to the cosmic wisdom of the universe. They are seen as the keepers of ancient knowledge and are often called upon to help us reconnect with our own origins and spiritual heritage. Their energy is pioneering, encouraging exploration and the pursuit of higher understanding. The Lyrans' influence can be felt in our quests for knowledge, adventure, and the expansion of consciousness.

The Spiritual Significance of Lyrans

Lyrans play a vital role in our spiritual development by offering guidance that helps us reconnect with our ancient wisdom and encourages exploration. Here's how they contribute to our growth:

Connecting to Ancient Wisdom: Lyrans are often regarded as the guardians of ancient knowledge. They help us access and understand the deep spiritual truths that have been passed down through the ages. Their guidance can illuminate the mysteries of our origins and the greater cosmic plan.

Encouraging Exploration: With their pioneering spirit, Lyrans inspire us to explore both our inner and outer worlds. They encourage us to seek new experiences, expand our horizons, and embrace the journey of discovery. This exploration is not limited to physical travel but extends to the realms of ideas, spirituality, and personal growth.

Fostering Independence and Sovereignty: Lyrans are deeply connected to the concepts of personal power and sovereignty. They guide us in asserting our independence, standing in our truth, and taking responsibility for our own paths. Their influence helps us cultivate self-reliance and confidence in our abilities to shape our destinies.

Promoting Higher Learning and Enlightenment: As keepers of ancient wisdom, Lyrans emphasize the importance of higher learning and spiritual enlightenment. They support our endeavors to acquire knowledge, deepen our understanding of the universe, and evolve spiritually.

In my encounters with Lyran energy, I have found them to be profound guides who offer deep insights into the nature of the universe and our place within it. Their encouragement has led me to explore new dimensions of thought and spirituality, opening doors to greater wisdom and understanding.

Recognizing and Connecting with Lyrans

Connecting with Lyrans involves tuning into their distinctive energy of ancient wisdom and exploration. Here are some ways to recognize and establish a connection with these guiding beings:

Meditate on the Lyra Constellation: During meditation, focus on the constellation Lyra. Visualize its stars and feel the energy of the

Lyrans flowing into your space. Invite their presence and be open to any messages or insights they may offer.

Seek Knowledge and Wisdom: Engage in activities that promote learning and exploration. Whether it's studying ancient civilizations, delving into spiritual texts, or exploring new fields of knowledge, align yourself with the Lyran spirit of curiosity and discovery.

Embrace Your Inner Explorer: Lyrans are pioneers at heart. Embark on new adventures, try new things, and expand your comfort zones. Allow their energy to inspire you to explore both the external world and your inner landscape.

Pay Attention to Feline Symbols: Lyrans are often associated with feline traits and symbols. Notice if you frequently encounter images or themes related to cats or lions, as these could be signs of Lyran guidance.

Cultivate Independence: Practice standing in your personal power and asserting your sovereignty. Lyrans support us in being self-reliant and confident in our ability to navigate our own paths.

Prayer for Lyran Guidance: "Beings of Lyra, I invite your ancient wisdom and pioneering spirit into my life. Guide me in my quest for knowledge and exploration. Help me reconnect with my origins and embrace my journey of discovery. Thank you for your profound insights and support."

Historical Significance of Lyrans

The Lyrans have a rich and influential presence in various historical and cultural contexts, often seen as foundational beings in the lore of many star races and civilizations.

In Greek mythology, the Lyra constellation is associated with the myth of Orpheus, whose music had the power to charm all living things and even inanimate objects. This myth reflects the Lyrans' connection to deep, transformative knowledge and the power to influence through wisdom.

Many spiritual traditions and channeling sources regard the Lyrans as one of the earliest space-faring races. They are believed to have played a crucial role in seeding life and civilization across various star systems, including the Pleiades and Sirius. Their legacy is seen as foundational to the development of many advanced galactic societies.

In contemporary spiritual practices, the Lyrans are often invoked for their wisdom and guidance in navigating complex spiritual paths. They are seen as mentors and protectors, offering deep insights and encouraging personal and collective evolution.

These historical perspectives highlight the Lyrans' enduring influence as keepers of wisdom and pioneers of exploration. Their presence in myth, lore, and spiritual teachings underscores their role as guiding lights in humanity's quest for knowledge and enlightenment.

Embracing the Journey with Lyrans

Working with Lyrans offers an opportunity to align with beings who embody the principles of ancient wisdom and exploration. Their guidance can lead to transformative experiences and a deeper connection to the vast universe.

As you explore this connection, honor the wisdom and pioneering spirit of the Lyrans. Whether through meditation, seeking knowledge, or embracing new adventures, allow their energy to guide and inspire you. Embrace their presence with respect and curiosity, and let their ancient light illuminate your path toward greater understanding and growth.

Chapter 147

Zetas

The Zetas intrigued me due to their connection to advanced technology and extraterrestrial wisdom. Known for their enigmatic presence and deep curiosity about the universe, Zetas are believed to come from the Zeta Reticuli star system, located approximately 39 light-years from Earth. They are often associated with themes of evolution, genetic research, and the bridging of interstellar knowledge.

Zetas are extraterrestrial beings often described as having a humanoid form with distinct characteristics such as large heads and almond-shaped eyes. Their appearance has become iconic in modern UFO lore and spirituality. Despite their sometimes unsettling appearance, Zetas are considered to be highly intelligent, spiritually evolved, and deeply committed to the advancement of knowledge and understanding.

Zetas are known for their incredible scientific and technological prowess. They possess a keen interest in the evolutionary processes of different species, including humanity. This fascination is reflected in their frequent involvement in genetic research and their role in guiding the evolution of consciousness on Earth.

The Spiritual Significance of Zetas

Zetas play a unique and significant role in our spiritual and evolutionary journey. Here's how they contribute to our growth and understanding:

Advancing Technological Wisdom: Zetas are often seen as guardians of advanced technological knowledge. They inspire us to push the boundaries of science and technology, encouraging innovation that aligns with ethical and spiritual principles. Their influence helps bridge the gap between advanced technology and spiritual evolution.

Guiding Evolution: With their deep interest in genetic research, Zetas assists in understanding and guiding the evolutionary processes. They help humanity realize its potential for higher consciousness and spiritual development. Their guidance supports the integration of advanced genetic knowledge to improve health and expand human capabilities.

Promoting Interstellar Connections: Zetas encourages the exploration of interstellar relationships and the understanding of different star races. They help us see beyond Earth-centric perspectives and foster a sense of unity and cooperation with other beings in the cosmos.

Facilitating Personal Transformation: On a personal level, Zetas can assist individuals in navigating shifts in consciousness. Their energy supports the release of old patterns and the adoption of new, more evolved ways of thinking and being.

In my encounters with Zeta Energy, I have found them to be incredibly insightful guides who challenge conventional thinking and open new pathways to understanding. Their presence can be both disconcerting and enlightening, pushing us to expand our horizons and embrace new possibilities.

Recognizing and Connecting with Zetas

Connecting with Zetas involves tuning into their unique energy of curiosity and advanced wisdom. Here are some ways to recognize and establish a connection with these enigmatic beings:

Meditate on Advanced Technologies: During meditation, focus on the themes of advanced technology and evolution. Visualize connecting with the Zetas and inviting their insights into your meditative space. Be open to receiving innovative ideas and solutions.

Seek Knowledge in Science and Evolution: Engage in studies or activities related to genetics, technology, or evolutionary biology. Aligning yourself with these fields can attune you to the Zeta energy and open communication channels.

Explore Interstellar Concepts: Expand your understanding of the cosmos by studying astronomy, astrophysics, or the mythology of different star systems. This exploration helps create a bridge to the interstellar perspectives of the Zetas.

Pay Attention to Patterns and Symbols: Zetas are known to communicate through intricate patterns and symbols, often related to technology or genetics. Notice if you encounter recurring symbols or complex patterns in your daily life, as these could be signs of Zeta guidance.

Embrace Transformation: Be open to personal and spiritual transformations. The Zetas' energy often brings about significant changes and shifts. Embrace these changes as opportunities for growth and evolution.

Prayer for Zeta Guidance: "Beings of Zeta Reticuli, I invite your advanced wisdom and transformative energy into my life. Guide me in understanding the mysteries of technology and evolution. Help me embrace change and expand my consciousness. Thank you for your profound insights and support."

Historical Significance of Zetas

The Zetas have captured the imagination of many through their frequent appearance in both ancient and modern contexts.

Some ancient astronaut theories suggest that beings resembling Zetas have visited Earth throughout history, contributing to the development of human civilization. These theories are supported by interpretations of

855

ancient art and texts that depict beings with features similar to the Zetas.

In contemporary times, Zetas are often linked to UFO sightings and abduction phenomena. The famous incident of the "Grey" aliens, associated with the Zetas, has become a cornerstone of modern UFO lore. These encounters have sparked significant interest and research into extraterrestrial life and its influence on humanity.

In the realm of spirituality, many channels and mediums report receiving messages from Zeta beings. These communications often focus on themes of human evolution, advanced technology, and interstellar cooperation. Zetas are seen as guides who help humanity prepare for future advancements and integration with the broader cosmic community.

The depiction of Zeta-like beings in movies, literature, and art has become a cultural phenomenon. They represent the archetype of the "otherworldly visitor," symbolizing humanity's curiosity about life beyond Earth and the potential for advanced civilizations.

These historical perspectives highlight the Zetas' enduring influence as guides and pioneers of knowledge. Their presence in both ancient and modern narratives underscores their role in expanding our understanding of the universe and our place within it.

Embracing the Journey with Zetas

Working with Zetas offers a unique opportunity to align with beings who embody the principles of advanced wisdom and evolutionary transformation. Their guidance can lead to great innovations, helping us navigate the complexities of modern life and the mysteries of the cosmos.

As you explore this connection, honor the Zetas' commitment to advancing knowledge and fostering personal and collective evolution. Whether through meditation, scientific exploration, or embracing change, allow their energy to guide and inspire you. Embrace their presence with respect and curiosity, and let their advanced wisdom

Guided by Spirits

illuminate your path toward greater understanding and growth.

Alex McCann Johnson

Chapter 148
Draconians

In my journey exploring the vast landscape of galactic beings, I encountered the Draconians. Initially, like many, I perceived them as beings solely driven by power and control, often viewed through the lens of fear and negativity. However, my experiences and deeper explorations revealed a more nuanced reality. Draconians, especially those aligned with the light, can be profound healers and guides, offering unique perspectives into energy healing.

Draconians originate from the star system Alpha Draconis and are often depicted as reptilian beings with a commanding presence. Their appearance is characterized by a strong, dragon-like form, symbolizing power and strength. Draconians are known for their complex societal structures and a deep understanding of energy and cosmic laws.

These beings possess a strong connection to the earth and its ley lines, understanding the intricate balance and energy flow that sustains our planet. Draconians are often seen as guardians of ancient wisdom, particularly related to earth's hidden energies and the deep-rooted knowledge of the cosmos.

The Spiritual Significance of Draconians

Despite the fear-based narratives surrounding them, Draconians aligned with the light play crucial roles in spiritual growth and healing. They embody the transformative power of facing and integrating our shadows, helping us understand and harness our personal and collective power.

Transformative Healing: Draconians are masters of transformative healing. They can guide individuals through deep-seated fears and traumas, offering insights into the nature of power and control. Their energy is potent and can catalyze significant personal and spiritual growth.

Guardians of Ancient Wisdom: Draconians hold vast reservoirs of ancient wisdom. They are guardians of knowledge related to earth's energies and cosmic principles. Their guidance can help us reconnect with the earth, understand its energy flows, and tap into the ancient wisdom that sustains our existence.

Empowerment and Self-Mastery: Working with Draconians can be a journey into empowerment and self-mastery. They teach us to embrace our strength, face our shadows, and transform our challenges into sources of power and growth. Their influence encourages us to take control of our lives with integrity and wisdom.

Balancing Light and Shadow: Draconians excel at balancing light and shadow. They help us integrate all aspects of our being, fostering a deeper understanding of our motivations and the dynamics of power. This integration is essential for achieving harmony and alignment in our spiritual journey.

In my interactions with Draconian energy, I have found them to be formidable yet compassionate guides. Their presence is both challenging and uplifting, pushing me to confront and transcend my limitations.

Recognizing and Connecting with Draconians

Establishing a connection with Draconians involves openness to their powerful and sometimes intense energy. Here are ways to recognize and connect with Draconian guides:

Meditate on Earth Energies: Draconians have a deep connection to the earth. During meditation, focus on grounding and the energies of the earth. Visualize connecting with the ley lines and the earth's core, inviting Draconian guides to share their wisdom and healing.

Embrace Personal Power: Draconians teach about power and self-mastery. Reflect on areas of your life where you can embrace your strength and assertiveness. Ask your Draconian guides to assist in harnessing your personal power for positive transformation.

Seek Ancient Wisdom: Engage in studies or activities related to ancient knowledge and the earth's energies. This alignment can attune you to Draconian wisdom and open channels for communication.

Balance Light and Shadow: Draconians help balance light and shadow. Practice self-reflection and shadow work, inviting Draconian guidance to help integrate all aspects of your being.

Prayer for Draconian Guidance: "Mighty Draconian beings, I invite your wisdom and transformative energy into my life. Guide me in embracing my power and healing my shadows. Help me connect with the ancient wisdom of the earth and harness my strength for the highest good."

Historical Significance of Draconians

Draconians have a rich presence in various mythologies and historical narratives, often symbolizing both the protective and destructive aspects of power.

Many ancient cultures have dragon-like beings in their mythologies. For example, in Chinese culture, dragons are revered as powerful and benevolent creatures associated with wisdom, strength, and good fortune. Similarly, in European folklore, dragons often guard treasures and sacred sites, representing both the challenges and rewards of seeking deeper knowledge and truth.

In ancient Sumerian and Mesopotamian texts, there are references to reptilian gods and beings, such as the Anunnaki. These entities are often depicted as possessing great knowledge and power, influencing the development of human civilization.

In contemporary UFO and extraterrestrial narratives, Draconians are frequently mentioned. While some accounts portray them as domineering, others recognize the existence of benevolent Draconians committed to guiding humanity toward a balanced and empowered existence.

Within spiritual and esoteric traditions, Draconians are seen as guardians of ancient earth wisdom. They are believed to hold keys to understanding the deeper workings of the planet and the cosmos, offering guidance on harnessing and balancing earth energies.

These historical perspectives highlight the multifaceted nature of Draconians. They are beings of immense power and knowledge, guiding us to understand and balance the complex dynamics of power, wisdom, and transformation.

Embracing the Journey with Draconians

Working with Draconians offers a unique opportunity to engage with powerful energies that challenge and transform. Their guidance can lead to insights into personal power, healing, and the ancient wisdom of the earth.

As you explore this connection, honor the Draconians' depth of knowledge and their role in guiding transformation. Whether through meditation, grounding practices, or seeking ancient wisdom, allow their energy to inspire and empower you. Embrace their presence with respect and openness, and let their transformative power illuminate your path toward greater understanding and growth.

Chapter 149
Mintakan

From a young age, I was always fascinated by the idea of distant star systems and the beings that might inhabit them. Among these, the Mintakans, hailing from the star system of Mintaka in the constellation Orion, captivated my imagination. These beings are often described as pure, loving, and deeply connected to water, embodying the qualities of clarity, fluidity, and purity.

Mintakans are said to be beings of pure light and water, originating from a star system that is no longer in existence. It is believed that their planet, Mintaka, was composed mostly of water, making them intrinsically connected to this element. They are known for their high vibrational frequency, embodying love, purity, and clarity.

Mintakans are described as having a luminous presence, often seen as beings of light with an ethereal, almost transparent quality. They are associated with the qualities of fluidity and adaptability, much like water, which can take any shape and cleanse impurities. Their presence is often calming and soothing, providing a sense of peace and tranquility.

The Spiritual Significance of Mintakans

Mintakans hold a special place in spiritual teachings due to their association with purity, healing, and clarity. They are considered to be gentle yet powerful guides, helping individuals cleanse their energy, find clarity in their lives, and connect with their true selves.

Purity and Cleansing: Mintakans are often called upon to help cleanse and purify one's energy. Just as water washes away dirt and impurities, Mintakans assist in clearing negative energies and emotional blockages, helping individuals achieve a state of purity and balance.

Clarity and Insight: These beings are associated with clarity of thought and purpose. They help individuals see through confusion and fog, providing clear insights and understanding. Their guidance can be invaluable when making important decisions or seeking direction in life.

Connection to Water: The Mintakan connection to water is profound. They encourage individuals to connect with the healing and transformative properties of water. Whether through meditative practices by the sea, swimming, or simply drinking more water, Mintakans emphasize the importance of this element in our spiritual and physical well-being.

Healing and Tranquility: Mintakans are known for their healing abilities. Their gentle, soothing energy can help heal emotional wounds and bring a sense of peace and tranquility. They are excellent guides for those dealing with stress, anxiety, or emotional turmoil.

In my own spiritual journey, connecting with Mintakans has been a deeply healing and enlightening experience. Their energy brings a sense of calm and clarity, helping me navigate through life's challenges with a clearer perspective and a lighter heart.

Recognizing and Connecting with Mintakans

Connecting with Mintakans involves embracing the qualities of purity, clarity, and fluidity. Here are some ways to recognize and connect with Mintakan guides:

Meditate with Water: Incorporate water into your meditation practice. Sit by a body of water, visualize a flowing river, or simply hold a bowl of water in your hands. Invite the presence of Mintakans and focus on the qualities of purity and clarity.

Seek Clarity and Simplicity: Mintakans are drawn to simplicity and clarity. Clear your space of clutter, simplify your routines, and seek clarity in your thoughts and actions. This creates an inviting environment for Mintakans to connect with you.

Embrace Water Healing: Engage in practices that involve water healing, such as swimming, taking salt baths, or drinking plenty of clean water. Visualize water washing away negative energies and bringing a sense of purity and balance.

Pay Attention to Signs: Mintakans may communicate through signs related to water, such as finding shells, hearing the sound of waves, or feeling drawn to the sea. Be open to these signs and trust their guidance.

Prayer for Mintakan Guidance: "Mintakans of pure light and water, I invite your presence into my life. Help me cleanse and purify my energy, bring clarity to my thoughts and actions, and guide me with your healing and tranquil energy. Thank you for your loving and gentle support."

Historical Significance of Mintakans

Mintakans, while less commonly referenced than other star beings, hold a unique place in the tapestry of cosmic guides. Their association with the star system Mintaka in Orion links them to one of the most significant and recognizable constellations in the night sky.

The constellation Orion, home to the Mintakan star system, has been revered in various ancient cultures. In ancient Egypt, Orion was associated with Osiris, the god of the afterlife, and the pyramids were aligned with the stars in Orion's belt. This alignment symbolized the pharaohs' journey to the afterlife and their eternal connection to the cosmos.

In modern mysticism and spiritual teachings, Mintaka is often seen as a lost world of pure love and light. The idea that Mintakans originated from a world predominantly composed of water adds a layer of mystical allure and highlights their unique connection to the element of water and its healing properties.

In contemporary starseed communities, Mintakans are recognized as gentle, loving beings who have chosen to assist Earth in its time of transition. They are believed to bring the qualities of purity, clarity, and healing, offering their wisdom to those who seek to elevate their spiritual awareness.

The historical and cultural significance of Mintakans underscores their role as guides of purity, clarity, and healing. Their connection to Orion and the mystical associations with this constellation enrich their presence in spiritual traditions.

Embracing the Journey with Mintakans

Working with Mintakans offers a pathway to deeper clarity, healing, and spiritual purity. Their gentle and loving energy provides support and guidance, helping us navigate our spiritual journeys with a sense of peace and purpose.

As you explore your connection with Mintakans, approach with openness and respect. Whether through meditation, water healing practices, or seeking simplicity and clarity in your life, allow their guidance to illuminate your path. Embrace their teachings with gratitude and let their pure light inspire you to achieve greater spiritual balance and understanding.

Chapter 150
Blue Avians

In the expansive universe of spiritual guides, Blue Avians stand out with their unique and bird-like presence. Known for their deep wisdom and exceptional communication abilities, these ethereal beings resemble birds with a striking blue hue. My first encounter with Blue Avians was during energy work. Their presence felt like a serene wave of understanding and clarity, guiding me toward a deeper comprehension of the universe and my place within it.

Blue Avians are highly advanced beings often described as tall, bird-like figures with radiant blue feathers. Their eyes exude intelligence and kindness, reflecting their role as communicators and wisdom bearers in the cosmos. They originate from higher dimensions, making them accessible primarily through meditative and astral practices rather than physical encounters.

These beings are known for their ability to convey complex spiritual insights in an easily understandable manner. They are considered guardians of higher wisdom and play a pivotal role in helping humanity evolve spiritually. Blue Avians often communicate telepathically, delivering messages that resonate deeply within our consciousness.

The Spiritual Significance of Blue Avians

Blue Avians hold a special place in spiritual teachings, often associated with higher consciousness, wisdom, and enhanced communication abilities. Their influence can be deeply transformative, guiding individuals and communities towards greater understanding and spiritual enlightenment.

Higher Consciousness: Blue Avians are seen as ambassadors of higher consciousness. They assist in expanding our awareness beyond the physical realm, encouraging us to explore and embrace higher states of being. Their guidance helps us tap into our innate wisdom and align with the universal truth.

Wisdom and Insight: As bearers of ancient wisdom, Blue Avians provide insights into the nature of reality and our spiritual journey. They help unravel the mysteries of existence and offer perspectives that foster personal and collective growth.

Enhanced Communication: These beings excel in facilitating clear and effective communication. They encourage us to express our truths with clarity and compassion, bridging gaps in understanding and fostering harmonious relationships.

Guides of Transformation: Blue Avians are catalysts for personal and spiritual transformation. They guide us through periods of change and growth, offering support and clarity as we navigate the complexities of our evolving paths.

In my experience, Blue Avians have helped me access deeper layers of understanding and communication, both within myself and in my interactions with others. Their presence is calming yet invigorating, pushing me to explore new dimensions of thought and existence.

Recognizing and Connecting with Blue Avians

Connecting with Blue Avians requires an open heart and a willingness to engage with higher frequencies of wisdom and communication. Here are ways to recognize and connect with Blue Avian guides:

Meditate on Blue Light: During meditation, visualize a soothing blue light surrounding you. Invite the presence of Blue Avians and open yourself to their messages. Their energy often feels like a gentle, yet powerful, wave of peace and clarity.

Focus on Communication and Understanding: Blue Avians are known for their exceptional communication abilities. Pay attention to moments of heightened clarity in your thoughts and expressions. These can be signs of their influence.

Seek Higher Wisdom: Engage in practices and studies that expand your spiritual knowledge. Blue Avians often guide those who are in pursuit of higher truths and understanding.

Embrace Transformation: Be open to changes and growth in your life. Blue Avians often assist during transformative periods, helping us navigate through challenges and evolve spiritually.

Prayer for Blue Avian Guidance: "Blue Avians of wisdom and light, I invite your presence into my life. Guide me towards higher understanding and help me communicate with clarity and compassion. Illuminate my path with your spiritual insights and support my journey of transformation."

Historical Significance of Blue Avians

Blue Avians have captured the imagination and reverence of many cultures and spiritual traditions, often seen as messengers of divine wisdom and celestial knowledge.

In ancient Egypt, Thoth, the god of wisdom and communication, is sometimes depicted with avian features. Thoth's representation as a bird-headed deity aligns closely with the attributes of Blue Avians, emphasizing their role in conveying higher wisdom and guiding humanity.

Some Native American tribes honor bird spirits as messengers between the physical and spiritual worlds. These beings are revered for their ability to travel between realms and bring back insights and guidance from the divine.

In contemporary spiritual teachings, Blue Avians have been

highlighted as advanced beings working to assist humanity's spiritual evolution. They are often associated with the transmission of higher knowledge and the promotion of peace and understanding on a global scale.

Various esoteric and channeled sources describe Blue Avians as part of the higher-dimensional beings guiding the earth through periods of transition and enlightenment. Their role in these teachings underscores their importance in facilitating communication and wisdom on a cosmic level.

The historical and cultural references to avian beings underscore the timeless and universal nature of Blue Avians as guides of wisdom and communication. Their influence continues to inspire and uplift those seeking higher truths and deeper connections.

Embracing the Journey with Blue Avians

Working with Blue Avians offers a pathway to deeper understanding, clearer communication, and transformation. Their presence invites us to elevate our consciousness and embrace the wisdom that transcends ordinary perception.

As you explore your connection with Blue Avians, approach with openness and respect. Whether through meditation, seeking higher knowledge, or enhancing your communication abilities, allow their guidance to illuminate your path. Embrace their teachings with gratitude and let their light inspire you to reach new heights of understanding and spiritual growth.

Chapter 151

Hadarians

In the expansiveness of galactic beings, the Hadarians stand out as emissaries of pure love and harmony. My journey into understanding the Hadarians began when I was exploring different star systems and their connections to human spirituality. Known for their ability to embody and spread unconditional love, Hadarians come from the Beta Centauri star system, also known as Hadar. These beings are dedicated to fostering deep connections and promoting peace and harmony among all beings.

Hadarians are beings of pure love and harmony. Originating from the Beta Centauri star system, they are often described as deeply compassionate, gentle, and nurturing. Their primary mission is to spread love and foster unity, making them powerful guides in matters of relationships and community building.

Hadarians are said to resonate at a very high frequency, embodying the essence of unconditional love. They often manifest their presence through feelings of warmth, peace, and profound connection. When they are around, you might feel an overwhelming sense of calm and acceptance, as if you are enveloped in a loving embrace.

In my interactions with Hadarian guides, I have experienced a deep sense of peace and an urge to cultivate more loving and compassionate relationships. They have helped me see the importance of community and the power of love to heal and transform.

Alex McCann Johnson

The Spiritual Significance of Hadarians

Hadarians hold a unique place in the realm of spiritual guides due to their connection to love and harmony. They are invaluable allies in promoting unity, healing relationships, and creating harmonious communities. Here are some key aspects of their spiritual significance:

Embodying Unconditional Love: Hadarians are known for their ability to embody and spread unconditional love. They teach us to love ourselves and others without conditions or judgments. Their guidance helps us open our hearts and embrace a more compassionate way of being.

Healing Relationships: One of the Hadarians' core missions is to heal and nurture relationships. Whether it's between family members, friends, or romantic partners, they offer support to help us cultivate deeper, more meaningful connections.

Promoting Peace and Unity: Hadarians work tirelessly to foster peace and unity. They inspire us to see beyond our differences and recognize the common bonds that unite us. Their influence encourages us to build communities based on love, respect, and mutual understanding.

Encouraging Compassion and Empathy: Hadarians help us develop greater compassion and empathy for others. They guide us to understand and share the feelings of others, fostering a sense of connectedness and mutual support.

Supporting Community Building: Hadarians are excellent guides for those involved in community building or humanitarian work. They offer wisdom and support to help create environments where people feel valued, respected, and loved.

In my experience, connecting with Hadarians has influenced my approach to relationships and community. Their guidance has helped me foster deeper connections and cultivate a more loving and compassionate outlook.

Recognizing and Connecting with Hadarians

Recognizing and connecting with Hadarians involves embracing the qualities of love, harmony, and compassion. Here are some ways to recognize and connect with Hadarian guides:

Feelings of Warmth and Peace: Hadarians often manifest their presence through feelings of warmth, peace, and a sense of being loved. Pay attention to these feelings, especially in moments of quiet reflection or meditation.

Sudden Urges to Connect: You might feel an unexpected urge to reach out and connect with others or to resolve conflicts and build bridges. This can be a sign of Hadarians encouraging you to foster deeper relationships and community.

Encounters with Symbols of Love: Hadarians may communicate through symbols associated with love and harmony, such as hearts, flowers, or doves. Notice if these symbols appear frequently in your life.

A Deep Sense of Compassion: If you find yourself feeling unusually compassionate or empathetic towards others, it could be a sign that Hadarians are guiding you. They often amplify these feelings to help you connect more deeply with those around you.

Meditative Visualization: Visualize yourself surrounded by a soft, glowing light, filled with love and peace. Invite the presence of Hadarian guides and be open to the messages and feelings that arise.

Prayer for Hadarian Guidance: "Hadarian beings of pure love and harmony, I invite your presence into my life. Help me embody unconditional love, heal my relationships, and foster peace and unity. Guide me to build compassionate connections and create harmonious communities. Thank you for your loving guidance and support."

Historical Significance of Hadarians

Hadarians, although less commonly known than other galactic beings, have a significant place in various spiritual traditions and modern starseed communities. Their connection to Beta Centauri, a prominent star in the southern hemisphere, links them to ancient cultures that revered the stars and the wisdom they believed emanated from these celestial bodies.

The southern skies, where Beta Centauri is located, were important to many ancient cultures. Indigenous peoples of Australia and South America, for example, often looked to these stars for guidance and inspiration. While Hadarians themselves may not be explicitly mentioned, their home star's significance in navigation and storytelling reflects their guiding role.

In contemporary spiritual teachings, Hadarians are seen as bearers of pure, unconditional love. They are often associated with the emerging global consciousness that emphasizes unity, compassion, and the interconnectedness of all beings. Their influence is recognized in movements that advocate for social harmony, peace, and the nurturing of communities.

In starseed communities, Hadarians are celebrated for their high vibrational energy and their mission to spread love and harmony. These communities view Hadarians as exemplars of how to live in alignment with love and unity, offering guidance to those who resonate with their energy. The historical significance of Hadarians highlights their enduring role as emissaries of love and harmony, guiding humanity towards a more compassionate and unified existence.

Embracing the Journey with Hadarians

Working with Hadarians offers a path to deeper love, harmony, and community. Their gentle and nurturing energy helps us cultivate more compassionate relationships and build stronger, more loving communities.

As you explore your connection with Hadarians, approach them with openness and a willingness to embrace their teachings of love and unity. Whether through meditation, community work, or simply cultivating compassion in your daily interactions, allow their guidance to transform your life. Embrace the wisdom and support of Hadarians, and let their pure love inspire you to create a more harmonious and connected world.

Alex McCann Johnson

Chapter 152
Galactic Federation

The Galactic Federation, often referred to in spiritual and metaphysical circles, is a coalition of advanced extraterrestrial beings committed to promoting peace, unity, and the evolution of consciousness throughout the galaxy. My journey into understanding the Galactic Federation began when I encountered teachings about cosmic alliances and their roles in guiding humanity's spiritual progress. This concept opened my mind to the possibility of interstellar cooperation and the profound wisdom these beings offer.

The Galactic Federation is believed to be an alliance of various star civilizations, including beings from the Pleiades, Sirius, Arcturus, Andromeda, and many others. These civilizations are said to have reached a high level of spiritual and technological advancement, allowing them to operate in harmony and support less evolved species, like humanity, in their growth and development.

The members of the Galactic Federation are often depicted as beings who have transcended their own planetary conflicts and now work together to foster peace and cooperation across the galaxy. They are dedicated to assisting planets that are undergoing significant transitions, particularly those moving from lower to higher states of consciousness. Their primary mission is to ensure that these transitions occur smoothly and peacefully, providing guidance and support where needed.

In my interactions and studies about the Galactic Federation, I have found them to be a source of immense wisdom and reassurance. Their guidance has helped me understand the broader cosmic context in which our spiritual evolution takes place and the importance of cooperation and unity in achieving higher states of being.

The Spiritual Significance of the Galactic Federation

The Galactic Federation holds spiritual significance for those who believe in their existence and mission. They represent a vision of what is possible when beings from different worlds come together in harmony and mutual respect. Here are some key aspects of their spiritual significance:

Promoting Universal Peace: One of the core missions of the Galactic Federation is to promote peace across the galaxy. They work to prevent and resolve conflicts, ensuring that different civilizations can coexist harmoniously. Their efforts remind us of the importance of peace and unity in our own lives and communities.

Supporting Spiritual Evolution: The Galactic Federation assists planets and their inhabitants in their spiritual evolution. They provide guidance and support to help beings move towards higher levels of consciousness and enlightenment. This role emphasizes the interconnectedness of all life and the shared journey of spiritual growth.

Encouraging Cooperation and Unity: By exemplifying cooperation and unity among diverse star civilizations, the Galactic Federation encourages us to foster these qualities in our own world. They teach us that working together and embracing our differences can lead to greater harmony and progress.

Offering Advanced Wisdom and Technology: The members of the Galactic Federation are often depicted as possessing advanced knowledge and technology, which they used to assist less developed civilizations. This symbolizes the potential for wisdom and innovation to transform our lives and world.

Guiding Planetary Transitions: The Galactic Federation plays a crucial role in guiding planets through significant transitions, such as shifts in consciousness or major evolutionary changes. Their involvement highlights the importance of support during times of change.

Connecting with the Galactic Federation has broadened my perspective on our place in the universe and the potential for collective growth and transformation. Their teachings inspire me to strive for greater peace, cooperation, and spiritual advancement.

Recognizing and Connecting with the Galactic Federation

Connecting with the Galactic Federation involves opening yourself to the possibility of interstellar guidance and embracing the values of peace, unity, and cooperation. Here are some ways to recognize and connect with the Galactic Federation:

Feelings of Universal Unity: If you experience a deep sense of connection with the universe and an awareness of the interconnectedness of all life, it may be a sign that the Galactic Federation is reaching out to you. These feelings often accompany a desire to work towards global peace and cooperation.

Sudden Insights into Cosmic Matters: You might receive intuitive insights or inspirations related to the broader universe and the role of humanity within it. These moments of clarity can be indicators of guidance from the Galactic Federation.

Encounters with Symbols of Unity and Peace: Pay attention to recurring symbols that represent unity, peace, or interstellar cooperation. These might appear in dreams, meditations, or even in your daily life as a way of signaling the Federation's presence.

Meditative Visualization: During meditation, visualize a vast, star-filled space where beings from various star systems gather in harmony. Invite the presence of the Galactic Federation and be open to any messages or feelings that come through.

Prayer for Galactic Guidance: "Galactic Federation of Light, I invite your presence into my life. Guide me towards peace, unity, and higher understanding. Help me embody the values of cooperation and harmony in my daily actions. Thank you for your wisdom and support."

Historical Significance of the Galactic Federation

The concept of the Galactic Federation has its roots in various ancient and modern sources, reflecting humanity's enduring fascination with the possibility of interstellar alliances and cosmic cooperation.

References to advanced beings guiding humanity can be found in many ancient texts and myths. For example, the Sumerians spoke of the Anunnaki, beings from the stars who influenced human civilization. Similarly, ancient Indian texts describe the Vimana, flying chariots used by gods and advanced beings.

The idea of the Galactic Federation gained prominence in the 20th century through the works of various spiritual teachers and channelers. These individuals claimed to receive messages from beings belonging to a cosmic federation dedicated to aiding humanity's evolution. Such teachings have influenced the New Age movement and the broader discourse on extraterrestrial intelligence and spiritual growth.

The notion of a galactic federation or alliance has also been popularized by science fiction literature and media. Stories like "Star Trek" envision a future where different species and civilizations work together for the common good, echoing the ideals attributed to the Galactic Federation.

In recent decades, many people claim to have channeled messages from the Galactic Federation, offering guidance on spiritual growth, planetary ascension, and global peace. These messages emphasize the importance of unity and cooperation in overcoming the challenges facing humanity.

The historical significance of the Galactic Federation lies in its representation of humanity's hope for a future where peace, unity, and cooperation prevail, both on Earth and among the stars. This concept has inspired countless individuals to strive for a better world and to look beyond our planet for guidance and wisdom.

Embracing the Journey with the Galactic Federation

Working with the Galactic Federation offers a pathway to greater understanding, peace, and unity. Their guidance helps us navigate the complexities of our world and the broader universe, encouraging us to embrace our role as part of a larger cosmic community.

As you explore your connection with the Galactic Federation, approach with an open heart and a willingness to learn and grow. Whether through meditation, study, or daily actions, allow their values of peace and cooperation to guide you. Embrace the wisdom and support of the Galactic Federation, and let their vision of unity inspire you to contribute to a more harmonious and enlightened world.

Alex McCann Johnson

Chapter 153

Integrating Galactic Insight

Working with galactic guides has been an enlightening experience for me. Initially, I encountered skepticism and misconceptions about certain extraterrestrial beings. For instance, I often heard that Draconians were inherently malevolent. However, my personal experiences have shown that these beings are perhaps misunderstood. I've felt their presence during healing sessions and have witnessed their unique approach to energy work. As young and evolving beings, we have much to learn from our galactic counterparts. They genuinely want to see us succeed and grow.

Practical Applications of Galactic Wisdom

Integrating the teachings of galactic guides into our daily lives can bring about personal and collective transformation. Here are some practical ways to incorporate their wisdom into your routines:

Daily Meditation and Connection: Setting aside time each day for meditation can help establish a strong connection with galactic guides. Begin by creating a quiet space where you won't be disturbed. Focus on your breath, and set the intention to connect with your galactic guide. Visualize the guide's presence and open yourself to receive their guidance. Over time, this practice can deepen your connection and make their wisdom more accessible.

Energy Healing Practices: Galactic guides, such as the Arcturians, are known for their advanced healing techniques. Integrating these practices into your healing sessions can enhance your overall well-being. For example, the Arcturian Healing Method involves using sacred geometry and light frequencies to clear energy blockages and balance the chakras. Incorporate these techniques into your self-healing routines or share them with others to promote collective healing.

Mindful Living and Higher Awareness: The teachings of the Pleiadians often emphasize the importance of living mindfully and with higher awareness. Practice mindfulness throughout your day by staying present in each moment, whether you're eating, walking, or working. This heightened awareness can help you attune to the subtle energies and messages from your galactic guides, leading to more insightful and inspired actions.

Intentional Dream Work: Dreams are a powerful way for galactic guides to communicate. Before going to bed, set the intention to connect with your guide and receive their wisdom through your dreams. Keep a dream journal by your bedside to record any significant dreams or symbols. Reflecting on these entries can reveal deeper meanings and guidance from your galactic guides.

Creating Sacred Spaces: Designate a space in your home as a sacred area for connecting with galactic guides. Adorn this space with items that resonate with the energy of your guides, such as crystals, star maps, or images of celestial beings. Spend time in this space for meditation, reflection, or simply to feel the presence of your guides.

Examples from Personal Experience

Draconian Healing Wisdom: Despite their controversial reputation, my experiences with Draconian guides have been unexpectedly positive. During a particularly challenging healing session, a Draconian guide appeared, bringing a sense of strength and resilience. Their energy was intense yet deeply healing, helping to release deep-seated fears and blockages. This experience taught me not to judge any being based on preconceived notions but to remain open to the unique gifts they bring.

Arcturian Energy Balancing: In one of my sessions, I called upon an Arcturian guide to assist with energy balancing. I visualized intricate geometric patterns and vibrant light infusing my energy field. The sensation was incredibly soothing, and afterward, I felt a sense of clarity and alignment. This method has since become a staple in my energy healing practice, helping me maintain balance and harmony.

Embracing Further Exploration

The journey of integrating galactic wisdom is ongoing and ever-evolving. Here are a few ways to continue exploring and deepening your connection with galactic guides:

Seek Community and Shared Experiences: Join groups or forums of like-minded individuals who are also exploring connections with galactic guides. Sharing experiences and insights can provide support, validation, and new perspectives on your journey.

Stay Curious and Open: Approach each new experience with curiosity and openness. Galactic guides often bring unexpected lessons and insights. By staying open, you allow yourself to fully receive and integrate their wisdom.

Document Your Journey: Keep a journal of your interactions with galactic guides, including meditations, dreams, and synchronicities. This documentation can help you track patterns, recognize guidance, and reflect on your growth over time.

Expand Your Knowledge: Continuously seek out new information and teachings about galactic guides. Read books, attend workshops, and explore various resources to broaden your understanding and deepen your connection.

The wisdom and guidance of galactic guides offer an opportunity for personal and collective transformation. By integrating their teachings into your daily life and remaining open to further exploration, you can embark on a journey of deep spiritual growth and enlightenment. May your path be filled with light, love, and the boundless wisdom of the cosmos. Embracing the teachings of these celestial beings can lead to a richer, more connected existence, helping you navigate life's challenges with grace and insight.

Chapter 154

Integration of All Guides

As we find ourselves in the midst of a collective awakening, the boundaries between different spiritual realms are dissolving, revealing a vast and interconnected network of guidance and support. This evolution in our consciousness is inviting us to recognize and integrate the wisdom of spirit guides from various traditions and dimensions, enriching our spiritual journey. Whether our guides are angels, ancestors, deities, ascended masters, galactic beings, or elementals, their presence is becoming increasingly accessible and vital as we navigate this transformative period.

In this era of awakening, we are beginning to understand that spirit guides are not confined to the frameworks of any single religion or spiritual tradition. They exist beyond these human-made distinctions, offering their support to all who seek it, regardless of their beliefs or cultural backgrounds. This universal nature of spirit guides highlights the unity and interconnectedness of all spiritual beings. Each guide, whether rooted in ancient folklore or cosmic dimensions, contributes to our growth and helps us align with our true selves.

In my personal experience, integrating the diverse energies and wisdom of these guides has been the greatest and most transformative experience. I've felt the protective embrace of guardian angels, the enlightened insights of ascended masters, the nurturing presence of ancestral spirits, and the expansive perspectives of galactic beings. Each guide brings its own unique qualities, enhancing my spiritual practice and providing new ways to navigate life's challenges and opportunities.

This awakening is a shared journey, and as we collectively raise our vibrations, we are opening up to greater access to the spiritual realm. This access is not reserved for a select few but is available to everyone willing to explore and connect. We are learning to trust our intuition, to heed the subtle nudges of our guides, and to recognize the signs and synchronicities that affirm we are on the right path. This requires a willingness to expand beyond the confines of traditional beliefs and to explore the rich tapestry of guidance that the universe offers.

One of the most important realizations in integrating various guides into our spiritual practice is understanding that they all operate within a larger, cohesive spiritual ecosystem. Each guide, from angels to ancestors to galactic beings, has a specific role in supporting our growth and evolution. They work synergistically, often in ways we might not fully comprehend, to help us align with our highest purpose. This holistic perspective helps us see our spiritual journey not as a series of disjointed experiences but as a unified and harmonious path.

For instance, the teachings of ascended masters, with their emphasis on wisdom and enlightenment, can complement the nurturing and grounding support of ancestral spirits. The vast, cosmic perspectives offered by galactic beings can enrich our understanding of the elemental forces that shape our physical world. By embracing this integrative approach, we allow ourselves to benefit from the full spectrum of spiritual guidance available, creating a more balanced and enriched spiritual practice.

As we navigate this evolutionary process, intention becomes a crucial component. Our intentions shape the type of guidance we attract and how we interpret it. When we engage with our spiritual practices with a pure heart and a sincere desire for growth, we align ourselves with higher frequencies and attract benevolent and supportive guides. This alignment ensures that the guidance we receive is in our best interest and conducive to our spiritual evolution.

We are moving into a time where spirituality is becoming more inclusive and expansive. This inclusivity allows us to blend elements from various traditions and belief systems into our spiritual practices.

Guided by Spirits

Whether we participate in religious ceremonies, meditate, connect with nature, or explore the cosmos through astral journeys, the core of our spiritual journey remains the same: to deepen our connection with the divine and to live in harmony with the universe.

In this era of awakening, we are also learning to honor the diversity of spiritual paths. There is no singular path to connecting with our guides or pursuing spiritual growth. Each person's journey is unique and shaped by their experiences, beliefs, and aspirations. By respecting and celebrating this diversity, we foster a more inclusive and supportive spiritual community.

As we continue to evolve and awaken, the integration of all types of guides into our spiritual practice becomes increasingly important. These guides, transcending individual belief systems, are here to support us in our journey toward greater spiritual awareness and fulfillment. By embracing their wisdom and working with them intentionally, we can navigate this time of great awakening with grace and confidence. The future holds immense potential for profound growth and connection, and our guides are here to assist us every step of the way. As we open ourselves to their guidance, we contribute to the collective awakening and the creation of a more harmonious and enlightened world.

Alex McCann Johnson

Chapter 155

Becoming a Spirit Guide Medium

Embarking on the journey to become a spirit guide medium can be one of the most transformative and enriching experiences of your life. As a spirit guide medium, you open yourself up to a connection with the spiritual realm, allowing you to receive guidance, wisdom, and support from higher beings. This path not only deepens your own spiritual growth but also enables you to help others navigate their life journeys with greater clarity and purpose. Here are some compelling reasons why you should consider becoming a spirit guide medium:

Deepening Your Spiritual Connection

Becoming a spirit guide medium allows you to forge a deeper connection with the spiritual world. This connection fosters a sense of unity with the universe and a greater understanding of the interconnectedness of all life. By regularly communicating with spirit guides, you develop a heightened awareness of the subtle energies around you and a stronger intuition. This spiritual sensitivity can lead to a more meaningful and enriched life.

In my own experience, the journey to mediumship began with an innate curiosity and a series of transformative encounters. Over time, these experiences developed into a deep and sustained relationship with various guides. Each interaction brought a deeper understanding of the universe and my place within it. This connection not only provides a sense of comfort and reassurance but also serves as a foundation for continuous spiritual exploration and growth.

Personal Growth and Healing

The journey to becoming a spirit guide medium is inherently transformative. As you open yourself to the guidance of spirit guides, you embark on a path of continuous self-discovery and personal growth. Spirit guides can help you uncover and address deep-seated emotional wounds, limiting beliefs, and past traumas. Through their guidance, you can achieve significant healing and release old patterns that no longer serve you. This healing process not only benefits you but also enhances your ability to support others on their healing journeys.

My path has been influenced by the healing I've received from my guides. They have helped me navigate through personal challenges and uncover aspects of myself that needed attention and love. This process of healing and self-discovery has been pivotal in my growth, providing me with the tools to support others on their paths.

Enhancing Intuition and Psychic Abilities

As a spirit guide medium, you cultivate and enhance your intuitive and psychic abilities. This development allows you to receive and interpret messages from the spiritual realm with greater clarity and accuracy. Strengthening your intuition can improve your decision-making process, help you navigate life's challenges more effectively, and provide valuable insights into your personal and professional life. Your heightened psychic abilities can also serve as a powerful tool for helping others.

The development of these abilities often begins subtly. You may start noticing a stronger gut feeling or a sense of knowing that wasn't as pronounced before. Over time, as you trust and refine these abilities, they become invaluable in both your life and in your work as a medium. The clarity and insight that comes from a well-honed intuition are remarkable tools for personal empowerment and helping others.

Providing Guidance and Support to Others

One of the most fulfilling aspects of being a spirit guide medium is the ability to help others. By acting as a conduit for spirit guides, you can offer guidance, comfort, and clarity to those seeking answers. Whether through personal readings, workshops, or public speaking, you have the opportunity to make a positive impact on the lives of others. Your ability to connect with spirit guides can provide solace to those dealing with grief, direction to those feeling lost, and inspiration to those seeking purpose.

Helping others through spirit guide mediumship is a rewarding experience. Seeing the relief that people gain from these connections is deeply satisfying. It is a privilege to be able to offer this kind of support and to be a part of someone's journey towards greater clarity and peace.

Fostering a Sense of Purpose and Fulfillment

Many people find a deep sense of purpose and fulfillment in becoming a spirit guide medium. The knowledge that you are contributing to the spiritual growth and well-being of others can be incredibly rewarding. This sense of purpose can bring joy and satisfaction to your life, knowing that you are making a difference in the world. By aligning with your spiritual calling, you create a life that is rich in meaning and aligned with your highest values.

For me, the sense of purpose that comes from this work is unmatched. Knowing that I am playing a part in helping others find their way and connect with their own guides fills my life with meaning. It's a calling that aligns deeply with my values and gives me fulfillment.

Developing a Greater Understanding of Life and Death

As a spirit guide medium, you gain a deeper understanding of the mysteries of life and death. Communicating with spirit guides often involves connecting with souls who have transitioned to the other side, offering you unique insights into the afterlife and the nature of existence. This understanding can alleviate fears and uncertainties about death. It also reinforces the continuity of life and the eternal nature of the soul.

This deeper understanding transforms the way you perceive life's transitions and challenges. It brings a sense of peace and perspective that extends beyond the mundane, helping you to see life as a continuous journey rather than a series of isolated events.

Cultivating Compassion and Empathy

The work of a spirit guide medium requires a high level of compassion and empathy. As you connect with spirit guides and the individuals seeking your help, you develop a deeper sense of compassion for the human experience. This empathy extends beyond your work as a medium, enriching your personal relationships and interactions with others. Cultivating these qualities can lead to more meaningful connections in all areas of your life.

Working as a medium, you often encounter people at their most vulnerable. This work teaches you to hold space with compassion and to offer guidance with empathy. These qualities naturally extend into all areas of your life, enhancing your personal relationships and your overall approach to the world.

Embracing a Lifelong Journey of Learning

Becoming a spirit guide medium is not a destination but a continuous journey of learning and growth. The spiritual realm is vast and ever-evolving, offering endless opportunities for discovery. As you deepen your practice, you will encounter new guides, receive different types of messages, and expand your understanding of the spiritual world. This lifelong journey keeps your spiritual practice dynamic and engaging, ensuring that you are always learning and evolving.

The journey of mediumship is ever-changing. Each day brings new opportunities to connect, learn, and grow. The spiritual realm offers endless depth and complexity, ensuring that there is always more to explore.

Guided by Spirits

Becoming a spirit guide medium offers a multitude of benefits that can enhance your life and the lives of others. From deepening your spiritual connection to providing guidance and fostering a sense of purpose, the journey of a spirit guide medium is rich with rewards. By embracing this path, you open yourself to a world of wisdom, healing, and transformation, making a lasting impact on the spiritual landscape and contributing to the greater good of humanity.

Alex McCann Johnson

Chapter 156
The Path Ahead

I am deeply honored that you have chosen to join me on this journey of exploring spirit guide mediumship. As someone who is passionate about knowledge and has a deep appreciation for history, I find immense joy in sharing these insights and experiences. I encourage you to continue learning and growing, for the quest to connect with spirit is a personal adventure. This path is not about achieving fame or seeking recognition; rather, it's about cultivating a unique and intimate relationship with the universe that can transform your life and the lives of those around you.

The journey to becoming a spirit guide medium is one of self-discovery and spiritual awakening. It begins with a sincere desire to understand the unseen forces that shape our existence and a willingness to open ourselves to the guidance of higher beings. This path is not about accolades or public acknowledgment; it's about developing a relationship with the spiritual realm that is meaningful. It's about listening to the subtle whispers of the universe and trusting the wisdom that comes from beyond our immediate experience.

As you deepen your connection with spirit, your perspective on the world expands. You start to see the intricate interconnections that bind all life together and realize that your actions, thoughts, and intentions ripple out into the universe, influencing the collective consciousness. This awareness brings a heightened sense of responsibility, motivating you to live a life imbued with service and compassion. Such a connection drives you to contribute positively to the greater good and support the spiritual evolution of all beings.

The beauty of connecting with spirit lies in the profound transformation it brings to your life. It imbues you with a sense of peace and clarity, helping you navigate life's challenges and uncertainties with grace and confidence. As you trust in the guidance of your spirit guides and align with your highest good, you learn to release fear and doubt, embracing life's flow with an open heart and a willing spirit.

Developing your connection with spirit also leads to a deeper understanding of your soul's purpose. You start to see the unique gifts and talents you possess and understand how you can use them to serve others. This realization is liberating, allowing you to step into your true potential and live an authentic and fulfilling life. You no longer seek validation from external sources because you know that your worth and purpose come from within and that your true calling is to serve the universe in your unique way.

The journey of a spirit guide medium is one of continuous learning and growth. Each interaction with the spiritual realm offers new insights and opportunities for expansion. You become more attuned to the subtle energies around you and more skilled at interpreting the messages you receive. This ongoing development keeps your spiritual practice vibrant and engaging, ensuring that you are always evolving and deepening your connection to spirit.

Connecting with spirit also nurtures a sense of gratitude and appreciation for the beauty and wonder of life. You become more aware of the everyday miracles and more attuned to the synchronicities that guide your path. This sense of gratitude opens your heart and mind, allowing you to receive even more blessings and share them generously with others. It creates a cycle of giving and receiving that enriches your life and the lives of those you touch.

As you embark on this path, remember that the ultimate goal is to leave the world a little better than you found it. Each step you take on your spiritual journey brings you closer to this goal, enriching not only your own life but also the lives of those around you. This is the true beauty of connecting with spirit and living a life dedicated to the greater good. Embrace this journey with an open heart, and let the wisdom and

Guided by Spirits

love of the universe guide you every step of the way.

Alex McCann Johnson

Chapter 157

Gratitude to Our Spirit Guides

Thank you to all the spirit guides out there. This chapter is for you. My heart and gratitude are with you. You guide the way and support others as they move forward. You do it for all that is good, and you do so lovingly and unconditionally.

Reflecting on my spiritual journey, I am continually humbled and inspired by the presence and guidance of spirit guides. Whether they are angels, ancestors, deities, ascended masters, galactic beings, or elemental spirits, their influence has been profound. Each step of the way, these guides have provided wisdom, protection, and unconditional love, helping me navigate the complexities of life and align more fully with my true purpose.

Spirit guides are the unseen allies who walk with us through the ups and downs of life. They are the whisper in the wind that nudges us in the right direction, the feeling of warmth and comfort during difficult times, and the spark of inspiration that ignites our passions. Their presence is a testament to the interconnectedness of all things and the benevolent nature of the universe.

Throughout life, I have felt the gentle touch of guardian angels, the profound insights of ascended masters, the nurturing embrace of ancestors, and the expansive consciousness of galactic beings. Each type of guide has brought its unique qualities and strengths to my life, enriching my spiritual practice and offering new perspectives on the challenges and opportunities I face. Their diverse energies blend seamlessly, creating a harmonious support system that guides me toward greater awareness and fulfillment.

It is important to recognize that spirit guides work tirelessly behind the scenes, often without recognition or acknowledgment. They operate from a place of pure love and selflessness, dedicated to our growth and well-being. Their guidance is always aligned with our highest good, even when it challenges us to step out of our comfort zones or confront difficult truths.

As we move into a time of great awakening, the role of spirit guides becomes even more significant. This period of heightened awareness and spiritual evolution is an opportunity for us to deepen our connection with these benevolent beings and to integrate their wisdom into our daily lives. By doing so, we not only enhance our own spiritual journey but also contribute to the collective awakening of humanity.

The key to this deepened connection is gratitude. When we express our appreciation for the guidance and support we receive, we strengthen our bond with our spirit guides. Gratitude opens our hearts and raises our vibrational frequency, making it easier for us to receive and interpret their messages. It is a simple yet powerful practice that can transform our relationship with the spiritual realm.

In my own practice, I have found that taking a few moments each day to thank my spirit guides brings a sense of alignment. Whether through prayer, meditation, or a simple, heartfelt acknowledgment, this expression of gratitude reinforces the connection and reminds me that I am never alone on my journey. It is a way of honoring the invisible threads that weave through our lives, connecting us to higher wisdom and divine love.

Spirit guides, this chapter is dedicated to you. Your unwavering support and unconditional love are the foundation upon which we build our spiritual paths. You guide us with patience and compassion, illuminating the way forward even in the darkest of times. Your presence is a constant reminder that we are part of something much greater than ourselves and that our journey has purpose and meaning.

Guided by Spirits

To all those who are just beginning to explore their connection with spirit guides, know that these beings are always with you, ready to offer their support. Open your heart, express your gratitude, and trust in the process. The journey of connecting with spirit guides is personal, but it is also one of the most rewarding aspects of the spiritual path.

As we continue to evolve and awaken, let us carry this sense of gratitude with us. Let us honor our spirit guides by living in alignment with their teachings, embodying the principles of love, compassion, and unity. In doing so, we not only transform our own lives but also contribute to the creation of a more harmonious and enlightened world.

Thank you, spirit guides, for your endless love and guidance. My heart and gratitude are with you always. You are the silent champions of our journey, and this entire book is a tribute to your unwavering dedication to all that is good.

Alex McCann Johnson

Chapter 158

Goodbye and Safe Journeys

As we come to the end of this exploration into the world of spirit guides and the many dimensions of spiritual awakening, I want to express my deepest gratitude for joining me on this journey. Whether you are just beginning to explore your connection with spirit guides or have been on this path for years, I hope that the insights shared here have enriched your understanding and inspired your spiritual growth.

Embarking on a spiritual journey is a profound experience. It requires courage, curiosity, and a willingness to explore the unknown. As you continue on your path, remember that you are supported by a diverse and loving community of guides who are dedicated to your well-being and evolution. Each step you take, each new guide you meet, and each moment of insight and connection brings you closer to the essence of your true self and to the vast, interconnected tapestry of the universe.

Keep your heart open and your spirit curious. Embrace the wisdom of your guides, whether they are angels, ancestors, deities, ascended masters, galactic beings, or the elemental forces of nature. Trust in the guidance you receive and know that you are always surrounded by love, support, and divine light.

As you journey forward, may you find joy in your discoveries, peace in your connections, and strength in your growing awareness. May your path be illuminated with the wisdom of the ages and the love of the universe. Remember, the journey of spiritual awakening is never-ending; it is a beautiful and continuous unfolding of who you are and

Alex McCann Johnson

the limitless possibilities that lie ahead.

Goodbye for now, and may your travels be filled with magic and wonder.

Safe journeys, Alex McCann Johnson

www.ingramcontent.com/pod-product-compliance
Lightning Source LLC
Chambersburg PA
CBHW071129130626
46553CB00004B/1316